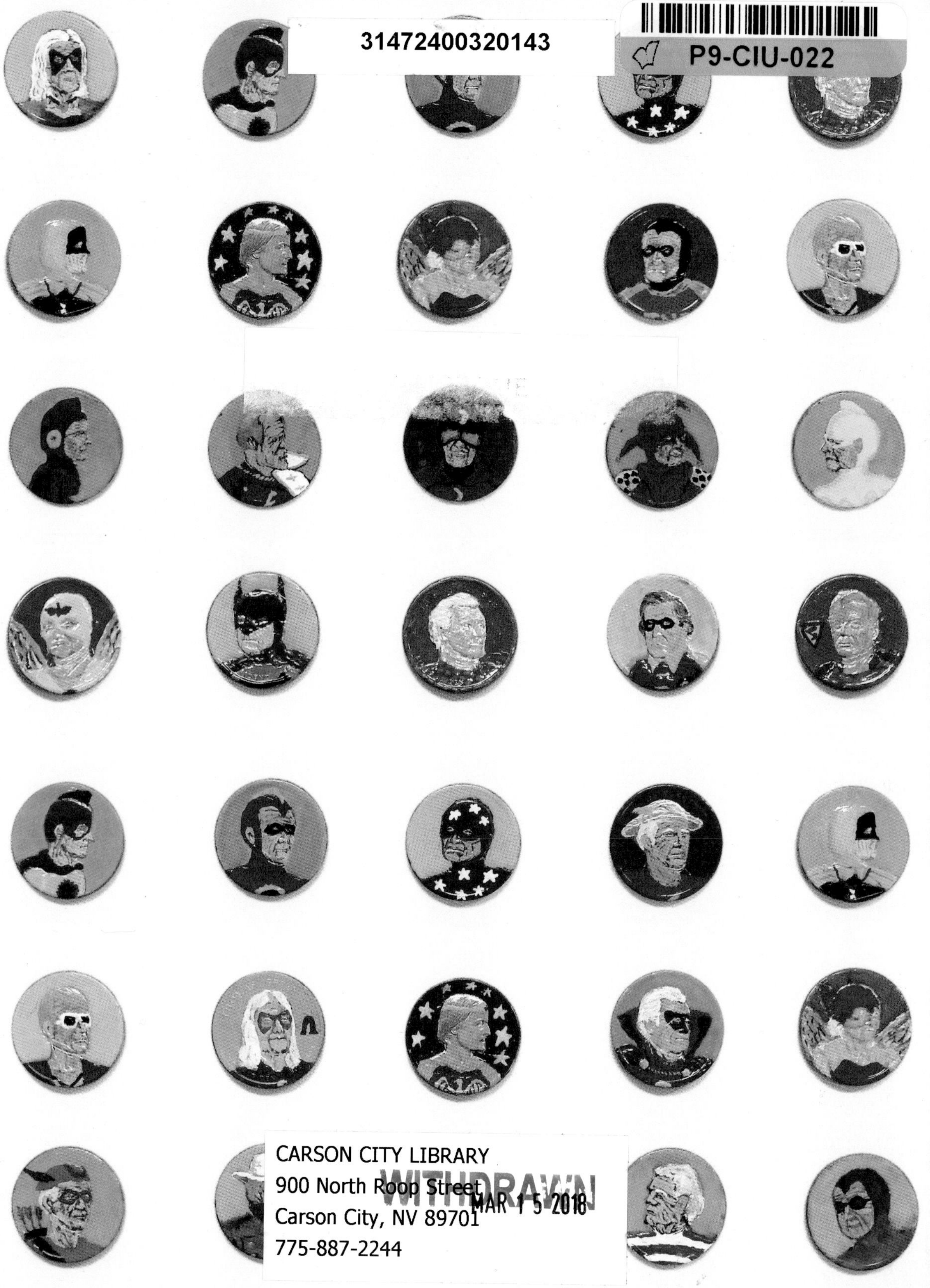

THE BEST AMERICAN

# Comics 2017

GUEST EDITORS OF THE
BEST AMERICAN COMICS

2006 HARVEY PEKAR
2007 CHRIS WARE
2008 LYNDA BARRY
2009 CHARLES BURNS
2010 NEIL GAIMAN
2011 ALISON BECHDEL
2012 FRANÇOISE MOULY
2013 JEFF SMITH
2014 SCOTT McCLOUD
2015 JONATHAN LETHEM
2016 ROZ CHAST
2017 BEN KATCHOR

THE BEST AMERICAN

# Comics

## 2017

EDITED *and* INTRODUCED

*by* Ben Katchor

BILL KARTALOPOULOS,
*series editor*

HOUGHTON MIFFLIN HARCOURT
BOSTON · NEW YORK · 2017

www.hmhco.com

*Library of Congress Cataloging-in-Publication Data is available.*

ISSN 1941-6385 (print)        ISSN 2573-3869 (ebook)
ISBN 978-0-544-75036-4 (print)    ISBN 978-0-544-75055-5 (ebook)

Book design: David Futato        Cover art: Matthew Thurber
Endpaper art: Oscar Azmitia       Cover art direction: Christopher Moisan

PRINTED IN THE UNITED STATES OF AMERICA

DOC 10 9 8 7 6 5 4 3 2 1

Permissions credits are located on page 376.

# Contents

# Foreword

Making comics is not a career.

It is true that many people have built careers by making comics, but in the United States, those artists who support themselves entirely through their comics work are a small group. They are rare exceptions among the countless others who also support themselves with day jobs, freelance work, teaching, original art sales, commissions, illustration, animation, graphic design, and in countless other ways. Artists must often budget their time as they seek to achieve a balance between passion projects and paying work.

The field of comics has changed radically in the past twenty years, as robust graphic novel sections have appeared in most bookstores and libraries. I think it could be easy for young artists entering the field now to see so much professionalized output and imagine a broader set of economic possibilities than actually exists. The truth is that most authors of graphic novels—like most authors of prose novels—cannot subsist on modest advances and royalties alone. They are a drop in the bucket relative to the many months—often years—of focused labor required to produce a book-length work in the comics form. Some countries like Canada and France have grant programs that support artists and publishers in order to develop and promote culture, but the United States has few such public programs. The notion that society should invest in humanizing culture has little traction here, and unfortunately seems at the time of this writing to be rapidly losing already meager ground. Comics remain healthier as a category of culture than as a category of commerce.

There's no question that circumstances now are better for comics than they were twenty years ago, when incredible work had little chance of gaining notice outside of niche circles. There are many wonderful benefits to being published and distributed through mainstream channels, despite the sometimes low compensation. It's not at all my goal to paint a dour picture of contemporary comics publishing. Rather, I wish to celebrate the fact that our current vital era of comics still exists *against all odds*. It is an uphill climb to make this work, with no true guarantees and little expectation of steady reward. Comics exist because artists are passionate about the art form and its possibilities for personal expression.

Precisely because those odds are so daunting, artists entering the field should engage the medium and take risks: expressive risks and artistic risks. In a field with no guarantees, compromising one's work to meet a perceived marketplace is a much riskier gamble than wholehearted, incautious engagement. The odds of financial success are always low, but if an artist pushes his or her work as far as it can go, the chances for personal satisfaction and growth climb exponentially. Personal creative ambition is a safer bet, on its own terms, than a career plan.

The artists who have broken through to mainstream attention in the biggest ways have often done so by making the work that they were motivated to make *despite* the lack of an obvious market or audience. Art Spiegelman serialized *Maus* in the comics anthology magazine he self-published with Françoise Mouly at a time when no publisher on earth was looking for a graphic novel about the Holocaust featuring cats and mice. Raina Telgemeier self-published the work that would become *Smile* in black-and-white photocopied form before children's book publishers became interested in comics. Alison Bechdel serialized her cult comic strip *Dykes to Watch Out For* for years in the alternative press before *Fun Home* made her a household name among readers. The world did not know that it needed this work until artists made it.

When artists resist limitations, readers gain a fuller and truer picture of everything the art form is capable of. It takes a little vision for artists to see beyond the edges of what comics have been to imagine what they could be. Readers can share this kind of vision, too. Certainly many who do function as critics, scholars, editors, and curators. But it's not necessary to be professionally involved with comics to share this vision. It only requires some thought, some curiosity, some imagination, and an open mind. This is the posture shared by artists, critics, and engaged readers that keeps us all open and primed and ready to appreciate new expressions as they emerge, no matter how alien they may appear to be upon first contact. *A culture will die* without readers who are willing to read adventurously, to push beyond their own comfort zones so that artists may push beyond theirs.

It's not surprising that great artists often make interesting critics. People who have spent a lifetime developing their own unique way of making comics tend to perceive the field uniquely. This is why we typically invite renowned artists to guest edit the Best American Comics each year, and I am especially excited that Ben Katchor has brought his perspective to the series this year.

Ben Katchor has always seen comics differently than anyone else I've ever met. In discussing the history of comics, Ben traces an alternate genealogy for the form reaching back to cultural artifacts like medieval European broadside ballads—illustrated song sheets—and other international formats that combine images with spoken or sung oral narratives. Ben prizes the ephemerality of performance, just as his own work prizes the ephemerality of urban spaces. Ben and his work look back to the entire history of figurative art and literature for inspiration, but these references provide Ben's work with fuel that pushes his comics forward into exciting new directions.

Ben's comics first gained notice in the ephemeral format of the alternative weekly newspaper, an outlet that flourished in the 1980s and '90s. These publications mixed art together with daily life in a post-punk collage of features—comics and illustrations intermingled with local news, opinion pieces, reviews, and classified ads. Alt-weekly newspapers physically brought art into the streets of the American cities where they were once freely available. This format gave artists like Ben, Matt Groening, Lynda Barry, Bechdel, and others a regular, visible, (low) paying platform for their work, combined with the opportunity for total creative freedom. Ben exercised his freedom so powerfully that his work in these now yellowing newspapers earned him a 1993 *New Yorker* profile, and in 2000 he became the first cartoonist to ever win a prestigious MacArthur Foundation grant—the so-called Genius Award.

If Ben is a genius as an artist making comics, I think he is also a bit of a genius when it comes to looking at comics, too. In our discussions this past year, Ben encouraged us to imagine all the comics that might exist far outside of the professional, constructed, visible field of comics and to think appreciatively about how different and unexpected they might be: comics by students, comics by people who have never made comics before, comics by incarcerated persons, comics existing within specific subcultures, instructional art, and propaganda. Ben in particular took a keen interest in seeking out comics by so-called "outsider" artists. His searching efforts in this regard allowed us to include several relevant comics by artists working at centers for adults making art across the spectrum of mental and physical abilities. These works have been seen principally in exhibition settings as well as in printed catalogs and online, but they exist outside the comics field as it's typically constructed. In this way, they fit into the category of "paracomics," which I described in my foreword to the 2015 edition of this series: comics produced by artists working outside of the field of comics, sometimes for exhibition rather than for conventional publication. I am so grateful that Ben has brought such an expansive vision to this project and has revealed for all of us that the field of comics itself is still—and is always—bigger and more surprising than we can imagine.

*The Best American Comics 2017* represents a selection of outstanding work published between September 1, 2015, and August 31, 2016. Many of the comics we considered came to us through our open submission process. Additionally, I sought out work for consideration at comic book stores, at comics festivals, online, and through recommendations from trusted colleagues. I amassed and considered a large pool of comics, and selected approximately 120 pieces to forward to our guest editor, who made the final selections from this pool of work, while, as always, retaining the flexibility to bring in some works he discovered on his own. In addition to the work we have reprinted here, I've assembled a lengthy list of Notable Comics that appears at the back of this book. If you have enjoyed any of the comics in this volume, the works listed in our Notable Comics list are all also worth seeking out. I have posted a version of this list to my website (on-panel.com) that includes links to sites where you can learn more about those comics.

We are always seeking work to consider for the Best American Comics. Any artist or publisher is encouraged to submit work, including self-published and online work. The continuing robust diversity of Best American Comics is greatly dependent upon these submissions. Work can be sent at any time to our public postal address:

Bill Kartalopoulos
Series Editor
The Best American Comics
Houghton Mifflin Harcourt
3 Park Avenue, 19th floor
New York, NY 10016

By the time this book is published, we will be seeking new, North American work published between September 1, 2017, and August 31, 2018, for consideration for *The Best American Comics 2019*.

Thanks as always to our in-house editor at Houghton Mifflin Harcourt, Nicole Angeloro, who manages and coordinates the many moving parts behind this challenging annual book project with efficiency and equanimity. Thanks to art director Christopher Moisan, who works with our artists on the cover and endpapers for each volume. Thanks to David Futato, our indefatigable interior designer (who is, sadly for us, moving on to bigger and better things), and to Beth Burleigh Fuller, for managing the complex production behind this book. Thanks as well to Mary Dalton-Hoffman, who secures the crucial rights and permissions for each year's volume. Many thanks to all of my colleagues who offered helpful suggestions, advice, and guidance as I worked on this volume.

Thanks to Oscar Azmitia for our excellent endpapers, which bring art, culture, and daily life together in such a delightful way.

And thanks finally to Matthew Thurber for crafting a cover that so succinctly captures the spirit of the moment in which it was drawn. It is strange to hope that this cover will be less timely when this book appears in physical form. I sometimes tell people that it's odd for us to put so much work into an annual book that has an expiration date written on the cover. Each year's volume enjoys a window of visibility before it is replaced by the next book in the series. Each volume *is* a statement about the past year in comics, but it's worth remembering that all of the artists included make work that is built to last, wherever and whenever it is found. And I think that each year's expression of our guest editor's critical point of view also retains great value beyond the annual cycle.

When the year 1984 came and went—and again in 1989 when the Berlin Wall came down—it may have been tempting to toss George Orwell's *1984* down the memory hole, to treat the book's dystopian projection as itself having passed some expiration date. But elements of Orwell's analysis were *always* timeless, particularly his vivid illustration of the ways in which power structures abuse language to manipulate the public (see: The Patriot Act, Citizens United, "right to work" laws, etc.). And citizens of other countries, under more oppressive regimes, would not have had the luxury of consigning Orwell's image of political suppression to the backlist of history.

In 2017 Orwell's *1984* struck many in the United States as suddenly relevant again, gaining new currency as a new government took power here, declaring unfavorable news stories "fake news" and calling the free press "the enemy of the people." Ignore the date on Orwell's cover: timeless ideas return eternally, and we are unfortunately urgently reminded that we are not yet done with the work of rendering his cautionary vision merely historical.

My earlier exhortation for artistic risk-taking may seem inconsequential or trivial in the face of larger issues, but it's not. In politics, in life, and in art, the stakes are always high, and we are periodically called to remember this. Hopefully not too infrequently, lest we lose hard-won ground.

We hope that you will freely read and engage all of the works in this year's volume in the spirit of free writing, free drawing, and free thinking in which they were all created.

BILL KARTALOPOULOS

# Introduction

BEN KATCHOR

**U.S. Chamber of Comics**
**Standing Up for American Cartoonists**
**1909 Q Street, Washington, DC 20065**

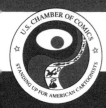

# The Triumph of American Comics!

THE book you hold in your hands, *The Best American* Comics 2017*, offers conclusive evidence of the greatness of today's American comics. Although many of the cartoonists included in this anthology come from obscure ethnic backgrounds, they have all willingly jumped onboard the American train to glory.

The comics industry under our present administration is booming — $1.03 billion in sales and growing! The cartoonists represented in this book are not only wonderful artist-authors, they are winning players in the casino of American culture. The image of the struggling alternative cartoonist living on ramen noodles and TV dinners is a thing of the past — today's cartoonist is a successful artist-entrepreneur negotiating multiple publishing and film deals, planning a line of toys and other merchandise, and receiving literary and academic accolades while comfortably ensconced in an upper-middle-class, or higher, lifestyle surrounded by loving family and jealous friends.

Today's cartoonist stands firmly with one foot planted in popular culture and the other in the blue-chip galleries and museums of the international art world. The cartoonist's feet are bathed in the twin revenue streams of low- and high-brow production. From the innocent child to the doddering, gray-haired comics fan — everyone is a potential paying customer. Money needed for food and medical care is gladly diverted to buy a few moments of comic-strip bliss. Even the small-press publisher — once the laughingstock of the media world — feeds from the same trough as his big brothers in the world of multinational corporate media.

That American comics have come to dominate the world's graphic-novel reading market is no accident. As an imperial military and economic power, the aura of American cultural products strikes both fear and admiration in the literate and illiterate peoples of the developing world. At the risk of drowning in provincialism, readers around the world must accommodate themselves to the consumption of American cultural products as they have since the end of the last great World War. The American sense of humor becomes their sense of humor; the American idea of comics becomes their idea of comics. The printing presses of Shenzhen and Shanghai are kept busy with American orders for cheap color printing.

Cartoonists also play an important role in our current war efforts around the globe. Our courageous drone operators in their leisure time leave their joysticks behind to relax in the fantasy world of comics; teenagers are inculcated with the pleasures of victimless violence through our biggest-selling superhero comics. Even small press art-comics do their bit to help the war effort. Through the depoliticization of comics into an "art object," they encourage young readers to accept the eternal values of "fine art" and the status quo of a free American society. We salute their efforts!

Regardless of your sexual orientation, your ethnic background, your religious delusions, or your dietary preferences, it's a great time to be an American cartoonist.

— Ben Katchor, Senior Vice-President Emeritus, International Strategy and Operations

* Unfortunately, we are contractually obliged to include Canada and Mexico in this anthology — countries that represent sluggish backwaters in this otherwise glorious industry.

*The U.S. Chamber of Comics is a nonprofit membership organization representing the unified interests of U.S. cartoonists before Congress, government agencies, and the courts.*

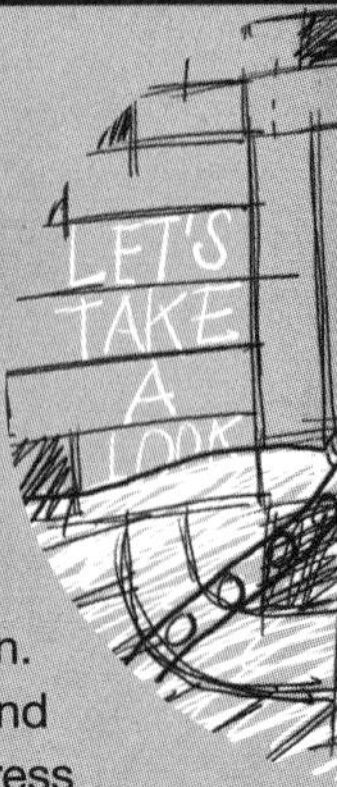
LET'S
TAKE
A

## An Introduction

With the newfound validation of comic art as a serious literary/art form, the number of practitioners has reached epidemic proportions in North America. One publisher estimates 6,000, but the actual number is probably closer to a million. Like the countless would-be poets and short-story writers filling the small-press magazines in the 1950s and '60s, young people are today turning to comics as a "serious" form of self-expression. We all want to encourage free artistic expression, but this unchecked expression has an incalculable impact upon the spouses, relatives, friends, and children of the practitioner. Understanding the urges behind various forms of cartooning is the first step toward a healthy coexistence.

In the popular press, a pernicious idea has been promulgated: that successful comic strips often arise from an alchemical combination of less than stellar writing and drawing. This creative license has led many young people who have experienced failure in other art forms — writing, painting, music, etc. — to turn to comics as a last resort for artistic expression and a career in the arts. It's important for family and friends to understand that they're often dealing with a would-be artist with a "chip" on his or her shoulder.

In a society that looks upon the manual trades: baking, carpentry, plumbing, etc., as being inferior to white-collar activities: the art world, the stock market, banking, etc., young people are driven to enroll in university courses that seem to guarantee an entry into these more prestigious and lucrative fields. In fact, these fields are glutted and the average annual salary in the arts amounts to a poverty wage. This economic reality explains the fact that most would-be cartoonists are born into the upper-middle class and want to stay there.

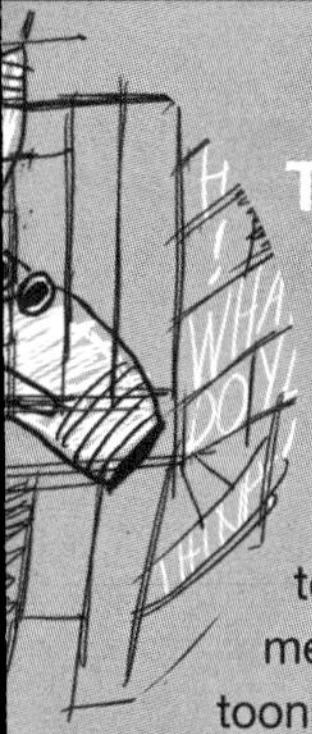

## The Comic Strip as "Contemporary Art"

In those years of the early 20th century when the comic strip was an actual business, the field attracted entertainers and vaudevillians who were able to translate their skills into the print medium. A number of contemporary cartoonists, seeing no demand for their work in today's diminished publishing world, have come to think of themselves as avant-garde artists. They labor under the discredited ideas of high-modernism, medium specificity, the purification of art forms, and other nonsense promulgated by ex-Trotskyite writers desperately trying to distance themselves from Soviet Realism and the traditions of figurative art that were intertwined with storytelling and theatrics.

If your loved one falls into this category, their theoretical inclinations might respond to reason and the suggestion that they deepen their understanding of cultural history. As they see other "fine" artists commanding obscene prices for their work, it's understandable that they believe that it's just a matter of time before comics, and more specifically *their* comics, are recognized and embraced by the art-industrial complex. Try to explain to them that comic strip imagery in the "art world" is old hat and to think about making comic strips for "this" world.

## "Real" or Mainstream Comics

Around 1938, the comic strip form was packaged into cheap, saddle-stitched pamphlets and marketed to children, teenagers, and semi-literate adults. These mass-marketed comic books, with their antisocial expressions of violence and vigilanteism delivered via simplistic narratives, account for the prejudice that most adults have against the form to this day.

Each year a number of young men dedicate their lives to the perpetuation of the genres of adventure, superhero, and crime comics. These young men take up bodybuilding and in their private lives adopt various neo-fascist beliefs. For those unfortunates who fail to outgrow these themes, it's common, by the age of 30, to use the form as a vehicle for a type of softcore pornography aimed at their aging peers. Children are usually repulsed by these comics and instead retreat into the world of video games and masturbation.

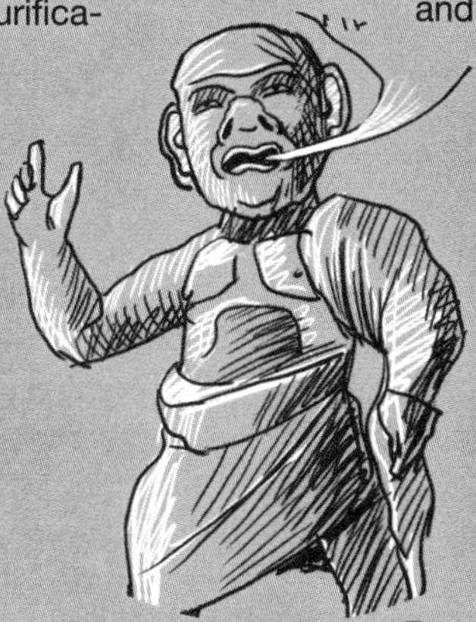

The prognosis for these mainstream comic book practitioners, trapped in a web of infantile aesthetics, is poor. The antisocial expression usually impacts their interpersonal relationships, leading to divorce, drugs, alcohol, and violent outbursts.

## Autobiographical Comic Strips

For comic strip makers with underdeveloped imaginative faculties, it's common to turn to a regurgitation of the details of their own life. The more pathetic or embarrassing the details the better. Following the validated model of "alternative" comic strip drawing — a banal, schematized, cartoonlike image — these individuals are oblivious to the pain their autobiographical comics might cause people in their social sphere. Like the obsessive diarist who can't leave home for fear of falling hopelessly behind in his diary, these individuals reduce their own lives to a narrow, circumscribed field of activity — making comics is their life and so the self-aggrandizement of their lifestyle spirals into ever narrower concerns.

Psychotherapy can be helpful in getting these individuals to look beyond themselves. In fortunate cases, a violent encounter with one of their subjects will awaken them from their delusion.

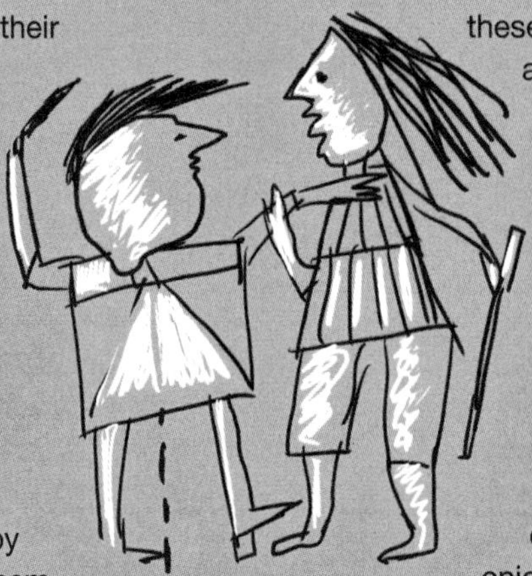

## Pseudo-Primitives and Outsider Comics

A number of young cartoonists have adopted, on a superficial level, the tortured handwriting and stylistic quirks of so-called primitive or untrained picture-makers. Some are driven to this choice by a pretentious desire to affiliate themselves with the supposed honesty of the untutored; others, lacking the energy to acquire the techniques of Western drawing or having failed in an attempt to do so, fall back upon a faux naive style in which all of their errors in drawing and thought are seen as an entertaining asset. The anemic quality of such work can usually be improved through a change in diet and vitamin supplements.

## The Mash-Up Style

At the height of delusion, we find a number of individuals who believe that they are living at "the end of history." All styles have been exhausted and the only option open to them is to engage in the avowed combination of the styles of cartoonists and writers of the past. In their eyes, the work of the cartoonists of the past is simply a matter of surface affectation that can be easily mimicked to result in a new and profound result. The prognosis for these individuals is not much better than their colleagues in the "mainstream" — they are hopelessly trapped in the past.

## The Politically Engaged Cartoonist

With the best of intentions, these individuals affiliate themselves with the social and economic underdogs of the world. Their comic strips aim to selflessly publicize the plight of the oppressed and downtrodden. Unfortunately, the tone and approach of these justifiably angry cartoonists alienates the readers most in need of their message. Unwittingly, they tend to adopt the crudest commercial drawing styles of the very capitalist system they are trying to undermine, and so repulse the connoisseurs of comic art. Because of their strong political opinions, these cartoonists resist all therapeutic approaches. After thirty years, their work takes on a quaint historical patina and can be enjoyed as social history.

## Toward a Brighter Future

We hope that this little brochure offers family and friends of cartoonists an unbiased view of the contemporary field of comic strip work and can serve as a basis for understanding the self-destructive decisions and strange impetus behind the work. For a cartoonist to toil in obscurity and with little remuneration over decades, often through the prime years of their life, requires a degree of self-delusion greater than most of us operate under. To the outside viewer, the work may seem meaningless, unintelligible, and superfluous in the context of contemporary culture. For these reasons, cartoonists do not take criticism lightly and so it's best to bring them into a therapeutic setting where trained professionals, with no prejudice against the comic strip form, can give them the help they need.

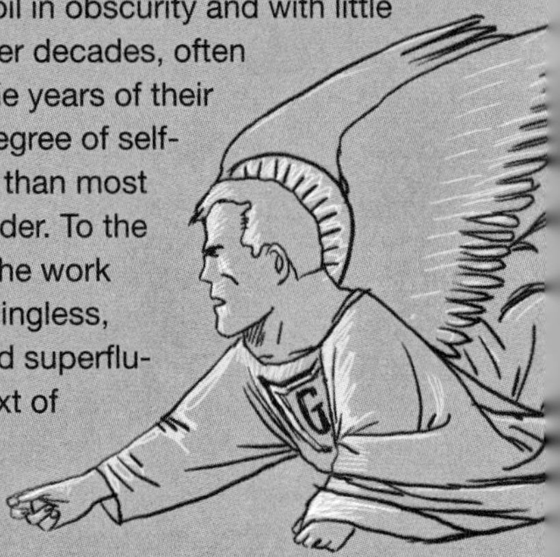
G

*For more help, contact:* **The National Society for the Prevention of Cruelty to Cartoonists**. *Bulletin #259.*

# I am
# a Cartoonist
# not
# a Mental Health
# Problem.

*Living with cartoonists in the*
*second Golden Age of comics.*

*NSPCC Bulletin #259.*

**From:** Ben Katchor <katchor@halvah.com>
**Date:** Tues. Jan. 3, 2017 at 5:41 PM
**Subject:** Best American Comics
**To:** Bill Kartalopoulos <bill@heraclitus.com>

Hi Bill,
Is there any way to extend the deadline for BAC? I'm still awaiting word from the director of that art workshop in Maybelline Penitentiary in Georgia. Some are minors who won't want to be identified as inmates. They're doing some interesting work. Let me know.
- Ben

---------------------------------------------------

**From:** Ben Katchor <katchor@halvah.com>
**Date:** Thur. Jan. 5, 2017 at 11:13 PM
**Subject:** Re: Best American Comics
**To:** Bill Kartalopoulos <bill@heraclitus.com>

Hi Bill,
And there's that troubled boy in Newark, NJ, who's drawing comic strips with feces on the walls of his parents' rent-controlled apartment. They've promised photos.
- Ben

---------------------------------------------------

**From:** Ben Katchor <katchor@halvah.com>
**Date:** Sun. Jan. 8, 2017 at 2:41 AM
**Subject:** Re: Best American Comics
**To:** Bill Kartalopoulos <bill@heraclitus.com>

Hi Bill,
I'm tracking down a collection of narrative doodles made in the margins of log books by transatlantic pilots at 30,000 feet above the ocean. It sounds great! By the way, that Inuit artist did produce a few comic strips, but they're currently lost.
- Ben

----------------------------------

**From:** Ben Katchor <katchor@halvah.com>
**Date:** Tues. Jan. 10, 2017 at 3:21 PM
**Subject:** Best American Comics
**To:** Bill Kartalopoulos <bill@heraclitus.com>

Bill,
I feel that we've only scratched the surface of this year's comic strip work -- mainly "career cartoonists" -- but I'm convinced that there's more going on. Most of this other work is not easily seen. The Mexican brothel cartoonists are not easy to work with as their strips are considered illegal. So, please, let's try to extend the deadline so that we can include some of these cartoonists -- otherwise, it's not fair.

# FEDS RAID "BEST OF" RACKET EDITORIAL LOVE NEST

## *Guest Editor of Art-Comics Bunco Scheme Begs for Mercy*

**NEW YORK (AAP)** In an early morning raid, the "guest" editor of "Best American Comics" was arrested in a cheap eatery on the Upper West Side of Manhattan. The annual publication claims to present the past year's "best comics."

A subpoena issued by the Federal Trade Commission was brought to night court and an immediate arrest warrant was issued for Ben Moishe Dovid Katchor, the legal "guest editor" of the current edition. The indictment for racketeering—that is, "the act of offering a dishonest service (a "racket") to solve a problem that wouldn't otherwise exist without the enterprise offering the service"—involved public misrepresentation and twenty counts of fraudulent literary activity in the publication of this annual book.

Each year a special "guest editor" is contracted and his, or her, name is advertised on the book's cover. The craftily written terms of these "guest editor" contracts absolves the Houghton Mifflin Harcourt Publishing Company of all responsibility for claims made by the publication.

Vasilios "Bill" Kartalopoulos, the so-called "series editor," traded upon his reputation as a comics historian, educator, and "organizer" to act as a middleman in this literary bunco scheme. Surveillance videos show Kartalopoulos transferring countless canvas tote bags filled with printed material to Katchor's office. The work, solicited through a variety of disreputable means, is purported to be, according to Kartalopoulos' "taste," the best work done in the comic strip field over the past year. Through these deliveries, Kartalopoulos had hoped to influence the contents of the book. In testimony, it was discovered that Kartalopoulos had close professional, and, in some cases, psycho-dependent relationships with many of the authors included in each year's selection. Katchor, an "award-winning" cartoonist in his own right, is suspected of accepting unspecified favors from a number of desperate young cartoonists in exchange for inclusion in the book.

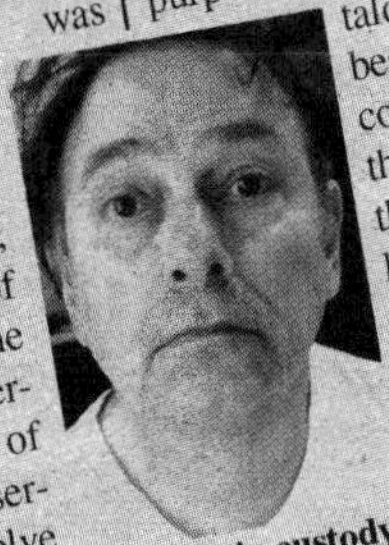

**Katchor in custody.**

Katchor, a first-generation American of Polish-Jewish-Communist origins, was paid tens of thousands of dollars for his "guest editorial" services. The "anointed" contributors to this highly regarded volume were to be paid less than the state's minimum hourly wage considering the repetitive hand labor involved in making such comics.

Night court Judge Marshall Buckram was visibly disgusted by the scale and blatant nature of this fraudulent operation. "How, in a free country, could such an ongoing debasement of the idea of 'the best,' be allowed to be published, sold in bookstores, and lapped up by naive readers," he said.

To immediately halt the production of the 2017 edition, an arrest warrant was issued that same evening. Laptop computers bearing the digital submissions and piles of cheaply printed comics slated for appearance in the upcoming volume were confiscated, brought to police headquarters, and destroyed.

Kartalopoulos was reportedly on a "business" trip to Greece. Katchor was chased from his apartment to a nearby 24-hour coffee shop and cornered in the ladies' room, where he fell to his knees and begged for mercy. "How could I turn down a chance to be paid for reading comics," he cried.

Katchor faces a stiff prison sentence with no chance of parole.

### *Killers Make Comic Strips in Upstate Penitentiary*

**FISTULA, NY (AP)** An innovative program encouraging long-term inmates at Maybelline State Penitentiary to try their hand at producing comic strips has led to positive results. The workshop, run by an inmate and once popular cartoonist, Ben Katchor, supplies incarcerated men with harmless ball-point pen fillers and soft erasers. They spend thousands of hours writing and drawing comic strips that express remorse for their heinous crimes and graphically notate their fond memories of family and pornographic celebrities in the outside world.

Katchor, recently arrested for overseeing a fraudulent literary publishing scheme, hopes to atone for his own

THE BEST AMERICAN

# Comics 2017

# The Future of Art 25 Years Hence

GARY PANTER

*originally published in*

*frieze*, no. 181

FRIEZE PUBLISHING LTD.

9.05 × 11.8 inches • 200 pages

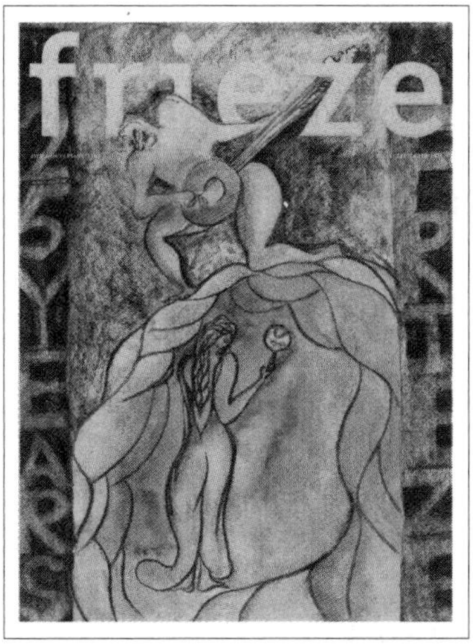
frieze

## Biography

Gary Panter is an artist living in Brooklyn, New York. He works in many mediums, including drawing, painting, music, cartoon narratives, and crafts such as candlemaking. His work grows out of the art and cultures of the Sixties.
garypanter.com

## Statement

My piece is an argument for the preservation of the analog and personal.

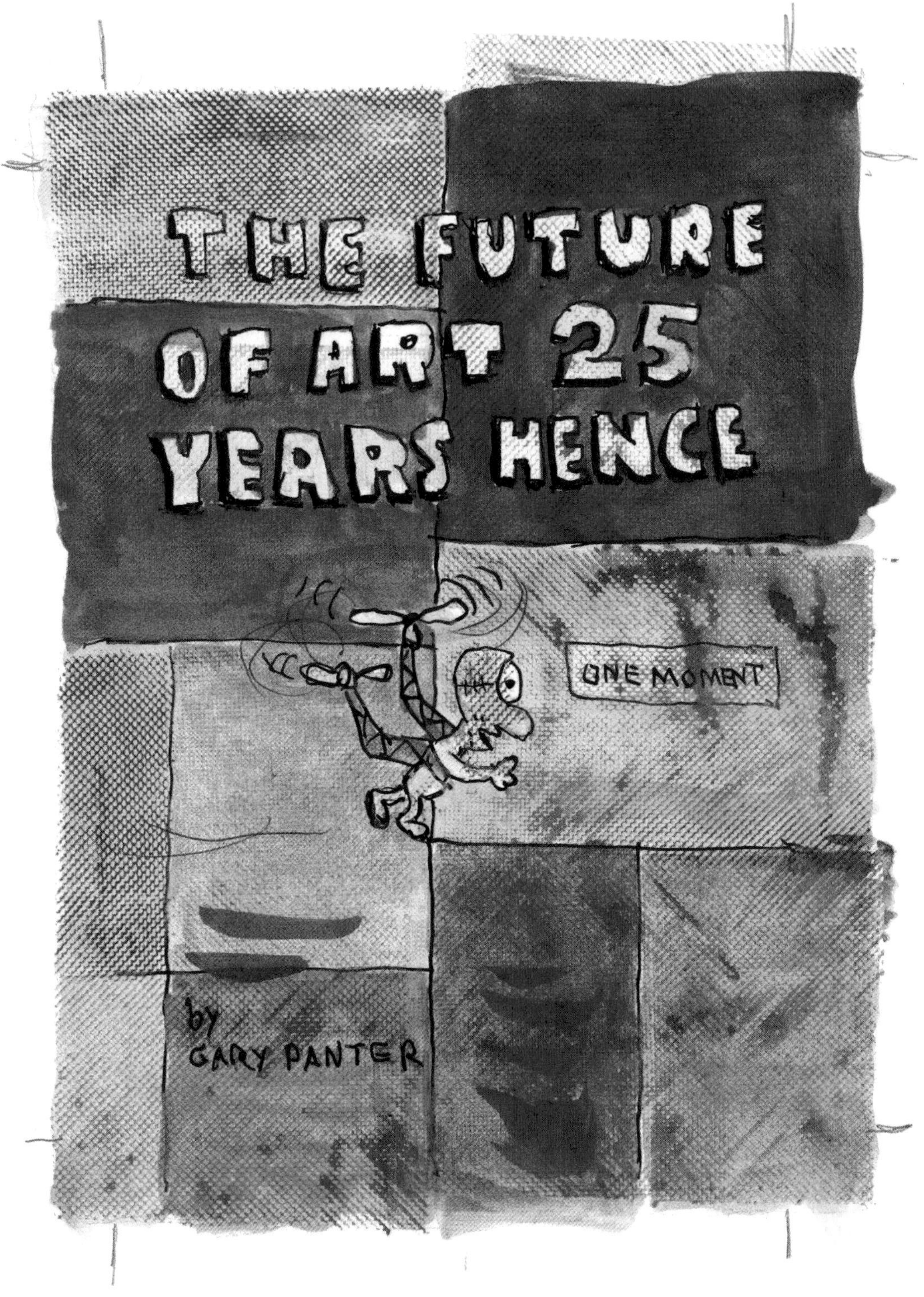
THE FUTURE OF ART 25 YEARS HENCE
ONE MOMENT
by GARY PANTER

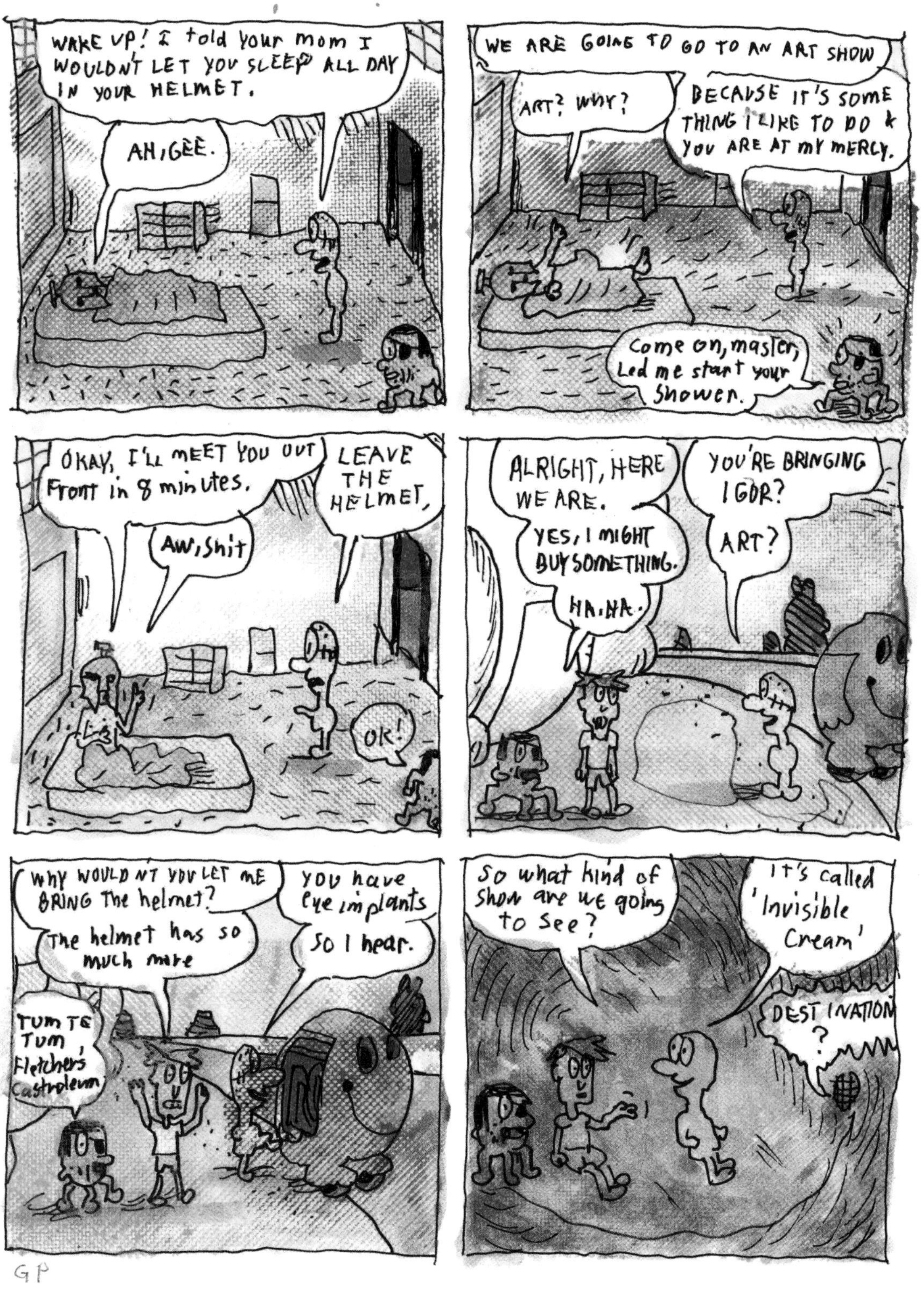
WAKE UP! I told your mom I WOULDN'T LET YOU SLEEP ALL DAY IN YOUR HELMET.
AH, GEE.
WE ARE GOING TO GO TO AN ART SHOW
ART? WHY?
BECAUSE IT'S SOME THING I LIKE TO DO & YOU ARE AT MY MERCY.
Come on, master, Led me start your shower.
OKAY, I'LL MEET YOU OUT Front in 8 minutes.
LEAVE THE HELMET.
AW, Shit
OK!
ALRIGHT, HERE WE ARE.
YOU'RE BRINGING IGOR?
YES, I MIGHT BUY SOMETHING.
ART?
HA, HA.
Why WOULDN'T YOU LET ME BRING The helmet?
You have eye implants
The helmet has so much more
So I hear.
TUM TE TUM, Fletcher's Castroleum
So what kind of show are we going to see?
It's called 'Invisible Cream'
DESTINATION?
GP

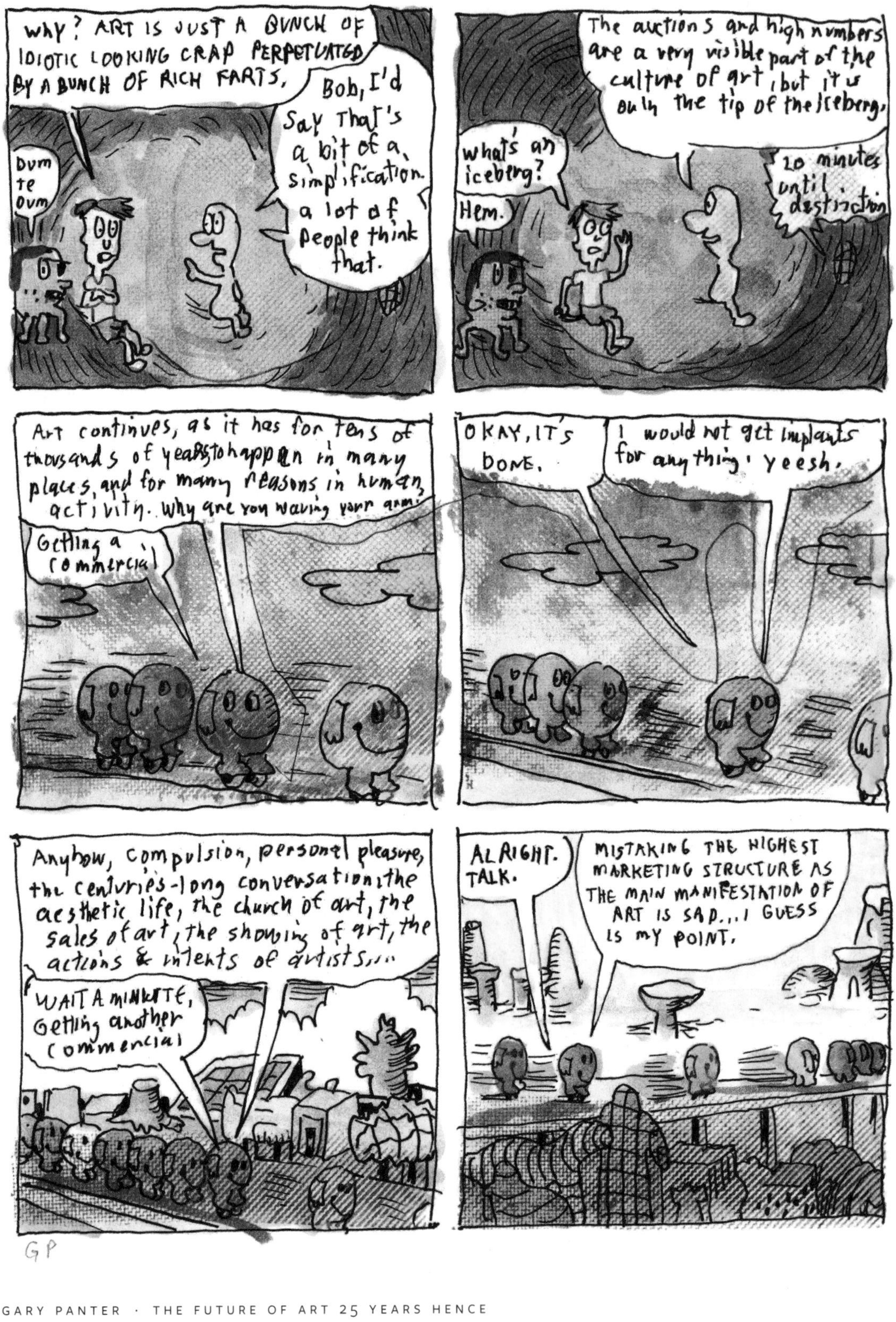

why? ART IS JUST A BUNCH OF IDIOTIC LOOKING CRAP PERPETUATED BY A BUNCH OF RICH FARTS.
Dum te dum
Bob, I'd say That's a bit of a simplification. a lot of people think that.
The auctions and high numbers are a very visible part of the culture of art, but it is only the tip of the iceberg.
what's an iceberg?
Hem.
20 minutes until destruction
Art continues, as it has for tens of thousands of years, to happen in many places, and for many reasons in human activity. Why are you waving your arm?
Getting a commercial
OKAY, IT'S DONE.
I would not get implants for anything! yeesh.
Anyhow, compulsion, personal pleasure, the centuries-long conversation, the aesthetic life, the church of art, the sales of art, the showing of art, the actions & intents of artists...
WAIT A MINUTE, Getting another commercial
ALRIGHT. TALK.
MISTAKING THE HIGHEST MARKETING STRUCTURE AS THE MAIN MANIFESTATION OF ART IS SAD... I GUESS IS MY POINT.
GP

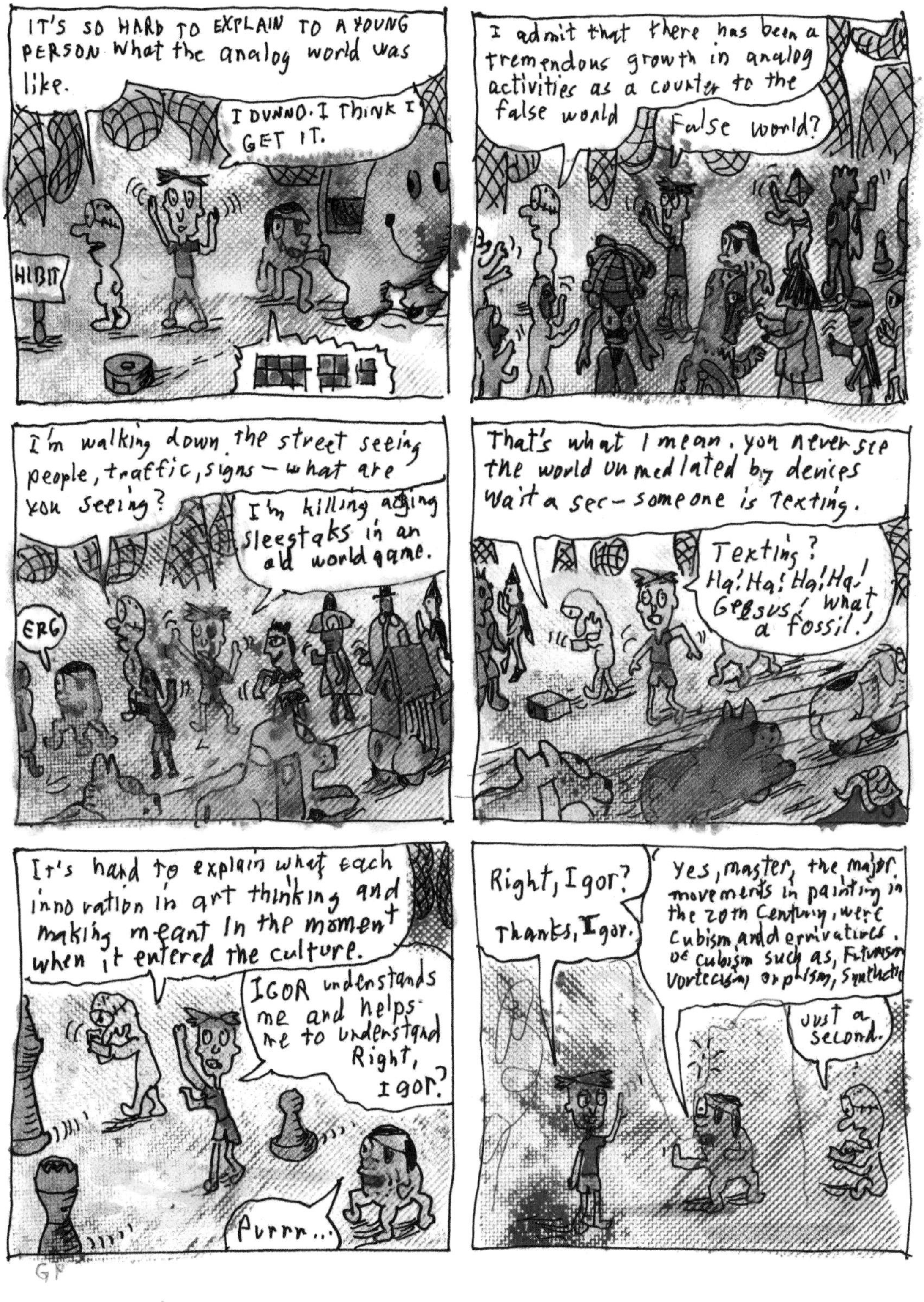
IT'S SO HARD TO EXPLAIN TO A YOUNG PERSON what the analog world was like.
I DUNNO. I THINK I GET IT.
I admit that there has been a tremendous growth in analog activities as a counter to the false world
False world?
I'm walking down the street seeing people, traffic, signs — what are you seeing?
I'm killing aging sleestaks in an old world game.
ERG
That's what I mean. you never see the world unmediated by devices wait a sec — someone is texting.
Texting? Ha! Ha! Ha! Ha! Geesus! what a fossil!
It's hard to explain what each innovation in art thinking and making meant in the moment when it entered the culture.
IGOR understands me and helps me to understand Right, Igor?
Purrr...
Right, Igor?
Thanks, Igor.
Yes, master, the major movements in painting in the 20th Century, were Cubism and derivatives of cubism such as, Futurism Vorticism, orphism, Synthetic
Just a second.
GP

Art is affected by climate and the mutating technical climate is playing out in bizarre ways.

...ll

Grrr...

Grrr...

A thing that you see in everyday life and art and in the shared ground is repetition, scaling and slave labor. And television fabric.

And live imagery.

...ll = ll =

EAT

And the peculiarity of the world makes a lot of art in museums invisible.

What's it do?

PROVOCATIONS BECAME THE NORM.

But if you can envision a world without these innovations in action, and you might be able to see the initial peculiarity of these artifacts.

Hard to imagine.

You can almost imagine it by looking at the resurgence of shaker style,

Well, I can see that the world looks complicated. O.K.

Can you turn that game off for a while so you stop waving?

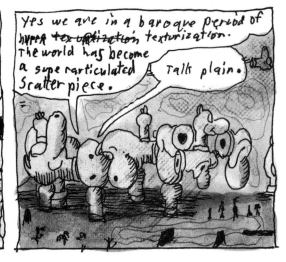

Yes we are in a baroque period of hyper tex articization texturization. The world has become a super articulated scatter piece.

Talk plain.

G.P

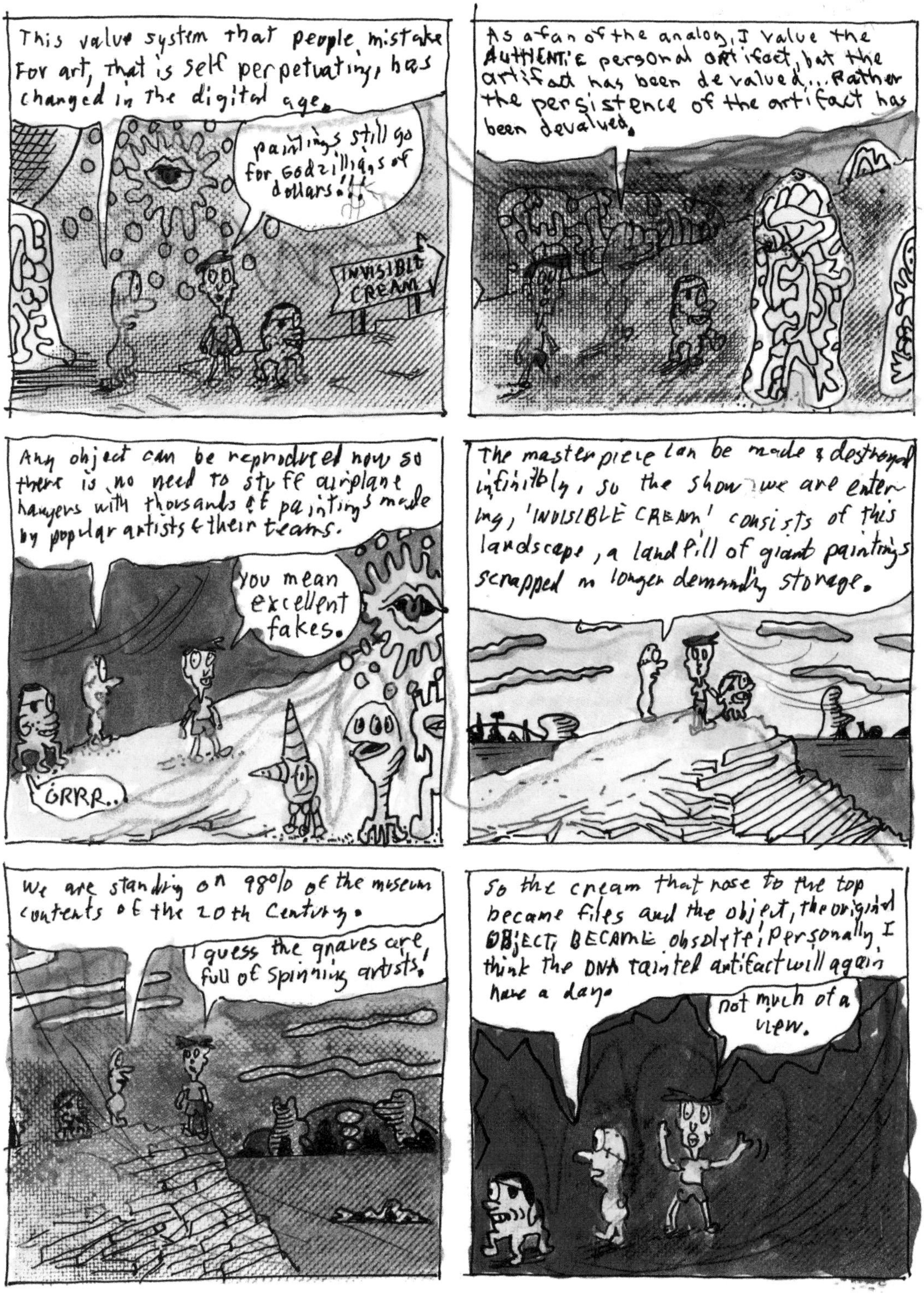
This value system that people mistake For art, that is self perpetuating, has changed in the digital age.
paintings still go for Godzilliags of dollars!!!
INVISIBLE CREAM
As a fan of the analog, I value the AUTHENTIC personal artifact, but the artifact has been devalued... Rather the persistence of the artifact has been devalued.
Any object can be reproduced now so there is no need to stuff airplane hangers with thousands of paintings made by popular artists & their teams.
You mean excellent fakes.
GRRR..
The masterpiece can be made & destroyed infinitbly, so the show we are entering, 'INVISIBLE CREAM' consists of this landscape, a landfill of giant paintings scrapped no longer demanding storage.
We are standing on 98% of the museum contents of the 20th Century.
I guess the graves are full of spinning artists!
So the cream that rose to the top became files and the object, the original OBJECT, BECAME obsolete; Personally, I think the DNA tainted artifact will again have a day.
not much of a view.

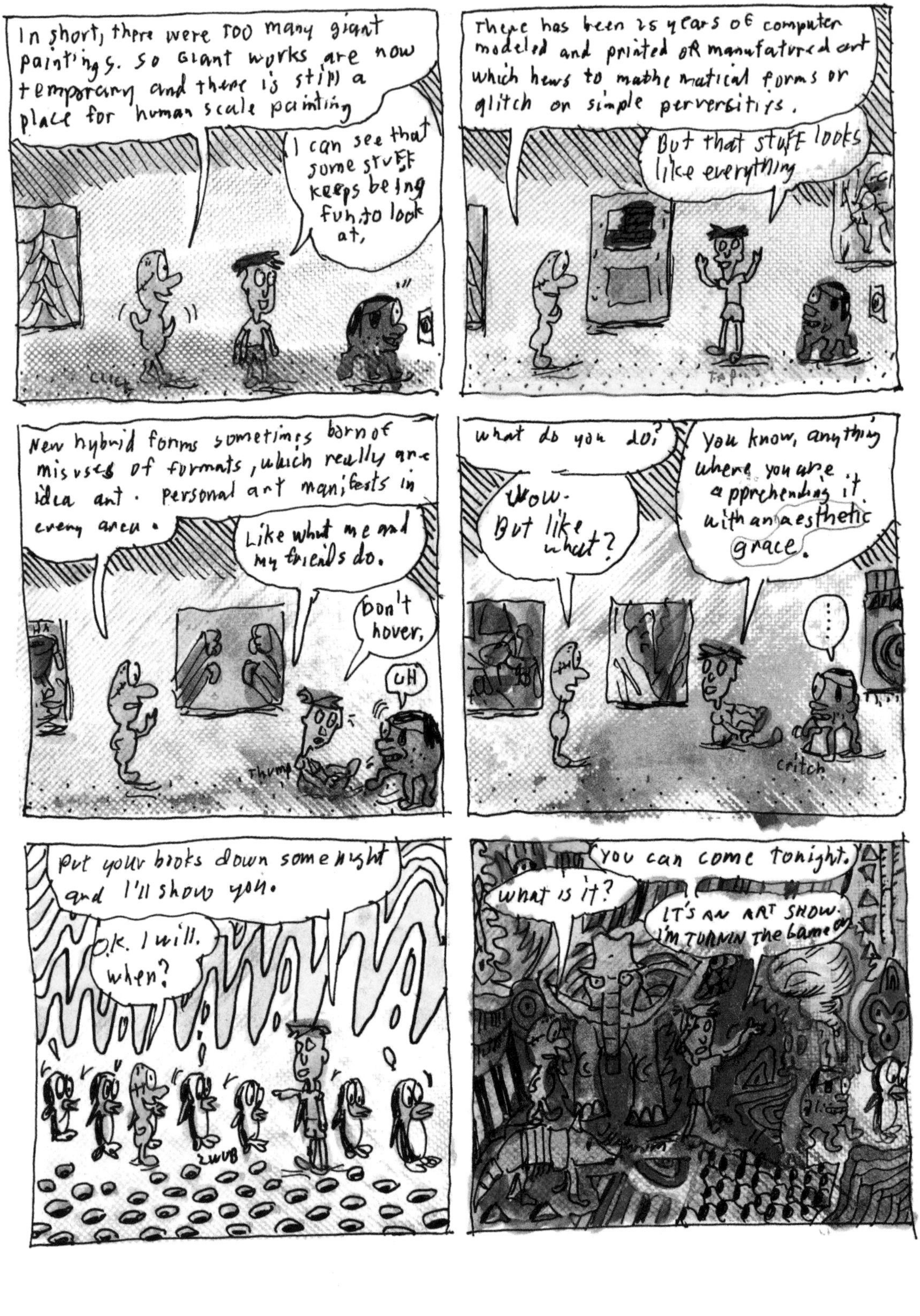
In short, there were TOO many giant paintings. So GIANT works are now temporary and there is still a place for human scale painting
I can see that some STUFF keeps being fun to look at,
CLICK
There has been 25 years of computer modeled and printed OR manufatured art which hews to mathematical forms or glitch on simple perversities.
But that STUFF looks like everything
TAP
New hybrid forms sometimes born of misuses of formats, which really are idea art. personal art manifests in every area.
Like what me and my friends do.
Don't hover,
UH
Thump
what do you do?
Wow. But like what?
You know, anything where you are apprehending it with an aesthetic grace.
.....
critch
Put your books down some night and I'll show you.
O.K. I will. when?
ZWUB
You can come tonight.
what is it?
IT'S AN ART SHOW. I'M TURNIN The Game on

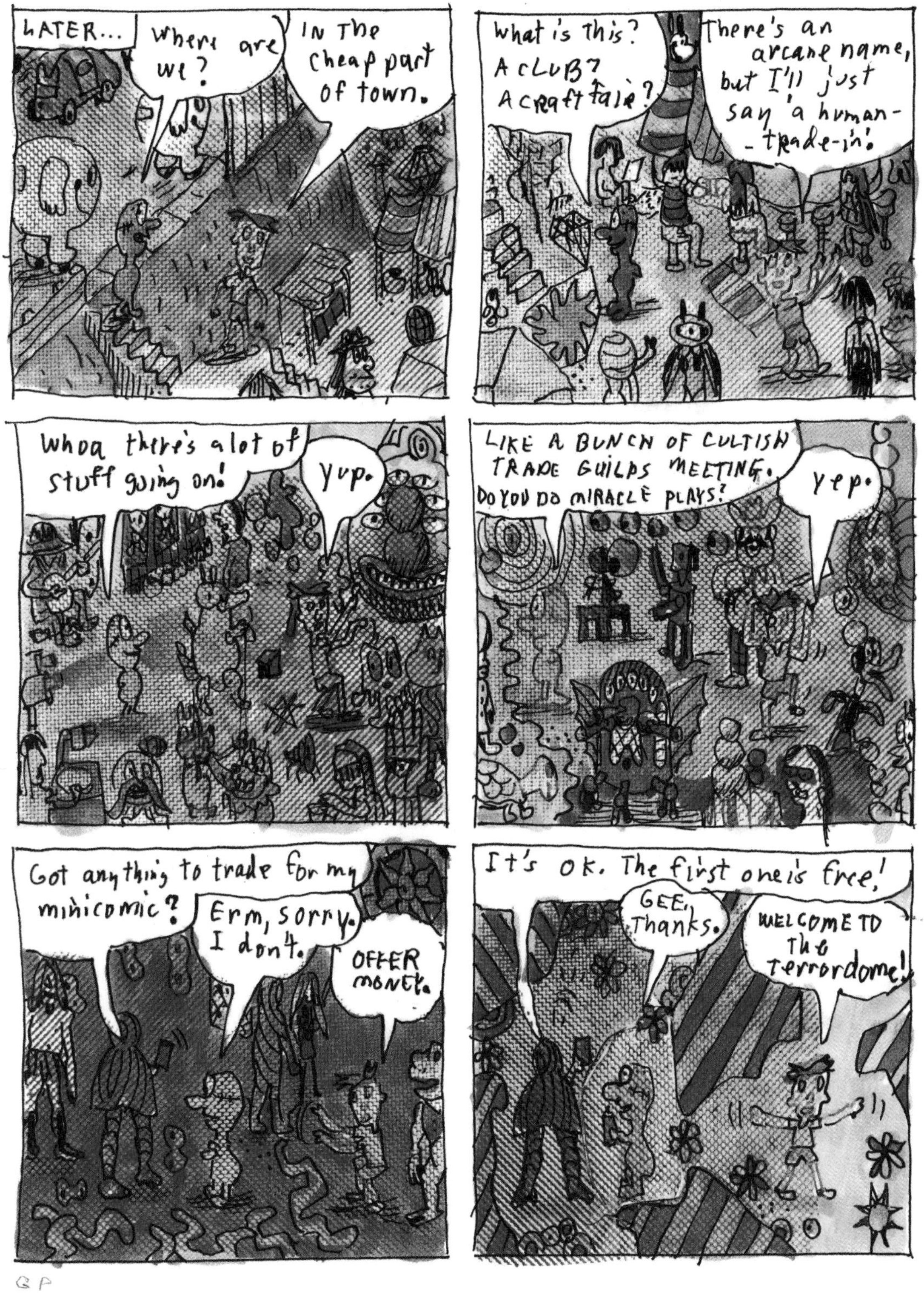
LATER...
Where are we?
In the cheap part of town.
What is this? A CLUB? A craft fair?
There's an arcane name, but I'll just say 'a human-trade-in'.
Whoa there's alot of stuff going on!
yup.
LIKE A BUNCH OF CULTISH TRADE GUILDS MEETING. DO YOU DO MIRACLE PLAYS?
yep.
Got anything to trade for my minicomic?
Erm, sorry. I don't.
OFFER MONEY.
It's OK. The first one is free!
GEE, Thanks.
WELCOME TO THE terrordome!
GP

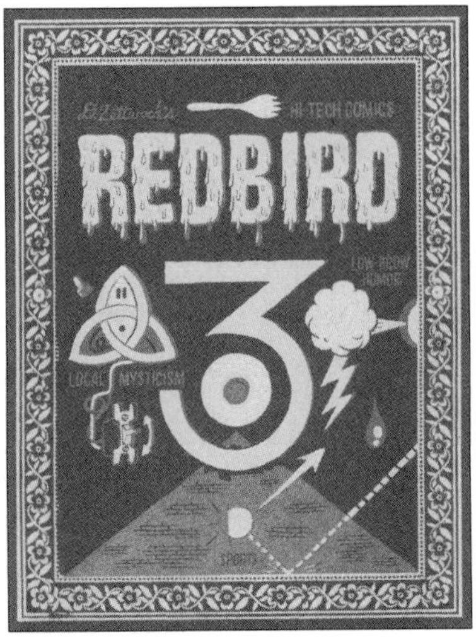
HI-TECH COMICS
REDBIRD
LOW-BROW HUMOR
LOCAL MYSTICISM
SPORTS

# Communications Workers of America AND Coffee Lids of Greater Old Red Falls

DAN ZETTWOCH

*originally published in*

*Redbird #3*

SELF-PUBLISHED

8.5 × 11 inches • 32 pages

## Biography

Dan Zettwoch makes slice-of-life comics, goofball illustrations, how-to diagrams, and folksy art in his house in St. Louis, Missouri. His books include *Birdseye Bristoe* (Drawn & Quarterly), *Amazing Facts & Beyond* (Uncivilized Books), and lots of self-published minicomics.
danzettwoch.com

## Statement

These strips are vignettes from Old Red River Falls, a fictional mid-southern American town founded on the banks of an ancient river and a modern interstate trucking route. Change has come to town in the form of cell-phone towers, big chain gas stations, corporate live-bait shops, and megachurches. Some local residents are trying to figure out how it all works.

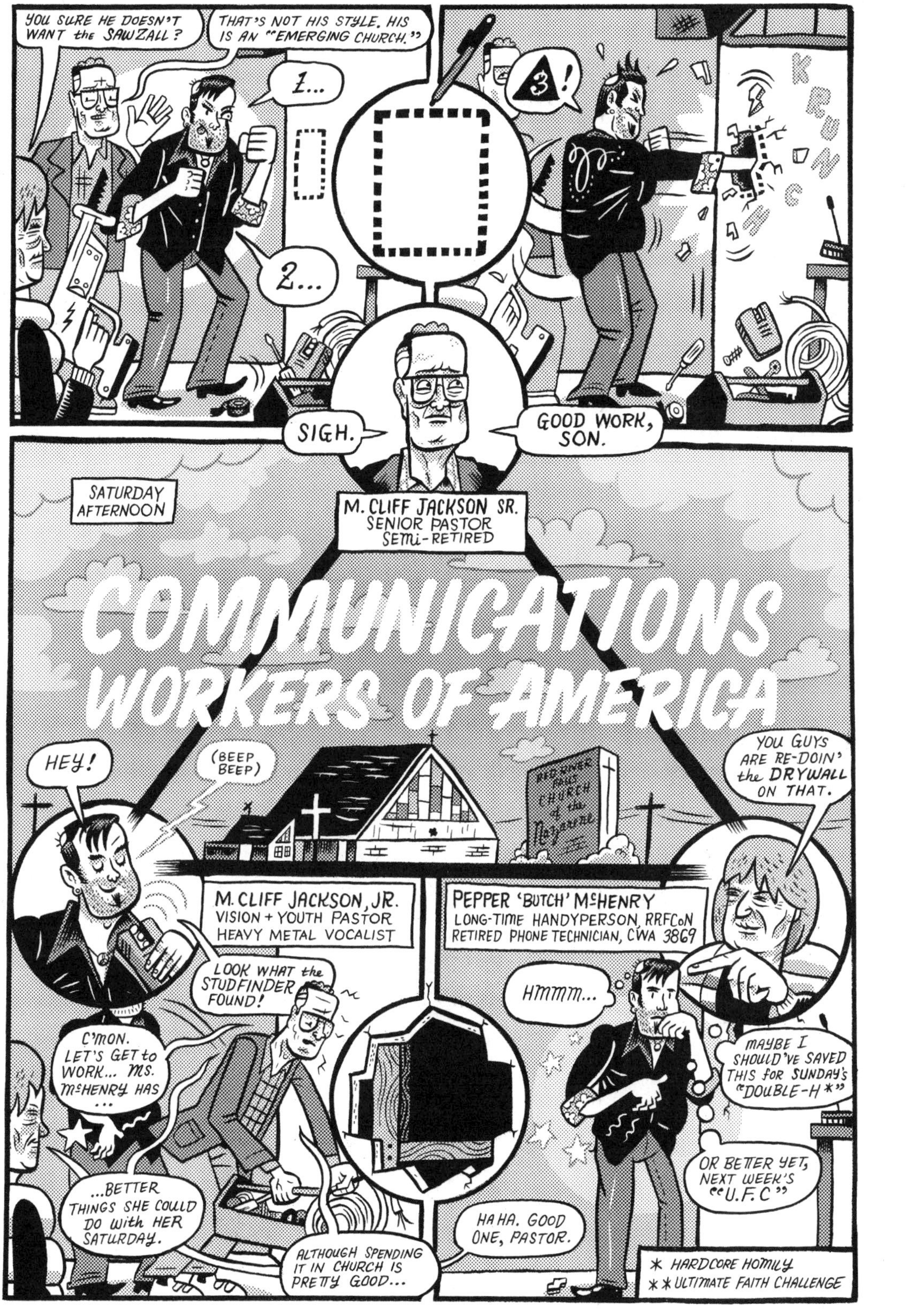

YOU SURE HE DOESN'T WANT the SAWZALL?
THAT'S NOT HIS STYLE. HIS IS AN "EMERGING CHURCH."
1...
2...
3!
KRUNCH
SIGH.
GOOD WORK, SON.
M. CLIFF JACKSON SR. SENIOR PASTOR SEMI-RETIRED
SATURDAY AFTERNOON
COMMUNICATIONS WORKERS OF AMERICA
RED RIVER FALLS CHURCH of the Nazarene
HEY!
(BEEP BEEP)
YOU GUYS ARE RE-DOIN' the DRYWALL ON THAT.
M. CLIFF JACKSON, JR. VISION + YOUTH PASTOR HEAVY METAL VOCALIST
PEPPER 'BUTCH' McHENRY LONG-TIME HANDYPERSON, RRFCoN RETIRED PHONE TECHNICIAN, CWA 3869
LOOK WHAT the STUDFINDER FOUND!
HMMM...
C'MON. LET'S GET to WORK... MS. McHENRY HAS ...
...BETTER THINGS SHE COULD DO with HER SATURDAY.
ALTHOUGH SPENDING IT IN CHURCH IS PRETTY GOOD...
MAYBE I SHOULD'VE SAVED THIS for SUNDAY's "DOUBLE-H*"
OR BETTER YET, NEXT WEEK'S "U.F.C**"
HA HA. GOOD ONE, PASTOR.
* HARDCORE HOMILY
** ULTIMATE FAITH CHALLENGE

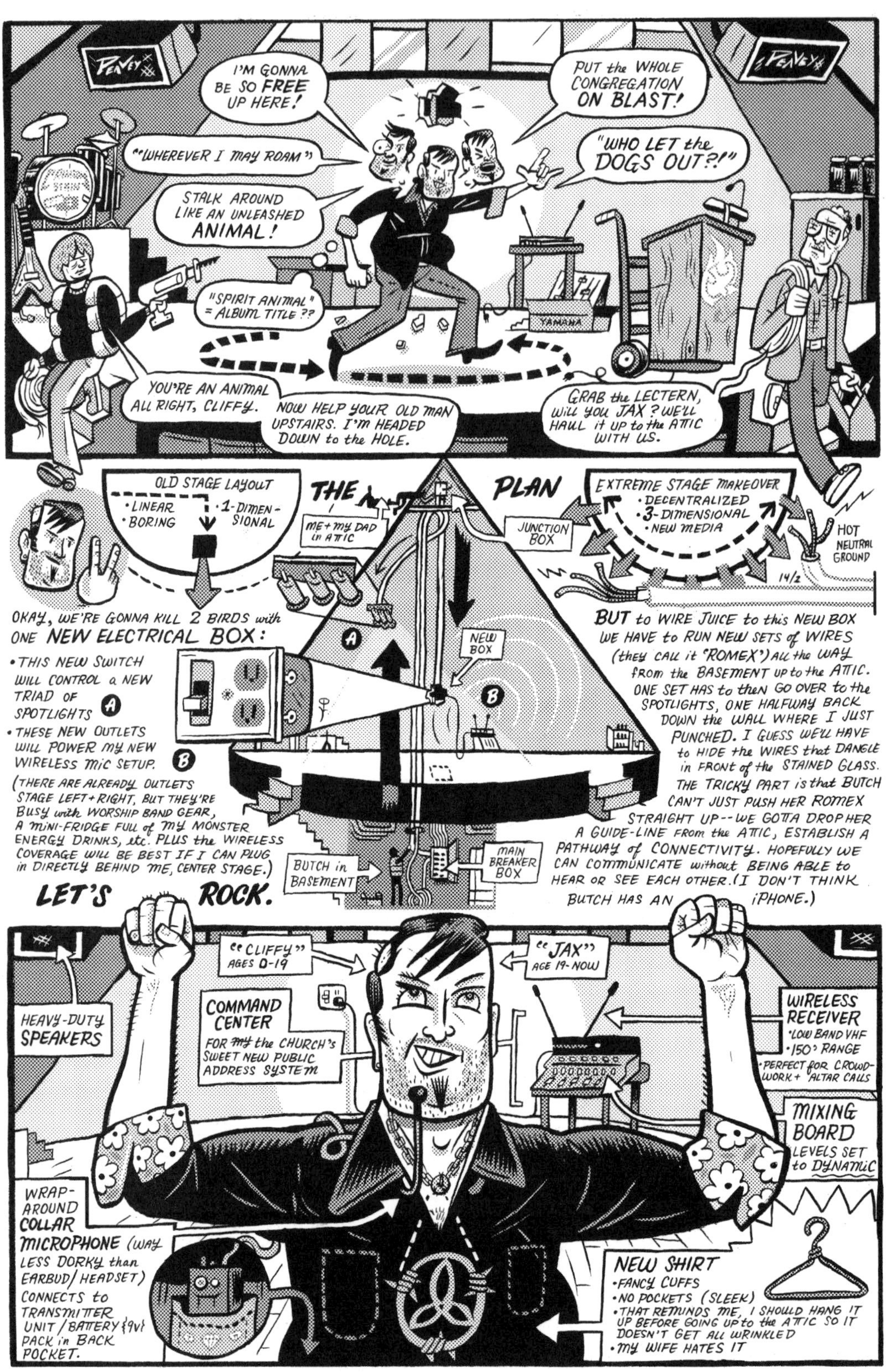

PEAVEY
I'M GONNA BE SO FREE UP HERE!
PUT the WHOLE CONGREGATION ON BLAST!
"WHEREVER I MAY ROAM"
"WHO LET the DOGS OUT?!"
STALK AROUND LIKE AN UNLEASHED ANIMAL!
"SPIRIT ANIMAL" = ALBUM TITLE ??
YAMAHA
YOU'RE AN ANIMAL ALL RIGHT, CLIFFY.
NOW HELP YOUR OLD MAN UPSTAIRS. I'M HEADED DOWN to the HOLE.
GRAB the LECTERN, WILL YOU JAX? WE'LL HAUL it UP to the ATTIC WITH US.
THE PLAN
OLD STAGE LAYOUT
·LINEAR ·BORING ·1-DIMENSIONAL
EXTREME STAGE MAKEOVER
·DECENTRALIZED ·3-DIMENSIONAL ·NEW MEDIA
ME + MY DAD in ATTIC
JUNCTION BOX
HOT NEUTRAL GROUND
14/2
OKAY, WE'RE GONNA KILL 2 BIRDS with ONE NEW ELECTRICAL BOX:
•THIS NEW SWITCH WILL CONTROL a NEW TRIAD OF SPOTLIGHTS A
•THESE NEW OUTLETS WILL POWER MY NEW WIRELESS MIC SETUP. B
(THERE ARE ALREADY OUTLETS STAGE LEFT + RIGHT, BUT THEY'RE BUSY with WORSHIP BAND GEAR, A MINI-FRIDGE FULL of MY MONSTER ENERGY DRINKS, etc. PLUS the WIRELESS COVERAGE WILL BE BEST IF I CAN PLUG in DIRECTLY BEHIND ME, CENTER STAGE.)
NEW BOX
A
B
BUT to WIRE JUICE to this NEW BOX WE HAVE to RUN NEW SETS of WIRES (they call it "ROMEX") ALL the WAY from the BASEMENT UP to the ATTIC. ONE SET HAS to then GO OVER to the SPOTLIGHTS, ONE HALFWAY BACK DOWN the WALL WHERE I JUST PUNCHED. I GUESS WE'LL HAVE to HIDE the WIRES that DANGLE in FRONT of the STAINED GLASS. THE TRICKY PART is that BUTCH CAN'T JUST PUSH HER ROMEX STRAIGHT UP--WE GOTTA DROP HER A GUIDE-LINE from the ATTIC, ESTABLISH A PATHWAY of CONNECTIVITY. HOPEFULLY WE CAN COMMUNICATE without BEING ABLE to HEAR OR SEE EACH OTHER. (I DON'T THINK BUTCH HAS AN iPHONE.)
BUTCH in BASEMENT
MAIN BREAKER BOX
LET'S ROCK.
"CLIFFY" AGES 0-19
"JAX" AGE 19-NOW
HEAVY-DUTY SPEAKERS
COMMAND CENTER
FOR MY the CHURCH'S SWEET NEW PUBLIC ADDRESS SYSTEM
WIRELESS RECEIVER
·LOW BAND VHF
·150' RANGE
·PERFECT for CROWD-WORK + ALTAR CALLS
MIXING BOARD LEVELS SET to DYNAMIC
WRAP-AROUND COLLAR MICROPHONE (WAY LESS DORKY than EARBUD/HEADSET) CONNECTS to TRANSMITTER UNIT/BATTERY {9V} PACK in BACK POCKET.
NEW SHIRT
•FANCY CUFFS
•NO POCKETS (SLEEK)
•THAT REMINDS ME, I SHOULD HANG IT UP BEFORE GOING UP to the ATTIC SO IT DOESN'T GET ALL WRINKLED
•MY WIFE HATES IT

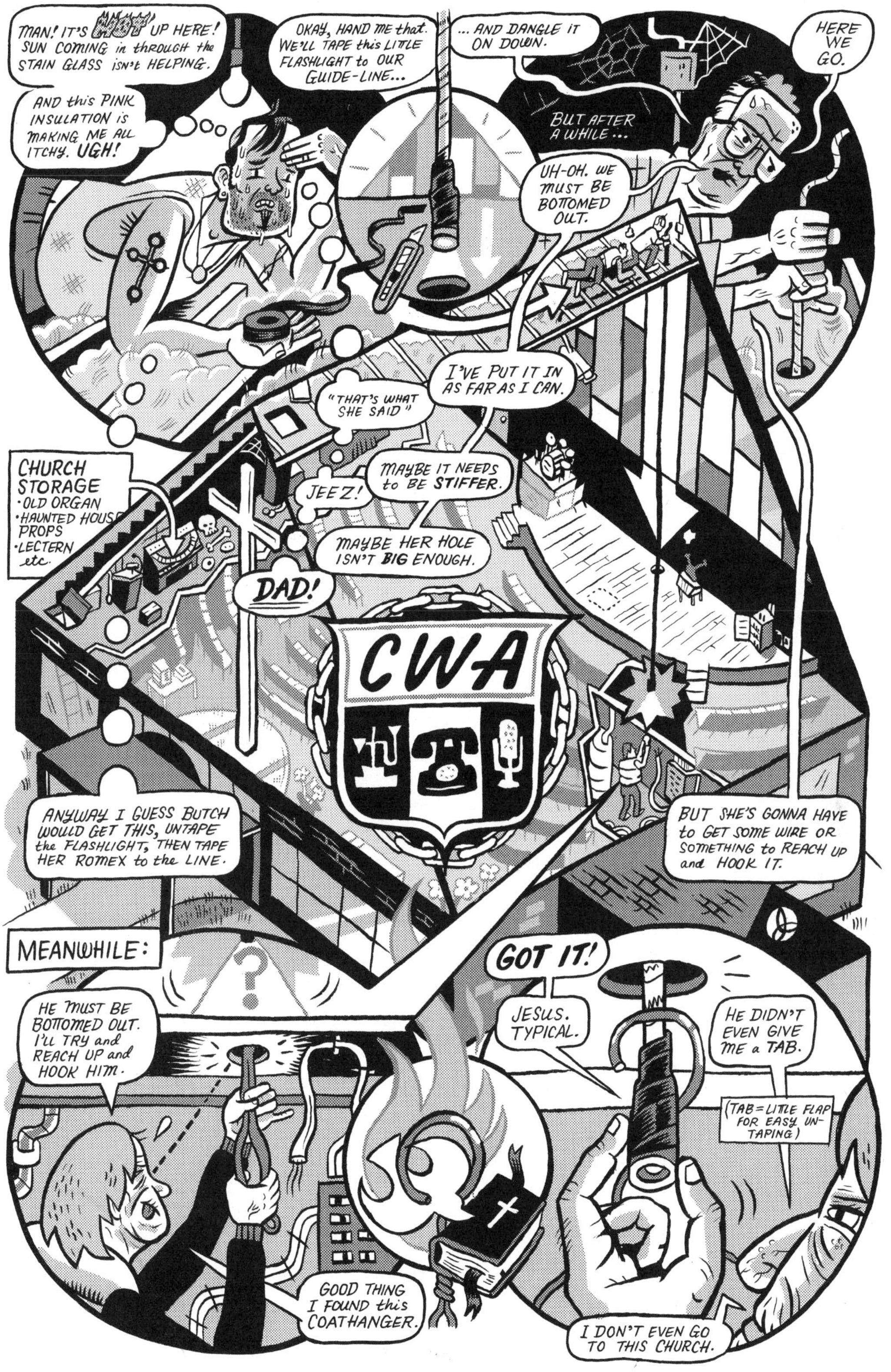
MAN! IT'S HOT UP HERE! SUN COMING in through the STAIN GLASS isn't HELPING.
AND this PINK INSULATION is MAKING ME ALL ITCHY. UGH!
OKAY, HAND ME that. WE'LL TAPE this LITTLE FLASHLIGHT to OUR GUIDE-LINE...
...AND DANGLE IT ON DOWN.
BUT AFTER A WHILE...
HERE WE GO.
UH-OH. WE MUST BE BOTTOMED OUT.
I'VE PUT IT IN AS FAR AS I CAN.
"THAT'S WHAT SHE SAID"
CHURCH STORAGE
•OLD ORGAN
•HAUNTED HOUSE PROPS
•LECTERN
etc.
JEEZ!
MAYBE IT NEEDS to BE STIFFER.
MAYBE HER HOLE ISN'T BIG ENOUGH.
DAD!
CWA
ANYWAY I GUESS BUTCH WOULD GET THIS, UNTAPE the FLASHLIGHT, THEN TAPE HER ROMEX to the LINE.
BUT SHE'S GONNA HAVE to GET SOME WIRE OR SOMETHING to REACH UP and HOOK IT.
MEANWHILE:
HE MUST BE BOTTOMED OUT. I'LL TRY and REACH UP and HOOK HIM.
GOT IT!
JESUS. TYPICAL.
HE DIDN'T EVEN GIVE ME a TAB.
(TAB = LITTLE FLAP FOR EASY UN-TAPING)
GOOD THING I FOUND this COATHANGER.
I DON'T EVEN GO TO THIS CHURCH.

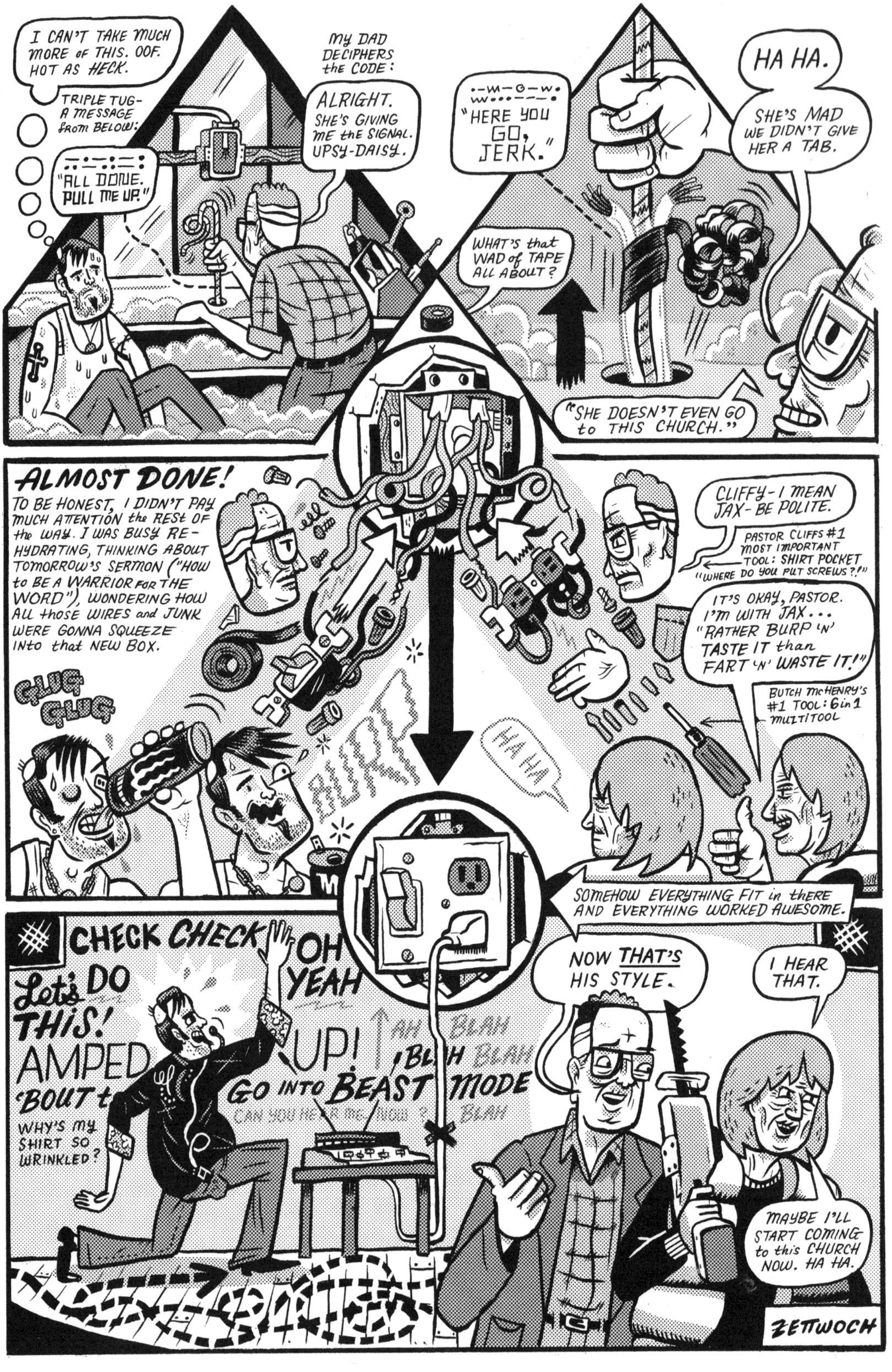
I CAN'T TAKE MUCH MORE OF THIS. OOF. HOT AS HECK.
TRIPLE TUG- A MESSAGE FROM BELOW:
"ALL DONE. PULL ME UP."
MY DAD DECIPHERS THE CODE:
ALRIGHT. SHE'S GIVING ME THE SIGNAL. UPSY-DAISY.
"HERE YOU GO, JERK."
HA HA.
SHE'S MAD WE DIDN'T GIVE HER A TAB.
WHAT'S THAT WAD OF TAPE ALL ABOUT?
"SHE DOESN'T EVEN GO TO THIS CHURCH."
ALMOST DONE!
TO BE HONEST, I DIDN'T PAY MUCH ATTENTION THE REST OF THE WAY. I WAS BUSY RE-HYDRATING, THINKING ABOUT TOMORROW'S SERMON ("HOW TO BE A WARRIOR FOR THE WORD"), WONDERING HOW ALL THOSE WIRES AND JUNK WERE GONNA SQUEEZE INTO THAT NEW BOX.
CLIFFY- I MEAN JAX- BE POLITE.
PASTOR CLIFFS #1 MOST IMPORTANT TOOL: SHIRT POCKET "WHERE DO YOU PUT SCREWS?!"
IT'S OKAY, PASTOR. I'M WITH JAX... "RATHER BURP 'N' TASTE IT THAN FART 'N' WASTE IT!"
BUTCH MCHENRY'S #1 TOOL: 6 IN 1 MULTITOOL
GLUG GLUG
BURP
HA HA
SOMEHOW EVERYTHING FIT IN THERE AND EVERYTHING WORKED AWESOME.
CHECK CHECK
OH YEAH
LET'S DO THIS!
AMPED 'BOUT
WHY'S MY SHIRT SO WRINKLED?
UP!
AH BLAH
BLAH BLAH
GO INTO BEAST MODE
CAN YOU HEAR ME NOW?
NOW THAT'S HIS STYLE.
I HEAR THAT.
MAYBE I'LL START COMING TO THIS CHURCH NOW. HA HA.
ZETTWOCH

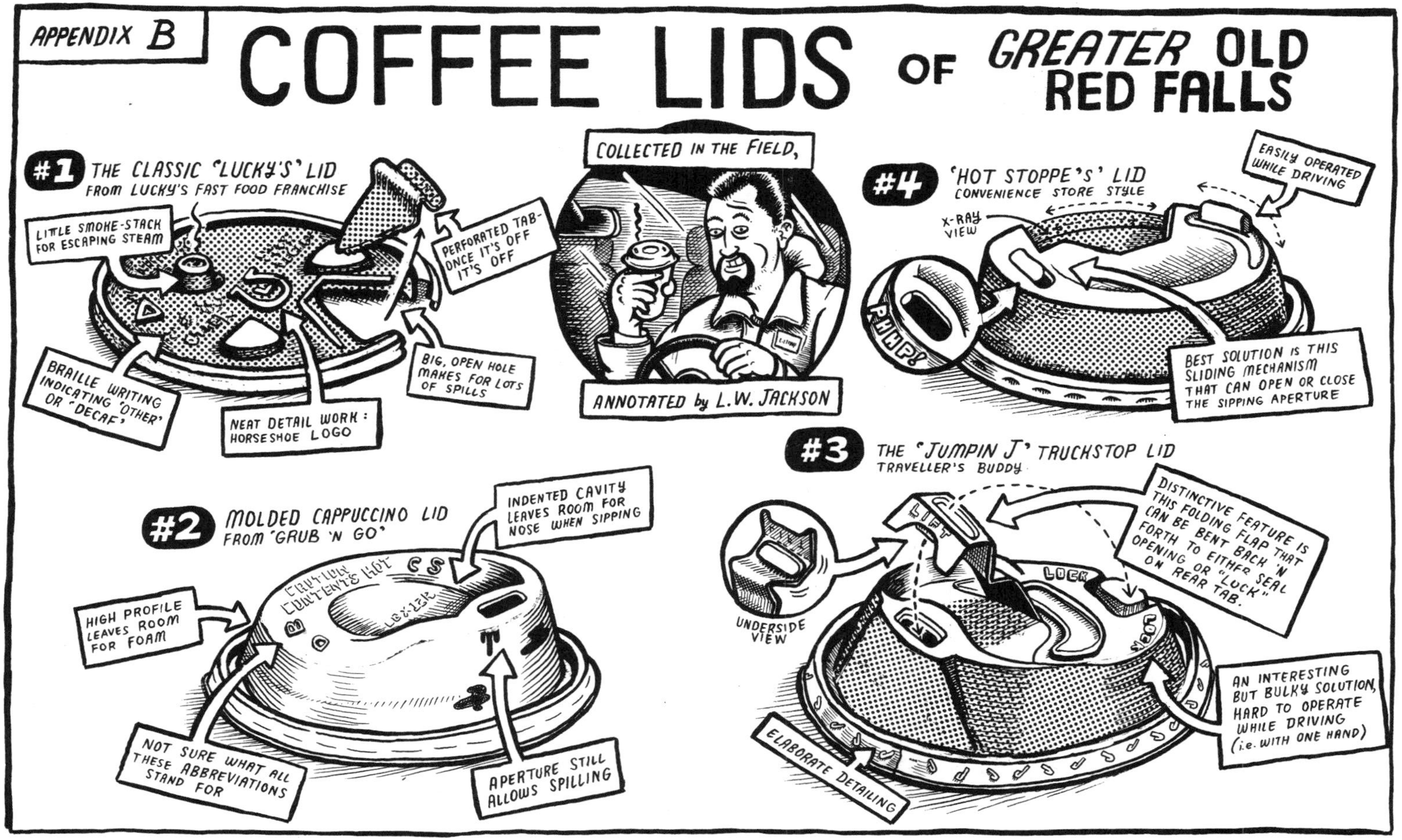
APPENDIX B
COFFEE LIDS OF GREATER OLD RED FALLS
#1 THE CLASSIC 'LUCKY'S' LID
FROM LUCKY'S FAST FOOD FRANCHISE
LITTLE SMOKE-STACK FOR ESCAPING STEAM
PERFORATED TAB- ONCE IT'S OFF IT'S OFF
BRAILLE WRITING INDICATING 'OTHER' OR 'DECAF'
NEAT DETAIL WORK: HORSESHOE LOGO
BIG, OPEN HOLE MAKES FOR LOTS OF SPILLS
COLLECTED IN THE FIELD,
ANNOTATED by L.W. JACKSON
#4 'HOT STOPPE'S' LID
CONVENIENCE STORE STYLE
X-RAY VIEW
EASILY OPERATED WHILE DRIVING
PHWP!
BEST SOLUTION IS THIS SLIDING MECHANISM THAT CAN OPEN OR CLOSE THE SIPPING APERTURE
#2 MOLDED CAPPUCCINO LID
FROM 'GRUB 'N GO'
INDENTED CAVITY LEAVES ROOM FOR NOSE WHEN SIPPING
HIGH PROFILE LEAVES ROOM FOR FOAM
CAUTION CONTENTS HOT
CS
NOT SURE WHAT ALL THESE ABBREVIATIONS STAND FOR
APERTURE STILL ALLOWS SPILLING
#3 THE 'JUMPIN J' TRUCKSTOP LID
TRAVELLER'S BUDDY
DISTINCTIVE FEATURE IS THIS FOLDING FLAP THAT CAN BE BENT BACK 'N FORTH TO EITHER SEAL OPENING OR "LOCK" ON REAR TAB.
LIFT
LOCK
UNDERSIDE VIEW
AN INTERESTING BUT BULKY SOLUTION, HARD TO OPERATE WHILE DRIVING (i.e. WITH ONE HAND)
ELABORATE DETAILING

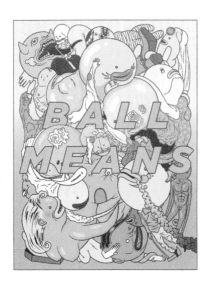

# Get In Where U Fit In AND Molt

## BEN DUNCAN

*originally published in*

*Ball Means*, vol. 1
SELF-PUBLISHED
9 × 12 inches · 64 pages

## Biography

Ben Duncan is an artist out of Vancouver, Canada. His narratives of transformation and metamorphosis include thematic outings such as large-scale entities being overrun by tiny arbiters, continued existence in extreme physical and mental states that initially seemed convincingly fatal, and heinous monsters revealing their own insecurities and affirmations through surprisingly tender displays of articulation. He presents the beauty of what lies on the inside of a sentient being, either by showing it split down the middle with its body halved and flopped open butterfly-style, or by the honest effort of its own expression. Often the former is conveyed with more ease, but it is the latter that lies at the heart of his most ardent desire as a creator.
benduncanmadeit.com

## Statement

These two comics, both reprinted from a personal anthology of short strips (*Ball Means* #1), tackle issues of metamorphoses in different ways. "Get In Where U Fit In" presents a lighthearted take on a debaucherous orgy in which a nervous protagonist ponders his ability to rise to the occasion; "Molt," on the other hand, depicts a man's personal paradigm shift as a result of biological reconfiguration.

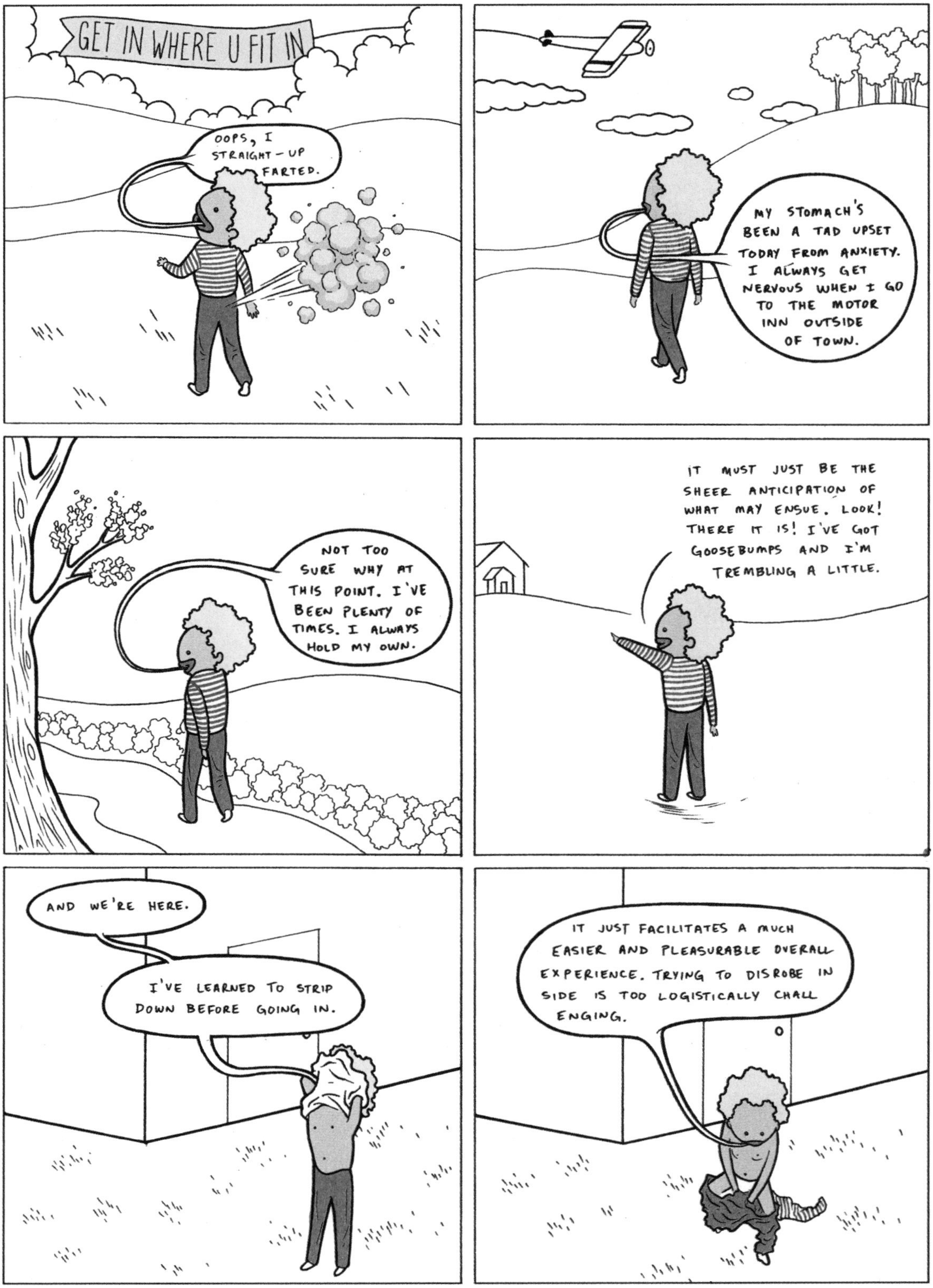
GET IN WHERE U FIT IN
OOPS, I STRAIGHT-UP FARTED.
MY STOMACH'S BEEN A TAD UPSET TODAY FROM ANXIETY. I ALWAYS GET NERVOUS WHEN I GO TO THE MOTOR INN OUTSIDE OF TOWN.
NOT TOO SURE WHY AT THIS POINT. I'VE BEEN PLENTY OF TIMES. I ALWAYS HOLD MY OWN.
IT MUST JUST BE THE SHEER ANTICIPATION OF WHAT MAY ENSUE. LOOK! THERE IT IS! I'VE GOT GOOSEBUMPS AND I'M TREMBLING A LITTLE.
AND WE'RE HERE.
I'VE LEARNED TO STRIP DOWN BEFORE GOING IN.
IT JUST FACILITATES A MUCH EASIER AND PLEASURABLE OVERALL EXPERIENCE. TRYING TO DISROBE IN SIDE IS TOO LOGISTICALLY CHALL ENGING.

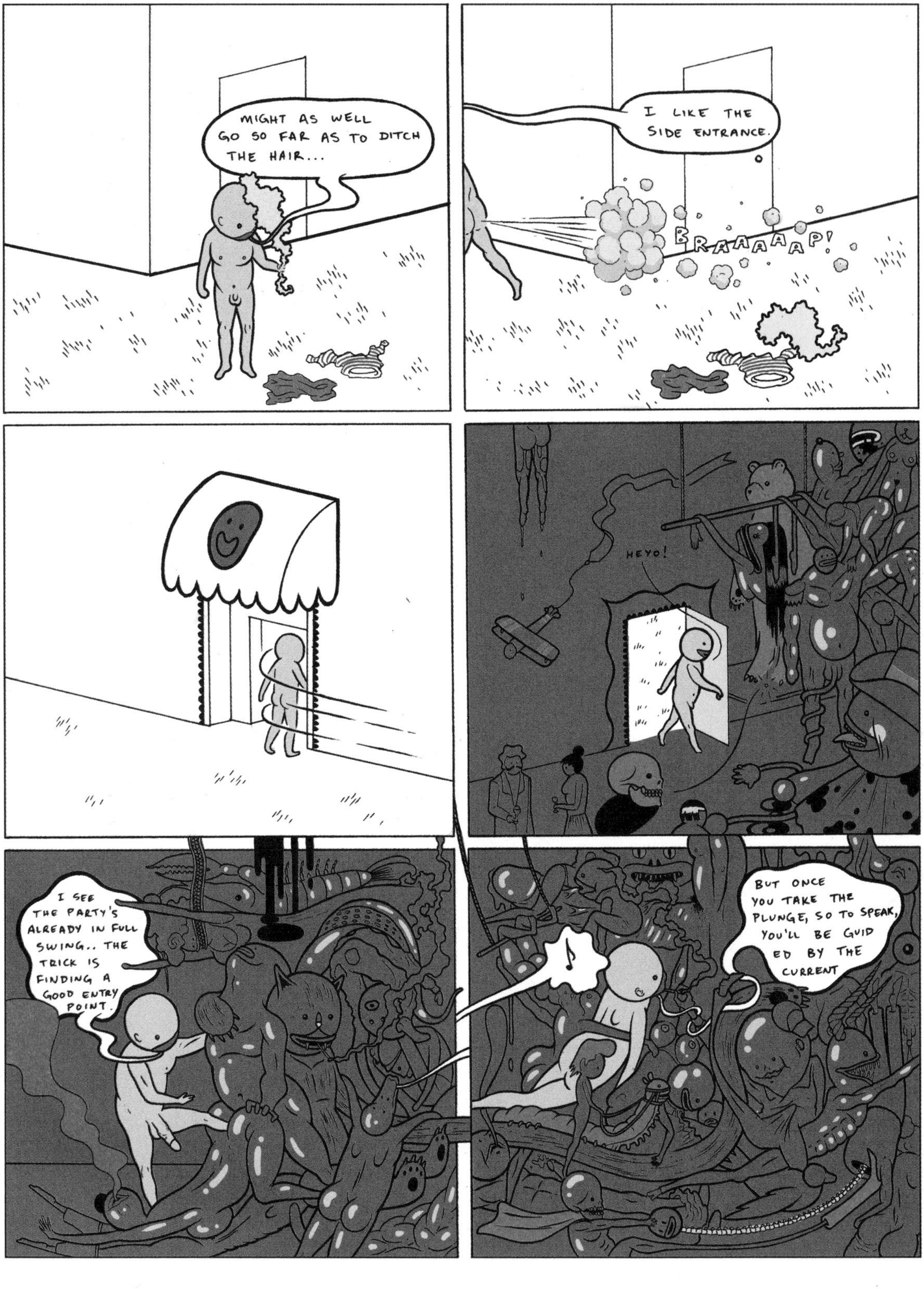
MIGHT AS WELL GO SO FAR AS TO DITCH THE HAIR...
I LIKE THE SIDE ENTRANCE.
BRAAAAAAP!
HEYO!
I SEE THE PARTY'S ALREADY IN FULL SWING.. THE TRICK IS FINDING A GOOD ENTRY POINT.
BUT ONCE YOU TAKE THE PLUNGE, SO TO SPEAK, YOU'LL BE GUIDED BY THE CURRENT

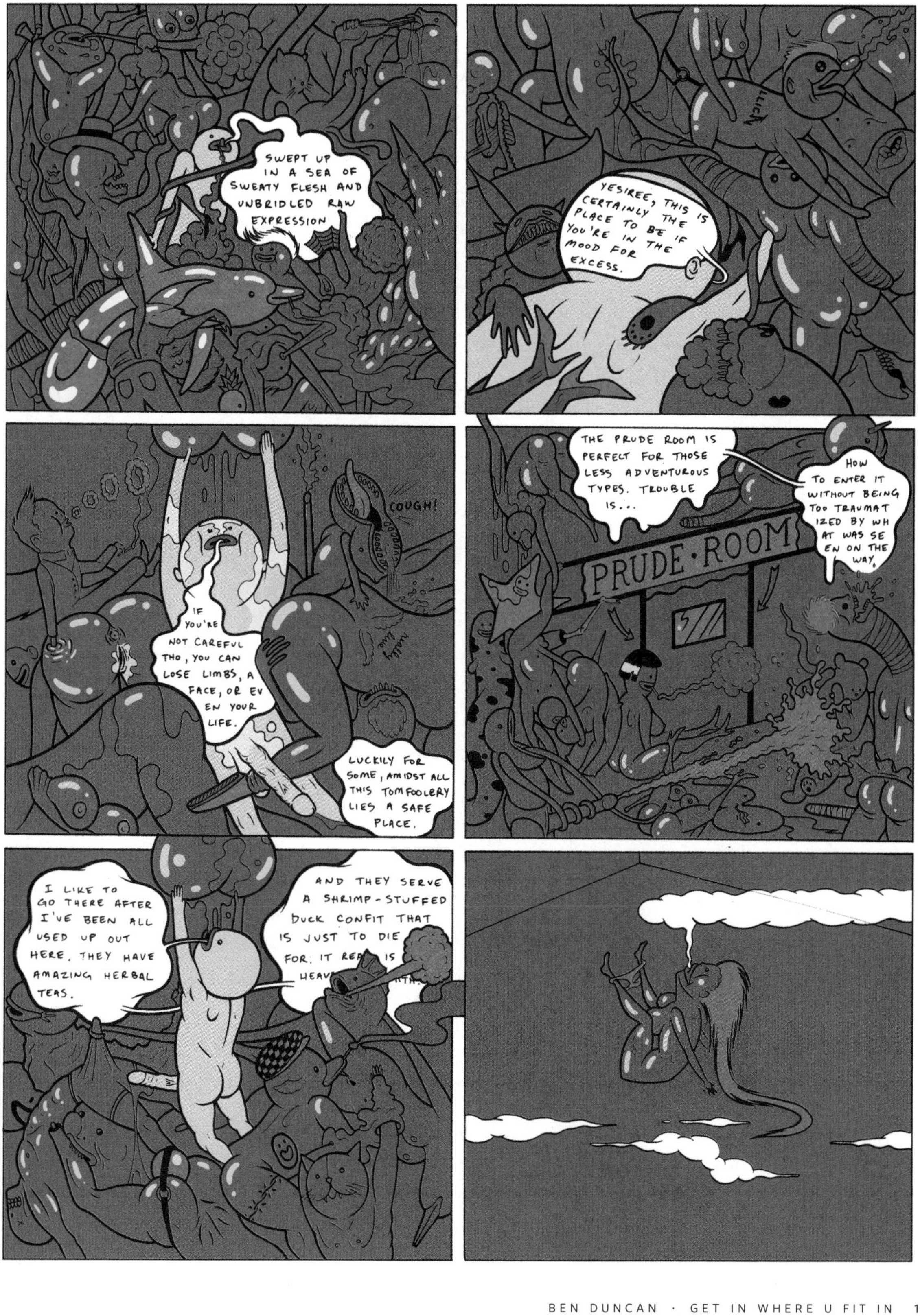
SWEPT UP IN A SEA OF SWEATY FLESH AND UNBRIDLED RAW EXPRESSION
YESIREE, THIS IS CERTAINLY THE PLACE TO BE IF YOU'RE IN THE MOOD FOR EXCESS.
COUGH!
IF YOU'RE NOT CAREFUL THO, YOU CAN LOSE LIMBS, A FACE, OR EV EN YOUR LIFE.
LUCKILY FOR SOME, AMIDST ALL THIS TOMFOOLERY LIES A SAFE PLACE.
THE PRUDE ROOM IS PERFECT FOR THOSE LESS ADVENTUROUS TYPES. TROUBLE IS...
HOW TO ENTER IT WITHOUT BEING TOO TRAUMAT IZED BY WH AT WAS SE EN ON THE WAY.
PRUDE • ROOM
I LIKE TO GO THERE AFTER I'VE BEEN ALL USED UP OUT HERE. THEY HAVE AMAZING HERBAL TEAS.
AND THEY SERVE A SHRIMP-STUFFED DUCK CONFIT THAT IS JUST TO DIE FOR.

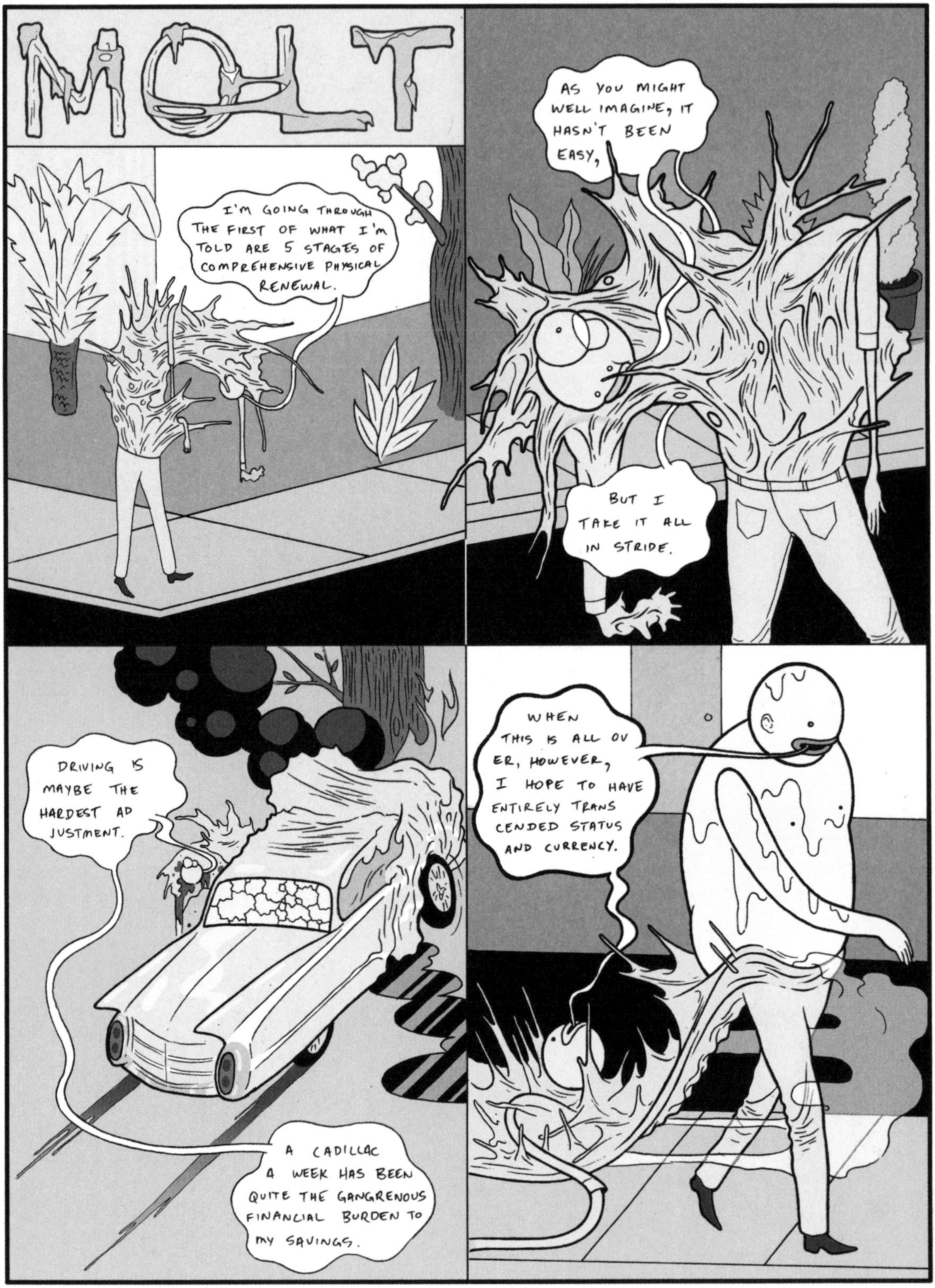
MOLT
I'M GOING THROUGH THE FIRST OF WHAT I'M TOLD ARE 5 STAGES OF COMPREHENSIVE PHYSICAL RENEWAL.
AS YOU MIGHT WELL IMAGINE, IT HASN'T BEEN EASY,
BUT I TAKE IT ALL IN STRIDE.
DRIVING IS MAYBE THE HARDEST AD JUSTMENT.
A CADILLAC A WEEK HAS BEEN QUITE THE GANGRENOUS FINANCIAL BURDEN TO MY SAVINGS.
WHEN THIS IS ALL OV ER, HOWEVER, I HOPE TO HAVE ENTIRELY TRANS CENDED STATUS AND CURRENCY.

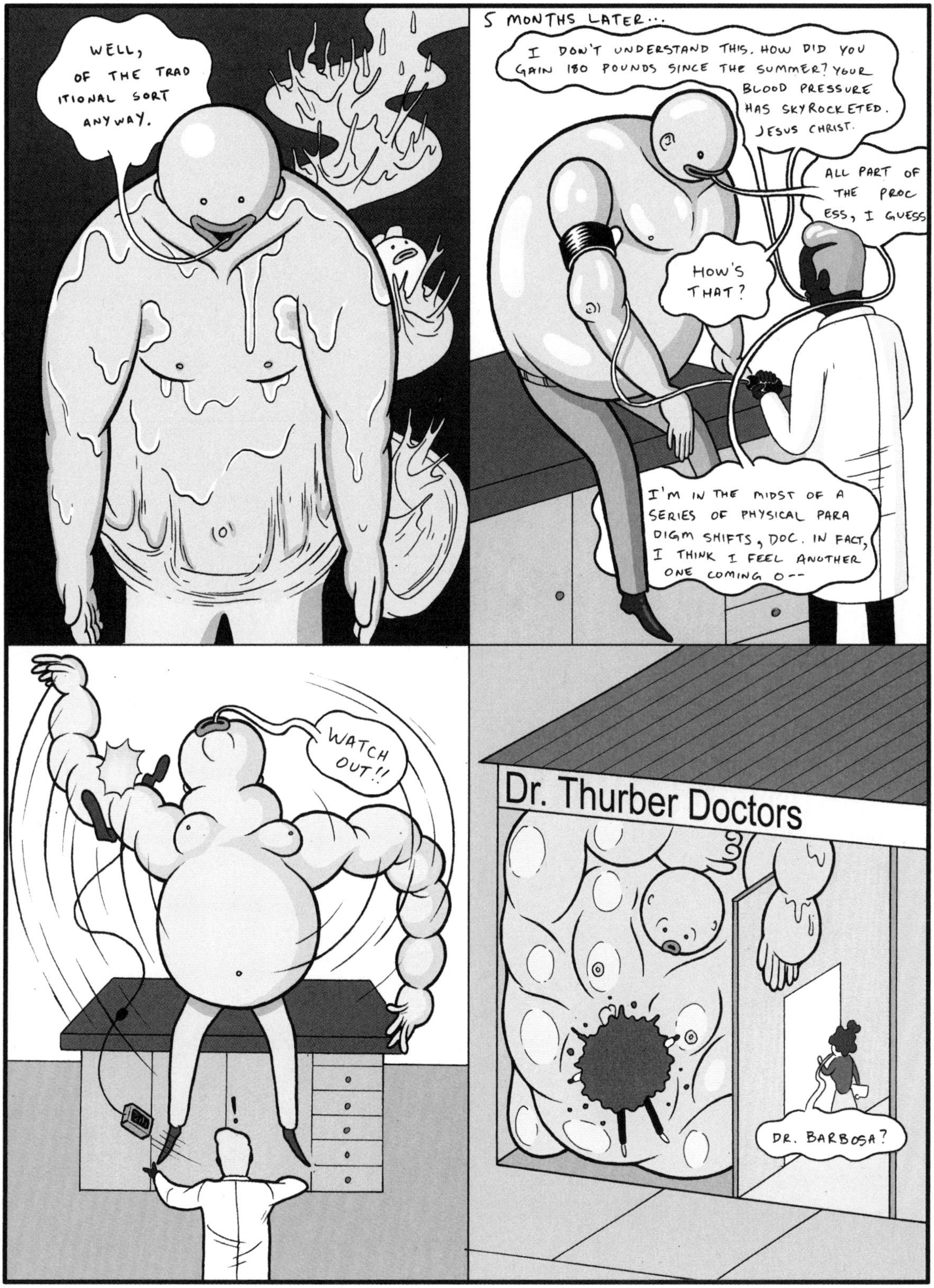
WELL, OF THE TRAD ITIONAL SORT ANYWAY.
5 MONTHS LATER...
I DON'T UNDERSTAND THIS. HOW DID YOU GAIN 180 POUNDS SINCE THE SUMMER? YOUR BLOOD PRESSURE HAS SKYROCKETED. JESUS CHRIST.
ALL PART OF THE PROC ESS, I GUESS
HOW'S THAT?
I'M IN THE MIDST OF A SERIES OF PHYSICAL PARA DIGM SHIFTS, DOC. IN FACT, I THINK I FEEL ANOTHER ONE COMING O--
WATCH OUT!!
!
Dr. Thurber Doctors
DR. BARBOSA?

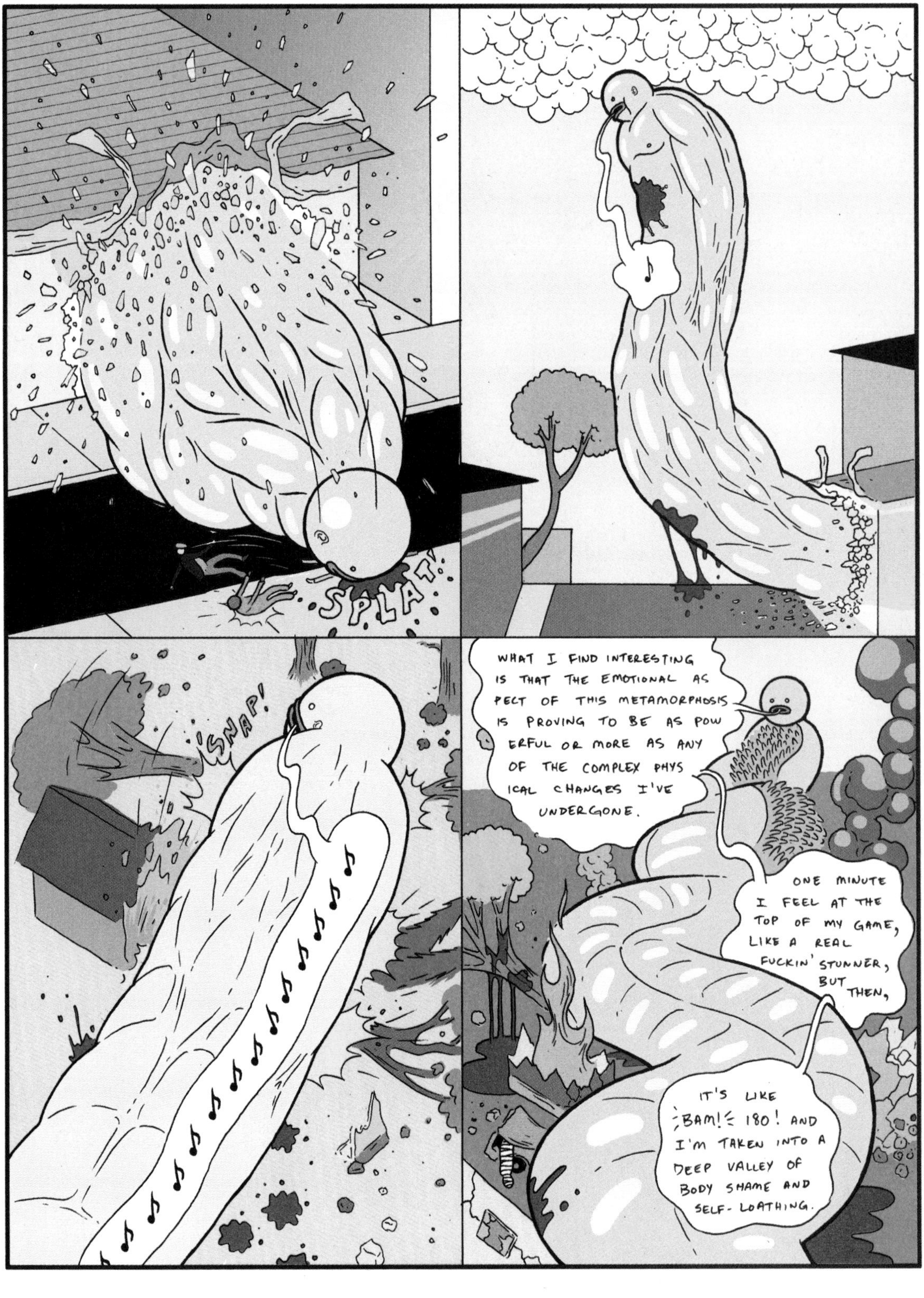
SPLAT
SNAP!
WHAT I FIND INTERESTING IS THAT THE EMOTIONAL AS PECT OF THIS METAMORPHOSIS IS PROVING TO BE AS POW ERFUL OR MORE AS ANY OF THE COMPLEX PHYS ICAL CHANGES I'VE UNDERGONE.
ONE MINUTE I FEEL AT THE TOP OF MY GAME, LIKE A REAL FUCKIN' STUNNER, BUT THEN,
IT'S LIKE BAM! 180! AND I'M TAKEN INTO A DEEP VALLEY OF BODY SHAME AND SELF-LOATHING.

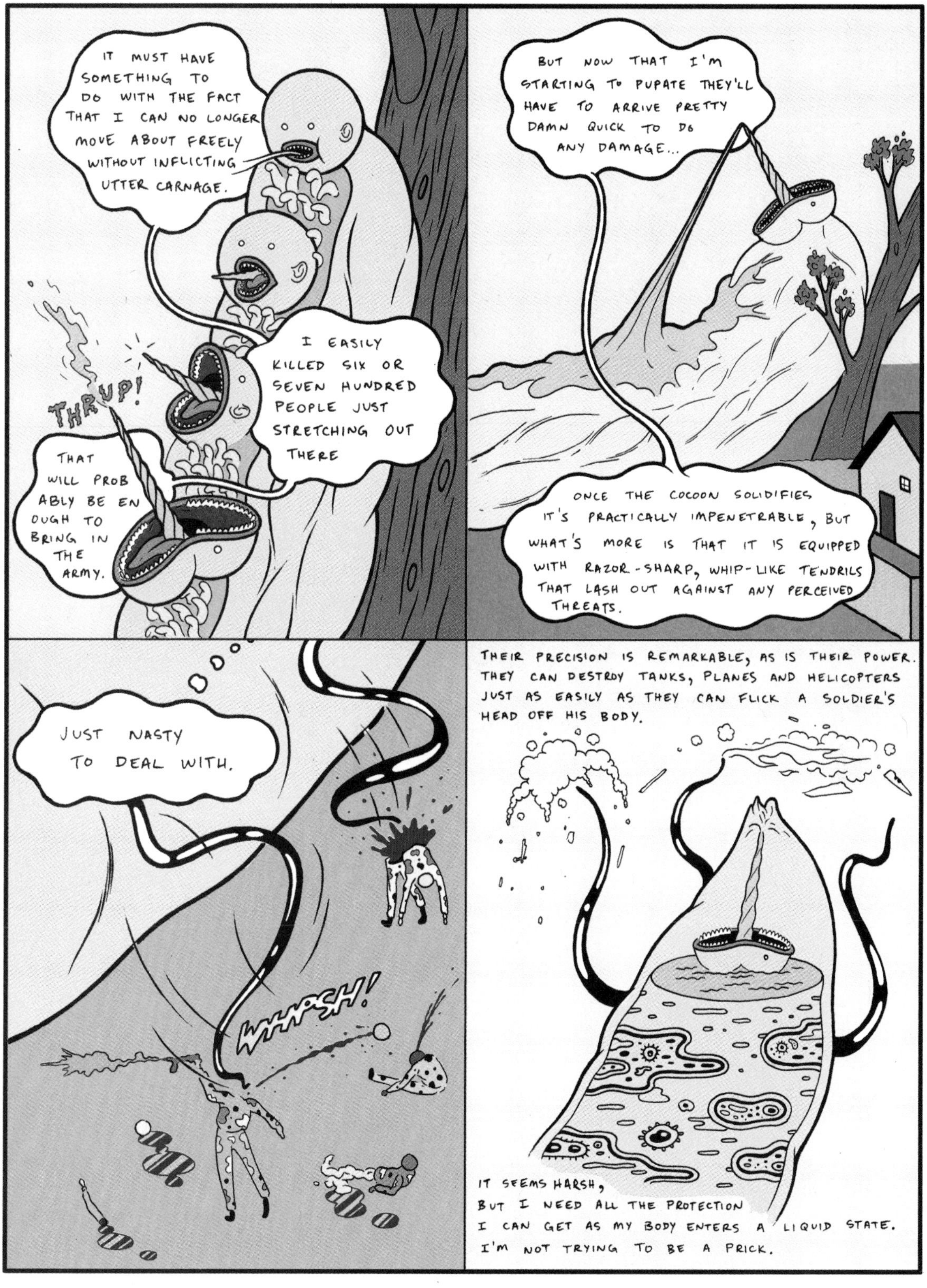
IT MUST HAVE SOMETHING TO DO WITH THE FACT THAT I CAN NO LONGER MOVE ABOUT FREELY WITHOUT INFLICTING UTTER CARNAGE.
THRUP!
I EASILY KILLED SIX OR SEVEN HUNDRED PEOPLE JUST STRETCHING OUT THERE
THAT WILL PROBABLY BE ENOUGH TO BRING IN THE ARMY.
BUT NOW THAT I'M STARTING TO PUPATE THEY'LL HAVE TO ARRIVE PRETTY DAMN QUICK TO DO ANY DAMAGE...
ONCE THE COCOON SOLIDIFIES IT'S PRACTICALLY IMPENETRABLE, BUT WHAT'S MORE IS THAT IT IS EQUIPPED WITH RAZOR-SHARP, WHIP-LIKE TENDRILS THAT LASH OUT AGAINST ANY PERCEIVED THREATS.
JUST NASTY TO DEAL WITH.
WHPSH!
THEIR PRECISION IS REMARKABLE, AS IS THEIR POWER. THEY CAN DESTROY TANKS, PLANES AND HELICOPTERS JUST AS EASILY AS THEY CAN FLICK A SOLDIER'S HEAD OFF HIS BODY.
IT SEEMS HARSH,
BUT I NEED ALL THE PROTECTION
I CAN GET AS MY BODY ENTERS A LIQUID STATE.
I'M NOT TRYING TO BE A PRICK.

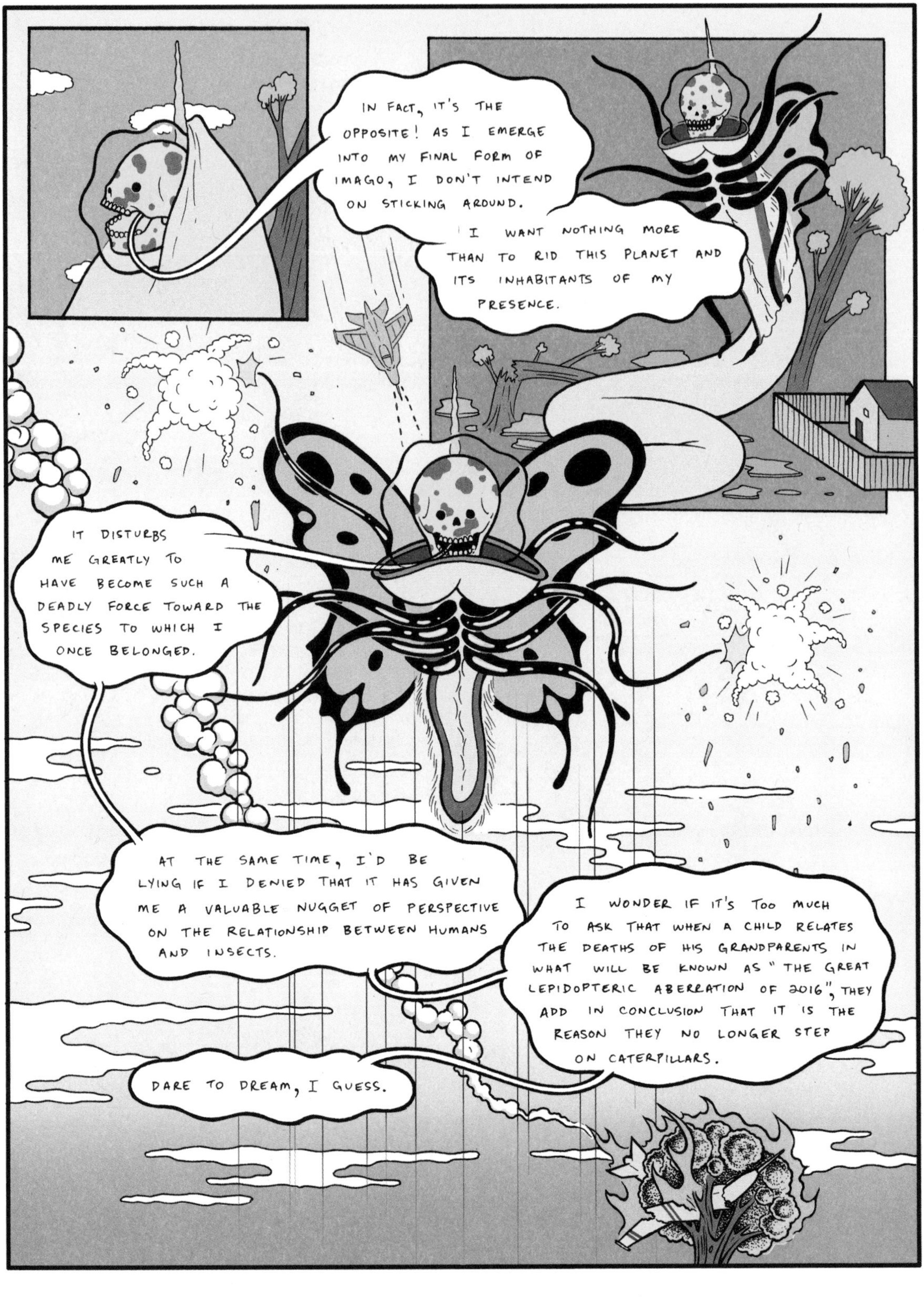
IN FACT, IT'S THE OPPOSITE! AS I EMERGE INTO MY FINAL FORM OF IMAGO, I DON'T INTEND ON STICKING AROUND.
I WANT NOTHING MORE THAN TO RID THIS PLANET AND ITS INHABITANTS OF MY PRESENCE.
IT DISTURBS ME GREATLY TO HAVE BECOME SUCH A DEADLY FORCE TOWARD THE SPECIES TO WHICH I ONCE BELONGED.
AT THE SAME TIME, I'D BE LYING IF I DENIED THAT IT HAS GIVEN ME A VALUABLE NUGGET OF PERSPECTIVE ON THE RELATIONSHIP BETWEEN HUMANS AND INSECTS.
I WONDER IF IT'S TOO MUCH TO ASK THAT WHEN A CHILD RELATES THE DEATHS OF HIS GRANDPARENTS IN WHAT WILL BE KNOWN AS "THE GREAT LEPIDOPTERIC ABERRATION OF 2016", THEY ADD IN CONCLUSION THAT IT IS THE REASON THEY NO LONGER STEP ON CATERPILLARS.
DARE TO DREAM, I GUESS.

# Shrine of the Monkey God

KIM DEITCH

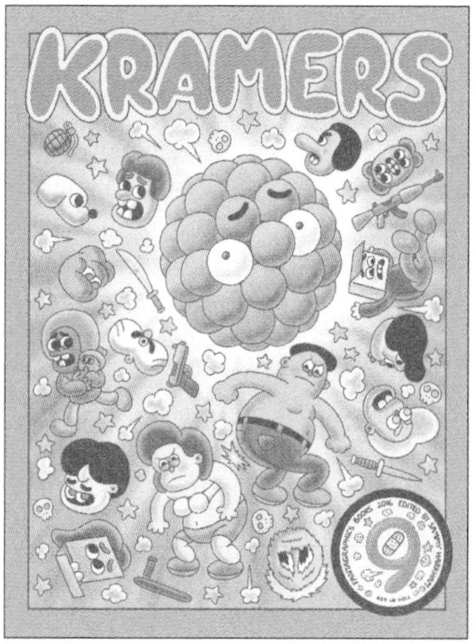
KRAMERS
9

*originally published in*

*Kramers Ergot*, vol. 9
FANTAGRAPHICS BOOKS
9 × 11.75 inches • 296 pages

## Biography

I was born in Los Angeles many moons ago. I came from an artistic background and was first published way back in 1967. I am still highly excited to be doing this sort of work. I am married to the best wife ever and I live with her and two cats in New York City. I am currently working on a book called *Reincarnation Stories*, which the story in this book will eventually appear in.
facebook.com/kimpam

## Statement

This was the first story I did for my next book, *Reincarnation Stories*. It kind of tickles me that with its publication here, it will have been twice printed before it will appear in the book that it is intended for. I take that as a good sign.

There's a macabre timelessness about those old stuffed animal dioramas at New York's Museum of Natural History. One of them shows 15 odd looking monkeys high in the African tree tops!

WHITE MANTLED COLUBUS

Even at age 7, I was troubled and yet fascinated by this one. I mean, think about it; an entire monkey community callously murdered for the "education" of the biggest monkeys of all; **us**, the so called human race.

And there was another thing that caught my eye. One little monkey, way up top; seemed to be staring right down at me! There was something rather unsettling about it.

# Shrine of the Monkey God!

The time locked quality of those dioramas was really brought home to me recently when my wife and I visited the old museum.

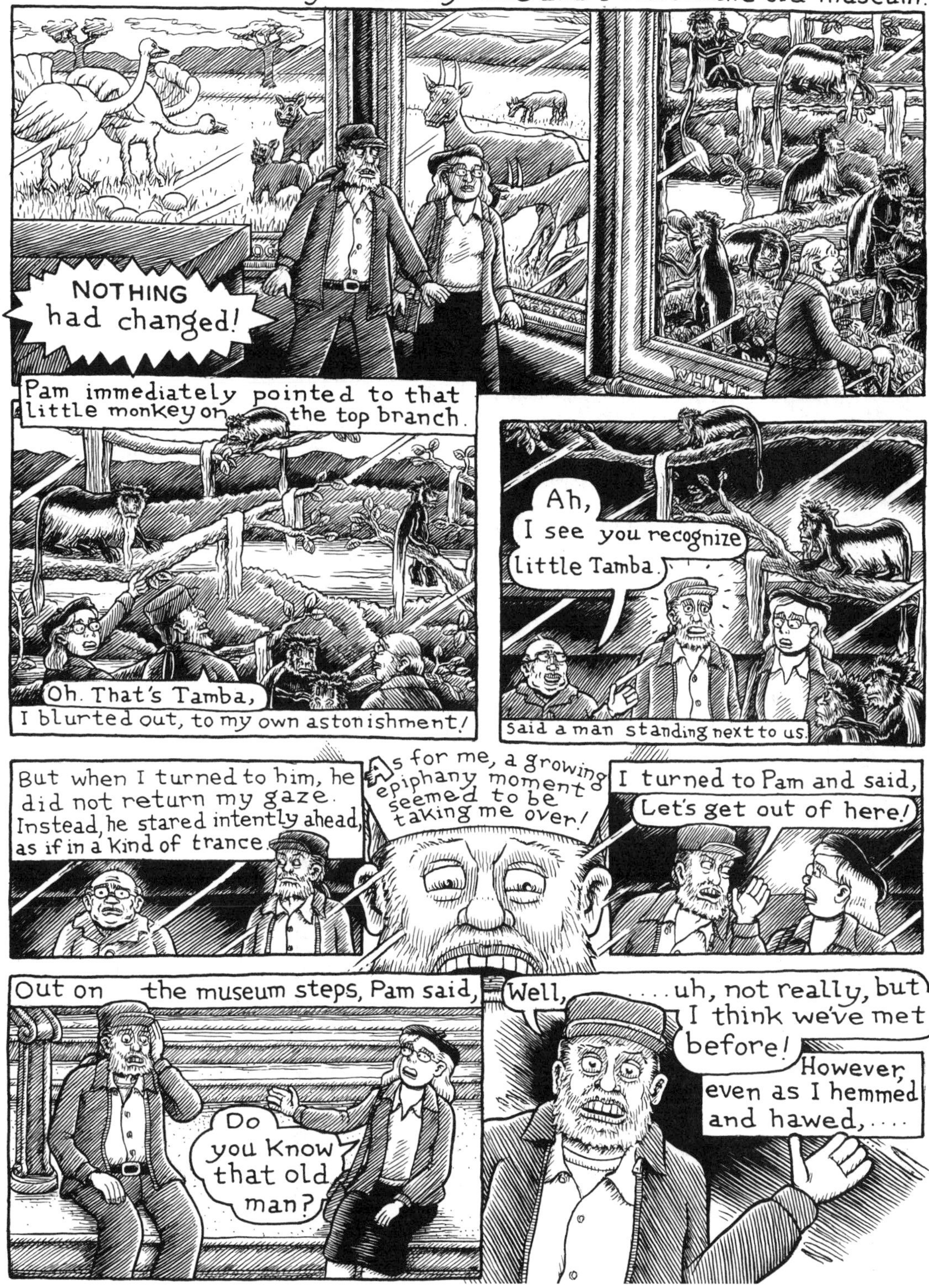

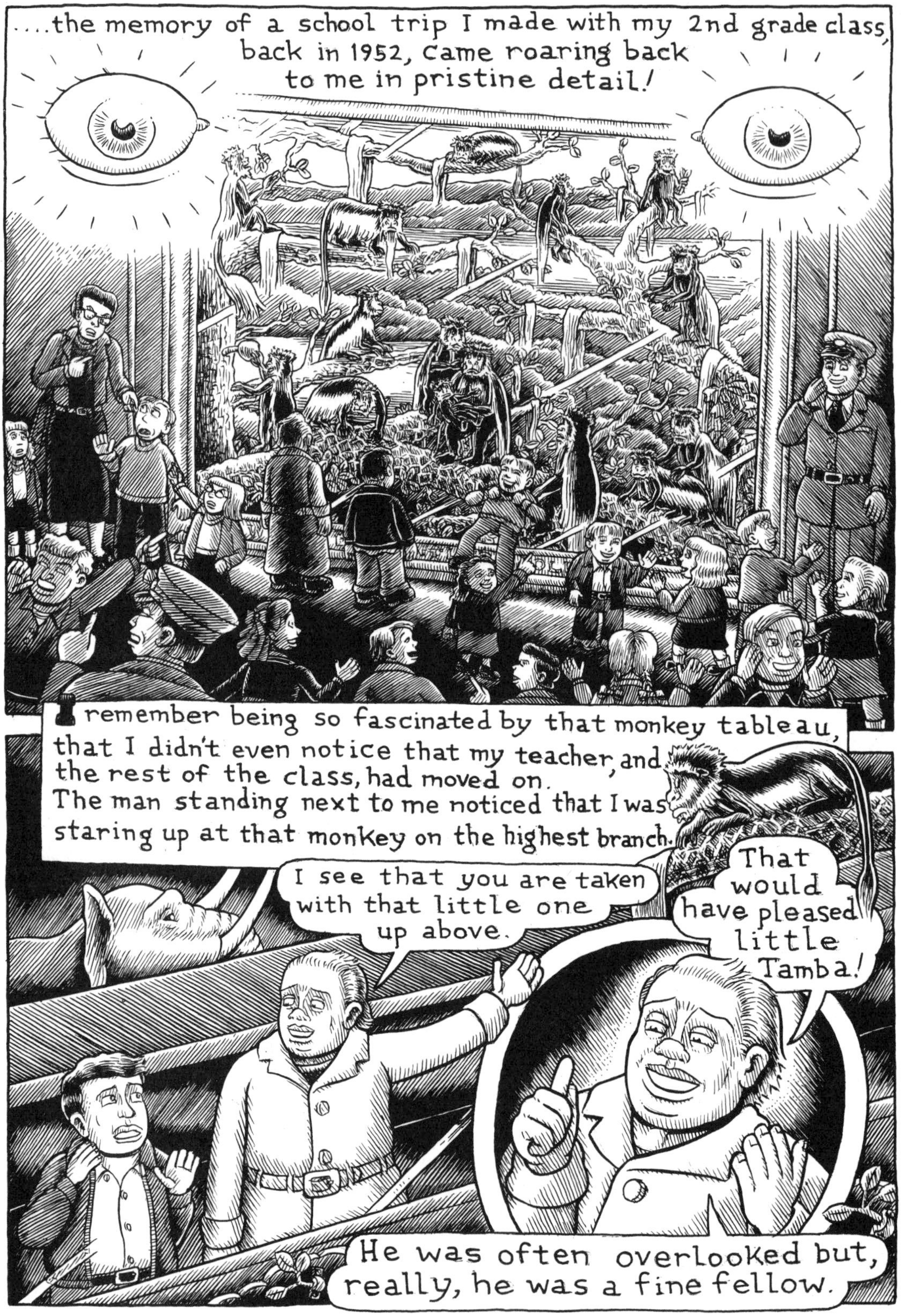
....the memory of a school trip I made with my 2nd grade class, back in 1952, came roaring back to me in pristine detail!
I remember being so fascinated by that monkey tableau, that I didn't even notice that my teacher, and the rest of the class, had moved on.
The man standing next to me noticed that I was staring up at that monkey on the highest branch.
I see that you are taken with that little one up above.
That would have pleased little Tamba!
He was often overlooked but, really, he was a fine fellow.

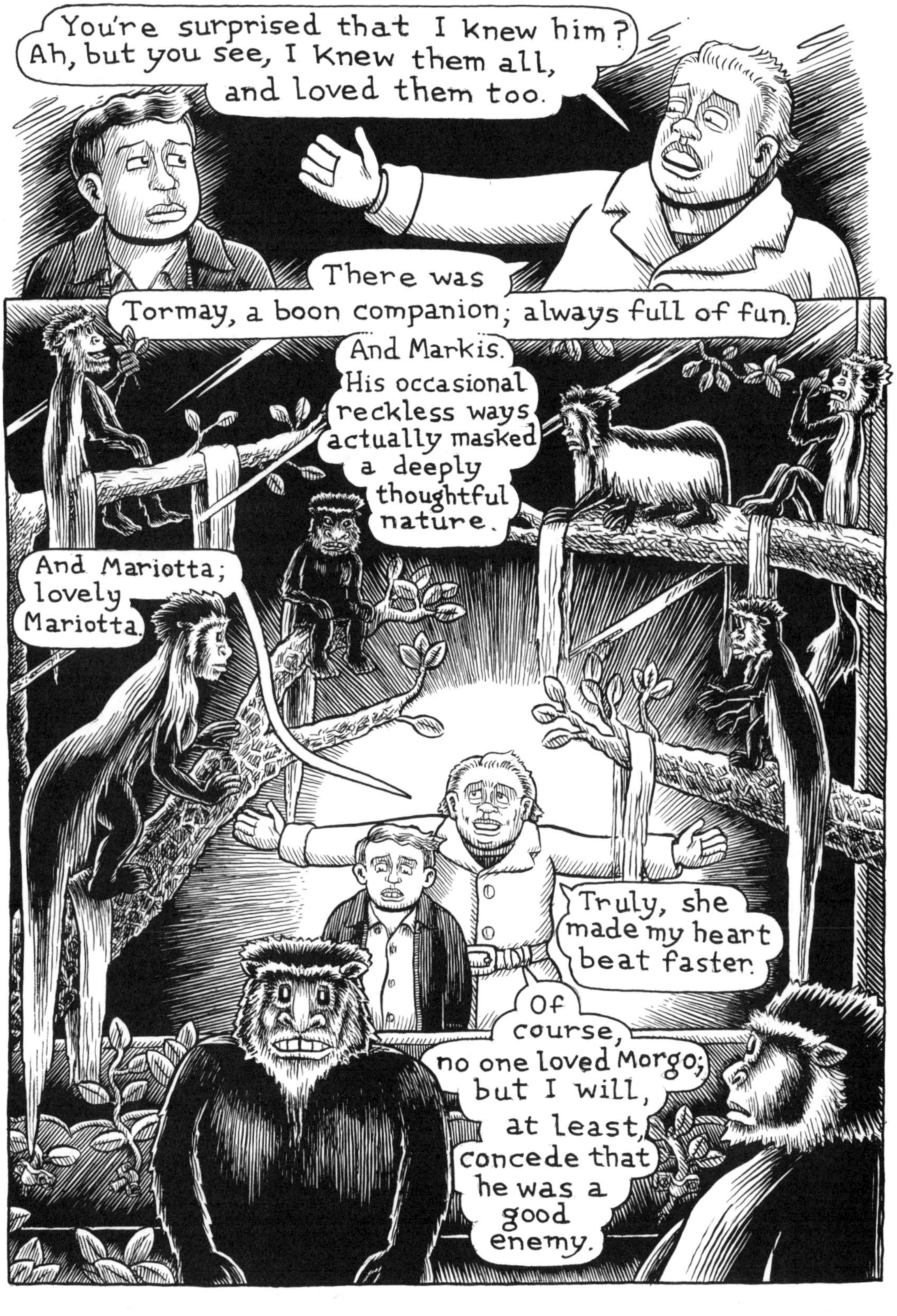
You're surprised that I knew him? Ah, but you see, I knew them all, and loved them too.
There was Tormay, a boon companion; always full of fun.
And Markis. His occasional reckless ways actually masked a deeply thoughtful nature.
And Mariotta; lovely Mariotta.
Truly, she made my heart beat faster.
Of course, no one loved Morgo; but I will, at least, concede that he was a good enemy.

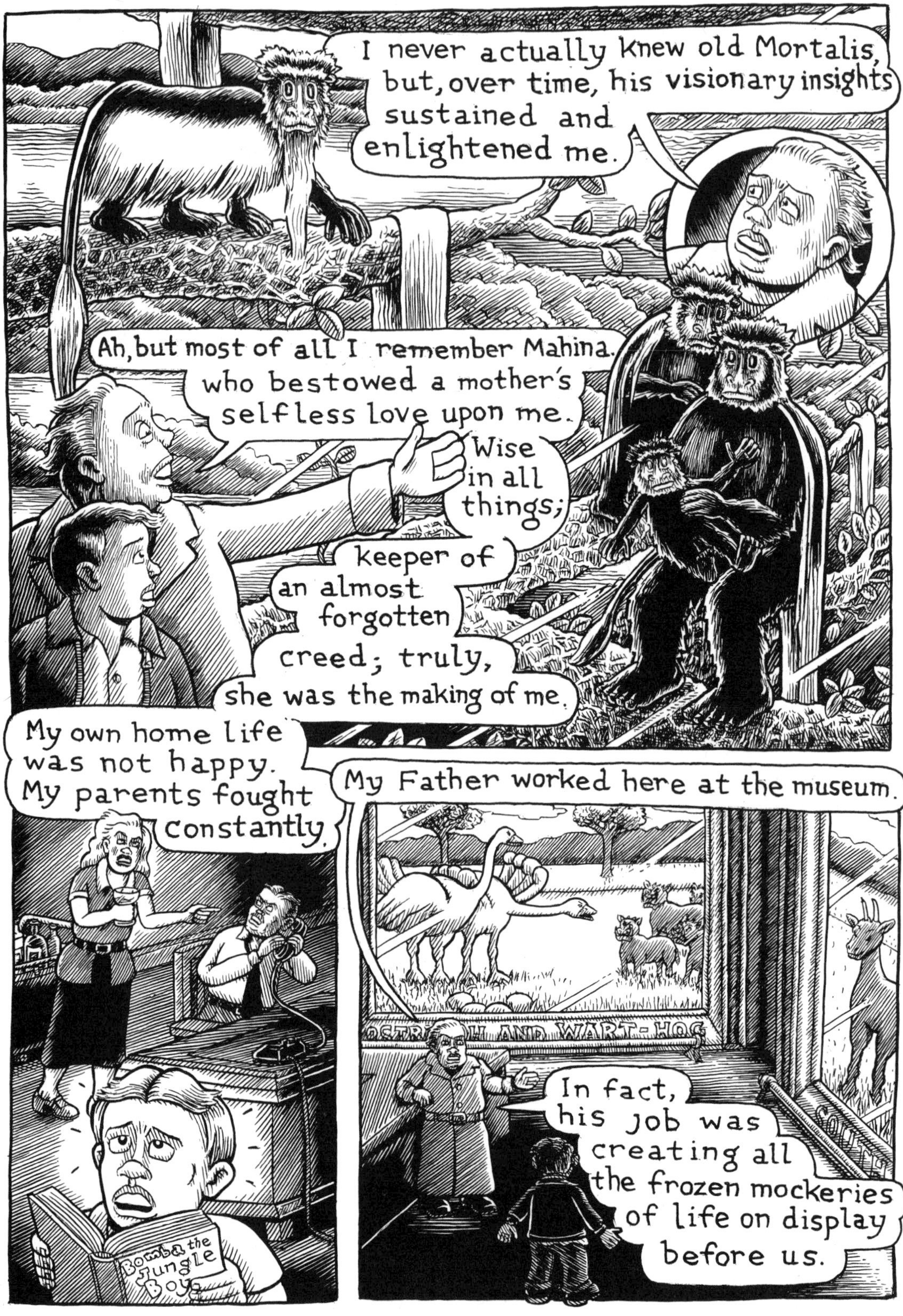

I never actually knew old Mortalis, but, over time, his visionary insights sustained and enlightened me.
Ah, but most of all I remember Mahina. who bestowed a mother's selfless love upon me.
Wise in all things;
keeper of an almost forgotten
creed; truly, she was the making of me.
My own home life was not happy. My parents fought constantly.
Bomba the Jungle Boy
My Father worked here at the museum.
OSTRICH AND WART-HOG
In fact, his job was creating all the frozen mockeries of life on display before us.

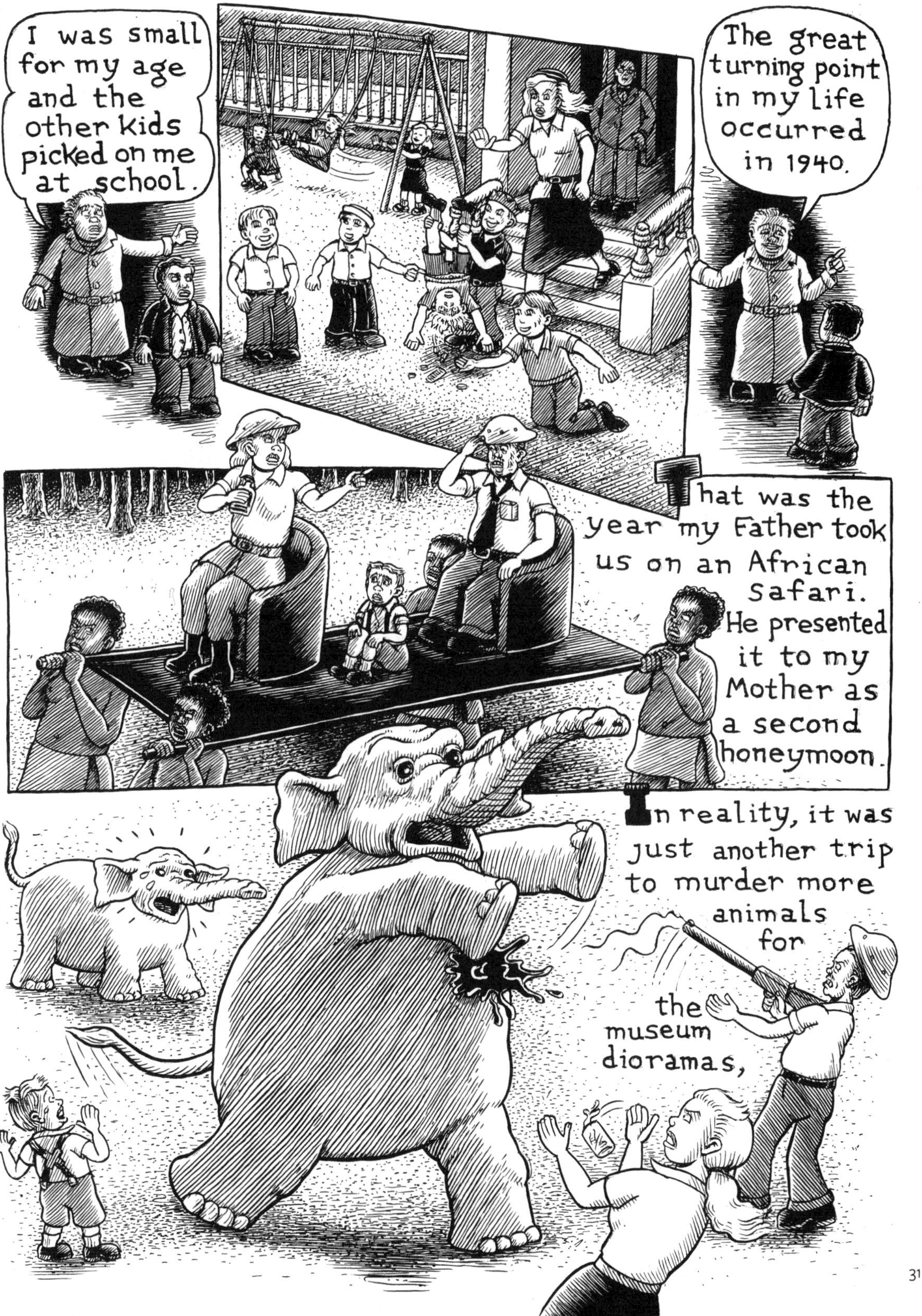
I was small for my age and the other kids picked on me at school.
The great turning point in my life occurred in 1940.
That was the year my Father took us on an African Safari. He presented it to my Mother as a second honeymoon.
In reality, it was just another trip to murder more animals for the museum dioramas,

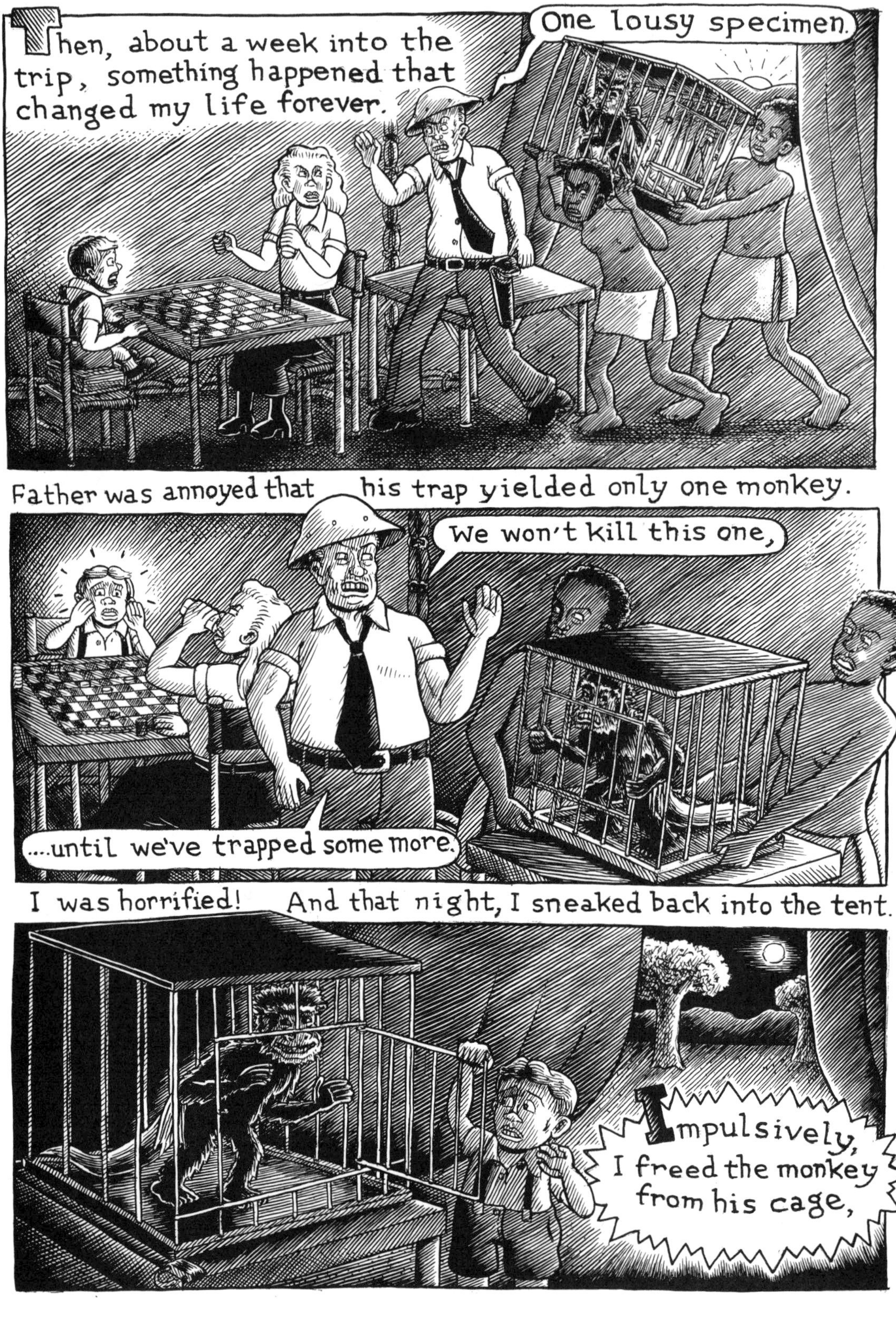
Then, about a week into the trip, something happened that changed my life forever.
One lousy specimen.
Father was annoyed that
his trap yielded only one monkey.
We won't kill this one,
....until we've trapped some more.
I was horrified!
And that night, I sneaked back into the tent.
Impulsively, I freed the monkey from his cage,

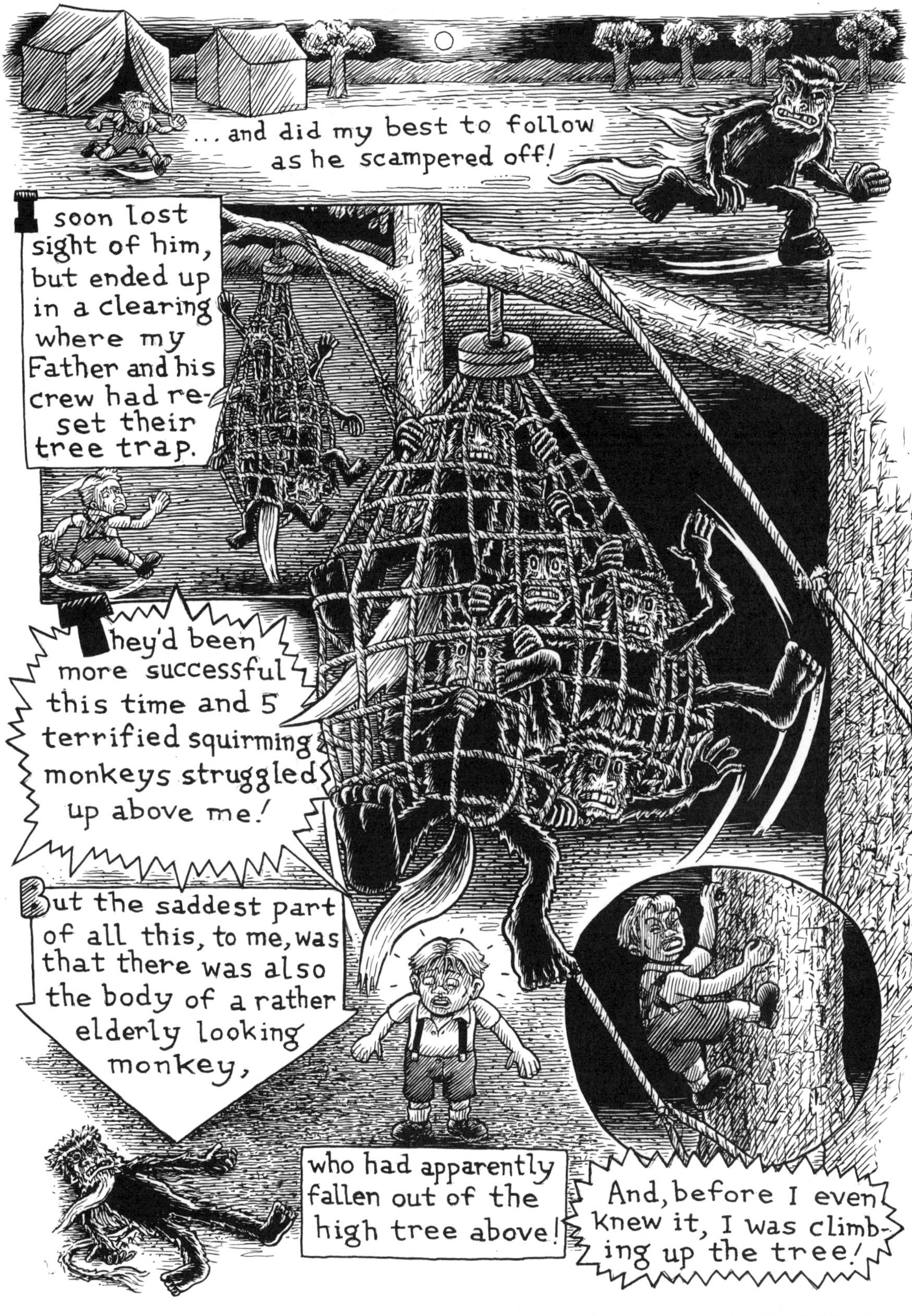

...and did my best to follow as he scampered off!
I soon lost sight of him, but ended up in a clearing where my Father and his crew had re-set their tree trap.
They'd been more successful this time and 5 terrified squirming monkeys struggled up above me!
But the saddest part of all this, to me, was that there was also the body of a rather elderly looking monkey,
who had apparently fallen out of the high tree above!
And, before I even knew it, I was climbing up the tree!

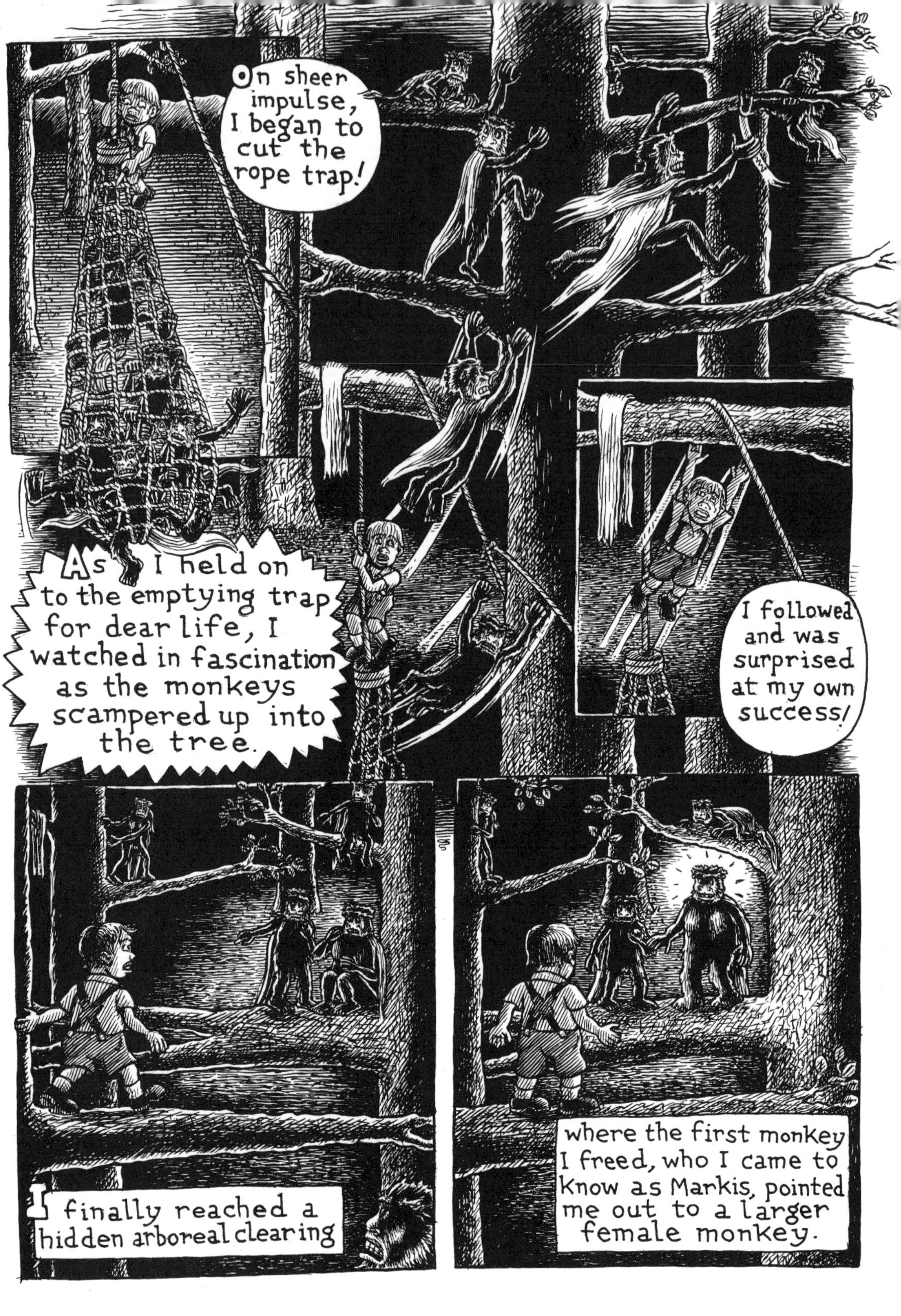
On sheer impulse, I began to cut the rope trap!
As I held on to the emptying trap for dear life, I watched in fascination as the monkeys scampered up into the tree.
I followed and was surprised at my own success!
I finally reached a hidden arboreal clearing
where the first monkey I freed, who I came to know as Markis, pointed me out to a larger female monkey.

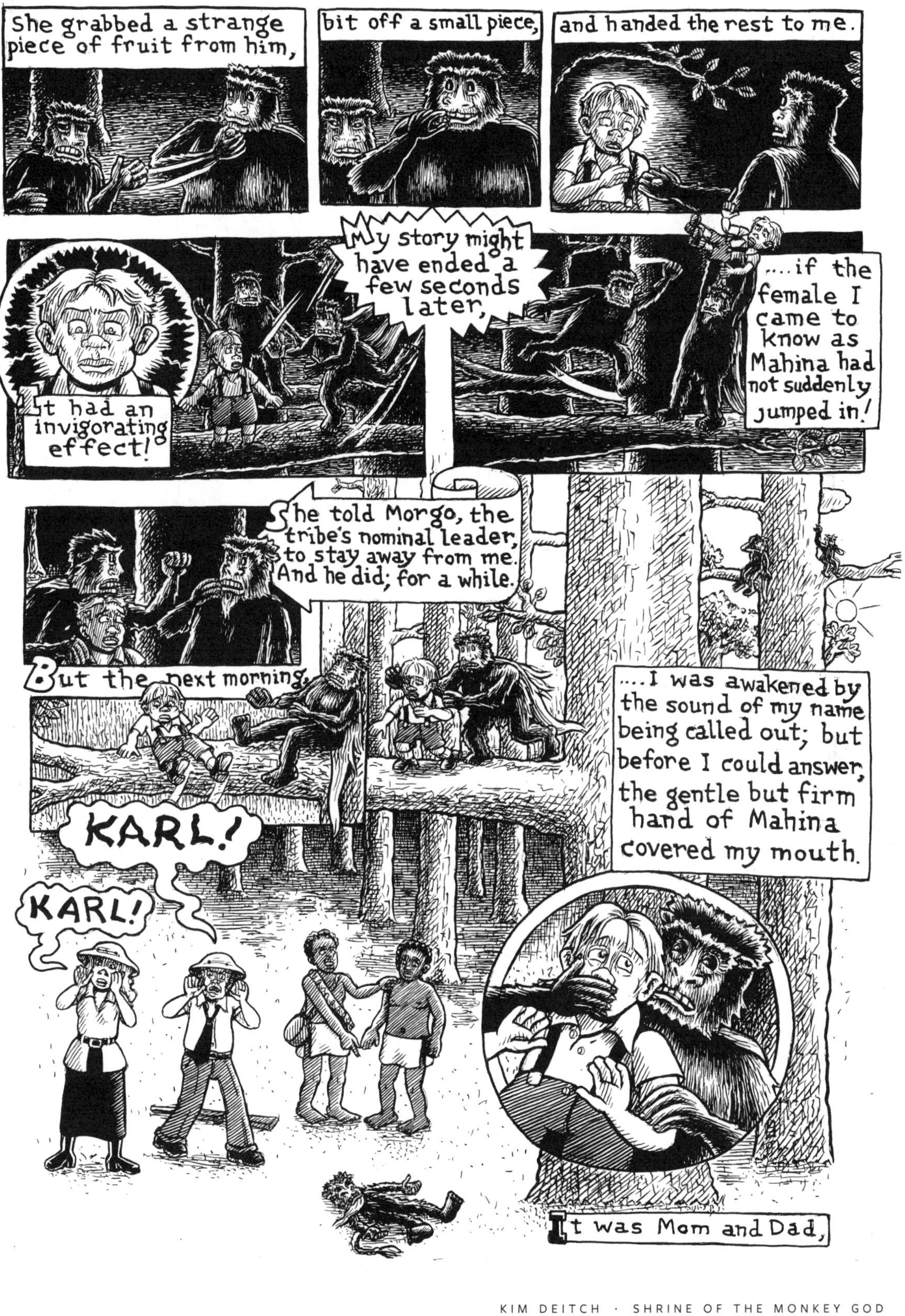
She grabbed a strange piece of fruit from him,
bit off a small piece,
and handed the rest to me.
It had an invigorating effect!
My story might have ended a few seconds later,
....if the female I came to know as Mahina had not suddenly jumped in!
She told Morgo, the tribe's nominal leader, to stay away from me. And he did; for a while.
But the next morning,
....I was awakened by the sound of my name being called out; but before I could answer, the gentle but firm hand of Mahina covered my mouth.
KARL!
KARL!
It was Mom and Dad,

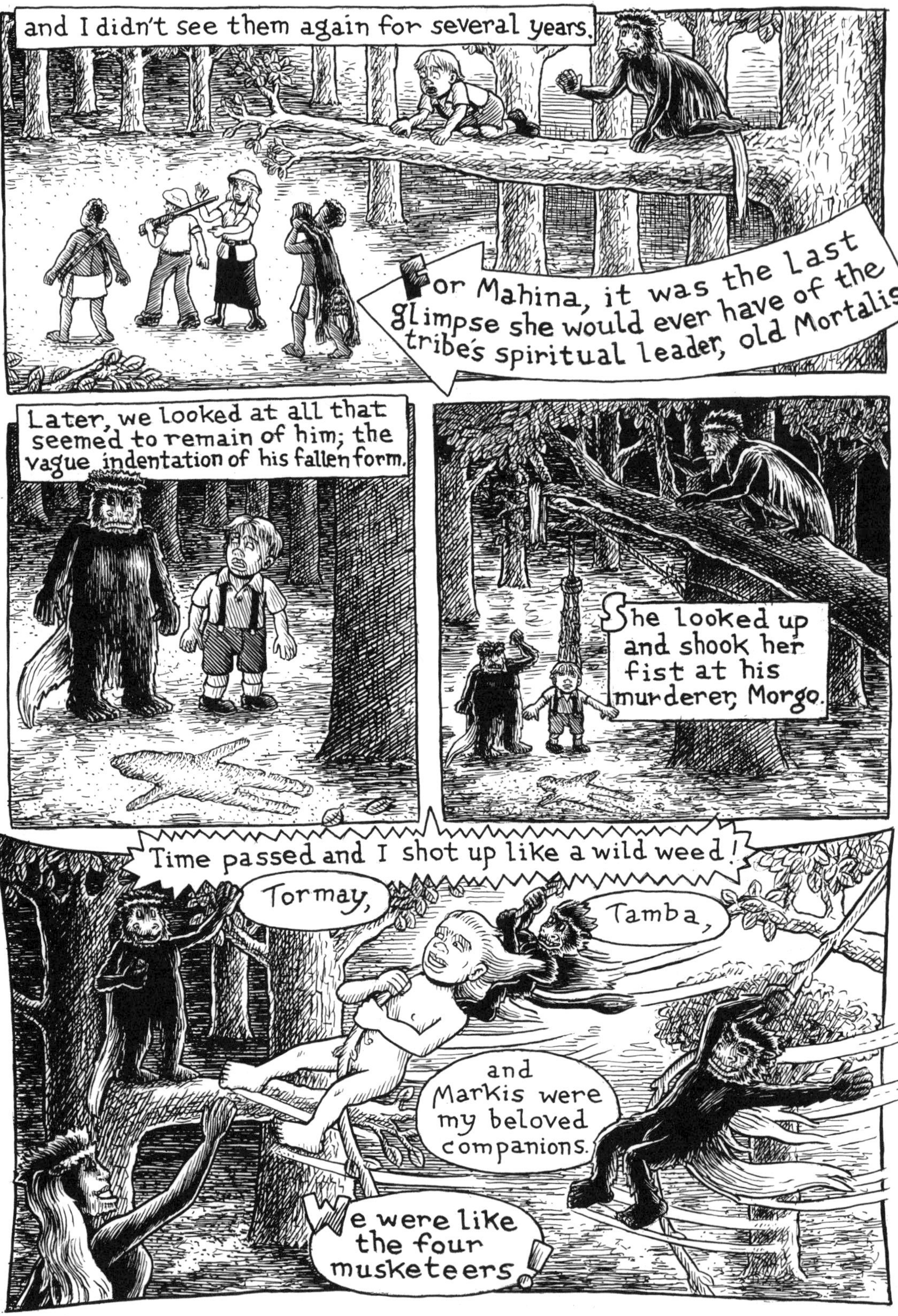

and I didn't see them again for several years.
For Mahina, it was the last glimpse she would ever have of the tribe's spiritual leader, old Mortalis.
Later, we looked at all that seemed to remain of him; the vague indentation of his fallen form.
She looked up and shook her fist at his murderer, Morgo.
Time passed and I shot up like a wild weed!
Tormay,
Tamba,
and Markis were my beloved companions.
We were like the four musketeers!

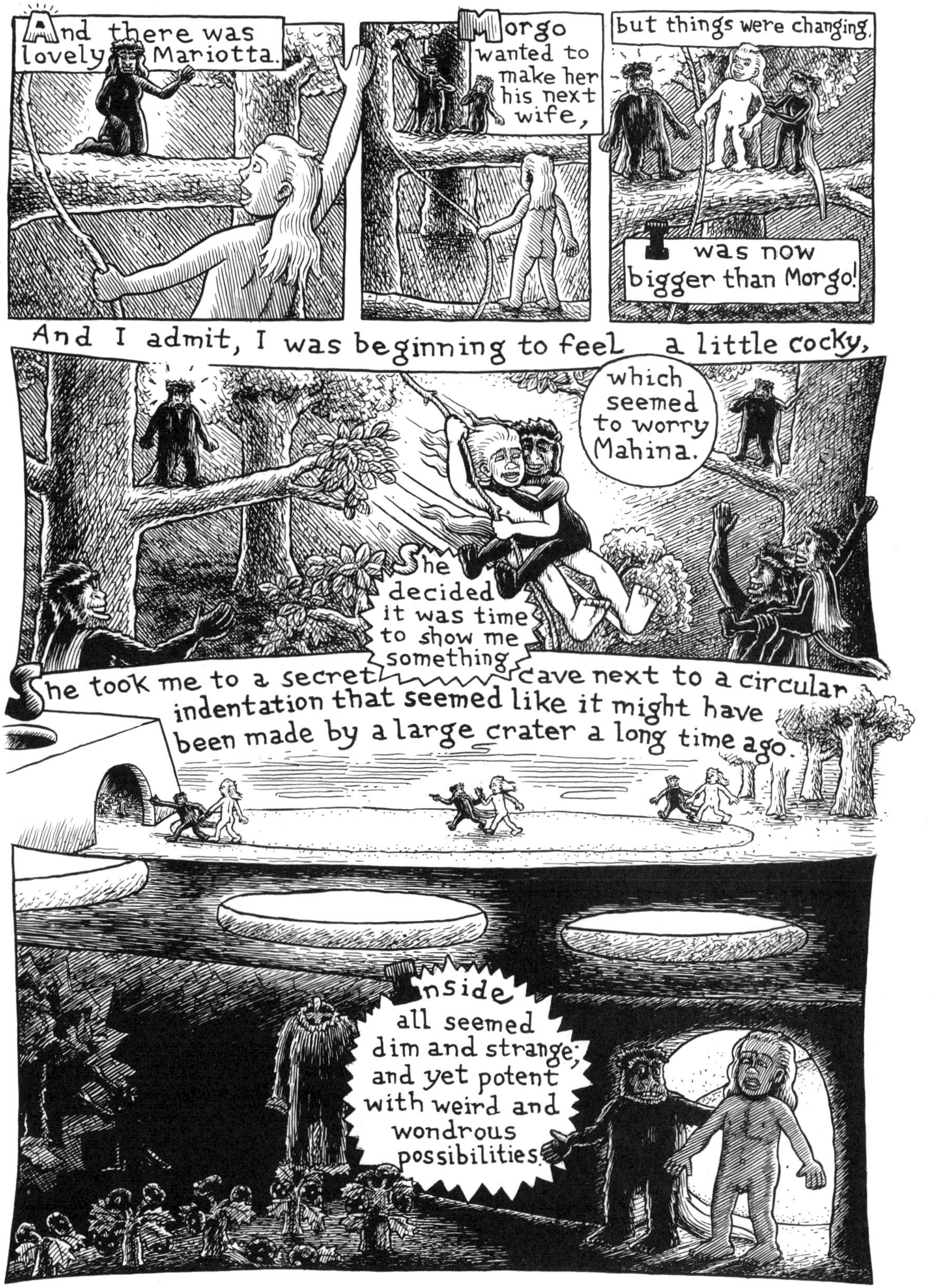
And there was lovely Mariotta.
Morgo wanted to make her his next wife,
but things were changing.
I was now bigger than Morgo!
And I admit, I was beginning to feel a little cocky,
which seemed to worry Mahina.
She decided it was time to show me something
She took me to a secret cave next to a circular indentation that seemed like it might have been made by a large crater a long time ago.
Inside all seemed dim and strange; and yet potent with weird and wondrous possibilities.

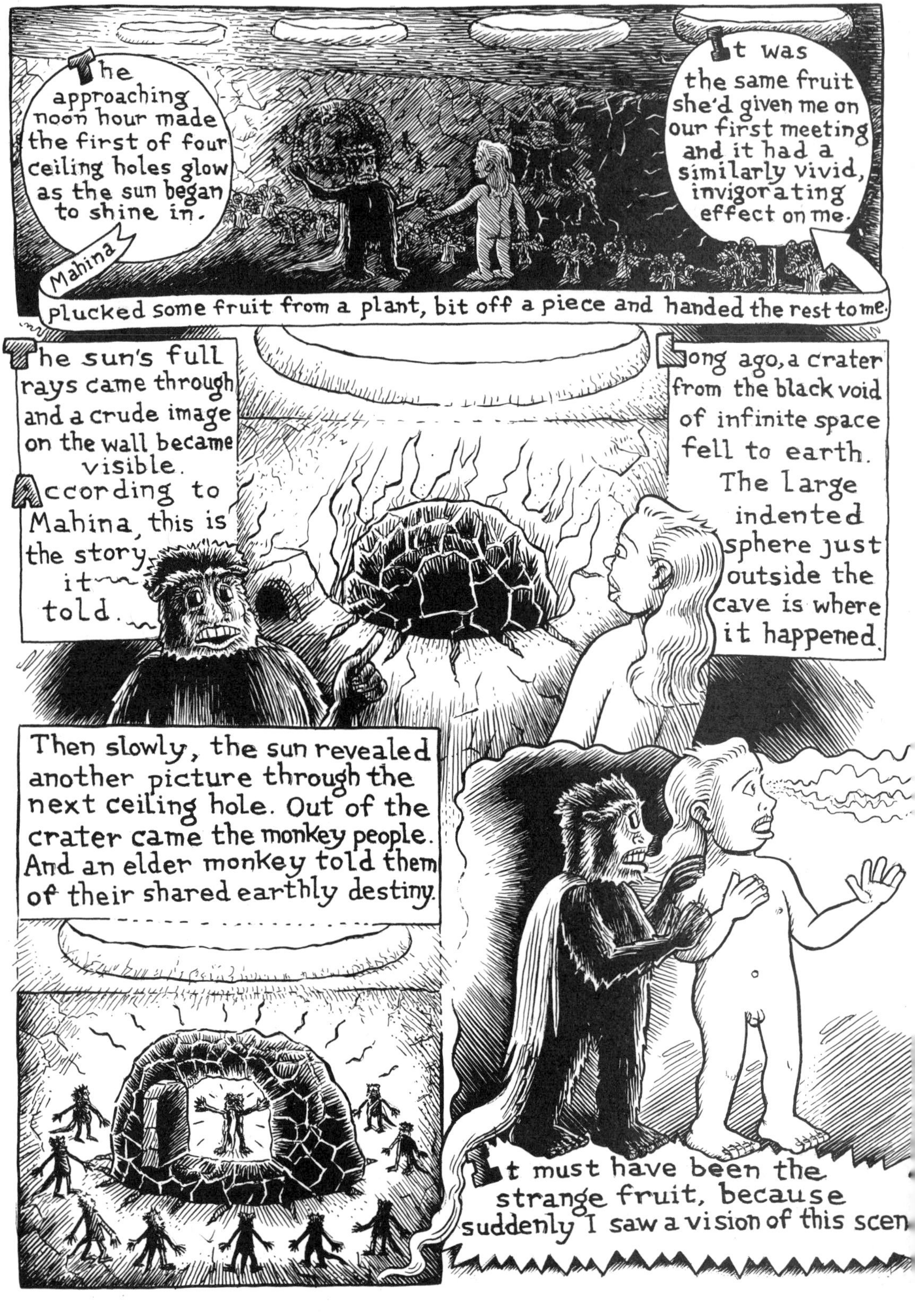
The approaching noon hour made the first of four ceiling holes glow as the sun began to shine in.
It was the same fruit she'd given me on our first meeting and it had a similarly vivid, invigorating effect on me.
Mahina plucked some fruit from a plant, bit off a piece and handed the rest to me.
The sun's full rays came through and a crude image on the wall became visible. According to Mahina, this is the story it told.
Long ago, a crater from the black void of infinite space fell to earth. The large indented sphere just outside the cave is where it happened.
Then slowly, the sun revealed another picture through the next ceiling hole. Out of the crater came the monkey people. And an elder monkey told them of their shared earthly destiny.
It must have been the strange fruit, because suddenly I saw a vision of this scen

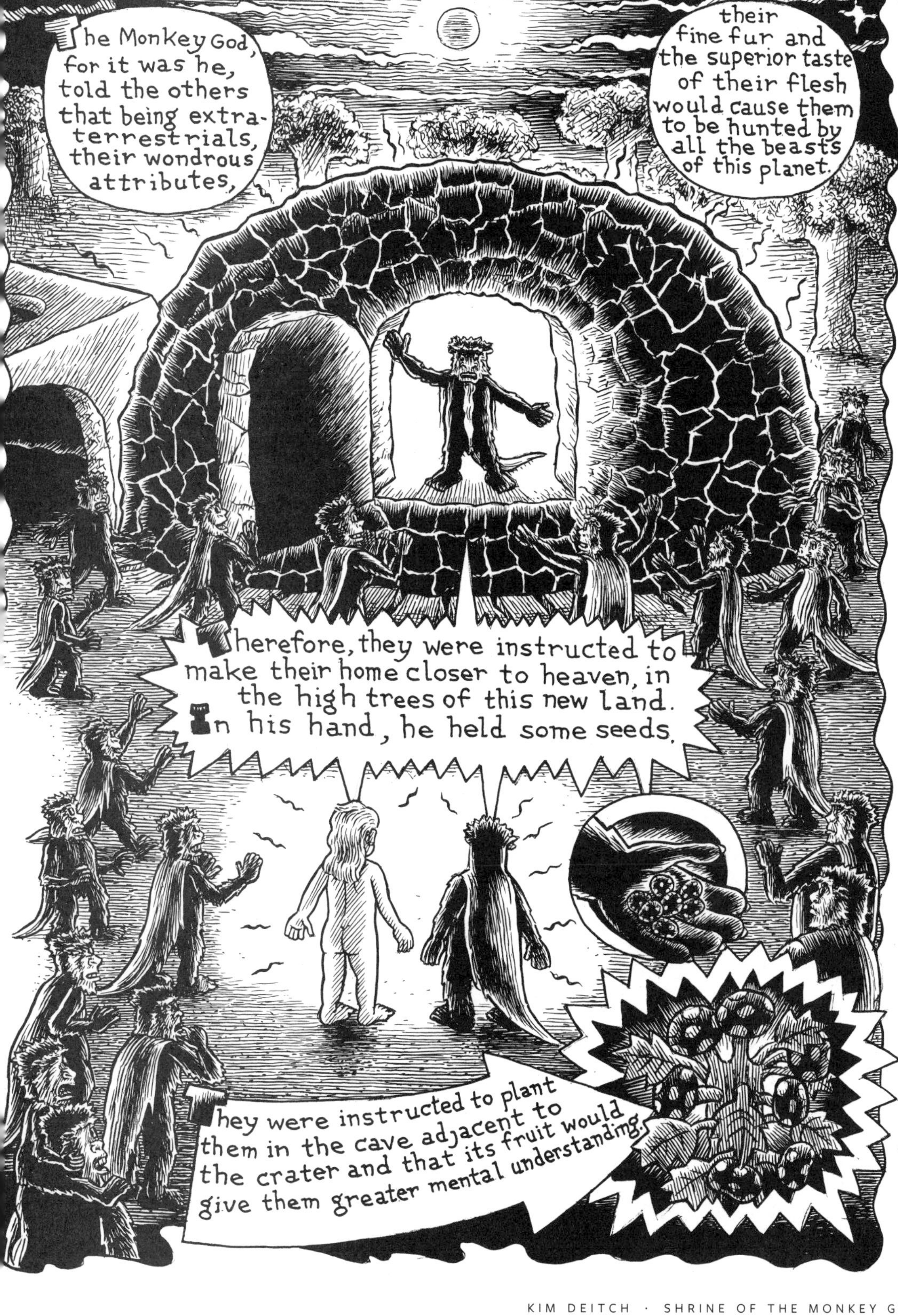
The Monkey God, for it was he, told the others that being extra-terrestrials, their wondrous attributes,
their fine fur and the superior taste of their flesh would cause them to be hunted by all the beasts of this planet.
Therefore, they were instructed to make their home closer to heaven, in the high trees of this new land. In his hand, he held some seeds.
They were instructed to plant them in the cave adjacent to the crater and that its fruit would give them greater mental understanding.

The moving sun hit the 3rd hole and the story shifted to things yet to come.

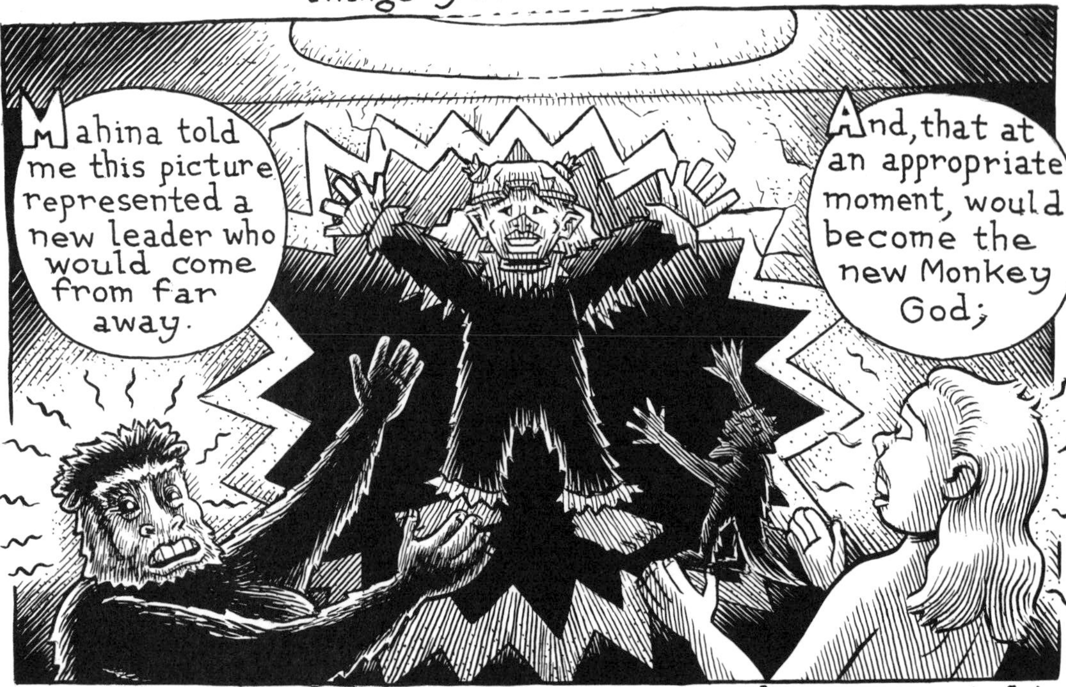
Mahina told me this picture represented a new leader who would come from far away.
And, that at an appropriate moment, would become the new Monkey God;

that the new God would cause them to be transported to a new place, where they would be together always.

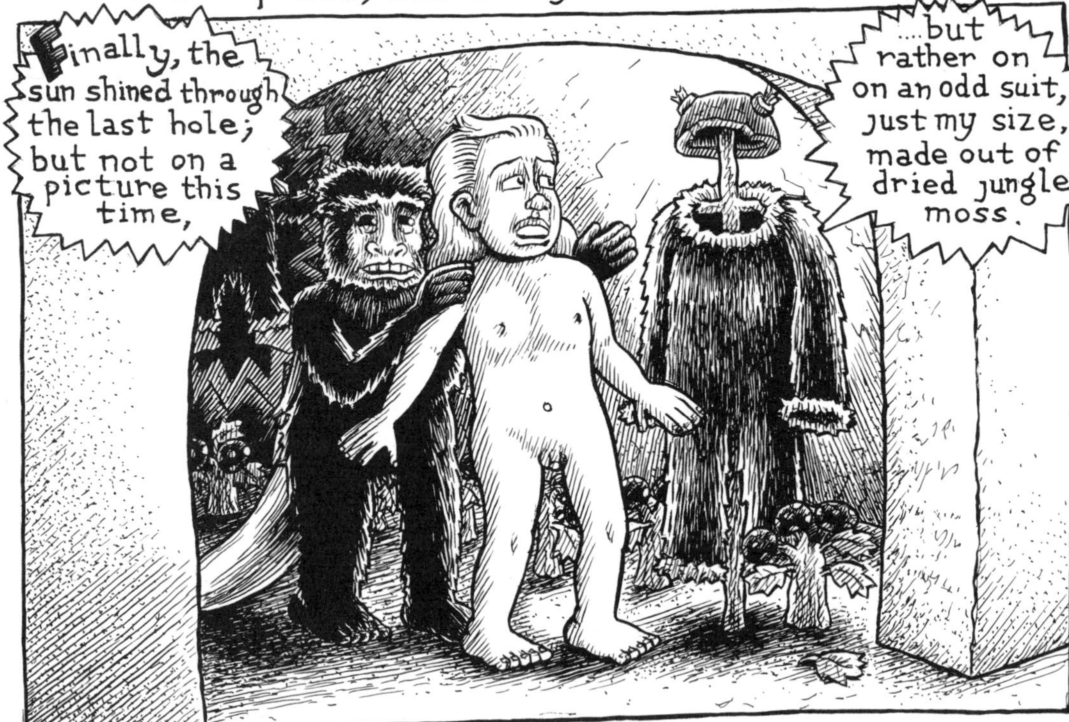
Finally, the sun shined through the last hole; but not on a picture this time,
...but rather on on an odd suit, just my size, made out of dried jungle moss.

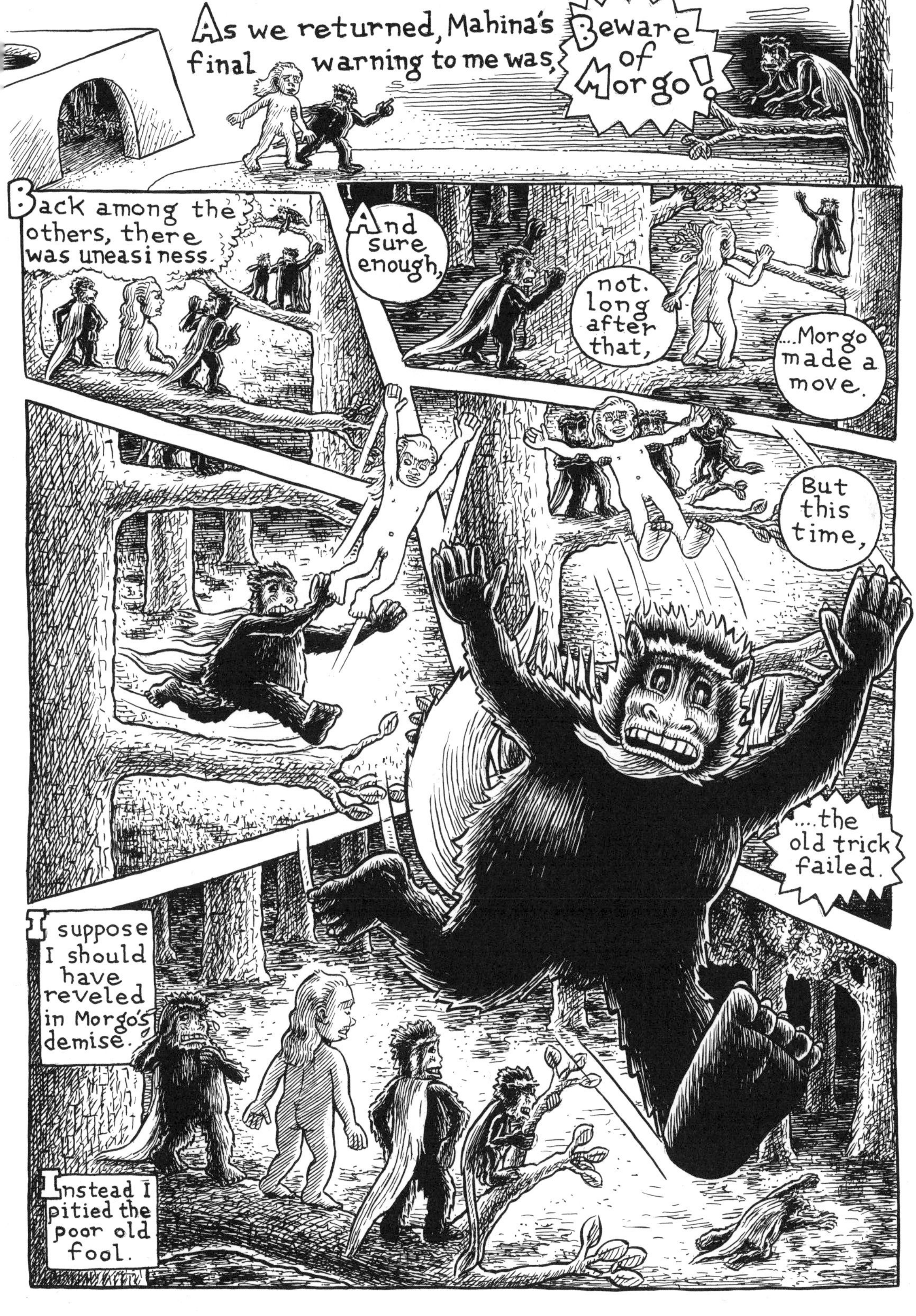
As we returned, Mahina's final warning to me was,
Beware of Morgo!
Back among the others, there was uneasiness.
And sure enough,
not. long after that,
....Morgo made a move.
But this time,
....the old trick failed.
I suppose I should have reveled in Morgo's demise.
Instead I pitied the poor old fool.

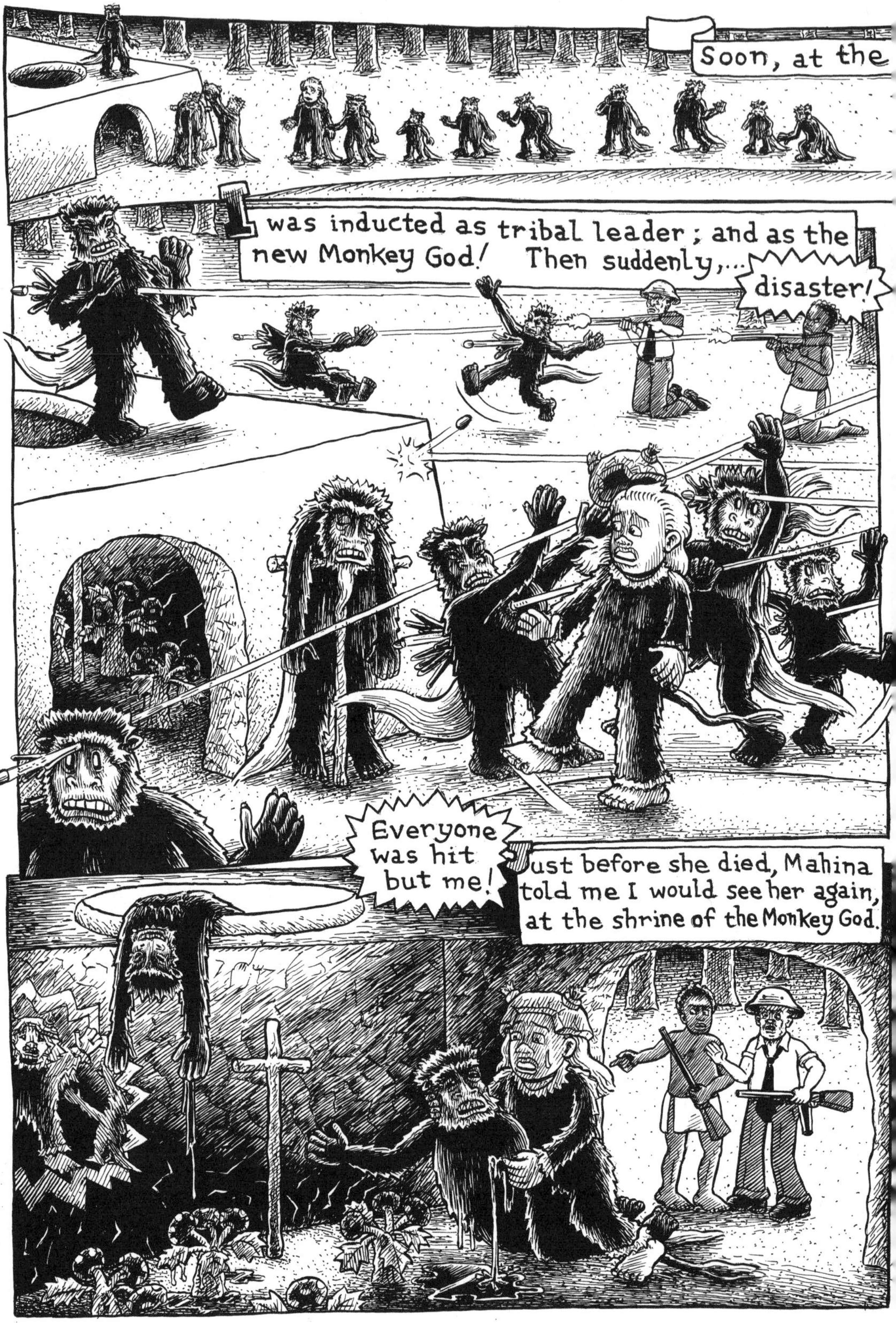
Soon, at the
I was inducted as tribal leader; and as the new Monkey God! Then suddenly,...
disaster!
Everyone was hit but me!
Just before she died, Mahina told me I would see her again, at the shrine of the Monkey God.

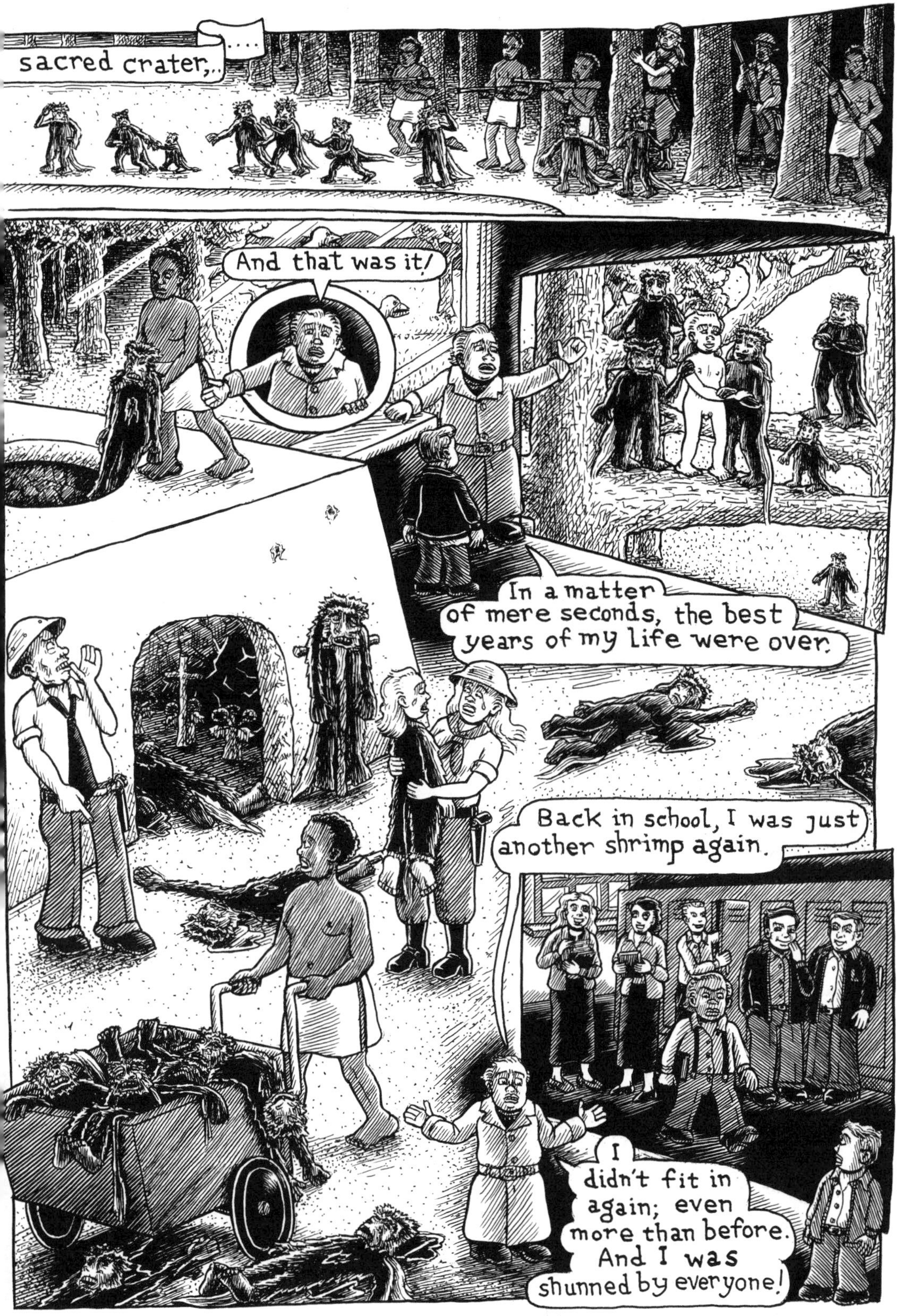
....
sacred crater,..
And that was it!
In a matter of mere seconds, the best years of my life were over.
Back in school, I was just another shrimp again.
I didn't fit in again; even more than before. And I was shunned by everyone!

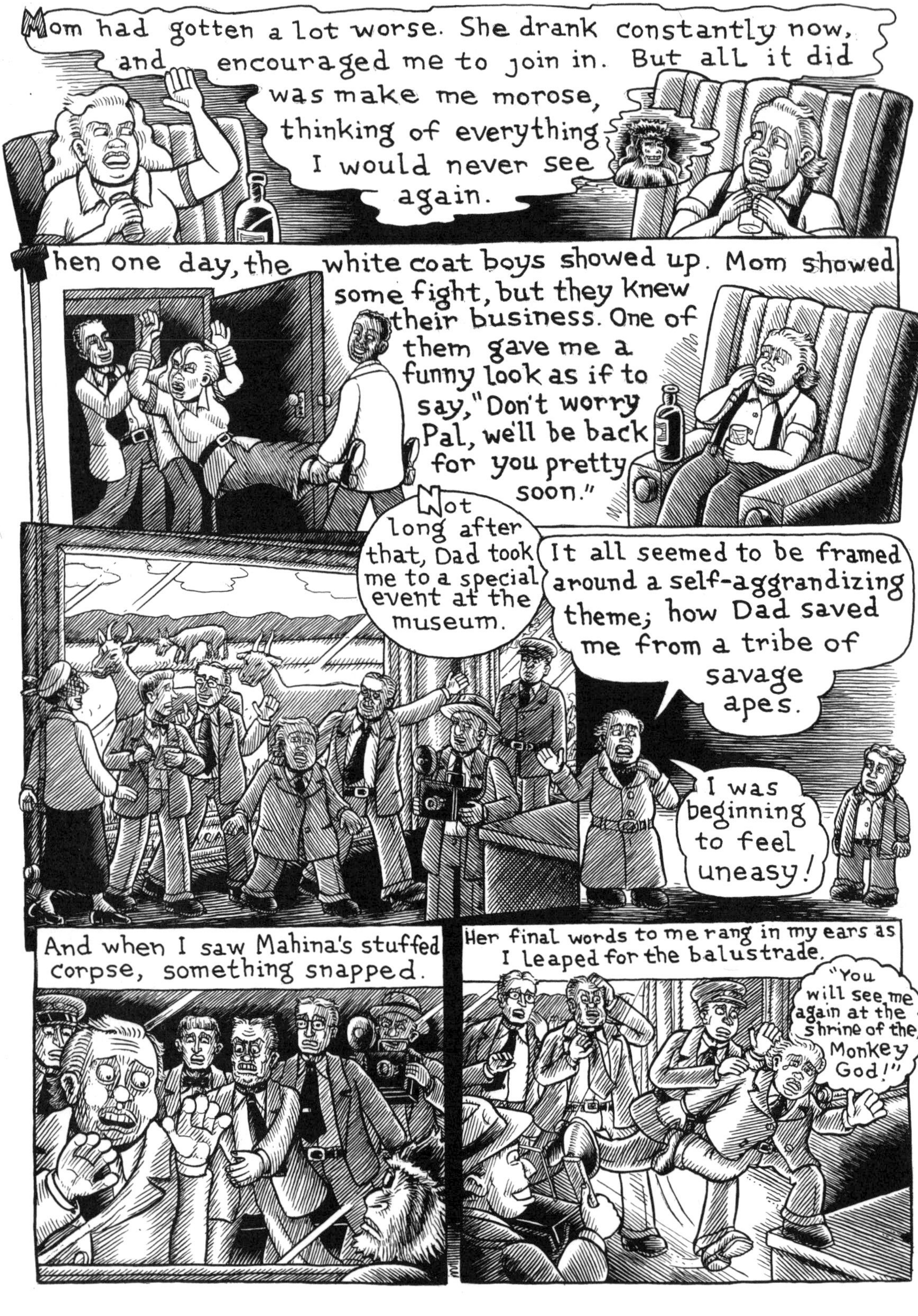
Mom had gotten a lot worse. She drank constantly now, and encouraged me to join in. But all it did was make me morose, thinking of everything I would never see again.
Then one day, the white coat boys showed up. Mom showed some fight, but they knew their business. One of them gave me a funny look as if to say, "Don't worry Pal, we'll be back for you pretty soon."
Not long after that, Dad took me to a special event at the museum.
It all seemed to be framed around a self-aggrandizing theme; how Dad saved me from a tribe of savage apes.
I was beginning to feel uneasy!
And when I saw Mahina's stuffed corpse, something snapped.
Her final words to me rang in my ears as I leaped for the balustrade.
"You will see me again at the shrine of the Monkey God!"

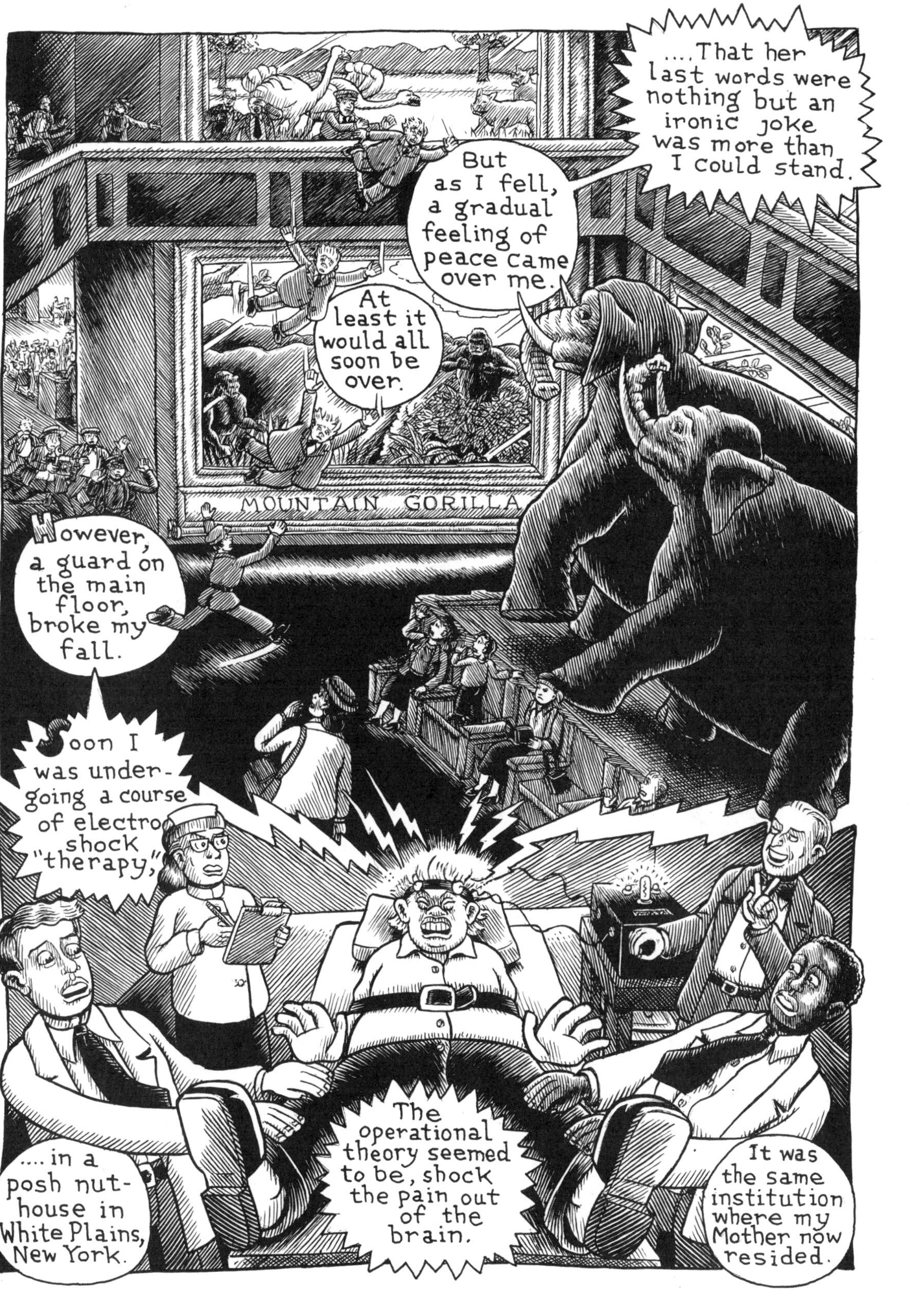
....That her last words were nothing but an ironic joke was more than I could stand.
But as I fell, a gradual feeling of peace came over me.
At least it would all soon be over.
MOUNTAIN GORILLA
However, a guard on the main floor, broke my fall.
Soon I was undergoing a course of electro shock "therapy,"
....in a posh nuthouse in White Plains, New York.
The operational theory seemed to be, shock the pain out of the brain.
It was the same institution where my Mother now resided.

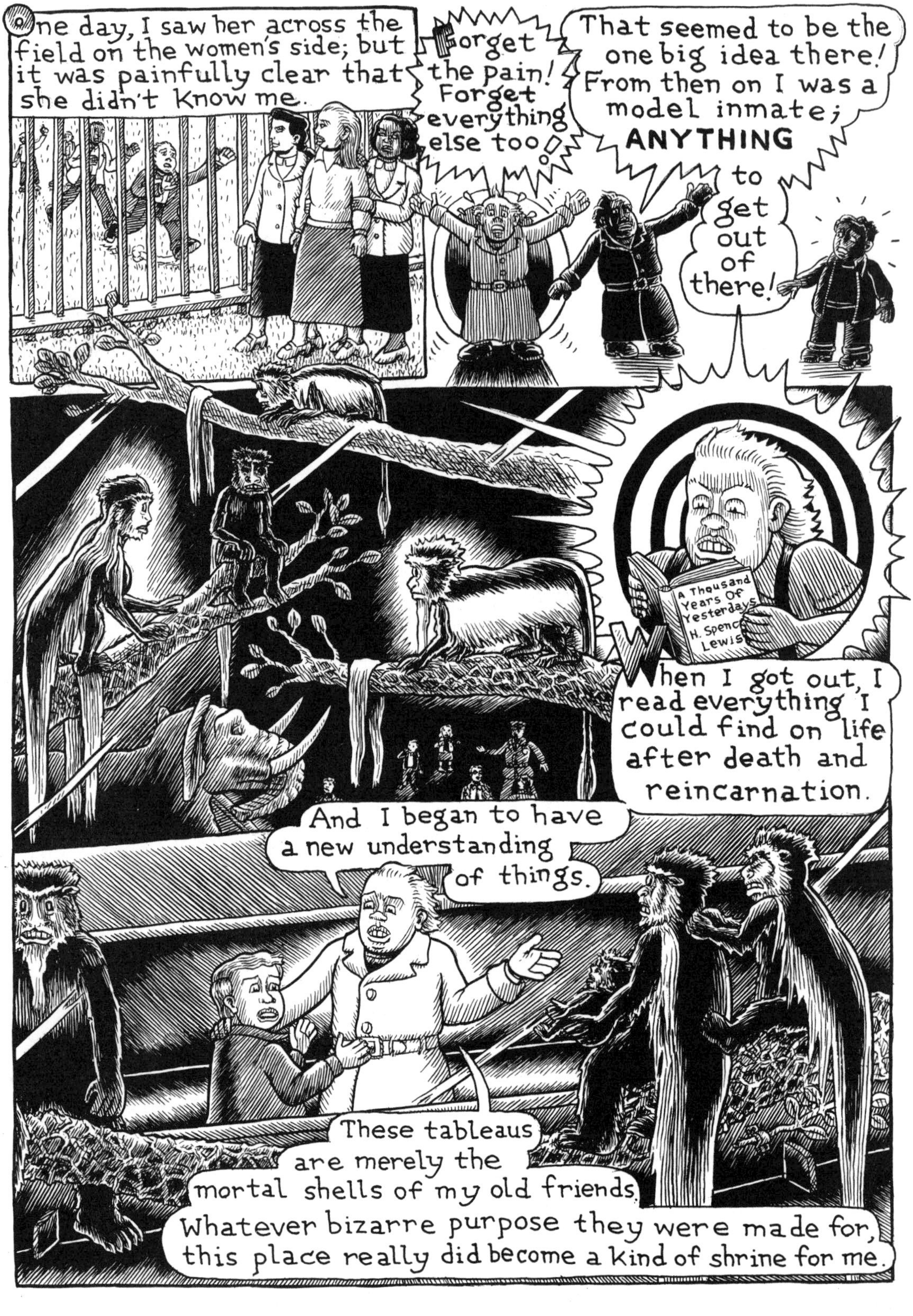
One day, I saw her across the field on the women's side; but it was painfully clear that she didn't know me.
Forget the pain! Forget everything else too!
That seemed to be the one big idea there! From then on I was a model inmate; ANYTHING to get out of there!
A Thousand Years Of Yesterdays H. Spenc Lewis
When I got out, I read everything I could find on life after death and reincarnation.
And I began to have a new understanding of things.
These tableaus are merely the mortal shells of my old friends.
Whatever bizarre purpose they were made for, this place really did become a kind of shrine for me.

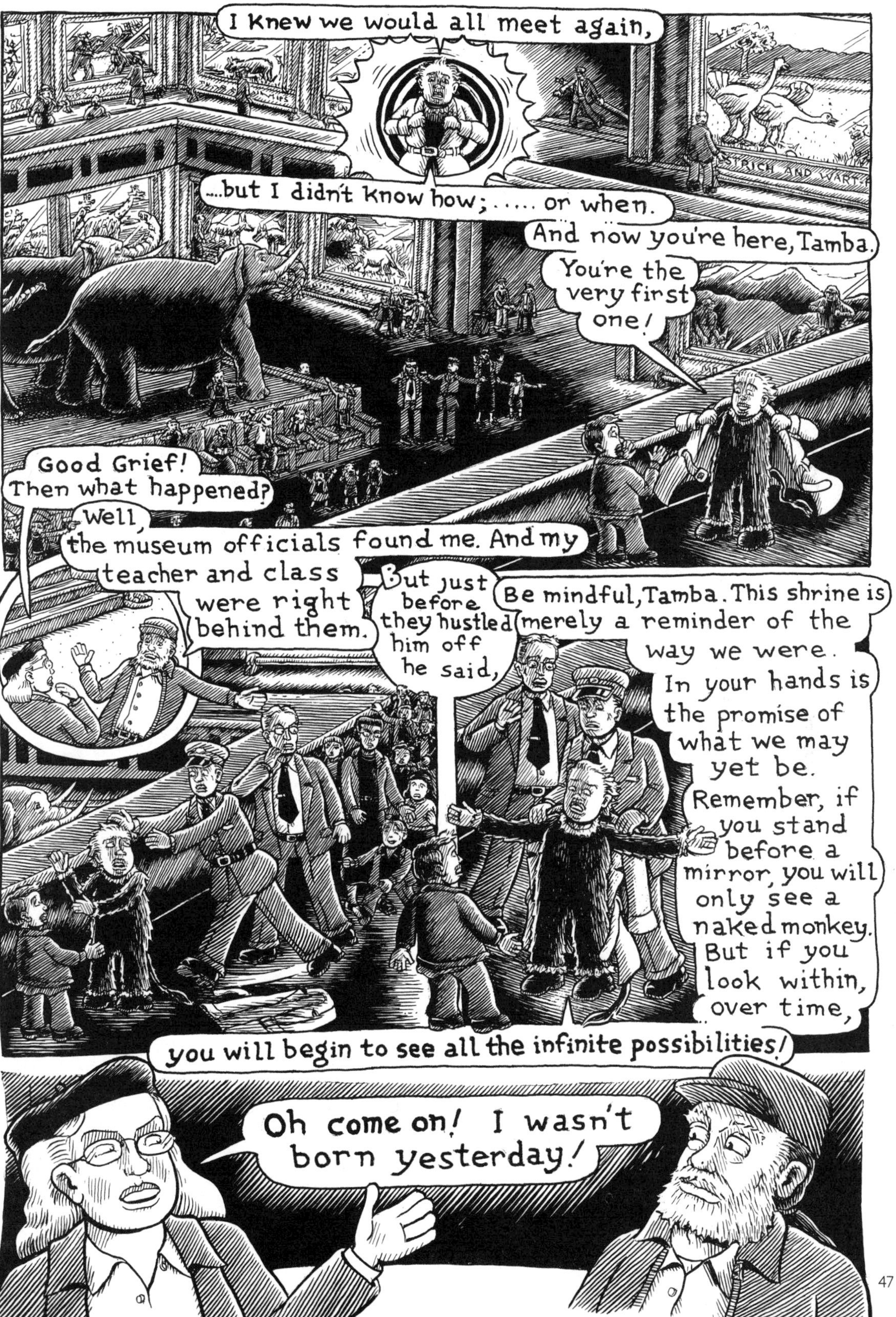

I knew we would all meet again,
...but I didn't know how; ..... or when.
And now you're here, Tamba.
You're the very first one!
STRICH AND WART
Good Grief! Then what happened?
Well, the museum officials found me. And my teacher and class were right behind them.
But just before they hustled him off he said,
Be mindful, Tamba. This shrine is merely a reminder of the way we were.
In your hands is the promise of what we may yet be.
Remember, if you stand before a mirror, you will only see a naked monkey.
But if you look within, over time,
you will begin to see all the infinite possibilities!
Oh come on! I wasn't born yesterday!

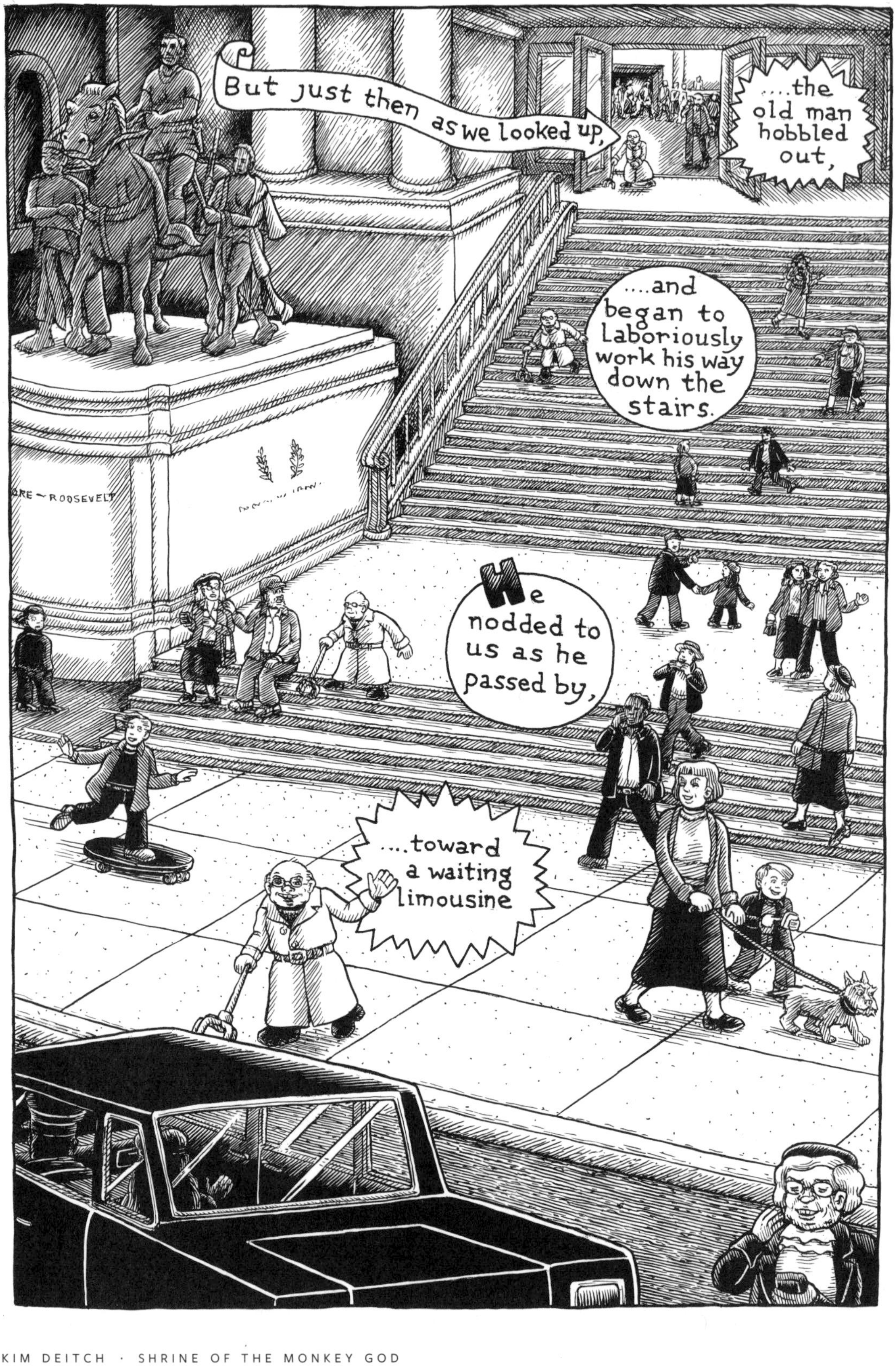

But just then as we looked up,
....the old man hobbled out,
....and began to laboriously work his way down the stairs.
He nodded to us as he passed by,
....toward a waiting limousine

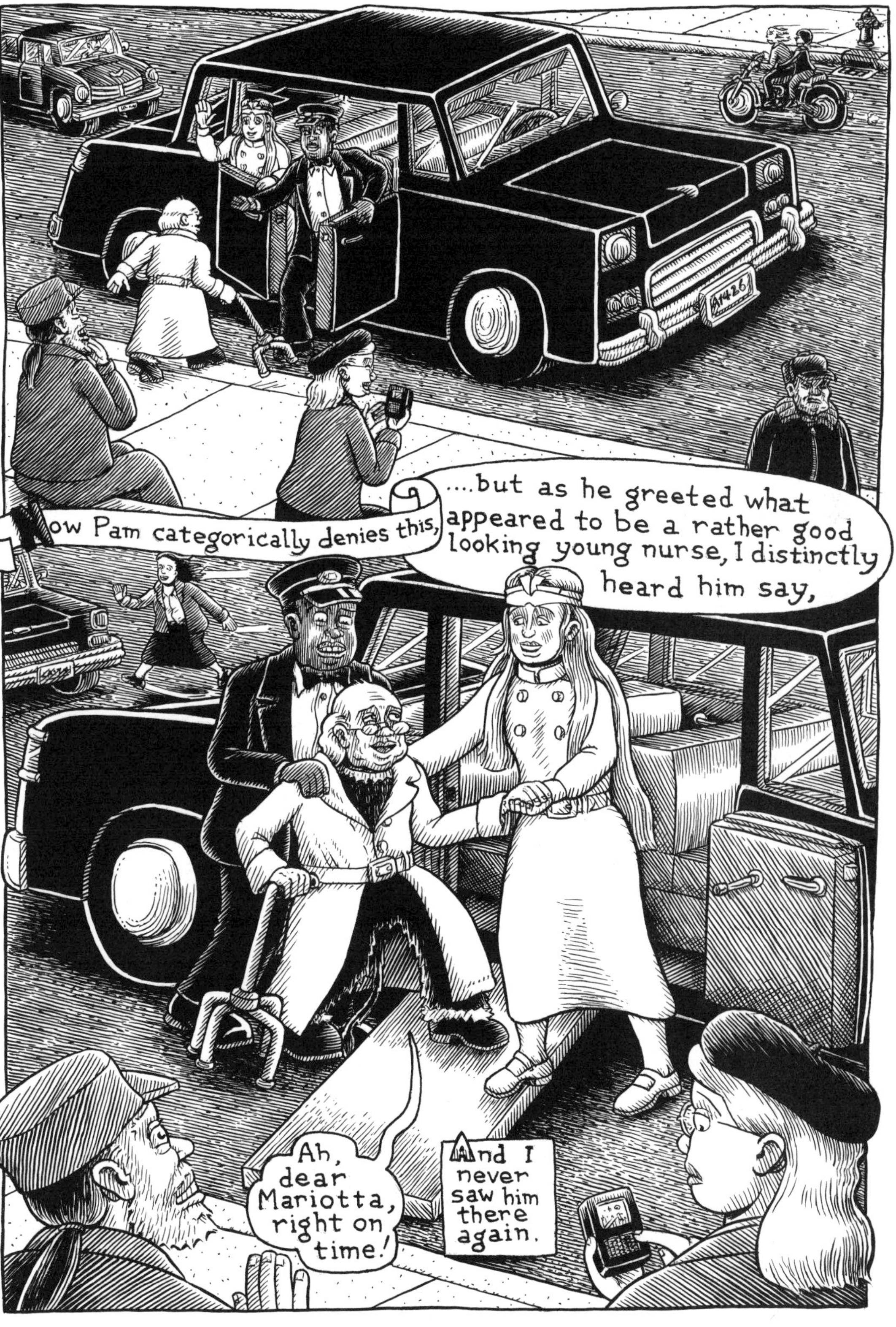

Now Pam categorically denies this,
...but as he greeted what appeared to be a rather good looking young nurse, I distinctly heard him say,
Ah, dear Mariotta, right on time!
And I never saw him there again.

# Willem de Kooning.
(Geniuses are nothing if not complicated in their methods.)

DEB SOKOLOW

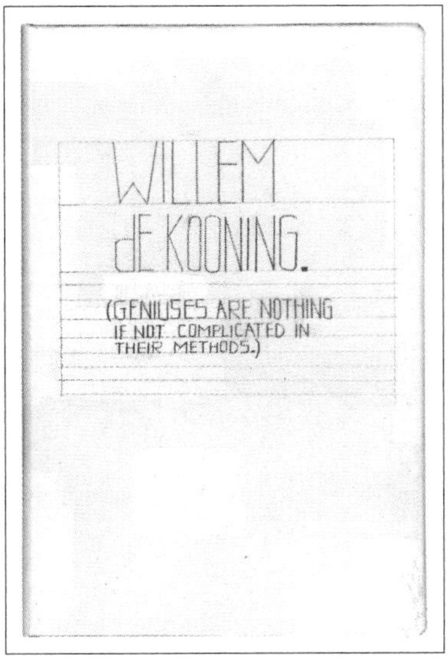
WILLEM
dE KOONING.
(GENIUSES ARE NOTHING
IF NOT COMPLICATED IN
THEIR METHODS.)

SELF-PUBLISHED

9 × 6 inches folded; 9 × 44 inches unfolded
Unique edition of three, one artist's proof

## Biography

Deb Sokolow is a Chicago-based artist and writer. Her work has been included in exhibitions at the Drawing Center in New York, Museum für Gegenwartskunst Siegen in Germany, Van Abbemuseum in the Netherlands, Institute of Contemporary Art in Philadelphia, and Western Exhibitions in Chicago. Her work has been reviewed in the *New York Times*, *Artforum.com*, and the *Washington Post* and reproduced for *Vitamin D2*, a survey on contemporary drawing. Sokolow's drawings and books are in several permanent collections, including the Los Angeles County Museum of Art and the Thomas J. Watson Library at the Metropolitan Museum of Art, New York.
www.debsokolow.com

## Statement

This is a work of fiction about artist Willem de Kooning, inspired by various anecdotes relayed in the 2004 biography *de Kooning: An American Master,* by Mark Stevens and Annalyn Swan.

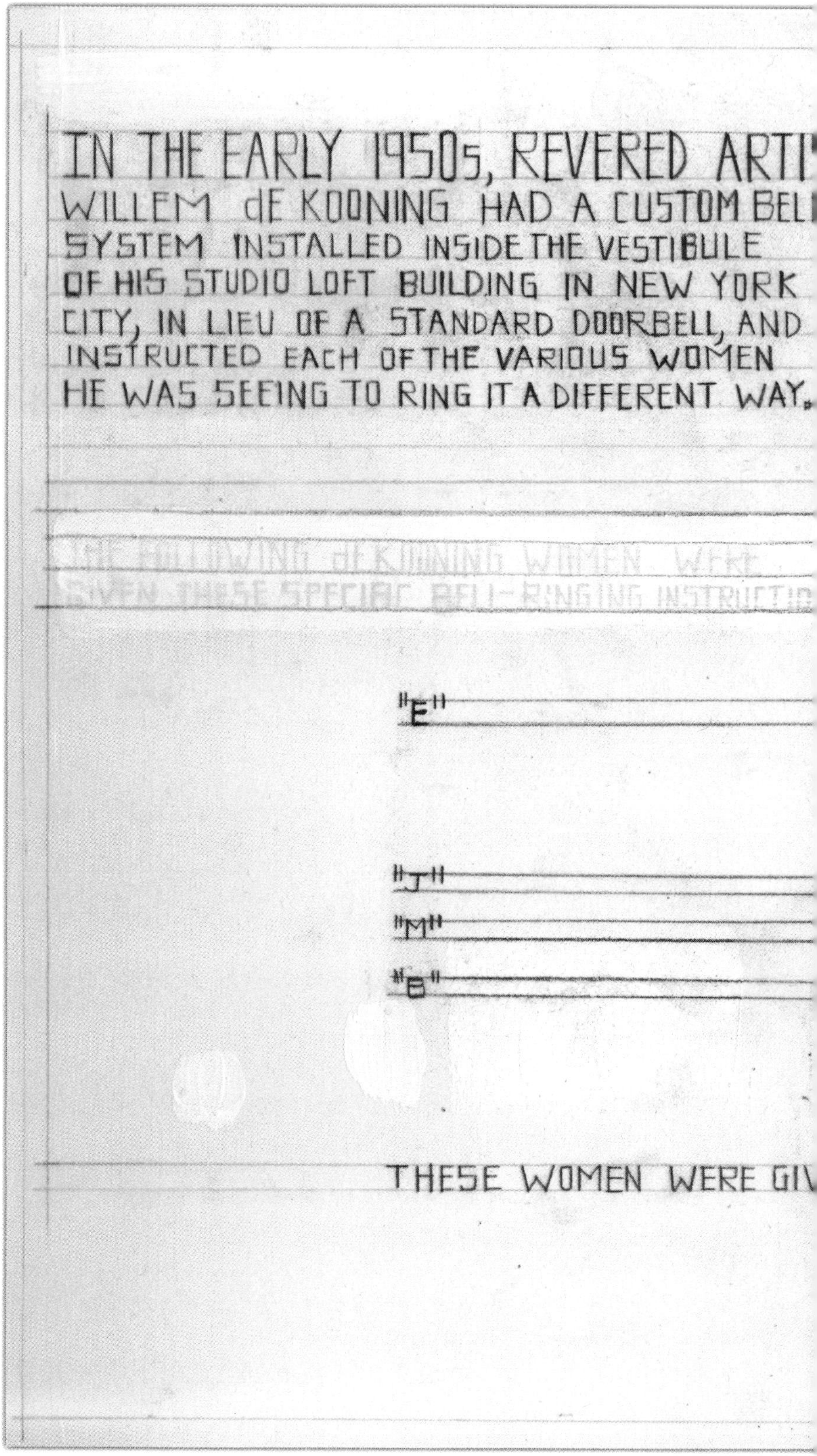
IN THE EARLY 1950s, REVERED ARTI
WILLEM dE KOONING HAD A CUSTOM BEL
SYSTEM INSTALLED INSIDE THE VESTIBULE
OF HIS STUDIO LOFT BUILDING IN NEW YORK
CITY, IN LIEU OF A STANDARD DOORBELL, AND
INSTRUCTED EACH OF THE VARIOUS WOMEN
HE WAS SEEING TO RING IT A DIFFERENT WAY.
THE FOLLOWING dE KOONING WOMEN WERE
GIVEN THESE SPECIAL BELL-RINGING INSTRUCTIO
"E"
"J"
"M"
"B"
THESE WOMEN WERE GIV

HIS WAY, IF HE WAS IN THE STUDIO
WITH ONE LADY AND ONE OF THE OTHER
ADIES WAS DOWNSTAIRS RINGING THE
ELL, HE'D BE ABLE TO MAKE A WELL-
NFORMED DECISION ABOUT WHETHER TO
UT SHORT THE IN-PROGRESS RENDEZVOUS
R CARRY ON WHILE IGNORING THE BELL
INGER BELOW.

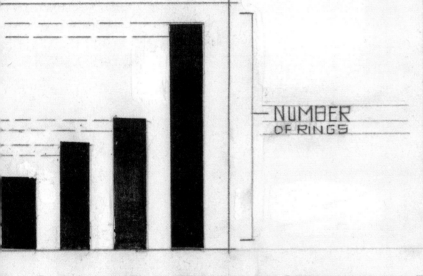

NUMBER
OF RINGS

CIFIC BELL-RINGING INSTRUCTIONS.

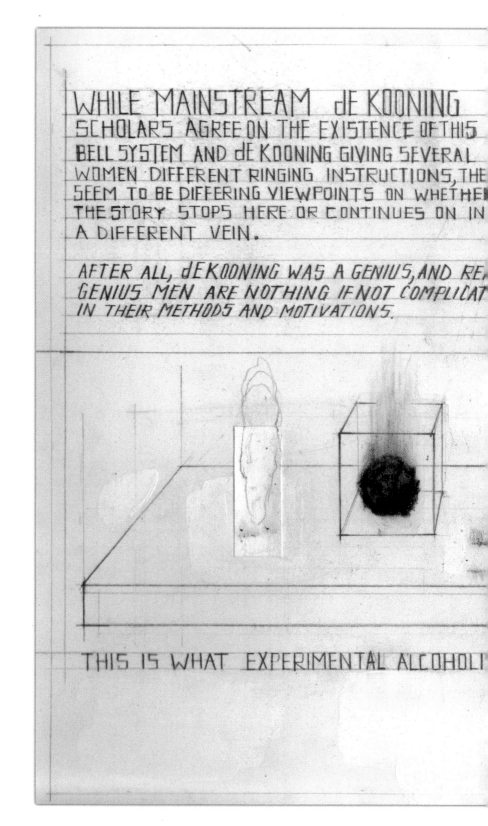

WHILE MAINSTREAM dE KOONING SCHOLARS AGREE ON THE EXISTENCE OF THIS BELL SYSTEM AND dE KOONING GIVING SEVERAL WOMEN DIFFERENT RINGING INSTRUCTIONS, THE SEEM TO BE DIFFERING VIEWPOINTS ON WHETHE THE STORY STOPS HERE OR CONTINUES ON IN A DIFFERENT VEIN.

AFTER ALL, dEKOONING WAS A GENIUS, AND RE GENIUS MEN ARE NOTHING IF NOT COMPLICAT IN THEIR METHODS AND MOTIVATIONS.

THIS IS WHAT EXPERIMENTAL ALCOHOLI

SEVERAL SOURCES CLAIM de KOONING
NEVER BEDDED AS MANY WOMEN AS WAS
GENERALLY ASSUMED, BUT THAT THERE WAS
A SERIOUS AMOUNT OF PRESSURE FOR de KOONING
TO CONSTRUCT BOTH A REPUTATION FOR SEXUAL
PROMISCUITY AND FOR EXPERIMENTAL
ALCOHOLISM THAT WOULD ENSURE HIS
STATUS AS ONE OF THE GREATEST ABSTRACT
EXPRESSIONIST ARTISTS OF ALL TIME.

ACCORDING TO THESE SOURCES, de KOONING WOULD
ENGAGE IN A DAILY RITUAL OF BED DISHEVELMENT
AND APPLE JUICE CONSUMPTION.
*(DOCTORED TO SMELL LIKE THE VILEST OF WHISKEYS)*

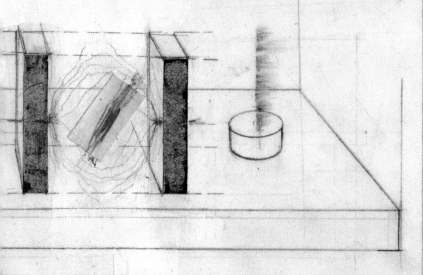

KS LIKE.

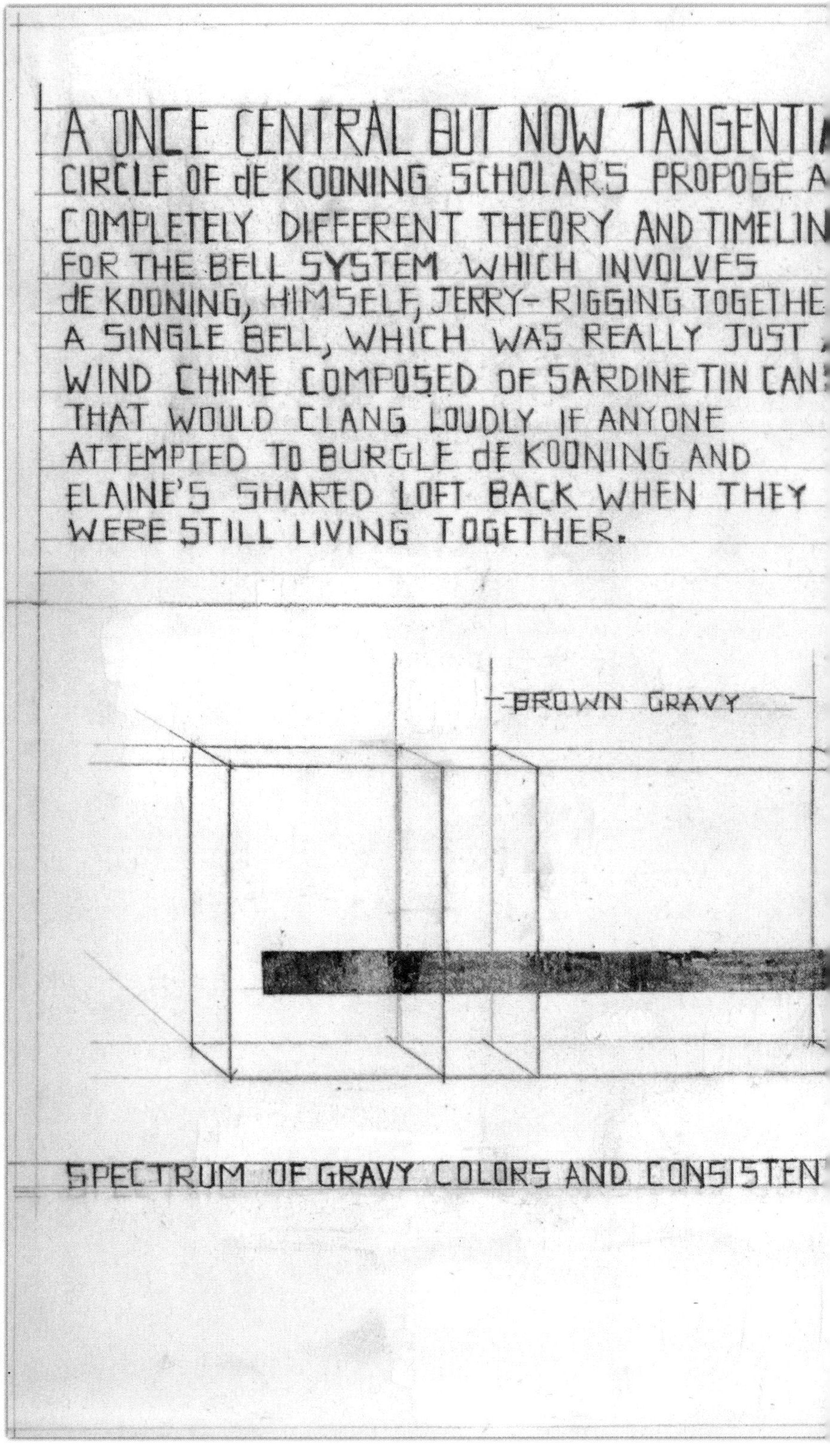

A ONCE CENTRAL BUT NOW TANGENTI
CIRCLE OF dE KOONING SCHOLARS PROPOSE A
COMPLETELY DIFFERENT THEORY AND TIMELIN
FOR THE BELL SYSTEM WHICH INVOLVES
dE KOONING, HIMSELF, JERRY-RIGGING TOGETHE
A SINGLE BELL, WHICH WAS REALLY JUST
WIND CHIME COMPOSED OF SARDINE TIN CAN
THAT WOULD CLANG LOUDLY IF ANYONE
ATTEMPTED TO BURGLE dE KOONING AND
ELAINE'S SHARED LOFT BACK WHEN THEY
WERE STILL LIVING TOGETHER.

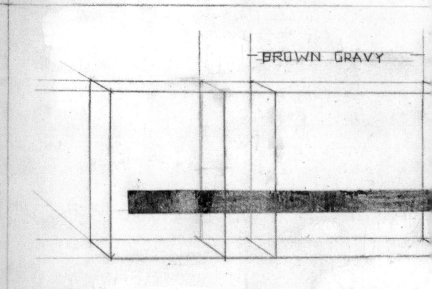

BROWN GRAVY

SPECTRUM OF GRAVY COLORS AND CONSISTEN

MYSTERIOUSLY DWINDLING SUPPLY OF
RAVY IN THEIR PANTRY LED dE KOONING TO
SSUME THAT SOMEONE WAS BREAKING IN
ND STEALING THE THICK BROWN (SOMETIMES
REY) SUBSTANCE, WHICH WAS OFTEN THE ONLY
HING THEY COULD AFFORD TO EAT IN THOSE
TORIED DAYS OF POVERTY.

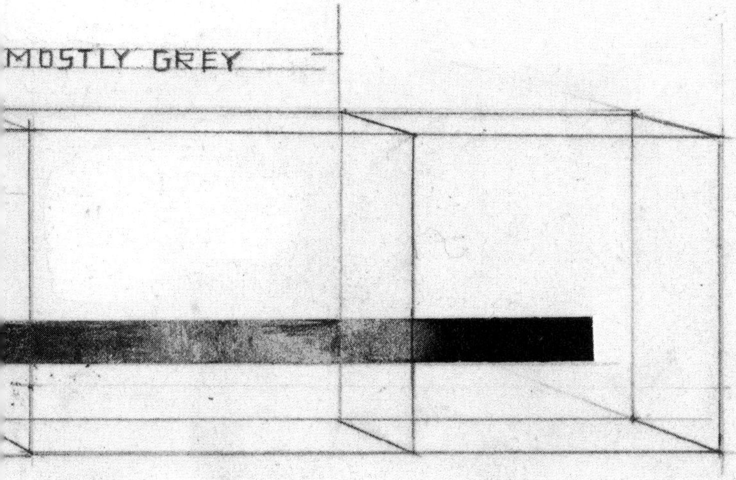
MOSTLY GREY

SED IN THE dE KOONING'S PANTRY

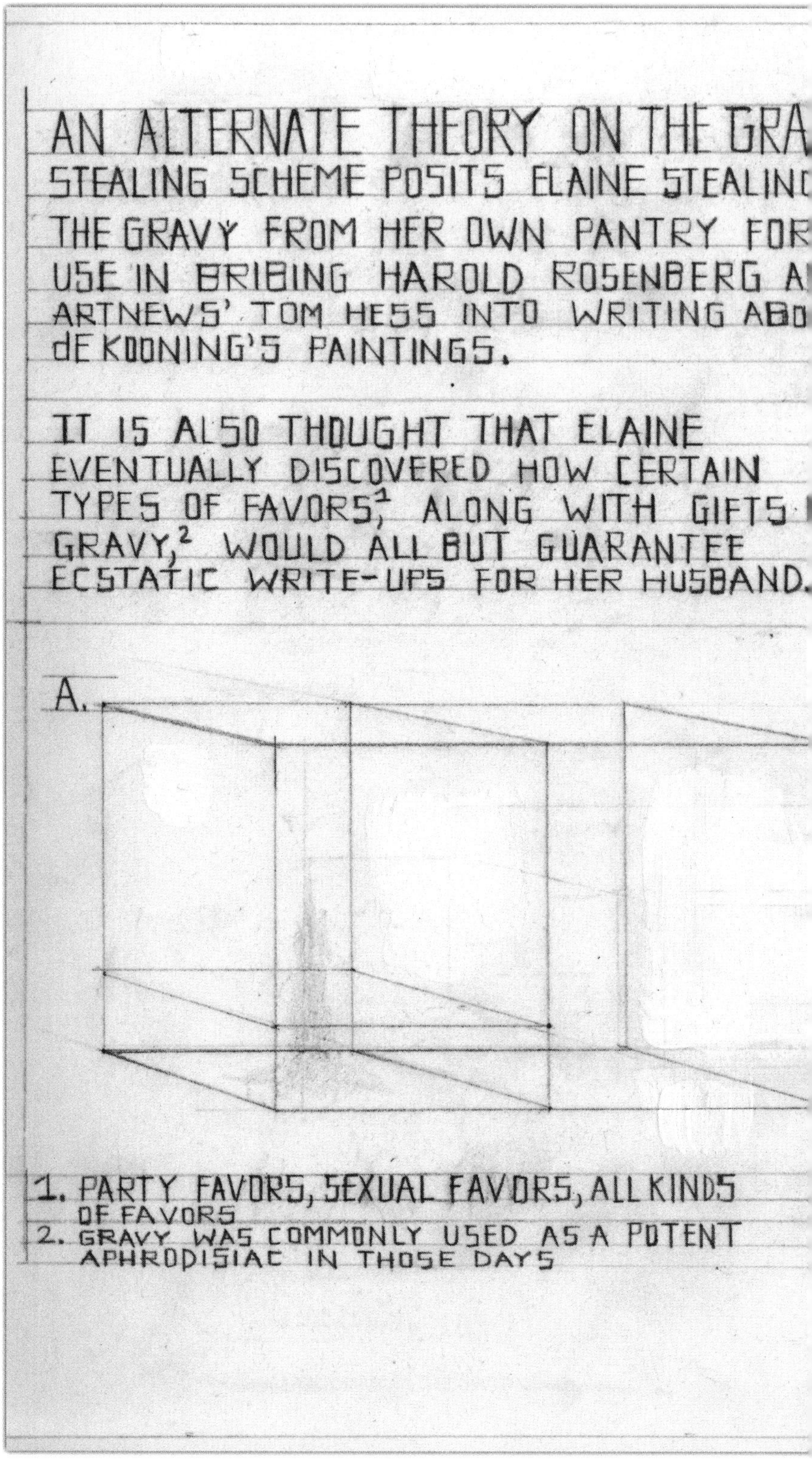

AN ALTERNATE THEORY ON THE GRA
STEALING SCHEME POSITS ELAINE STEALING
THE GRAVY FROM HER OWN PANTRY FOR
USE IN BRIBING HAROLD ROSENBERG AI
ARTNEWS' TOM HESS INTO WRITING ABO
dE KOONING'S PAINTINGS.

IT IS ALSO THOUGHT THAT ELAINE
EVENTUALLY DISCOVERED HOW CERTAIN
TYPES OF FAVORS[1], ALONG WITH GIFTS
GRAVY,[2] WOULD ALL BUT GUARANTEE
ECSTATIC WRITE-UPS FOR HER HUSBAND.

A.

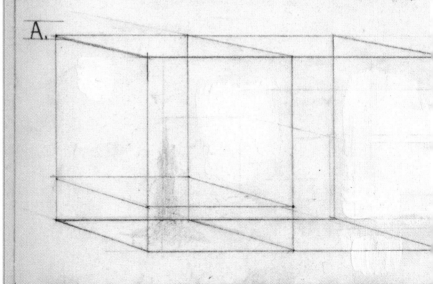

1. PARTY FAVORS, SEXUAL FAVORS, ALL KINDS
   OF FAVORS
2. GRAVY WAS COMMONLY USED AS A POTENT
   APHRODISIAC IN THOSE DAYS

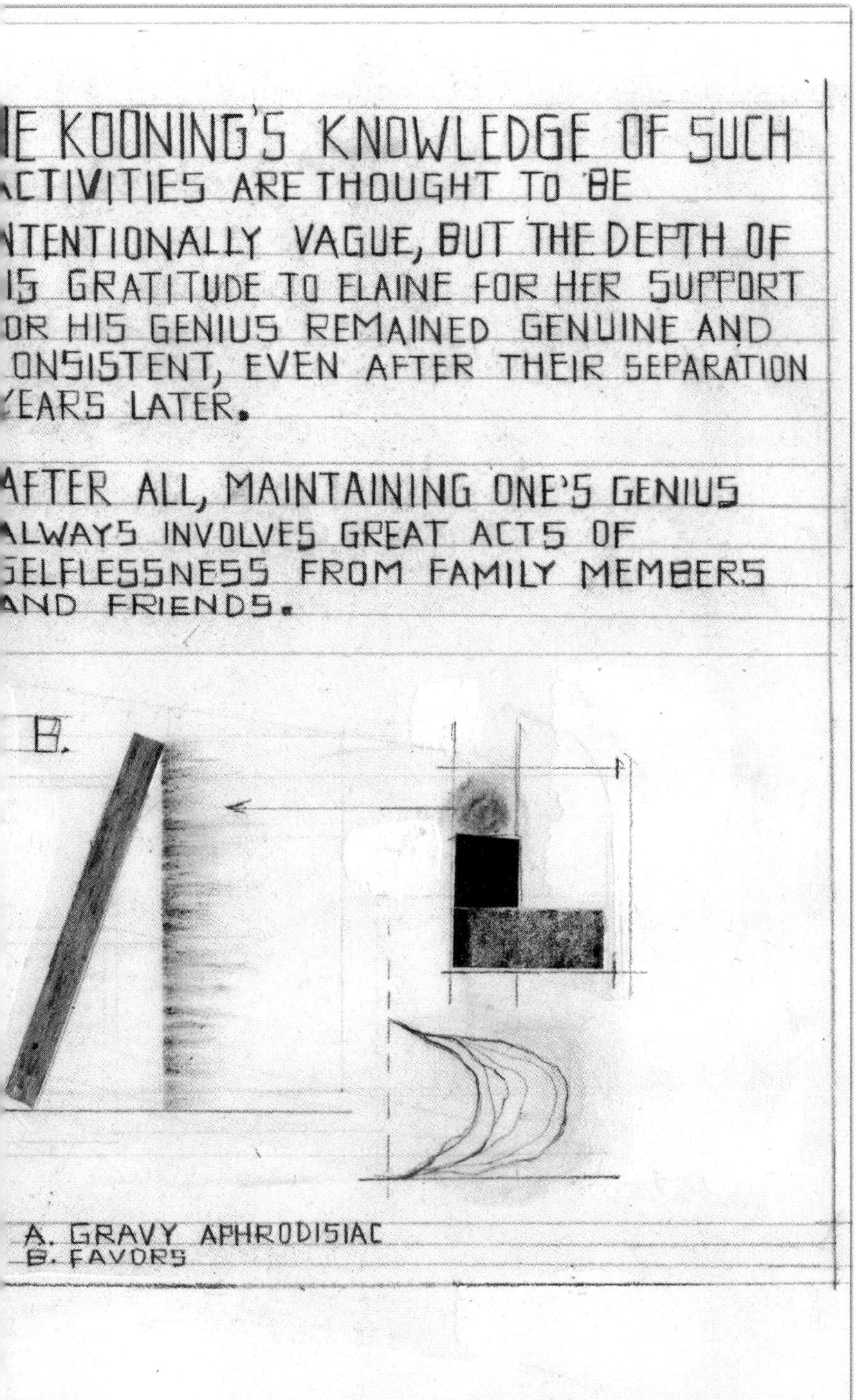

E KOONING'S KNOWLEDGE OF SUCH
ACTIVITIES ARE THOUGHT TO BE
NTENTIONALLY VAGUE, BUT THE DEPTH OF
IS GRATITUDE TO ELAINE FOR HER SUPPORT
OR HIS GENIUS REMAINED GENUINE AND
ONSISTENT, EVEN AFTER THEIR SEPARATION
YEARS LATER.

AFTER ALL, MAINTAINING ONE'S GENIUS
ALWAYS INVOLVES GREAT ACTS OF
SELFLESSNESS FROM FAMILY MEMBERS
AND FRIENDS.

B.

A. GRAVY APHRODISIAC
B. FAVORS

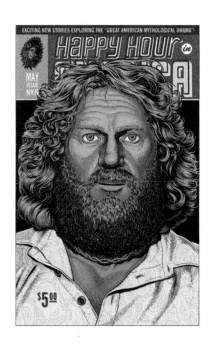

EXCITING NEW STORIES EXPLORING THE "GREAT AMERICAN MYTHOLOGICAL DRAMA"!
HAPPY HOUR in
MAY
ISSUE
Nº6
$5.00

# Remembering the Millionaire Hobo

## TIM LANE

*originally published in*

*The Riverfront Times*

and

*Happy Hour in America*, no. 6

SELF-PUBLISHED

6.63 × 10.19 inches • 28 pages

### Biography

Tim Lane is a graphic novelist and freelance illustrator. He is the author of *Abandoned Cars* (2007) and *The Lonesome Go* (2014), both published by Fantagraphics Books. He is also the creator of the comic book *Happy Hour in America* and produces graphic feature stories for the *Riverfront Times*.
jackienoname.com

### Statement

"Remembering the Millionaire Hobo" is a graphic feature story I produced for the *Riverfront Times* about the unusual and extraordinary life of James Eads How.

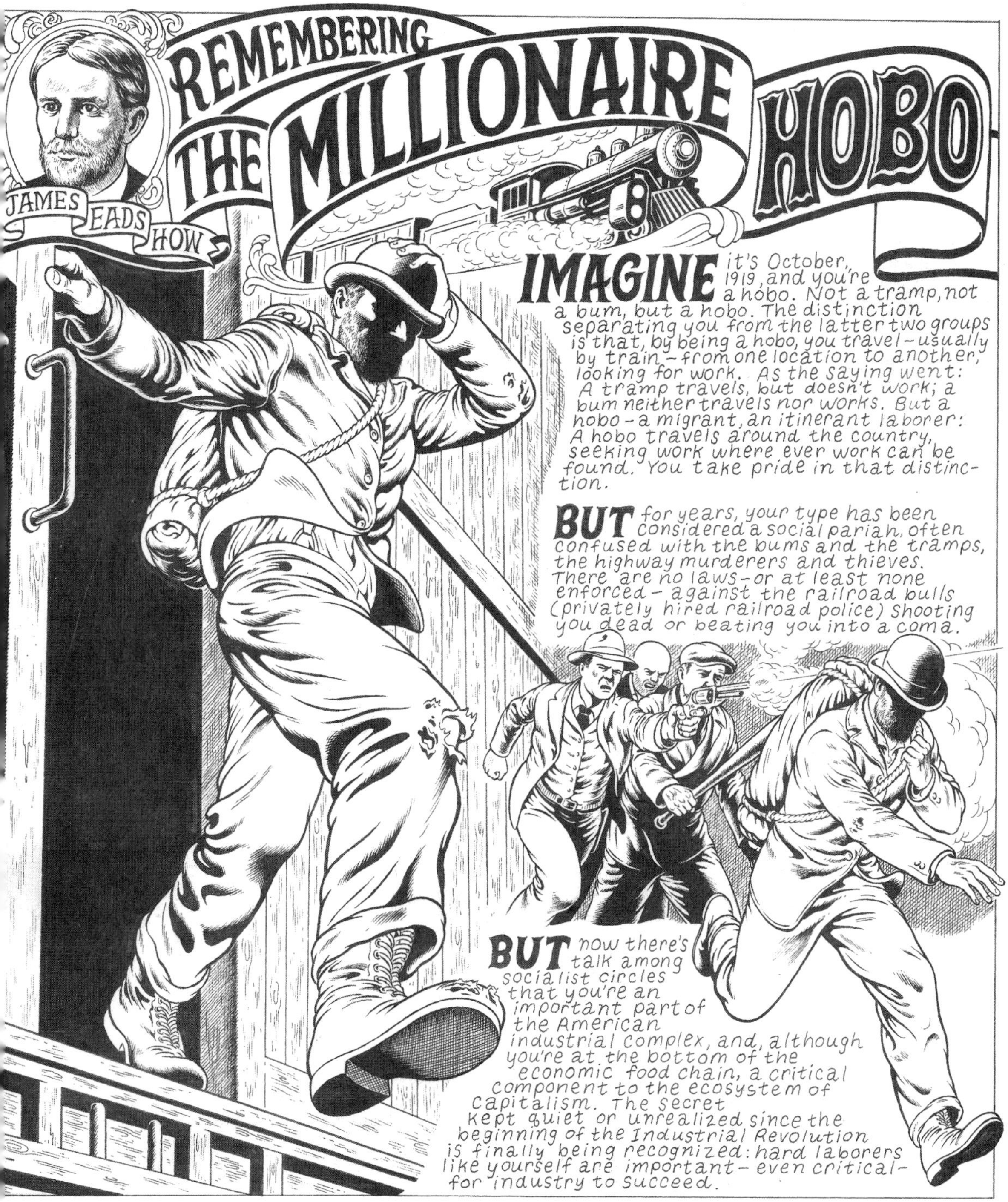
REMEMBERING THE MILLIONAIRE HOBO
JAMES EADS HOW
IMAGINE it's October, 1919, and you're a hobo. Not a tramp, not a bum, but a hobo. The distinction separating you from the latter two groups is that, by being a hobo, you travel—usually by train—from one location to another, looking for work. As the saying went: A tramp travels, but doesn't work; a bum neither travels nor works. But a hobo—a migrant, an itinerant laborer: A hobo travels around the country, seeking work where ever work can be found. You take pride in that distinction.
BUT for years, your type has been considered a social pariah, often confused with the bums and the tramps, the highway murderers and thieves. There are no laws—or at least none enforced—against the railroad bulls (privately hired railroad police) shooting you dead or beating you into a coma.
BUT now there's talk among socialist circles that you're an important part of the American industrial complex, and, although you're at the bottom of the economic food chain, a critical component to the ecosystem of capitalism. The secret kept quiet or unrealized since the beginning of the Industrial Revolution is finally being recognized: hard laborers like yourself are important—even critical—for industry to succeed.

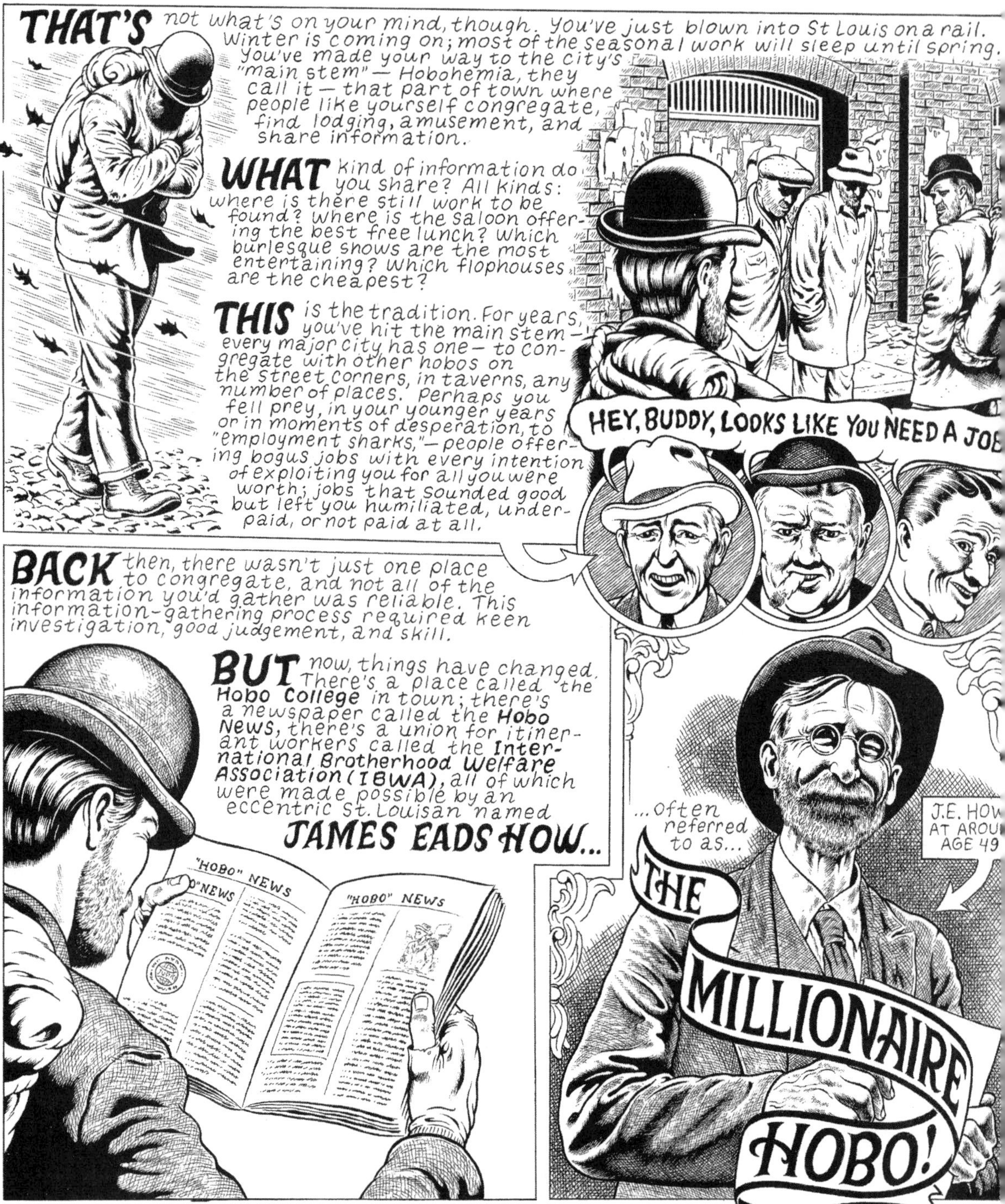
THAT'S not what's on your mind, though. You've just blown into St Louis on a rail. Winter is coming on; most of the seasonal work will sleep until spring. You've made your way to the city's "main stem" — Hobohemia, they call it — that part of town where people like yourself congregate, find lodging, amusement, and share information.
WHAT kind of information do you share? All kinds: where is there still work to be found? Where is the saloon offering the best free lunch? Which burlesque shows are the most entertaining? Which flophouses are the cheapest?
THIS is the tradition. For years, you've hit the main stem — every major city has one — to congregate with other hobos on the street corners, in taverns, any number of places. Perhaps you fell prey, in your younger years or in moments of desperation, to "employment sharks," — people offering bogus jobs with every intention of exploiting you for all you were worth; jobs that sounded good but left you humiliated, underpaid, or not paid at all.
HEY, BUDDY, LOOKS LIKE YOU NEED A JOB
BACK then, there wasn't just one place to congregate, and not all of the information you'd gather was reliable. This information-gathering process required keen investigation, good judgement, and skill.
BUT now, things have changed. There's a place called the Hobo College in town; there's a newspaper called the Hobo News, there's a union for itinerant workers called the International Brotherhood Welfare Association (IBWA), all of which were made possible by an eccentric St. Louisan named JAMES EADS HOW...
"HOBO" NEWS
"HOBO" NEWS
...often referred to as...
J.E. HOW AT AROU AGE 49
THE MILLIONAIRE HOBO!

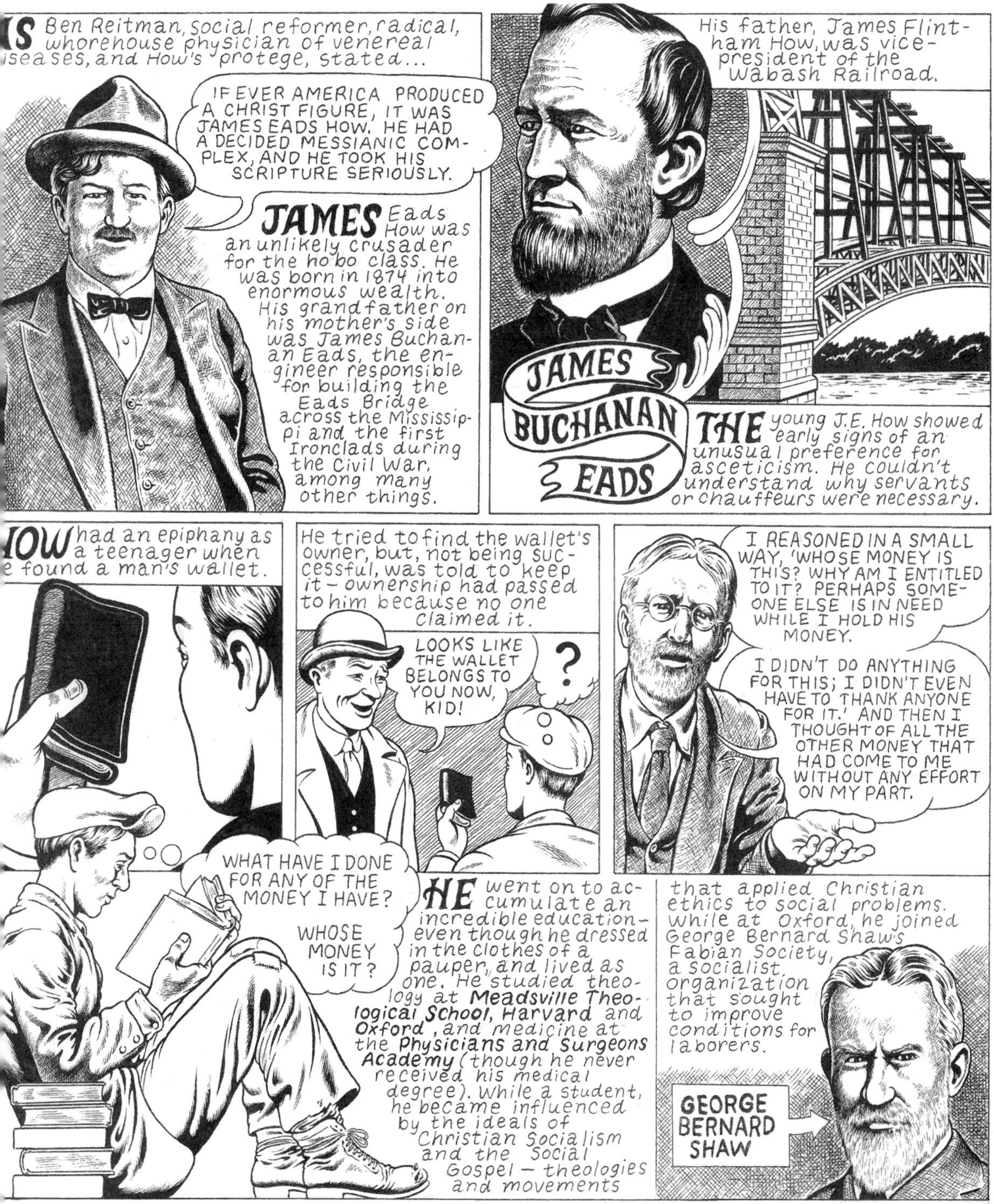

[A]S Ben Reitman, social reformer, radical, whorehouse physician of venereal [d]iseases, and How's protege, stated...
IF EVER AMERICA PRODUCED A CHRIST FIGURE, IT WAS JAMES EADS HOW. HE HAD A DECIDED MESSIANIC COMPLEX, AND HE TOOK HIS SCRIPTURE SERIOUSLY.
JAMES Eads How was an unlikely crusader for the hobo class. He was born in 1874 into enormous wealth. His grandfather on his mother's side was James Buchanan Eads, the engineer responsible for building the Eads Bridge across the Mississippi and the first Ironclads during the Civil War, among many other things.
His father, James Flintham How, was vice-president of the Wabash Railroad.
JAMES BUCHANAN EADS
THE young J.E. How showed early signs of an unusual preference for asceticism. He couldn't understand why servants or chauffeurs were necessary.
[H]OW had an epiphany as a teenager when [h]e found a man's wallet.
He tried to find the wallet's owner, but, not being successful, was told to keep it—ownership had passed to him because no one claimed it.
LOOKS LIKE THE WALLET BELONGS TO YOU NOW, KID!
?
I REASONED IN A SMALL WAY, 'WHOSE MONEY IS THIS? WHY AM I ENTITLED TO IT? PERHAPS SOMEONE ELSE IS IN NEED WHILE I HOLD HIS MONEY.
I DIDN'T DO ANYTHING FOR THIS; I DIDN'T EVEN HAVE TO THANK ANYONE FOR IT.' AND THEN I THOUGHT OF ALL THE OTHER MONEY THAT HAD COME TO ME WITHOUT ANY EFFORT ON MY PART.
WHAT HAVE I DONE FOR ANY OF THE MONEY I HAVE?
WHOSE MONEY IS IT?
HE went on to accumulate an incredible education—even though he dressed in the clothes of a pauper, and lived as one. He studied theology at Meadsville Theological School, Harvard and Oxford, and medicine at the Physicians and Surgeons Academy (though he never received his medical degree). While a student, he became influenced by the ideals of Christian Socialism and the Social Gospel—theologies and movements
that applied Christian ethics to social problems. While at Oxford, he joined George Bernard Shaw's Fabian Society, a socialist organization that sought to improve conditions for laborers.
GEORGE BERNARD SHAW

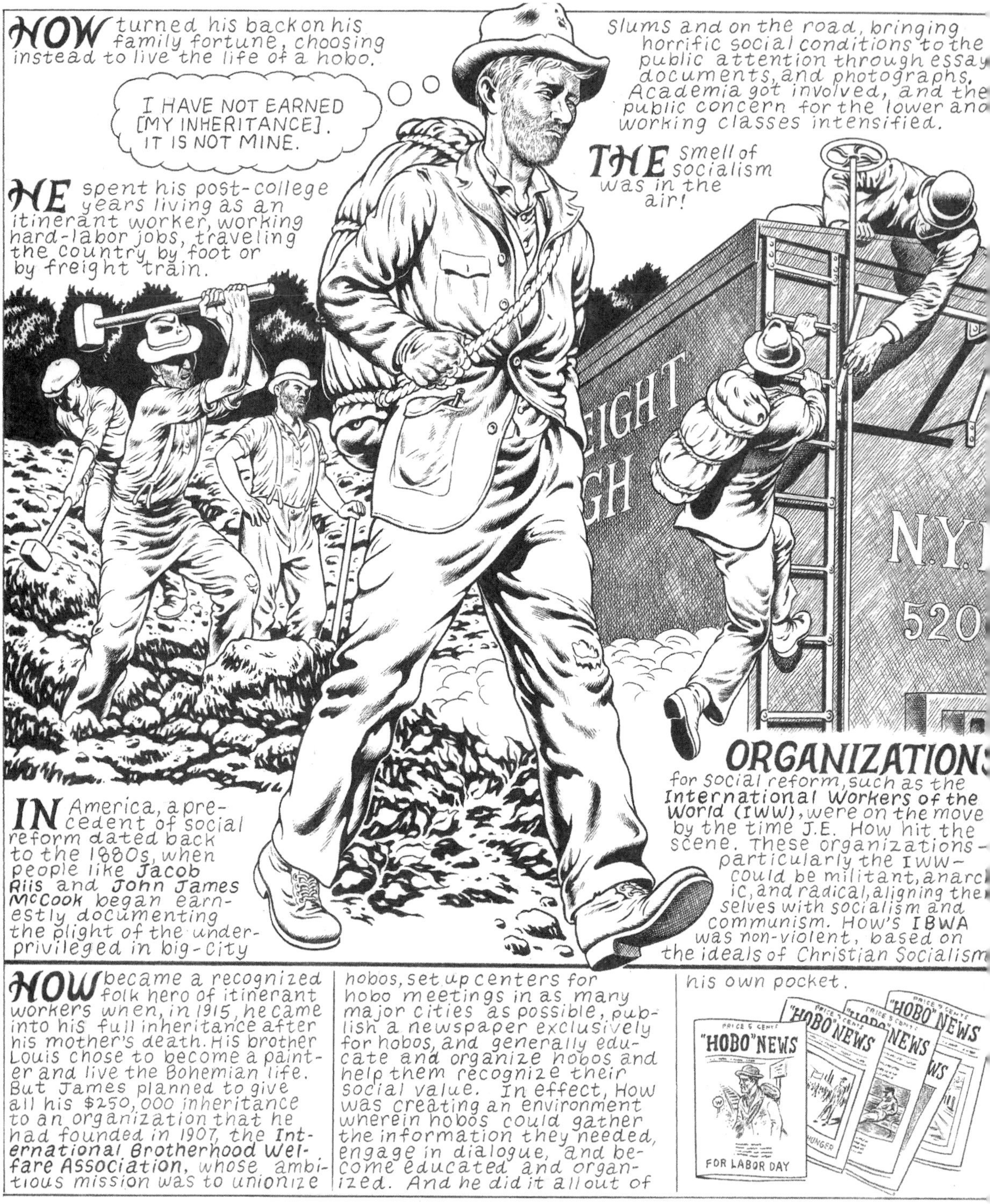
HOW turned his back on his family fortune, choosing instead to live the life of a hobo.
I HAVE NOT EARNED [MY INHERITANCE]. IT IS NOT MINE.
HE spent his post-college years living as an itinerant worker, working hard-labor jobs, traveling the country by foot or by freight train.
IN America, a precedent of social reform dated back to the 1880s, when people like Jacob Riis and John James McCook began earnestly documenting the plight of the underprivileged in big-city
slums and on the road, bringing horrific social conditions to the public attention through essays, documents, and photographs. Academia got involved, and the public concern for the lower and working classes intensified.
THE smell of socialism was in the air!
EIGHT
GH
N.Y.
520
ORGANIZATIONS
for social reform, such as the International Workers of the World (IWW), were on the move by the time J.E. How hit the scene. These organizations—particularly the IWW—could be militant, anarchic, and radical, aligning themselves with socialism and communism. How's IBWA was non-violent, based on the ideals of Christian Socialism.
HOW became a recognized folk hero of itinerant workers when, in 1915, he came into his full inheritance after his mother's death. His brother Louis chose to become a painter and live the Bohemian life. But James planned to give all his $250,000 inheritance to an organization that he had founded in 1907, the International Brotherhood Welfare Association, whose ambitious mission was to unionize
hobos, set up centers for hobo meetings in as many major cities as possible, publish a newspaper exclusively for hobos, and generally educate and organize hobos and help them recognize their social value. In effect, How was creating an environment wherein hobos could gather the information they needed, engage in dialogue, and become educated and organized. And he did it all out of
his own pocket.
PRICE 5 CENTS
"HOBO" NEWS
FOR LABOR DAY
"HOBO" NEWS
"HOBO" NEWS
"HOBO" NEWS

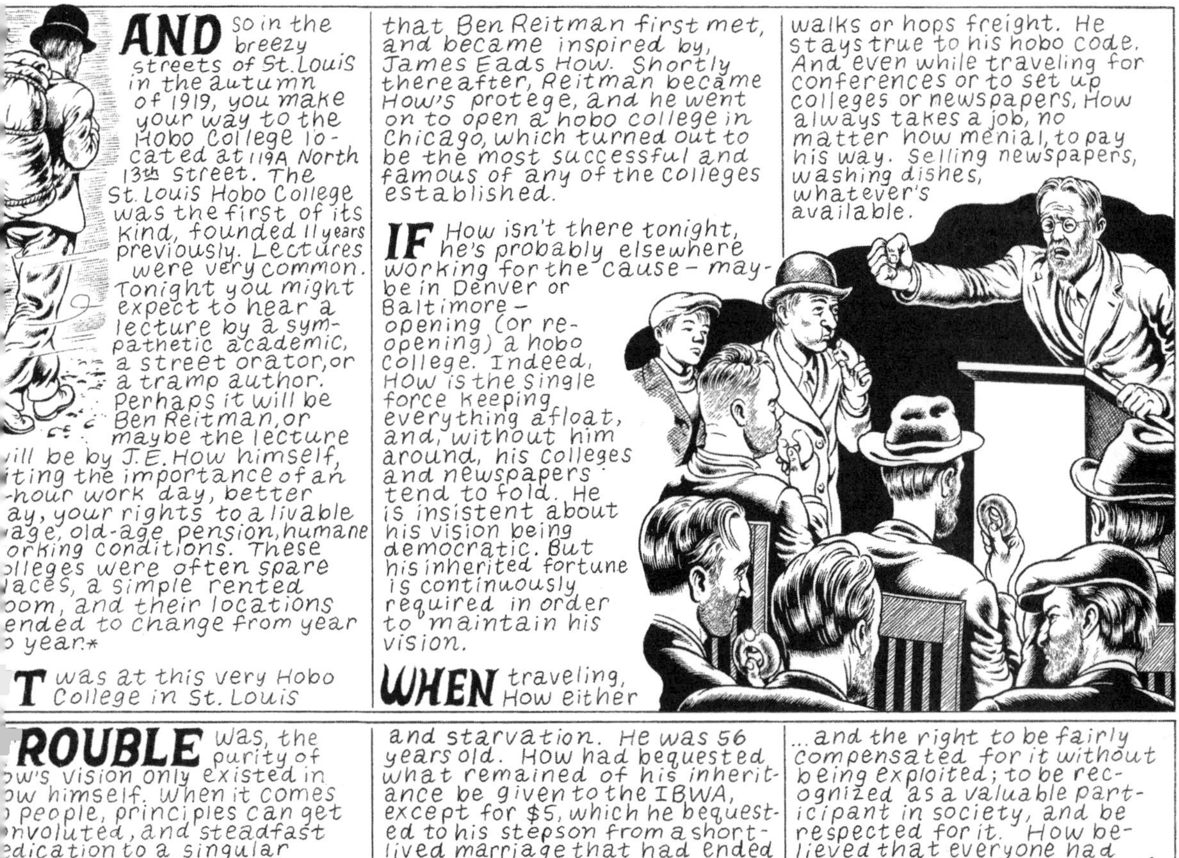

**AND** so in the breezy streets of St. Louis in the autumn of 1919, you make your way to the Hobo College located at 119A North 13th Street. The St. Louis Hobo College was the first of its kind, founded 11 years previously. Lectures were very common. Tonight you might expect to hear a lecture by a sympathetic academic, a street orator, or a tramp author. Perhaps it will be Ben Reitman, or maybe the lecture will be by J.E. How himself, stating the importance of an 8-hour work day, better pay, your rights to a livable wage, old-age pension, humane working conditions. These colleges were often spare places, a simple rented room, and their locations tended to change from year to year.*

**IT** was at this very Hobo College in St. Louis that Ben Reitman first met, and became inspired by, James Eads How. Shortly thereafter, Reitman became How's protégé, and he went on to open a hobo college in Chicago, which turned out to be the most successful and famous of any of the colleges established.

**IF** How isn't there tonight, he's probably elsewhere working for the cause — maybe in Denver or Baltimore — opening (or re-opening) a hobo college. Indeed, How is the single force keeping everything afloat, and, without him around, his colleges and newspapers tend to fold. He is insistent about his vision being democratic. But his inherited fortune is continuously required in order to maintain his vision.

**WHEN** traveling, How either walks or hops freight. He stays true to his hobo code. And even while traveling for conferences or to set up colleges or newspapers, How always takes a job, no matter how menial, to pay his way. Selling newspapers, washing dishes, whatever's available.

**TROUBLE** was, the purity of How's vision only existed in How himself. When it comes to people, principles can get convoluted, and steadfast dedication to a singular ideal is a lonely and alienating occupation. J.E. How was taken advantage of by his own people, and, if it weren't for his deep pockets, it's unlikely that any of the colleges or papers would have stayed in operation. How's critics commented cynically that the only thing attracting itinerant workers to his colleges, meetings, and lectures were the doughnuts and stale bread on offer. Despite this, How doggedly remained true to his ideals and his cause, unintimidated by his critics.

**JAMES** Eads How died on July 2, 1930, shortly after collapsing in Cincinnati's Union Station. The causes of death were reportedly pneumonia and starvation. He was 56 years old. How had bequeathed what remained of his inheritance be given to the IBWA, except for $5, which he bequeathed to his stepson from a short-lived marriage that had ended two years previously. But thanks to legal shenanigans, How's stepson received the full inheritance; the IBWA was left to fend for itself.

**HOW'S** legacy is still significant: He fought for an enriched appreciation for the work someone does...

...and the right to be fairly compensated for it without being exploited; to be recognized as a valuable participant in society, and be respected for it. How believed that everyone had the right to their own piece of the American Dream — an issue as important today as it was then, and also just as polarizing.

According to issues of the **HOBO NEWS**, the IBWA local for St. Louis in 1919 was located at 119A North 13th Street. However, in 1918, it was at 617 Elm Street; in 1917, 1113 Clark Avenue; and in 1916, it was at 26-28 South 12th Street.

# The Kanibul Ball

LALE WESTVIND

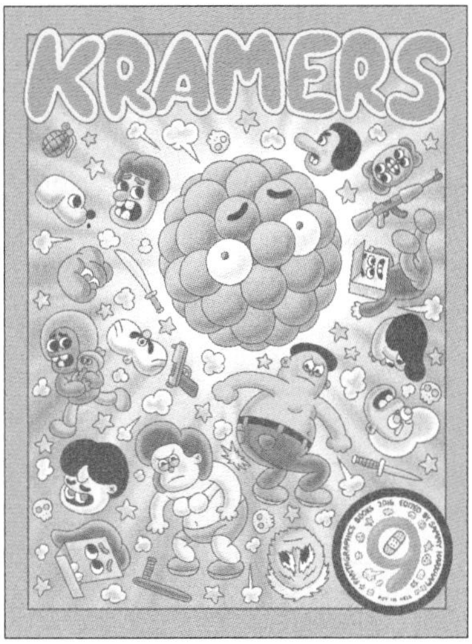
KRAMERS
9

*originally published in*

*Kramers Ergot*, vol. 9

FANTAGRAPHICS BOOKS

9 × 11.75 inches • 296 pages

## Biography

Lale Westvind is an artist working in comics, animation, and painting. She is currently teaching as an adjunct professor at the Parsons School of Design whilst working to complete as much work as time allows.
lalewestvind.tumblr.com

## Statement

I was trying to imagine a ritual to make sense of all the pain in the universe, a kind of absolute empathetic exchange, and I wanted to place a down-and-out person there, as representative for the human race, someone who couldn't even care for themselves, let alone others. The character is warped by the encounter, by their inability to transcend the ritual, into something angry and violent. They become a devotee of Chaos, isolated in the coldest, darkest wood.

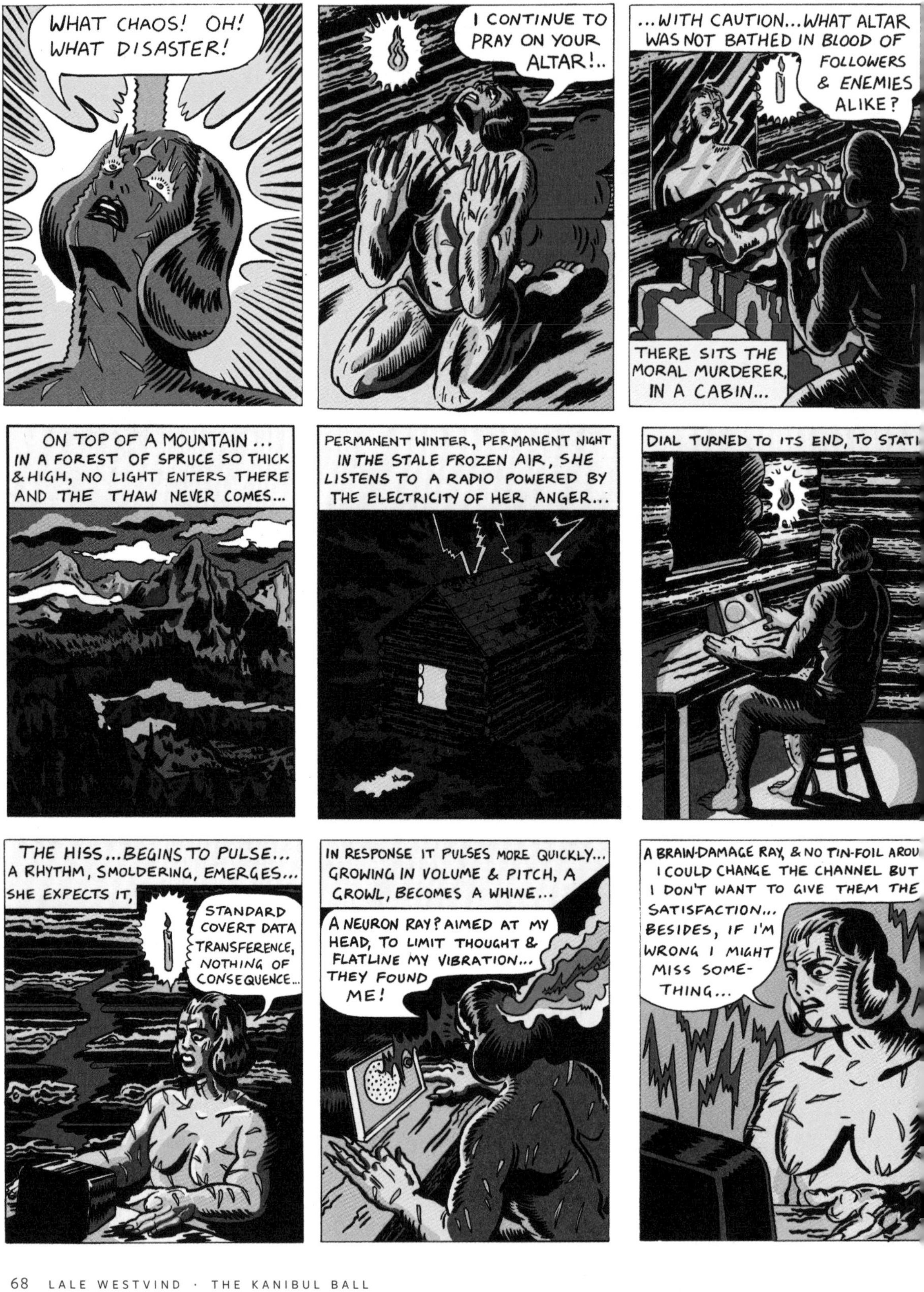
WHAT CHAOS! OH! WHAT DISASTER!
I CONTINUE TO PRAY ON YOUR ALTAR!..
...WITH CAUTION...WHAT ALTAR WAS NOT BATHED IN BLOOD OF FOLLOWERS & ENEMIES ALIKE?
THERE SITS THE MORAL MURDERER, IN A CABIN...
ON TOP OF A MOUNTAIN ... IN A FOREST OF SPRUCE SO THICK & HIGH, NO LIGHT ENTERS THERE AND THE THAW NEVER COMES...
PERMANENT WINTER, PERMANENT NIGHT IN THE STALE FROZEN AIR, SHE LISTENS TO A RADIO POWERED BY THE ELECTRICITY OF HER ANGER...
DIAL TURNED TO ITS END, TO STATI
THE HISS...BEGINS TO PULSE... A RHYTHM, SMOLDERING, EMERGES...
SHE EXPECTS IT,
STANDARD COVERT DATA TRANSFERENCE, NOTHING OF CONSEQUENCE...
IN RESPONSE IT PULSES MORE QUICKLY... GROWING IN VOLUME & PITCH, A GROWL, BECOMES A WHINE...
A NEURON RAY? AIMED AT MY HEAD, TO LIMIT THOUGHT & FLATLINE MY VIBRATION... THEY FOUND ME!
A BRAIN-DAMAGE RAY, & NO TIN-FOIL AROU
I COULD CHANGE THE CHANNEL BUT I DON'T WANT TO GIVE THEM THE SATISFACTION... BESIDES, IF I'M WRONG I MIGHT MISS SOMETHING...

AND SO...

MEANWHILE, IN ANOTHER WORLD, ON ANOTHER PLANE... DEEP IN THE JUNGLE, BENEATH THE VOLCANO, A TEN-MILE-HIGH TOWER OF CHROME & STAINLESS STEEL, RISING UP FROM AN IMMENSE CRATER...

INSIDE THE TOWER A CEREMONY OF INTIMATE FEASTING & DISCUSSION IS TAKING PLACE...

ANIMALS GATHER AT THE EDGE OF THE CRATER TO GOSSIP DETAILS OF THE EVENT...

"THEY" SET THE TABLE FIRST... BANQUET STYLE...

WHAT DO YOU MEAN?

THE KANIBUL BALL

PLATES & SILVERWARE! ALL LIKE A ROYAL BANQUET 'CEPT THE KNIVES ARE SHARP ENOUGH TO SLICE BONE! AND THE TABLE CLOTH IS DYED... IN BLOOD!

WHO CLEANS UP THE MESS AFTERWARDS?

OH IT DON'T GET TOO MESSY, THEY GET SO HUNGRY IN THERE...

THEY LICK THE PLACE CLEAN!

I BET IT REEKS OF SALIVA !

THAT MUST BE WHY THEY TORCH THE ROOM AFTERWARDS!

THEY TORCH THE WHOLE TOWER!

WITH PLASMA BEAMS FROM SPACE!..

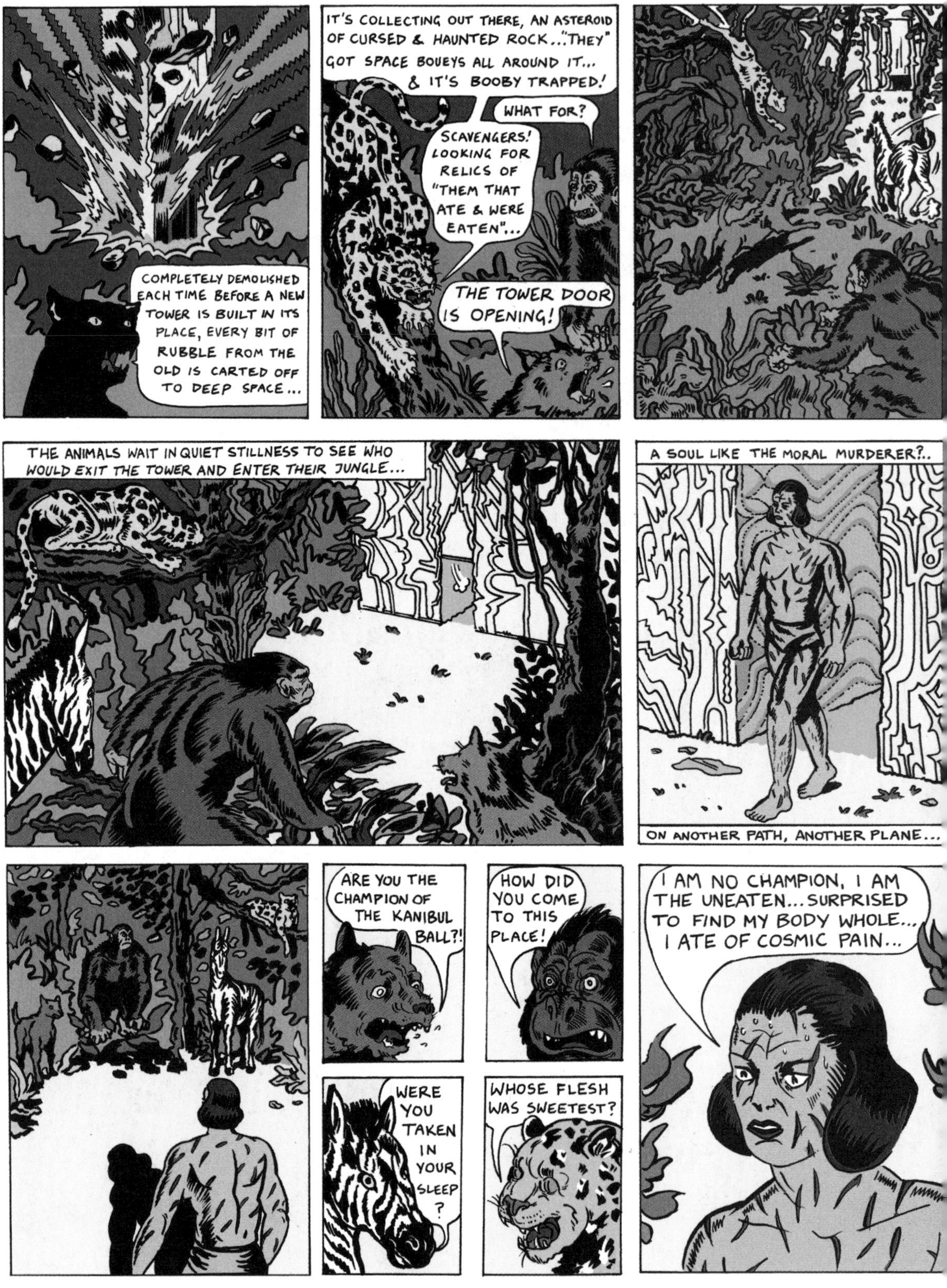
COMPLETELY DEMOLISHED EACH TIME BEFORE A NEW TOWER IS BUILT IN ITS PLACE, EVERY BIT OF RUBBLE FROM THE OLD IS CARTED OFF TO DEEP SPACE...
IT'S COLLECTING OUT THERE, AN ASTEROID OF CURSED & HAUNTED ROCK..."THEY" GOT SPACE BOUEYS ALL AROUND IT... & IT'S BOOBY TRAPPED!
WHAT FOR?
SCAVENGERS! LOOKING FOR RELICS OF "THEM THAT ATE & WERE EATEN"...
THE TOWER DOOR IS OPENING!
THE ANIMALS WAIT IN QUIET STILLNESS TO SEE WHO WOULD EXIT THE TOWER AND ENTER THEIR JUNGLE...
A SOUL LIKE THE MORAL MURDERER?..
ON ANOTHER PATH, ANOTHER PLANE...
ARE YOU THE CHAMPION OF THE KANIBUL BALL?!
HOW DID YOU COME TO THIS PLACE!
WERE YOU TAKEN IN YOUR SLEEP?
WHOSE FLESH WAS SWEETEST?
I AM NO CHAMPION, I AM THE UNEATEN... SURPRISED TO FIND MY BODY WHOLE... I ATE OF COSMIC PAIN...

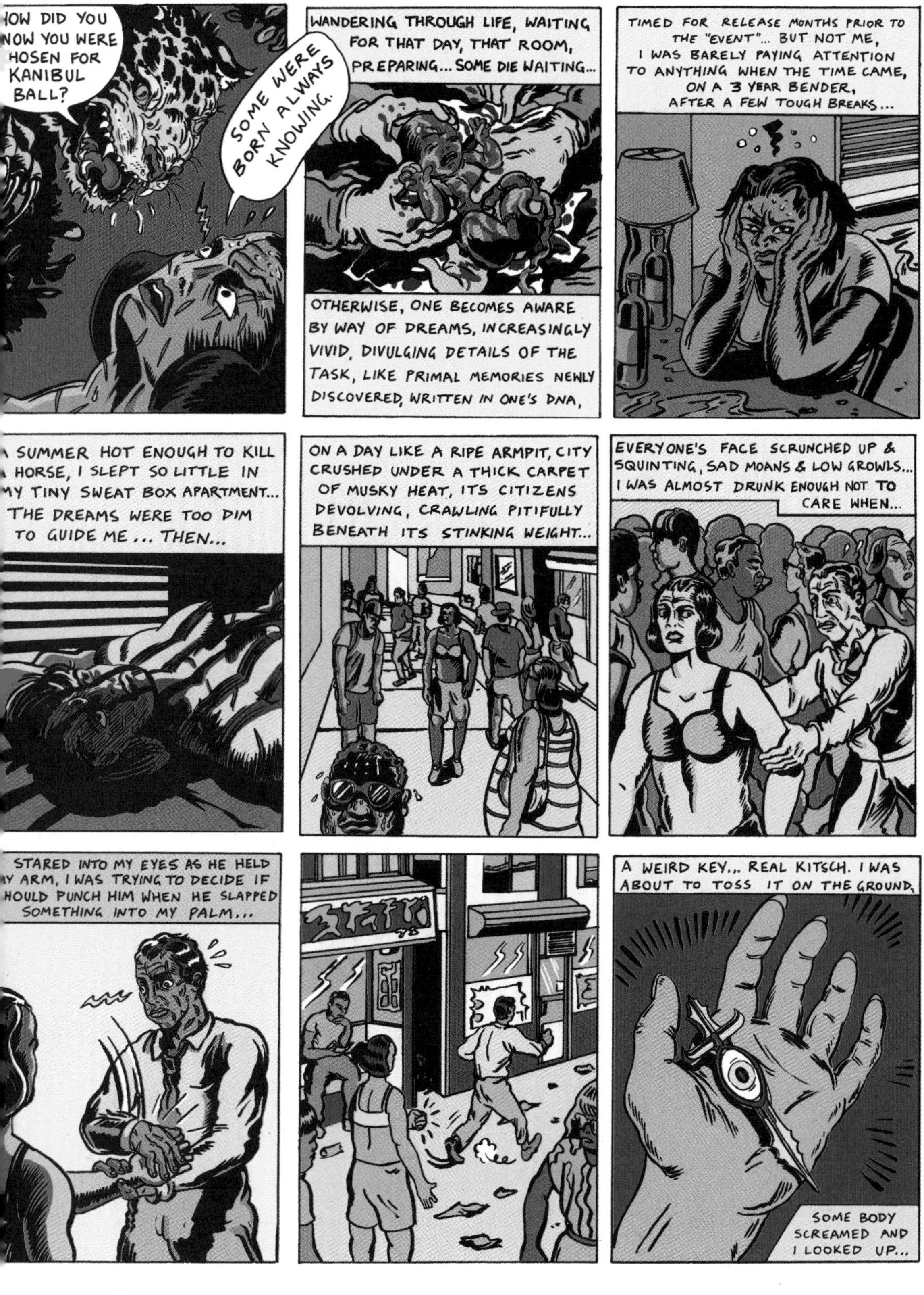

OW DID YOU NOW YOU WERE HOSEN FOR KANIBUL BALL?
SOME WERE BORN ALWAYS KNOWING.
WANDERING THROUGH LIFE, WAITING FOR THAT DAY, THAT ROOM, PREPARING... SOME DIE WAITING...
OTHERWISE, ONE BECOMES AWARE BY WAY OF DREAMS, INCREASINGLY VIVID, DIVULGING DETAILS OF THE TASK, LIKE PRIMAL MEMORIES NEWLY DISCOVERED, WRITTEN IN ONE'S DNA,
TIMED FOR RELEASE MONTHS PRIOR TO THE "EVENT"... BUT NOT ME, I WAS BARELY PAYING ATTENTION TO ANYTHING WHEN THE TIME CAME, ON A 3 YEAR BENDER, AFTER A FEW TOUGH BREAKS...
SUMMER HOT ENOUGH TO KILL HORSE, I SLEPT SO LITTLE IN MY TINY SWEAT BOX APARTMENT... THE DREAMS WERE TOO DIM TO GUIDE ME... THEN...
ON A DAY LIKE A RIPE ARMPIT, CITY CRUSHED UNDER A THICK CARPET OF MUSKY HEAT, ITS CITIZENS DEVOLVING, CRAWLING PITIFULLY BENEATH ITS STINKING WEIGHT...
EVERYONE'S FACE SCRUNCHED UP & SQUINTING, SAD MOANS & LOW GROWLS... I WAS ALMOST DRUNK ENOUGH NOT TO CARE WHEN...
STARED INTO MY EYES AS HE HELD Y ARM, I WAS TRYING TO DECIDE IF HOULD PUNCH HIM WHEN HE SLAPPED SOMETHING INTO MY PALM...
A WEIRD KEY... REAL KITSCH. I WAS ABOUT TO TOSS IT ON THE GROUND,
SOME BODY SCREAMED AND I LOOKED UP...

AN ASTEROID

EXCUSE ME,

DO YOU HAVE THE TIME?

NO, DON'T YOU?

HE BORE A STRIKING RESEMBLANCE TO THE OTHER MAN, DISTRACTED...

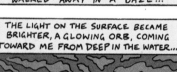

I PUT THE KEY IN MY POCKET AND WALKED AWAY IN A DAZE...

I GRABBED A BAGGER 'N' WENT DOWN TO RIVER PARK TO SIT ON A BENCH & WATCH JOGGERS GO BY, THOSE FUCKERS,

WASTIN' ALL THAT ENERGY...

THERE I WAS, BUZZ STARTIN', ROCKING SLOWLY TO THE RHYTHM OF INTOXICATION STARIN' AT THE WATER, AT THE SETTING SUN'S REFLECTION...

THE LIGHT ON THE SURFACE BECAME BRIGHTER, A GLOWING ORB, COMING TOWARD ME FROM DEEP IN THE WATER...

AFTER A WHILE I LOOKED AROUND... IT WAS SUDDENLY DARK, NOT A SOUL IN SIGHT, I TURNED BACK TOWARDS THE GLOW...

I IMAGINED MY FACE, SEEN FROM THE OTHER SIDE OF THAT BEAM, A SWEATY RED MOON IN A SEA OF VELVET BLACK

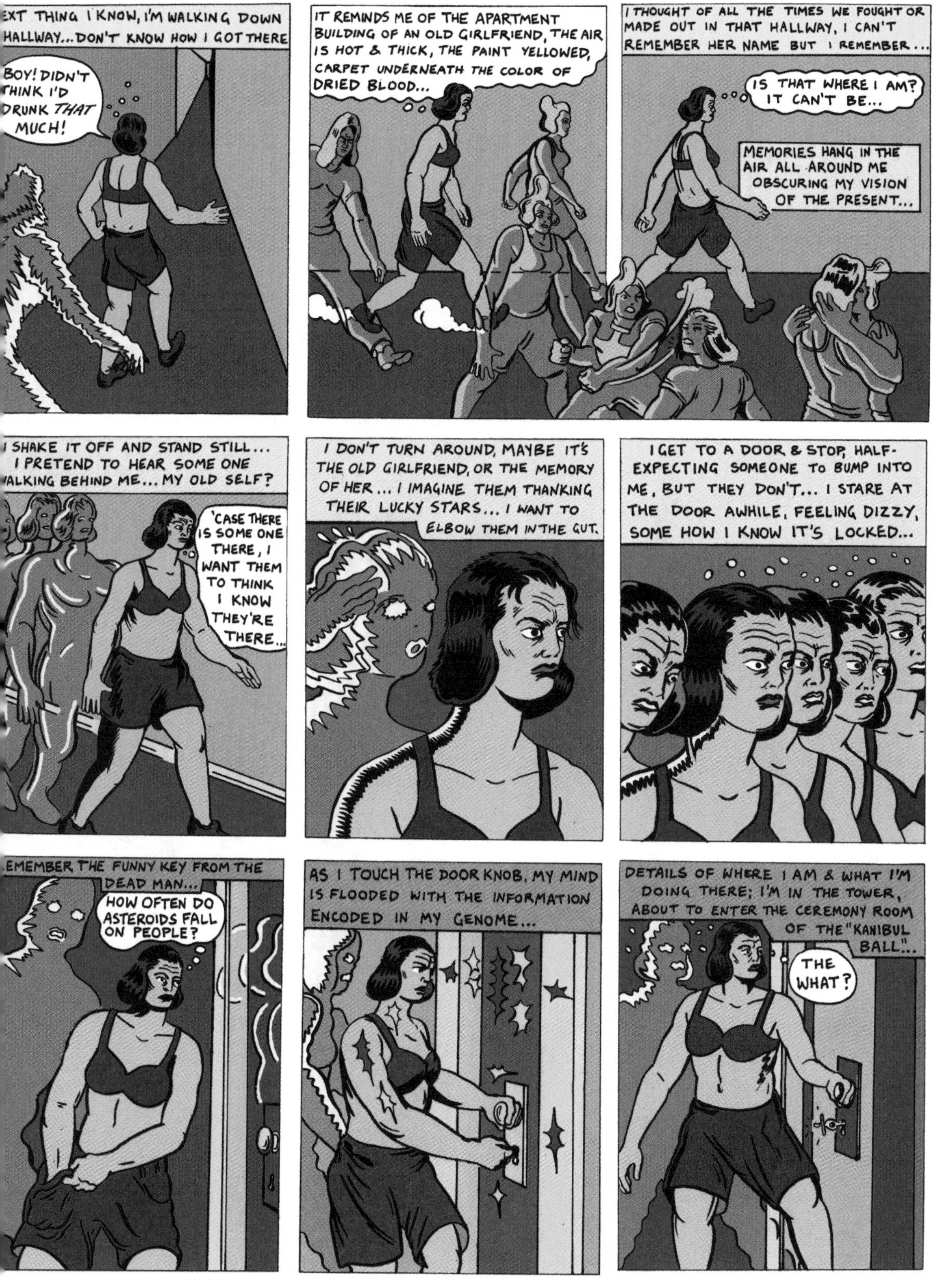
EXT THING I KNOW, I'M WALKING DOWN HALLWAY... DON'T KNOW HOW I GOT THERE
BOY! DIDN'T THINK I'D DRUNK *THAT* MUCH!
IT REMINDS ME OF THE APARTMENT BUILDING OF AN OLD GIRLFRIEND, THE AIR IS HOT & THICK, THE PAINT YELLOWED, CARPET UNDERNEATH THE COLOR OF DRIED BLOOD...
I THOUGHT OF ALL THE TIMES WE FOUGHT OR MADE OUT IN THAT HALLWAY, I CAN'T REMEMBER HER NAME BUT I REMEMBER...
IS THAT WHERE I AM? IT CAN'T BE...
MEMORIES HANG IN THE AIR ALL AROUND ME OBSCURING MY VISION OF THE PRESENT...
I SHAKE IT OFF AND STAND STILL... I PRETEND TO HEAR SOME ONE WALKING BEHIND ME... MY OLD SELF?
'CASE THERE IS SOME ONE THERE, I WANT THEM TO THINK I KNOW THEY'RE THERE...
I DON'T TURN AROUND, MAYBE IT'S THE OLD GIRLFRIEND, OR THE MEMORY OF HER... I IMAGINE THEM THANKING THEIR LUCKY STARS... I WANT TO ELBOW THEM IN THE GUT.
I GET TO A DOOR & STOP, HALF-EXPECTING SOMEONE TO BUMP INTO ME, BUT THEY DON'T... I STARE AT THE DOOR AWHILE, FEELING DIZZY, SOME HOW I KNOW IT'S LOCKED...
EMEMBER THE FUNNY KEY FROM THE DEAD MAN...
HOW OFTEN DO ASTEROIDS FALL ON PEOPLE?
AS I TOUCH THE DOOR KNOB, MY MIND IS FLOODED WITH THE INFORMATION ENCODED IN MY GENOME...
DETAILS OF WHERE I AM & WHAT I'M DOING THERE; I'M IN THE TOWER, ABOUT TO ENTER THE CEREMONY ROOM OF THE "KANIBUL BALL"...
THE WHAT?

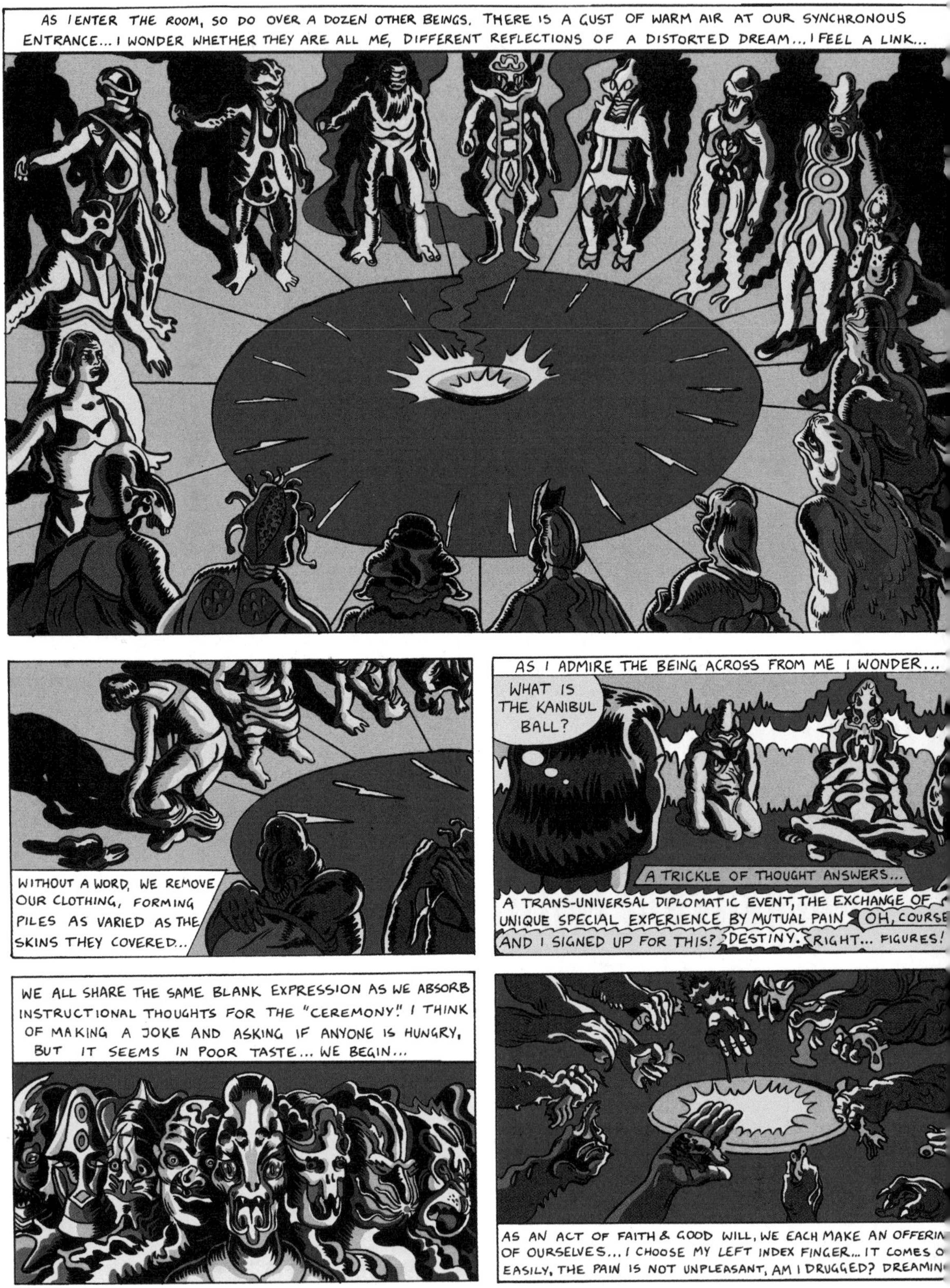
AS I ENTER THE ROOM, SO DO OVER A DOZEN OTHER BEINGS. THERE IS A GUST OF WARM AIR AT OUR SYNCHRONOUS ENTRANCE... I WONDER WHETHER THEY ARE ALL ME, DIFFERENT REFLECTIONS OF A DISTORTED DREAM... I FEEL A LINK...
WITHOUT A WORD, WE REMOVE OUR CLOTHING, FORMING PILES AS VARIED AS THE SKINS THEY COVERED...
AS I ADMIRE THE BEING ACROSS FROM ME I WONDER...
WHAT IS THE KANIBUL BALL?
A TRICKLE OF THOUGHT ANSWERS...
A TRANS-UNIVERSAL DIPLOMATIC EVENT, THE EXCHANGE OF UNIQUE SPECIAL EXPERIENCE BY MUTUAL PAIN
OH, COURSE
AND I SIGNED UP FOR THIS?
DESTINY.
RIGHT... FIGURES!
WE ALL SHARE THE SAME BLANK EXPRESSION AS WE ABSORB INSTRUCTIONAL THOUGHTS FOR THE "CEREMONY." I THINK OF MAKING A JOKE AND ASKING IF ANYONE IS HUNGRY, BUT IT SEEMS IN POOR TASTE... WE BEGIN...
AS AN ACT OF FAITH & GOOD WILL, WE EACH MAKE AN OFFERIN OF OURSELVES... I CHOOSE MY LEFT INDEX FINGER... IT COMES O EASILY, THE PAIN IS NOT UNPLEASANT, AM I DRUGGED? DREAMIN

OUR TOKEN OFFERINGS BURN UP QUICKLY IN A SUDDEN TOWER OF FLAME...

WORDS OF RITUAL GREETING COME TO MIND OUT OF THE THOUGHT STREAM... I SAY THEM ALOUD TO THE CREATURE ACROSS FROM ME

I WILL EAT OF YOU...

IN ANOTHER SETTING I MIGHT HAVE FOUND THE STATEMENT EROTIC, BUT HERE, ECHOED BY INHUMAN VOICES, IT'S DEADLY SERIOUS.

THEY RESPOND...

WE WILL EAT OF EACHOTHER.

I MANAGE NOT TO BLUSH...

AND WONDER AGAIN WHETHER WE ARE NOT ALL REFLECTIONS OF A SINGLE BEING, DRESSED IN DIFFERENT FLESH, FLESH WE WILL SOON BE...

BEFORE I CAN FINISH THE THOUGHT THE ROOM DARKENS, ALIEN FACES STILL HANGING IN MY MIND...

I FEEL SOMETHING TOUCH ME BUT I'M NOT SURE, THEN IT HAPPENS AGAIN, AT THE BASE OF MY NECK, CREST OF MY SHOULDER BLADE... WARM AND WET, TONGUE-LIKE...I BECOME AROUSED...

I REACH OUT AND FIND NOTHING... I BECOME NERVOUS...

AM I ALONE IN THE ROOM NOW? NO... I CAN HEAR BREATHING... MOVEMENT... CHEWING? WHERE'S THAT KNIFE?..

A THOUGHT FROM THE ETHER...

STRANGE CEREMONY INDEED!

I CAN ONLY RESPOND VERBALLY...

MY VOICE SOUNDS ABSURD IN THE DARK AMIDST ALL THE SLURPING...

NONSENSE! THINK FREELY!

CAN EVERYONE HERE COMMUNICATE THIS WAY?

THEY ANSWER IN UNISON WITH A MENTAL NOD THAT FEELS MORE THAN ANYTHING LIKE A PUFF OF WARM AIR ROLLING OVER ME...

THE DARKNESS SEEMS TO FACILITATE THE SUBTLER DIMENSIONS OF THE TELEPATHIC STATE...

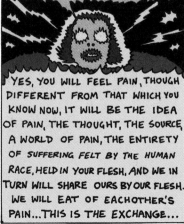

WILL I FEEL THE PAIN OF YOUR KNIVES AND TEETH ON MY FLESH?

YES, YOU WILL FEEL PAIN, THOUGH DIFFERENT FROM THAT WHICH YOU KNOW NOW, IT WILL BE THE IDEA OF PAIN, THE THOUGHT, THE SOURCE, A WORLD OF PAIN, THE ENTIRETY OF SUFFERING FELT BY THE HUMAN RACE, HELD IN YOUR FLESH, AND WE IN TURN WILL SHARE OURS BY OUR FLESH. WE WILL EAT OF EACHOTHER'S PAIN...THIS IS THE EXCHANGE...

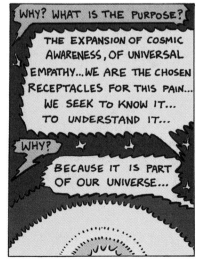

WHY? WHAT IS THE PURPOSE?

THE EXPANSION OF COSMIC AWARENESS, OF UNIVERSAL EMPATHY...WE ARE THE CHOSEN RECEPTACLES FOR THIS PAIN... WE SEEK TO KNOW IT... TO UNDERSTAND IT...

WHY?

BECAUSE IT IS PART OF OUR UNIVERSE...

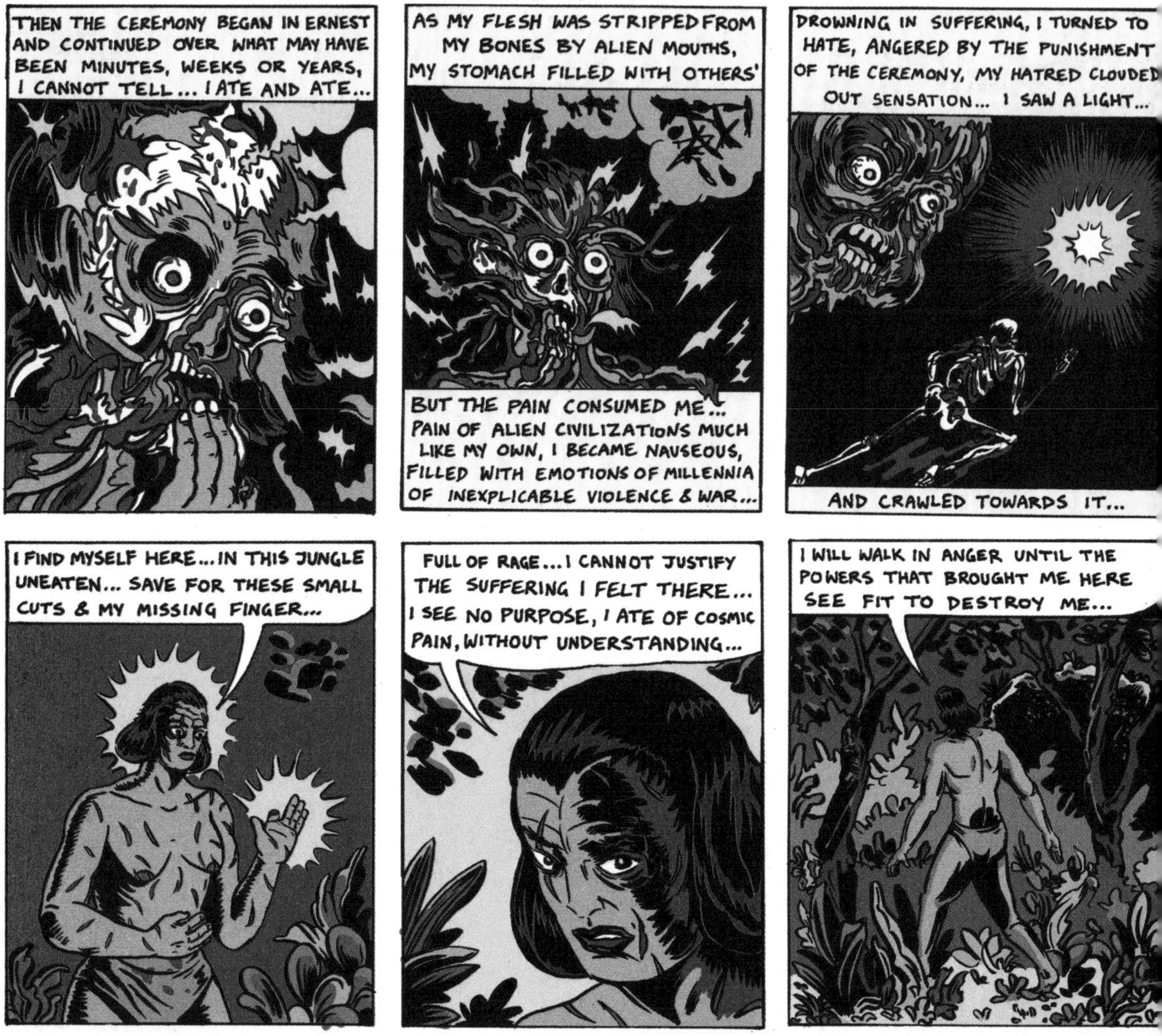
THEN THE CEREMONY BEGAN IN ERNEST AND CONTINUED OVER WHAT MAY HAVE BEEN MINUTES, WEEKS OR YEARS, I CANNOT TELL ... I ATE AND ATE ...
AS MY FLESH WAS STRIPPED FROM MY BONES BY ALIEN MOUTHS, MY STOMACH FILLED WITH OTHERS'
BUT THE PAIN CONSUMED ME ... PAIN OF ALIEN CIVILIZATIONS MUCH LIKE MY OWN, I BECAME NAUSEOUS, FILLED WITH EMOTIONS OF MILLENNIA OF INEXPLICABLE VIOLENCE & WAR ...
DROWNING IN SUFFERING, I TURNED TO HATE, ANGERED BY THE PUNISHMENT OF THE CEREMONY, MY HATRED CLOUDED OUT SENSATION ... I SAW A LIGHT ...
AND CRAWLED TOWARDS IT ...
I FIND MYSELF HERE ... IN THIS JUNGLE UNEATEN ... SAVE FOR THESE SMALL CUTS & MY MISSING FINGER ...
FULL OF RAGE ... I CANNOT JUSTIFY THE SUFFERING I FELT THERE ... I SEE NO PURPOSE, I ATE OF COSMIC PAIN, WITHOUT UNDERSTANDING ...
I WILL WALK IN ANGER UNTIL THE POWERS THAT BROUGHT ME HERE SEE FIT TO DESTROY ME ...
I AM A SHADOW CREATURE ...
ANOTHER WALKS AS BEFORE, CONSUMED BY SMALL MISERY ...
HUMANITY IS A YOUNG RACE ...
THEY CANNOT CARRY THE WEIGHT OF COSMIC DARKNESS ...

# Get Out Your Hankies (*Excerpt*)

FROM *July Diary 2016*

GABRIELLE BELL

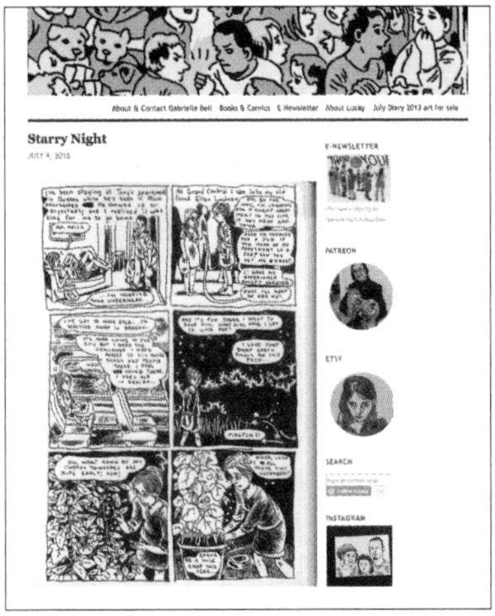
Starry Night

*originally published at*

gabriellebell.com

SELF-PUBLISHED

digital

## Biography

Gabrielle Bell's work has been has been featured in *McSweeney's*, *The Believer*, *Bookforum*, and *VICE* magazines. Her story "Cecil and Jordan in New York" was adapted for the film anthology *Tokyo!* by Bell and Michel Gondry. She has published several books and her latest, *Everything Is Flammable*, was released in April 2017. She lives in Brooklyn, New York.
gabriellebell.com

## Statement

I set myself the goal of drawing an unpenciled, unedited comic strip every day in July of 2016. These are some selections from that.

Starry Night

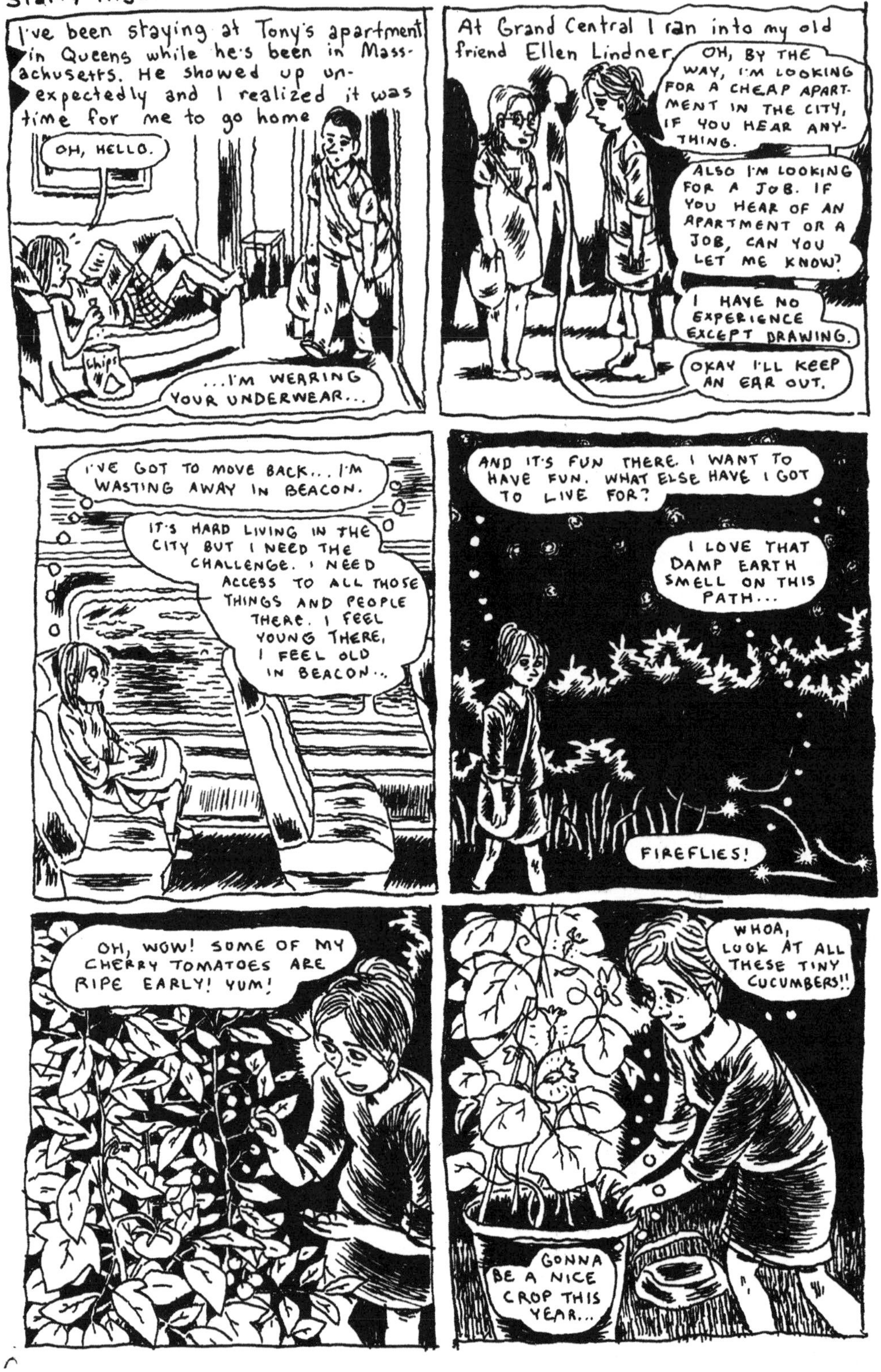
I've been staying at Tony's apartment in Queens while he's been in Massachusetts. He showed up unexpectedly and I realized it was time for me to go home
OH, HELLO.
...I'M WEARING YOUR UNDERWEAR...
Chips
At Grand Central I ran into my old friend Ellen Lindner
OH, BY THE WAY, I'M LOOKING FOR A CHEAP APARTMENT IN THE CITY, IF YOU HEAR ANYTHING.
ALSO I'M LOOKING FOR A JOB. IF YOU HEAR OF AN APARTMENT OR A JOB, CAN YOU LET ME KNOW?
I HAVE NO EXPERIENCE EXCEPT DRAWING.
OKAY I'LL KEEP AN EAR OUT.
I'VE GOT TO MOVE BACK... I'M WASTING AWAY IN BEACON.
IT'S HARD LIVING IN THE CITY BUT I NEED THE CHALLENGE. I NEED ACCESS TO ALL THOSE THINGS AND PEOPLE THERE. I FEEL YOUNG THERE, I FEEL OLD IN BEACON...
AND IT'S FUN THERE. I WANT TO HAVE FUN. WHAT ELSE HAVE I GOT TO LIVE FOR?
I LOVE THAT DAMP EARTH SMELL ON THIS PATH...
FIREFLIES!
OH, WOW! SOME OF MY CHERRY TOMATOES ARE RIPE EARLY! YUM!
WHOA, LOOK AT ALL THESE TINY CUCUMBERS!!
GONNA BE A NICE CROP THIS YEAR...

shame

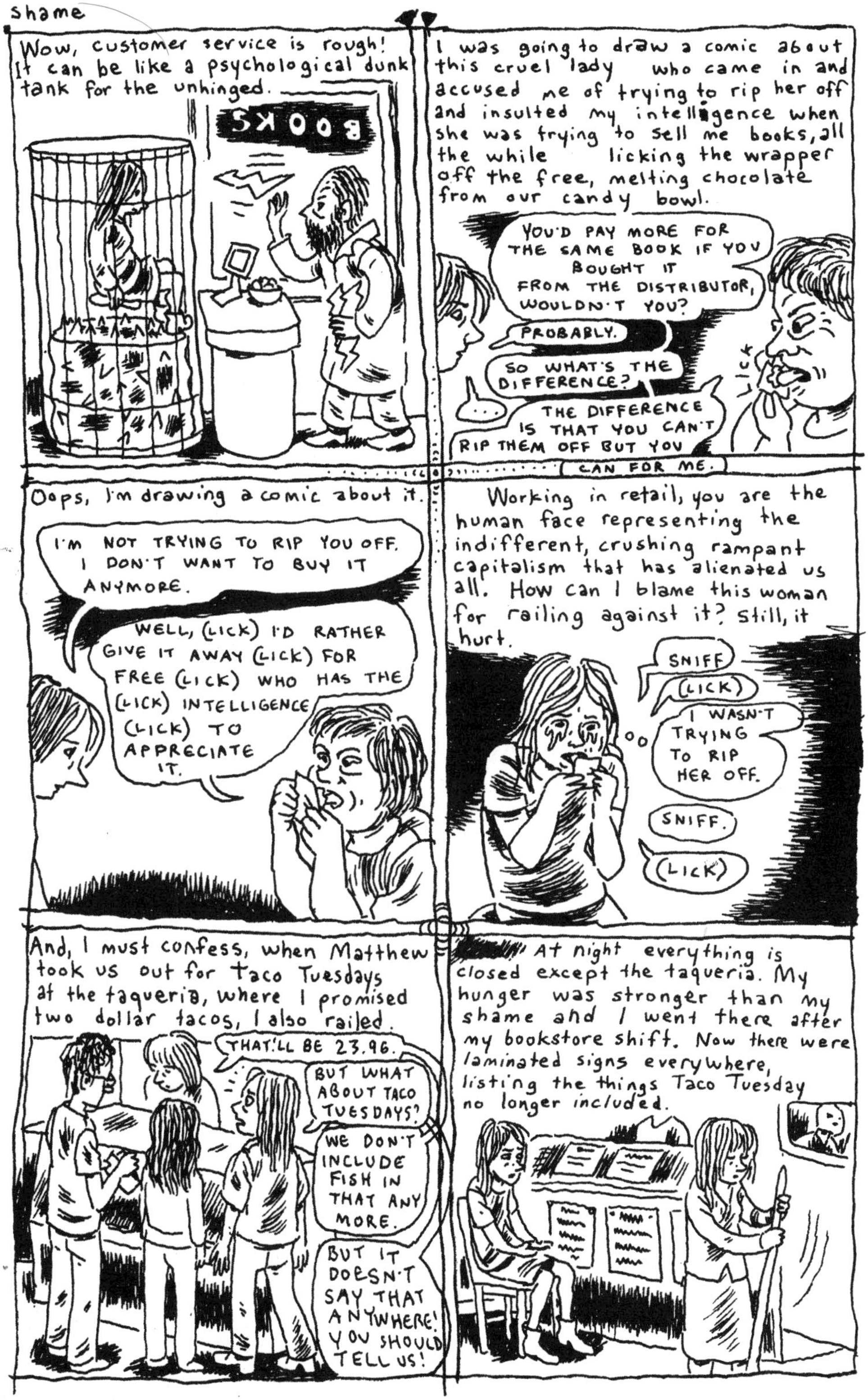
Wow, customer service is rough! It can be like a psychological dunk tank for the unhinged.
BOOKS
I was going to draw a comic about this cruel lady who came in and accused me of trying to rip her off and insulted my intelligence when she was trying to sell me books, all the while licking the wrapper off the free, melting chocolate from our candy bowl.
YOU'D PAY MORE FOR THE SAME BOOK IF YOU BOUGHT IT FROM THE DISTRIBUTOR, WOULDN'T YOU?
PROBABLY.
SO WHAT'S THE DIFFERENCE?
LICK
THE DIFFERENCE IS THAT YOU CAN'T RIP THEM OFF BUT YOU CAN FOR ME.
Oops, I'm drawing a comic about it.
I'M NOT TRYING TO RIP YOU OFF. I DON'T WANT TO BUY IT ANYMORE.
WELL, (LICK) I'D RATHER GIVE IT AWAY (LICK) FOR FREE (LICK) WHO HAS THE (LICK) INTELLIGENCE (LICK) TO APPRECIATE IT.
Working in retail, you are the human face representing the indifferent, crushing rampant capitalism that has alienated us all. How can I blame this woman for railing against it? Still, it hurt.
SNIFF
(LICK)
I WASN'T TRYING TO RIP HER OFF.
SNIFF.
(LICK)
And, I must confess, when Matthew took us out for Taco Tuesdays at the taqueria, where I promised two dollar tacos, I also railed.
THAT'LL BE 23.96.
BUT WHAT ABOUT TACO TUESDAYS?
WE DON'T INCLUDE FISH IN THAT ANY MORE.
BUT IT DOESN'T SAY THAT ANYWHERE! YOU SHOULD TELL US!
At night everything is closed except the taqueria. My hunger was stronger than my shame and I went there after my bookstore shift. Now there were laminated signs everywhere, listing the things Taco Tuesday no longer included.

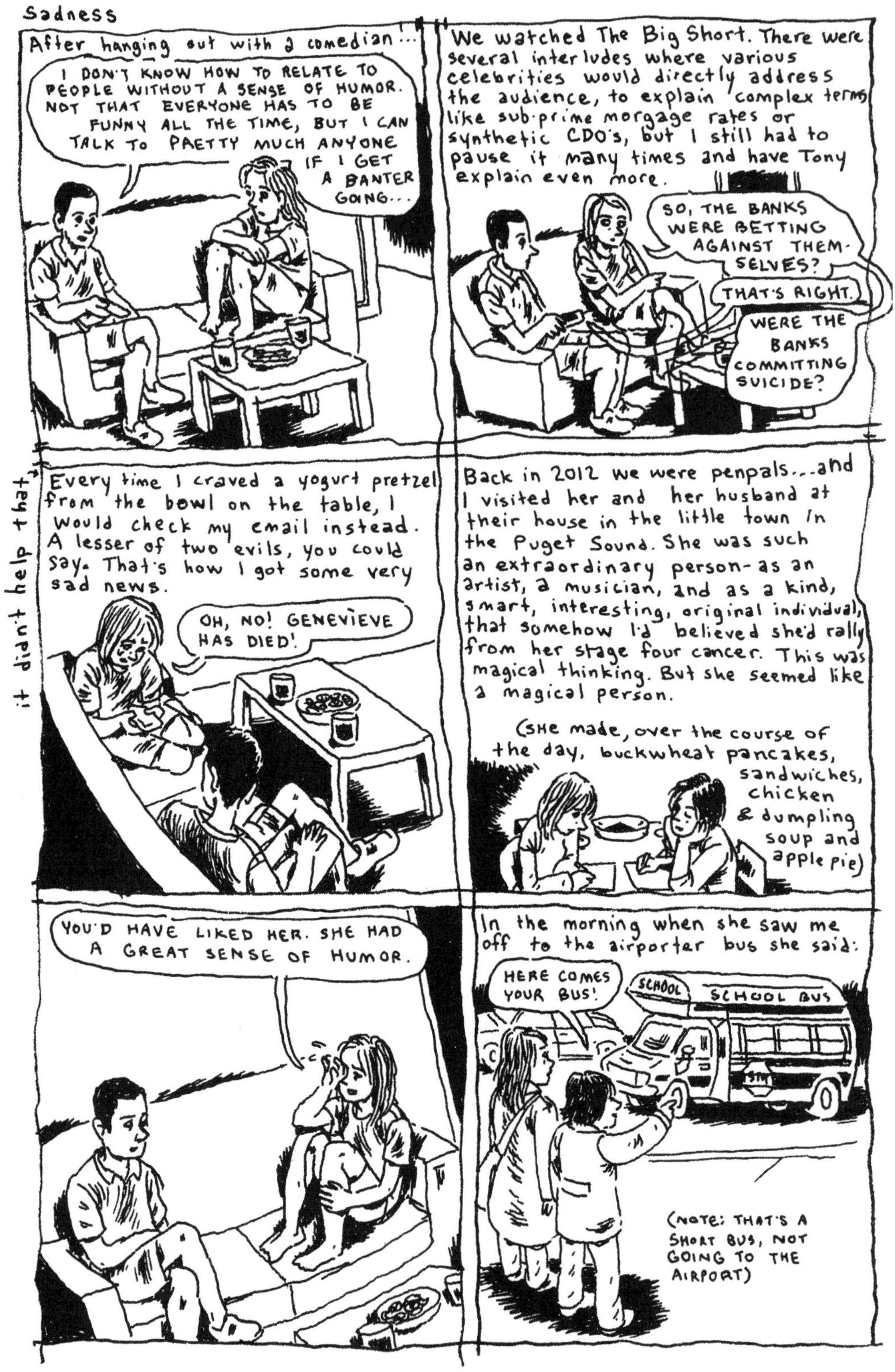
Sadness
After hanging out with a comedian!...
I DON'T KNOW HOW TO RELATE TO PEOPLE WITHOUT A SENSE OF HUMOR. NOT THAT EVERYONE HAS TO BE FUNNY ALL THE TIME, BUT I CAN TALK TO PRETTY MUCH ANYONE IF I GET A BANTER GOING...
We watched The Big Short. There were several interludes where various celebrities would directly address the audience, to explain complex terms like sub-prime morgage rates or synthetic CDO's, but I still had to pause it many times and have Tony explain even more.
SO, THE BANKS WERE BETTING AGAINST THEMSELVES?
THAT'S RIGHT.
WERE THE BANKS COMMITTING SUICIDE?
it didn't help that,
Every time I craved a yogurt pretzel from the bowl on the table, I would check my email instead. A lesser of two evils, you could say. That's how I got some very sad news.
OH, NO! GENEVIEVE HAS DIED!
Back in 2012 we were penpals...and I visited her and her husband at their house in the little town in the Puget Sound. She was such an extraordinary person- as an artist, a musician, and as a kind, smart, interesting, original individual, that somehow I'd believed she'd rally from her stage four cancer. This was magical thinking. But she seemed like a magical person.
(SHE made, over the course of the day, buckwheat pancakes, sandwiches, chicken & dumpling soup and apple pie)
YOU'D HAVE LIKED HER. SHE HAD A GREAT SENSE OF HUMOR.
In the morning when she saw me off to the airporter bus she said:
HERE COMES YOUR BUS!
SCHOOL
SCHOOL BUS
(NOTE: THAT'S A SHORT BUS, NOT GOING TO THE AIRPORT)

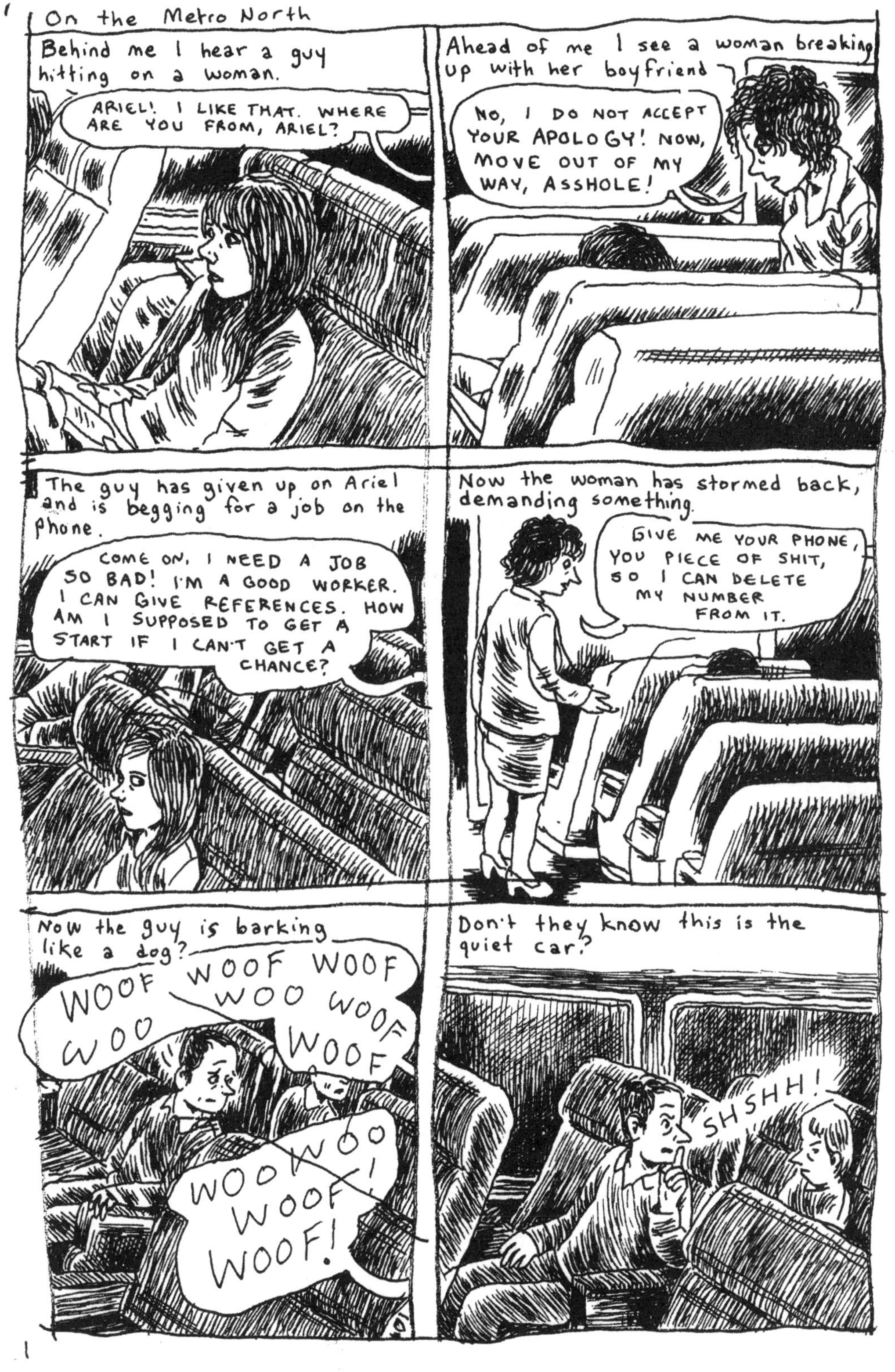
On the Metro North
Behind me I hear a guy hitting on a woman.
ARIEL! I LIKE THAT. WHERE ARE YOU FROM, ARIEL?
Ahead of me I see a woman breaking up with her boyfriend
NO, I DO NOT ACCEPT YOUR APOLOGY! NOW, MOVE OUT OF MY WAY, ASSHOLE!
The guy has given up on Ariel and is begging for a job on the phone.
COME ON, I NEED A JOB SO BAD! I'M A GOOD WORKER. I CAN GIVE REFERENCES. HOW AM I SUPPOSED TO GET A START IF I CAN'T GET A CHANCE?
Now the woman has stormed back, demanding something.
GIVE ME YOUR PHONE, YOU PIECE OF SHIT, SO I CAN DELETE MY NUMBER FROM IT.
Now the guy is barking like a dog?
WOOF WOOF WOOF WOO WOO WOOF WOO WOOF
WOO WOO WOOF! WOOF WOOF!
Don't they know this is the quiet car?
SHSHH!

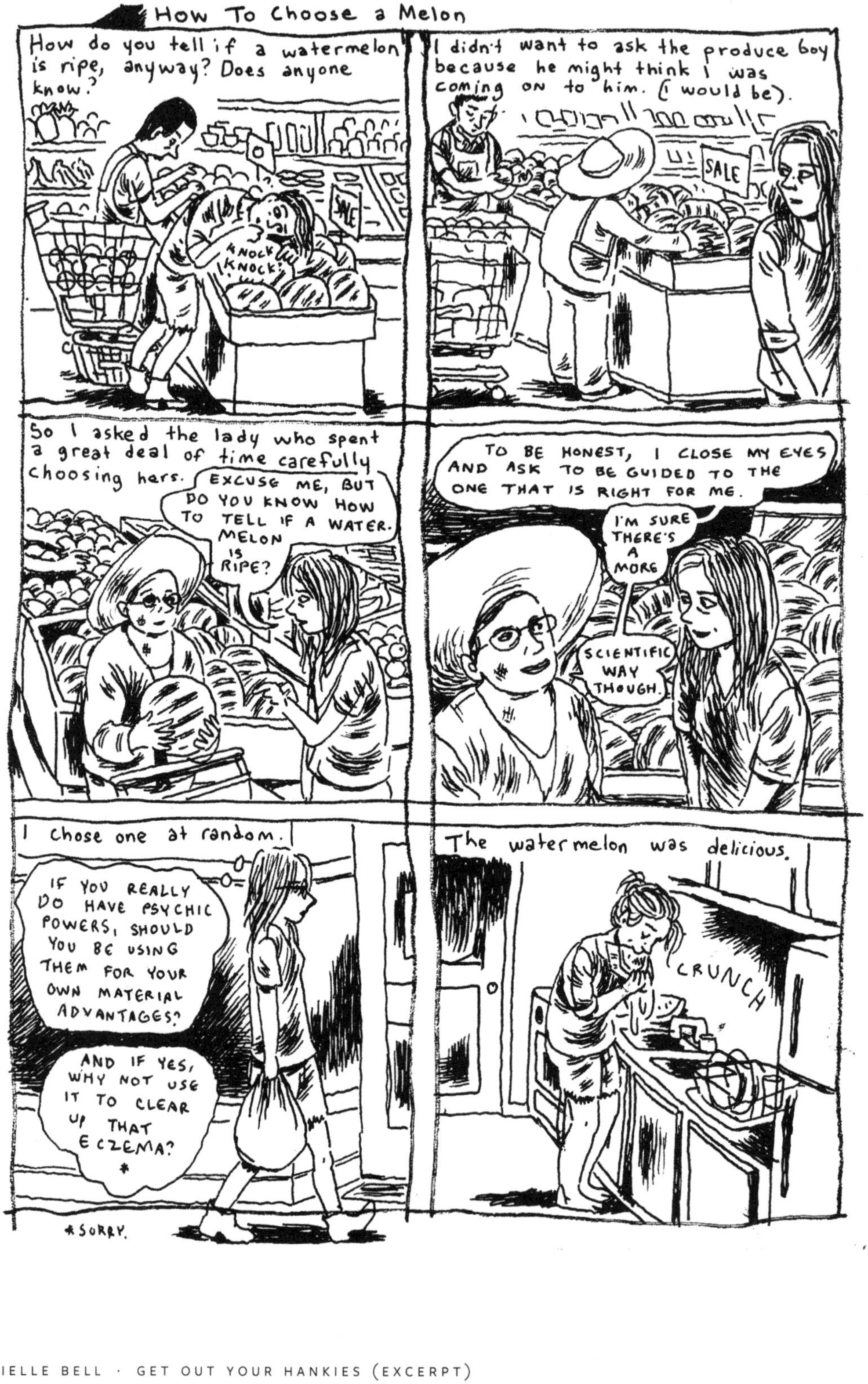
How To Choose a Melon
How do you tell if a watermelon is ripe, anyway? Does anyone know?
KNOCK KNOCK
SALE
I didn't want to ask the produce boy because he might think I was coming on to him. (I would be).
SALE
So I asked the lady who spent a great deal of time carefully choosing hers.
EXCUSE ME, BUT DO YOU KNOW HOW TO TELL IF A WATER-MELON IS RIPE?
TO BE HONEST, I CLOSE MY EYES AND ASK TO BE GUIDED TO THE ONE THAT IS RIGHT FOR ME.
I'M SURE THERE'S A MORE
SCIENTIFIC WAY THOUGH.
I chose one at random.
IF YOU REALLY DO HAVE PSYCHIC POWERS, SHOULD YOU BE USING THEM FOR YOUR OWN MATERIAL ADVANTAGES?
AND IF YES, WHY NOT USE IT TO CLEAR UP THAT ECZEMA? *
*SORRY.
The watermelon was delicious.
CRUNCH

# Technology

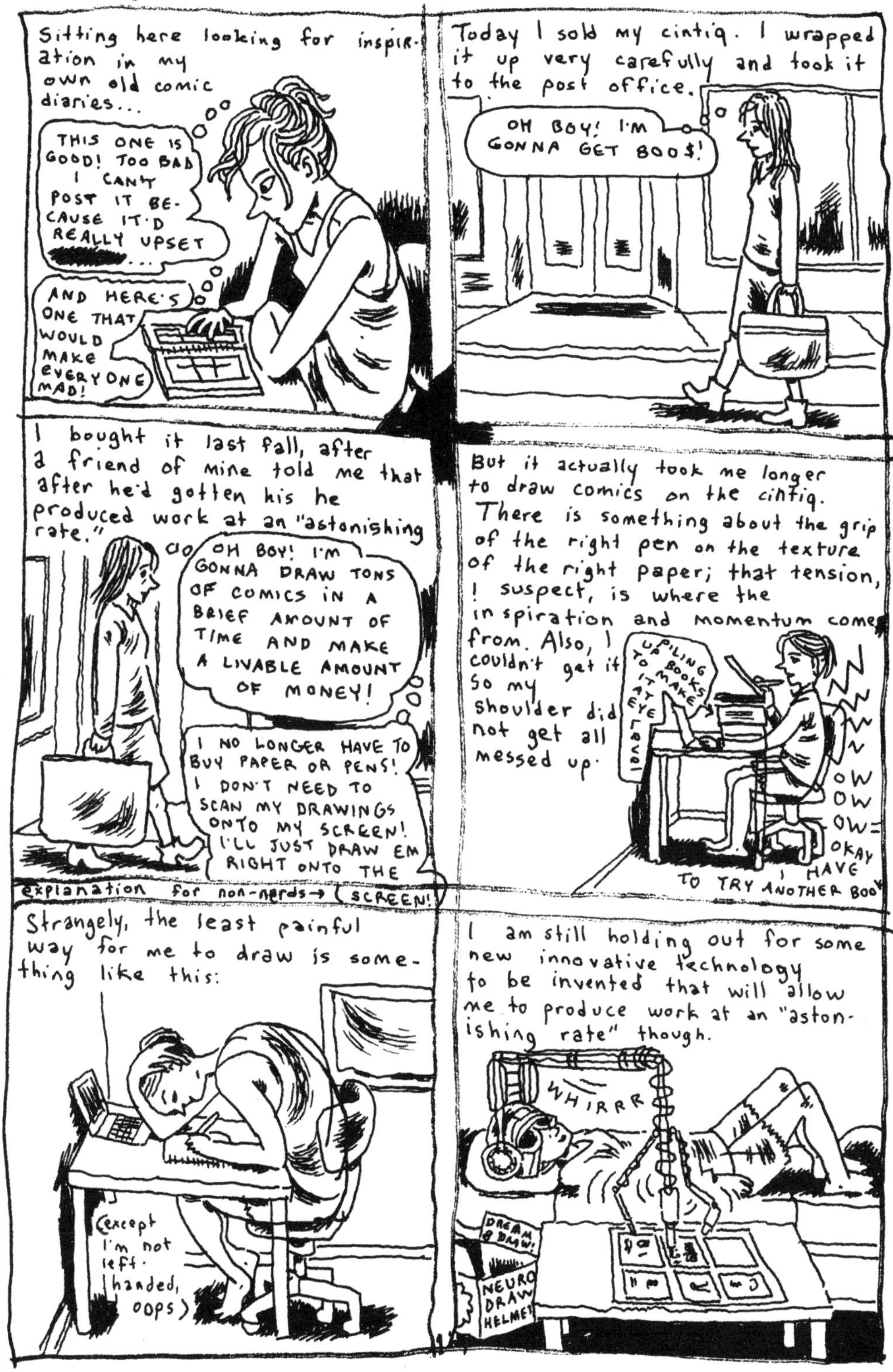

Sitting here looking for inspiration in my own old comic diaries...
THIS ONE IS GOOD! TOO BAD I CAN'T POST IT BECAUSE IT'D REALLY UPSET [redacted]...
AND HERE'S ONE THAT WOULD MAKE EVERYONE MAD!
Today I sold my cintiq. I wrapped it up very carefully and took it to the post office.
OH BOY! I'M GONNA GET BOO$!
I bought it last fall, after a friend of mine told me that after he'd gotten his he produced work at an "astonishing rate."
OH BOY! I'M GONNA DRAW TONS OF COMICS IN A BRIEF AMOUNT OF TIME AND MAKE A LIVABLE AMOUNT OF MONEY!
I NO LONGER HAVE TO BUY PAPER OR PENS! I DON'T NEED TO SCAN MY DRAWINGS ONTO MY SCREEN! I'LL JUST DRAW EM RIGHT ONTO THE SCREEN!
explanation for non-nerds →
But it actually took me longer to draw comics on the cintiq. There is something about the grip of the right pen on the texture of the right paper; that tension, I suspect, is where the inspiration and momentum comes from. Also, I couldn't get it so my shoulder did not get all messed up.
PILING UP BOOKS TO MAKE IT AT EYE LEVEL
OW OW OW— OKAY I HAVE TO TRY ANOTHER BOOK
Strangely, the least painful way for me to draw is something like this:
(except I'm not left-handed, oops)
I am still holding out for some new innovative technology to be invented that will allow me to produce work at an "astonishing rate" though.
WHIRRR
DREAM & DRAW!
NEURO DRAW HELMET

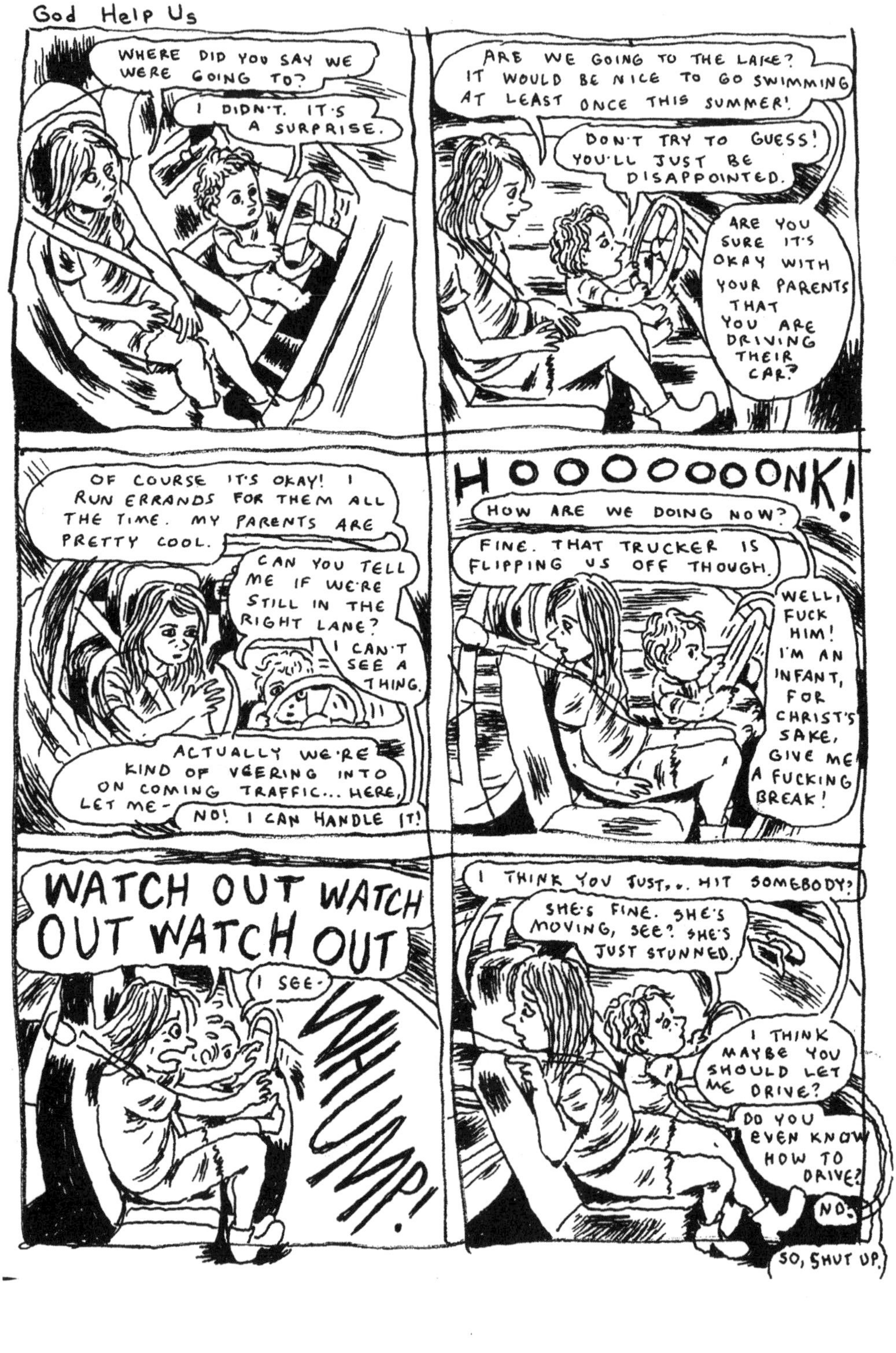
God Help Us
WHERE DID YOU SAY WE WERE GOING TO?
I DIDN'T. IT'S A SURPRISE.
ARE WE GOING TO THE LAKE? IT WOULD BE NICE TO GO SWIMMING AT LEAST ONCE THIS SUMMER!
DON'T TRY TO GUESS! YOU'LL JUST BE DISAPPOINTED.
ARE YOU SURE IT'S OKAY WITH YOUR PARENTS THAT YOU ARE DRIVING THEIR CAR?
OF COURSE IT'S OKAY! I RUN ERRANDS FOR THEM ALL THE TIME. MY PARENTS ARE PRETTY COOL.
CAN YOU TELL ME IF WE'RE STILL IN THE RIGHT LANE?
I CAN'T SEE A THING.
ACTUALLY WE'RE KIND OF VEERING INTO ON COMING TRAFFIC... HERE, LET ME-
NO! I CAN HANDLE IT!
HOOOOOOONK!
HOW ARE WE DOING NOW?
FINE. THAT TRUCKER IS FLIPPING US OFF THOUGH.
WELL FUCK HIM! I'M AN INFANT, FOR CHRIST'S SAKE, GIVE ME A FUCKING BREAK!
WATCH OUT WATCH OUT WATCH OUT WATCH OUT
I SEE-
WHUMP!
I THINK YOU JUST... HIT SOMEBODY?
SHE'S FINE. SHE'S MOVING, SEE? SHE'S JUST STUNNED.
I THINK MAYBE YOU SHOULD LET ME DRIVE?
DO YOU EVEN KNOW HOW TO DRIVE?
NO.
SO, SHUT UP.

# De Hooch

JOHN HANKIEWICZ

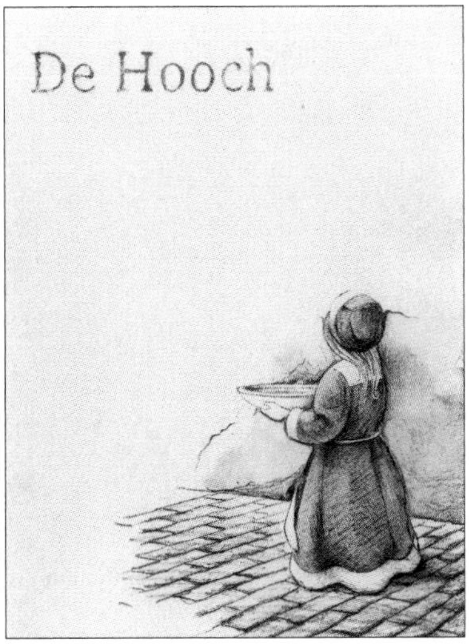
De Hooch

*originally published as*

*De Hooch*

SELF-PUBLISHED

8.5 × 11 inches • 17 pages

## Biography

John Hankiewicz was born in Chicago in 1971. He has self-published several comics since the mid-1990s, including the series *Tepid* and the book-length *Education*. A collection of his short comics, *Asthma*, was published by Sparkplug in 2006. He received an MFA in printmaking from Miami University, and his etchings and lithographs have appeared in several exhibitions.
hankiewicz.blogspot.com

## Statement

Pieter de Hooch's painting *The Courtyard of a House in Delft* inspired my comic. His pairing of deep and shallow spaces, in that piece and others, particularly moved me. On the one hand, there is the freedom of going deep into space, but this means disappearing into the architecture. On the other hand, the figures—usually women—fully delineated in the foreground are always caught up in some kind of routine. In this pessimistic interpretation, the paintings are about two kinds of anonymity, but are nevertheless beautiful.

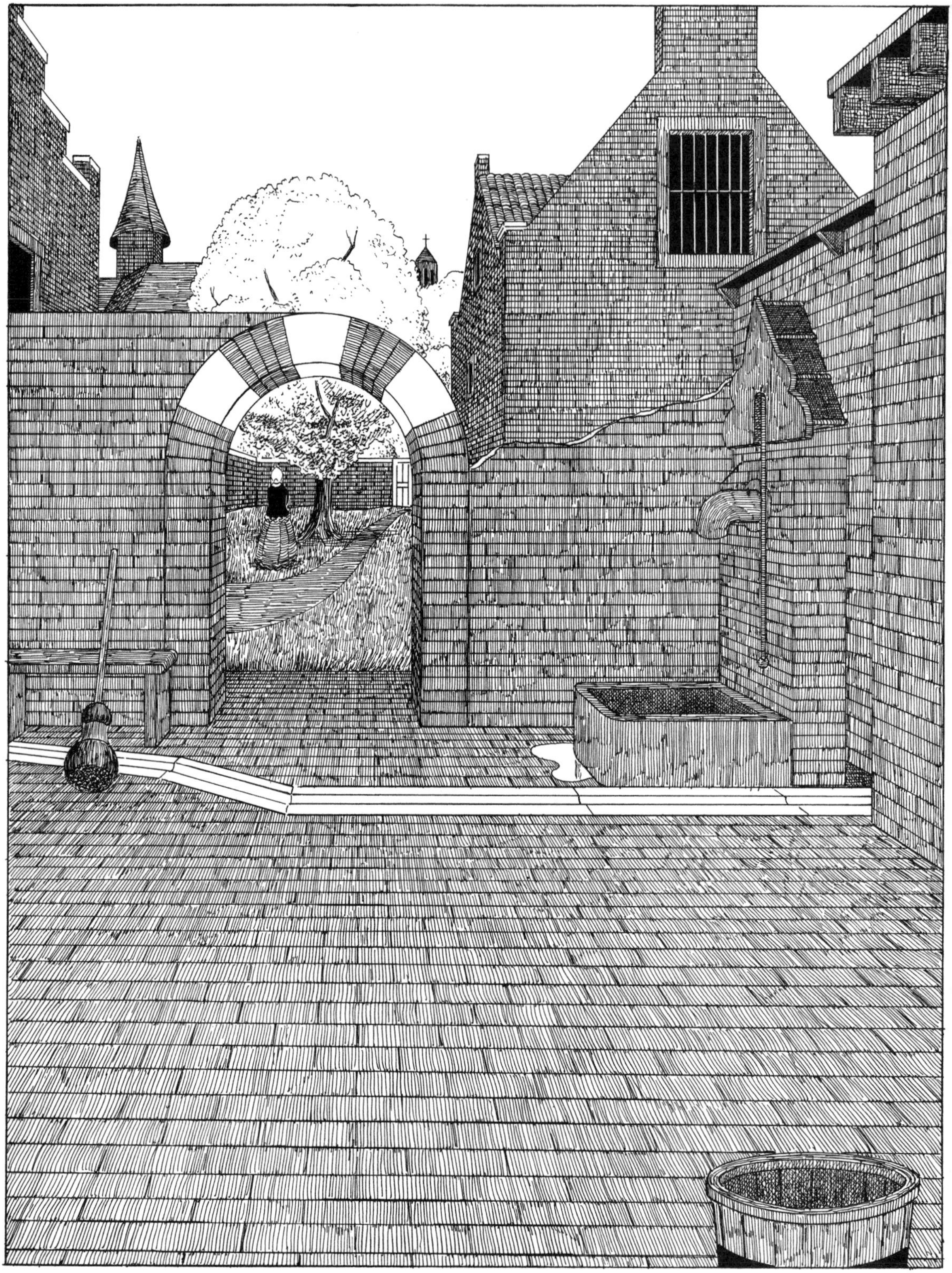

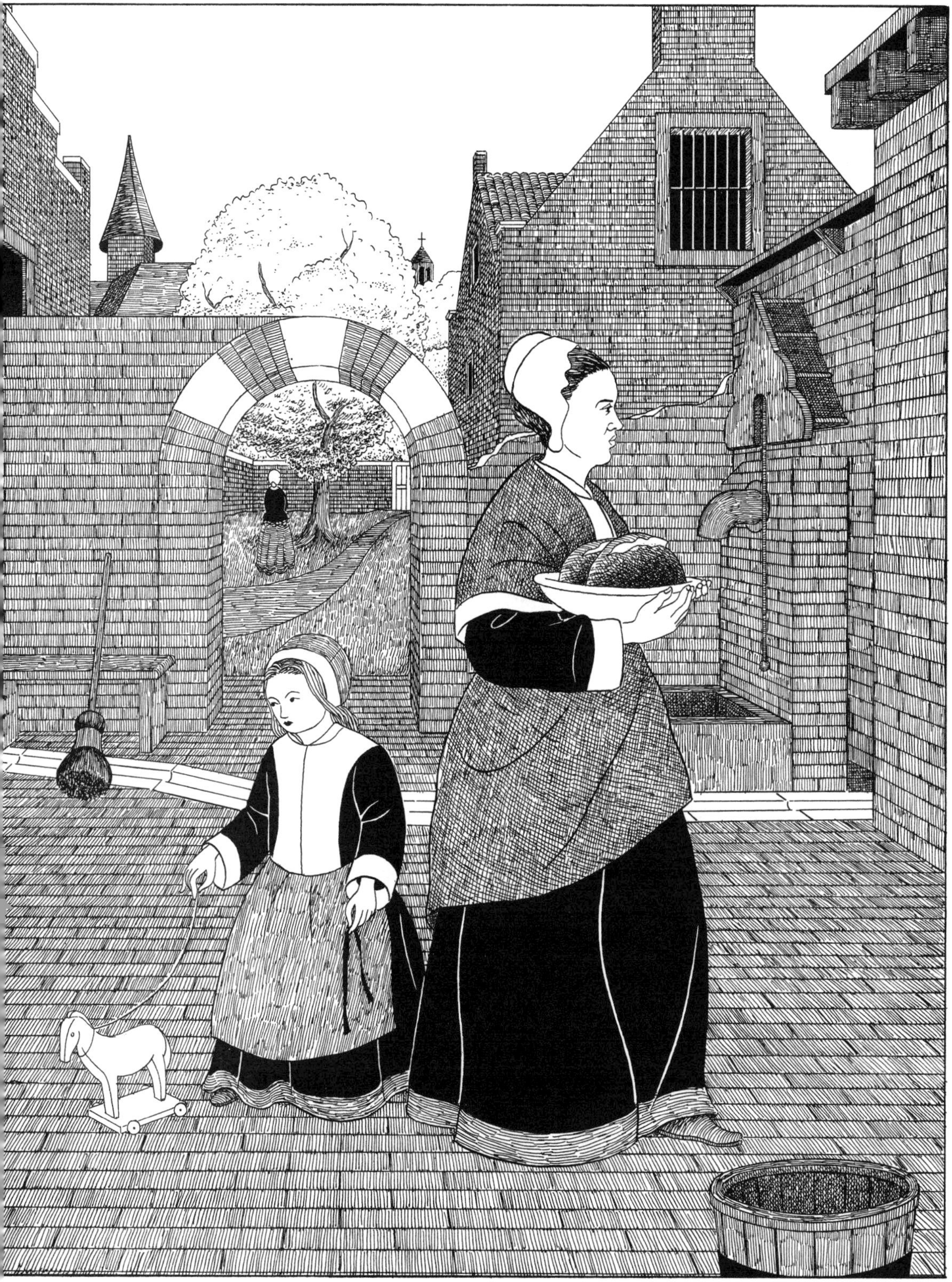

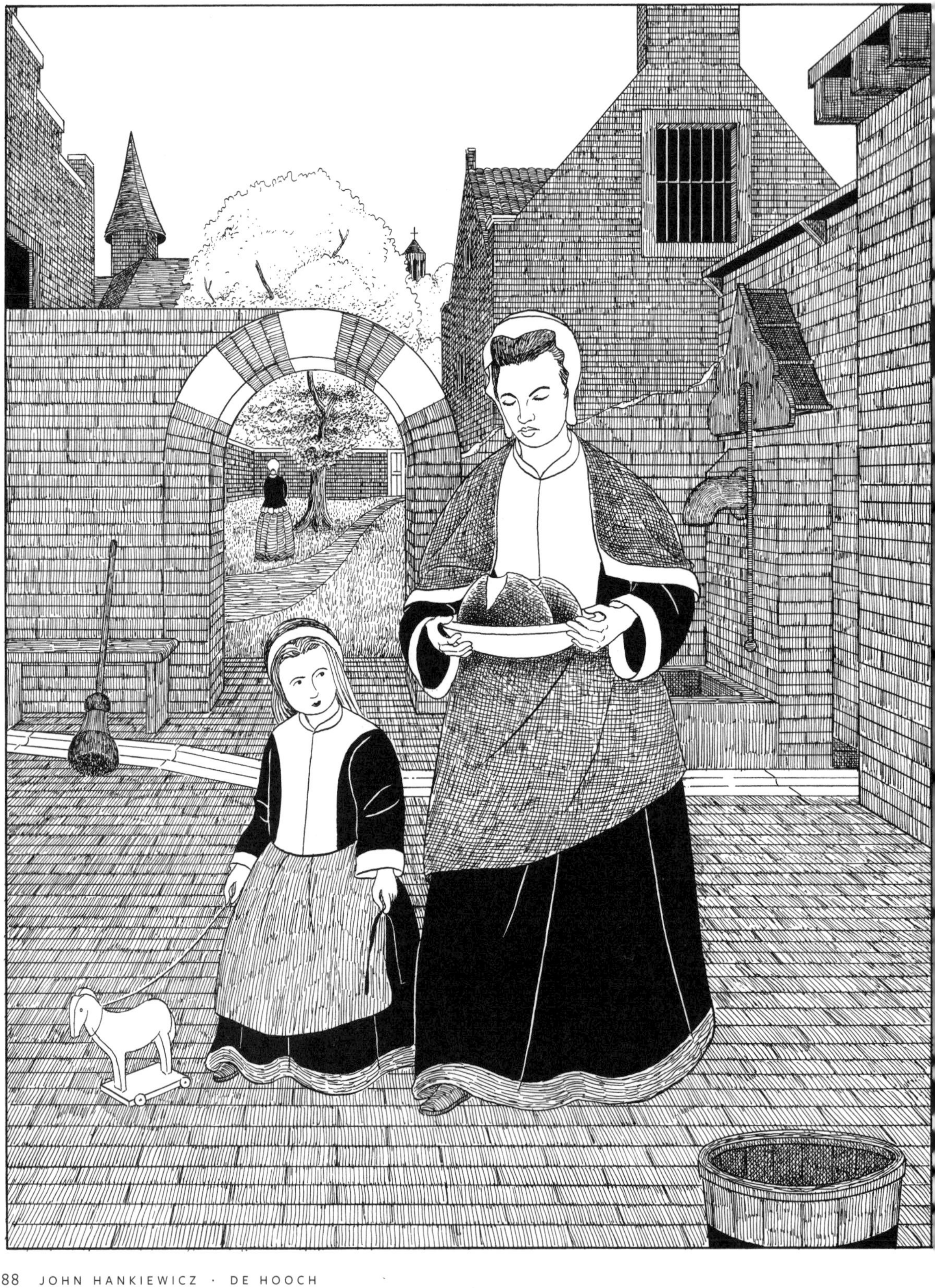

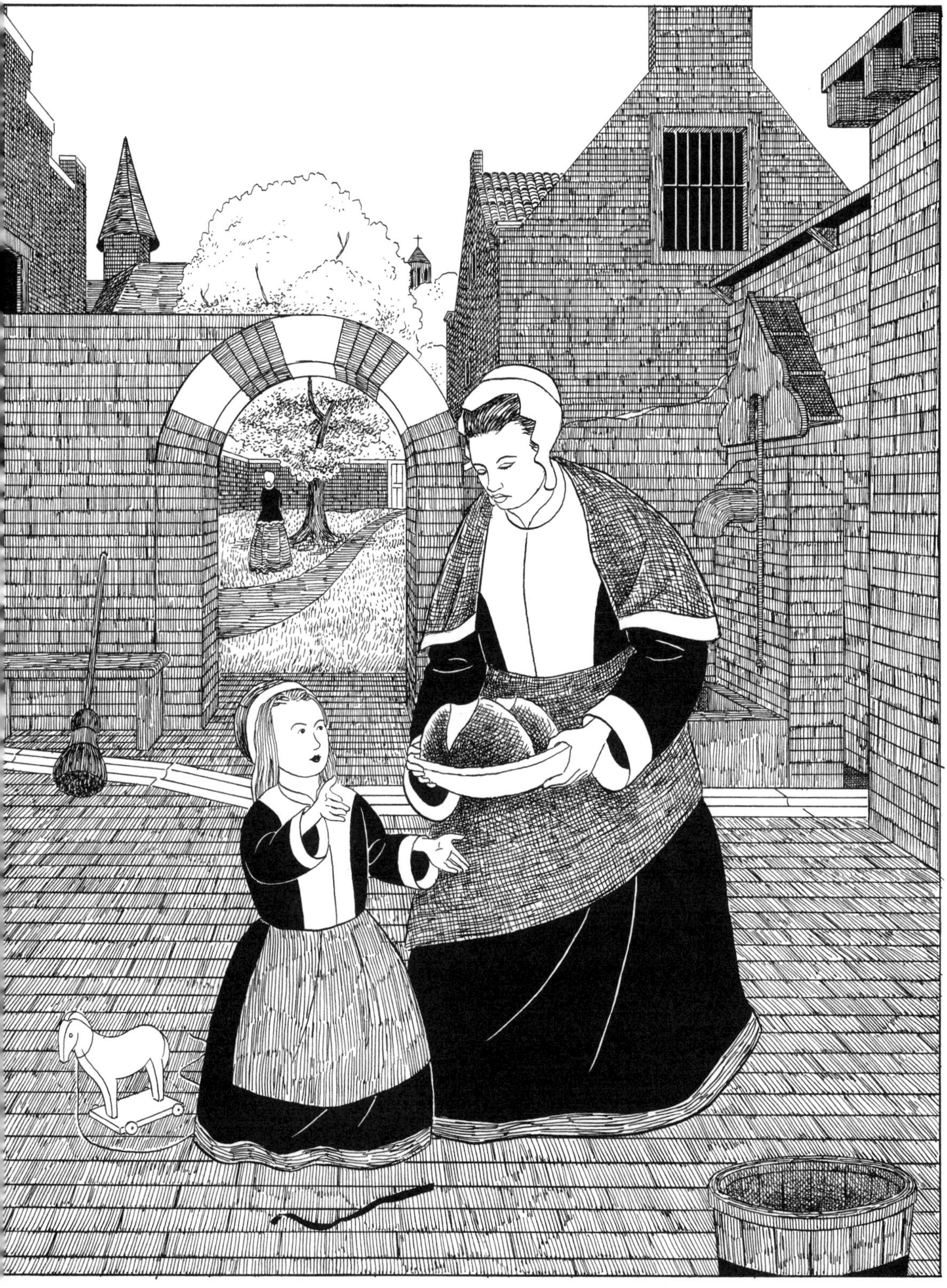

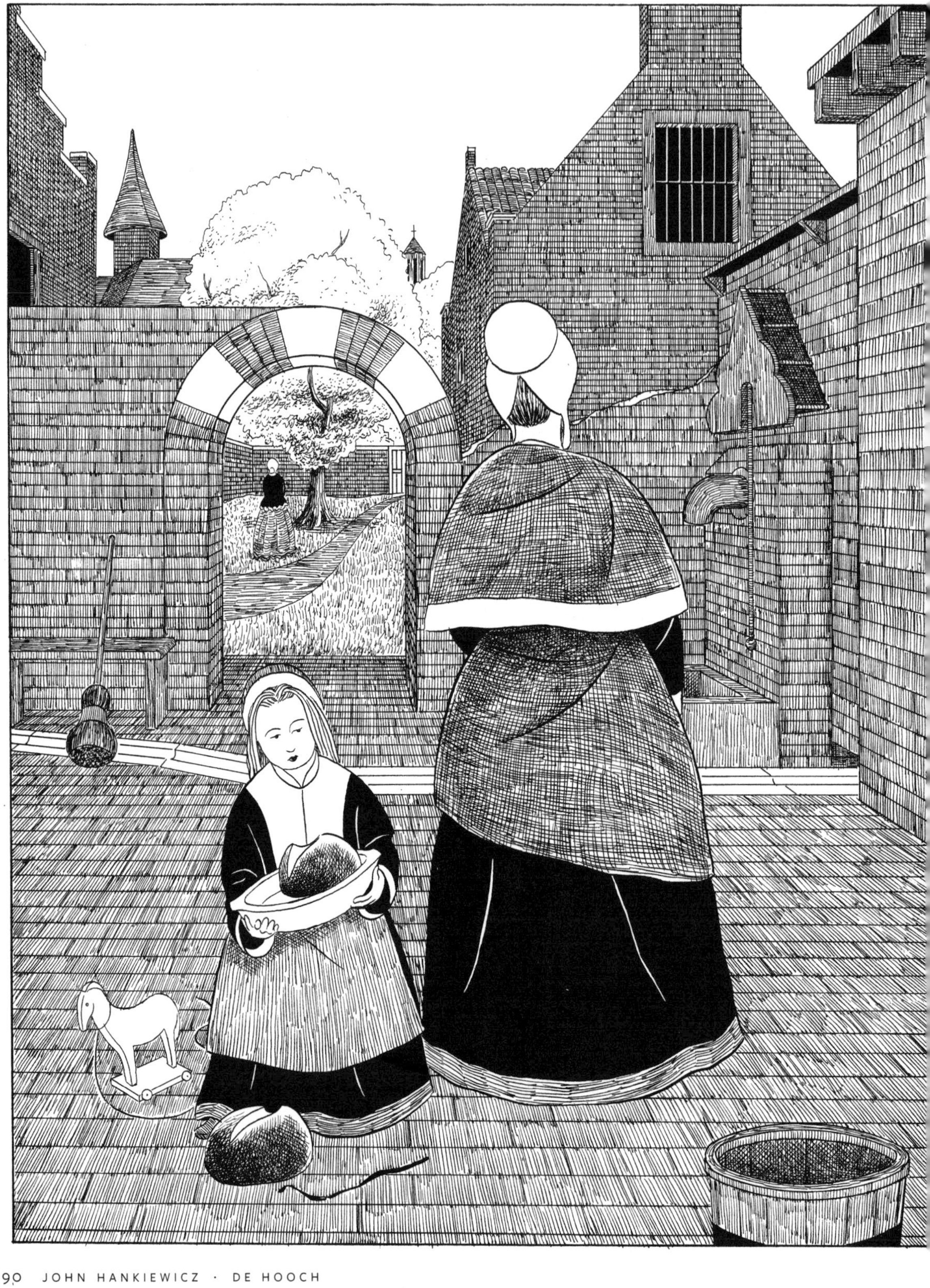

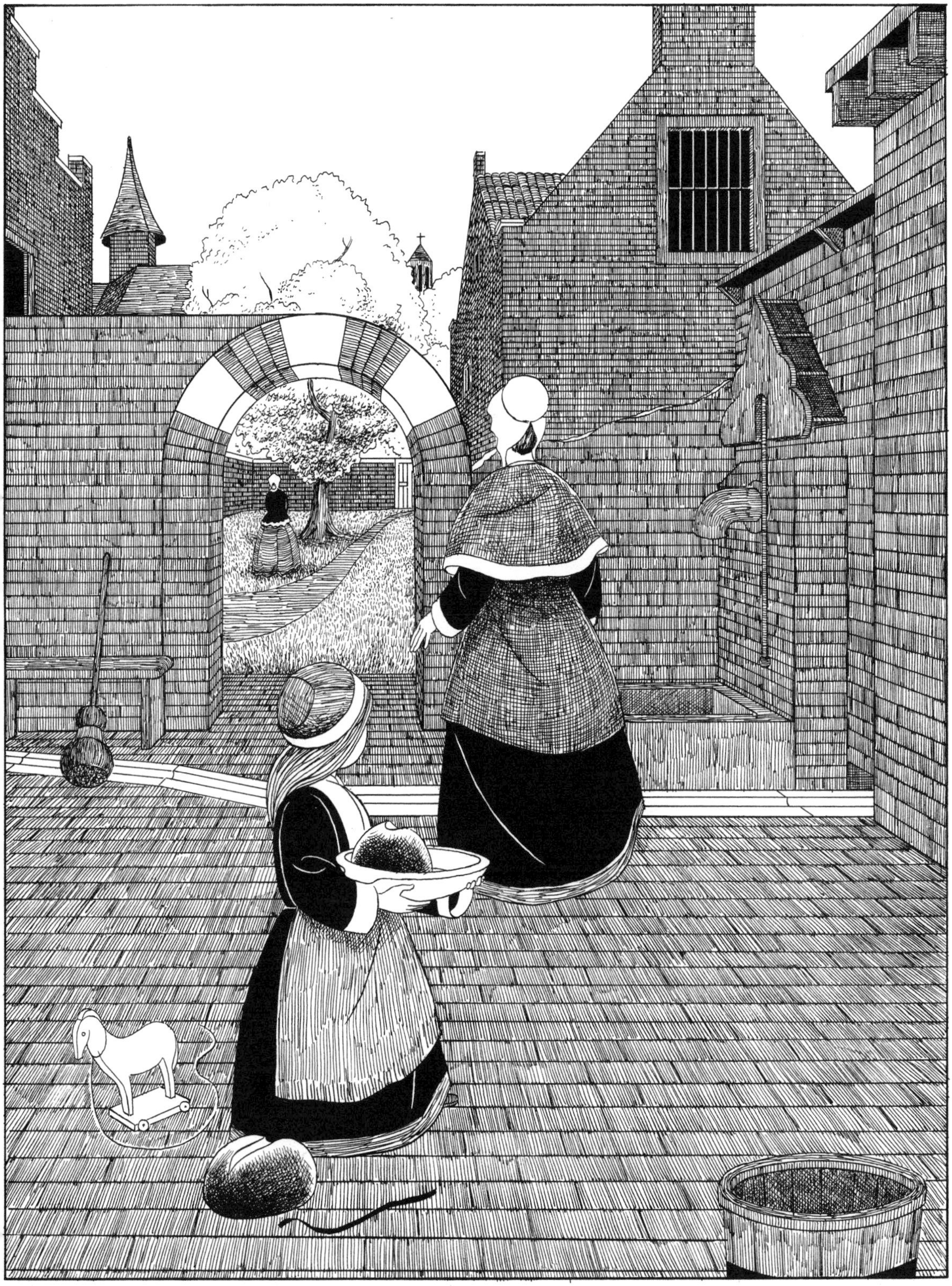

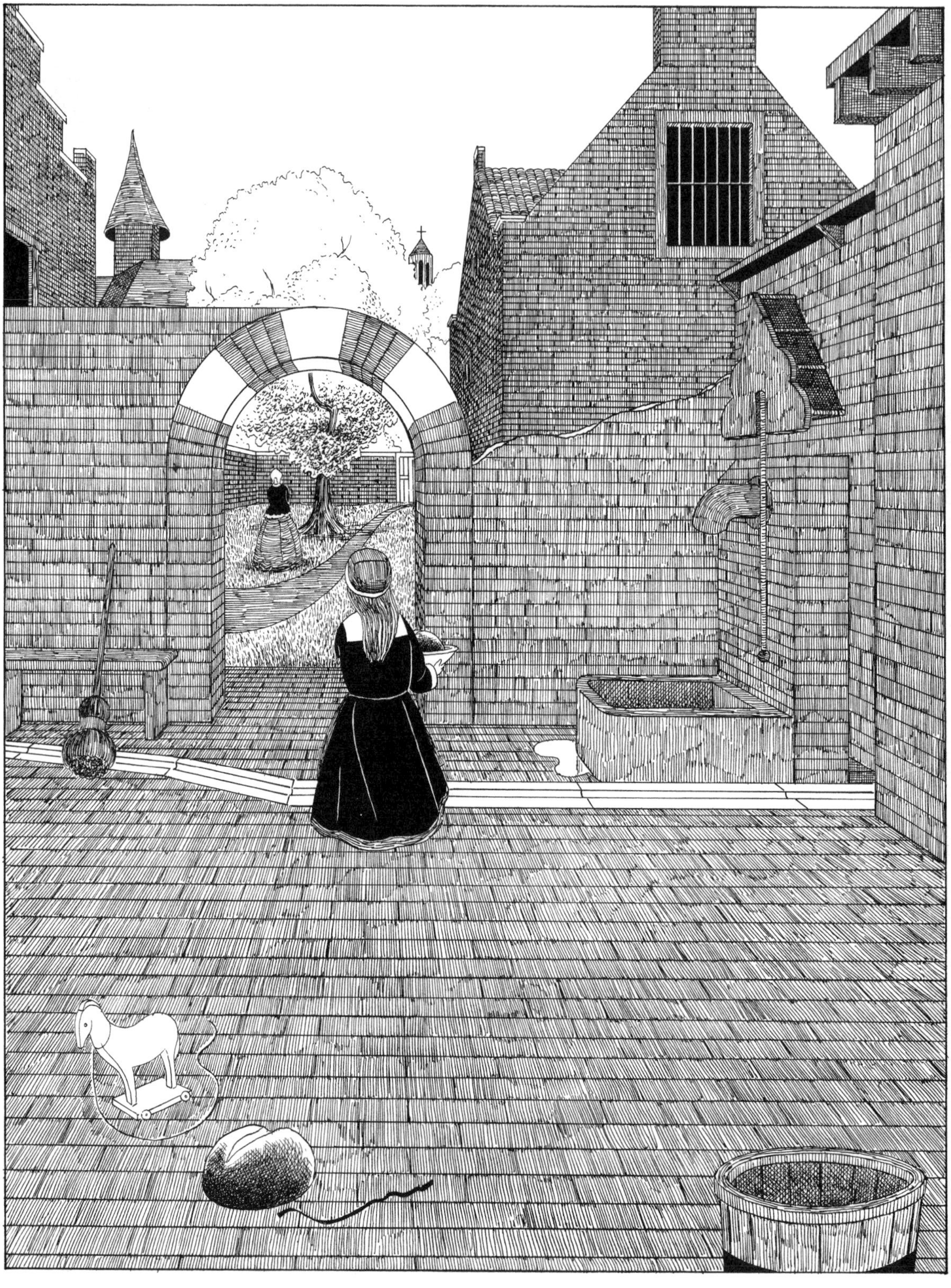

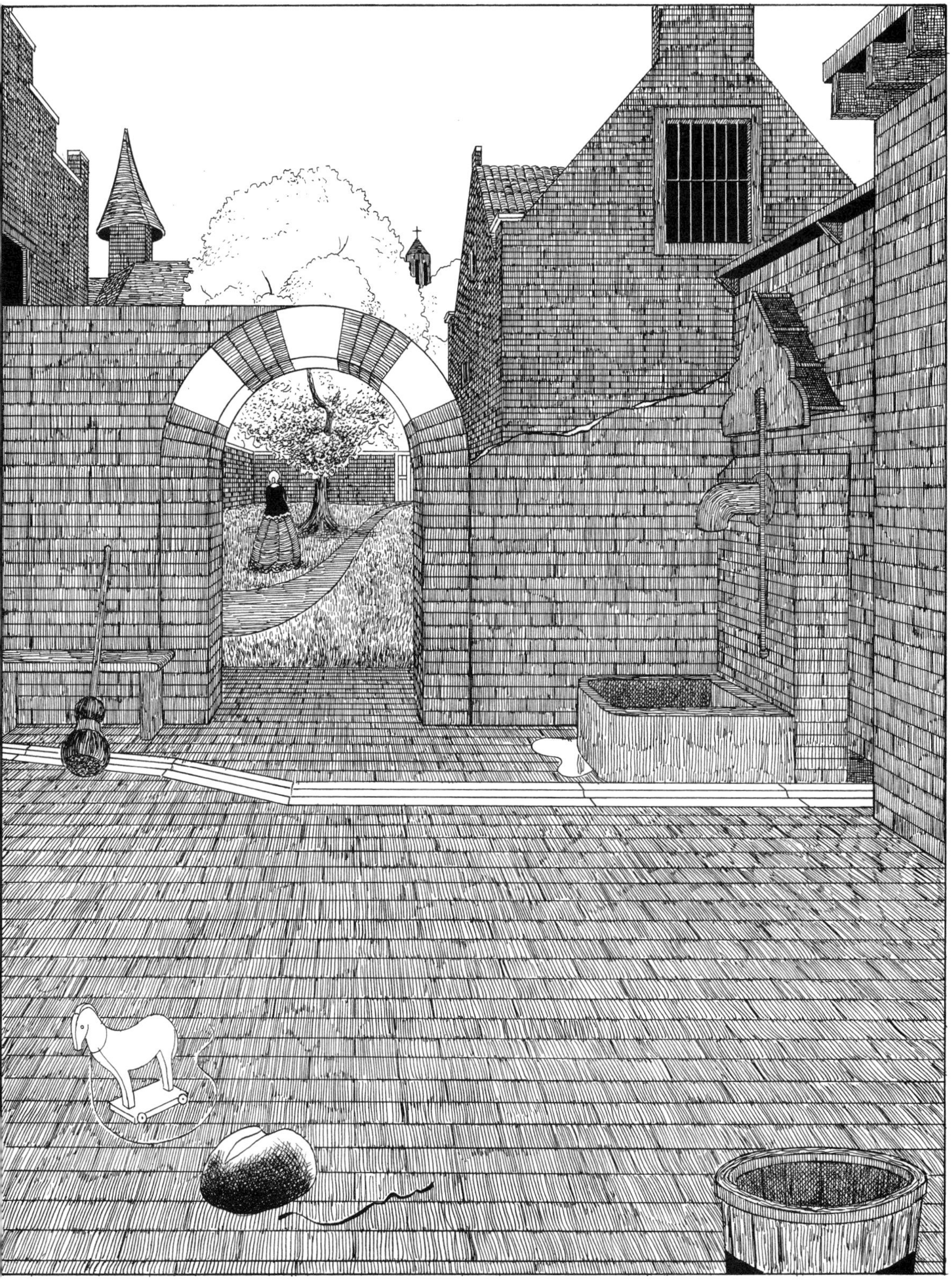

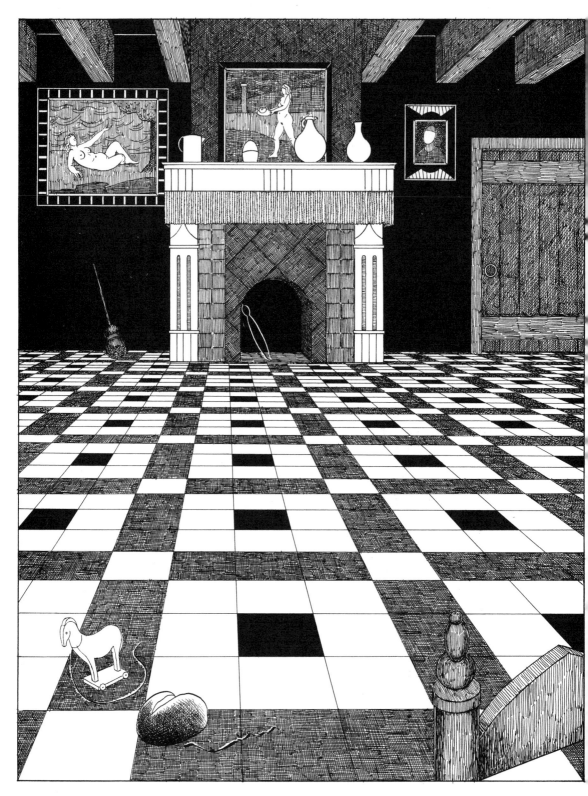

Where the courtyard or room was lacking, I would supply props, alter rooftops, lend extra color.

I would omit twigs and slop, invent patterns for the bricks and tiles.

When I finished, I would have a setting.

Then the figures.

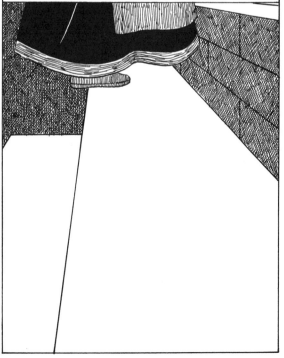

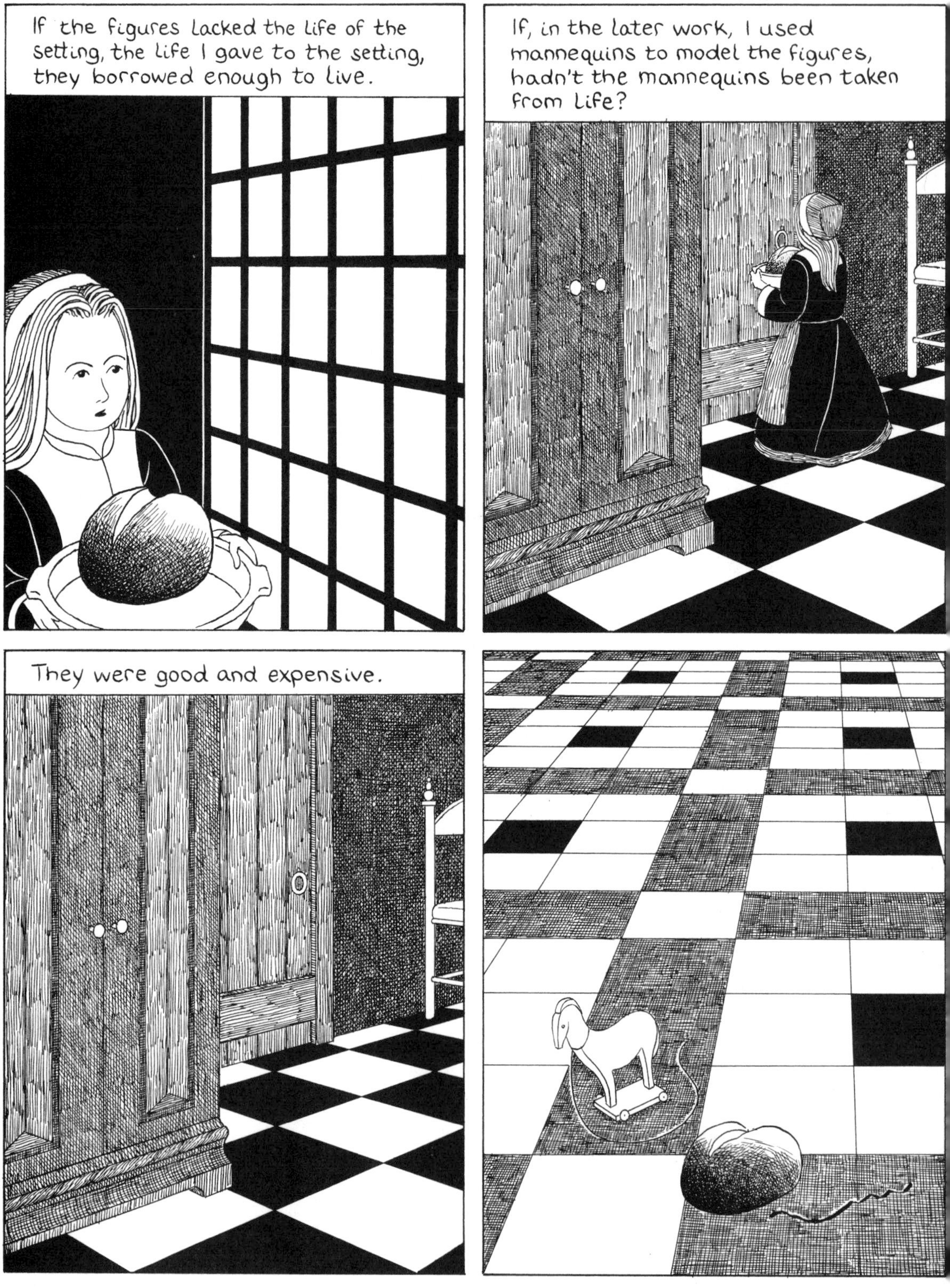
If the figures lacked the life of the setting, the life I gave to the setting, they borrowed enough to live.
If, in the later work, I used mannequins to model the figures, hadn't the mannequins been taken from life?
They were good and expensive.

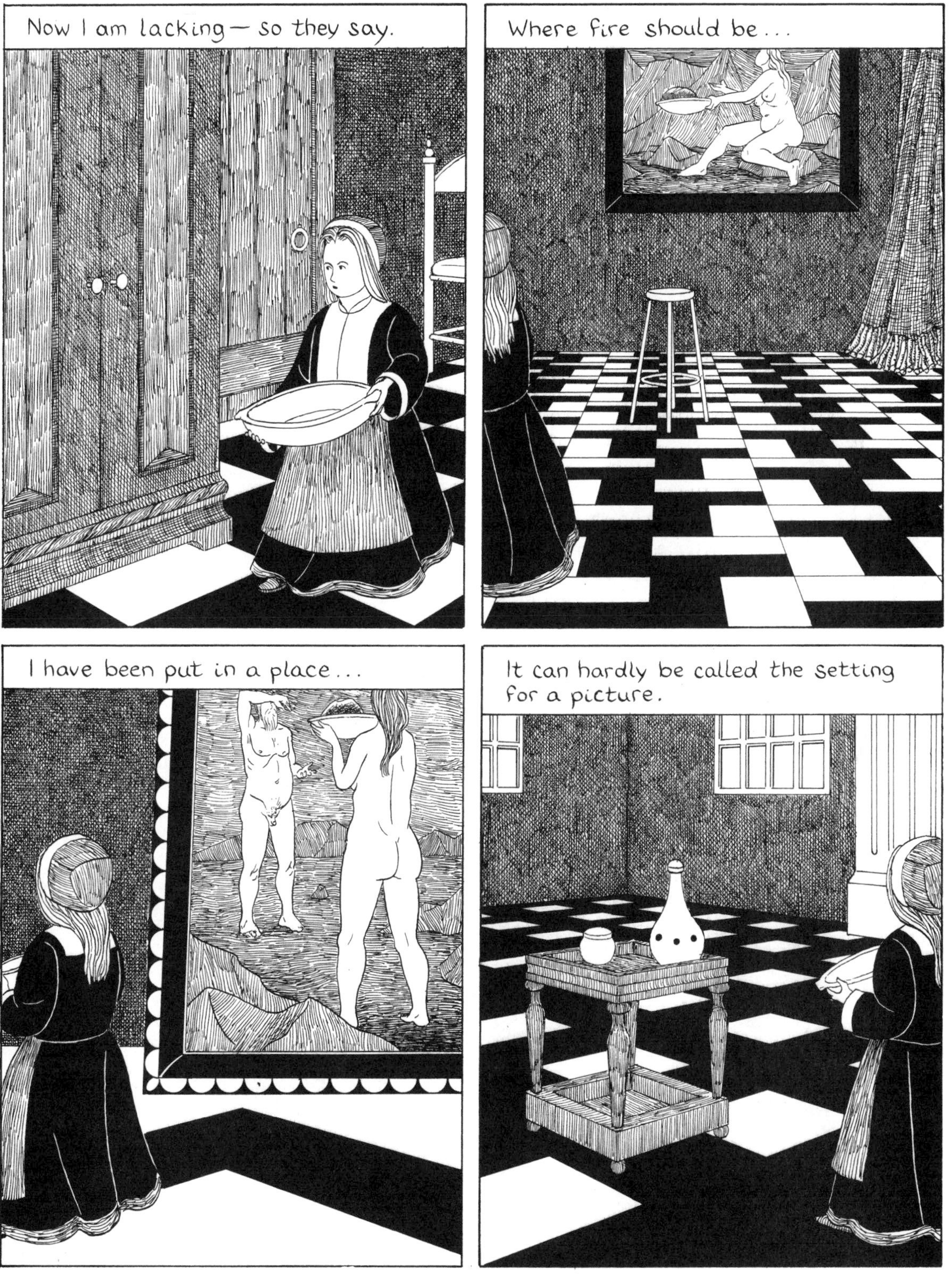
Now I am lacking— so they say.
Where fire should be...
I have been put in a place...
It can hardly be called the setting for a picture.

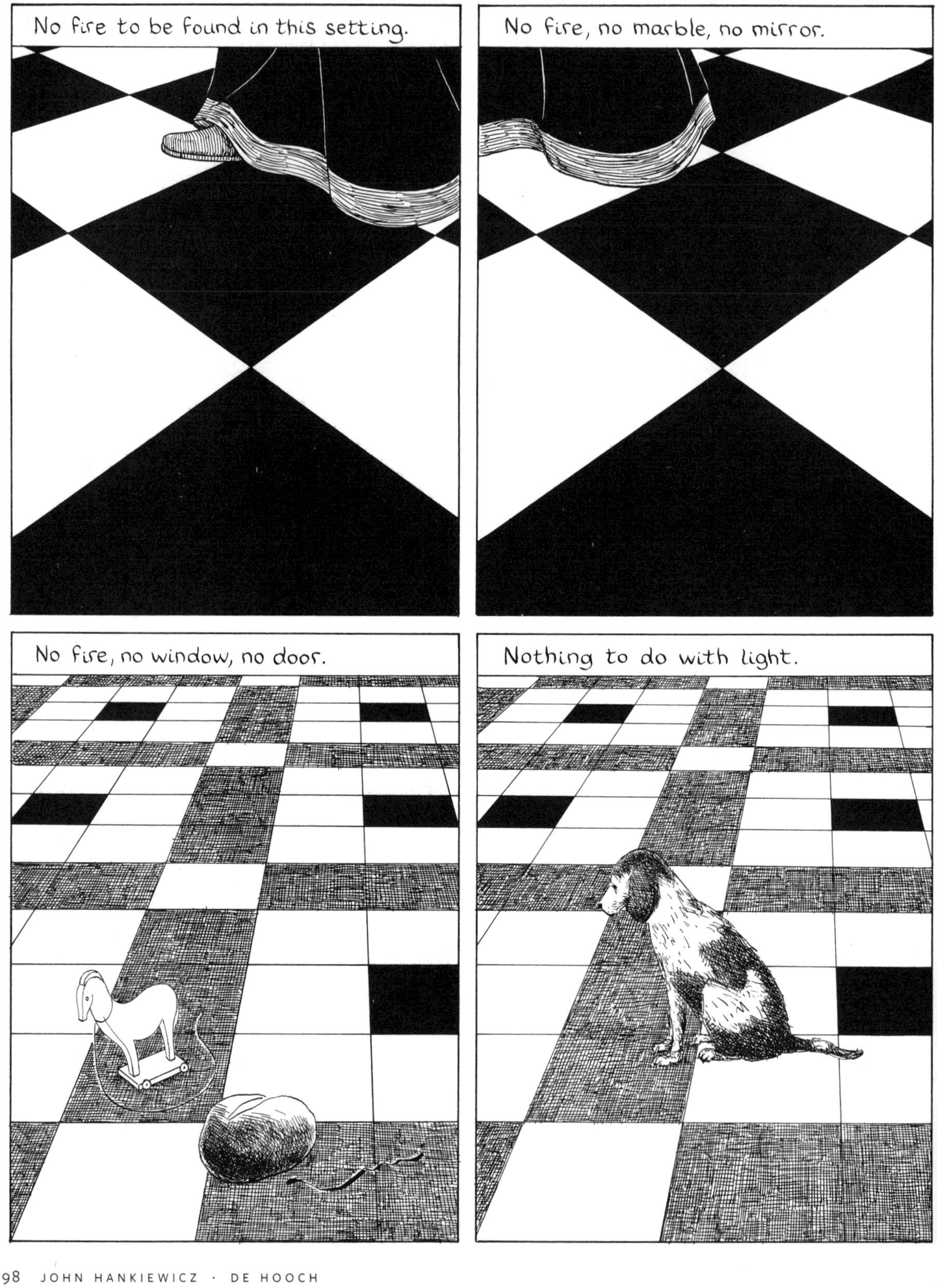
No fire to be found in this setting.
No fire, no marble, no mirror.
No fire, no window, no door.
Nothing to do with light.

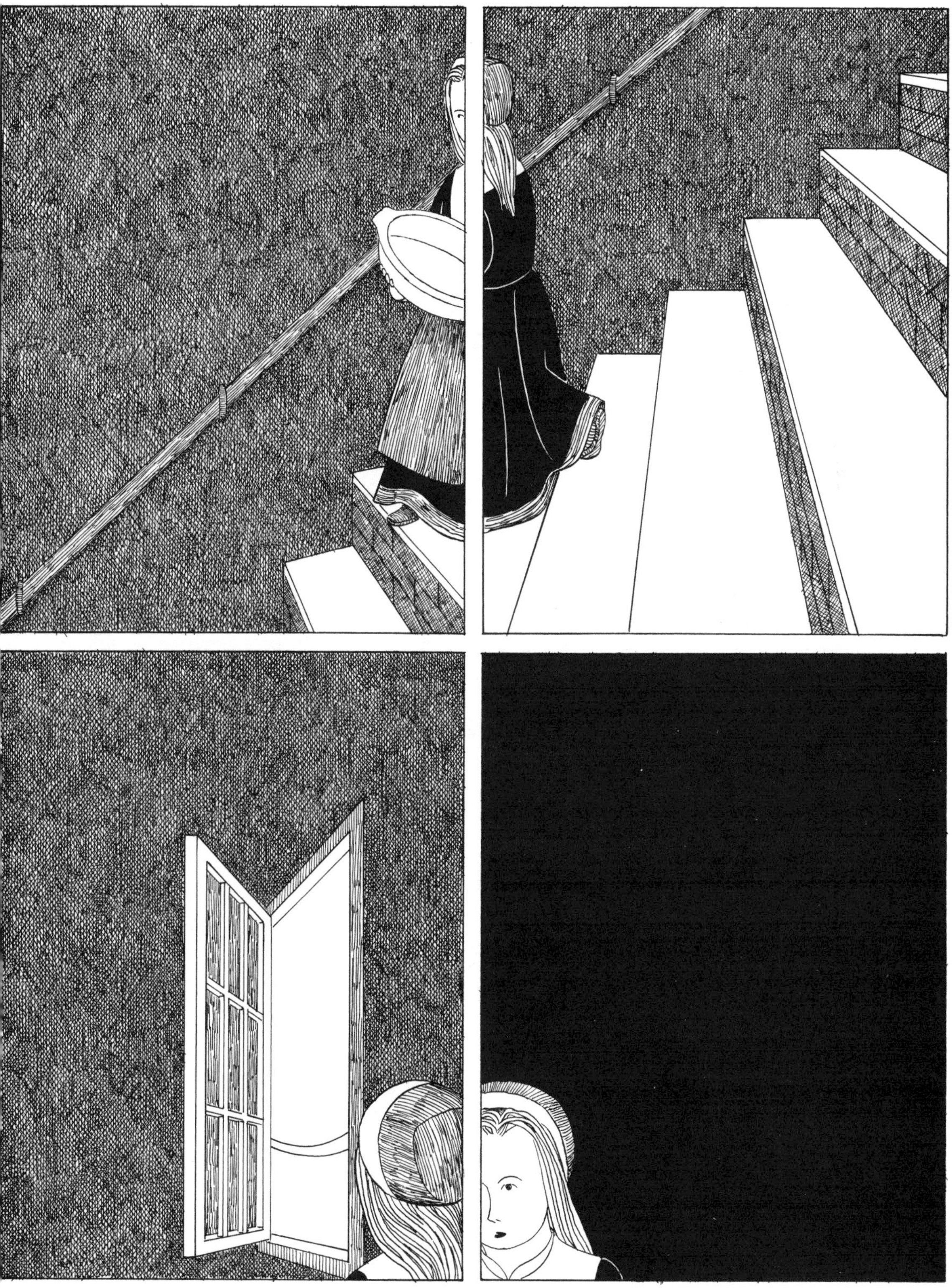

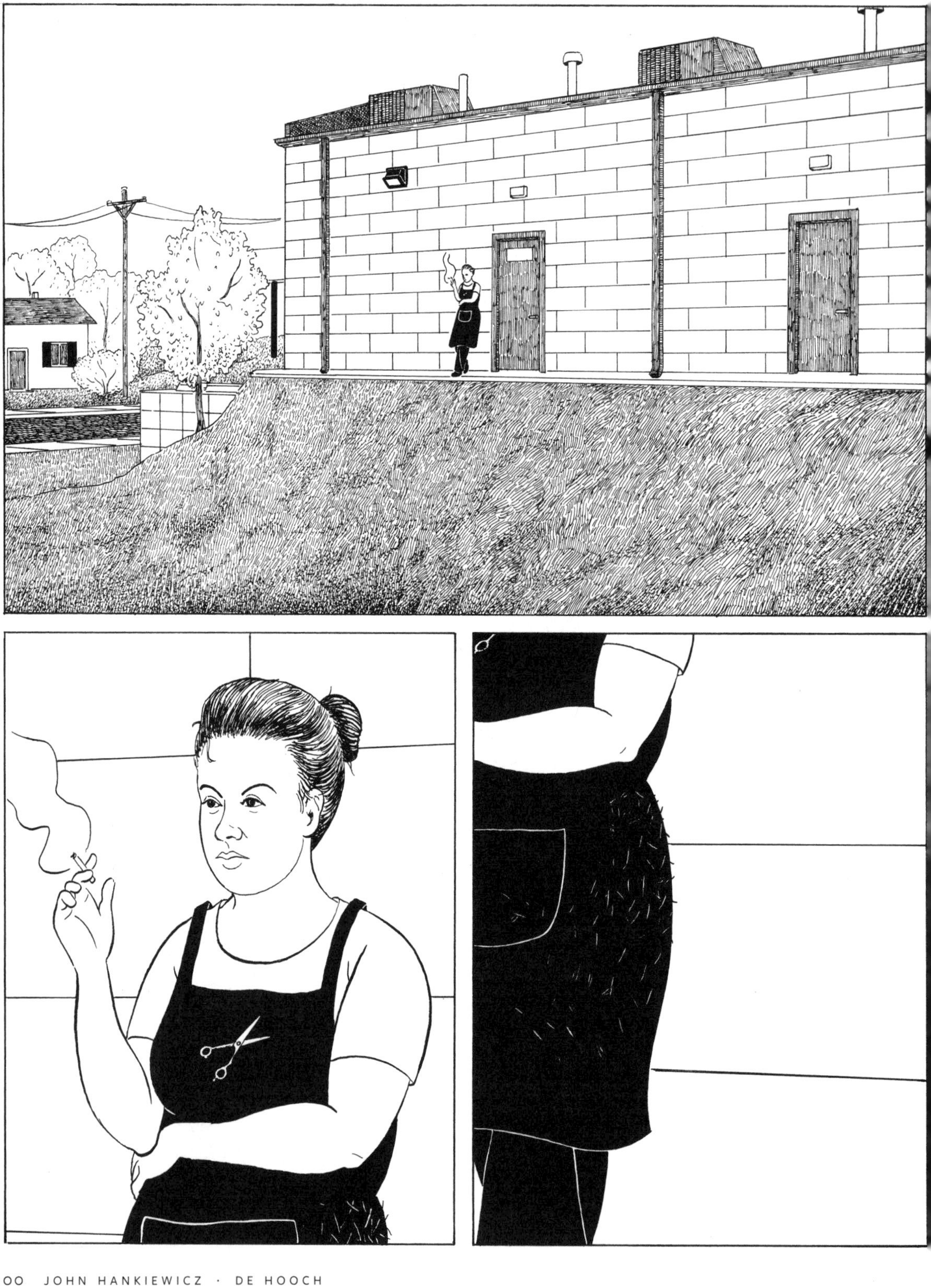

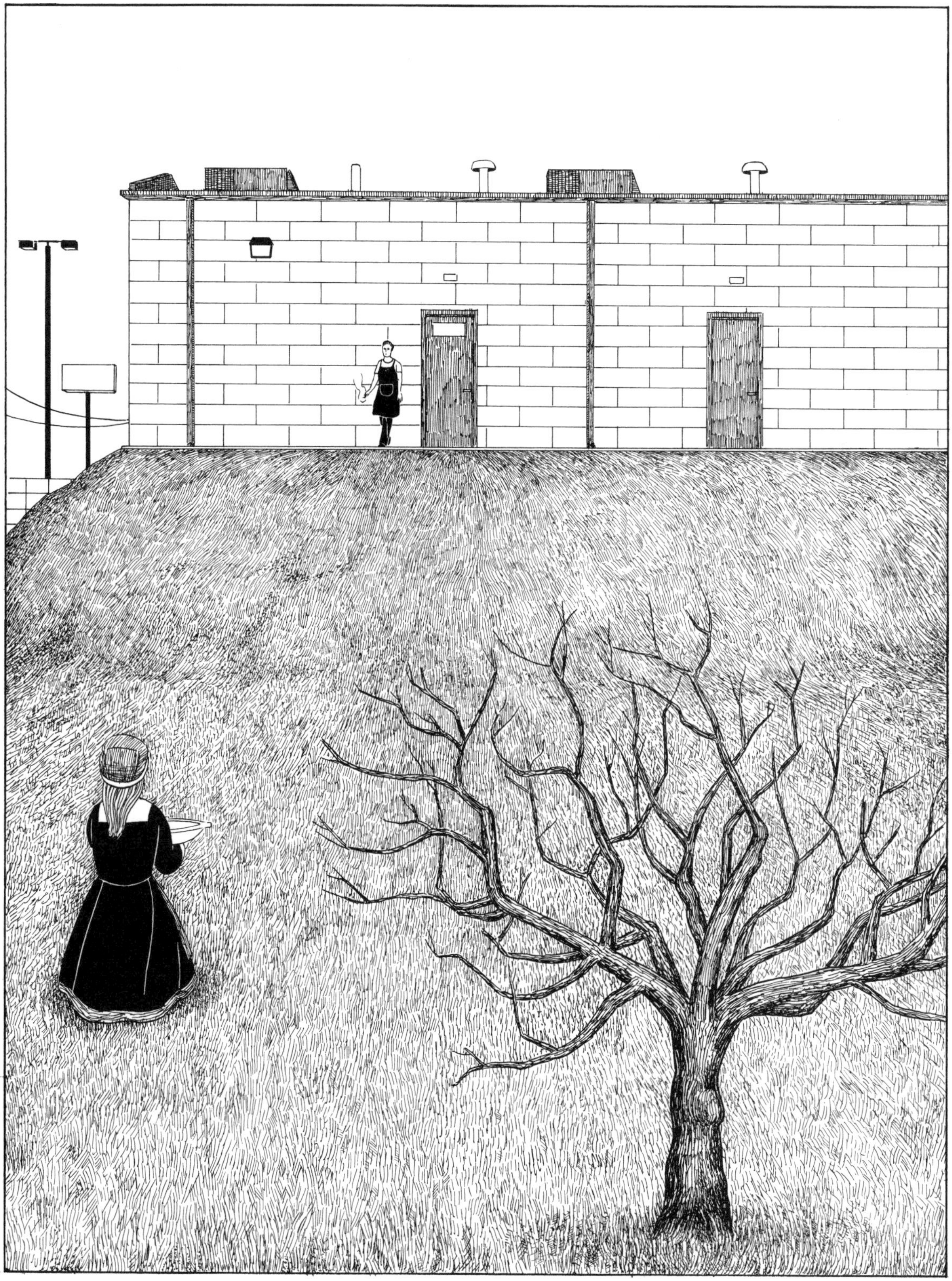

The women who surround me — who cut my hair, who carry bread — whisper in my ear:

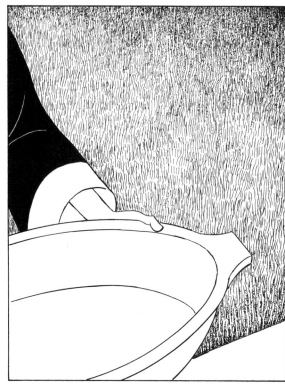

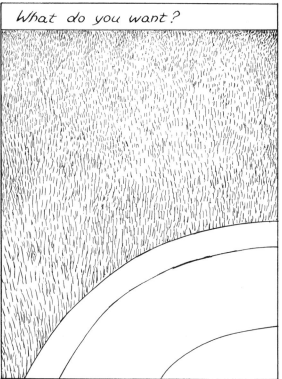

*What do you want?*

SELECTIONS FROM

# Hip Hop Family Tree

## ED PISKOR

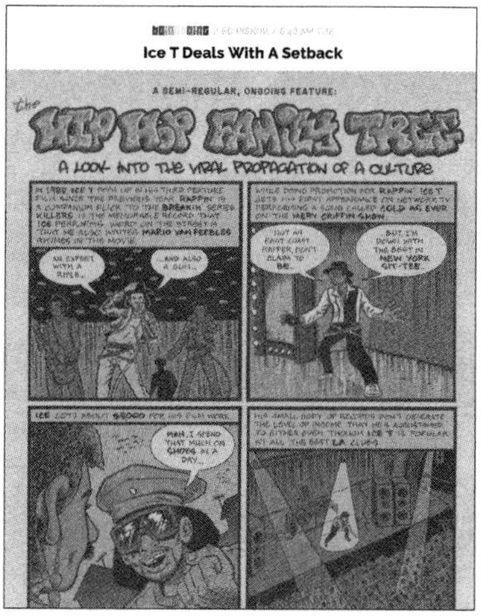
Ice T Deals With A Setback
A SEMI-REGULAR, ONGOING FEATURE:
A LOOK INTO THE VIRAL PROPAGATION OF A CULTURE

*originally published at*

*Boing Boing*

BOINGBOING.NET/TAG/HIP-HOP-FAMILY-TREE

digital • serial

### Biography

Ed Piskor cut his teeth drawing *American Splendor* strips for Harvey Pekar. They went on to create two graphic novels together, *Macedonia* (2005, Villard) and *The Beats* (2007, Hill and Wang). Piskor then went on to create his own comics, the first being *Wizzywig* (2012, Top Shelf). He now does *Hip Hop Family Tree* full-time, published by Fantagraphics.
edpiskor.com

### Statement

I consider myself an archaeologist and a curator as much as I consider myself a cartoonist on *Hip Hop Family Tree*. The idea is to excavate as much detail about every important moment in the culture as possible and compile it in one location.

IN **1985, ICE T** POPS UP IN HIS THIRD FEATURE FILM SINCE THE PREVIOUS YEAR. **RAPPIN'** IS A COMPANION FLICK TO THE **BREAKIN'** SERIES. **KILLERS** IS THE MEMORABLE RECORD THAT **ICE** PERFORMS. WORD ON THE STREET IS THAT HE ALSO WRITES **MARIO VAN PEEBLES** RHYMES IN THE MOVIE.

AN EXPERT WITH A RIFLE...

...AND ALSO A GUN...

WHILE DOING PROMOTION FOR **RAPPIN'**, **ICE T** GETS HIS FIRST APPEARANCE ON NETWORK TV PERFORMING A SONG CALLED **COLD AS EVER** ON THE **MERV GRIFFIN SHOW**.

NOT AN EAST COAST RAPPER, DON'T CLAIM TO BE...

...BUT, I'M DOWN WITH THE BEST IN **NEW YORK** SIT-TEE...

**ICE** GETS ABOUT **$5,000** FOR HIS FILM WORK.

**MAN**, I SPEND THAT MUCH ON **SHOES** IN A DAY...

HIS SMALL BODY OF RECORDS DON'T GENERATE THE LEVEL OF INCOME THAT HE'S ACCUSTOMED TO EITHER EVEN THOUGH **ICE T** IS POPULAR AT ALL THE BEST **LA** CLUBS.

**ICE** STILL HANGS OUT WITH A CRIMINAL ELEMENT TO MAKE ENDS MEET. HE HAS A BABY DAUGHTER TO PROVIDE FOR, AFTER ALL...

ONE NIGHT AFTER BURNING THE CANDLE AT BOTH ENDS...

zzzzz...

ZZZZZ
...

HONK

THE CAR ACCIDENT BROKE **ICE T'S** PELVIS, RIBS, AND LEFT FEMUR. WHILE BEING FELONIOUS, **ICE** WOULDN'T CARRY IDENTIFICATION SO WHEN HE GOT SCOOPED UP, HE WAS REGISTERED AS A **JOHN DOE** AND WAREHOUSED AT THE SHITTY COUNTY HOSPITAL...

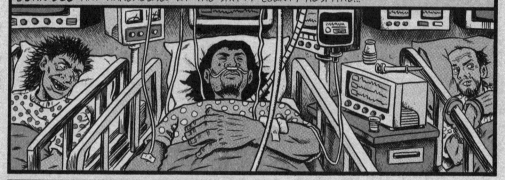

**ICE** ALSO HAD SEVERAL APARTMENTS ACROSS THE CITY AND WOULD MOVE AROUND A LOT. IT TOOK A WHILE BEFORE ANY OF HIS FRIENDS EVEN KNEW HE WAS MISSING.

HIS NAME'S **TRACY** SUMP'N OR OTHER...

WHEN IDENTIFIED, HIS FORMER AFFILIATION WITH THE **US ARMY** IS DISCOVERED **ICE T** IS IMMEDIATELY WHISKED AWAY TO RECOVER IN HIS OWN, PRIVATE ROOM AT THE **VA HOSPITAL.**

YO, **ICE**, THIS ARTICLE GOT YOU LABELLED AS A MOTHER FUCKIN' FATALITY, YO!

HA HA... **DAMN**

LOS ANGELES TIMES
FATAL ACCIDENT

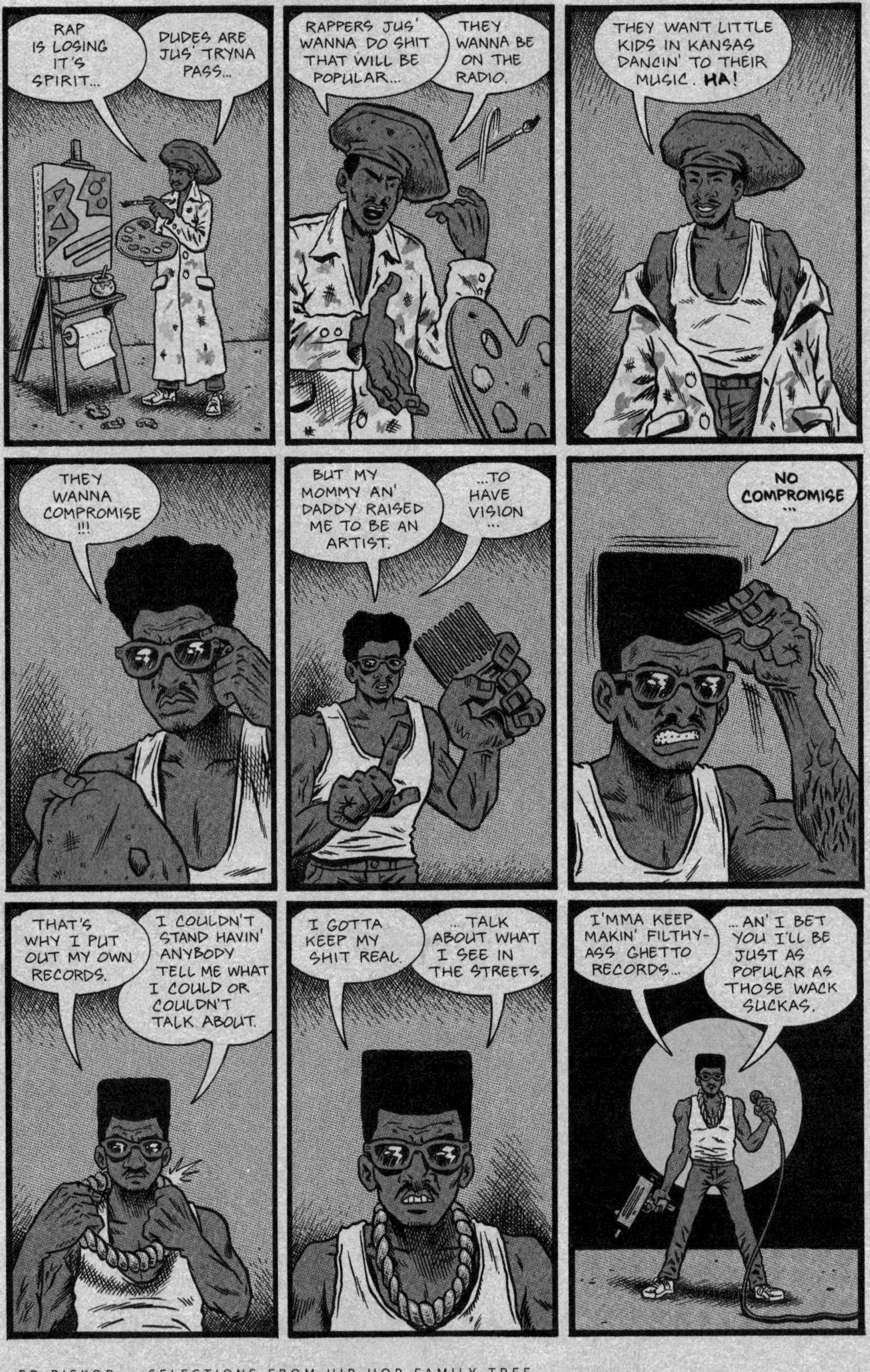
RAP IS LOSING IT'S SPIRIT...
DUDES ARE JUS' TRYNA PASS...
RAPPERS JUS' WANNA DO SHIT THAT WILL BE POPULAR...
THEY WANNA BE ON THE RADIO.
THEY WANT LITTLE KIDS IN KANSAS DANCIN' TO THEIR MUSIC. HA!
THEY WANNA COMPROMISE !!!
BUT MY MOMMY AN' DADDY RAISED ME TO BE AN ARTIST.
...TO HAVE VISION ...
NO COMPROMISE ...
THAT'S WHY I PUT OUT MY OWN RECORDS.
I COULDN'T STAND HAVIN' ANYBODY TELL ME WHAT I COULD OR COULDN'T TALK ABOUT.
I GOTTA KEEP MY SHIT REAL.
... TALK ABOUT WHAT I SEE IN THE STREETS.
I'MMA KEEP MAKIN' FILTHY-ASS GHETTO RECORDS...
... AN' I BET YOU I'LL BE JUST AS POPULAR AS THOSE WACK SUCKAS.

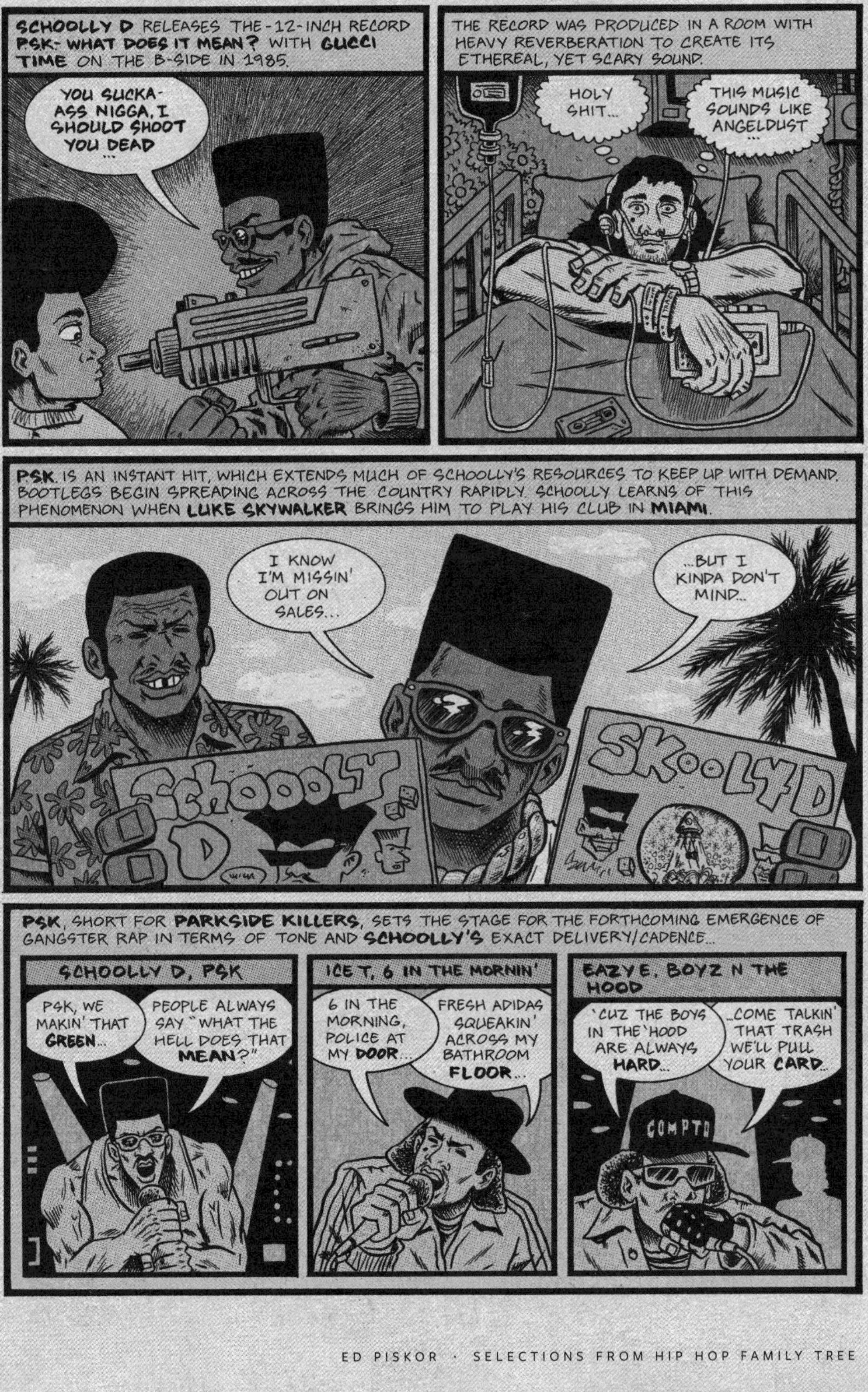
SCHOOLLY D RELEASES THE 12-INCH RECORD P.S.K.- WHAT DOES IT MEAN? WITH GUCCI TIME ON THE B-SIDE IN 1985.
YOU SUCKA-ASS NIGGA, I SHOULD SHOOT YOU DEAD...
THE RECORD WAS PRODUCED IN A ROOM WITH HEAVY REVERBERATION TO CREATE ITS ETHEREAL, YET SCARY SOUND.
HOLY SHIT...
THIS MUSIC SOUNDS LIKE ANGELDUST...
P.S.K. IS AN INSTANT HIT, WHICH EXTENDS MUCH OF SCHOOLLY'S RESOURCES TO KEEP UP WITH DEMAND. BOOTLEGS BEGIN SPREADING ACROSS THE COUNTRY RAPIDLY. SCHOOLLY LEARNS OF THIS PHENOMENON WHEN LUKE SKYWALKER BRINGS HIM TO PLAY HIS CLUB IN MIAMI.
I KNOW I'M MISSIN' OUT ON SALES...
...BUT I KINDA DON'T MIND...
PSK, SHORT FOR PARKSIDE KILLERS, SETS THE STAGE FOR THE FORTHCOMING EMERGENCE OF GANGSTER RAP IN TERMS OF TONE AND SCHOOLLY'S EXACT DELIVERY/CADENCE...
SCHOOLLY D, PSK
PSK, WE MAKIN' THAT GREEN...
PEOPLE ALWAYS SAY "WHAT THE HELL DOES THAT MEAN?"
ICE T, 6 IN THE MORNIN'
6 IN THE MORNING, POLICE AT MY DOOR...
FRESH ADIDAS SQUEAKIN' ACROSS MY BATHROOM FLOOR...
EAZY E, BOYZ N THE HOOD
'CUZ THE BOYS IN THE 'HOOD ARE ALWAYS HARD...
...COME TALKIN' THAT TRASH WE'LL PULL YOUR CARD...
COMPTO

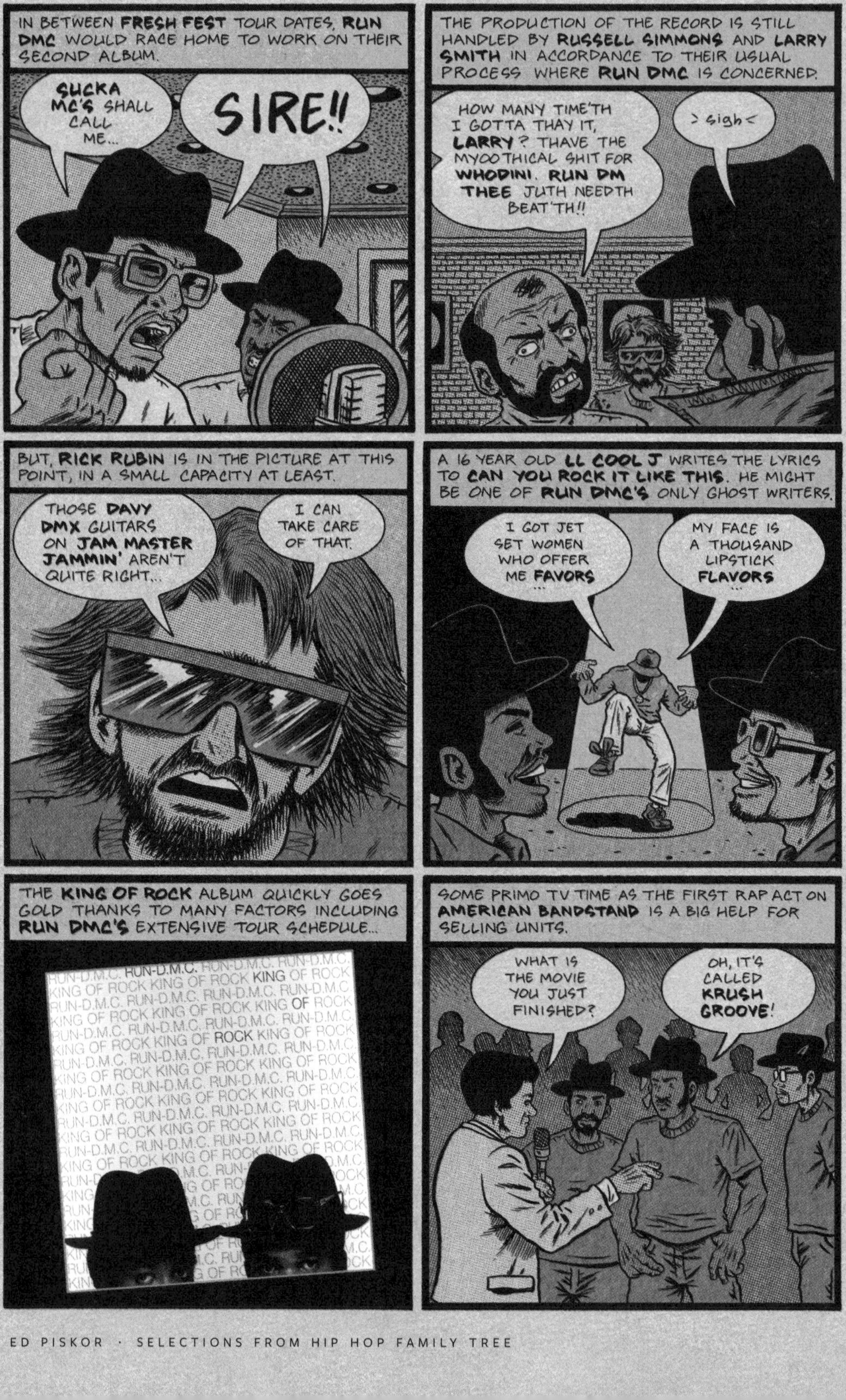
IN BETWEEN FRESH FEST TOUR DATES, RUN DMC WOULD RACE HOME TO WORK ON THEIR SECOND ALBUM.
SUCKA MC'S SHALL CALL ME...
SIRE!!
THE PRODUCTION OF THE RECORD IS STILL HANDLED BY RUSSELL SIMMONS AND LARRY SMITH IN ACCORDANCE TO THEIR USUAL PROCESS WHERE RUN DMC IS CONCERNED.
HOW MANY TIME'TH I GOTTA THAY IT, LARRY? THAVE THE MYOOTHICAL SHIT FOR WHODINI. RUN DM THEE JUTH NEEDTH BEAT'TH!!
>sigh<
BUT, RICK RUBIN IS IN THE PICTURE AT THIS POINT, IN A SMALL CAPACITY AT LEAST.
THOSE DAVY DMX GUITARS ON JAM MASTER JAMMIN' AREN'T QUITE RIGHT...
I CAN TAKE CARE OF THAT.
A 16 YEAR OLD LL COOL J WRITES THE LYRICS TO CAN YOU ROCK IT LIKE THIS. HE MIGHT BE ONE OF RUN DMC'S ONLY GHOST WRITERS.
I GOT JET SET WOMEN WHO OFFER ME FAVORS...
MY FACE IS A THOUSAND LIPSTICK FLAVORS...
THE KING OF ROCK ALBUM QUICKLY GOES GOLD THANKS TO MANY FACTORS INCLUDING RUN DMC'S EXTENSIVE TOUR SCHEDULE...
RUN-D.M.C. KING OF ROCK
SOME PRIMO TV TIME AS THE FIRST RAP ACT ON AMERICAN BANDSTAND IS A BIG HELP FOR SELLING UNITS.
WHAT IS THE MOVIE YOU JUST FINISHED?
OH, IT'S CALLED KRUSH GROOVE!

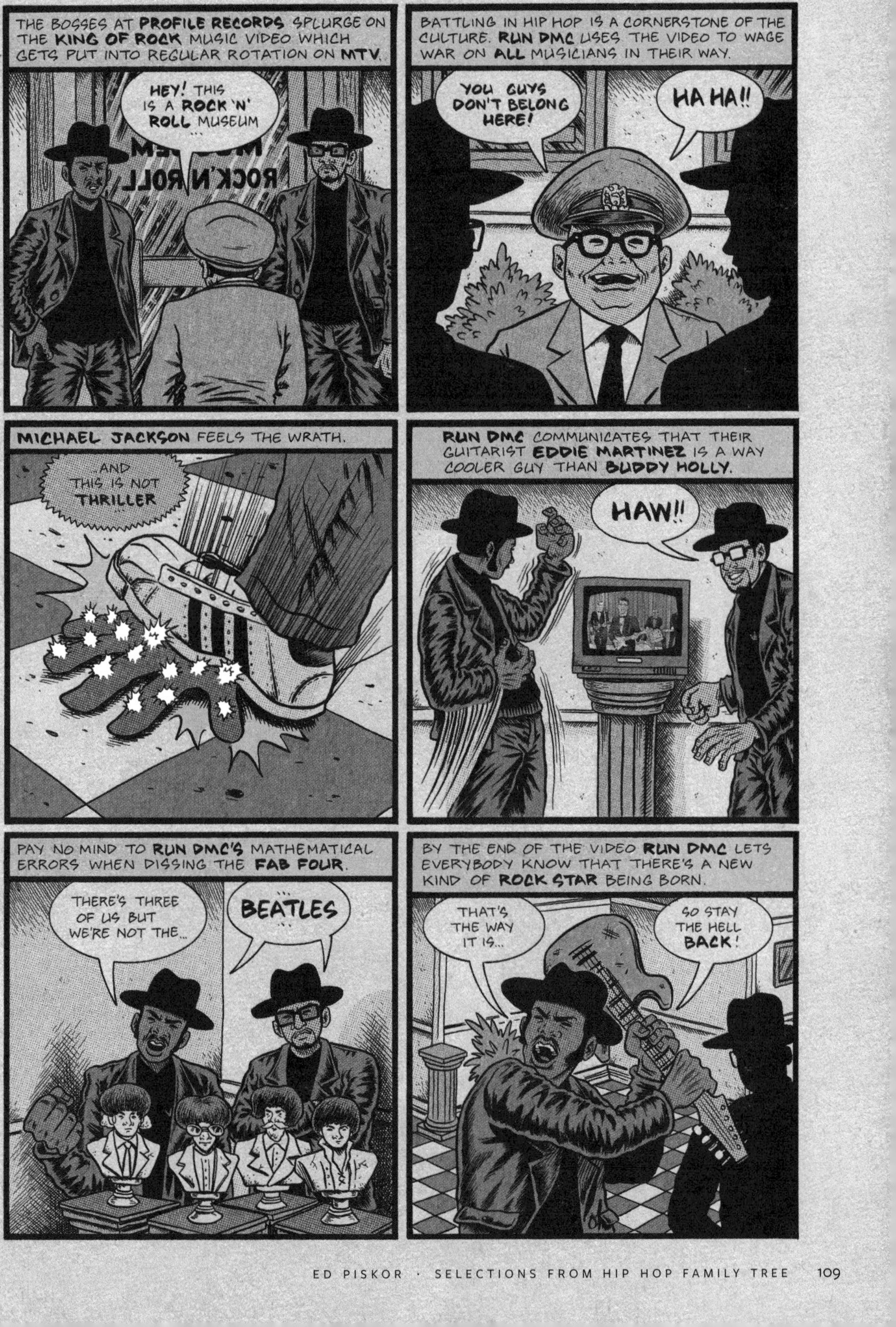
THE BOSSES AT PROFILE RECORDS SPLURGE ON THE KING OF ROCK MUSIC VIDEO WHICH GETS PUT INTO REGULAR ROTATION ON MTV.
HEY! THIS IS A ROCK 'N' ROLL MUSEUM ...
BATTLING IN HIP HOP IS A CORNERSTONE OF THE CULTURE. RUN DMC USES THE VIDEO TO WAGE WAR ON ALL MUSICIANS IN THEIR WAY.
YOU GUYS DON'T BELONG HERE!
HA HA!!
MICHAEL JACKSON FEELS THE WRATH.
...AND THIS IS NOT THRILLER
RUN DMC COMMUNICATES THAT THEIR GUITARIST EDDIE MARTINEZ IS A WAY COOLER GUY THAN BUDDY HOLLY.
HAW!!
PAY NO MIND TO RUN DMC'S MATHEMATICAL ERRORS WHEN DISSING THE FAB FOUR.
THERE'S THREE OF US BUT WE'RE NOT THE...
BEATLES
BY THE END OF THE VIDEO RUN DMC LETS EVERYBODY KNOW THAT THERE'S A NEW KIND OF ROCK STAR BEING BORN.
THAT'S THE WAY IT IS...
SO STAY THE HELL BACK!

YOU GOT THE **COOLEY HIGH** DIRECTOR INNERETH'TED IN MAKIN' THE **RUN DM THEE** FLICK! BET!

**RUSSELL** FEELS COMFORTABLE WITH DIRECTOR **MICHAEL SCHULTZ** ON THE STRENGTH OF HIS FILM COLLABORATIONS WITH RICHARD **PRYOR** AND HIS LATEST MOVIE **THE LAST DRAGON**.

THE BULK OF THE **RUN DMC** FILM'S NARRATIVE WAS UP FOR DEBATE AT THE BEGINNING.

A YOUNG STARLET GETS HELP FROM **RUN DMC** TO BREAK INTO THE MUSIC BIZ. WHATTAYA THINK?

WHAT IF WE MAKE A STORY ABOUT THE LIFE AN' DEATH OF **DJ JUNEBUG** FROM THE **FEVER**?

WE WANNA SHOOT SOME GUNS!

WE GOTTA GET ALL THE **GIRLS**.

IT WAS SETTLED THAT THE FILM, NOW TITLED **KRUSH GROOVE**, WOULD BE A HOLLYWOOD VERSION OF THE HUMBLE BEGINNINGS OF **RUN DMC**, **THE FAT BOYS**, AND **RICK** AND **RUSSELL**.

THEY'RE GONNA GET **FULL FORCE** TO PLAY THE GANGSTER HENCHMEN...

WE GET $15,000 A PEETH!

THE HOLLYWOOD GUYS MADE AN ARGUMENT THAT A FEMALE LOVE INTEREST WAS NEEDED FOR THE PICTURE.

I WANTED THUMWUN LIKE THE **REAL ROXANNE**.

THEY DIDN'T GET HER?

**SHEILA E.** THE **PRINCE** CHICK.

LYOR COHEN

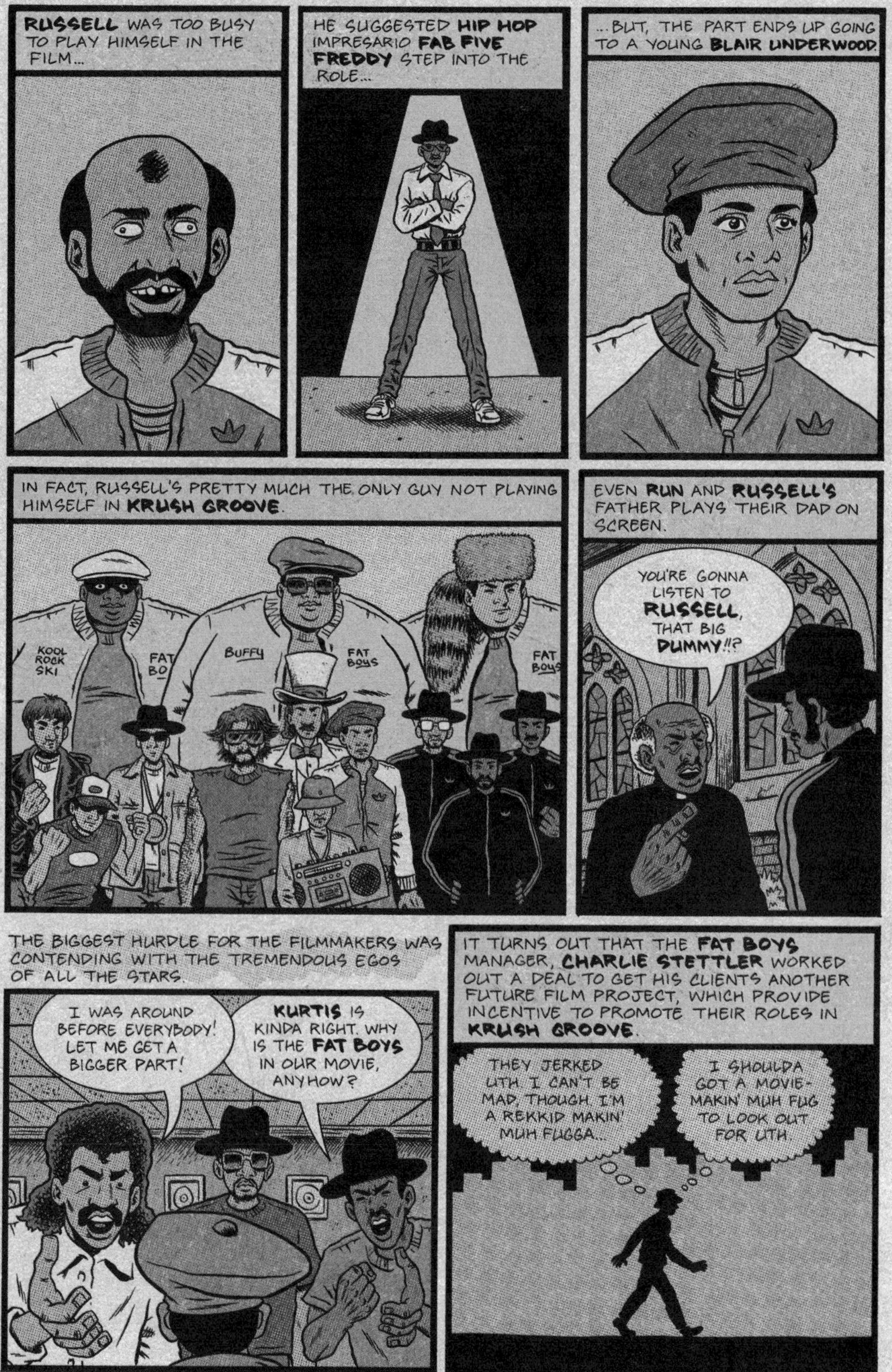
RUSSELL WAS TOO BUSY TO PLAY HIMSELF IN THE FILM...
HE SUGGESTED HIP HOP IMPRESARIO FAB FIVE FREDDY STEP INTO THE ROLE...
...BUT, THE PART ENDS UP GOING TO A YOUNG BLAIR UNDERWOOD.
IN FACT, RUSSELL'S PRETTY MUCH THE ONLY GUY NOT PLAYING HIMSELF IN KRUSH GROOVE.
KOOL ROCK SKI
FAT BO
BUFFY
FAT BOYS
FAT BOYS
EVEN RUN AND RUSSELL'S FATHER PLAYS THEIR DAD ON SCREEN.
YOU'RE GONNA LISTEN TO RUSSELL, THAT BIG DUMMY!!?
THE BIGGEST HURDLE FOR THE FILMMAKERS WAS CONTENDING WITH THE TREMENDOUS EGOS OF ALL THE STARS.
I WAS AROUND BEFORE EVERYBODY! LET ME GET A BIGGER PART!
KURTIS IS KINDA RIGHT. WHY IS THE FAT BOYS IN OUR MOVIE, ANYHOW?
IT TURNS OUT THAT THE FAT BOYS MANAGER, CHARLIE STETTLER WORKED OUT A DEAL TO GET HIS CLIENTS ANOTHER FUTURE FILM PROJECT, WHICH PROVIDE INCENTIVE TO PROMOTE THEIR ROLES IN KRUSH GROOVE.
THEY JERKED UTH I CAN'T BE MAD, THOUGH. I'M A REKKID MAKIN' MUH FUGGA...
I SHOULDA GOT A MOVIE-MAKIN' MUH FUG TO LOOK OUT FOR UTH.

THE BUDGET FOR **KRUSH GROOVE** IS AROUND **$3 MILLION.**

YOU SHOULD MAKE THAT GUY CALL THE UTHA DUDE A **MUTHA-FUCKA!!**

IF IT WERE UP TO YOU, **RUSSELL,** THEY'D SAY **FUCK** EVERY 2 MINUTES.

THE ARTIFICIAL REALITY OF THE MOVIE SET TOOK SOME GETTING USED TO.

**CUT!** RUSSELL WOULD NEVER DO IT THAT WAY!!

**RICK,** LISTEN, BUD. I'M THE DIRECTOR OF THIS PICTURE. YOU'RE MAKIN' ME LOOK BAD.

sigh...

DO IT LIKE RICK SUGGESTED. HE WAS RIGHT ABOUT THAT.

THERE WERE SOME PLOT POINTS THAT **RUN-DMC** HAD TROUBLE WITH.

IT WASN'T COOL WHEN **SHEILA** SOCKED **RUN** IN HIS JIB.

THAT PART WHERE WE GOT A NEW MANAGER WAS BULLSHIT. I'D NEVER GO BEHIND MY BROTHER'S BACK!

WHEN SHOOTING THE **SHEILA E** CHOREOGRAPHED SEQUENCES SHE'D SHOW UP TO THE SET SORE AND EXHAUSTED.

**PRINCE** AND I WERE REHEARSING ALL NIGHT. HE'S SUCH A PERFECTIONIST...

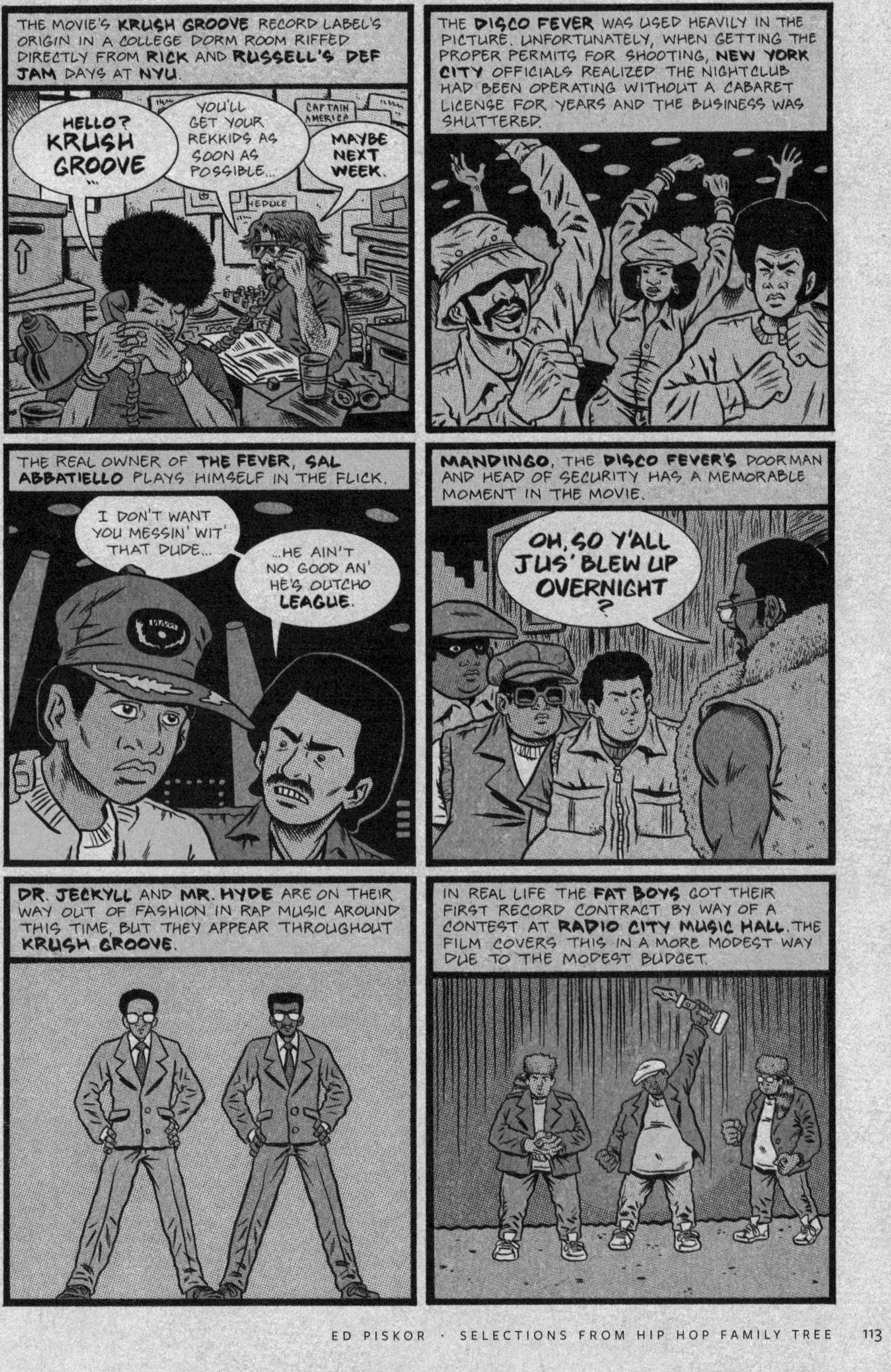
THE MOVIE'S KRUSH GROOVE RECORD LABEL'S ORIGIN IN A COLLEGE DORM ROOM RIFFED DIRECTLY FROM RICK AND RUSSELL'S DEF JAM DAYS AT NYU.
HELLO? KRUSH GROOVE...
YOU'LL GET YOUR REKKIDS AS SOON AS POSSIBLE...
MAYBE NEXT WEEK.
CAPTAIN AMERICA
THE DISCO FEVER WAS USED HEAVILY IN THE PICTURE. UNFORTUNATELY, WHEN GETTING THE PROPER PERMITS FOR SHOOTING, NEW YORK CITY OFFICIALS REALIZED THE NIGHTCLUB HAD BEEN OPERATING WITHOUT A CABARET LICENSE FOR YEARS AND THE BUSINESS WAS SHUTTERED.
THE REAL OWNER OF THE FEVER, SAL ABBATIELLO PLAYS HIMSELF IN THE FLICK.
I DON'T WANT YOU MESSIN' WIT' THAT DUDE...
...HE AIN'T NO GOOD AN' HE'S OUTCHO LEAGUE.
MANDINGO, THE DISCO FEVER'S DOORMAN AND HEAD OF SECURITY HAS A MEMORABLE MOMENT IN THE MOVIE.
OH, SO Y'ALL JUS' BLEW UP OVERNIGHT?
DR. JECKYLL AND MR. HYDE ARE ON THEIR WAY OUT OF FASHION IN RAP MUSIC AROUND THIS TIME, BUT THEY APPEAR THROUGHOUT KRUSH GROOVE.
IN REAL LIFE THE FAT BOYS GOT THEIR FIRST RECORD CONTRACT BY WAY OF A CONTEST AT RADIO CITY MUSIC HALL. THE FILM COVERS THIS IN A MORE MODEST WAY DUE TO THE MODEST BUDGET.

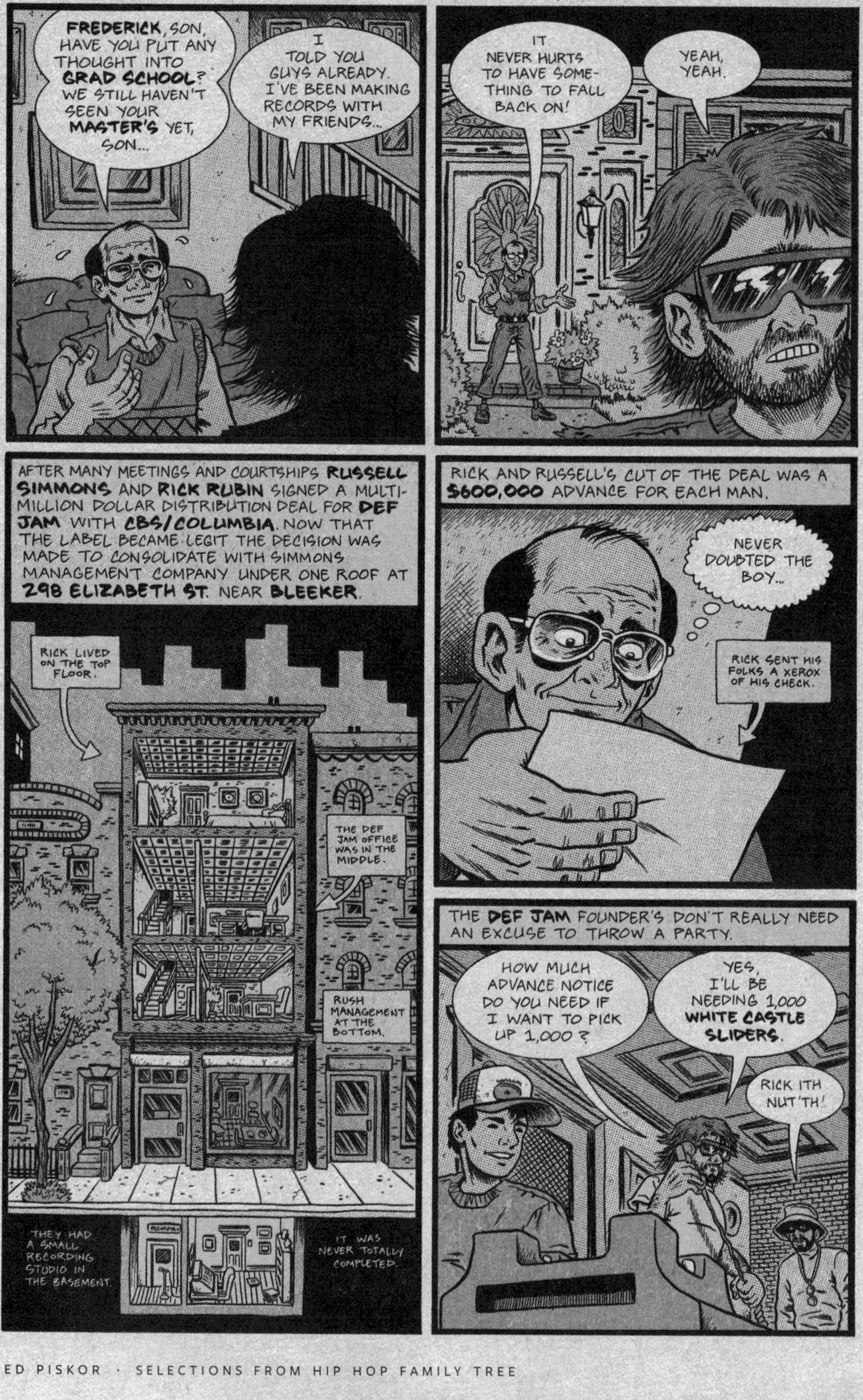
FREDERICK, SON, HAVE YOU PUT ANY THOUGHT INTO GRAD SCHOOL? WE STILL HAVEN'T SEEN YOUR MASTER'S YET, SON...
I TOLD YOU GUYS ALREADY. I'VE BEEN MAKING RECORDS WITH MY FRIENDS...
IT NEVER HURTS TO HAVE SOMETHING TO FALL BACK ON!
YEAH, YEAH.
AFTER MANY MEETINGS AND COURTSHIPS RUSSELL SIMMONS AND RICK RUBIN SIGNED A MULTI-MILLION DOLLAR DISTRIBUTION DEAL FOR DEF JAM WITH CBS/COLUMBIA. NOW THAT THE LABEL BECAME LEGIT THE DECISION WAS MADE TO CONSOLIDATE WITH SIMMONS MANAGEMENT COMPANY UNDER ONE ROOF AT 298 ELIZABETH ST. NEAR BLEEKER.
RICK LIVED ON THE TOP FLOOR.
THE DEF JAM OFFICE WAS IN THE MIDDLE.
RUSH MANAGEMENT AT THE BOTTOM.
THEY HAD A SMALL RECORDING STUDIO IN THE BASEMENT.
IT WAS NEVER TOTALLY COMPLETED.
RICK AND RUSSELL'S CUT OF THE DEAL WAS A $600,000 ADVANCE FOR EACH MAN.
NEVER DOUBTED THE BOY...
RICK SENT HIS FOLKS A XEROX OF HIS CHECK.
THE DEF JAM FOUNDER'S DON'T REALLY NEED AN EXCUSE TO THROW A PARTY.
HOW MUCH ADVANCE NOTICE DO YOU NEED IF I WANT TO PICK UP 1,000?
YES, I'LL BE NEEDING 1,000 WHITE CASTLE SLIDERS.
RICK ITH NUT'TH!

THE ROOFTOP OF THE SUPER-HOT CLUB **DANCETERIA** WAS THE LOCATION FOR **DEF JAM'S** BIG ANNOUNCEMENT.

THE **BEASTIE BOYS** SCREENED THEIR NEWLY COMPLETED MUSIC VIDEO, **SHE'S ON IT**, FOR THEIR CAPTIVE AUDIENCE...

...IF A PIRATE HAD A **DEF JAM** SHIRT...

YOU SEE THAT GUY OVER THERE? THAT'S **WALTER YETNIKOFF**. HE SAYS YOU'RE TOO MUCH OF A PUSSY TO THROW A HAMBURGER AT HIM...

LOTTA REPORTERS HERE...

FOOD FIGHT!

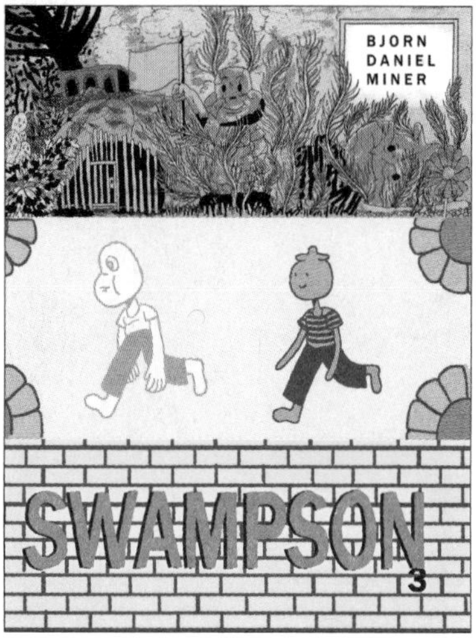
BJORN
DANIEL
MINER
SWAMPSON
3

# Daisies (*Excerpt*)

BJÖRN MINER

*originally published in*

*Swampson* 3

SELF-PUBLISHED

8 × 10 inches • 24 pages

## Biography

Björn is a cartoonist and printer living in Seattle, Washington.
swampson.com

## Statement

This story is from a series I draw called *Daisies/Swampson*. I'm trying to write and draw stories that are cute and fun, but grounded in the real world. Although all the characters in this story are strange-looking people, I want to convey they have emotions, dreams, and insecurities.

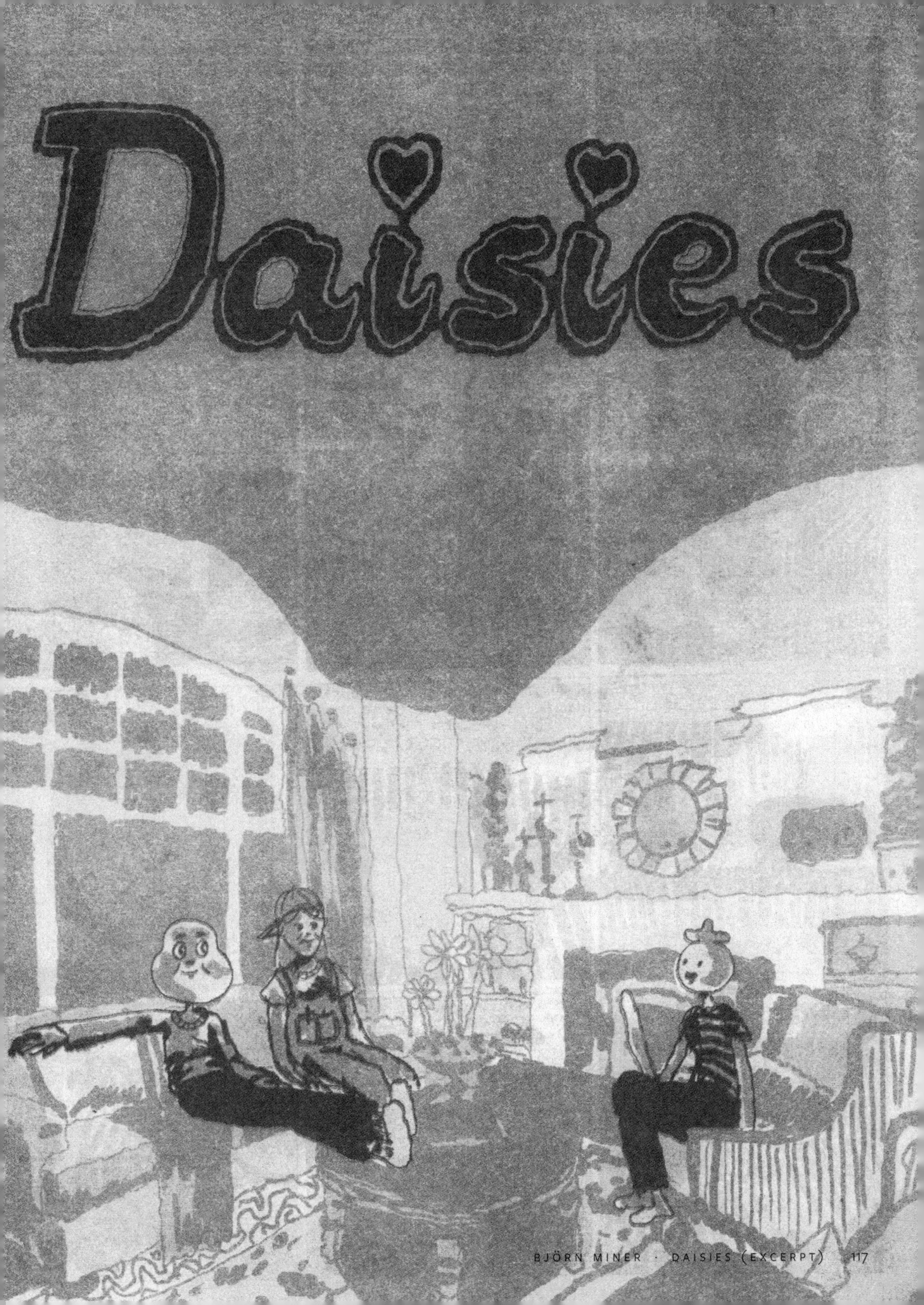
Daisies

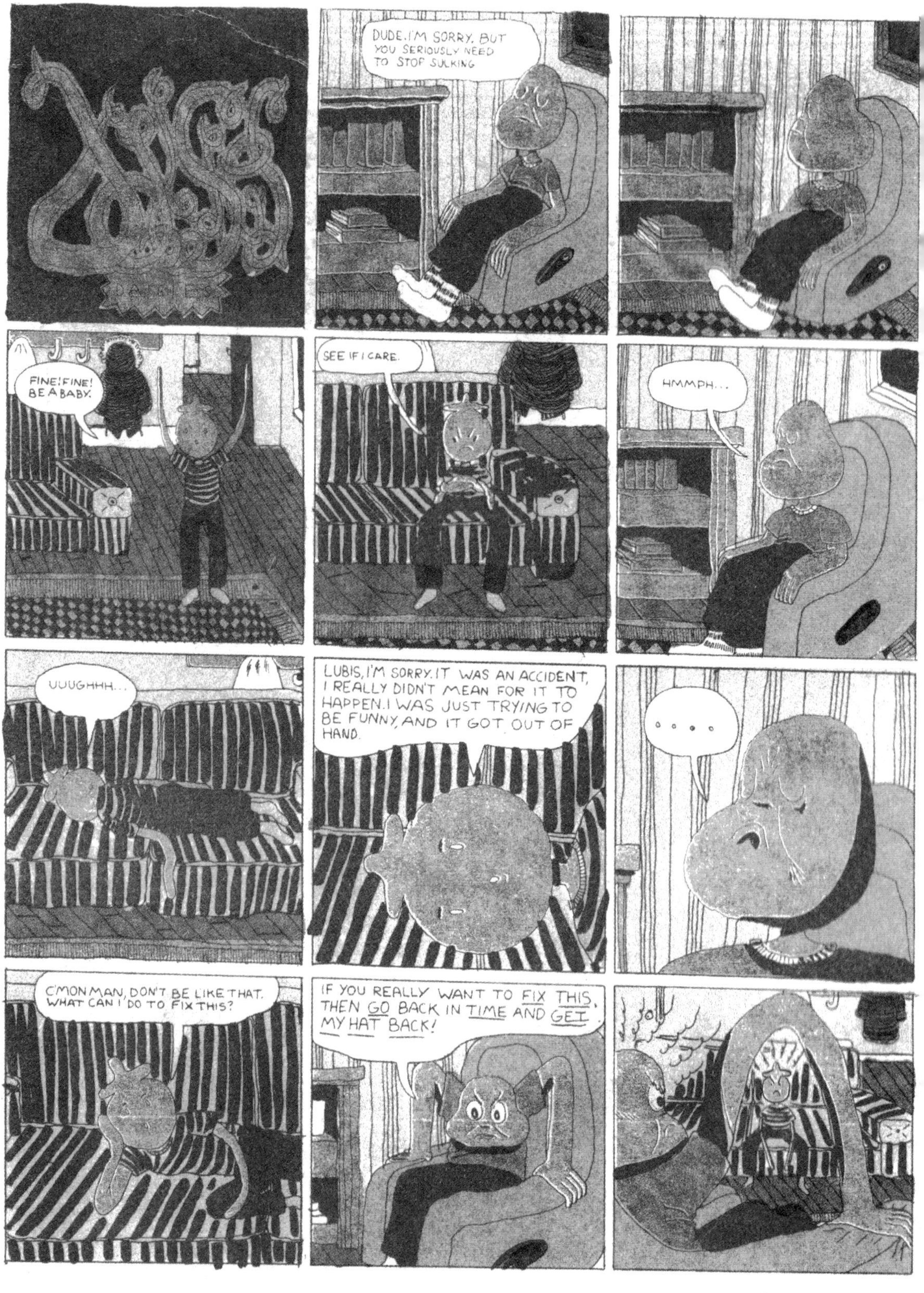

DUDE. I'M SORRY. BUT YOU SERIOUSLY NEED TO STOP SULKING
FINE! FINE! BE A BABY.
SEE IF I CARE.
HMMPH...
UUUGHHH...
LUBIS, I'M SORRY. IT WAS AN ACCIDENT, I REALLY DIDN'T MEAN FOR IT TO HAPPEN. I WAS JUST TRYING TO BE FUNNY, AND IT GOT OUT OF HAND.
. . . .
C'MON MAN, DON'T BE LIKE THAT. WHAT CAN I DO TO FIX THIS?
IF YOU REALLY WANT TO FIX THIS, THEN GO BACK IN TIME AND GET MY HAT BACK!

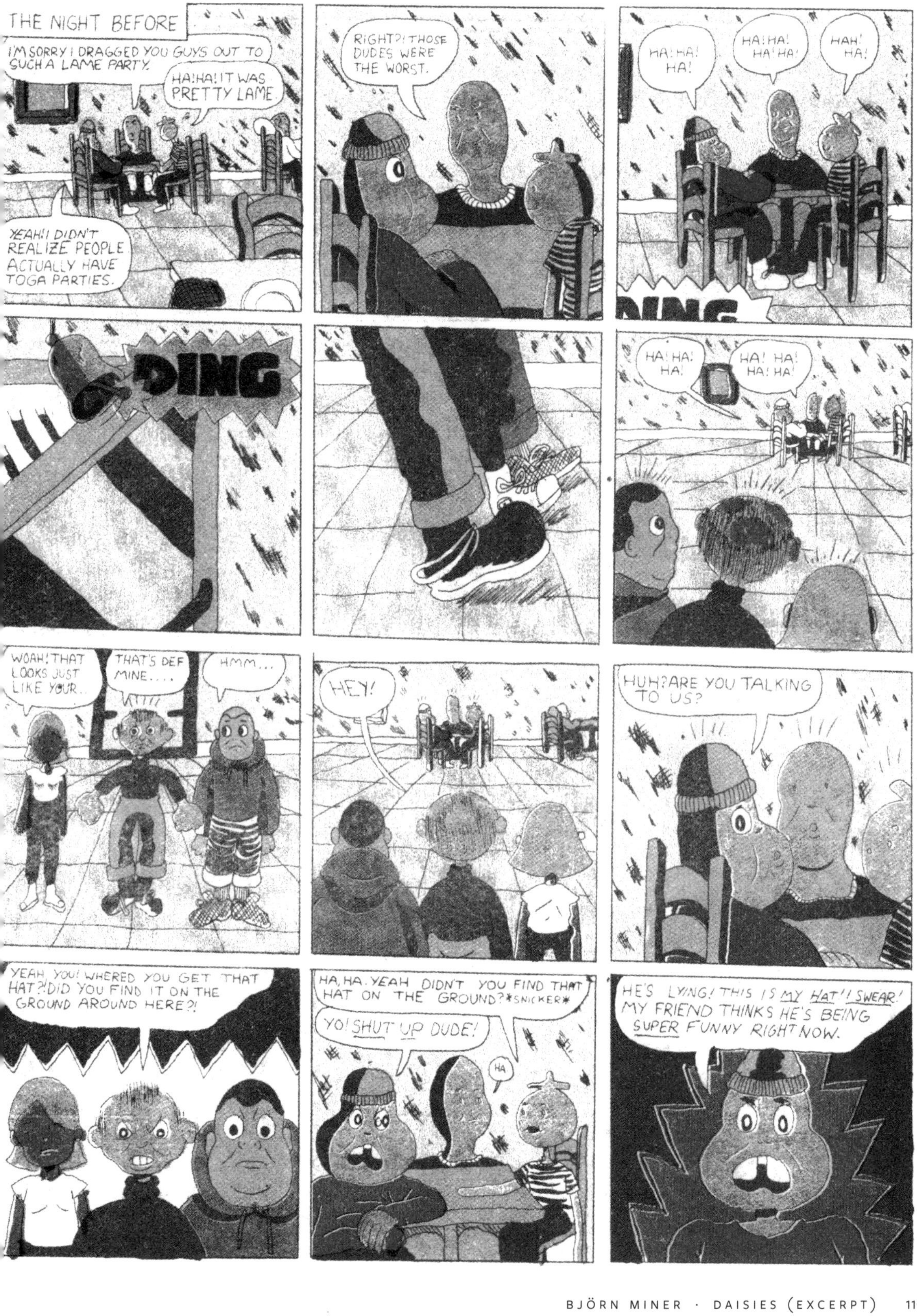
THE NIGHT BEFORE
I'M SORRY I DRAGGED YOU GUYS OUT TO SUCH A LAME PARTY.
HA! HA! IT WAS PRETTY LAME.
YEAH! I DIDN'T REALIZE PEOPLE ACTUALLY HAVE TOGA PARTIES.
RIGHT?! THOSE DUDES WERE THE WORST.
HA! HA! HA!
HA! HA! HA! HA!
HAH! HA!
DING
DING
HA! HA! HA!
HA! HA! HA! HA!
WOAH! THAT LOOKS JUST LIKE YOUR...
THAT'S DEF MINE....
HMM...
HEY!
HUH? ARE YOU TALKING TO US?
YEAH YOU! WHERED YOU GET THAT HAT?! DID YOU FIND IT ON THE GROUND AROUND HERE?!
HA, HA. YEAH DIDN'T YOU FIND THAT HAT ON THE GROUND? *SNICKER*
YO! SHUT UP DUDE!
HA
HE'S LYING! THIS IS MY HAT! I SWEAR! MY FRIEND THINKS HE'S BEING SUPER FUNNY RIGHT NOW.

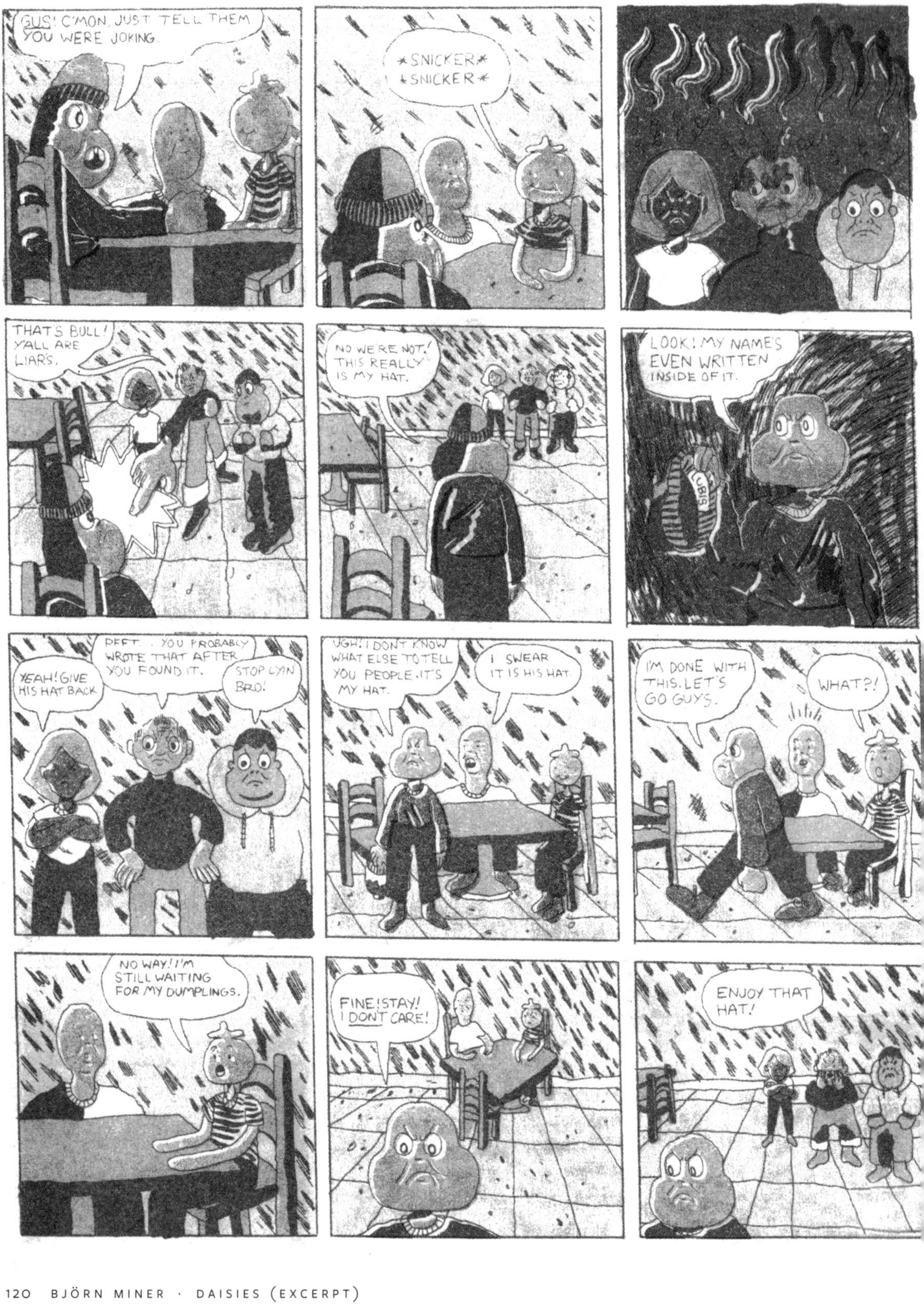
GUS! C'MON, JUST TELL THEM YOU WERE JOKING.
*SNICKER* *SNICKER*
THAT'S BULL! Y'ALL ARE LIAR'S.
NO WE'RE NOT! THIS REALLY IS MY HAT.
LOOK! MY NAME'S EVEN WRITTEN INSIDE OF IT.
GUS
YEAH! GIVE HIS HAT BACK
PFFT. . YOU PROBABLY WROTE THAT AFTER YOU FOUND IT.
STOP LYIN BRO!
UGH! I DONT KNOW WHAT ELSE TO TELL YOU PEOPLE. IT'S MY HAT.
I SWEAR IT IS HIS HAT.
I'M DONE WITH THIS. LET'S GO GUYS.
WHAT?!
NO WAY! I'M STILL WAITING FOR MY DUMPLINGS.
FINE! STAY! I DON'T CARE!
ENJOY THAT HAT!

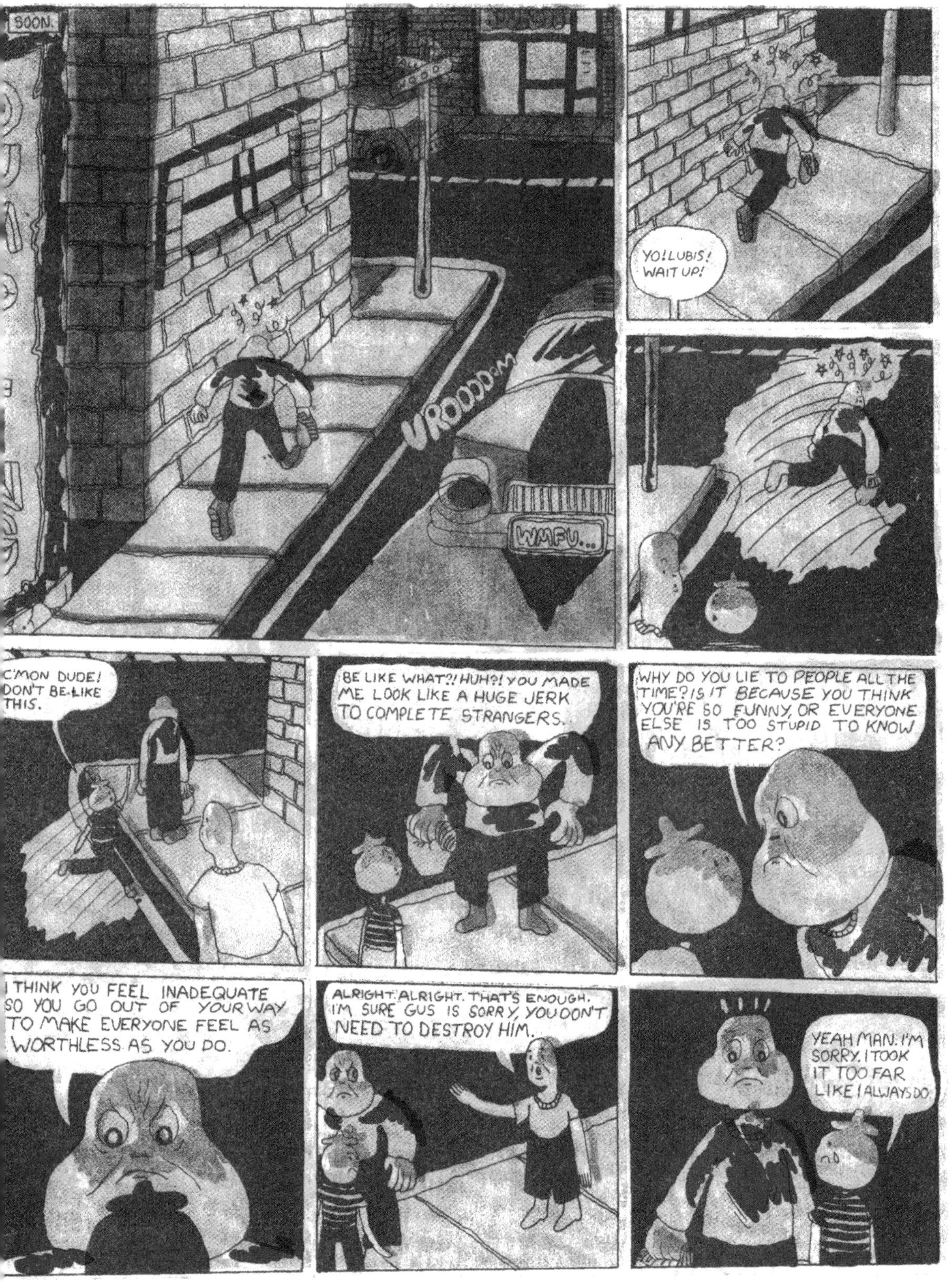
SOON.
UROOOOOM
WMFU...
YO! LUBIS! WAIT UP!
C'MON DUDE! DON'T BE LIKE THIS.
BE LIKE WHAT?! HUH?! YOU MADE ME LOOK LIKE A HUGE JERK TO COMPLETE STRANGERS.
WHY DO YOU LIE TO PEOPLE ALL THE TIME? IS IT BECAUSE YOU THINK YOU'RE SO FUNNY, OR EVERYONE ELSE IS TOO STUPID TO KNOW ANY BETTER?
I THINK YOU FEEL INADEQUATE SO YOU GO OUT OF YOUR WAY TO MAKE EVERYONE FEEL AS WORTHLESS AS YOU DO.
ALRIGHT. ALRIGHT. THAT'S ENOUGH. I'M SURE GUS IS SORRY, YOU DON'T NEED TO DESTROY HIM.
YEAH MAN. I'M SORRY. I TOOK IT TOO FAR LIKE I ALWAYS DO.

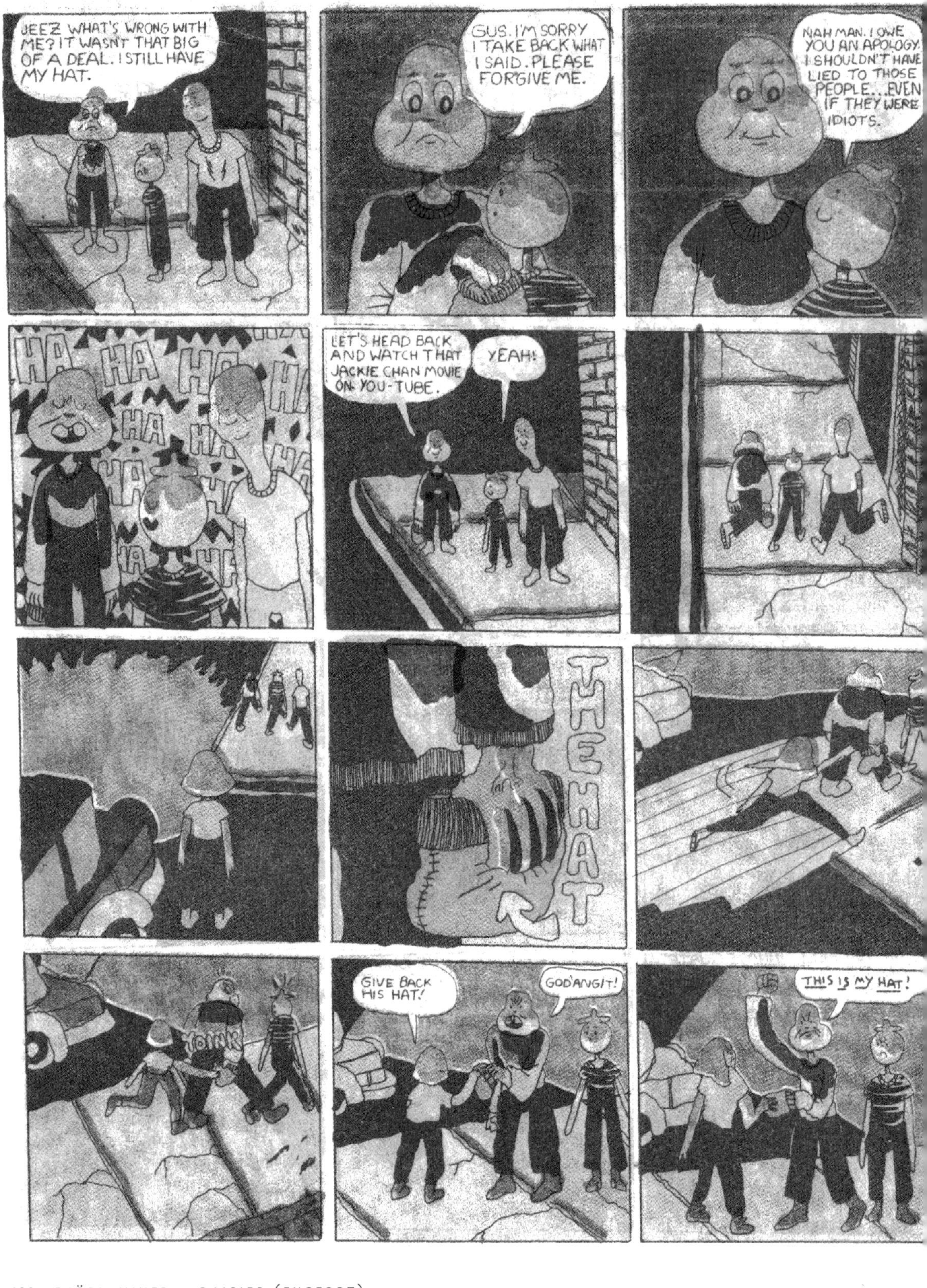

JEEZ WHAT'S WRONG WITH ME? IT WASN'T THAT BIG OF A DEAL. I STILL HAVE MY HAT.
GUS. I'M SORRY I TAKE BACK WHAT I SAID. PLEASE FORGIVE ME.
NAH MAN. I OWE YOU AN APOLOGY. I SHOULDN'T HAVE LIED TO THOSE PEOPLE...EVEN IF THEY WERE IDIOTS.
HA HA HA HA HA HA HA HA HA HA HA
LET'S HEAD BACK AND WATCH THAT JACKIE CHAN MOVIE ON YOU-TUBE.
YEAH!
THE HAT
YOINK
GIVE BACK HIS HAT!
GOD'ANGIT!
THIS IS MY HAT!

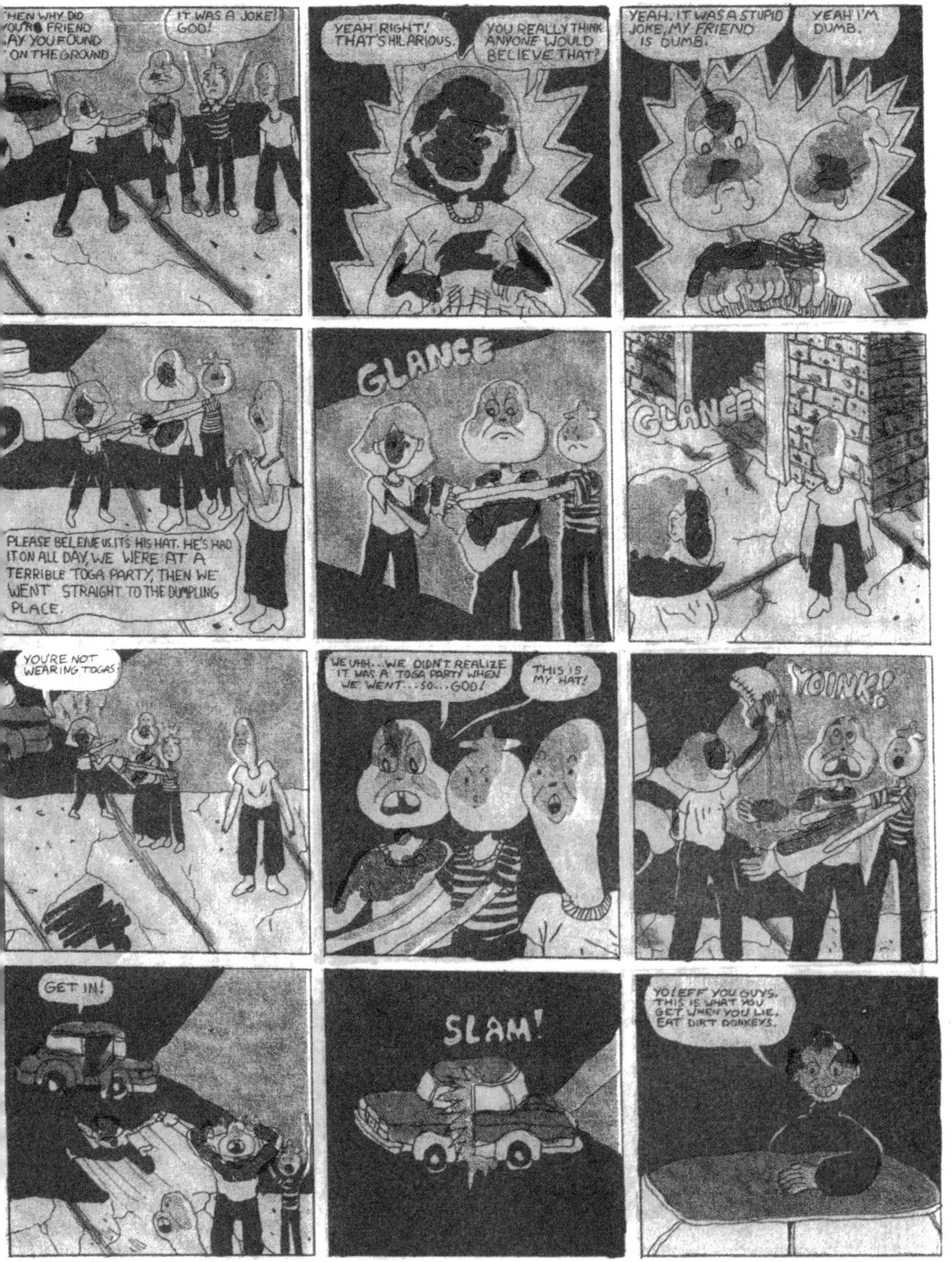

HEN WHY DID YOU'RE FRIEND AY YOU FOUND ON THE GROUND
IT WAS A JOKE! GOD!
YEAH RIGHT! THAT'S HILARIOUS.
YOU REALLY THINK ANYONE WOULD BELIEVE THAT?
YEAH. IT WAS A STUPID JOKE. MY FRIEND IS DUMB.
YEAH I'M DUMB.
PLEASE BELIEVE US. ITS HIS HAT. HE'S HAD IT ON ALL DAY, WE WERE AT A TERRIBLE TOGA PARTY, THEN WE WENT STRAIGHT TO THE DUMPLING PLACE.
GLANCE
GLANCE
YOU'RE NOT WEARING TOGAS!
WE UHH... WE DIDN'T REALIZE IT WAS A TOGA PARTY WHEN WE WENT... SO... GOD!
THIS IS MY HAT!
YOINK!
GET IN!
SLAM!
YO! EFF YOU GUYS. THIS IS WHAT YOU GET WHEN YOU LIE. EAT DIRT DONKEYS.

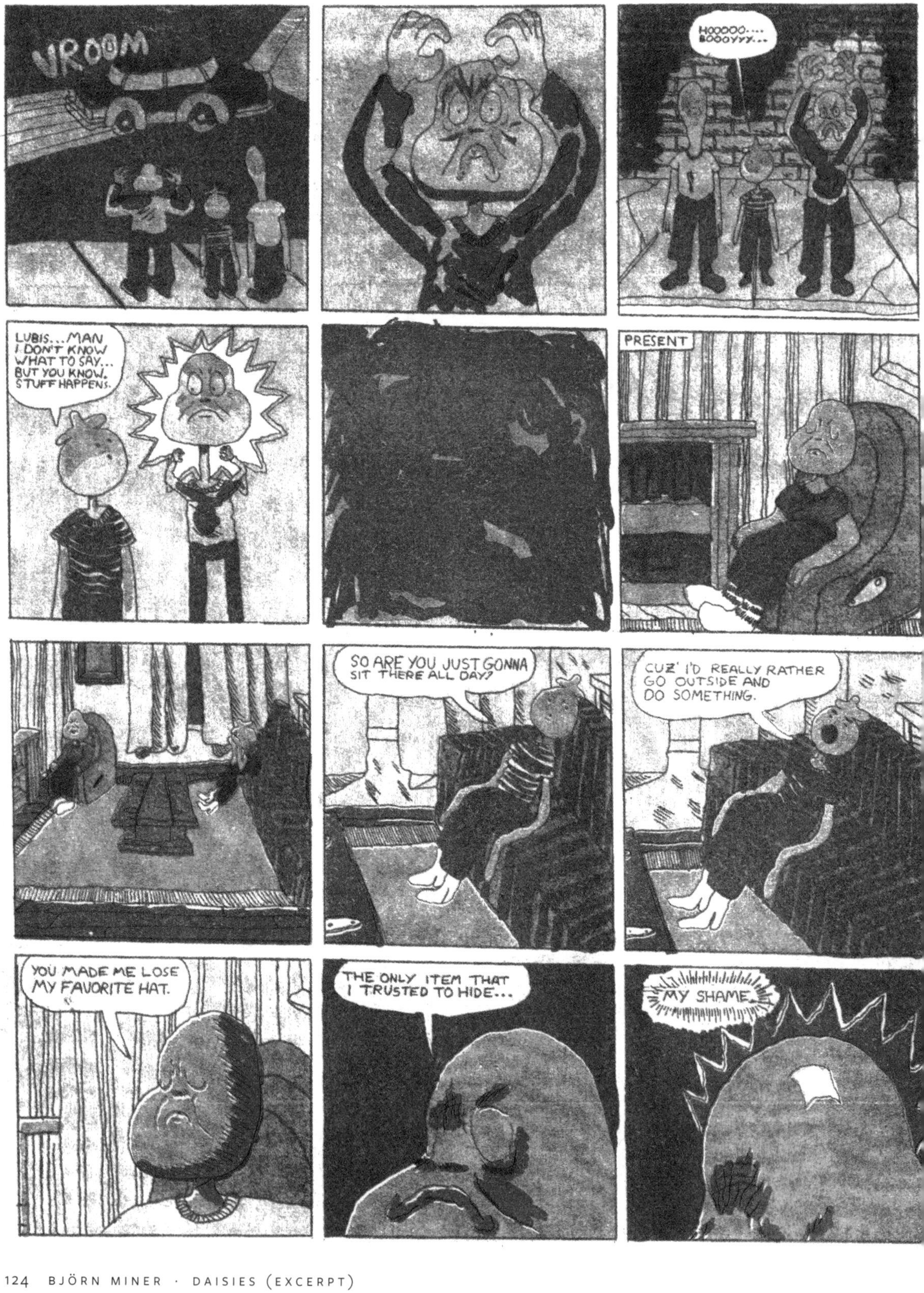
VROOM
HOOOOO....
BOOOYYY...
LUBIS...MAN I DON'T KNOW WHAT TO SAY... BUT YOU KNOW. STUFF HAPPENS.
PRESENT
SO ARE YOU JUST GONNA SIT THERE ALL DAY?
CUZ' I'D REALLY RATHER GO OUTSIDE AND DO SOMETHING.
YOU MADE ME LOSE MY FAVORITE HAT.
THE ONLY ITEM THAT I TRUSTED TO HIDE...
MY SHAME.

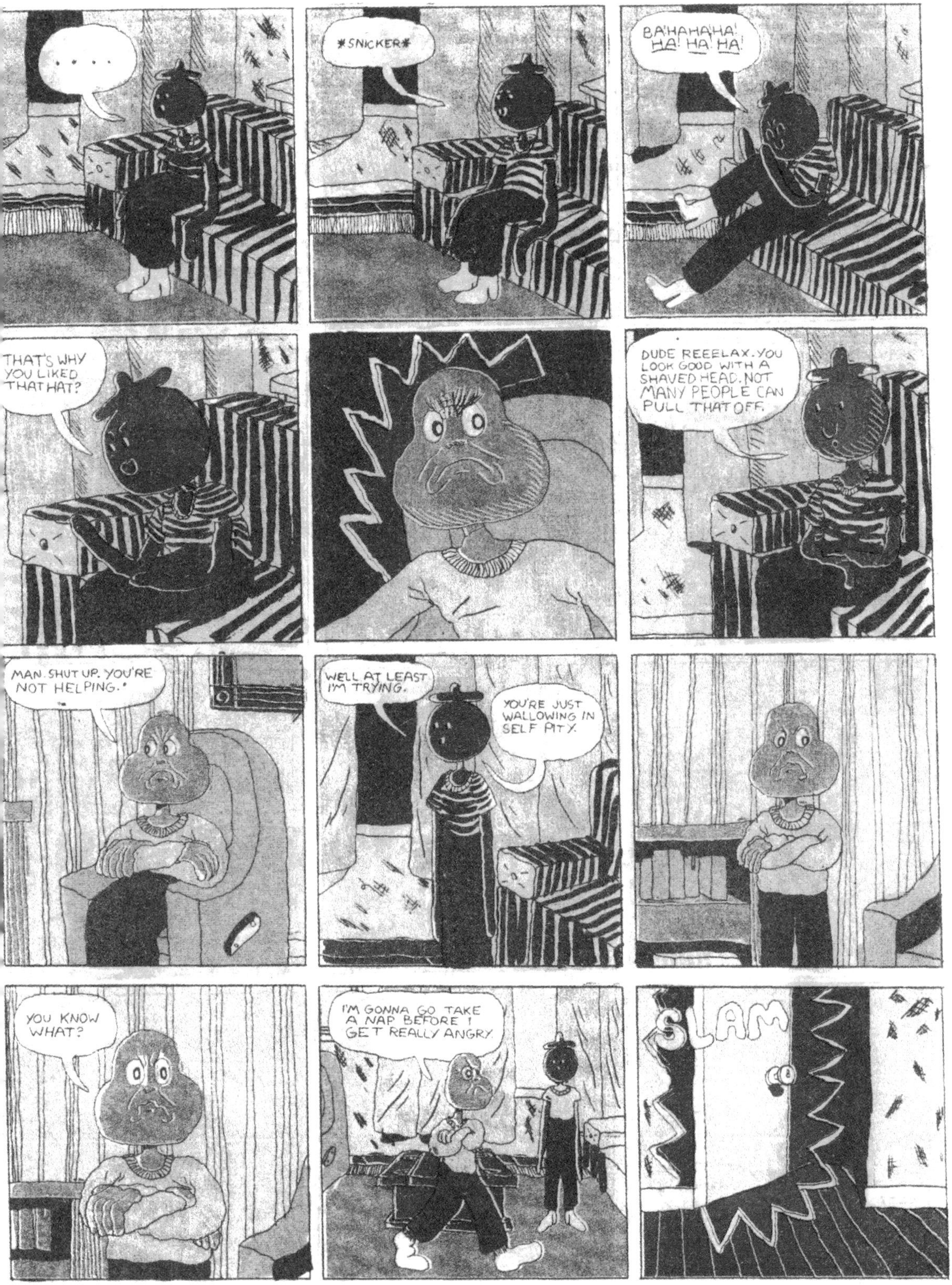
. . . . .
*SNICKER*
BA'HAHA'HA! HA! HA! HA!
THAT'S WHY YOU LIKED THAT HAT?
DUDE REEELAX. YOU LOOK GOOD WITH A SHAVED HEAD. NOT MANY PEOPLE CAN PULL THAT OFF.
MAN. SHUT UP. YOU'RE NOT HELPING.
WELL AT LEAST I'M TRYING.
YOU'RE JUST WALLOWING IN SELF PITY.
YOU KNOW WHAT?
I'M GONNA GO TAKE A NAP BEFORE I GET REALLY ANGRY.
SLAM

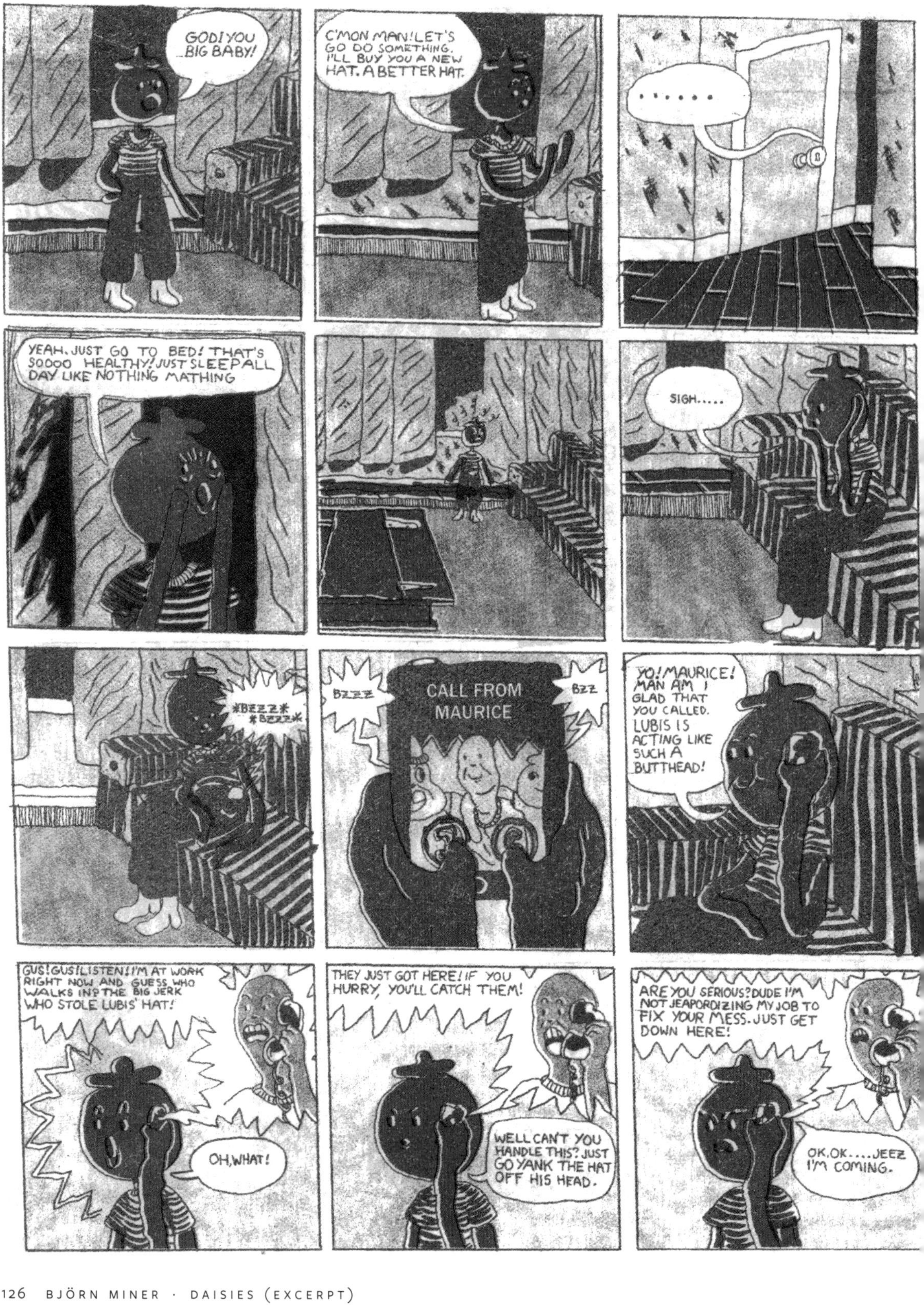
GOD! YOU BIG BABY!
C'MON MAN! LET'S GO DO SOMETHING. I'LL BUY YOU A NEW HAT. A BETTER HAT.
......
YEAH. JUST GO TO BED! THAT'S SOOOO HEALTHY! JUST SLEEP ALL DAY LIKE NOTHING MATHING
SIGH.....
*BZZZ* *BZZZ*
BZZZ
CALL FROM MAURICE
BZZ
YO! MAURICE! MAN AM I GLAD THAT YOU CALLED. LUBIS IS ACTING LIKE SUCH A BUTTHEAD!
GUS! GUS! LISTEN! I'M AT WORK RIGHT NOW AND GUESS WHO WALKS IN? THE BIG JERK WHO STOLE LUBIS' HAT!
OH, WHAT!
THEY JUST GOT HERE! IF YOU HURRY, YOU'LL CATCH THEM!
WELL CAN'T YOU HANDLE THIS? JUST GO YANK THE HAT OFF HIS HEAD.
ARE YOU SERIOUS? DUDE I'M NOT JEAPORDIZING MY JOB TO FIX YOUR MESS. JUST GET DOWN HERE!
OK, OK.... JEEZ I'M COMING.

# Rent Crisis

## JOE SACCO

*originally published by*

CHLOE FOR PORTLAND CAMPAIGN

6.63 × 10.25 inches • 6 pages

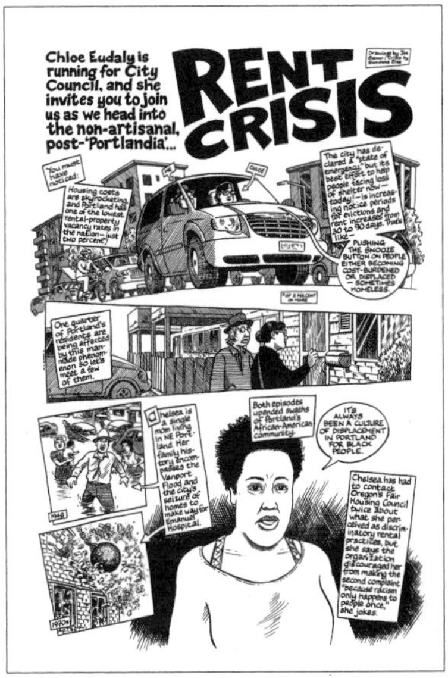

Chloe Eudaly is running for City Council, and she invites you to join us as we head into the non-artisanal, post-'Portlandia'...
RENT CRISIS
You must have noticed:
Housing costs are skyrocketing, and Portland has one of the lowest rental-property vacancy rates in the nation—just two percent*!
CHLOE
The city has declared a "state of emergency," but its best effort to help people facing loss of shelter now—today!—is increasing notice periods for evictions and rent increases from 30 to 90 days. That's like—
PUSHING THE SNOOZE BUTTON ON PEOPLE EITHER BECOMING COST-BURDENED OR DISPLACED—SOMETIMES HOMELESS.
One quarter of Portland's residents are being affected by this man-made phenomenon so let's meet a few of them.
Chelsea is a single mom living in NE Portland. Her family history encompasses the Vanport Flood and the city's seizure of homes to make way for Emanuel Hospital.
1948
1970s
Both episodes upended swaths of Portland's African-American community.
IT'S ALWAYS BEEN A CULTURE OF DISPLACEMENT IN PORTLAND FOR BLACK PEOPLE.
Chelsea has had to contact Oregon's Fair Housing Council twice about what she perceived as discriminatory rental practices, but she says the organization discouraged her from making the second complaint "because racism only happens to people once," she jokes.


## Biography

Joe Sacco is a cartoonist living in Portland, Oregon. Most of his work is journalistic in nature, though he has been known to pine for the good ol' days when he drew to make people laugh.

## Statement

"Rent Crisis" was a piece of campaign literature I drew for Chloe Eudaly, who ran for and won a seat on the city council of Portland, Oregon. It was printed up and distributed to the homes of voters. Drawing it was an explicit political act on behalf of someone trying to confront the neoliberal forces eating our neighborhoods.

Her current two-bedroom is rundown and rents for $1,300. Chelsea, who has a bachelor's degree and had a corporate job, could afford it, but she was laid off in May.

WITHOUT THE SUPPORT OF OTHER COST-BURDENED RENTERS WE WOULDN'T STILL BE HERE BECAUSE PEOPLE CAME TOGETHER AND RAISED ALMOST $800 FOR ME TO STAY...

I COVERED THE REST WITH MY UNEMPLOY-MENT.

IT'S REALLY A STRUGGLE FOR US.

IT'S VERY STRESS-FUL.

But now the greater crisis looms. A new property management company is issuing $3-400 monthly rent increases. One neighbor after another has moved out, and she expects to be notified of a similar rent increase in October as her lease runs out.

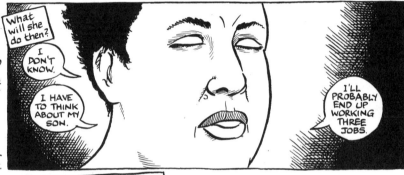

What will she do then?

I DON'T KNOW.

I HAVE TO THINK ABOUT MY SON.

I'LL PROBABLY END UP WORKING THREE JOBS.

Chloe points out that, technically, this apartment rents under Portland's going rate.

$1,400 FOR A ONE-BEDROOM IS AVERAGE RIGHT NOW, BUT THAT'S COMPLETELY SKEWED BY OVER-BUILDING OF MARKET- AND LUXURY-RATE APARTMENTS.

Chloe says that landlords of old and sub-standard properties are basing rent increases on what developers are squeezing out of new and fancier units.

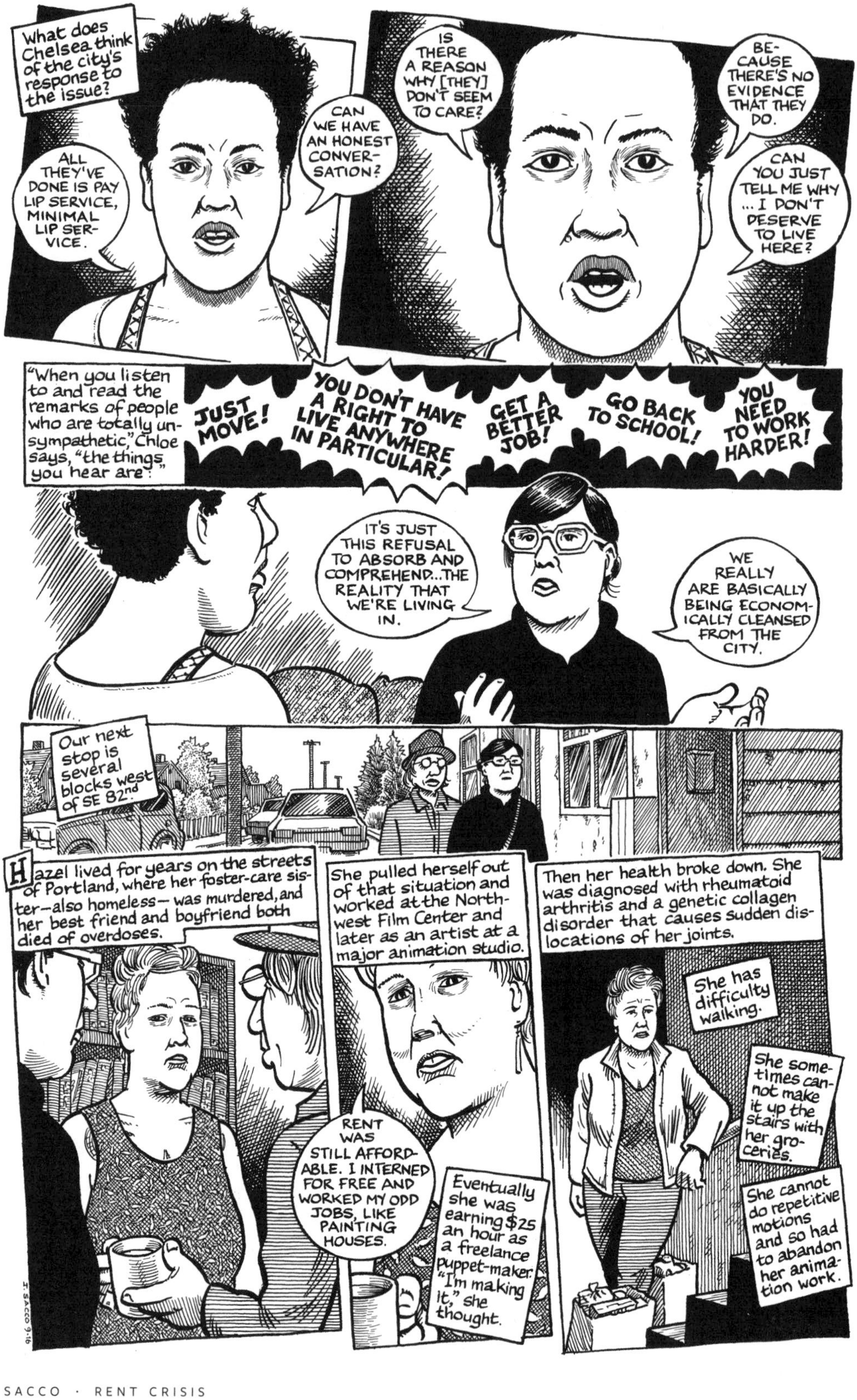

What does Chelsea think of the city's response to the issue?
ALL THEY'VE DONE IS PAY LIP SERVICE, MINIMAL LIP SERVICE.
CAN WE HAVE AN HONEST CONVERSATION?
IS THERE A REASON WHY [THEY] DON'T SEEM TO CARE?
BECAUSE THERE'S NO EVIDENCE THAT THEY DO.
CAN YOU JUST TELL ME WHY ... I DON'T DESERVE TO LIVE HERE?
"When you listen to and read the remarks of people who are totally unsympathetic," Chloe says, "the things you hear are:"
JUST MOVE!
YOU DON'T HAVE A RIGHT TO LIVE ANYWHERE IN PARTICULAR!
GET A BETTER JOB!
GO BACK TO SCHOOL!
YOU NEED TO WORK HARDER!
IT'S JUST THIS REFUSAL TO ABSORB AND COMPREHEND...THE REALITY THAT WE'RE LIVING IN.
WE REALLY ARE BASICALLY BEING ECONOMICALLY CLEANSED FROM THE CITY.
Our next stop is several blocks west of SE 82nd
Hazel lived for years on the streets of Portland, where her foster-care sister—also homeless—was murdered, and her best friend and boyfriend both died of overdoses.
She pulled herself out of that situation and worked at the Northwest Film Center and later as an artist at a major animation studio.
RENT WAS STILL AFFORDABLE. I INTERNED FOR FREE AND WORKED MY ODD JOBS, LIKE PAINTING HOUSES.
Eventually she was earning $25 an hour as a freelance puppet-maker. "I'm making it," she thought.
J. SACCO 9-16
Then her health broke down. She was diagnosed with rheumatoid arthritis and a genetic collagen disorder that causes sudden dislocations of her joints.
She has difficulty walking.
She sometimes cannot make it up the stairs with her groceries.
She cannot do repetitive motions and so had to abandon her animation work.

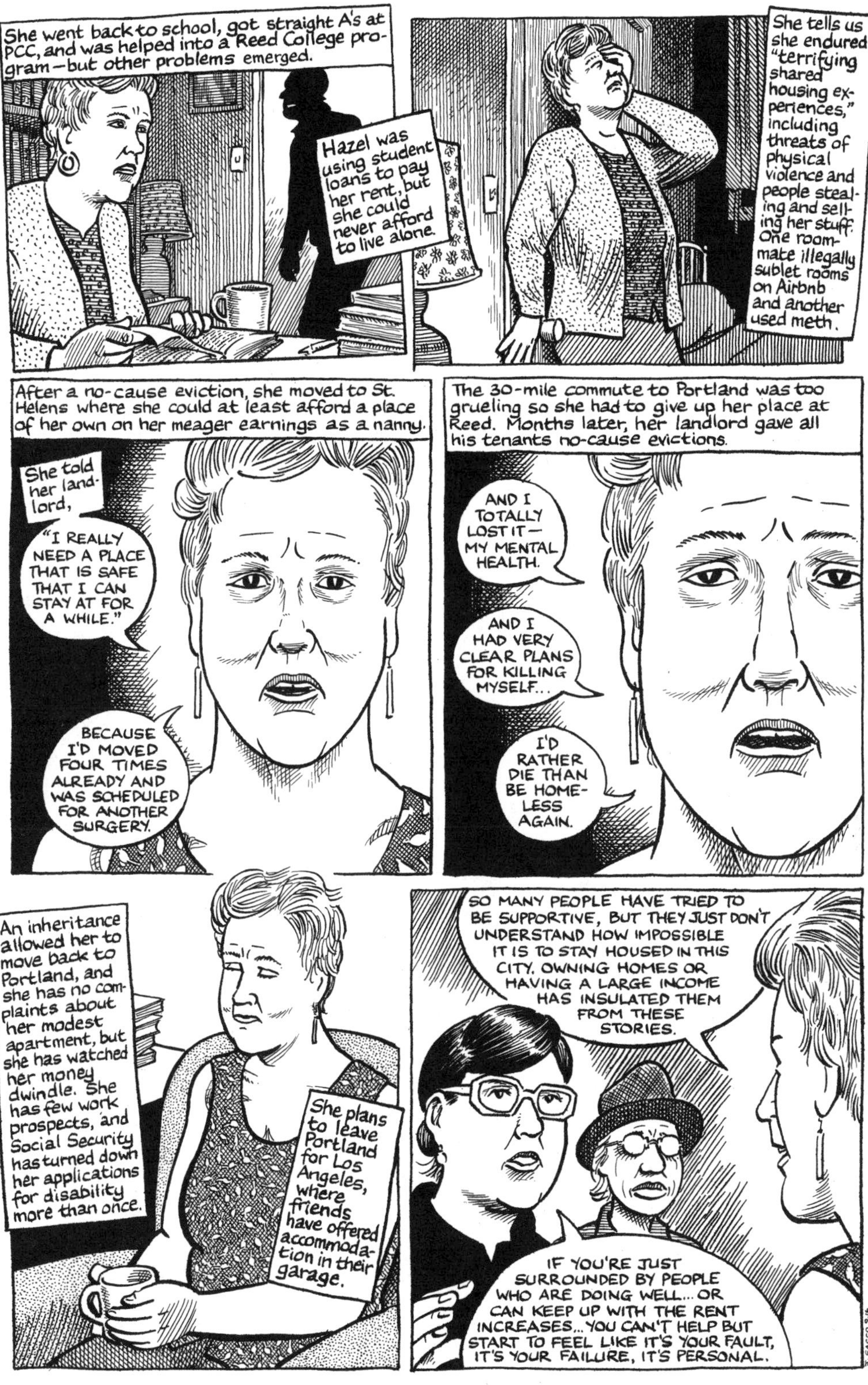
She went back to school, got straight A's at PCC, and was helped into a Reed College program—but other problems emerged.
Hazel was using student loans to pay her rent, but she could never afford to live alone.
She tells us she endured "terrifying shared housing experiences," including threats of physical violence and people stealing and selling her stuff. One roommate illegally sublet rooms on Airbnb and another used meth.
After a no-cause eviction, she moved to St. Helens where she could at least afford a place of her own on her meager earnings as a nanny.
She told her landlord,
"I REALLY NEED A PLACE THAT IS SAFE THAT I CAN STAY AT FOR A WHILE."
BECAUSE I'D MOVED FOUR TIMES ALREADY AND WAS SCHEDULED FOR ANOTHER SURGERY.
The 30-mile commute to Portland was too grueling so she had to give up her place at Reed. Months later, her landlord gave all his tenants no-cause evictions.
AND I TOTALLY LOST IT— MY MENTAL HEALTH.
AND I HAD VERY CLEAR PLANS FOR KILLING MYSELF...
I'D RATHER DIE THAN BE HOMELESS AGAIN.
An inheritance allowed her to move back to Portland, and she has no complaints about her modest apartment, but she has watched her money dwindle. She has few work prospects, and Social Security has turned down her applications for disability more than once.
She plans to leave Portland for Los Angeles, where friends have offered accommodation in their garage.
SO MANY PEOPLE HAVE TRIED TO BE SUPPORTIVE, BUT THEY JUST DON'T UNDERSTAND HOW IMPOSSIBLE IT IS TO STAY HOUSED IN THIS CITY. OWNING HOMES OR HAVING A LARGE INCOME HAS INSULATED THEM FROM THESE STORIES.
IF YOU'RE JUST SURROUNDED BY PEOPLE WHO ARE DOING WELL... OR CAN KEEP UP WITH THE RENT INCREASES... YOU CAN'T HELP BUT START TO FEEL LIKE IT'S YOUR FAULT, IT'S YOUR FAILURE, IT'S PERSONAL.
J. SACCO 9.16

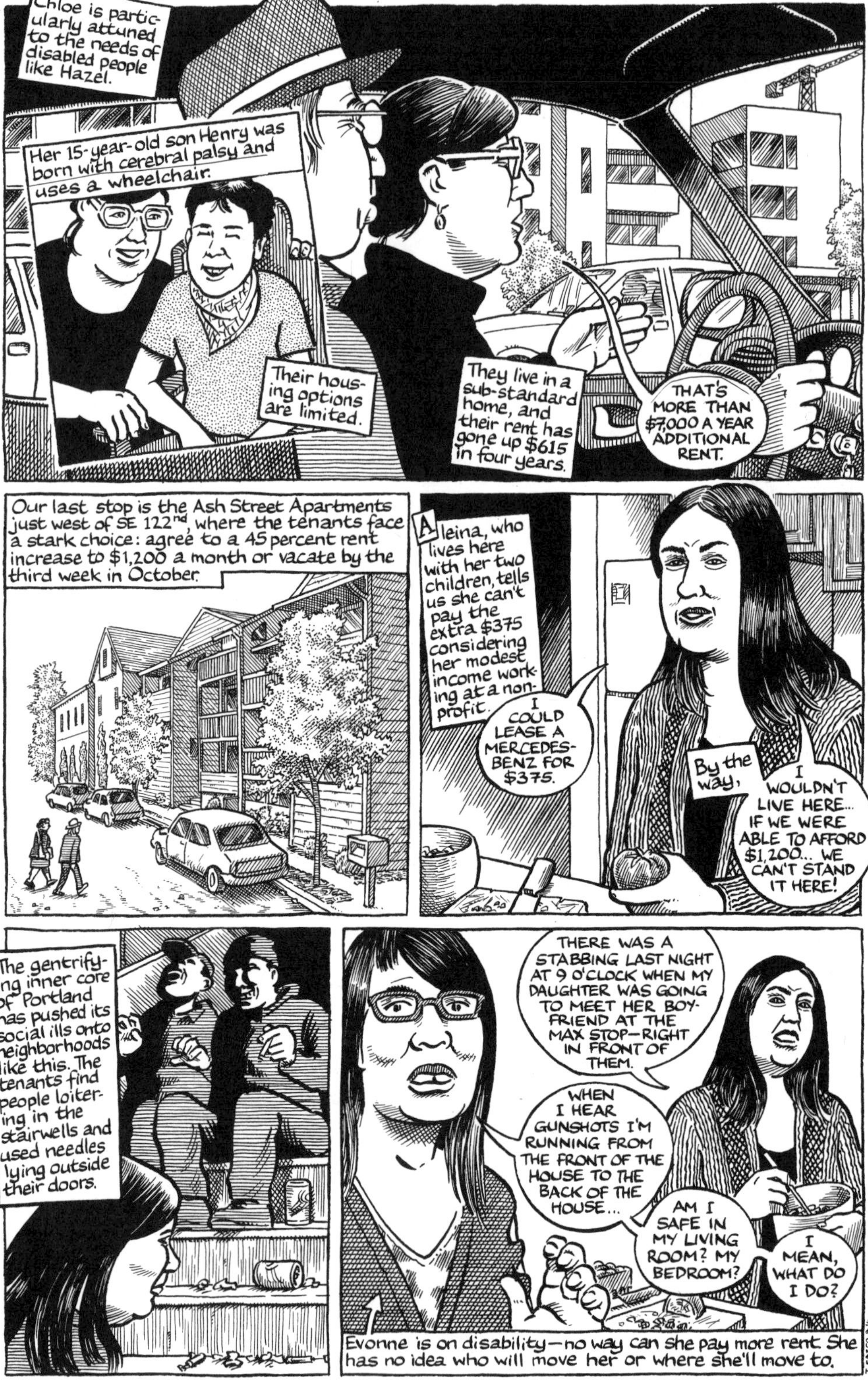

Chloe is particularly attuned to the needs of disabled people like Hazel.
Her 15-year-old son Henry was born with cerebral palsy and uses a wheelchair.
Their housing options are limited.
They live in a sub-standard home, and their rent has gone up $615 in four years.
THAT'S MORE THAN $7,000 A YEAR ADDITIONAL RENT.
Our last stop is the Ash Street Apartments just west of SE 122nd, where the tenants face a stark choice: agree to a 45 percent rent increase to $1,200 a month or vacate by the third week in October.
Aleina, who lives here with her two children, tells us she can't pay the extra $375 considering her modest income working at a non-profit.
I COULD LEASE A MERCEDES-BENZ FOR $375.
By the way,
I WOULDN'T LIVE HERE... IF WE WERE ABLE TO AFFORD $1,200... WE CAN'T STAND IT HERE!
The gentrifying inner core of Portland has pushed its social ills onto neighborhoods like this. The tenants find people loitering in the stairwells and used needles lying outside their doors.
THERE WAS A STABBING LAST NIGHT AT 9 O'CLOCK WHEN MY DAUGHTER WAS GOING TO MEET HER BOYFRIEND AT THE MAX STOP—RIGHT IN FRONT OF THEM.
WHEN I HEAR GUNSHOTS I'M RUNNING FROM THE FRONT OF THE HOUSE TO THE BACK OF THE HOUSE...
AM I SAFE IN MY LIVING ROOM? MY BEDROOM?
I MEAN, WHAT DO I DO?
Evonne is on disability—no way can she pay more rent. She has no idea who will move her or where she'll move to.

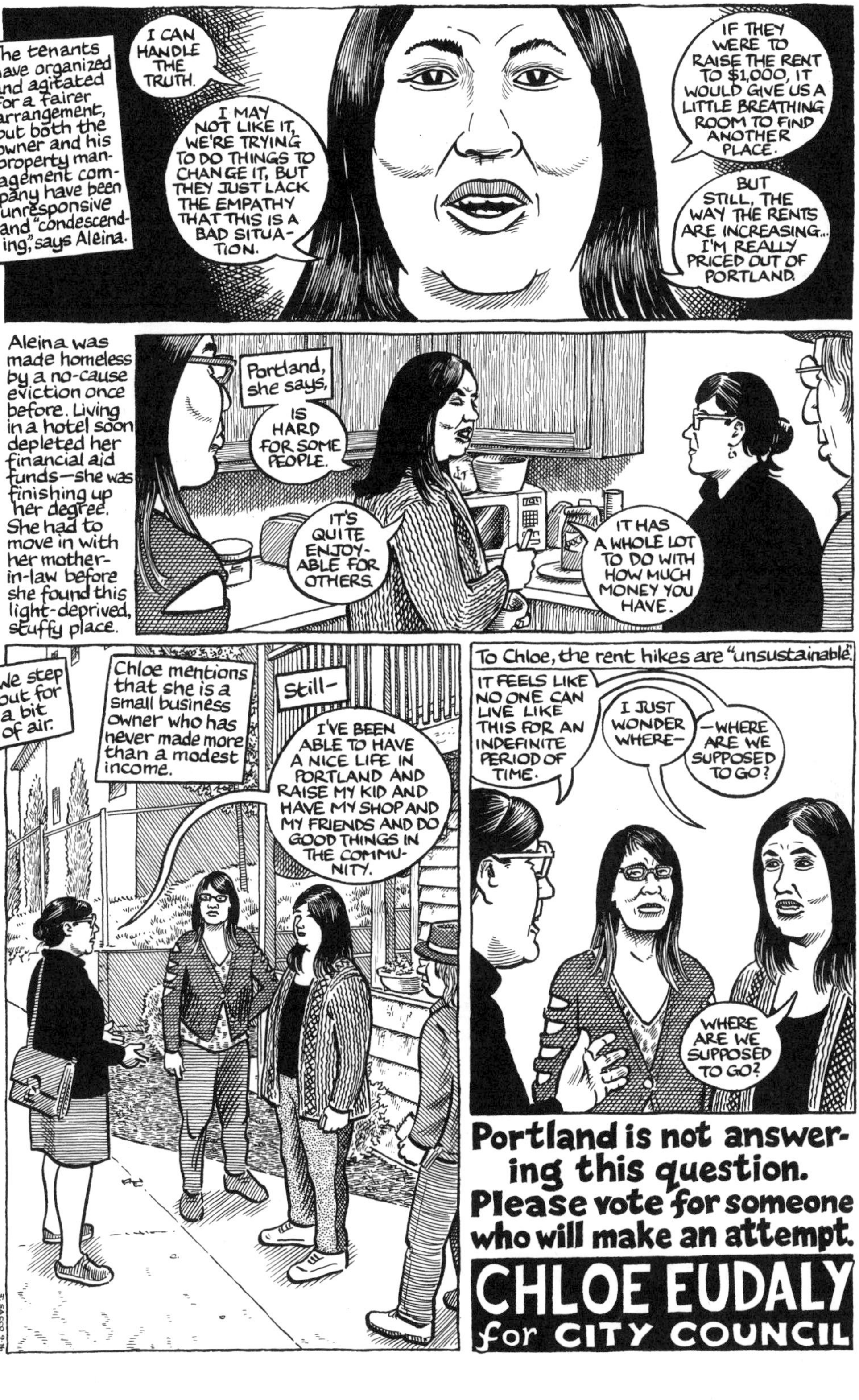
The tenants have organized and agitated for a fairer arrangement, but both the owner and his property management company have been unresponsive and "condescending," says Aleina.
I CAN HANDLE THE TRUTH.
I MAY NOT LIKE IT, WE'RE TRYING TO DO THINGS TO CHANGE IT, BUT THEY JUST LACK THE EMPATHY THAT THIS IS A BAD SITUATION.
IF THEY WERE TO RAISE THE RENT TO $1,000, IT WOULD GIVE US A LITTLE BREATHING ROOM TO FIND ANOTHER PLACE.
BUT STILL, THE WAY THE RENTS ARE INCREASING... I'M REALLY PRICED OUT OF PORTLAND.
Aleina was made homeless by a no-cause eviction once before. Living in a hotel soon depleted her financial aid funds—she was finishing up her degree. She had to move in with her mother-in-law before she found this light-deprived, stuffy place.
Portland, she says,
IS HARD FOR SOME PEOPLE.
IT'S QUITE ENJOYABLE FOR OTHERS.
IT HAS A WHOLE LOT TO DO WITH HOW MUCH MONEY YOU HAVE.
We step out for a bit of air.
Chloe mentions that she is a small business owner who has never made more than a modest income.
Still-
I'VE BEEN ABLE TO HAVE A NICE LIFE IN PORTLAND AND RAISE MY KID AND HAVE MY SHOP AND MY FRIENDS AND DO GOOD THINGS IN THE COMMUNITY.
To Chloe, the rent hikes are "unsustainable."
IT FEELS LIKE NO ONE CAN LIVE LIKE THIS FOR AN INDEFINITE PERIOD OF TIME.
I JUST WONDER WHERE-
—WHERE ARE WE SUPPOSED TO GO?
WHERE ARE WE SUPPOSED TO GO?
Portland is not answering this question.
Please vote for someone who will make an attempt.
CHLOE EUDALY
for CITY COUNCIL
J. SACCO 9-16

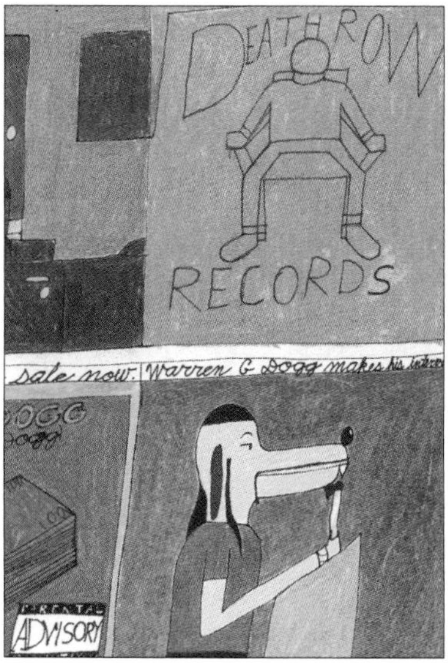
DEATH ROW
RECORDS
sale now: Warren G Dogg
ADVISORY

# Time To Get Paid, Sexual Chocolate, Women Only, No Men Allowed, AND Hong Fong Chuey

GERONE SPRUILL

*exhibited at*

CREATIVE GROWTH ART CENTER

30 × 22 inches / 30 × 22 inches / 30 × 22 inches / 8.5 × 11 inches • prismacolor and ink

## Biography

Born in 1973 and raised in Oakland, California, Gerone Spruill is an aspiring DJ with an encyclopedic music collection. Spruill's street-smart graphic sensibility illuminates his work, whose central hero is his foot-loving alias "DJ Disco Duck." His drawings take the form of extensive, if not epic comic-book narratives that chronicle the misadventures of his characters, memorably coiffed and infinitely cool, as they cruise Chocolate City in pursuit of rap stardom and other "satisfaction." Gerone has been an artist at Creative Growth Art Center since 1993. His work has been exhibited in New York, London, San Francisco, and the American Visionary Art Museum in Baltimore.
creativegrowth.org/artists/gerone-spruill

## Statement

I liked watching Hanna-Barbera cartoons and reading *Little Archie, Betty & Veronica,* and Marvel comics like *Spider-Man* and *Fantastic Four* when I was young. My cartoon characters are based on people I went to high school with and my friends. I'm really inspired by music and mainly the '70s album cover art by Overton Loyd and Pedro Bell for Parliament-Funkadelic. In my comics, the story comes first, then the illustrations. My character is "DJ Disco Duck" and he has a duck bill for a nose—he's the hero. Sir Noses is similar to Batman and Robin, but they stop crime and protect the smooth white chocolate city of San Jose. There's also The Prettyfeet Finder and Hong Fong Chuey, who is half black and half Chinese. MC G is a Technics turntable expert armed with a Footstranger Gun that converts foot-haters into kindred spirits.

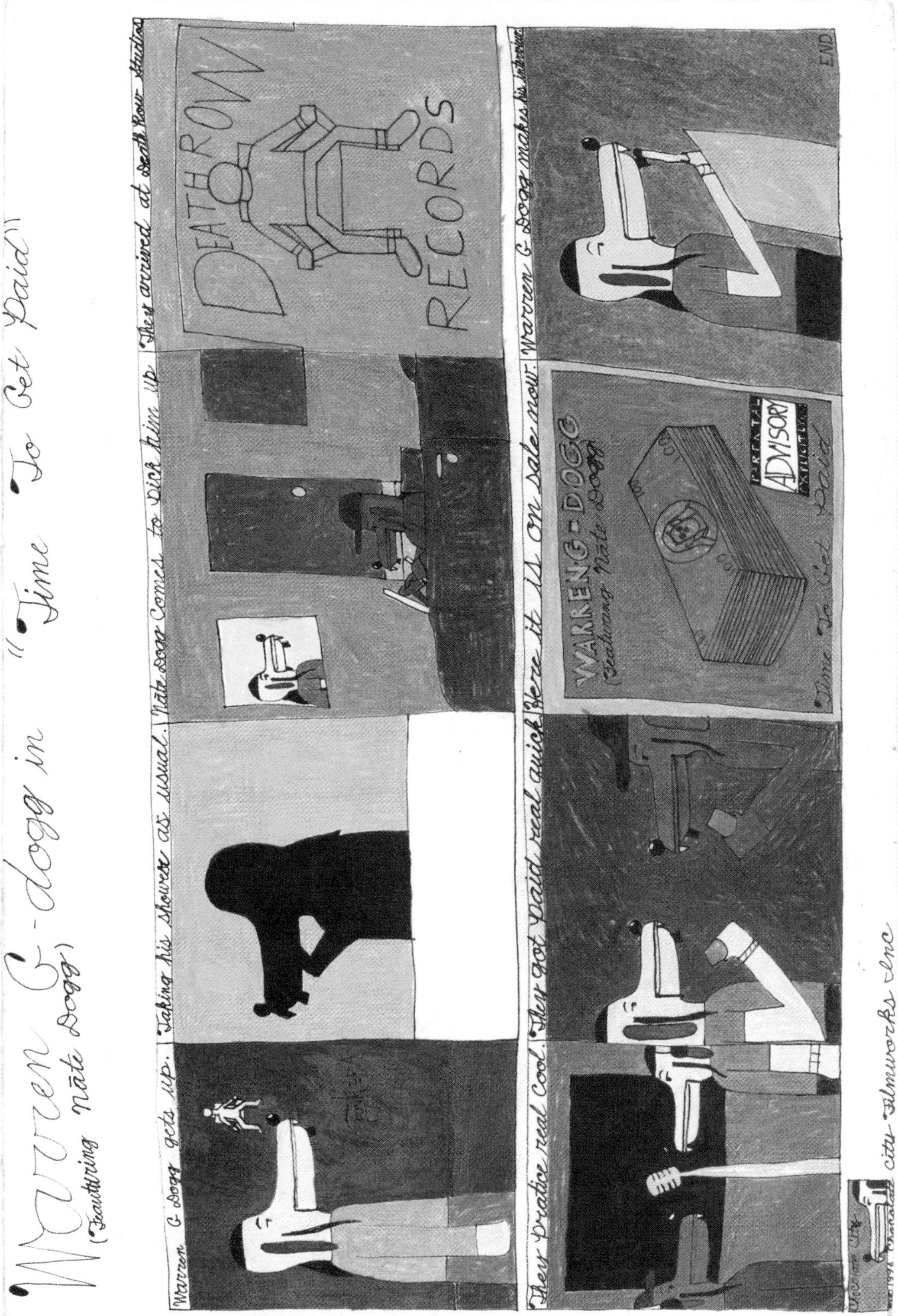
Warren G-dogg in "Time To Get Paid"
(Featuring Nate Dogg)
Warren G Dogg gets up.
Taking his shower as usual.
Nate Dogg Comes to Pick him up
They arrived at Death Row studios
DEATH ROW RECORDS
Their pratice real Cool.
They got Paid real quick
Here it is on sale now!
WARREN G-DOGG
(featuring Nate Dogg)
PARENTAL ADVISORY
Time To Get Paid
Warren G Dogg makes his interview
END
Chocolate city Filmworks Inc

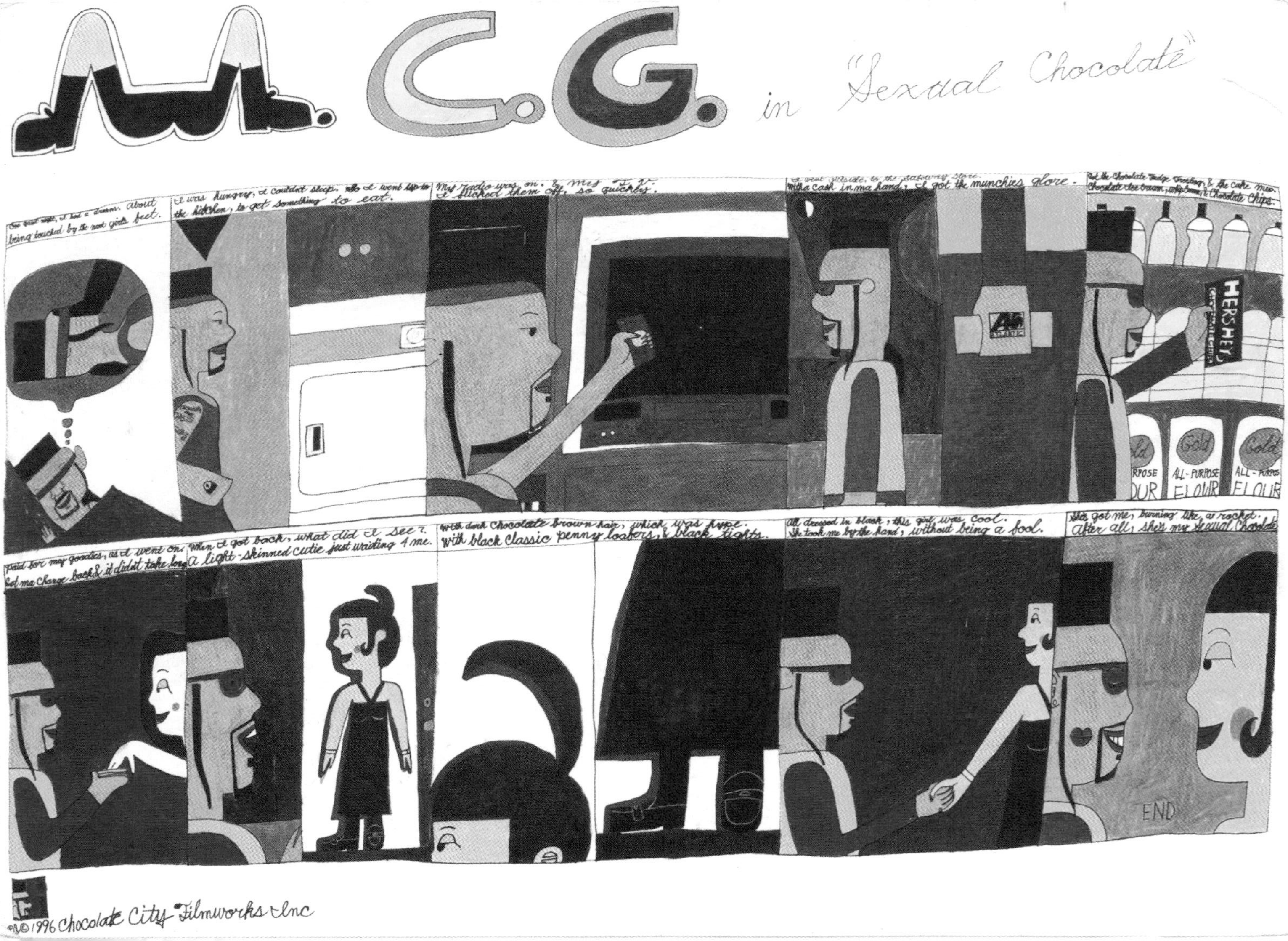
M.C.G. in "Sexual Chocolate"
being touched by the next girls feet.
I was hungry, I couldnt sleep, so I went to the kitchen, to get something to eat.
I clicked them off, so quickly.
With a cash in ma hand, I got the munchies galore.
HERSHEY'S
ALL-PURPOSE FLOUR
Gold
paid for my goodies, as I went on. Got ma change back & it didnt take long.
When I got back, what did I see? A light-skinned cutie just waiting 4 me.
with black classic penny loafers, & black tights.
All dressed in black, this girl was cool. She took me by the hand, without being a fool.
She's got me, burning like a rocket. After all, she's my Sexual Chocolate
END
© 1996 Chocolate City Filmworks Inc

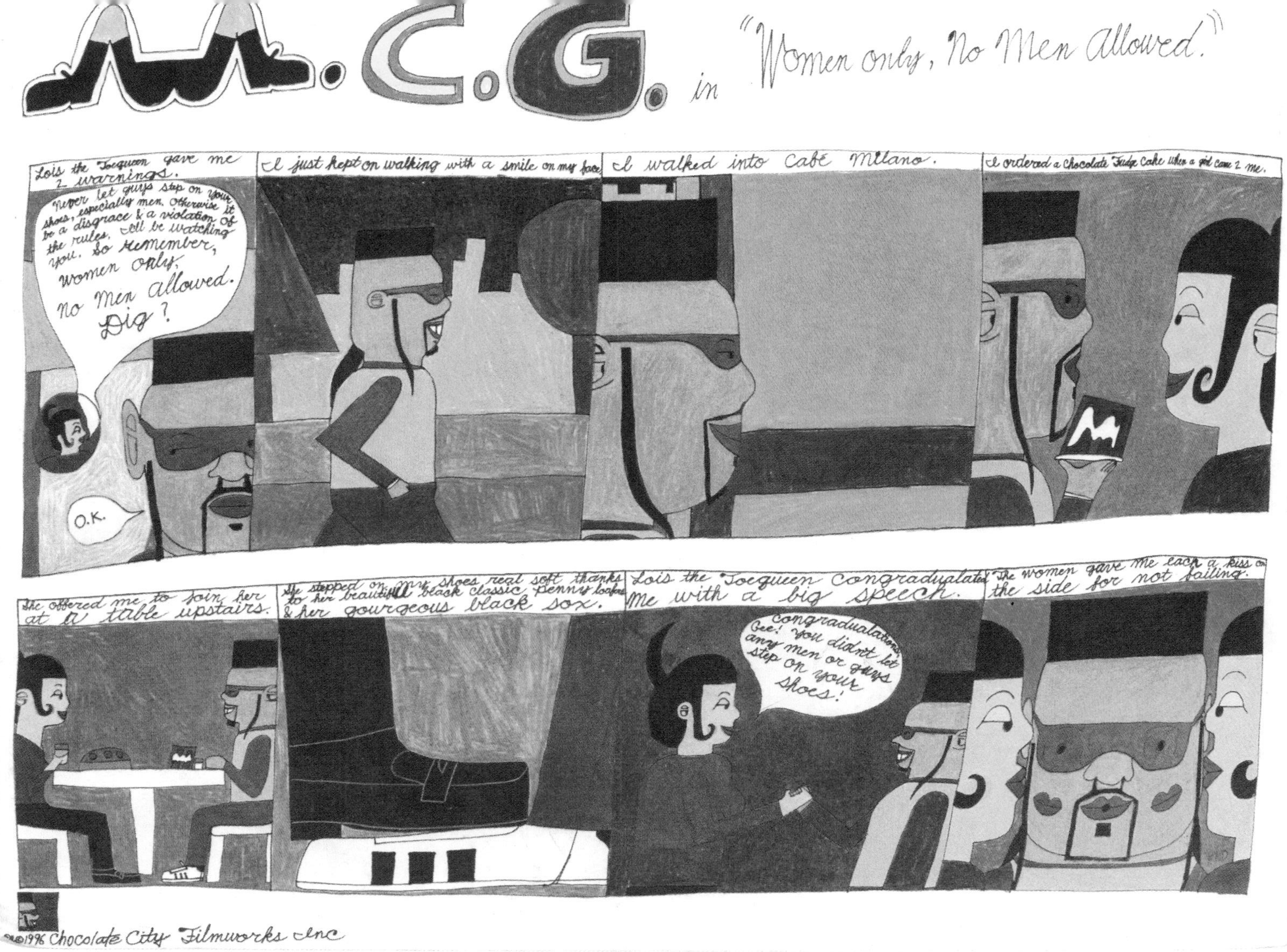
M.C.G. in "Women only, No Men Allowed."
Lois the Toequeen gave me 2 warnings.
Never let guys step on your shoes, especially men. Otherwise it be a disgrace & a violation of the rules. I'll be watching you. So remember, women only, no men allowed. Dig?
O.K.
I just kept on walking with a smile on my face.
I walked into Café Milano.
I ordered a Chocolate Fudge Cake when a girl came 2 me.
She offered me to join her at a table upstairs.
She stepped on my shoes real soft thanks to her beautiful black classic penny loafers & her gourgeous black sox.
Lois the Toequeen congradualated me with a big speech.
Congradualations! Gee! You didn't let any men or guys step on your shoes!
The women gave me each a kiss on the side for not failing.
©1996 Chocolate City Filmworks Inc

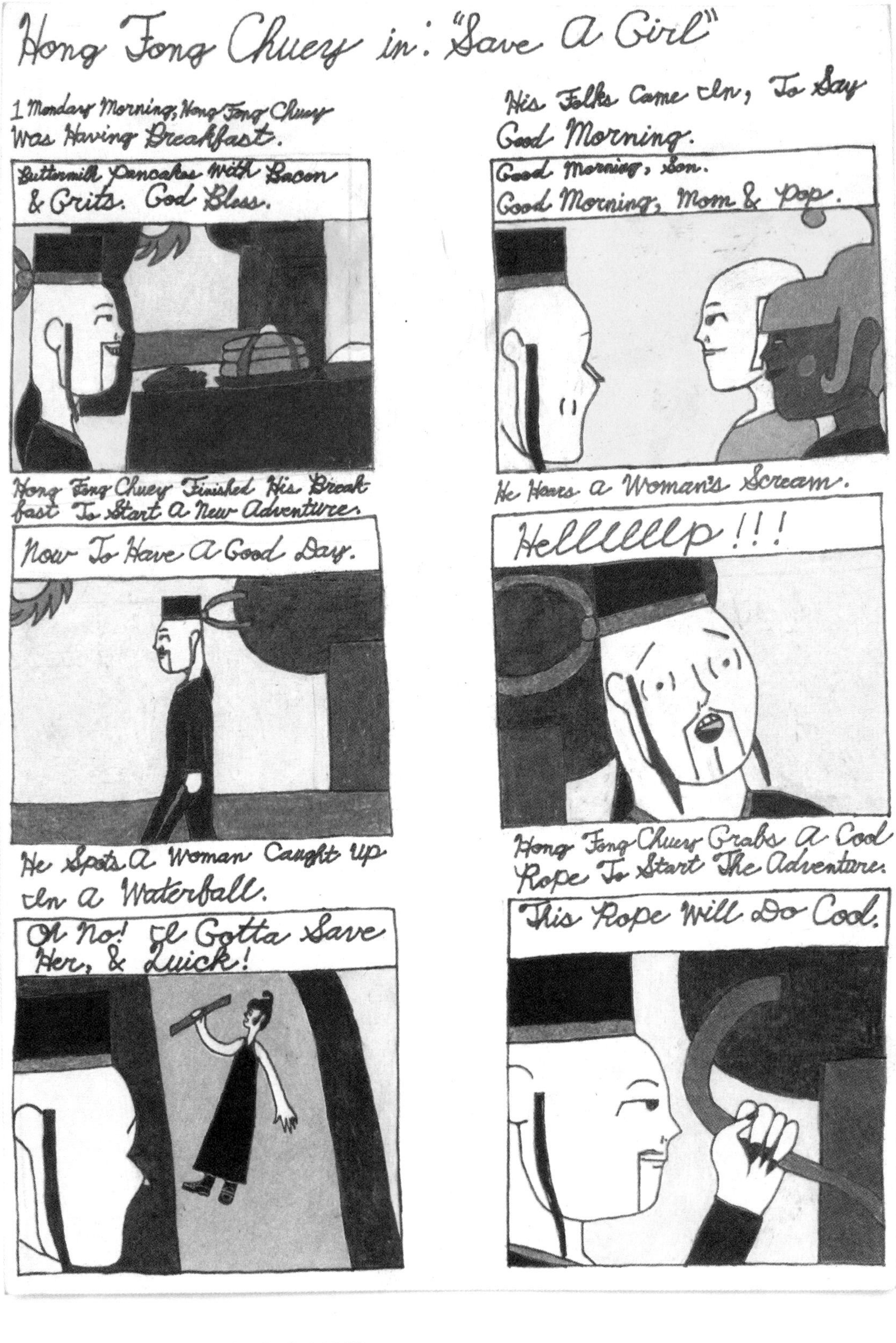
Hong Fong Chuey in: "Save A Girl"
1 Monday Morning, Hong Fong Chuey Was Having Breakfast.
Buttermilk Pancakes with Bacon & Grits. God Bless.
His Folks Came In, To Say Good Morning.
Good Morning, Son.
Good Morning, Mom & Pop.
Hong Fong Chuey Finished His Breakfast To Start A New Adventure.
Now To Have A Good Day.
He Hears a Woman's Scream.
Helllllp!!!
He Spots A Woman Caught up In a Waterfall.
Oh No! I Gotta Save Her, & Quick!
Hong Fong Chuey Grabs A Cool Rope To Start The Adventure.
This Rope Will Do Cool.

# Radio Silence

GRANT REYNOLDS

*originally published in*

*Lumpen*, no. 126
PUBLIC MEDIA INSTITUTE
8 × 10.5 inches • 80 pages

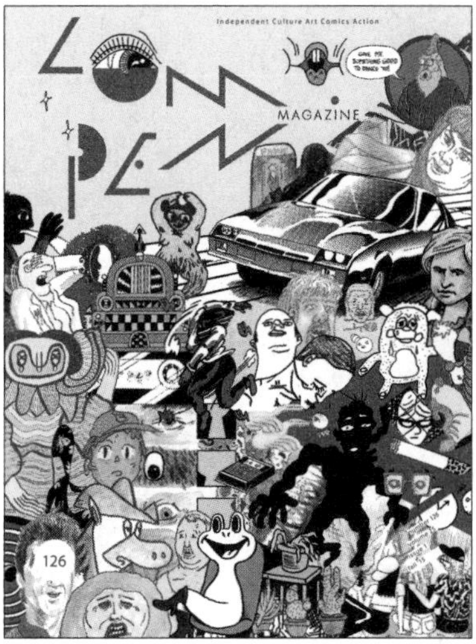
Independent Culture Art Comics Action
MAGAZINE
126

## Biography

Grant Reynolds lives in Chicago and has been self-publishing comics since the mid-'90s. His work is often characterized as "dreamlike," and concerns itself with themes of alcoholism/sobriety, physical abuse, depression, sexuality, feminism, and gender theory. grantreynolds.com

## Statement

"Radio Silence" was inspired by a prompt from a deck of Oblique Strategies: "Listen to the quiet voice." It was also a significant transitional comic for me, and the first that I made with brush and ink, rather than a Micron. At the time I had been suffering from debilitating chronic pain in both of my hands, which made it impossible for me to use a pen, so I began to experiment with alternative methods of mark-making. Accustomed to drawing my comics at print size, I found that I had to work at a much larger scale in order to retain some semblance of the detail I wanted from the brush. I really struggled while making "Radio Silence," but for all its resistance the end result represented a personal accomplishment, as well as a new direction for my work. I essentially taught myself how to draw again, and three subsequent brush and ink comics were eventually collected in my book *Corpus Distorta* (2016). In retrospect, "Radio Silence" was very much about the struggle I was going through at the time, and the deep depression caused by my inability to draw. Obsessive art-making has always defined me, and without a proper means of reliable creative self-expression I found myself grappling with my own personal identity, and started coming apart at the seams as a result. Just as I'd left my characters at the end of the comic, my life was bare to me in a way that it had never been before, and it was only then that I was able to start anew.

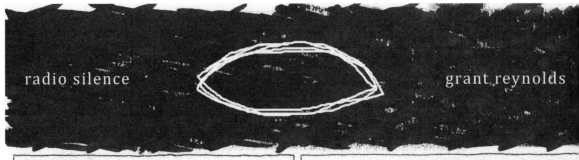

THE BEACON OF THE TRANSMITTER TOWER HERALDS ITS FOLLOWERS FROM MILES AWAY, SIGNALING TO THEM IN ALL DIRECTIONS, WITH THE SLOW & STEADY PULSE OF A LONE RED HEART.

ON BENDED KNEE THEY BESEECH ITS AIRWAVES, PRESSING SINGED & RINGING EARS, RUINED FROM THE BLAST, TO THE SIDES OF RECOVERED TRANSISTOR RADIOS, WHICH HUM TO THE TUNE OF OMNI-COVETED ALKALINE CELLS — THE WORLD'S LAST REMAINING AA BATTERIES.

SHAKY, DAMAGED FINGERS SCROLLING BACK & FORTH, CEASELESSLY, WITH BLIND DESPERATION — AT THIS POINT SO HABITUAL IT'S BECOME A RITUAL GESTURE, MORE SYMBOLIC THAN ANY REAL HOPE OF AN ACTUAL BROADCAST — THROUGH THE BANDS OF WAVERING STATIC, WHICH CRACKLE LIKE THE MEAGER FIRES THEY BUILD TO WARM THEIR WANING CAMPS AT NIGHTFALL, WHEN TEMPERATURES BEGIN TO DROP.

ALTHOUGH IT IS THE BEACON ON THE HORIZON THAT THEY LOOK TO, NONE SEEM CERTAIN OF WHO EXACTLY HAS BEEN MAINTAINING THE TOWER.

STILL, RUMORS PERSIST, WAFTING FROM THE CRACKED LIPS OF TOOTHLESS, SHAMBLING SCAVENGERS, THE WHITE OF THEIR HAUNTED, SHIFTY EYES PEERING LIDLESS FROM OUT DEEP & HOLLOW SOCKETS, KEEN & RAVENING, STARK IN CONTRAST TO THE SOOTY REMAINDER OF EACH INDIVIDUAL'S DEEPLY-WEATHERED & ULCEROUS FRAME.

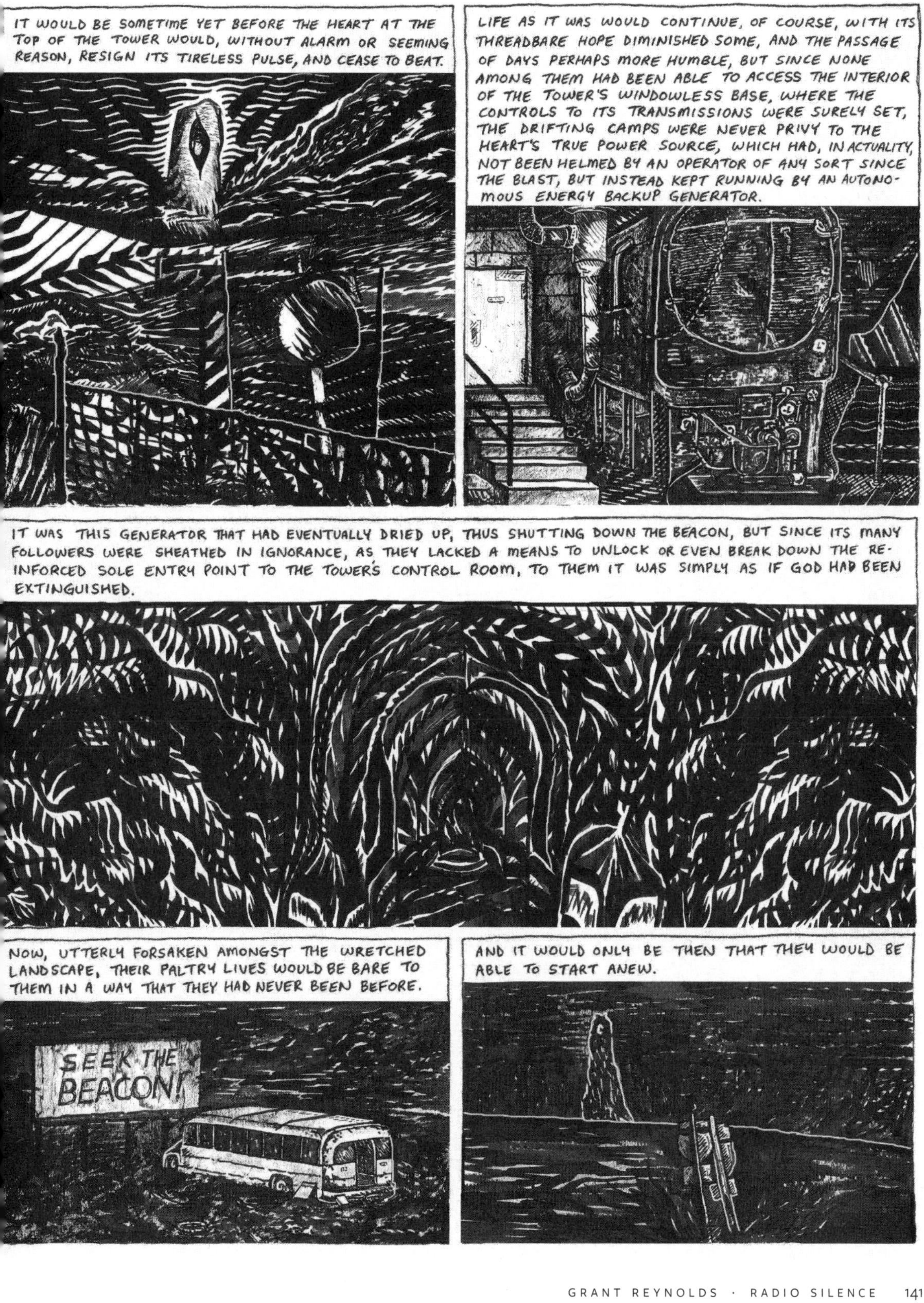
IT WOULD BE SOMETIME YET BEFORE THE HEART AT THE TOP OF THE TOWER WOULD, WITHOUT ALARM OR SEEMING REASON, RESIGN ITS TIRELESS PULSE, AND CEASE TO BEAT.
LIFE AS IT WAS WOULD CONTINUE, OF COURSE, WITH ITS THREADBARE HOPE DIMINISHED SOME, AND THE PASSAGE OF DAYS PERHAPS MORE HUMBLE, BUT SINCE NONE AMONG THEM HAD BEEN ABLE TO ACCESS THE INTERIOR OF THE TOWER'S WINDOWLESS BASE, WHERE THE CONTROLS TO ITS TRANSMISSIONS WERE SURELY SET, THE DRIFTING CAMPS WERE NEVER PRIVY TO THE HEART'S TRUE POWER SOURCE, WHICH HAD, IN ACTUALITY, NOT BEEN HELMED BY AN OPERATOR OF ANY SORT SINCE THE BLAST, BUT INSTEAD KEPT RUNNING BY AN AUTONOMOUS ENERGY BACKUP GENERATOR.
IT WAS THIS GENERATOR THAT HAD EVENTUALLY DRIED UP, THUS SHUTTING DOWN THE BEACON, BUT SINCE ITS MANY FOLLOWERS WERE SHEATHED IN IGNORANCE, AS THEY LACKED A MEANS TO UNLOCK OR EVEN BREAK DOWN THE REINFORCED SOLE ENTRY POINT TO THE TOWER'S CONTROL ROOM, TO THEM IT WAS SIMPLY AS IF GOD HAD BEEN EXTINGUISHED.
NOW, UTTERLY FORSAKEN AMONGST THE WRETCHED LANDSCAPE, THEIR PALTRY LIVES WOULD BE BARE TO THEM IN A WAY THAT THEY HAD NEVER BEEN BEFORE.
SEEK THE BEACON!
AND IT WOULD ONLY BE THEN THAT THEY WOULD BE ABLE TO START ANEW.

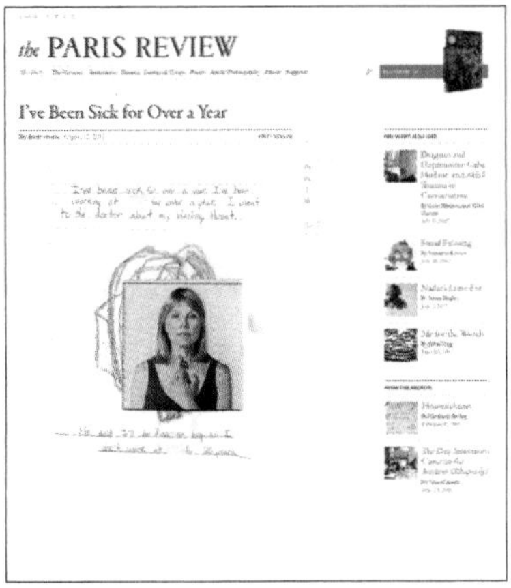
the PARIS REVIEW
I've Been Sick for Over a Year

# Untitled

BAILEY JEAN THOMAS

*originally published at*

*theparisreview.org*

THE PARIS REVIEW

digital

## Biography

Bailey Jean Thomas is a student from Louisville, Kentucky.

## Statement

This piece was a visual memoir of past work experiences.

I've been sick for over a year. I've been
working at _____ for over a year. I went
to the doctor about my bleeding throat.

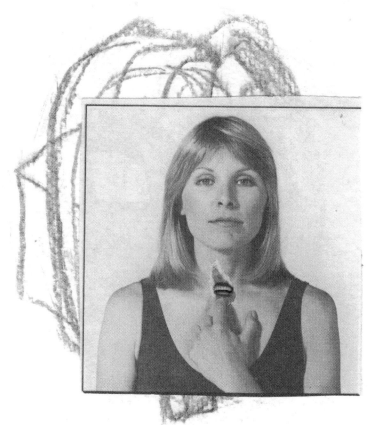

He said I'll be fine as long as I
don't work at _____ for 20 years.

When I
first started working there, it
seemed so surreal. I had never worked a job where
I was one out of hundreds, being shuffled
into trams like cattle. I had
never had to pass

through
security and metal detectors every day and
I started to view it like prison before

I remembered that I am free to

leave whenever I like.
Kind of.

It usually takes students about 8 years to graduate with a 4 year degree. You have to work every night to pay for school but if you dont make at least a "C" on the class they don't pay for it.

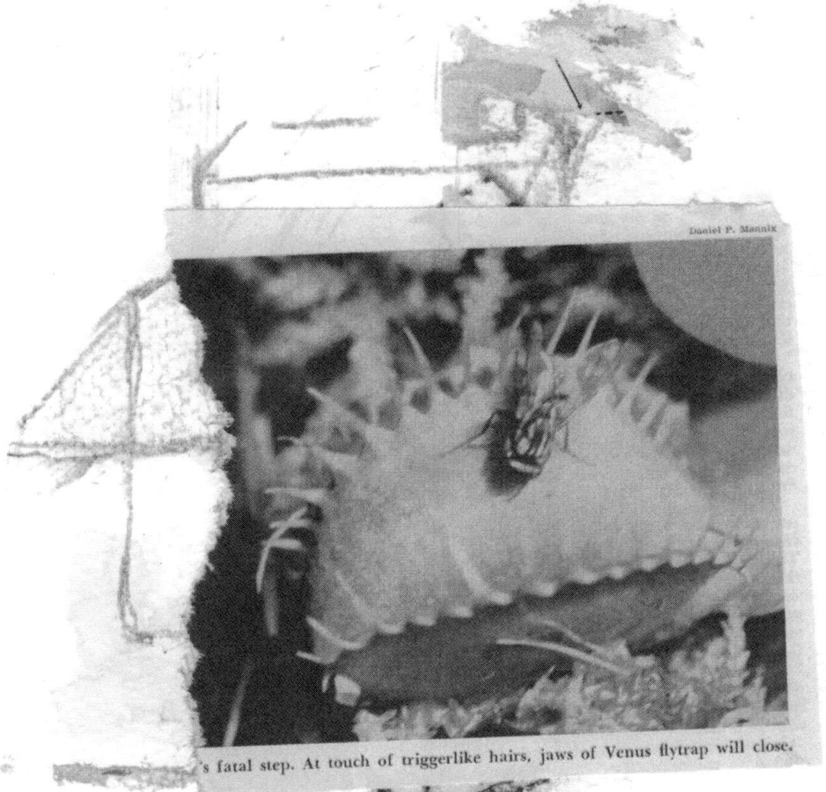
Daniel P. Mannix
's fatal step. At touch of triggerlike hairs, jaws of Venus flytrap will close.

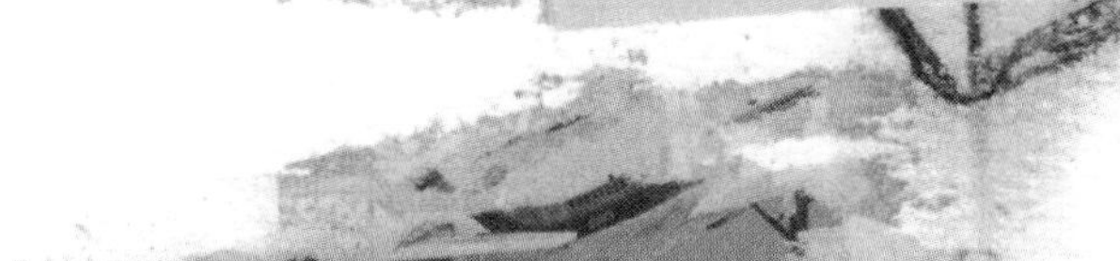

Even if you graduate college, you're likely to already have the best job you'll ever get So just stay at

There has been a corpse of a mouse laying on the warehouse floor for a few months now. The first day I saw it the little intestines were still kind of red. I try to go check on it every day. I started finding it in different locations because people were kicking it about.

I haven't seen it for weeks and I still look for it.

I annoy the shit out of myself while I'm working.

On a particularly
busy day my brain gets stuck on

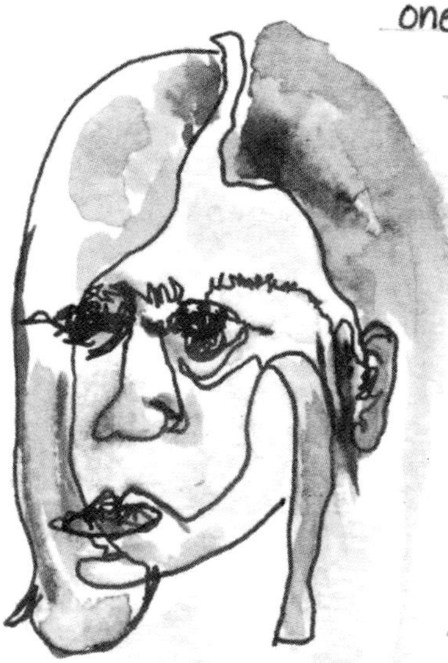

one question and I
just ask myself that

Same question everytime
I load a box.

With each box I
ask myself the
question a different
way... what comes out
earholes?

Does earwax count? Are earholes the
only holes in our bodies that aren't
involuntarily and routinely expelling some
sort of liquid?

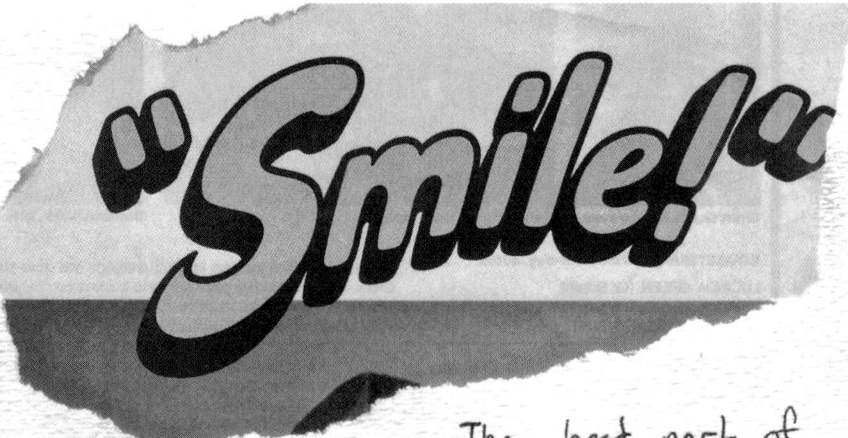
"Smile!"

The best part of being a loader is watching the drug dogs sniff the boxes. They seem so happy to do their job. Apparently they have the dogs sniff cocaine so that they know what it smells like and the dogs sometimes get addicted to it. I wonder why they don't make cocaine scented candles for them to sniff instead.

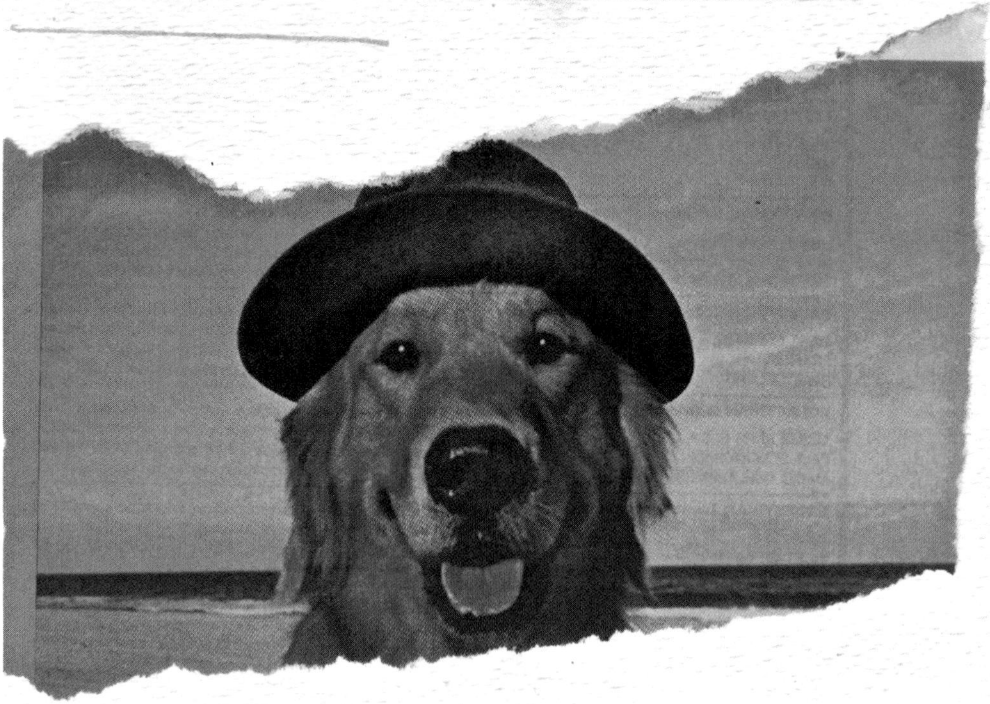

At least I get to have the illusion that it is possible to "work your way through school." As if I could pay for school with my income alone. But has to promise student free tuition because most of their employees are college students who will only last a few months before they decide it isn't worth it.

They are always understaffed. Too many packages of steak and bull semen coming in for people who have never thought about where it is coming from.

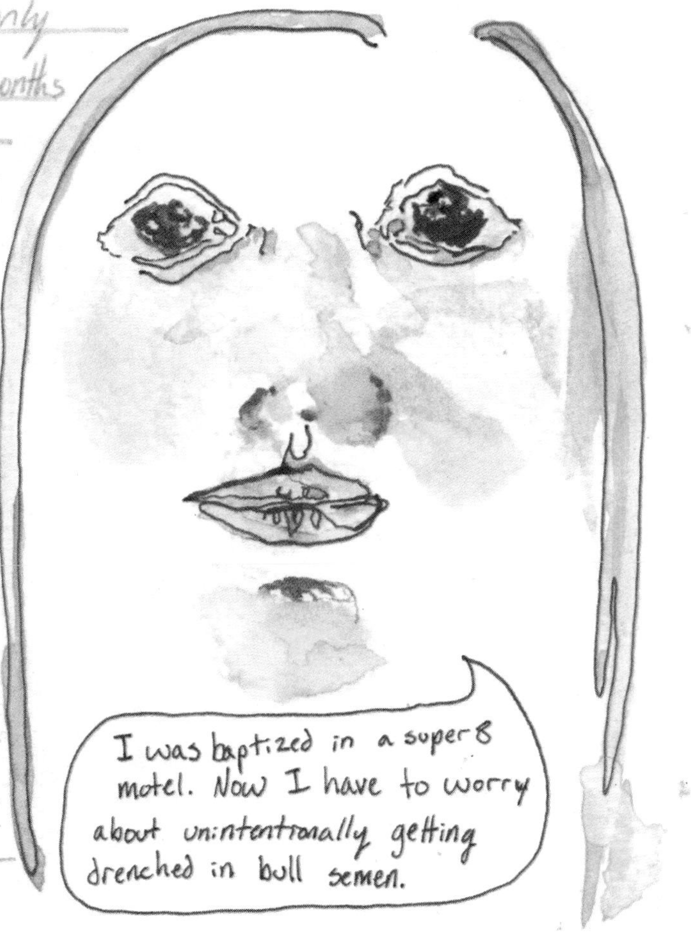
I was baptized in a super 8 motel. Now I have to worry about unintentionally getting drenched in bull semen.

It's sad.

Because our tedious, overlooked job can become so important so quickly.

Suddenly, a flammable liquid has been overlooked and a plane going to Dubai catches on fire.

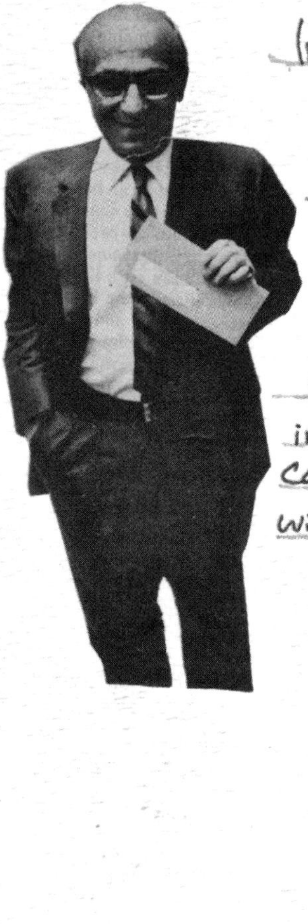

Or a tiny envelope is left in a can and a cancer patient is without medicine.

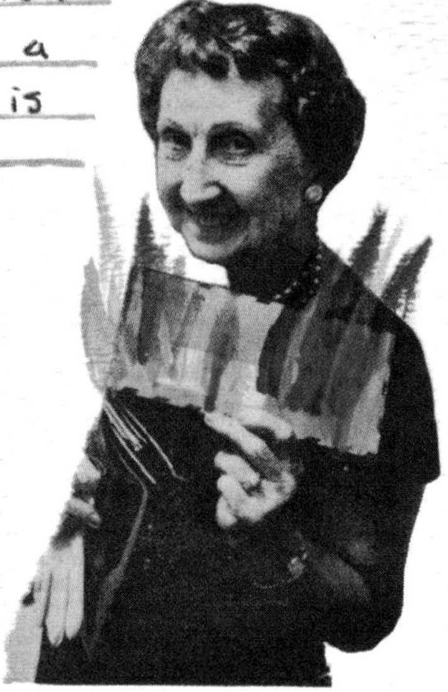

Customers write "fragile" and "please do not drop" on the boxes as if the warehouse equipment that sends them zipping around can read. The hundred-dollar orders crash down the chutes. There are so many boxes of tropical fish. How many fish are swimming in the sky right now?

FRAGILE
ORDER#
DEPT.#
ORDER#
DEPT.#

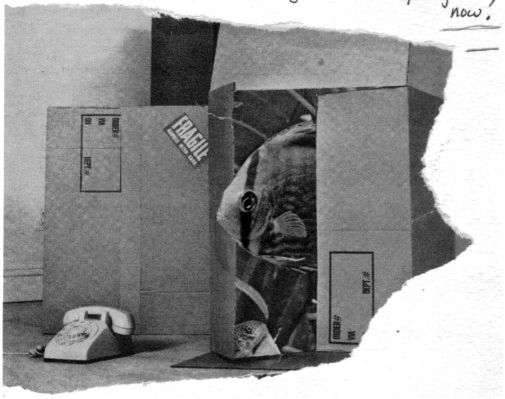

I know that I am lucky.

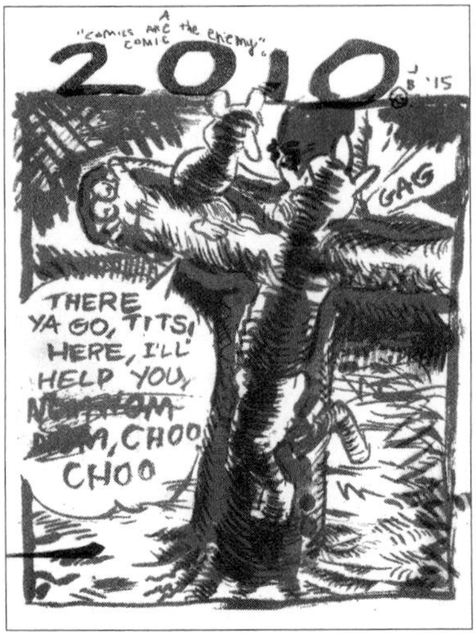
2010
GAG
THERE YA GO, TITS! HERE, I'LL HELP YOU,
CHOO CHOO

# 2010

## JOSH BAYER

*originally published as*

*2010*

IAMWAR/COMICS ARE THE ENEMY

8.5 × 11 inches • 20 pages

### Biography

Josh Bayer is the author of *Theth*, *Raw Power* #1 and 2, and the editor of the *Suspect Device* and *The Black Hood* anthologies. He is the writer and executive editor of *All Time Comics* from Fantagraphics Books. He teaches art and comics at the Parsons School of Design, 92Y, and many other New York–based schools.
joshbayer.com

### Statement

*2010* is a piece that was a continuation of work I started in 2010. It's a meditation on the call and response between an artist and the work they begin at one point and finish at a later point, creating a thread running from the past to the future.

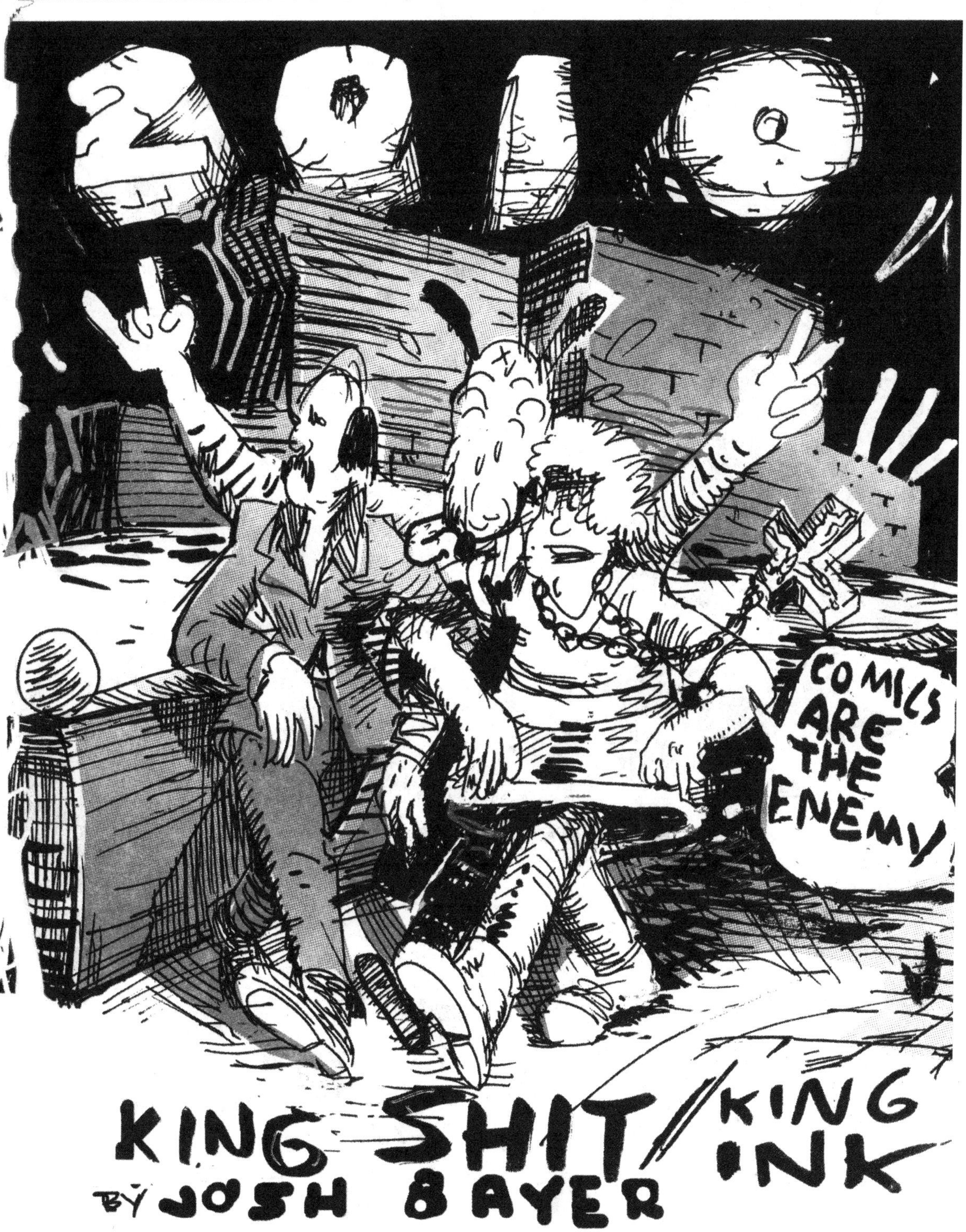
2010
COMICS ARE THE ENEMY
KING SHIT/KING INK
BY JOSH BAYER

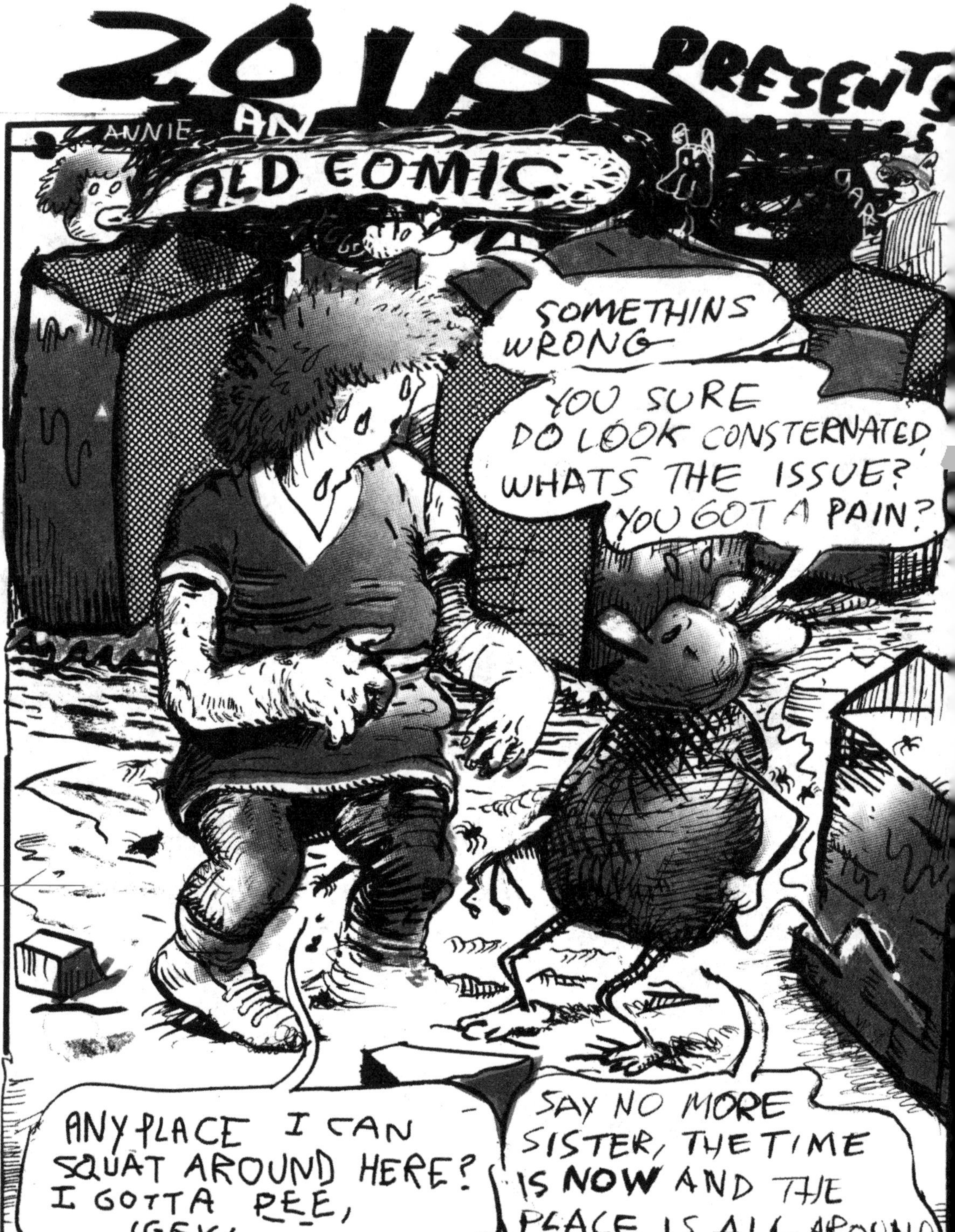
2010 PRESENTS
AN
OLD COMIC
ANNIE
SOMETHINS WRONG
YOU SURE DO LOOK CONSTERNATED, WHATS THE ISSUE? YOU GOT A PAIN?
ANY PLACE I CAN SQUAT AROUND HERE? I GOTTA PEE, IGGY!
SAY NO MORE SISTER, THE TIME IS NOW AND THE PLACE IS ALL AROUND

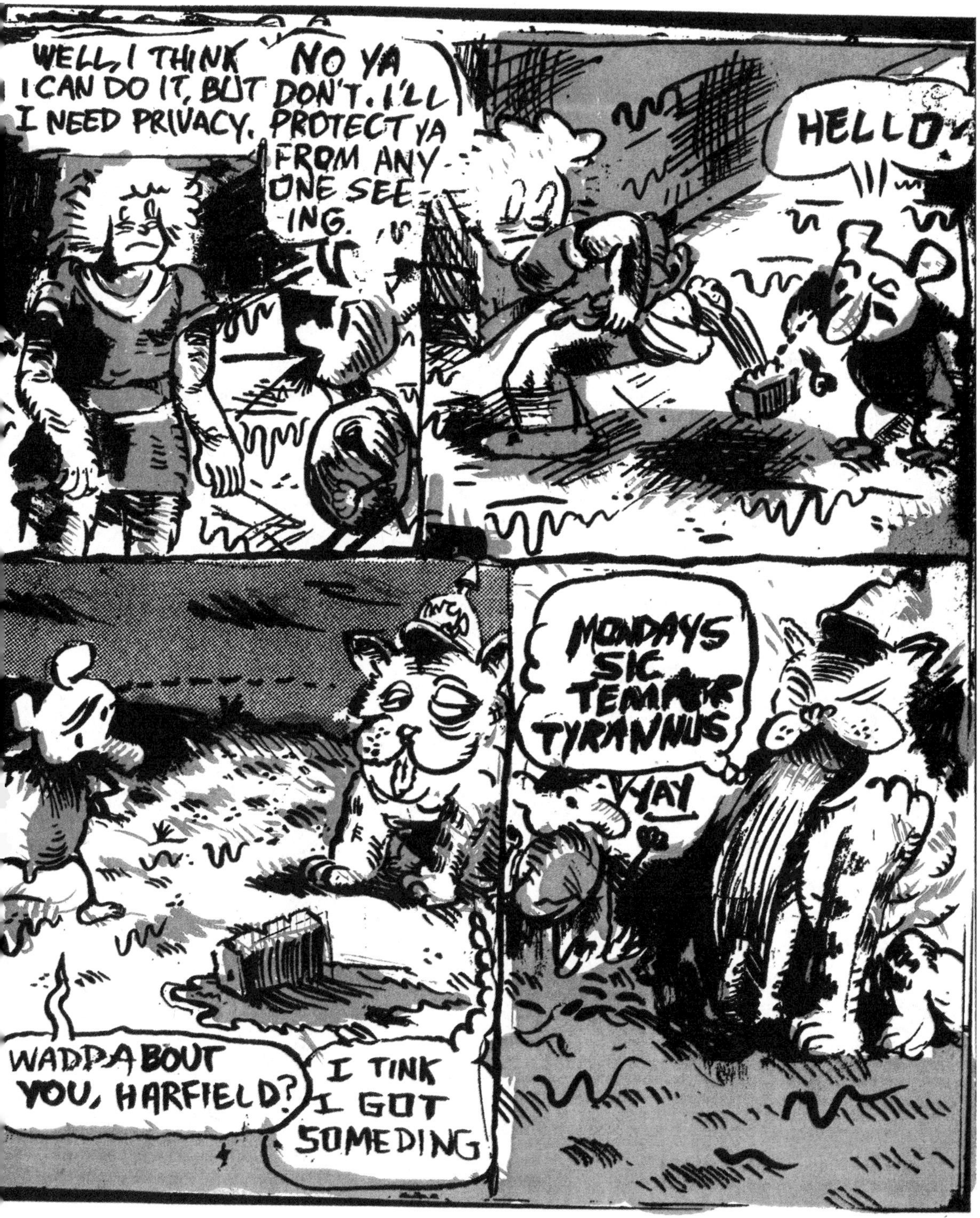
WELL, I THINK I CAN DO IT, BUT I NEED PRIVACY.
NO YA DON'T. I'LL PROTECT YA FROM ANY ONE SEE ING.
HELLO
MONDAYS SIC TEMPER TYRANNUS
YAY
WADDABOUT YOU, HARFIELD?
I TINK I GOT SOMEDING

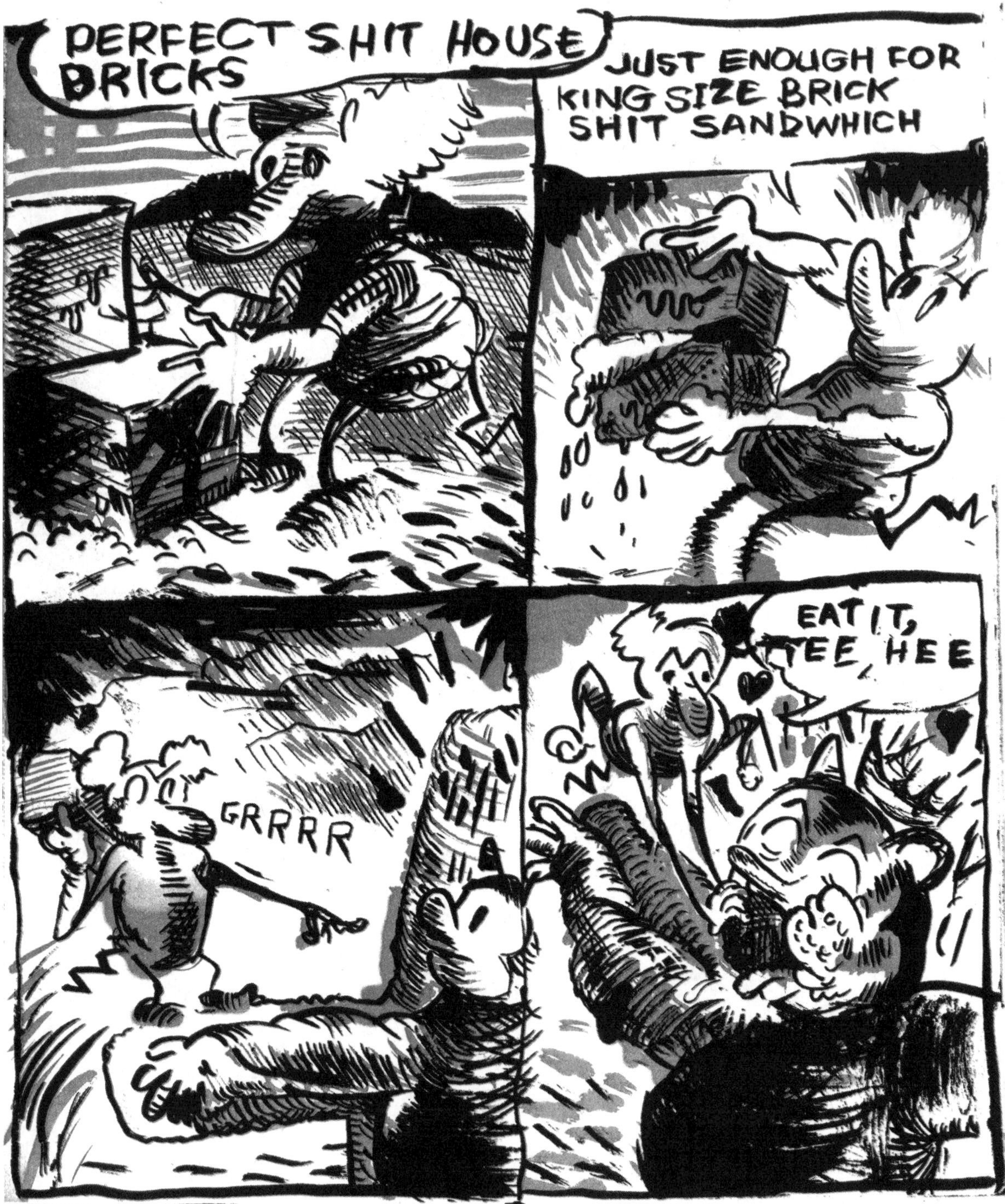
PERFECT SHIT HOUSE BRICKS
JUST ENOUGH FOR KING SIZE BRICK SHIT SANDWHICH
GRRRRR
EAT IT, TEE HEE

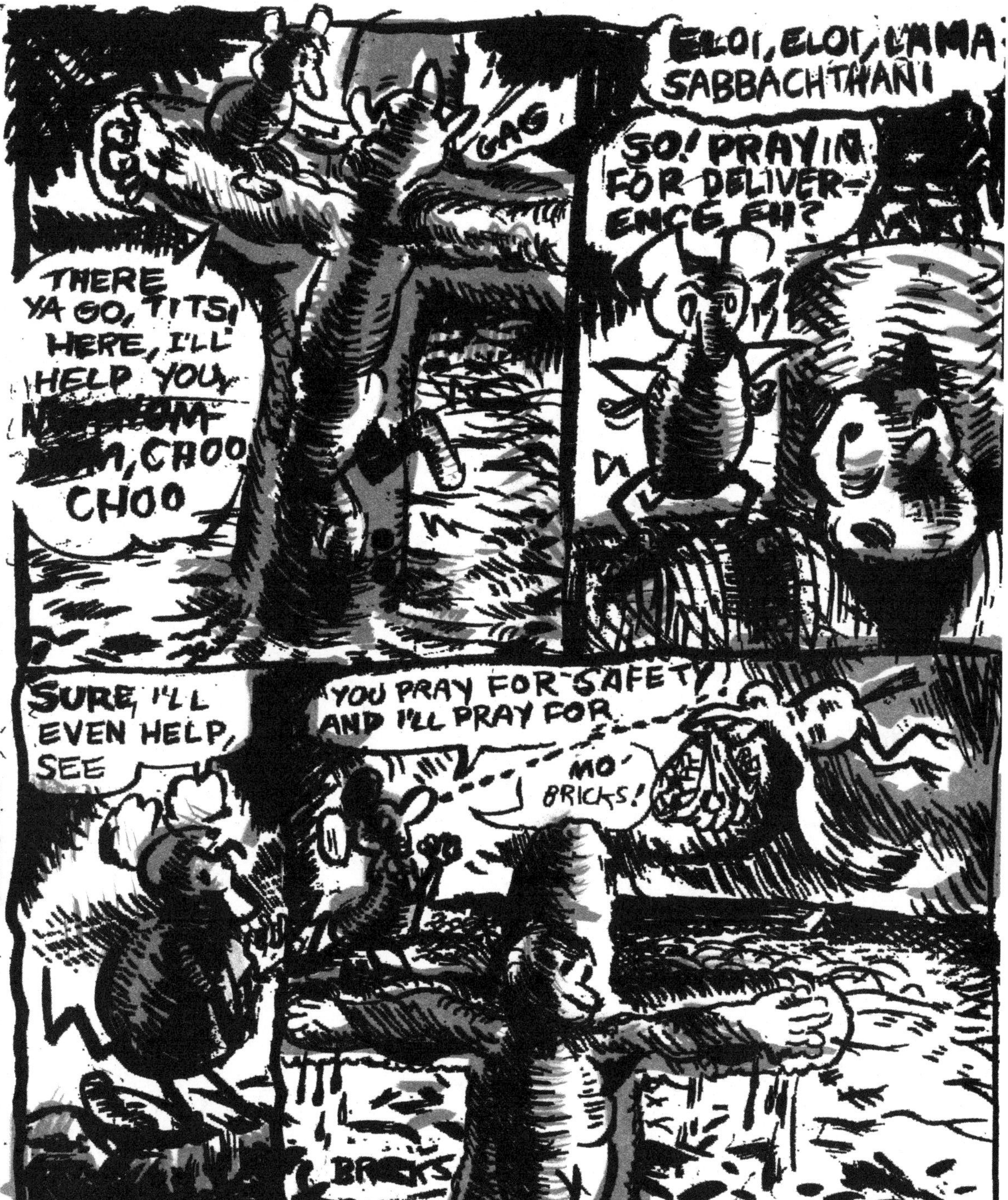
GAG
THERE YA GO, TITS! HERE, I'LL HELP YOU, [redacted], CHOO CHOO
ELOI, ELOI, LAMA SABBACHTHANI
SO! PRAYIN FOR DELIVER-ENCE EH?
SURE I'LL EVEN HELP SEE
YOU PRAY FOR SAFETY AND I'LL PRAY FOR
MO' BRICKS!
BRICKS

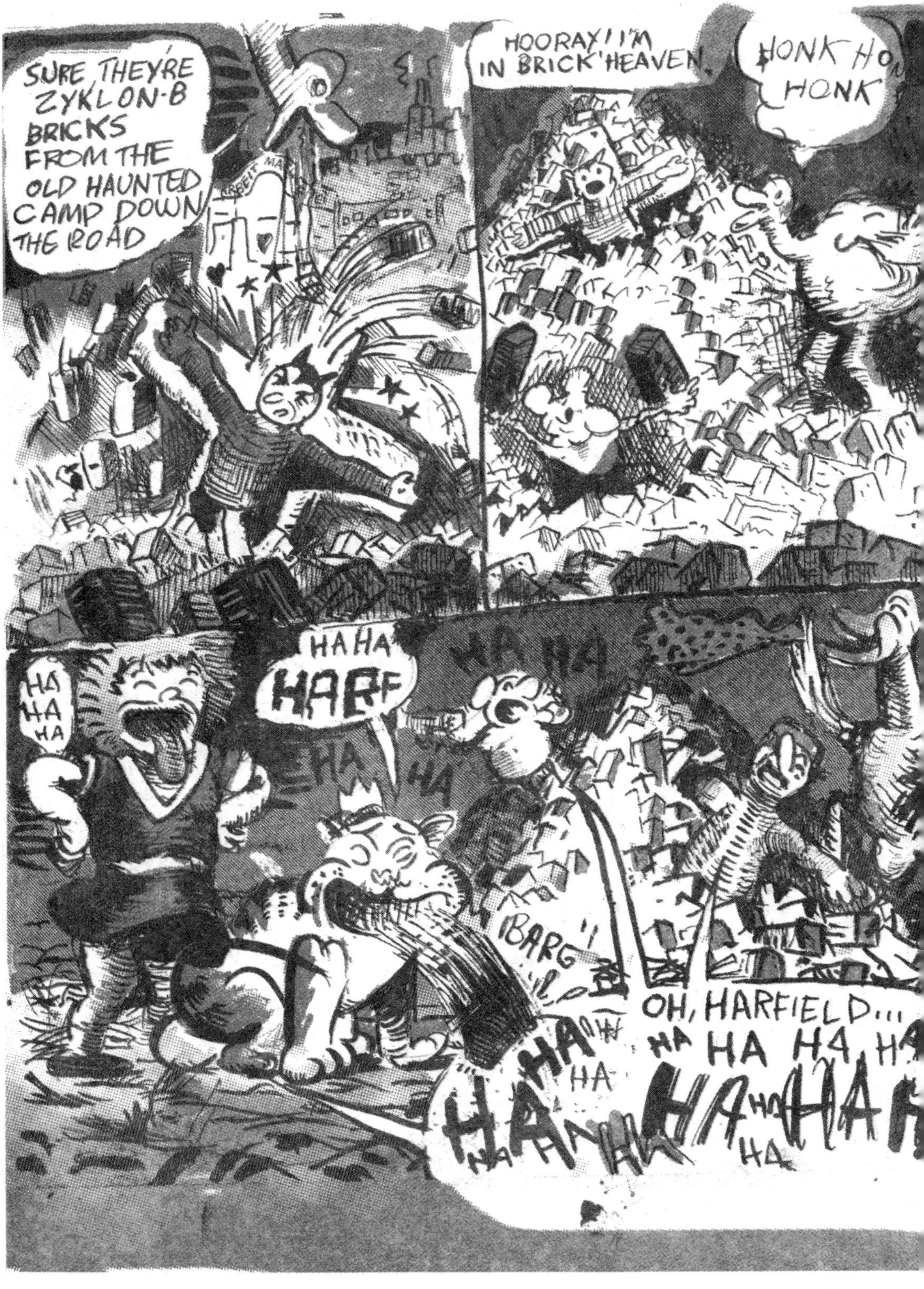
SURE THEY'RE ZYKLON-B BRICKS FROM THE OLD HAUNTED CAMP DOWN THE ROAD
HOORAY! I'M IN BRICK HEAVEN.
HONK HON HONK
HA HA HA
HA HA HARF
HA HA
HA
HA
BARG
OH, HARFIELD... HA HA HA H
HA HA
HA HA HA HA HA HA

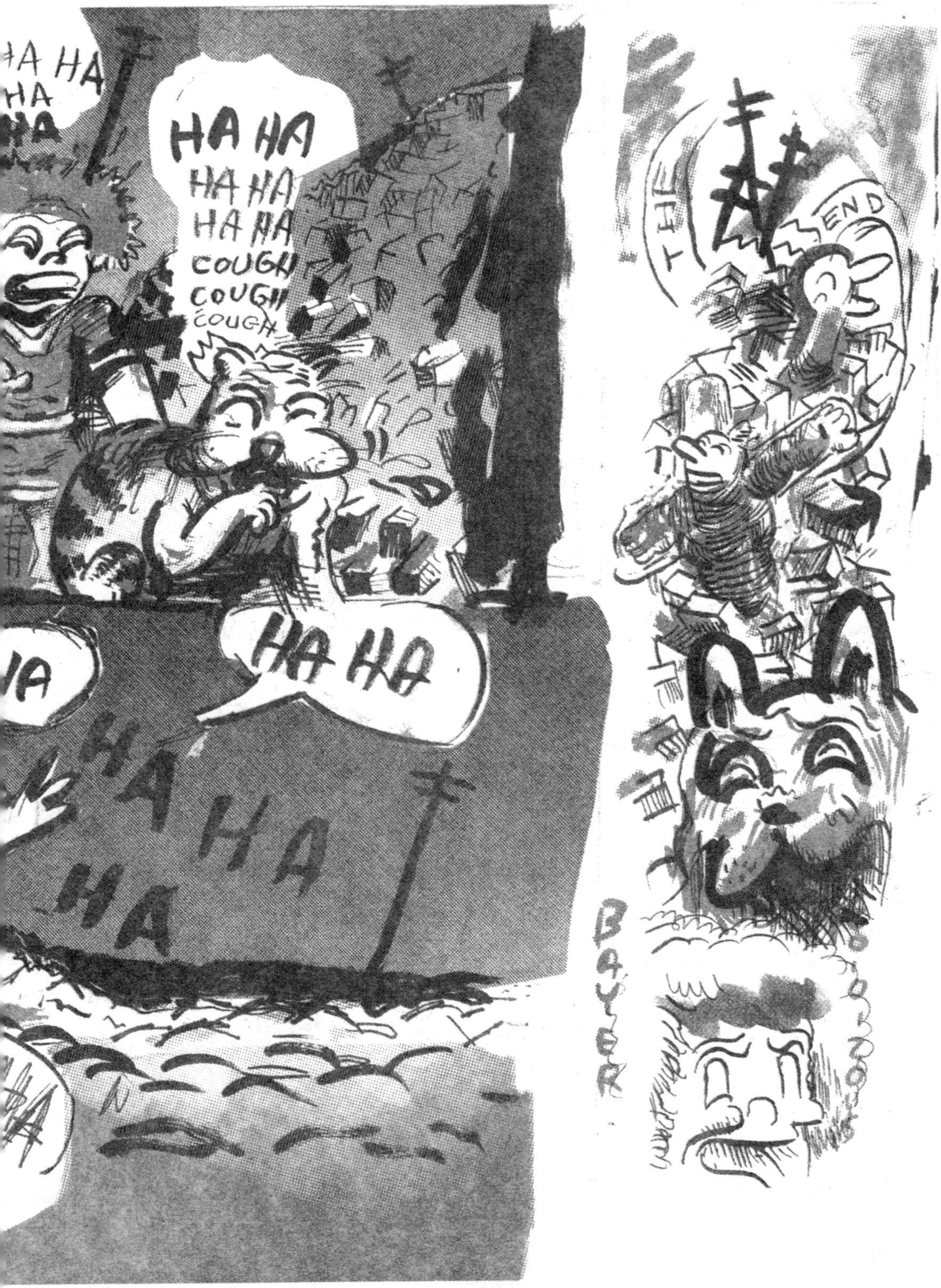
HA HA
HA
HA
HA HA
HA HA
HA HA
COUGH
COUGH
COUGH
HA HA
HA
HA
HA
HA
HA
THE END
BAYER

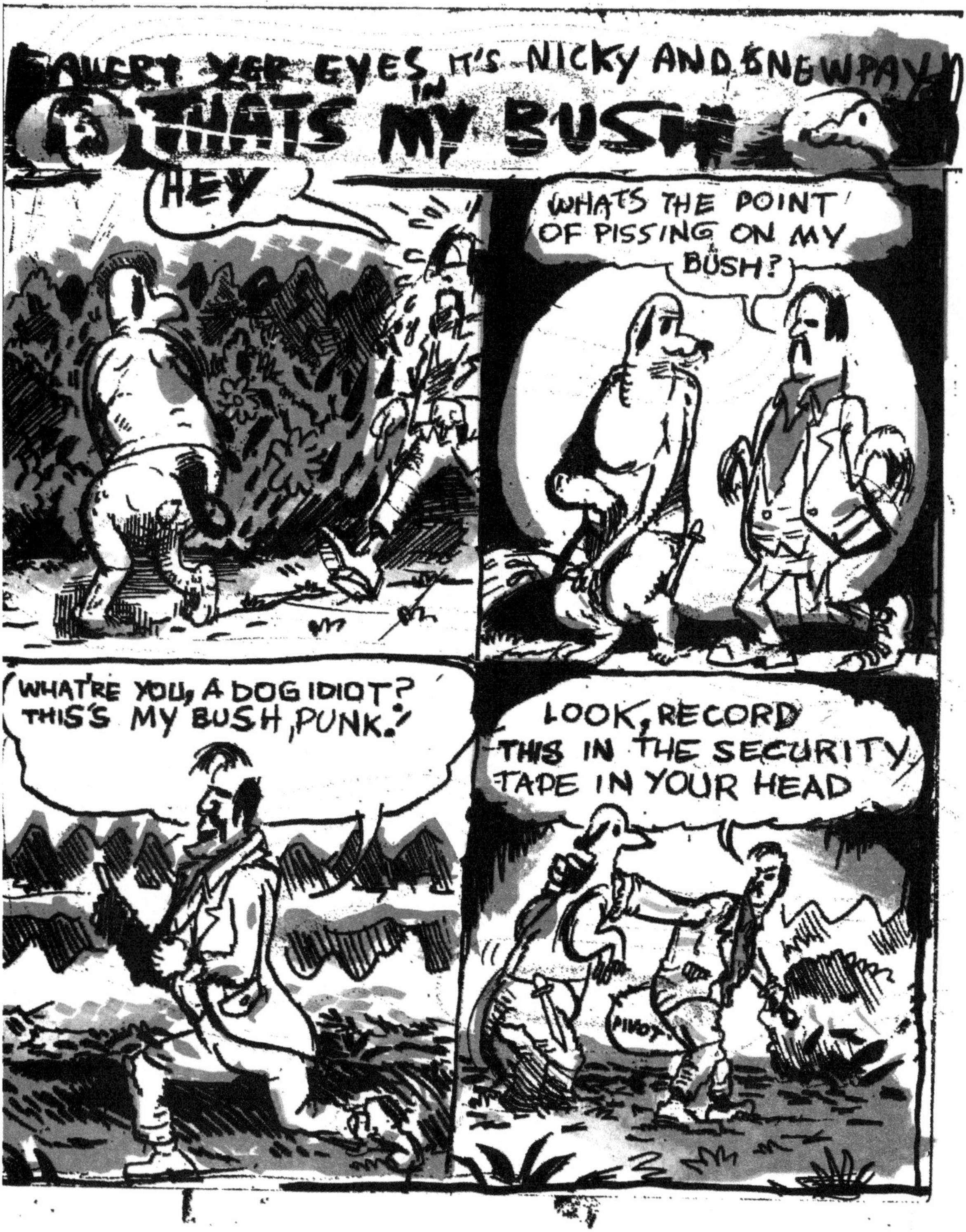
AVERT YER EYES, IT'S NICKY AND SNEWPAY IN
THATS MY BUSH
HEY
WHATS THE POINT OF PISSING ON MY BUSH?
WHAT'RE YOU, A DOG IDIOT? THIS'S MY BUSH, PUNK.
LOOK, RECORD THIS IN THE SECURITY TAPE IN YOUR HEAD
PIVOT

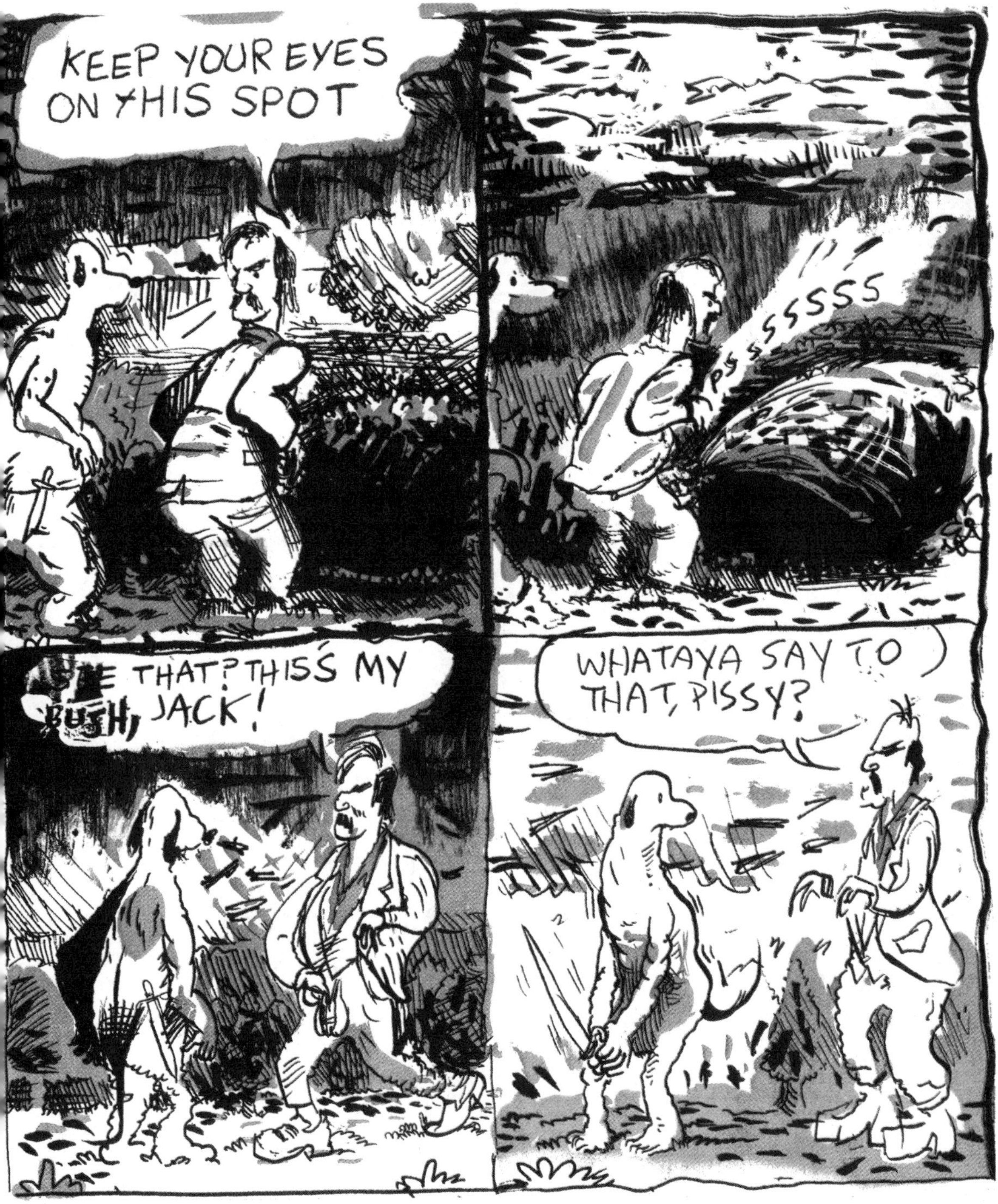
KEEP YOUR EYES ON THIS SPOT
PSSSSSSSS
THAT? THIS'S MY BUSH, JACK!
WHATAYA SAY TO THAT, PISSY?

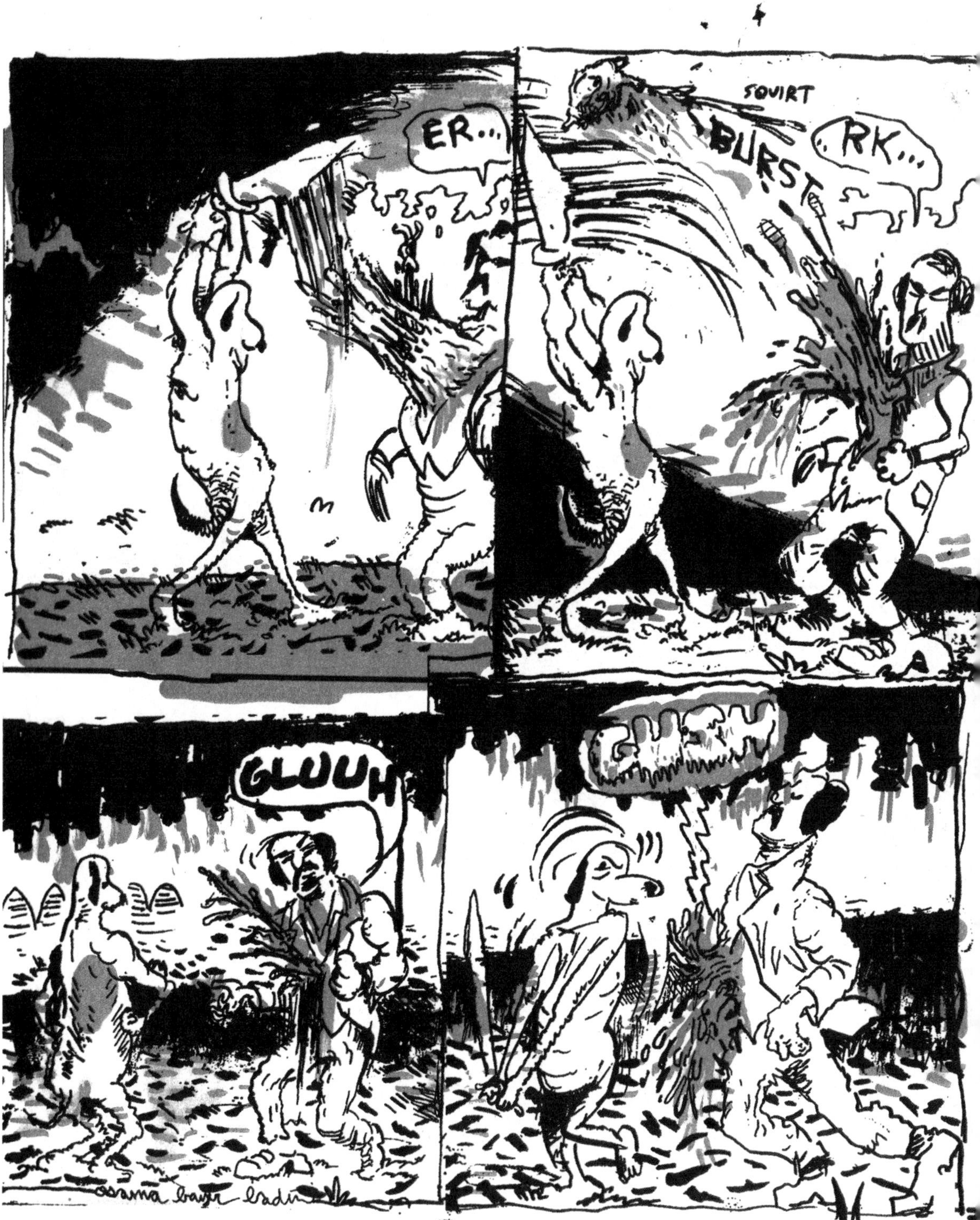
ER...
SQUIRT
BURST
RK...
GLUUH

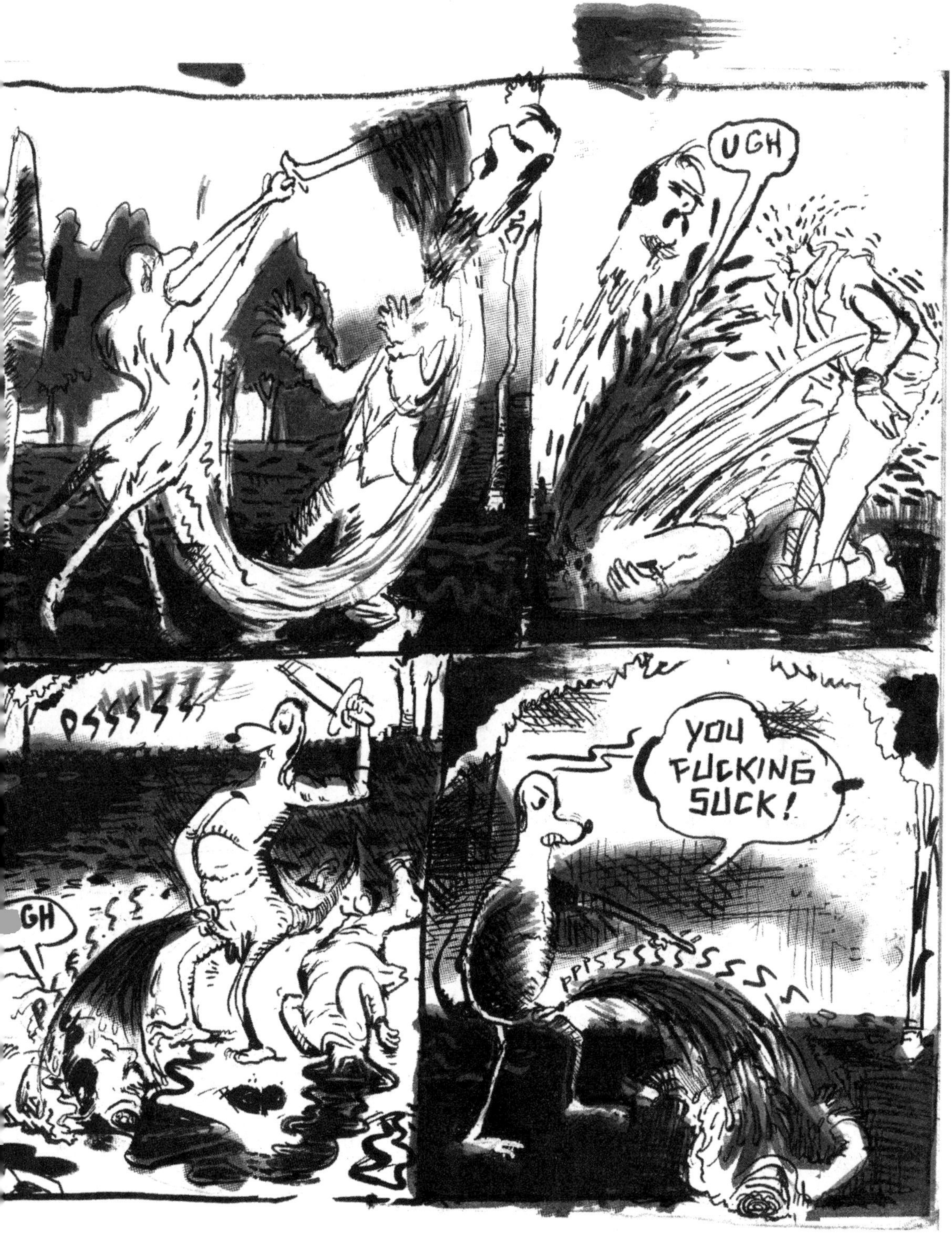
UGH
PSSSSSS
GH
YOU FUCKING SUCK!
PPPSSSSSSSSSS

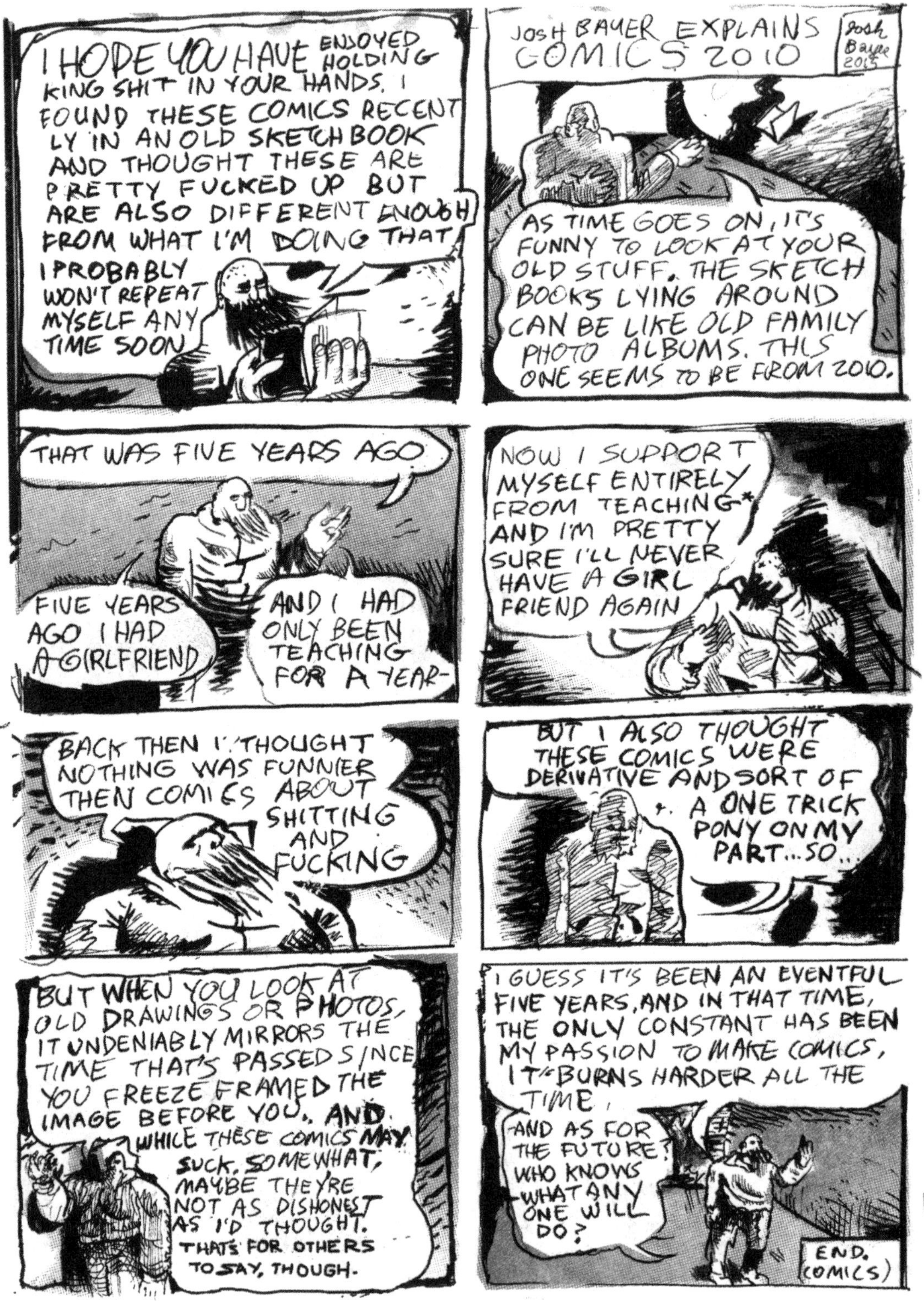
I HOPE YOU HAVE ENJOYED HOLDING KING SHIT IN YOUR HANDS. I FOUND THESE COMICS RECENTLY IN AN OLD SKETCHBOOK AND THOUGHT THESE ARE PRETTY FUCKED UP BUT ARE ALSO DIFFERENT ENOUGH FROM WHAT I'M DOING THAT I PROBABLY WON'T REPEAT MYSELF ANY TIME SOON
JOSH BAYER EXPLAINS COMICS 2010
Josh Bayer 2015
AS TIME GOES ON, IT'S FUNNY TO LOOK AT YOUR OLD STUFF. THE SKETCH BOOKS LYING AROUND CAN BE LIKE OLD FAMILY PHOTO ALBUMS. THIS ONE SEEMS TO BE FROM 2010.
THAT WAS FIVE YEARS AGO
FIVE YEARS AGO I HAD A GIRLFRIEND
AND I HAD ONLY BEEN TEACHING FOR A YEAR-
NOW I SUPPORT MYSELF ENTIRELY FROM TEACHING* AND I'M PRETTY SURE I'LL NEVER HAVE A GIRL FRIEND AGAIN
BACK THEN I THOUGHT NOTHING WAS FUNNIER THEN COMICS ABOUT SHITTING AND FUCKING
BUT I ALSO THOUGHT THESE COMICS WERE DERIVATIVE AND SORT OF A ONE TRICK PONY ON MY PART... SO...
BUT WHEN YOU LOOK AT OLD DRAWINGS OR PHOTOS, IT UNDENIABLY MIRRORS THE TIME THAT'S PASSED SINCE YOU FREEZE FRAMED THE IMAGE BEFORE YOU. AND WHILE THESE COMICS MAY SUCK, SOMEWHAT, MAYBE THEY'RE NOT AS DISHONEST AS I'D THOUGHT. THATS FOR OTHERS TO SAY, THOUGH.
I GUESS IT'S BEEN AN EVENTFUL FIVE YEARS, AND IN THAT TIME, THE ONLY CONSTANT HAS BEEN MY PASSION TO MAKE COMICS, IT BURNS HARDER ALL THE TIME.
AND AS FOR THE FUTURE? WHO KNOWS WHAT ANY ONE WILL DO?
END. (COMICS)

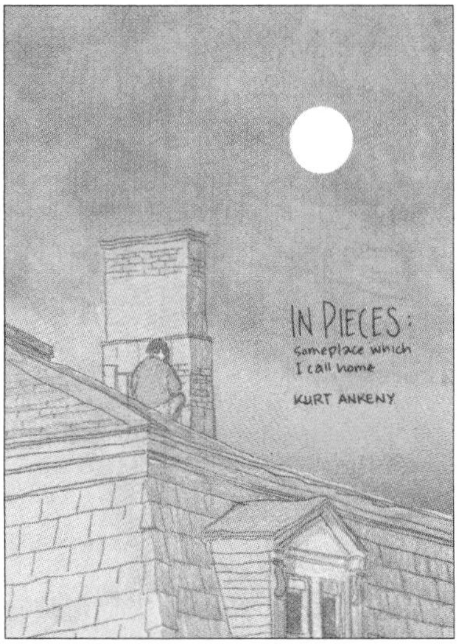
IN PIECES:
someplace which
I call home
KURT ANKENY

# In Pieces: Someplace Which I Call Home (*Excerpt*)

KURT ANKENY

*originally published in*

*In Pieces: Someplace Which I Call Home*

200 ZOO PRESS

6 × 8 inches • 120 pages

## Biography

Kurt Ankeny is an award-winning cartoonist and painter who returned to the medium of comics in 2014 after a decade-long exploration of oil painting. His work has appeared at the Society of Illustrators, at the Cape Ann Museum, and in Comics Workbook. He lives with his wife and son in Salem, Massachusetts.
kurtankeny.com

## Statement

*In Pieces* is intended to be a collage-portrait of the small New England town where I lived from 2011 to 2016. While it cannot help but include autobiographical detail, my aim was to distill the feeling of the small town and its citizens rather than offer glimpses into my quotidian life.

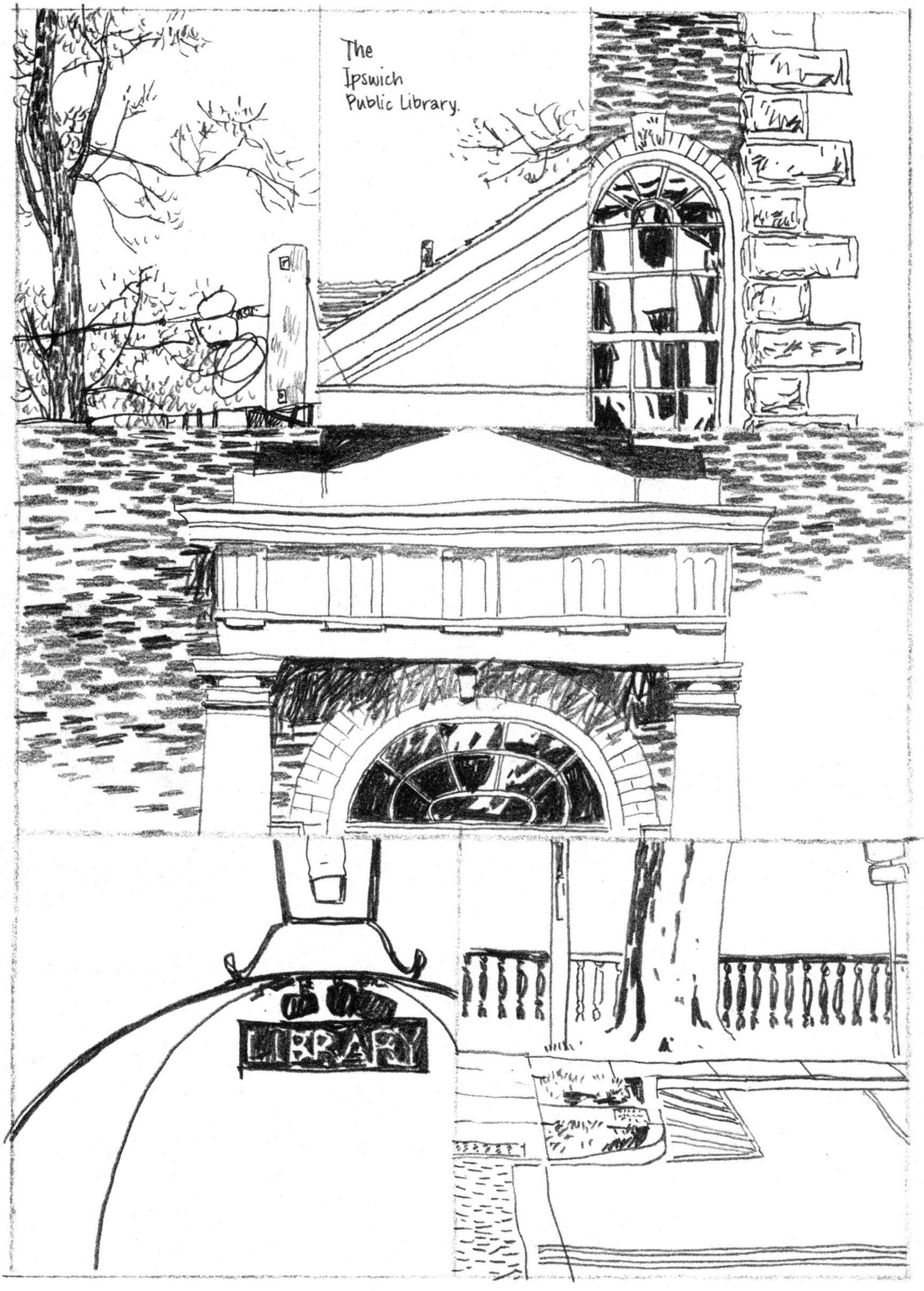
The Ipswich Public Library.
LIBRARY

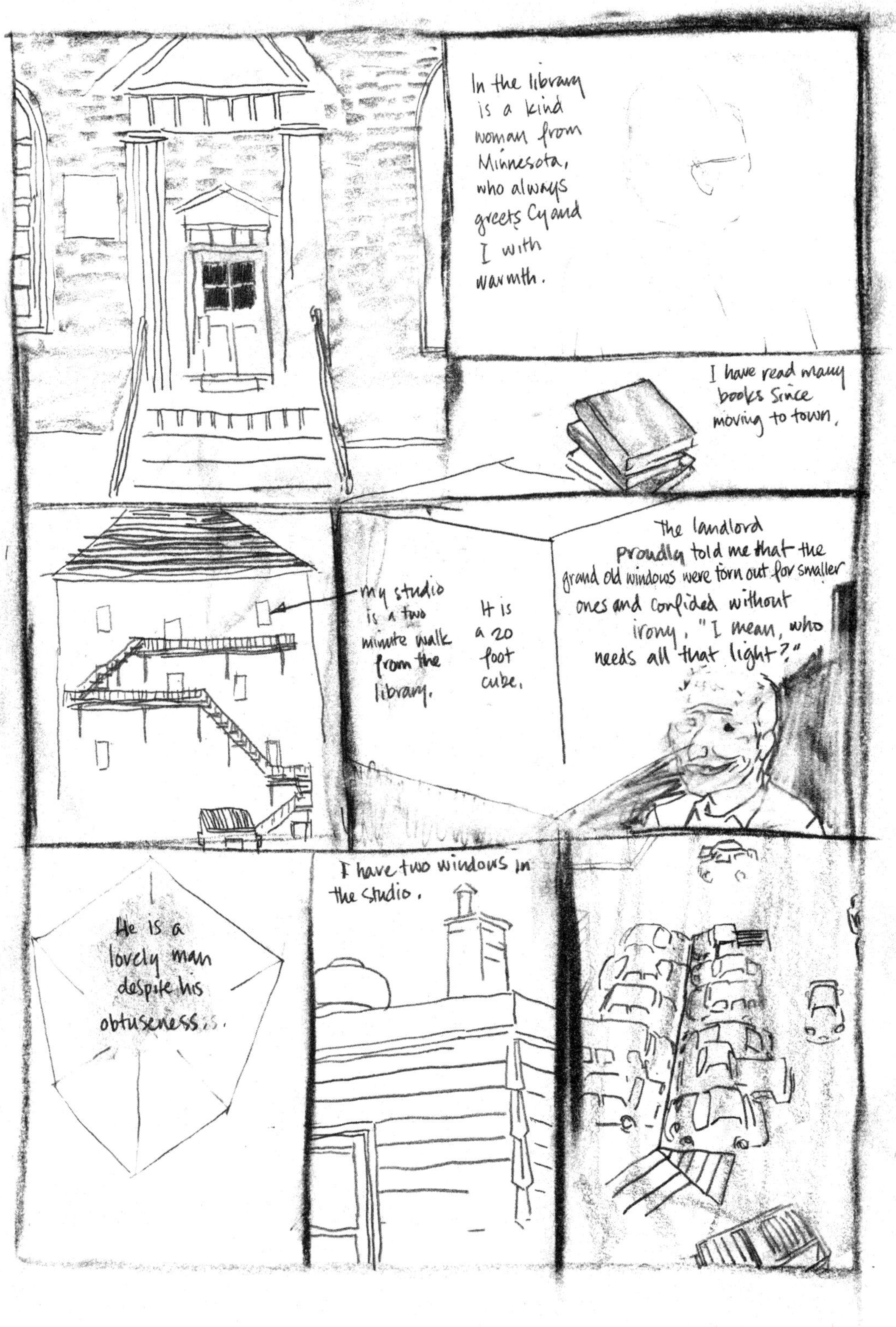
In the library is a kind woman from Minnesota, who always greets Cy and I with warmth.
I have read many books since moving to town.
my studio is a two minute walk from the library.
It is a 20 foot cube.
The landlord proudly told me that the grand old windows were torn out for smaller ones and confided without irony, "I mean, who needs all that light?"
He is a lovely man despite his obtuseness.
I have two windows in the studio.

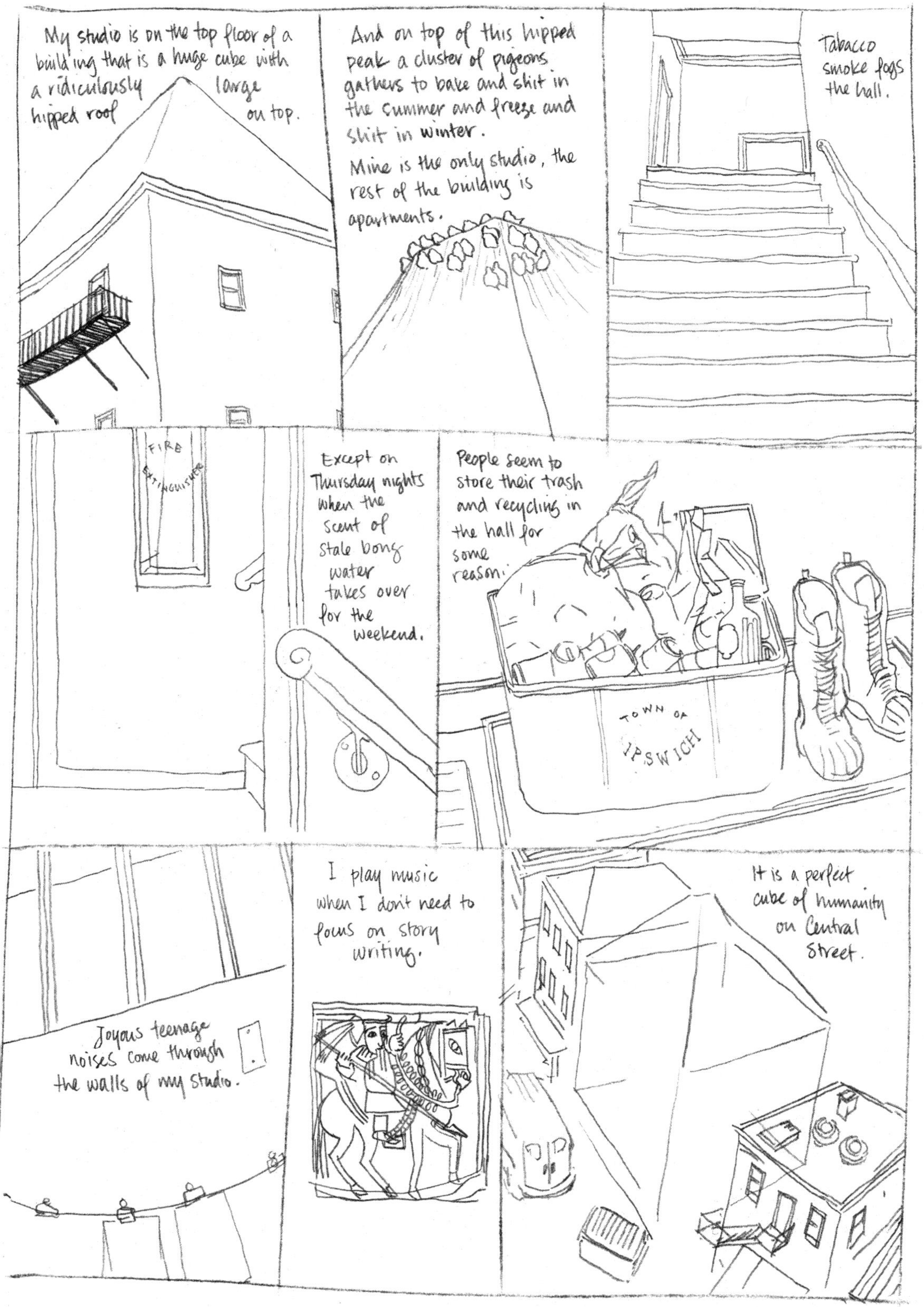
My studio is on the top floor of a building that is a huge cube with a ridiculously large hipped roof on top.
And on top of this hipped peak a cluster of pigeons gathers to bake and shit in the summer and freeze and shit in winter.
Mine is the only studio, the rest of the building is apartments.
Tabacco smoke fogs the hall.
FIRE EXTINGUISHER
Except on Thursday nights when the scent of stale bong water takes over for the weekend.
People seem to store their trash and recycling in the hall for some reason.
TOWN OF IPSWICH
Joyous teenage noises come through the walls of my studio.
I play music when I don't need to focus on story writing.
It is a perfect cube of humanity on Central Street.

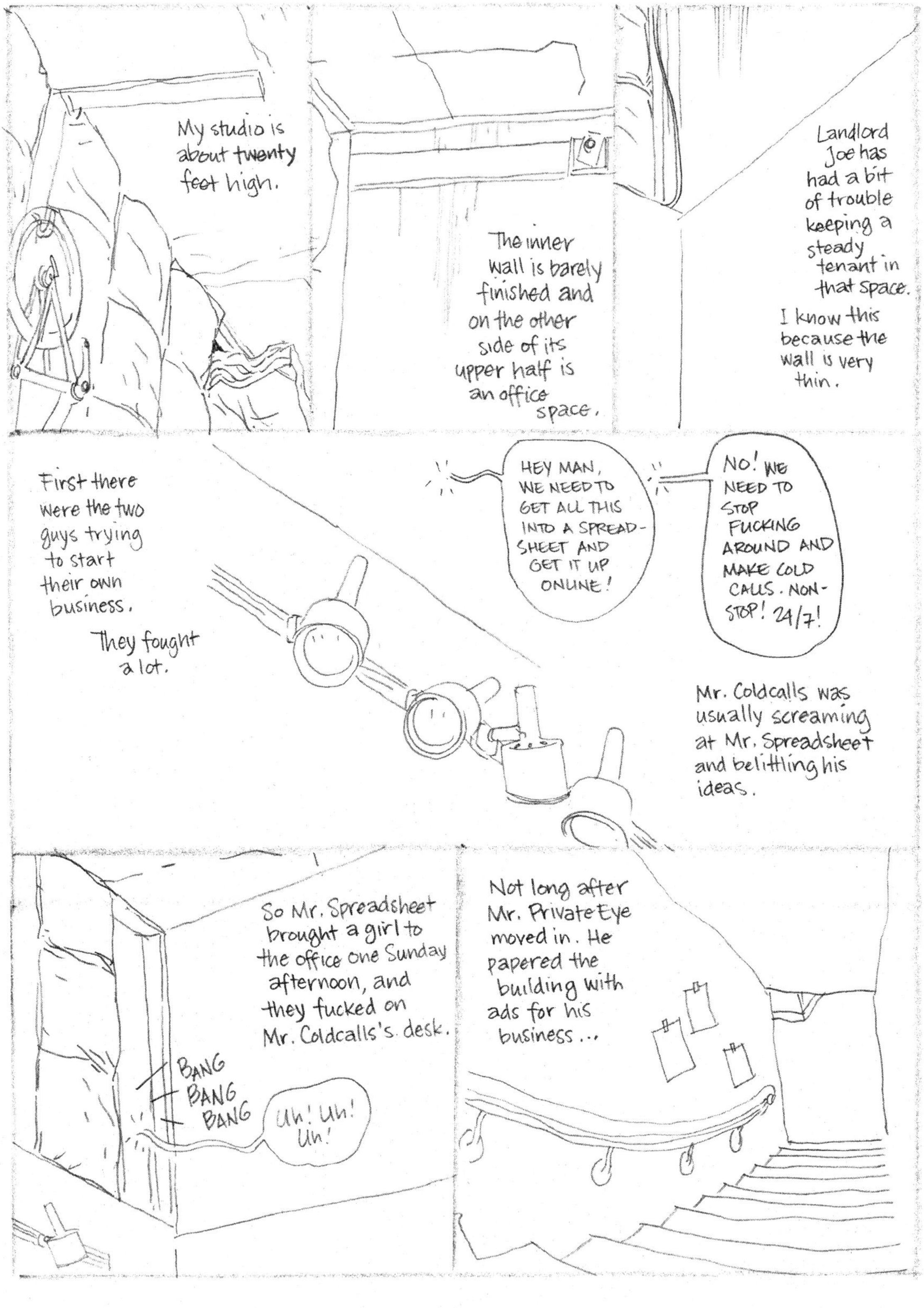
My studio is about twenty feet high.
The inner wall is barely finished and on the other side of its upper half is an office space.
Landlord Joe has had a bit of trouble keeping a steady tenant in that space.
I know this because the wall is very thin.
First there were the two guys trying to start their own business.
They fought a lot.
HEY MAN, WE NEED TO GET ALL THIS INTO A SPREAD-SHEET AND GET IT UP ONLINE!
NO! WE NEED TO STOP FUCKING AROUND AND MAKE COLD CALLS. NON-STOP! 24/7!
Mr. Coldcalls was usually screaming at Mr. Spreadsheet and belittling his ideas.
So Mr. Spreadsheet brought a girl to the office one Sunday afternoon, and they fucked on Mr. Coldcalls's desk.
BANG
BANG
BANG
Uh! Uh! Uh!
Not long after Mr. Private Eye moved in. He papered the building with ads for his business...

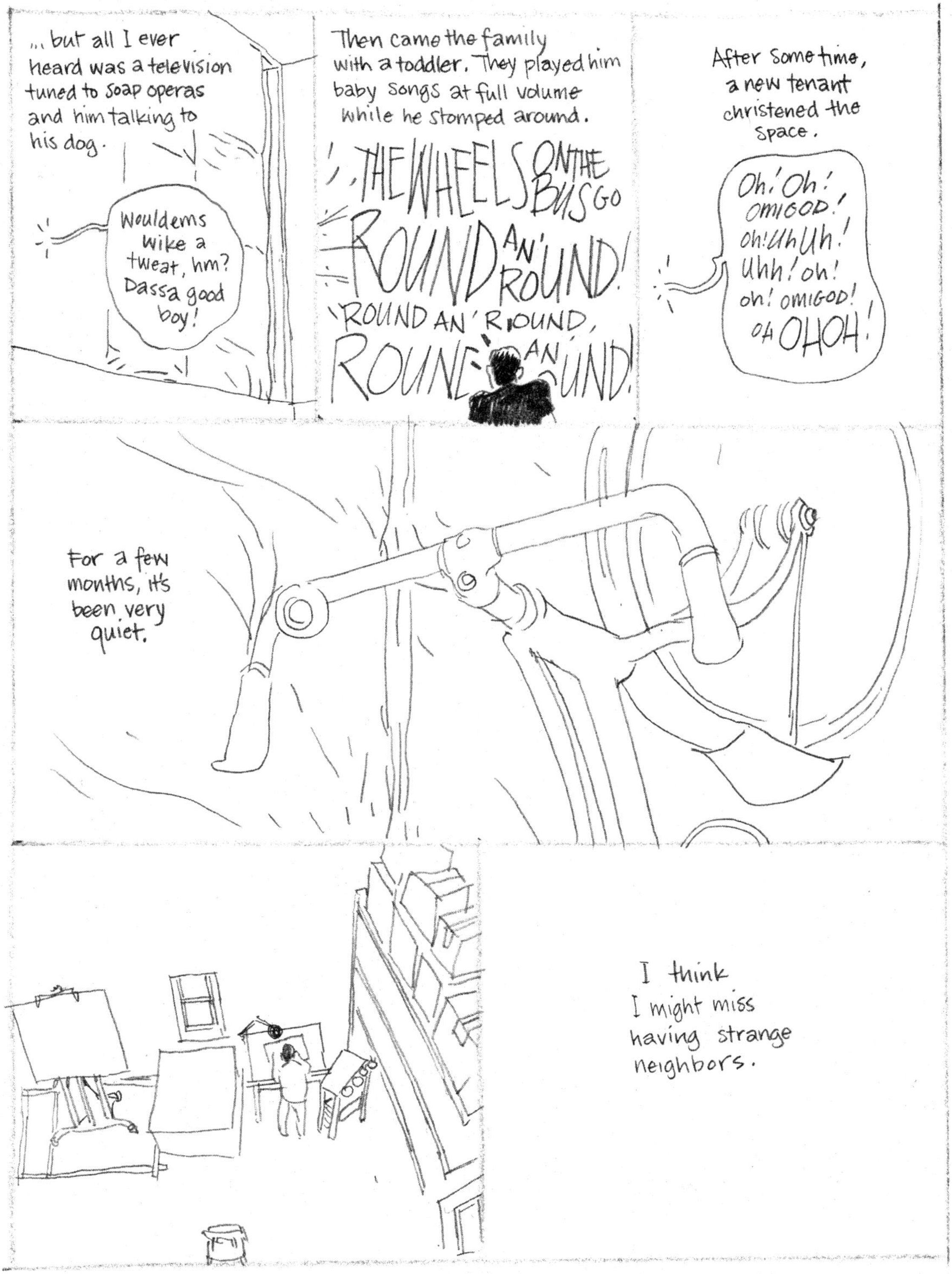

... but all I ever heard was a television tuned to soap operas and him talking to his dog.
Wouldems wike a tweat, hm? Dassa good boy!
Then came the family with a toddler. They played him baby songs at full volume while he stomped around.
THE WHEELS ON THE BUS GO ROUND AN' ROUND!
ROUND AN' ROUND,
After some time, a new tenant christened the space.
Oh! Oh! OMIGOD! Oh! Uh Uh! Uhh! Oh! Oh! OMIGOD! Oh OHOH!
For a few months, it's been very quiet.
I think I might miss having strange neighbors.

It is mid-spring.

A downpour is drying off the railing and the air is filled with chir-yawps from young sparrows, demanding to be fed.

These ones terrorize their parents, silent only while inhaling whatever offering has been presented in the last minute.

You can feel, even at a distance, the hot spark of survival that bounces within a ribcage made of bones no bigger than watch parts.

These young are still blissfully unaware of the eons of change that wrought these puffs of fire

from the lizard tyrants of the earth,

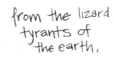

BIG
KIDS
MICHAEL
DEFORGE

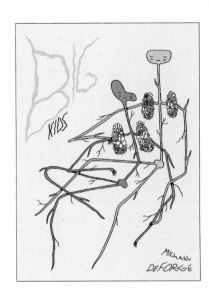

# Big Kids (*Excerpt*)

MICHAEL DeFORGE

*originally published in*

*Big Kids*

DRAWN AND QUARTERLY

4.5 × 5.8 inches • 96 pages

## Biography

Michael DeForge was born in 1987 and grew up in Ottawa, Canada. He is the author of *Sticks Angelica: Folk Hero*, *Big Kids*, *Dressing*, *Ant Colony*, *First Year Healthy*, *A Body Beneath*, and *Very Casual.*
michael-deforge.com

## Statement

While working on *Big Kids*, it was very important that the final book be able to fit in the back pocket of someone's jeans.

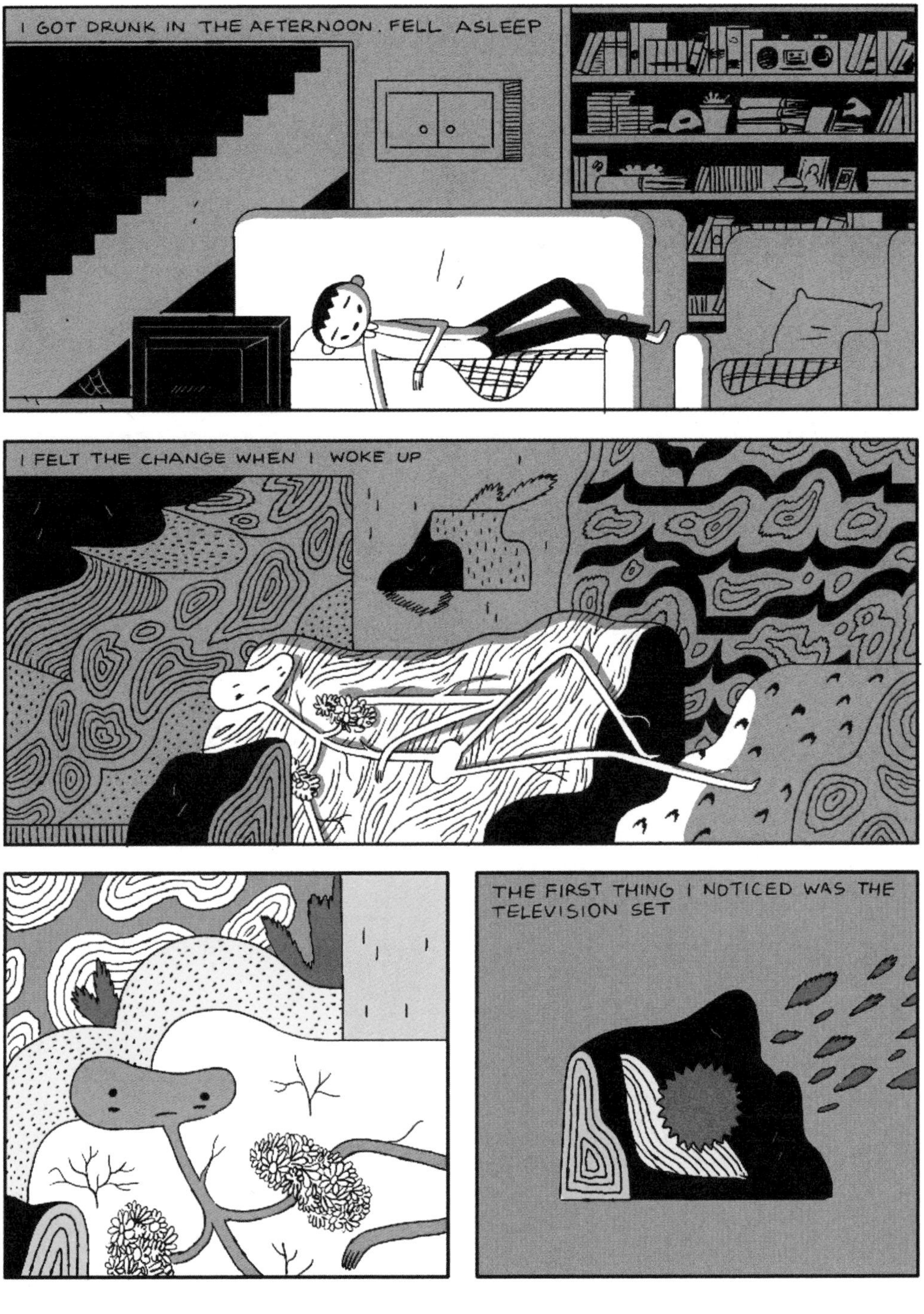
I GOT DRUNK IN THE AFTERNOON. FELL ASLEEP
I FELT THE CHANGE WHEN I WOKE UP
THE FIRST THING I NOTICED WAS THE TELEVISION SET

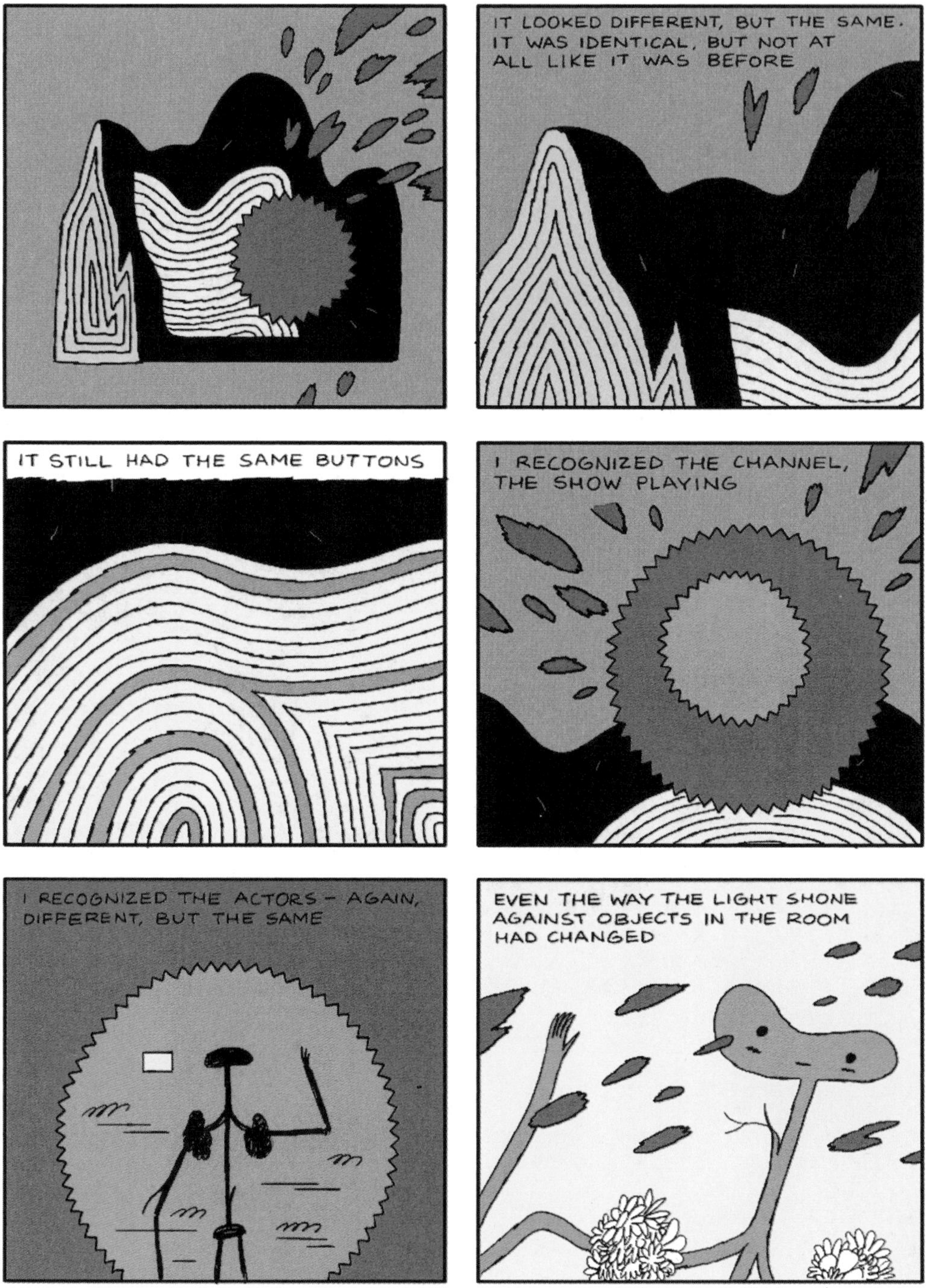
IT LOOKED DIFFERENT, BUT THE SAME. IT WAS IDENTICAL, BUT NOT AT ALL LIKE IT WAS BEFORE
IT STILL HAD THE SAME BUTTONS
I RECOGNIZED THE CHANNEL, THE SHOW PLAYING
I RECOGNIZED THE ACTORS – AGAIN, DIFFERENT, BUT THE SAME
EVEN THE WAY THE LIGHT SHONE AGAINST OBJECTS IN THE ROOM HAD CHANGED

I WALKED TO THE BATHROOM

IT WAS THE SAME THING IN THE MIRROR. I COULD TELL MY FACE WAS MY OWN

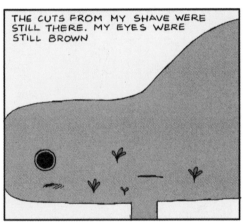

THE CUTS FROM MY SHAVE WERE STILL THERE. MY EYES WERE STILL BROWN

MY SHIRT WAS STILL YELLOW, WITH BUTTONS

MY HAIR WAS STILL THE DUMB-LOOKING CUT MY MOM GAVE ME

APRIL POKED HER HEAD IN FROM UPSTAIRS

YOUR PARENTS WANT YOU TO COME EAT DINNER

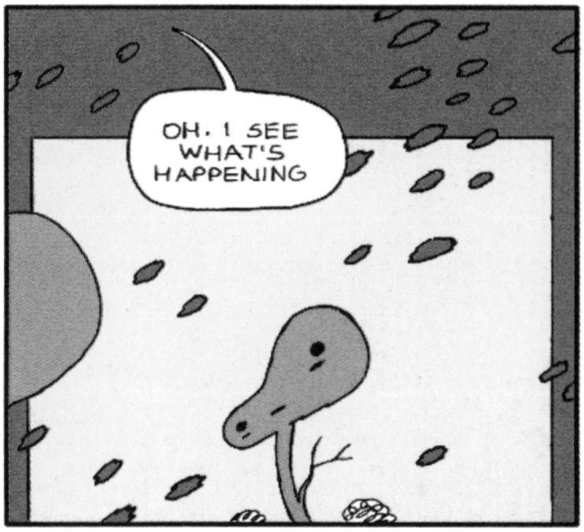
OH. I SEE WHAT'S HAPPENING

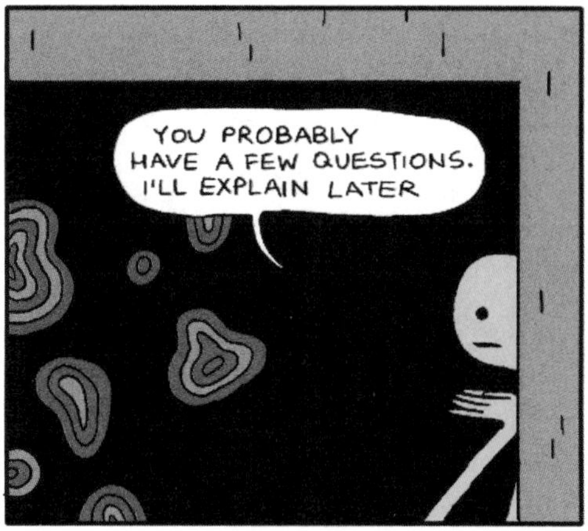
YOU PROBABLY HAVE A FEW QUESTIONS. I'LL EXPLAIN LATER

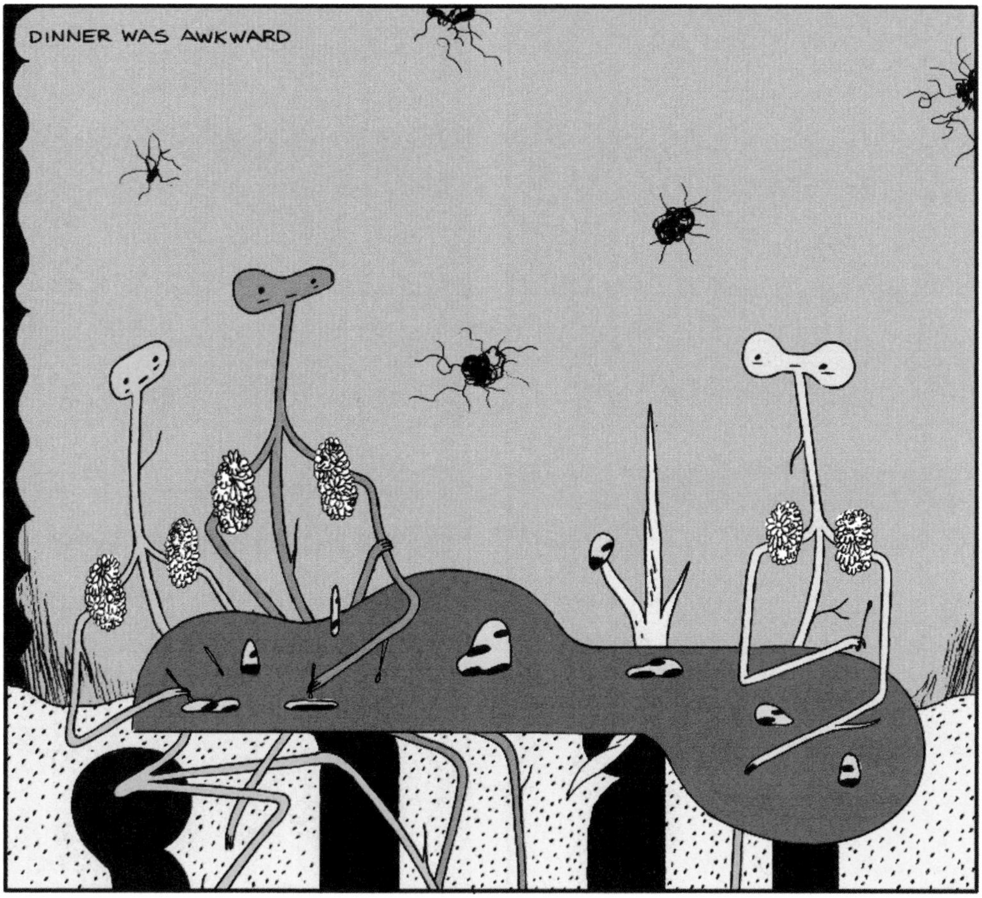
DINNER WAS AWKWARD

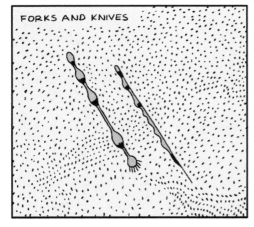

FORKS AND KNIVES

PLATES OF FOOD

THE WAY FOOD TASTED

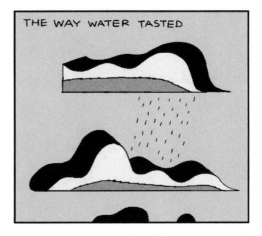

THE WAY WATER TASTED

MOM

I COULD TELL SHE WAS AVOIDING MY GAZE

APRIL. ALL THE STUDENTS IN MY CLASSES ARE VERY EXCITED ABOUT THE ATHLETIC CENTRE'S POOL BEING REOPENED. ARE YOU?
MAYBE YOU TWO SHOULD GO TO THE POOL
SHE WOULDN'T MAKE EYE CONTACT
THE LAMB IS ESPECIALLY GOOD TONIGHT
SHE SEEMED SO TENSE
THANK YOU
DAD
VERY, VERY GOOD

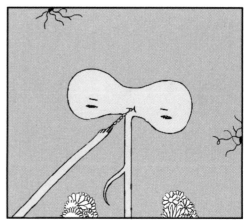

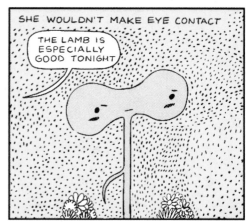

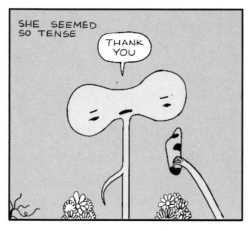

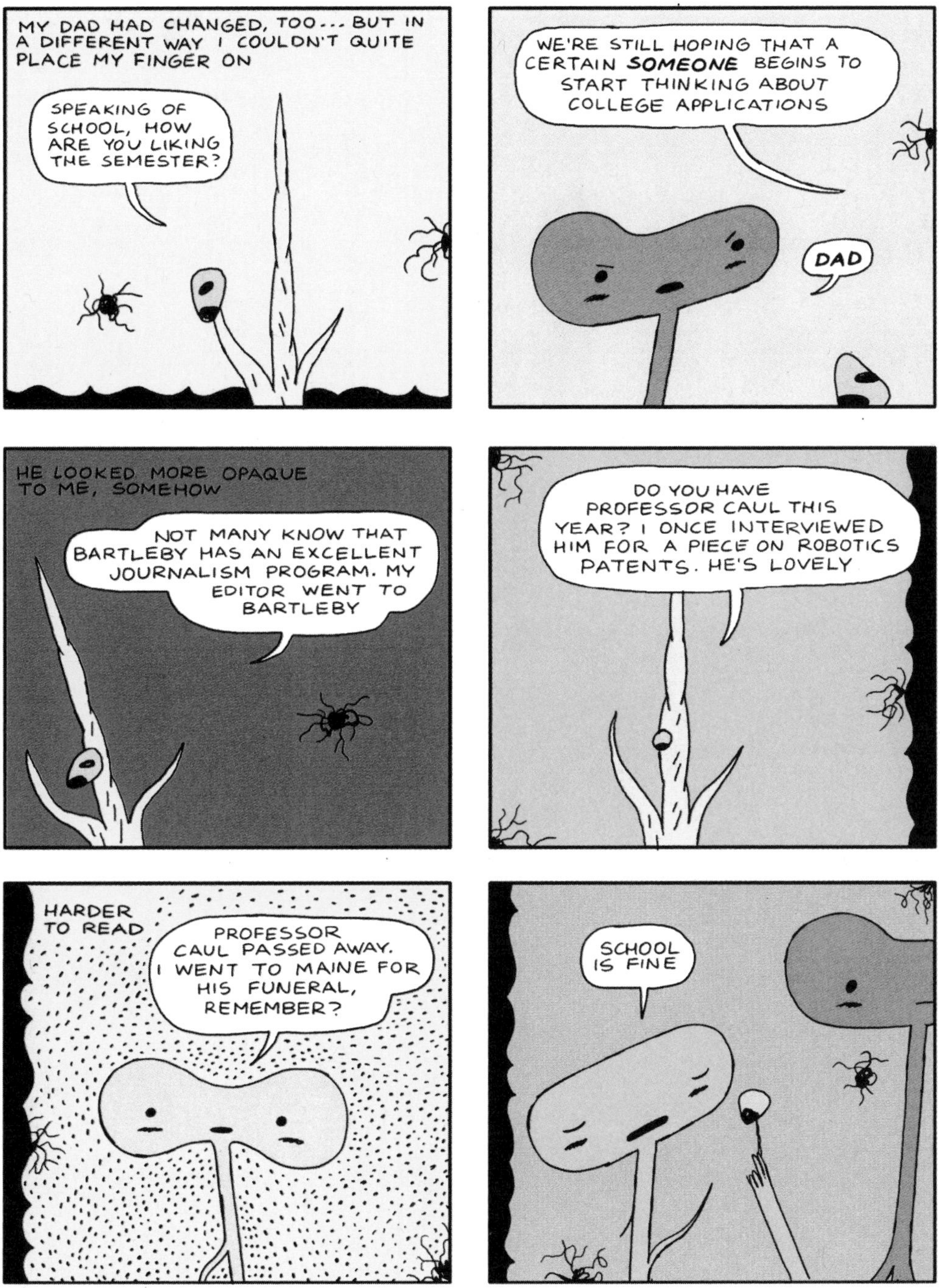

MY DAD HAD CHANGED, TOO... BUT IN A DIFFERENT WAY I COULDN'T QUITE PLACE MY FINGER ON
SPEAKING OF SCHOOL, HOW ARE YOU LIKING THE SEMESTER?
WE'RE STILL HOPING THAT A CERTAIN **SOMEONE** BEGINS TO START THINKING ABOUT COLLEGE APPLICATIONS
DAD
HE LOOKED MORE OPAQUE TO ME, SOMEHOW
NOT MANY KNOW THAT BARTLEBY HAS AN EXCELLENT JOURNALISM PROGRAM. MY EDITOR WENT TO BARTLEBY
DO YOU HAVE PROFESSOR CAUL THIS YEAR? I ONCE INTERVIEWED HIM FOR A PIECE ON ROBOTICS PATENTS. HE'S LOVELY
HARDER TO READ
PROFESSOR CAUL PASSED AWAY. I WENT TO MAINE FOR HIS FUNERAL, REMEMBER?
SCHOOL IS FINE

I BASICALLY KNOW ALL THE STUFF THEY'RE TEACHING ALREADY

REALLY? SASHA, IS THAT TRUE?

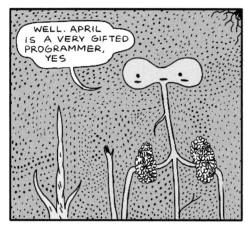

WELL. APRIL IS A VERY GIFTED PROGRAMMER, YES

TWO COMPUTER WHIZZES UNDER THE SAME ROOF! STILL THINKING OF TAKING UP YOUR MOTHER'S TRADE, ADAM?

I WAS MOSTLY JOKING

I BARELY KNOW HOW TO USE THOSE MACHINES

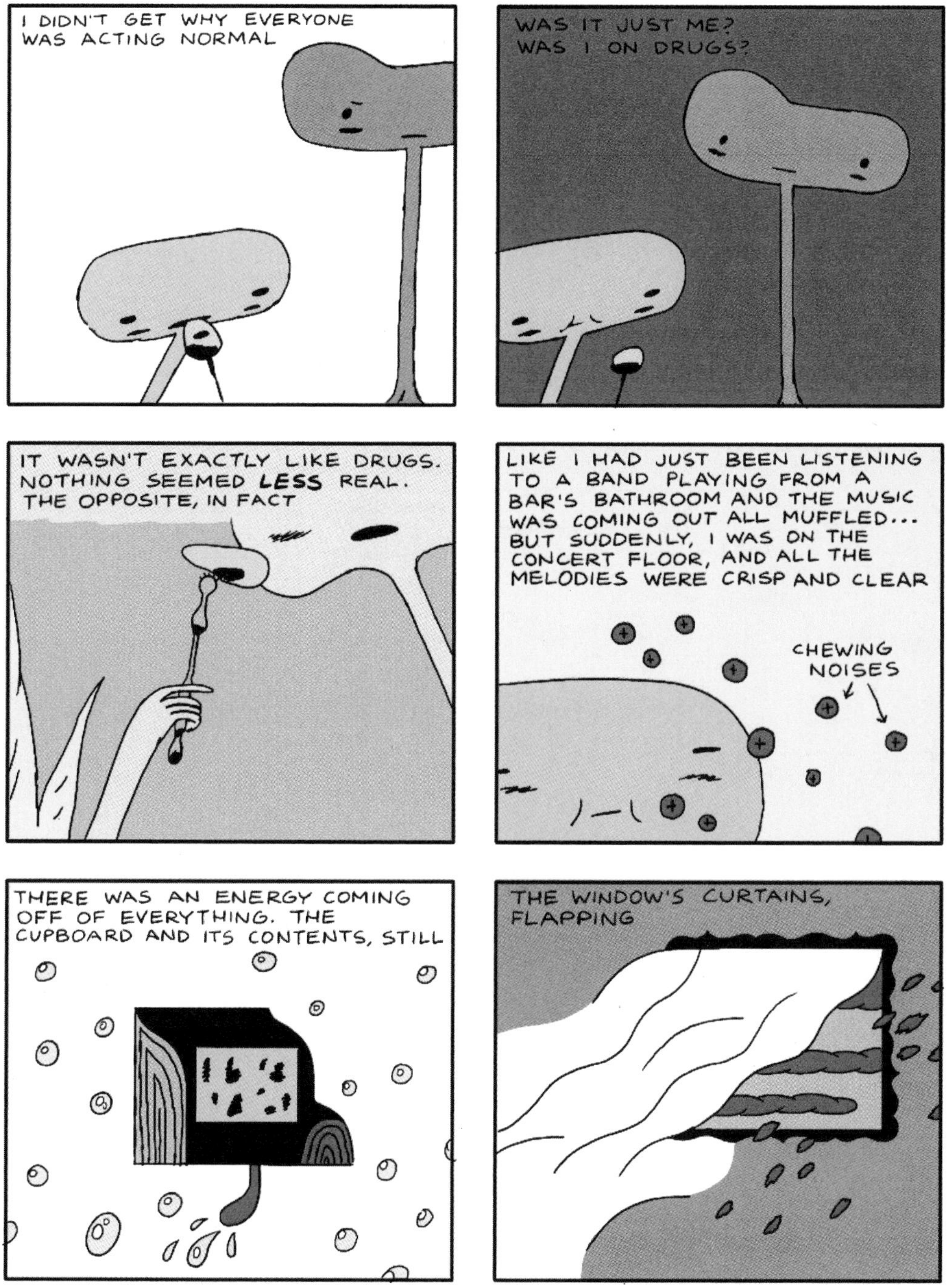

I DIDN'T GET WHY EVERYONE WAS ACTING NORMAL
WAS IT JUST ME? WAS I ON DRUGS?
IT WASN'T EXACTLY LIKE DRUGS. NOTHING SEEMED **LESS** REAL. THE OPPOSITE, IN FACT
LIKE I HAD JUST BEEN LISTENING TO A BAND PLAYING FROM A BAR'S BATHROOM AND THE MUSIC WAS COMING OUT ALL MUFFLED... BUT SUDDENLY, I WAS ON THE CONCERT FLOOR, AND ALL THE MELODIES WERE CRISP AND CLEAR
CHEWING NOISES
THERE WAS AN ENERGY COMING OFF OF EVERYTHING. THE CUPBOARD AND ITS CONTENTS, STILL
THE WINDOW'S CURTAINS, FLAPPING

AN ENERGY COMING OFF OF MY MOM, OFF OF ME, OFF OF APRIL

FUZZY LITTLE BEAMS THAT WORMED ONTO OUR BODIES

BURROWING INTO OUR FLOWER BEDS

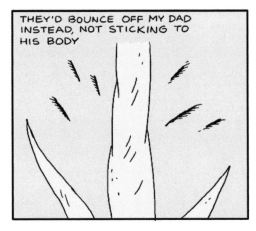

THEY'D BOUNCE OFF MY DAD INSTEAD, NOT STICKING TO HIS BODY

FORMING A HALO AROUND HIM

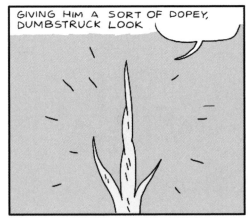

GIVING HIM A SORT OF DOPEY, DUMBSTRUCK LOOK

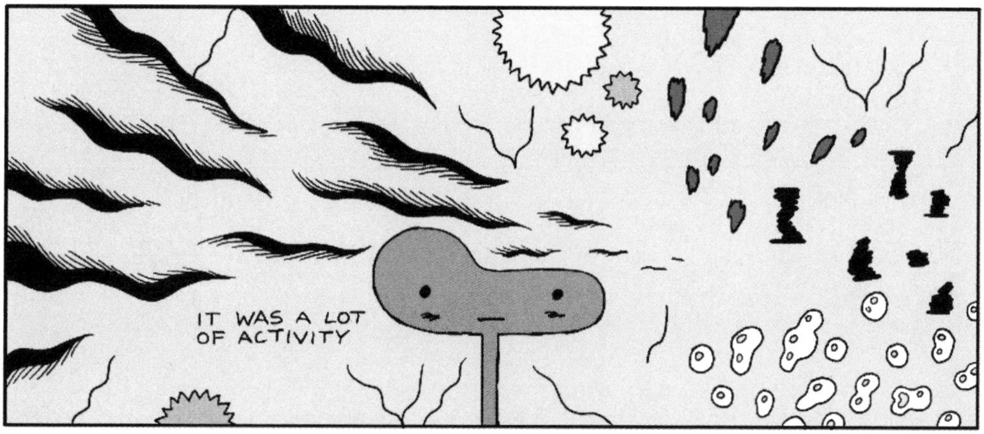
IT WAS A LOT
OF ACTIVITY

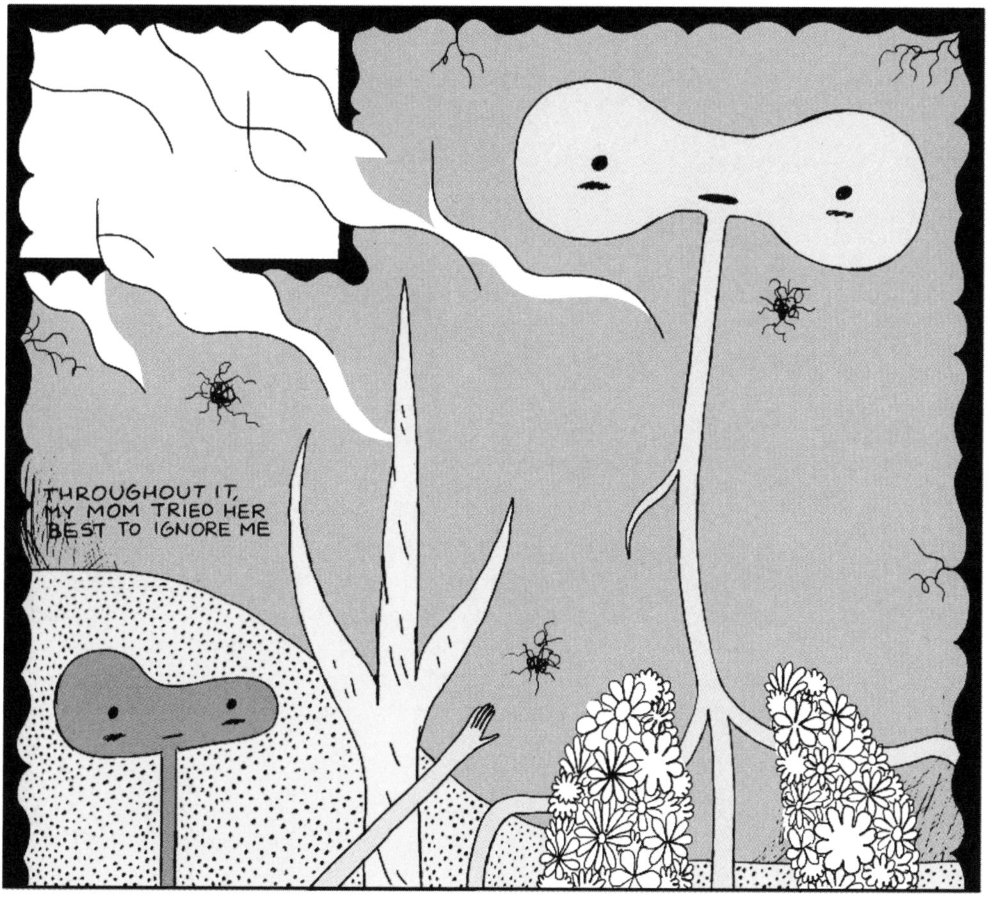
THROUGHOUT IT,
MY MOM TRIED HER
BEST TO IGNORE ME

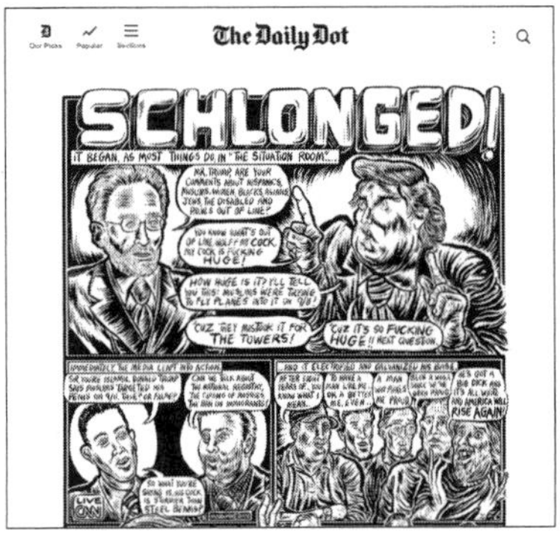
The Daily Dot
SCHLONGED!
IT BEGAN, AS MOST THINGS DO, IN "THE SITUATION ROOM"...
HUGE!
'CUZ THEY MISTOOK IT FOR THE TOWERS!
'CUZ IT'S SO FUCKING HUGE!! NEXT QUESTION
RISE AGAIN!
LIVE
CNN

# SCHLONGED!

ELI VALLEY

*originally published at*

*The Daily Dot* (dailydot.com)

BILLBOARD-HOLLYWOOD REPORTER MEDIA GROUP

digital

## Biography

Eli Valley is a writer and artist whose work has been featured in *The Nation*, the *New Republic*, the *Daily Beast*, the *Nib*, the *Village Voice*, *Gawker*, and elsewhere. He was the 2011–2013 Artist in Residence at the *Forward* newspaper, and his art has been labeled "ferociously repugnant" by *Commentary* and "hilarious" by the *Comics Journal*. Eli's comics collection, *Diaspora Boy: Comics on Crisis in America and Israel*, was released in 2017 from OR Books.
elivalley.com

## Statement

During Donald Trump's run for president, satire seemed redundant. In every respect, both personal and political, Trump exceeded the most ludicrous and offensive hyperbole. Given the multiple daily outrages, longer satirical narratives risked becoming stenography by the time they were finished. I wanted to make a comic that was both safe from this pitfall and that touched on the subtext to Trump's insecurity-laced braggadocio and race-obsessed demagoguery. A penis comic—one that tore away whatever patina of tastefulness still existed in the campaign, and that morphed into a psychosexual dreamscape involving a talking member—was the most alluring option. It would touch on Trump's serial lies as well as his ability to capture and articulate a dream that could inspire a mass movement, even if that dream was undergirded by violence, xenophobia, and racism. Besides, the fantasy didn't seem like much of a stretch: a builder of skyscrapers obsessed with reminding the world of his "hugeness," whose revulsion for the first black president touched on racial and sexual panic, isn't the most complicated analysand. Still, it felt like the single taboo that might exceed Trump's own vulgarity. But sure enough, seven weeks after the comic came out, during a Republican National Debate, I was startled to hear Trump acting out the comic: in response to taunts about the size of his hands, he started boasting, emphatically, about the size of his penis. "I guarantee you, there's no problem." Once again, he had neutralized the most extreme hyperbole (although I never confirmed whether his penis speaks and/or whether they have extended late-night arguments). I realized there's no satirical universe and no vile obscenity that won't be eclipsed by Trump's own degradations. But still, we have to try.

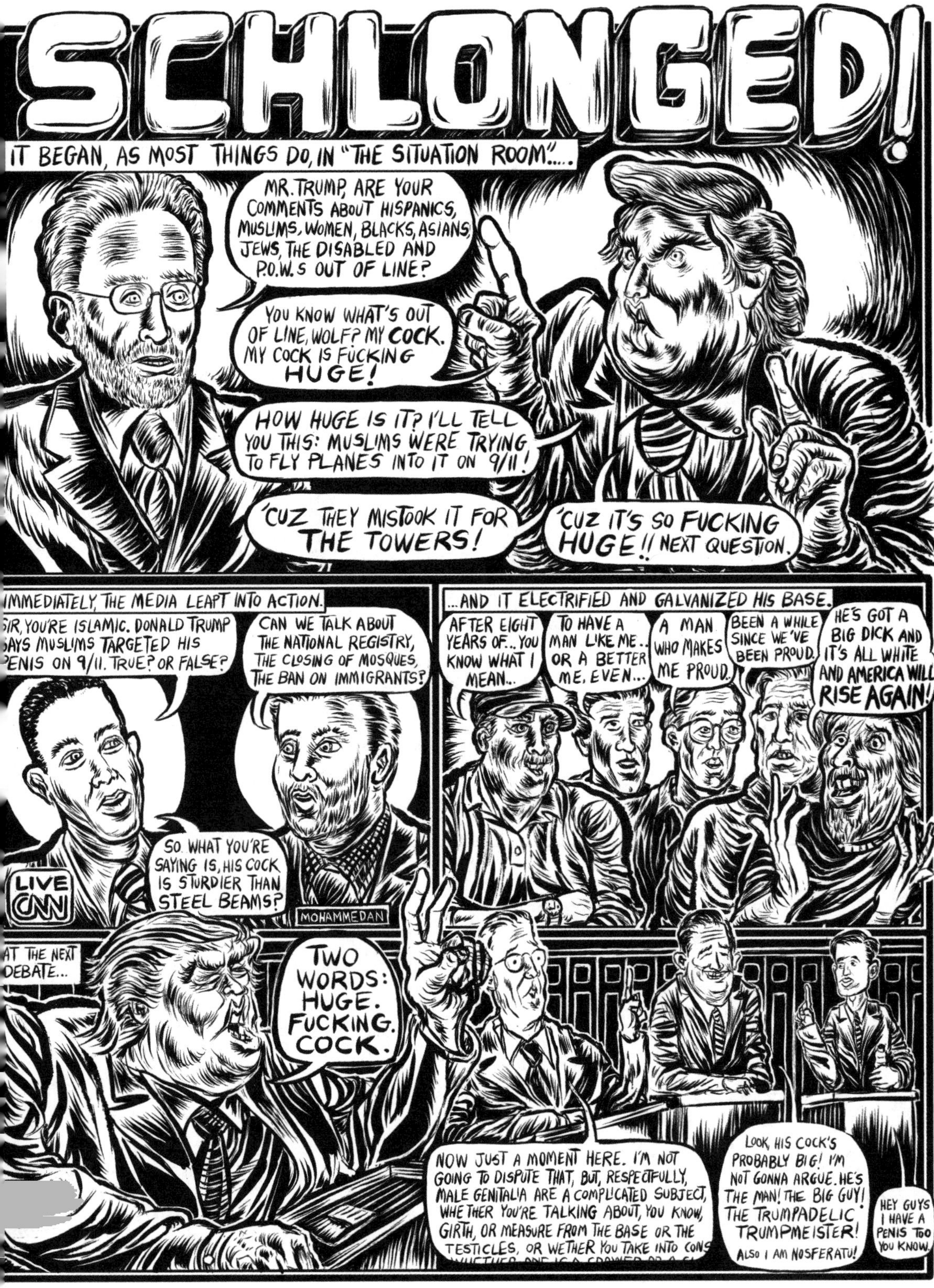
SCHLONGED!
IT BEGAN, AS MOST THINGS DO, IN "THE SITUATION ROOM"....
MR. TRUMP, ARE YOUR COMMENTS ABOUT HISPANICS, MUSLIMS, WOMEN, BLACKS, ASIANS, JEWS, THE DISABLED AND P.O.W.S OUT OF LINE?
YOU KNOW WHAT'S OUT OF LINE, WOLF? MY COCK. MY COCK IS FUCKING HUGE!
HOW HUGE IS IT? I'LL TELL YOU THIS: MUSLIMS WERE TRYING TO FLY PLANES INTO IT ON 9/11!
'CUZ THEY MISTOOK IT FOR THE TOWERS!
'CUZ IT'S SO FUCKING HUGE!! NEXT QUESTION.
IMMEDIATELY, THE MEDIA LEAPT INTO ACTION.
SIR, YOU'RE ISLAMIC. DONALD TRUMP SAYS MUSLIMS TARGETED HIS PENIS ON 9/11. TRUE? OR FALSE?
CAN WE TALK ABOUT THE NATIONAL REGISTRY, THE CLOSING OF MOSQUES, THE BAN ON IMMIGRANTS?
SO. WHAT YOU'RE SAYING IS, HIS COCK IS STURDIER THAN STEEL BEAMS?
LIVE
CNN
MOHAMMEDAN
...AND IT ELECTRIFIED AND GALVANIZED HIS BASE.
AFTER EIGHT YEARS OF... YOU KNOW WHAT I MEAN...
TO HAVE A MAN LIKE ME.. OR A BETTER ME, EVEN...
A MAN WHO MAKES ME PROUD.
BEEN A WHILE SINCE WE'VE BEEN PROUD.
HE'S GOT A BIG DICK AND IT'S ALL WHITE AND AMERICA WILL RISE AGAIN!
AT THE NEXT DEBATE...
TWO WORDS: HUGE. FUCKING. COCK.
NOW JUST A MOMENT HERE. I'M NOT GOING TO DISPUTE THAT, BUT, RESPECTFULLY, MALE GENITALIA ARE A COMPLICATED SUBJECT, WHETHER YOU'RE TALKING ABOUT, YOU KNOW, GIRTH, OR MEASURE FROM THE BASE OR THE TESTICLES, OR WETHER YOU TAKE INTO CONS
LOOK, HIS COCK'S PROBABLY BIG! I'M NOT GONNA ARGUE. HE'S THE MAN! THE BIG GUY! THE TRUMPADELIC TRUMPMEISTER! ALSO I AM NOSFERATU!
HEY GUYS I HAVE A PENIS TOO YOU KNOW.

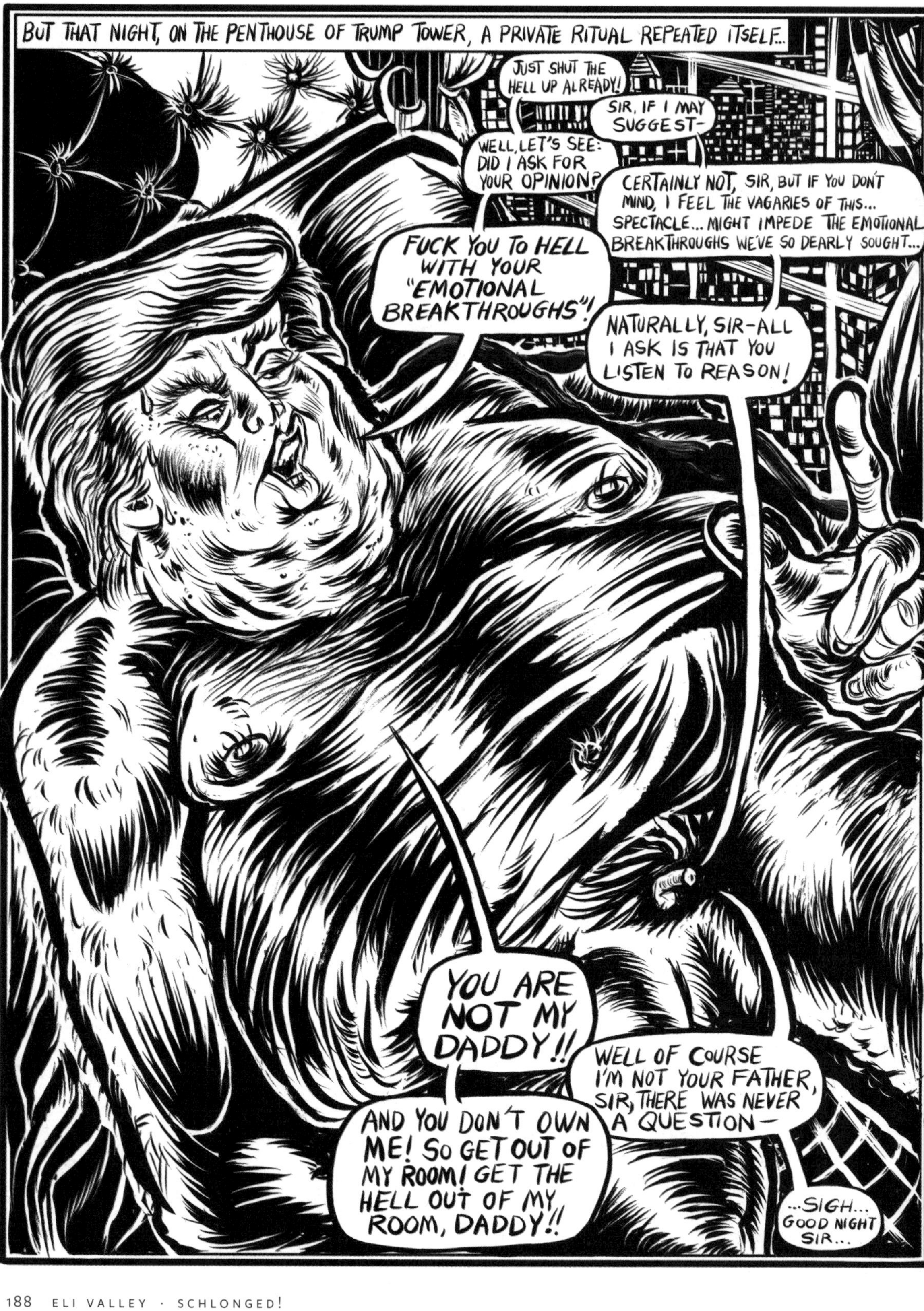
BUT THAT NIGHT, ON THE PENTHOUSE OF TRUMP TOWER, A PRIVATE RITUAL REPEATED ITSELF...
JUST SHUT THE HELL UP ALREADY!
SIR, IF I MAY SUGGEST-
WELL, LET'S SEE: DID I ASK FOR YOUR OPINION?
CERTAINLY NOT, SIR, BUT IF YOU DON'T MIND, I FEEL THE VAGARIES OF THIS... SPECTACLE... MIGHT IMPEDE THE EMOTIONAL BREAKTHROUGHS WE'VE SO DEARLY SOUGHT...
FUCK YOU TO HELL WITH YOUR "EMOTIONAL BREAKTHROUGHS"!
NATURALLY, SIR-ALL I ASK IS THAT YOU LISTEN TO REASON!
YOU ARE NOT MY DADDY!!
WELL OF COURSE I'M NOT YOUR FATHER, SIR, THERE WAS NEVER A QUESTION-
AND YOU DON'T OWN ME! SO GET OUT OF MY ROOM! GET THE HELL OUT OF MY ROOM, DADDY!!
...SIGH... GOOD NIGHT SIR...

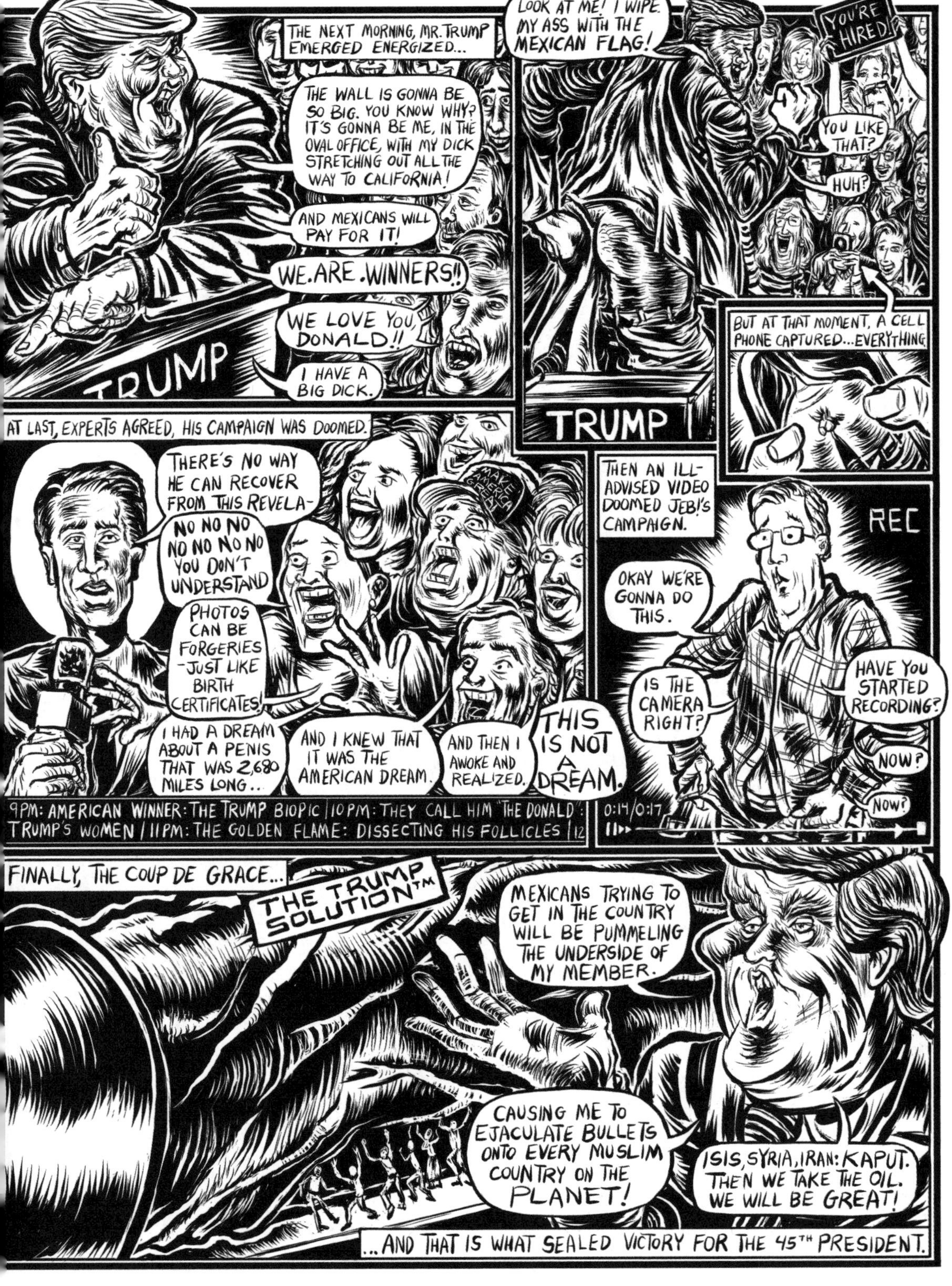
THE NEXT MORNING, MR. TRUMP EMERGED ENERGIZED...
THE WALL IS GONNA BE SO BIG. YOU KNOW WHY? IT'S GONNA BE ME, IN THE OVAL OFFICE, WITH MY DICK STRETCHING OUT ALL THE WAY TO CALIFORNIA!
AND MEXICANS WILL PAY FOR IT!
WE. ARE. WINNERS!!
WE LOVE YOU, DONALD!!
I HAVE A BIG DICK.
TRUMP
LOOK AT ME! I WIPE MY ASS WITH THE MEXICAN FLAG!
YOU'RE HIRED!
YOU LIKE THAT?
HUH?
TRUMP
BUT AT THAT MOMENT, A CELL PHONE CAPTURED...EVERYTHING.
AT LAST, EXPERTS AGREED, HIS CAMPAIGN WAS DOOMED.
THERE'S NO WAY HE CAN RECOVER FROM THIS REVELA-
NO NO NO NO NO NO NO YOU DON'T UNDERSTAND
MAKE AMERICA GREAT
PHOTOS CAN BE FORGERIES -JUST LIKE BIRTH CERTIFICATES!
I HAD A DREAM ABOUT A PENIS THAT WAS 2,680 MILES LONG..
AND I KNEW THAT IT WAS THE AMERICAN DREAM.
AND THEN I AWOKE AND REALIZED,
THIS IS NOT A DREAM.
9PM: AMERICAN WINNER: THE TRUMP BIOPIC | 10PM: THEY CALL HIM "THE DONALD": TRUMP'S WOMEN | 11PM: THE GOLDEN FLAME: DISSECTING HIS FOLLICLES | 12
THEN AN ILL-ADVISED VIDEO DOOMED JEB!'S CAMPAIGN.
REC
OKAY WE'RE GONNA DO THIS.
IS THE CAMERA RIGHT?
HAVE YOU STARTED RECORDING?
NOW?
NOW?
0:14/0:17
FINALLY, THE COUP DE GRACE...
THE TRUMP SOLUTION™
MEXICANS TRYING TO GET IN THE COUNTRY WILL BE PUMMELING THE UNDERSIDE OF MY MEMBER.
CAUSING ME TO EJACULATE BULLETS ONTO EVERY MUSLIM COUNTRY ON THE PLANET!
ISIS, SYRIA, IRAN: KAPUT. THEN WE TAKE THE OIL. WE WILL BE GREAT!
...AND THAT IS WHAT SEALED VICTORY FOR THE 45TH PRESIDENT.

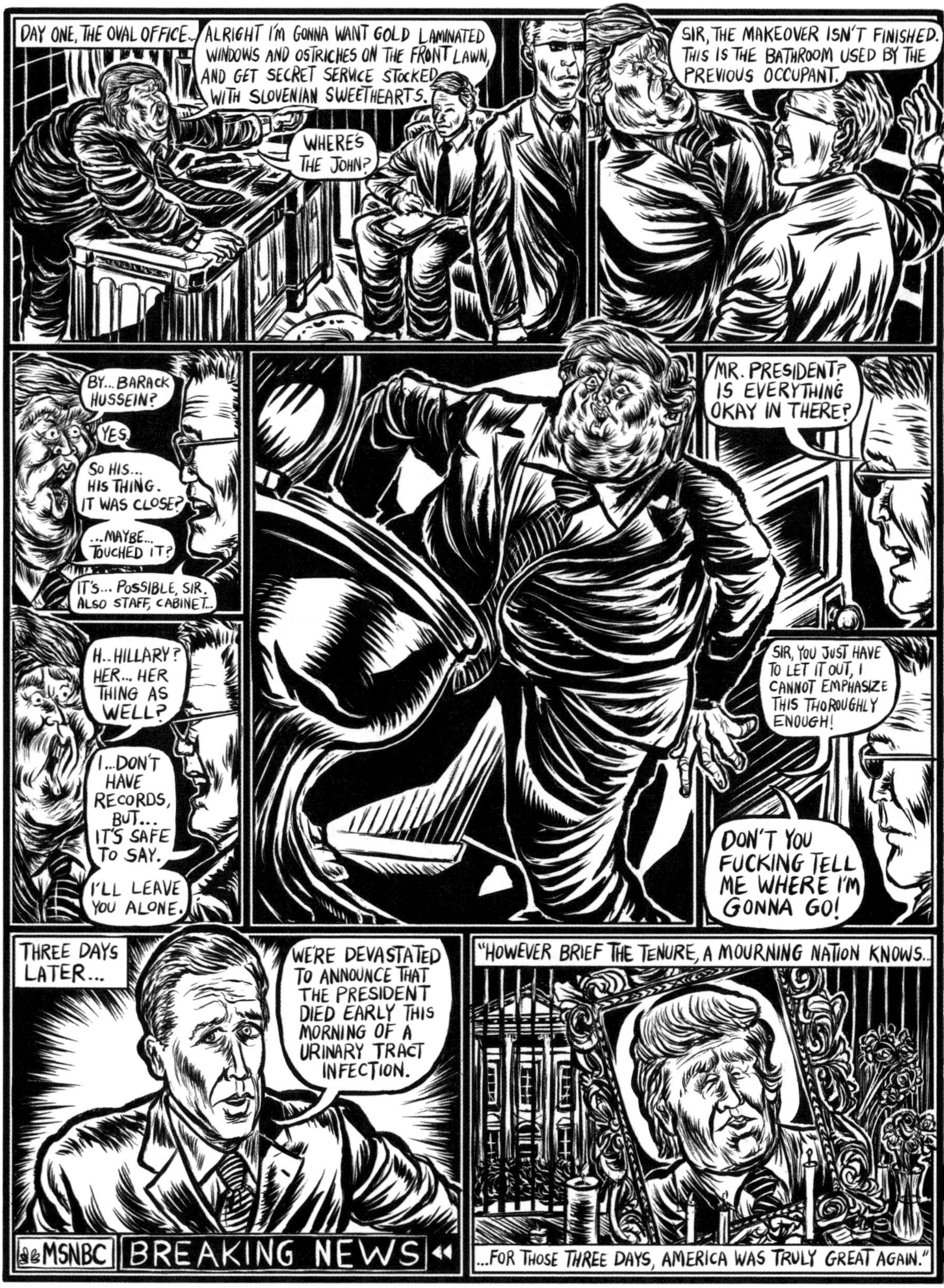
DAY ONE, THE OVAL OFFICE...
ALRIGHT I'M GONNA WANT GOLD LAMINATED WINDOWS AND OSTRICHES ON THE FRONT LAWN, AND GET SECRET SERVICE STOCKED WITH SLOVENIAN SWEETHEARTS.
WHERE'S THE JOHN?
SIR, THE MAKEOVER ISN'T FINISHED. THIS IS THE BATHROOM USED BY THE PREVIOUS OCCUPANT.
BY... BARACK HUSSEIN?
YES.
SO HIS... HIS THING. IT WAS CLOSE?
...MAYBE... TOUCHED IT?
IT'S... POSSIBLE, SIR. ALSO STAFF, CABINET...
H.. HILLARY? HER... HER THING AS WELL?
I...DON'T HAVE RECORDS, BUT... IT'S SAFE TO SAY.
I'LL LEAVE YOU ALONE.
MR. PRESIDENT? IS EVERYTHING OKAY IN THERE?
SIR, YOU JUST HAVE TO LET IT OUT, I CANNOT EMPHASIZE THIS THOROUGHLY ENOUGH!
DON'T YOU FUCKING TELL ME WHERE I'M GONNA GO!
THREE DAYS LATER...
WE'RE DEVASTATED TO ANNOUNCE THAT THE PRESIDENT DIED EARLY THIS MORNING OF A URINARY TRACT INFECTION.
MSNBC
BREAKING NEWS
"HOWEVER BRIEF THE TENURE, A MOURNING NATION KNOWS...
...FOR THOSE THREE DAYS, AMERICA WAS TRULY GREAT AGAIN."

# Good Haven High

## OSCAR AZMITIA

*exhibited at*

PURE VISION ARTS

22 × 11.5 inches / 9.5 × 13.5 inches / 10.5 × 12.5 inches • acrylic on wood

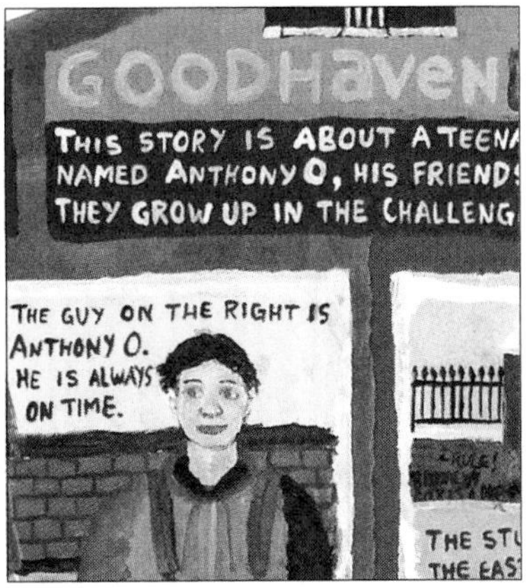
GOODHaven
THIS STORY IS ABOUT A TEEN
NAMED ANTHONY O, HIS FRIEND
THEY GROW UP IN THE CHALLENG
THE GUY ON THE RIGHT IS ANTHONY O. HE IS ALWAYS ON TIME.

### Biography

Oscar Azmitia was born in Manhattan in 1978 and raised in a very religious Christian family. He was home-schooled by his mother from ages 7 to 18. Part of his curriculum was studying and memorizing biblical scriptures and stories.

Azmitia has Asperger Syndrome, a high-functioning form of autism. He has drawn since he was a young child and is completely self-taught. He has created numerous acrylic paintings, which reflect his interests in storytelling, comic books, and popular culture.

Azmitia also paints on found objects such as coins and vintage record albums. His work has garnered an enthusiastic following and is included in numerous private collections and exhibitions.

purevisionarts.org/artists/oscar-azmitia

### Statement

My Good Haven High series is loosely autobiographical and based on the difficulties I had as a child attending New York City public and parochial schools. After those terrible educational experiences, I was then homeschooled for the rest of my education.

You see, I have Asperger Syndrome, which is a form of high-functioning autism. That made it hard to make friends, so I developed an imaginary world illustrating my feelings and memories in a comic-book style. As an adult, my paintings are a way to express the loneliness, fear, and sadness I have experienced. Humor is also important in my art and helps me get through life. In my comics, I can change the narrative and become a victorious hero interested in reconciliation instead of revenge and righting the wrongs of my past.

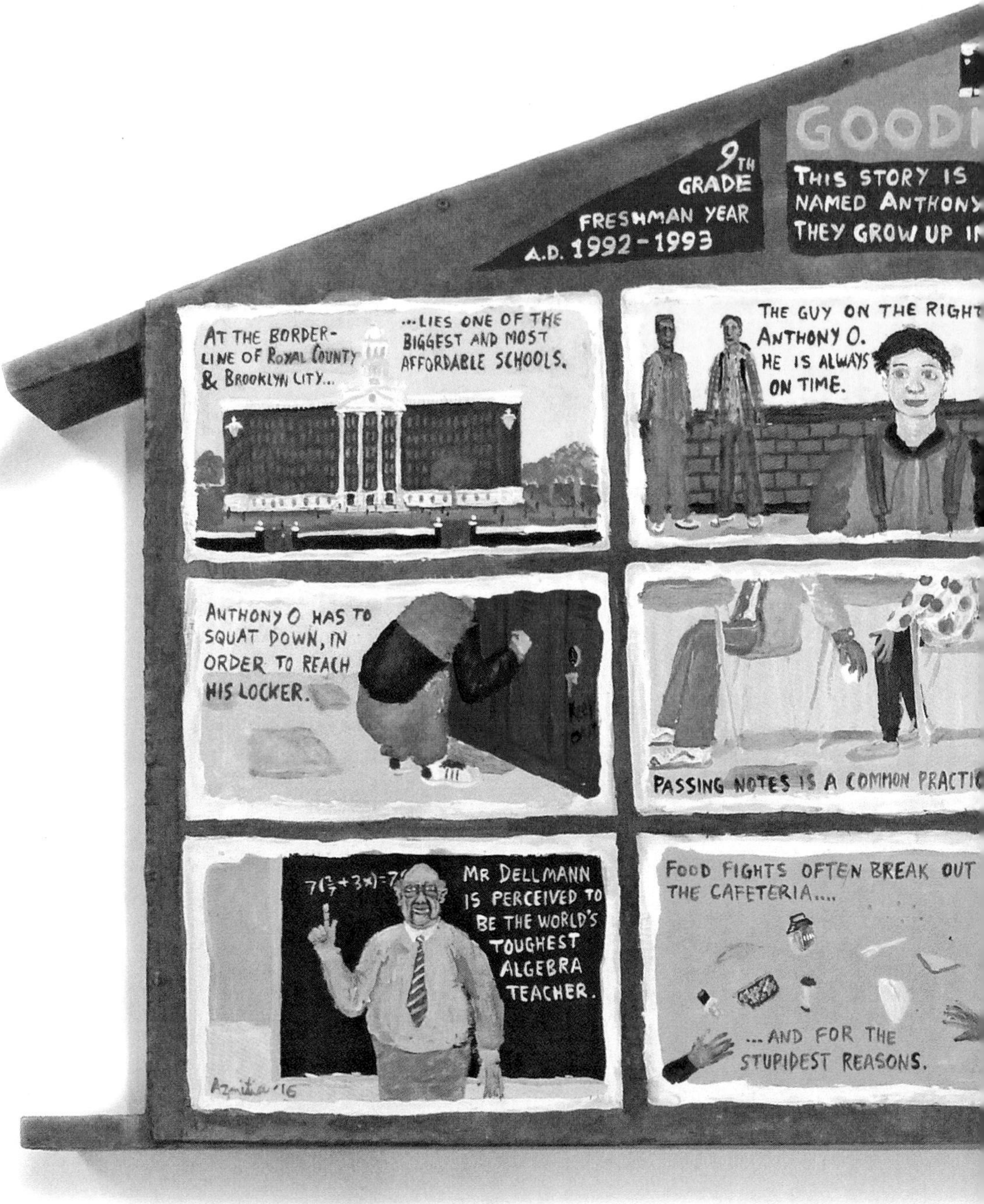
9TH GRADE
FRESHMAN YEAR
A.D. 1992-1993
GOOD
THIS STORY IS
NAMED ANTHONY
THEY GROW UP IN
AT THE BORDER-LINE OF ROYAL COUNTY & BROOKLYN CITY...
...LIES ONE OF THE BIGGEST AND MOST AFFORDABLE SCHOOLS.
THE GUY ON THE RIGHT
ANTHONY O.
HE IS ALWAYS ON TIME.
ANTHONY O HAS TO SQUAT DOWN, IN ORDER TO REACH HIS LOCKER.
PASSING NOTES IS A COMMON PRACTIC
MR DELLMANN IS PERCEIVED TO BE THE WORLD'S TOUGHEST ALGEBRA TEACHER.
FOOD FIGHTS OFTEN BREAK OUT
THE CAFETERIA....
...AND FOR THE STUPIDEST REASONS.
Azmitia '16

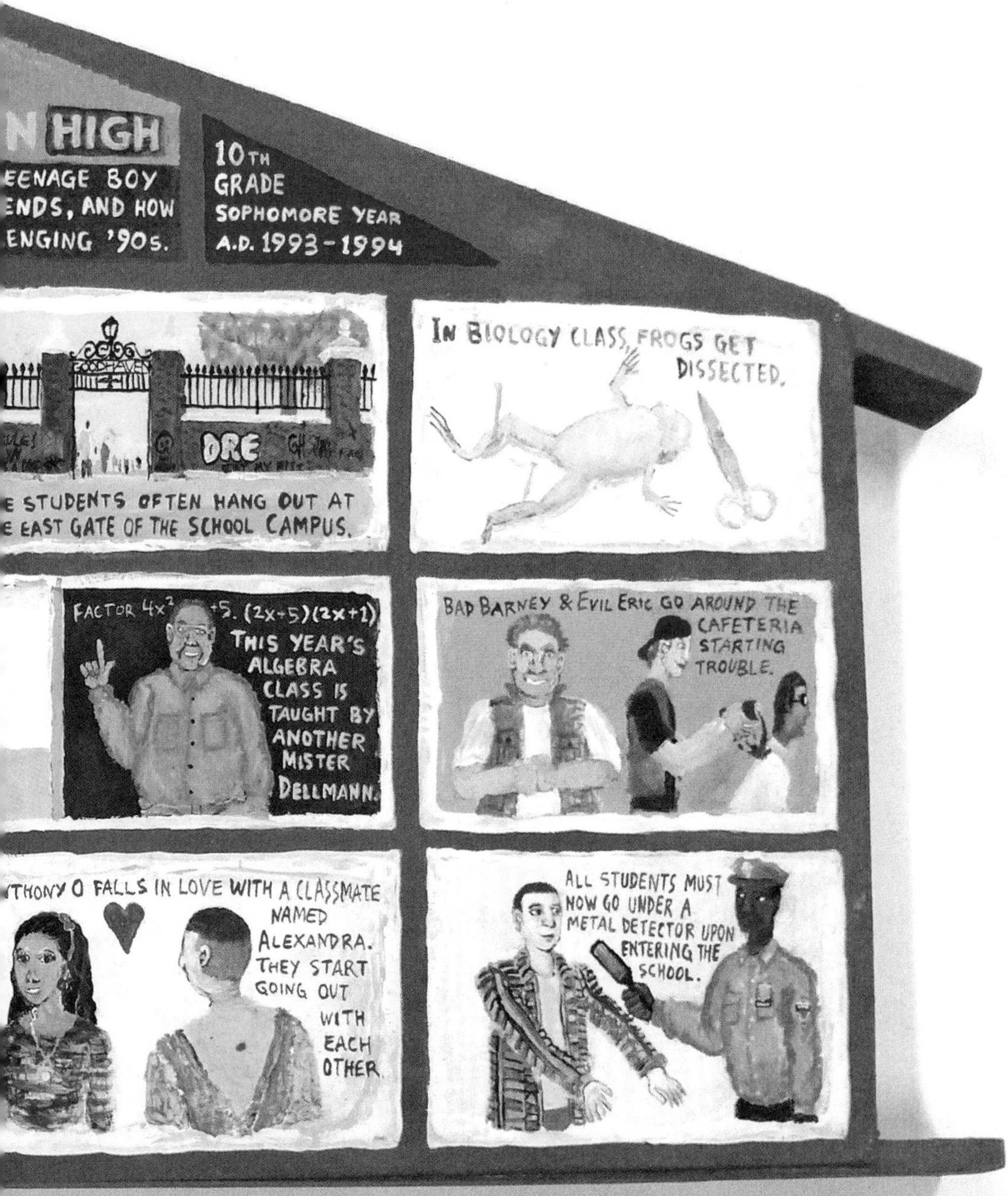
N HIGH
EENAGE BOY
ENDS, AND HOW
ENGING '90s.
10TH
GRADE
SOPHOMORE YEAR
A.D. 1993-1994
E STUDENTS OFTEN HANG OUT AT
E EAST GATE OF THE SCHOOL CAMPUS.
DRE
IN BIOLOGY CLASS, FROGS GET DISSECTED.
FACTOR 4x2 ... +5. (2x+5)(2x+1)
THIS YEAR'S ALGEBRA CLASS IS TAUGHT BY ANOTHER MISTER DELLMANN.
BAD BARNEY & EVIL ERIC GO AROUND THE CAFETERIA STARTING TROUBLE.
ITHONY O FALLS IN LOVE WITH A CLASSMATE NAMED ALEXANDRA. THEY START GOING OUT WITH EACH OTHER.
ALL STUDENTS MUST NOW GO UNDER A METAL DETECTOR UPON ENTERING THE SCHOOL.

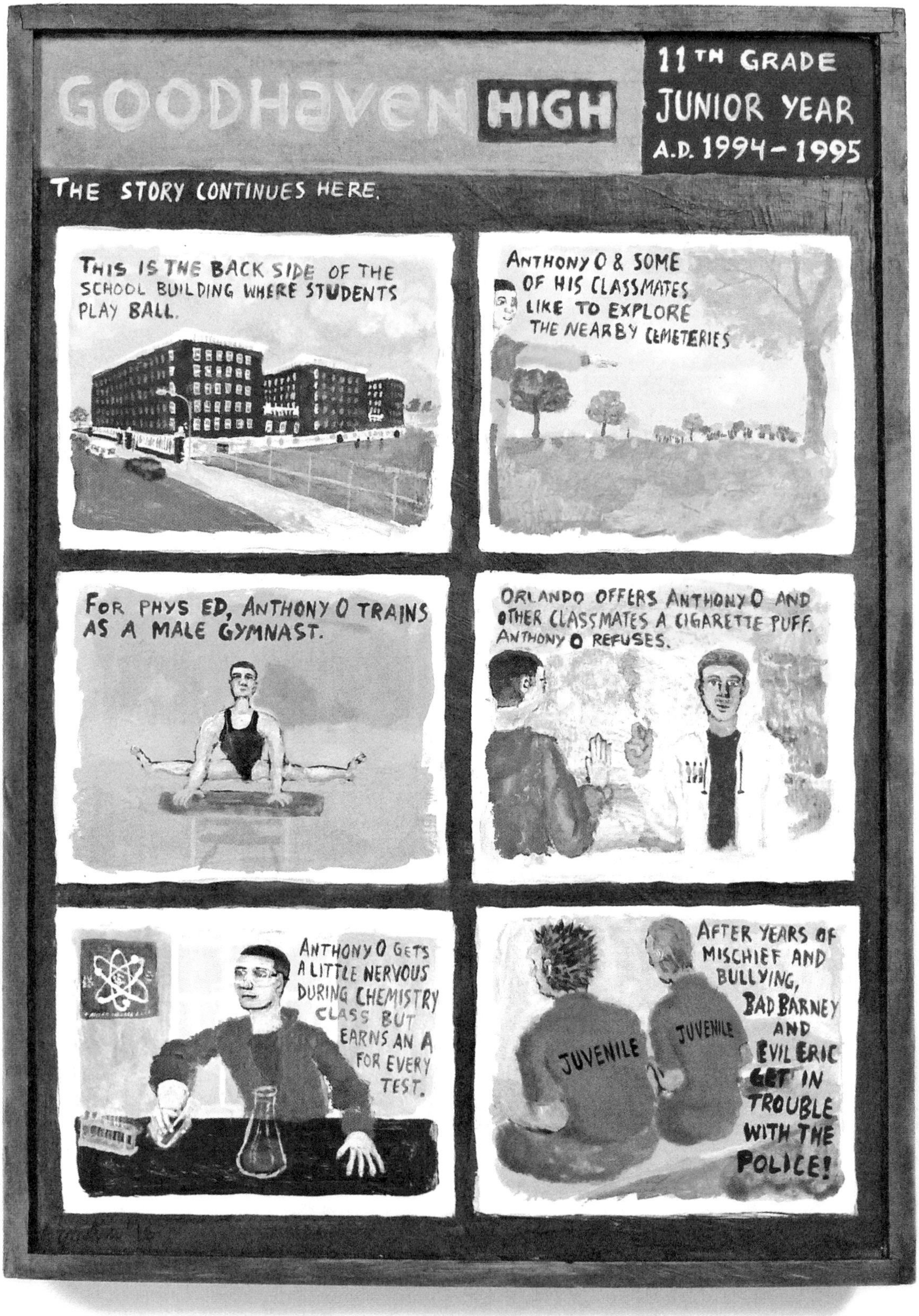
GOODHAVEN HIGH
11TH GRADE
JUNIOR YEAR
A.D. 1994 - 1995
THE STORY CONTINUES HERE.
THIS IS THE BACK SIDE OF THE SCHOOL BUILDING WHERE STUDENTS PLAY BALL.
ANTHONY O & SOME OF HIS CLASSMATES LIKE TO EXPLORE THE NEARBY CEMETERIES
FOR PHYS ED, ANTHONY O TRAINS AS A MALE GYMNAST.
ORLANDO OFFERS ANTHONY O AND OTHER CLASSMATES A CIGARETTE PUFF. ANTHONY O REFUSES.
ANTHONY O GETS A LITTLE NERVOUS DURING CHEMISTRY CLASS BUT EARNS AN A FOR EVERY TEST.
AFTER YEARS OF MISCHIEF AND BULLYING, BAD BARNEY AND EVIL ERIC GET IN TROUBLE WITH THE POLICE!
JUVENILE
JUVENILE

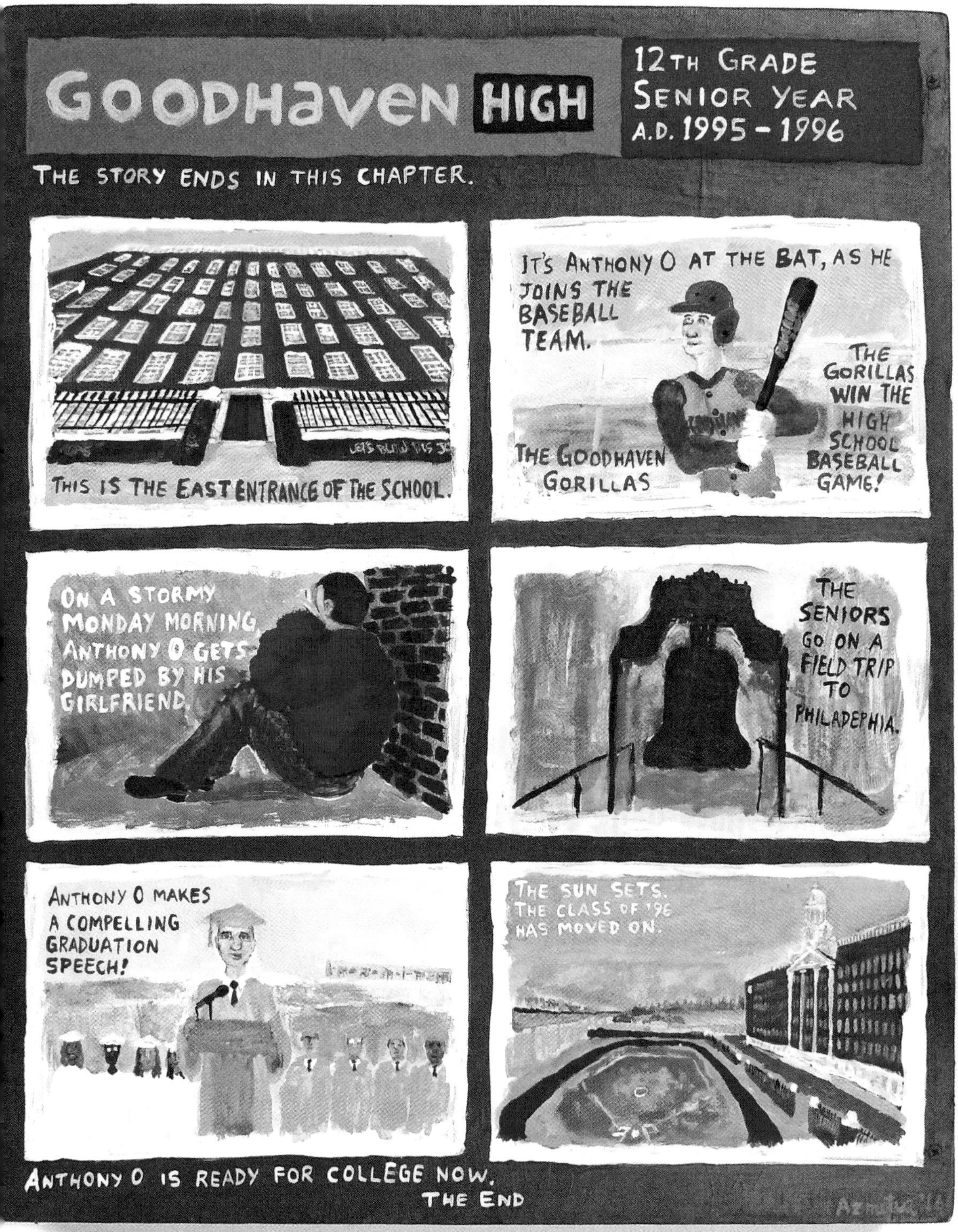
GOODHAVEN HIGH
12TH GRADE
SENIOR YEAR
A.D. 1995 - 1996
THE STORY ENDS IN THIS CHAPTER.
THIS IS THE EAST ENTRANCE OF THE SCHOOL.
IT'S ANTHONY O AT THE BAT, AS HE JOINS THE BASEBALL TEAM.
THE GOODHAVEN GORILLAS
THE GORILLAS WIN THE HIGH SCHOOL BASEBALL GAME!
ON A STORMY MONDAY MORNING, ANTHONY O GETS DUMPED BY HIS GIRLFRIEND.
THE SENIORS GO ON A FIELD TRIP TO PHILADEPHIA.
ANTHONY O MAKES A COMPELLING GRADUATION SPEECH!
THE SUN SETS. THE CLASS OF '96 HAS MOVED ON.
ANTHONY O IS READY FOR COLLEGE NOW.
THE END

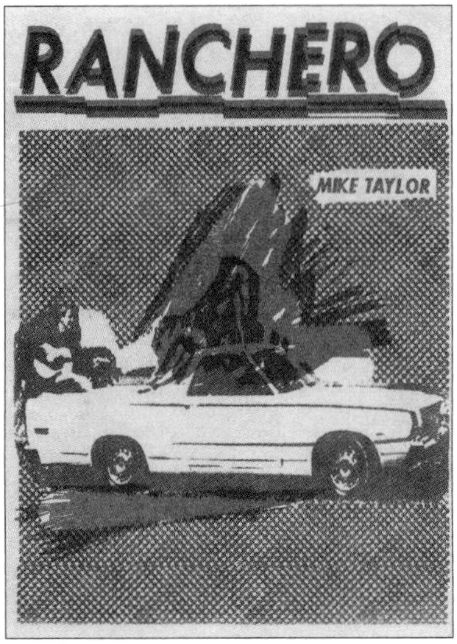
RANCHERO
MIKE TAYLOR

# Ranchero

MIKE TAYLOR

*originally published as*

*Ranchero*
PEGACORN PRESS
5.71 × 7.28 inches • 12 pages

## Biography

Besides putting out his 'zine, *Late Era Clash*, since 1994, Mike Taylor balances drawing, screen printing, and painting, trying to let each live within the other. His most recent work is a series of five screen-printed books involving the interplay of music, advertising, social media, and mind control: *No/Future*, *The Bigger Chill*, *Hammer of the Dogs*, *Unlike*, and *Love Song*.
miketaylorart.com

## Statement

*Ranchero* is based on a true story from my teenage years in a small town in Florida, but I wasn't around when it happened. I usually try to stay away from this kind of unmediated realism, but the story contains so many of the themes I work with—subculture, sexuality, authority, the secret lives of young people—that it just told itself. I now happily live with one of the delinquent girls from the story.

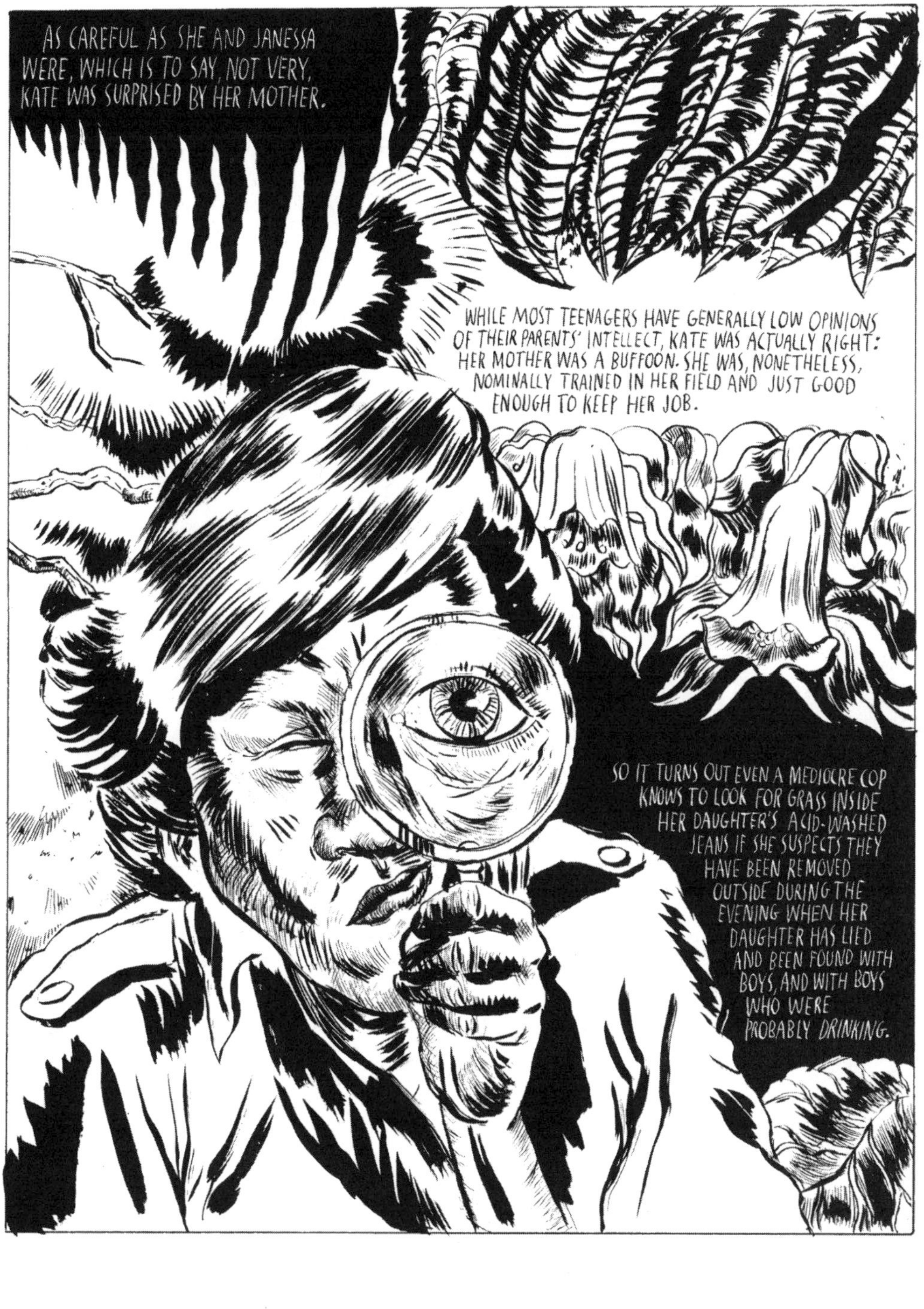
AS CAREFUL AS SHE AND JANESSA WERE, WHICH IS TO SAY, NOT VERY, KATE WAS SURPRISED BY HER MOTHER.
WHILE MOST TEENAGERS HAVE GENERALLY LOW OPINIONS OF THEIR PARENTS' INTELLECT, KATE WAS ACTUALLY RIGHT: HER MOTHER WAS A BUFFOON. SHE WAS, NONETHELESS, NOMINALLY TRAINED IN HER FIELD AND JUST GOOD ENOUGH TO KEEP HER JOB.
SO IT TURNS OUT EVEN A MEDIOCRE COP KNOWS TO LOOK FOR GRASS INSIDE HER DAUGHTER'S ACID-WASHED JEANS IF SHE SUSPECTS THEY HAVE BEEN REMOVED OUTSIDE DURING THE EVENING WHEN HER DAUGHTER HAS LIED AND BEEN FOUND WITH BOYS, AND WITH BOYS WHO WERE PROBABLY *DRINKING*.

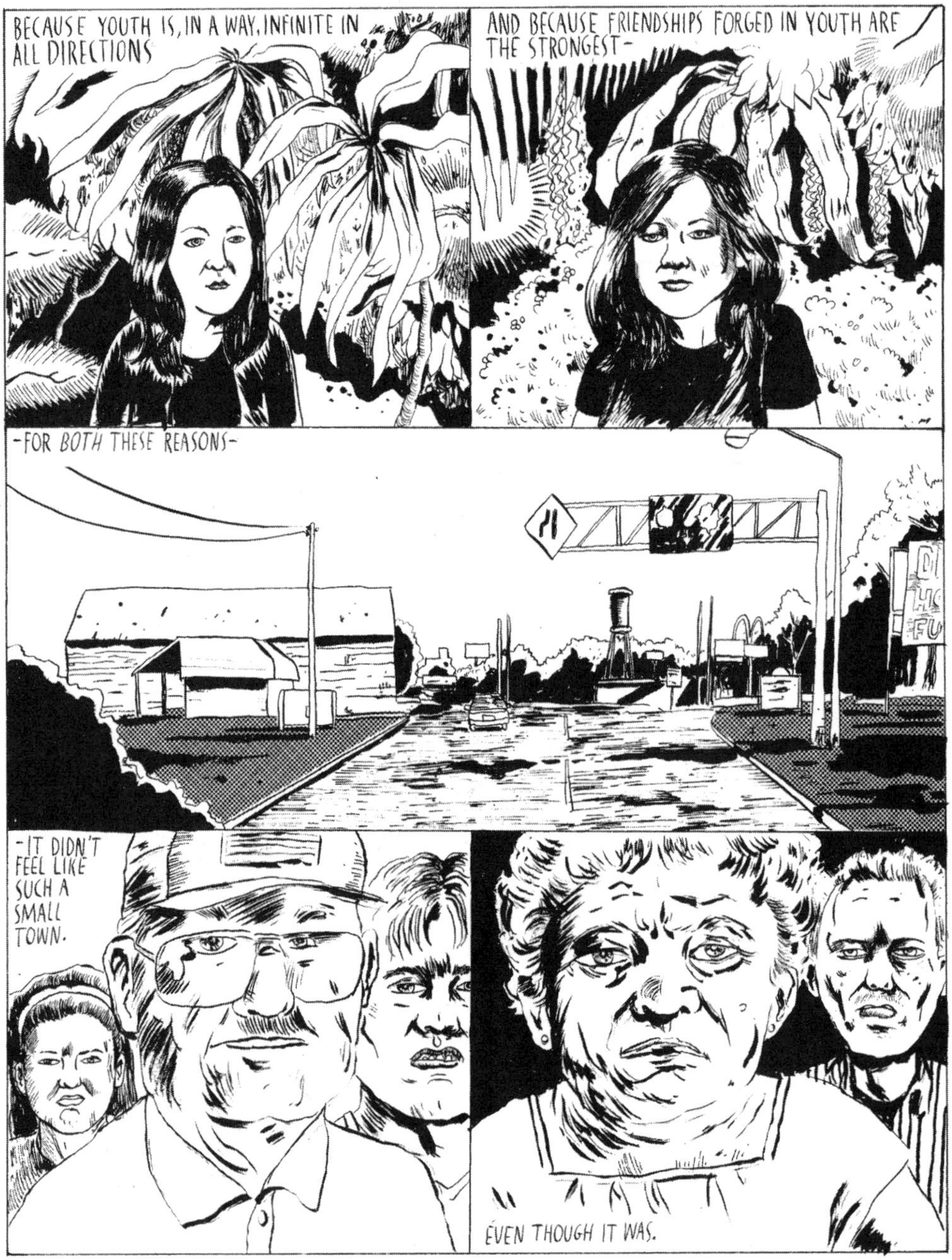
BECAUSE YOUTH IS, IN A WAY, INFINITE IN ALL DIRECTIONS
AND BECAUSE FRIENDSHIPS FORGED IN YOUTH ARE THE STRONGEST–
–FOR *BOTH* THESE REASONS–
–IT DIDN'T FEEL LIKE SUCH A SMALL TOWN.
EVEN THOUGH IT WAS.

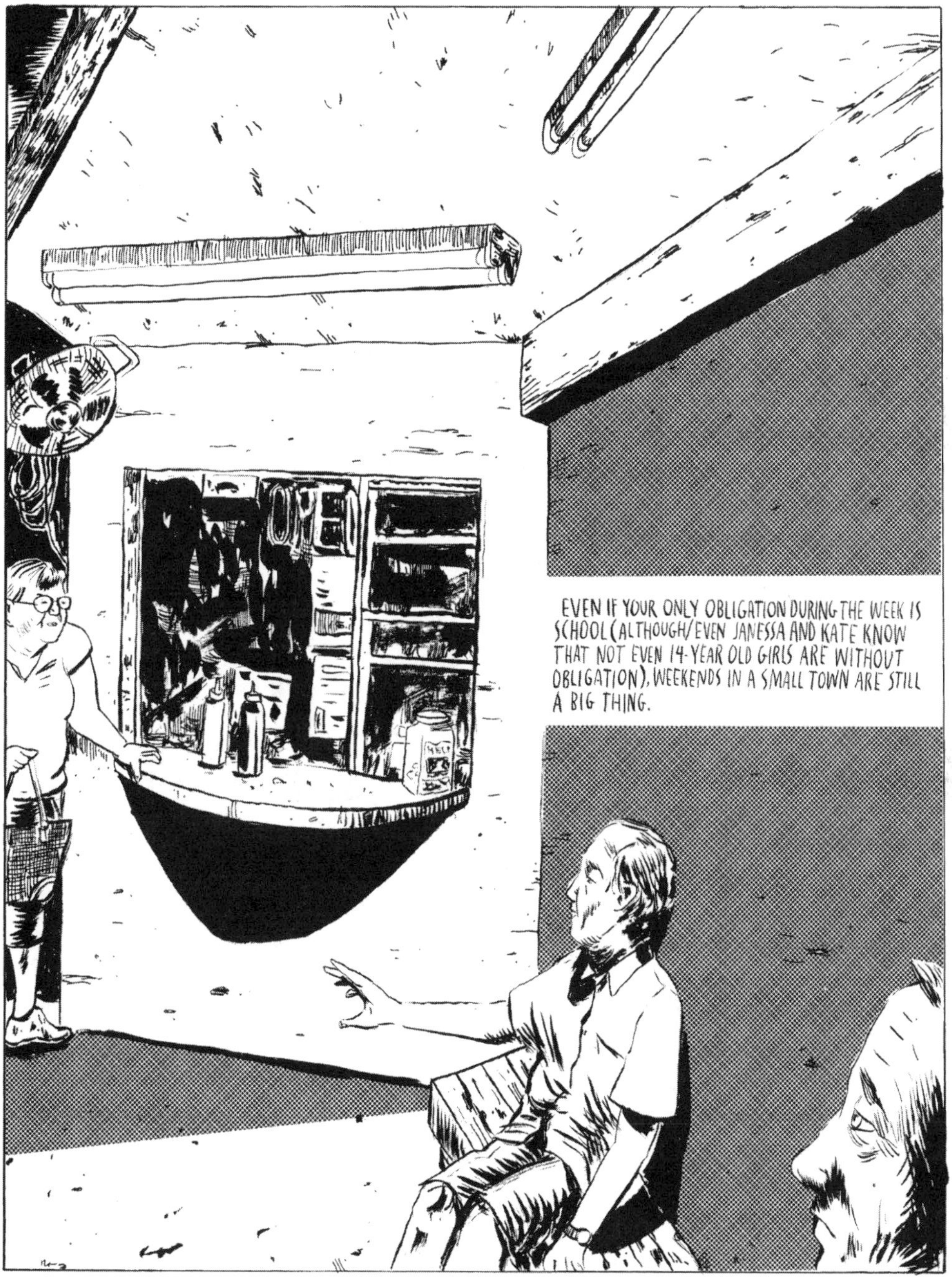
EVEN IF YOUR ONLY OBLIGATION DURING THE WEEK IS SCHOOL (ALTHOUGH/EVEN JANESSA AND KATE KNOW THAT NOT EVEN 14-YEAR OLD GIRLS ARE WITHOUT OBLIGATION), WEEKENDS IN A SMALL TOWN ARE STILL A BIG THING.

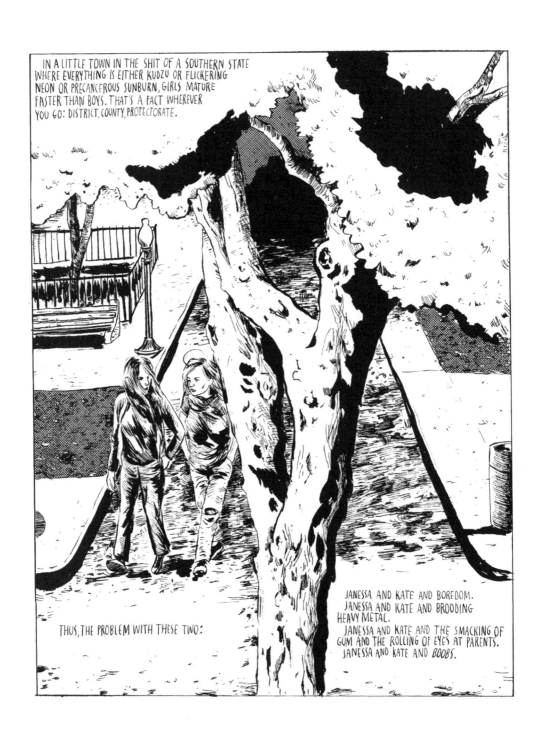

IN A LITTLE TOWN IN THE SHIT OF A SOUTHERN STATE WHERE EVERYTHING IS EITHER KUDZU OR FLICKERING NEON OR PRECANCEROUS SUNBURN, GIRLS MATURE FASTER THAN BOYS. THAT'S A FACT WHEREVER YOU GO: DISTRICT, COUNTY, PROTECTORATE.

THUS, THE PROBLEM WITH THESE TWO:

JANESSA AND KATE AND BOREDOM.
JANESSA AND KATE AND BROODING HEAVY METAL.
JANESSA AND KATE AND THE SMACKING OF GUM AND THE ROLLING OF EYES AT PARENTS.
JANESSA AND KATE AND *BOOBS*.

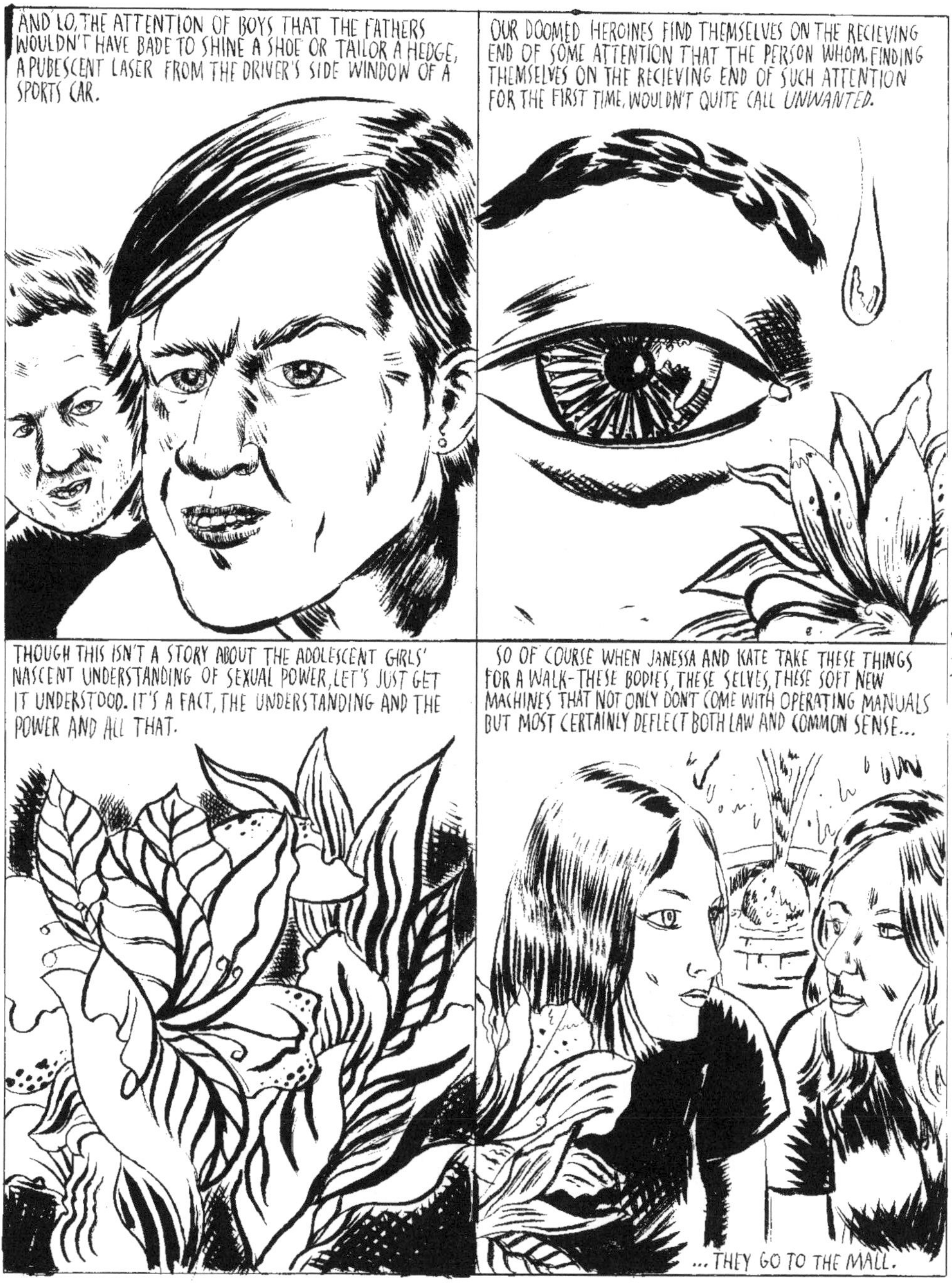
AND LO, THE ATTENTION OF BOYS THAT THE FATHERS WOULDN'T HAVE BADE TO SHINE A SHOE OR TAILOR A HEDGE, A PUBESCENT LASER FROM THE DRIVER'S SIDE WINDOW OF A SPORTS CAR.
OUR DOOMED HEROINES FIND THEMSELVES ON THE RECIEVING END OF SOME ATTENTION THAT THE PERSON WHOM, FINDING THEMSELVES ON THE RECIEVING END OF SUCH ATTENTION FOR THE FIRST TIME, WOULDN'T QUITE CALL UNWANTED.
THOUGH THIS ISN'T A STORY ABOUT THE ADOLESCENT GIRLS' NASCENT UNDERSTANDING OF SEXUAL POWER, LET'S JUST GET IT UNDERSTOOD. IT'S A FACT, THE UNDERSTANDING AND THE POWER AND ALL THAT.
SO OF COURSE WHEN JANESSA AND KATE TAKE THESE THINGS FOR A WALK-THESE BODIES, THESE SELVES, THESE SOFT NEW MACHINES THAT NOT ONLY DON'T COME WITH OPERATING MANUALS BUT MOST CERTAINLY DEFLECT BOTH LAW AND COMMON SENSE...
...THEY GO TO THE MALL.

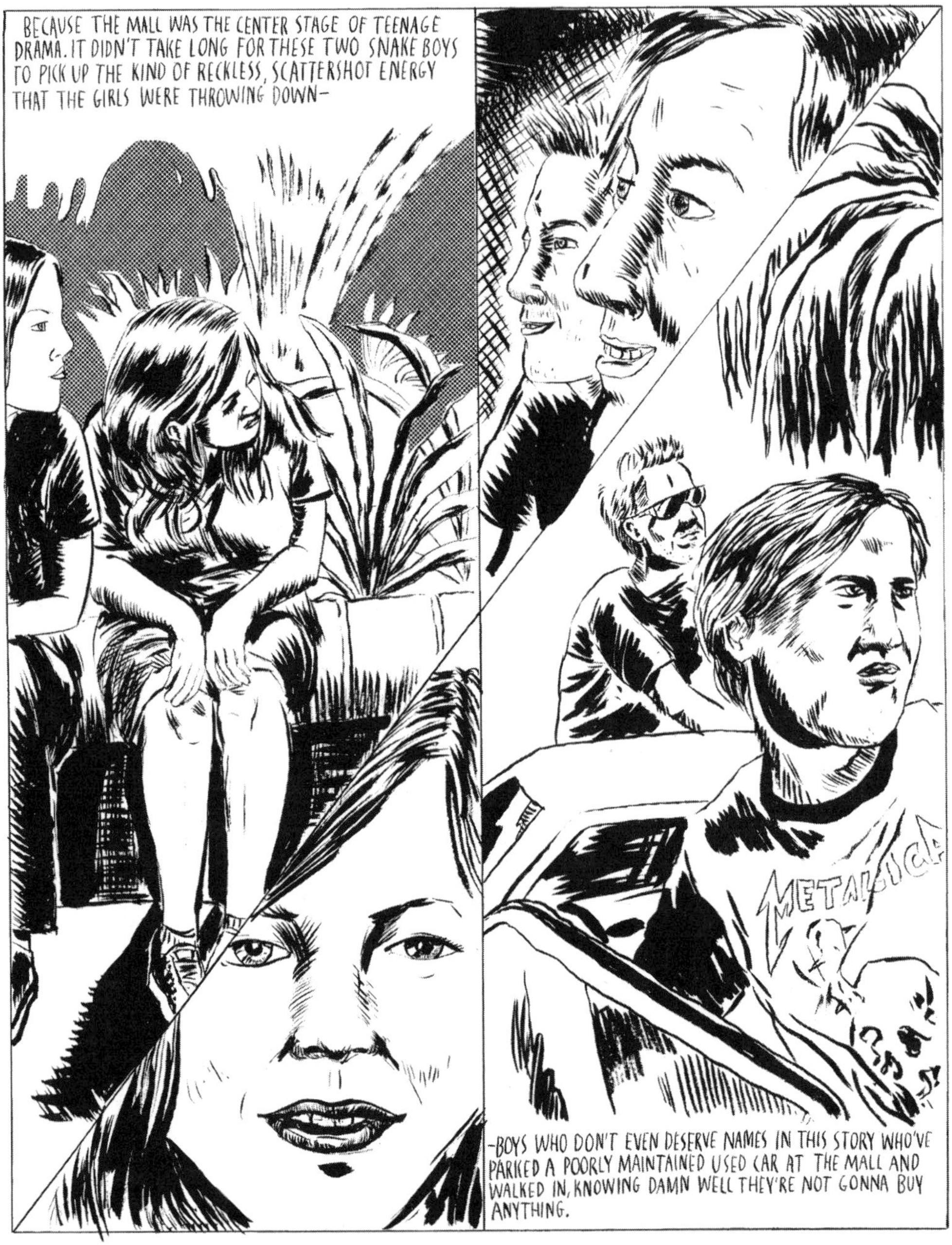
BECAUSE THE MALL WAS THE CENTER STAGE OF TEENAGE DRAMA. IT DIDN'T TAKE LONG FOR THESE TWO SNAKE BOYS TO PICK UP THE KIND OF RECKLESS, SCATTERSHOT ENERGY THAT THE GIRLS WERE THROWING DOWN–
–BOYS WHO DON'T EVEN DESERVE NAMES IN THIS STORY WHO'VE PARKED A POORLY MAINTAINED USED CAR AT THE MALL AND WALKED IN, KNOWING DAMN WELL THEY'RE NOT GONNA BUY ANYTHING.

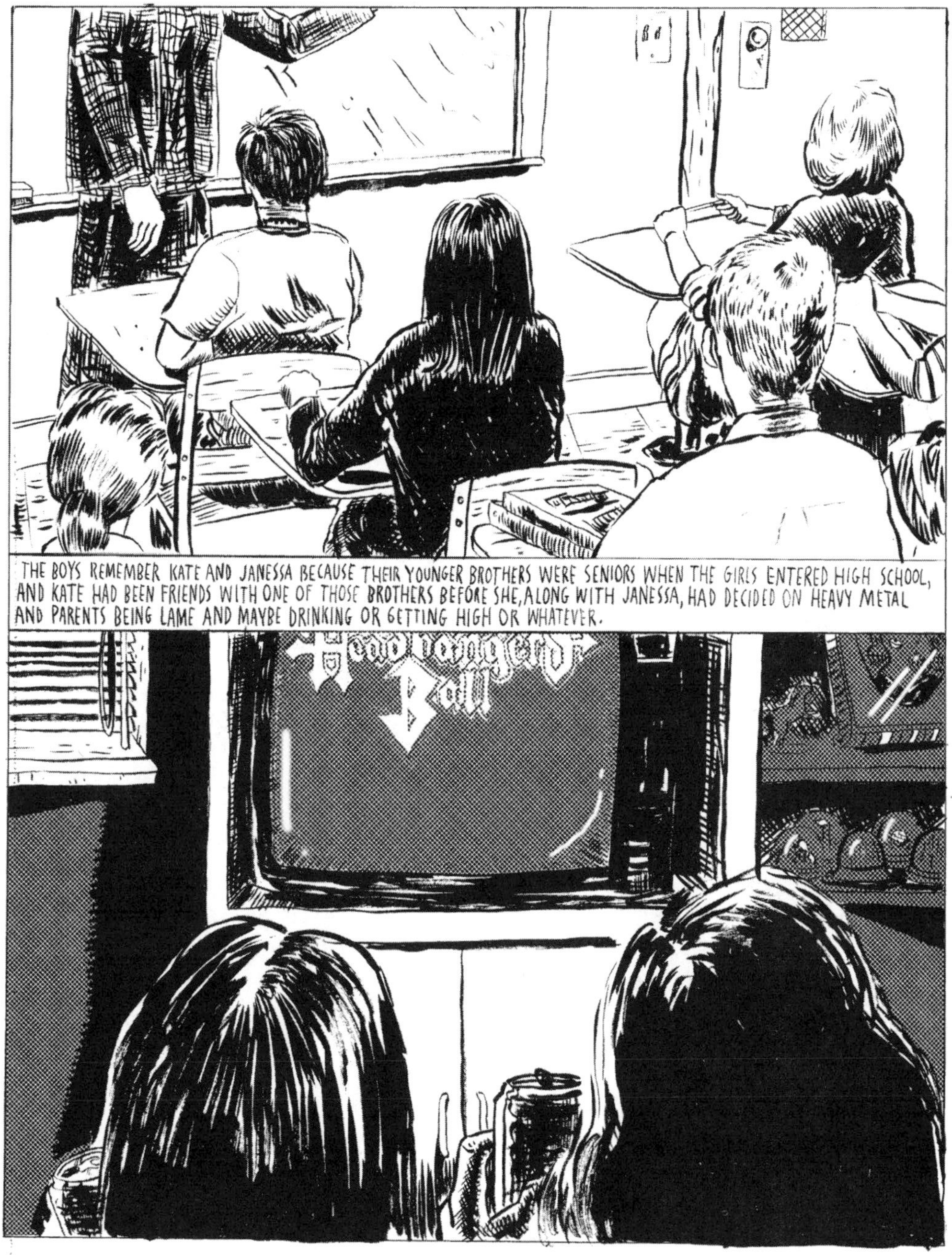
THE BOYS REMEMBER KATE AND JANESSA BECAUSE THEIR YOUNGER BROTHERS WERE SENIORS WHEN THE GIRLS ENTERED HIGH SCHOOL, AND KATE HAD BEEN FRIENDS WITH ONE OF THOSE BROTHERS BEFORE SHE, ALONG WITH JANESSA, HAD DECIDED ON HEAVY METAL AND PARENTS BEING LAME AND MAYBE DRINKING OR GETTING HIGH OR WHATEVER.

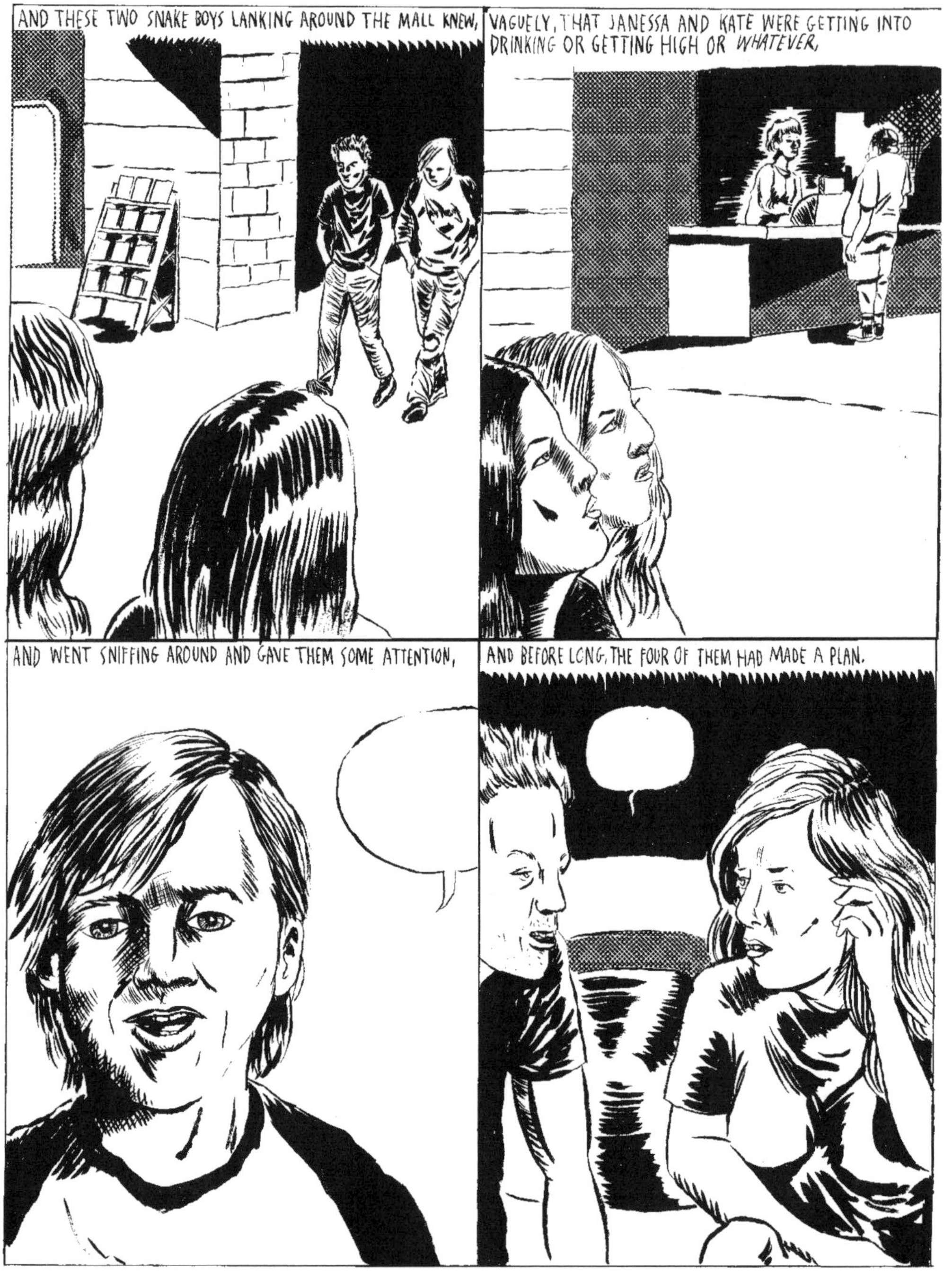
AND THESE TWO SNAKE BOYS LANKING AROUND THE MALL KNEW,
VAGUELY, THAT JANESSA AND KATE WERE GETTING INTO DRINKING OR GETTING HIGH OR WHATEVER,
AND WENT SNIFFING AROUND AND GAVE THEM SOME ATTENTION,
AND BEFORE LONG, THE FOUR OF THEM HAD MADE A PLAN.

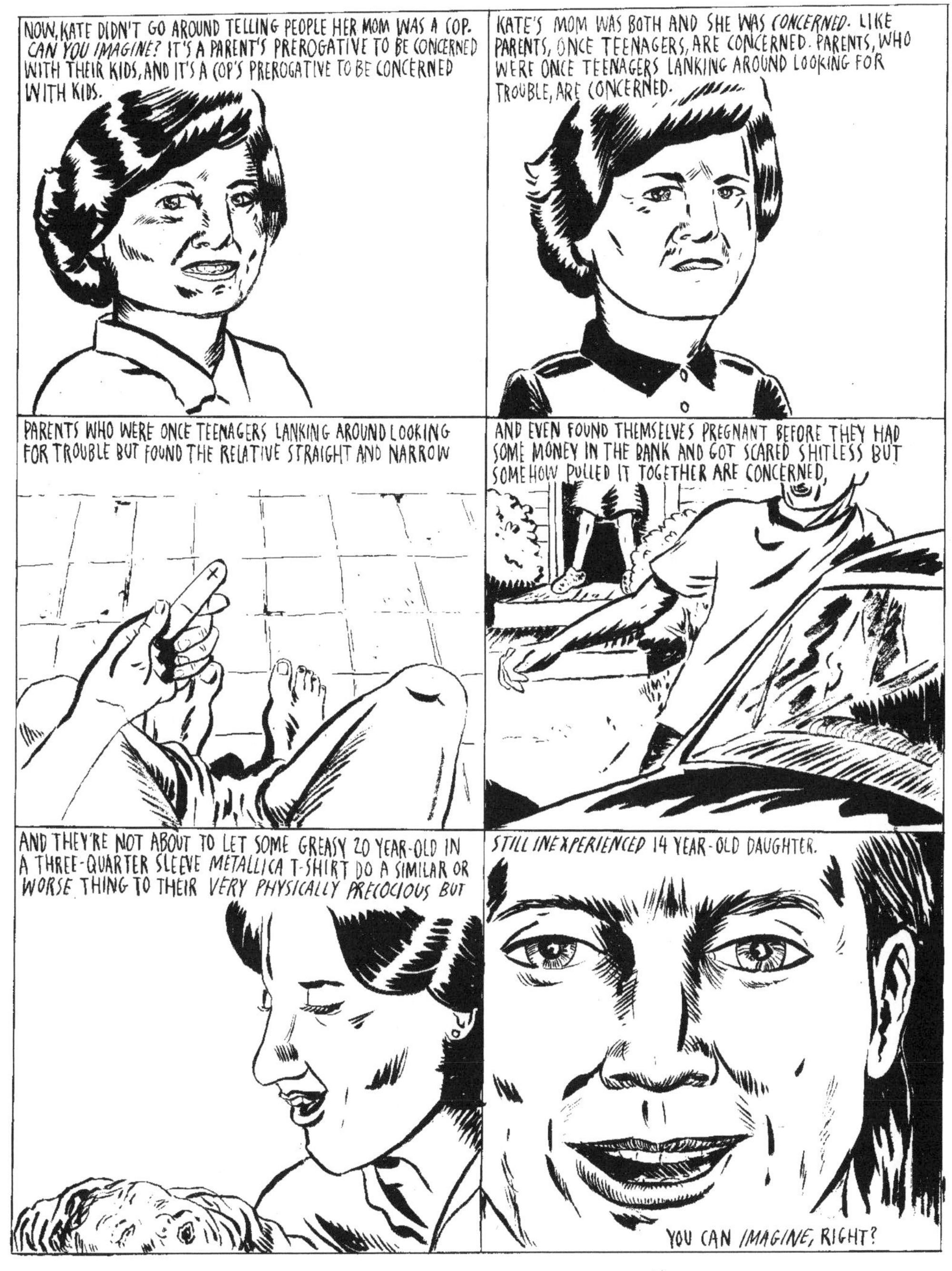
NOW, KATE DIDN'T GO AROUND TELLING PEOPLE HER MOM WAS A COP. CAN YOU IMAGINE? IT'S A PARENT'S PREROGATIVE TO BE CONCERNED WITH THEIR KIDS, AND IT'S A COP'S PREROGATIVE TO BE CONCERNED WITH KIDS.
KATE'S MOM WAS BOTH AND SHE WAS CONCERNED. LIKE PARENTS, ONCE TEENAGERS, ARE CONCERNED. PARENTS, WHO WERE ONCE TEENAGERS LANKING AROUND LOOKING FOR TROUBLE, ARE CONCERNED.
PARENTS WHO WERE ONCE TEENAGERS LANKING AROUND LOOKING FOR TROUBLE BUT FOUND THE RELATIVE STRAIGHT AND NARROW
AND EVEN FOUND THEMSELVES PREGNANT BEFORE THEY HAD SOME MONEY IN THE BANK AND GOT SCARED SHITLESS BUT SOMEHOW PULLED IT TOGETHER ARE CONCERNED,
AND THEY'RE NOT ABOUT TO LET SOME GREASY 20 YEAR-OLD IN A THREE-QUARTER SLEEVE METALLICA T-SHIRT DO A SIMILAR OR WORSE THING TO THEIR VERY PHYSICALLY PRECOCIOUS BUT
STILL INEXPERIENCED 14 YEAR-OLD DAUGHTER.
YOU CAN IMAGINE, RIGHT?

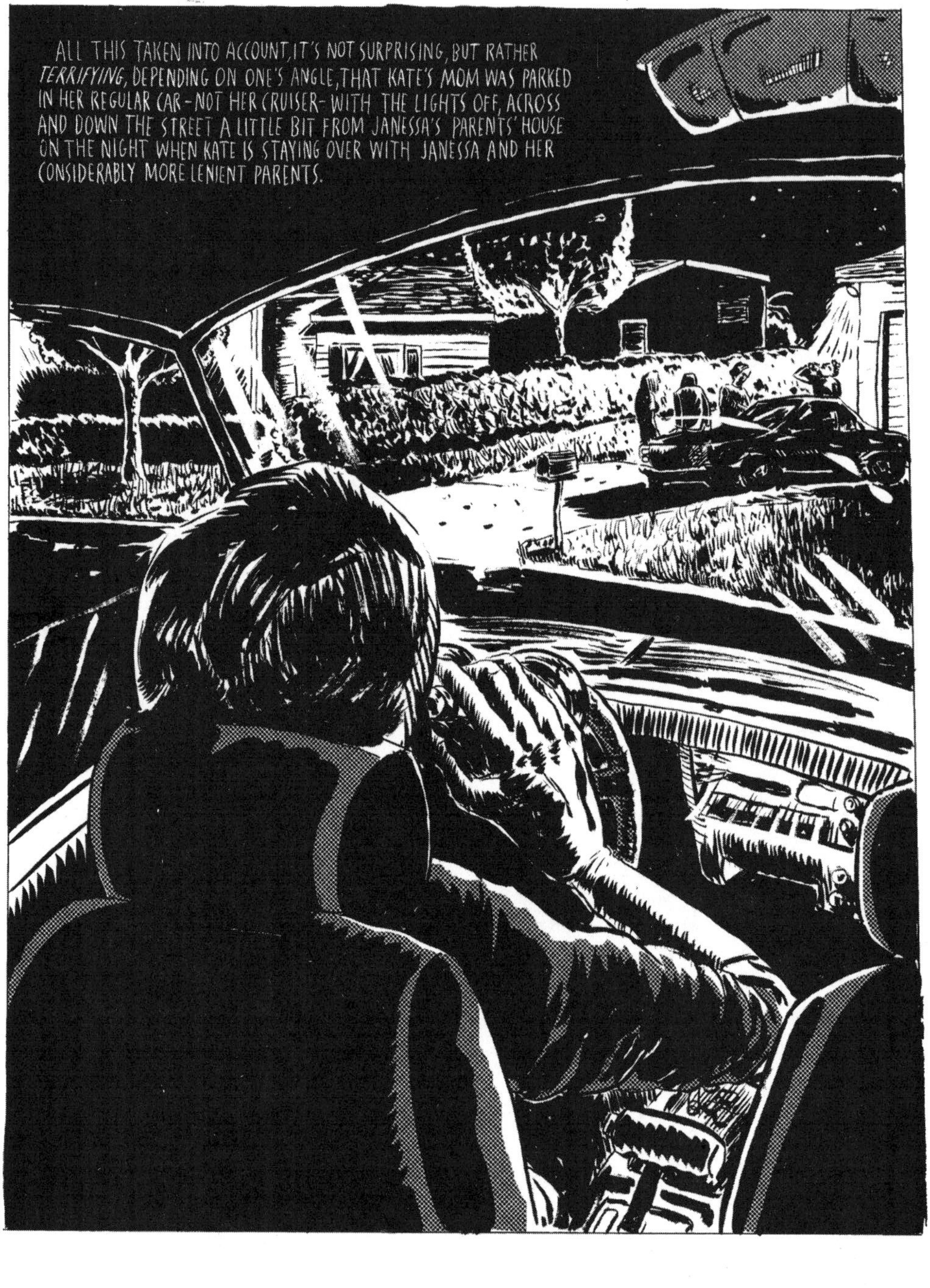
ALL THIS TAKEN INTO ACCOUNT, IT'S NOT SURPRISING, BUT RATHER *TERRIFYING*, DEPENDING ON ONE'S ANGLE, THAT KATE'S MOM WAS PARKED IN HER REGULAR CAR - NOT HER CRUISER - WITH THE LIGHTS OFF, ACROSS AND DOWN THE STREET A LITTLE BIT FROM JANESSA'S PARENTS' HOUSE ON THE NIGHT WHEN KATE IS STAYING OVER WITH JANESSA AND HER CONSIDERABLY MORE LENIENT PARENTS.

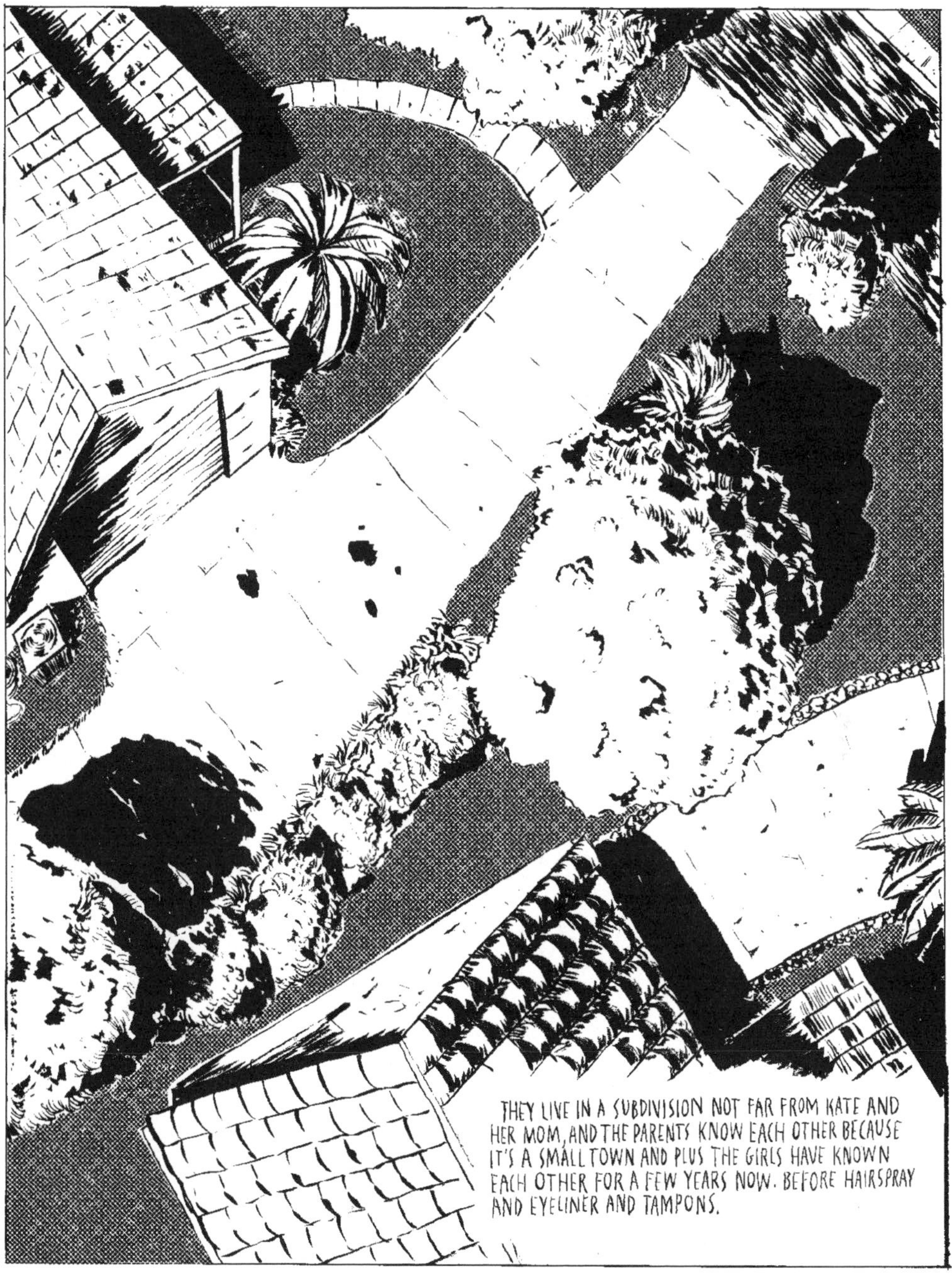
THEY LIVE IN A SUBDIVISION NOT FAR FROM KATE AND HER MOM, AND THE PARENTS KNOW EACH OTHER BECAUSE IT'S A SMALL TOWN AND PLUS THE GIRLS HAVE KNOWN EACH OTHER FOR A FEW YEARS NOW. BEFORE HAIRSPRAY AND EYELINER AND TAMPONS.

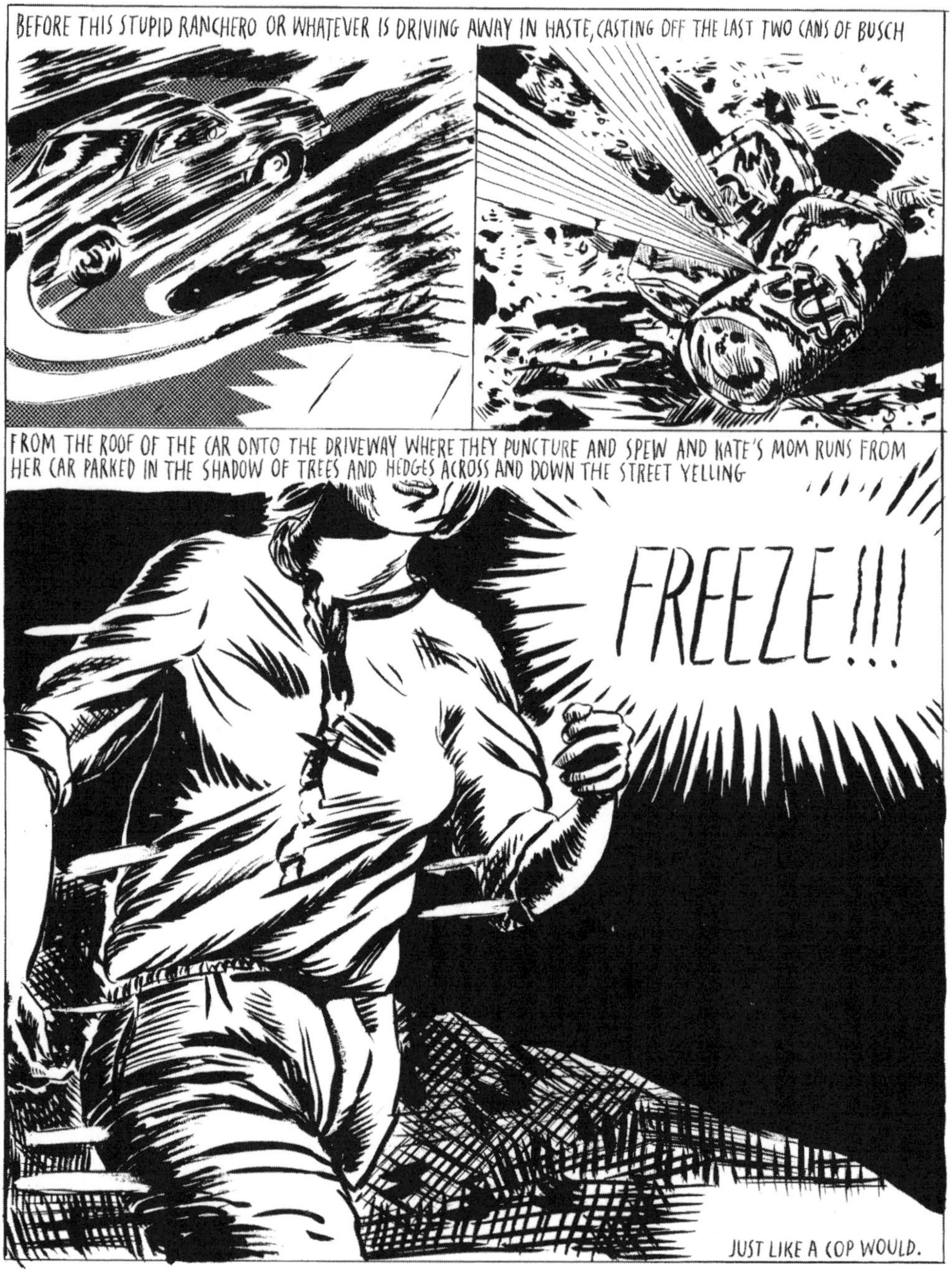
BEFORE THIS STUPID RANCHERO OR WHATEVER IS DRIVING AWAY IN HASTE, CASTING OFF THE LAST TWO CANS OF BUSCH
FROM THE ROOF OF THE CAR ONTO THE DRIVEWAY WHERE THEY PUNCTURE AND SPEW AND KATE'S MOM RUNS FROM HER CAR PARKED IN THE SHADOW OF TREES AND HEDGES ACROSS AND DOWN THE STREET YELLING
FREEZE!!!
JUST LIKE A COP WOULD.

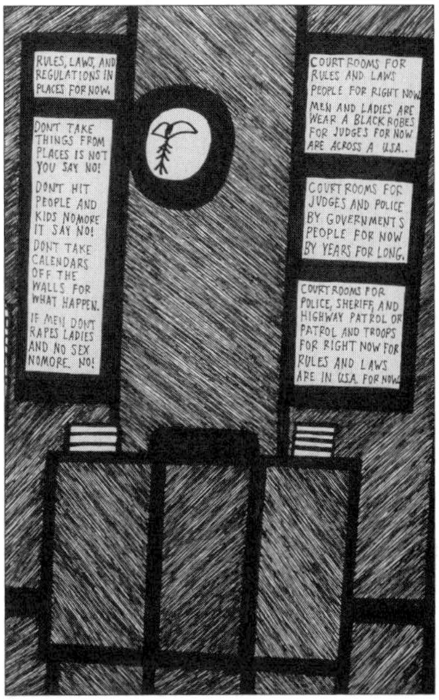
RULES, LAWS, AND REGULATIONS IN PLACES FOR NOW.
DONT TAKE THINGS FROM PLACES IS NOT YOU SAY NO!
DONT HIT PEOPLE AND KIDS NOMORE IT SAY NO!
DONT TAKE CALENDARS OFF THE WALLS FOR WHAT HAPPEN.
IF MEN DONT RAPES LADIES AND NO SEX NOMORE. NO!
COURT ROOMS FOR RULES AND LAWS PEOPLE FOR RIGHT NOW
MEN AND LADIES ARE WEAR A BLACK ROBES FOR JUDGES FOR NOW ARE ACROSS A USA..
COURT ROOMS FOR JUDGES AND POLICE BY GOVERNMENTS PEOPLE FOR NOW BY YEARS FOR LONG.
COURT ROOMS FOR POLICE, SHERIFF, AND HIGHWAY PATROL OR PATROL AND TROOPS FOR RIGHT NOW FOR RULES AND LAWS ARE IN USA. FOR NOW

# Four Untitled Pieces

## WILLIAM TYLER

*exhibited at*

CREATIVE GROWTH ART CENTER

30 × 22 inches / 22.5 × 15 inches / 30 × 22 inches / 22 × 15 inches • black marker on paper

### Biography

William Tyler was born in Cincinnati, Ohio, in 1954 and has been working at Creative Growth Art Center since 1978. His precise, ordered black marker drawings on paper reflect a fascination with fantasy and reality and the often thin line between the two. William draws images from both his personal experience and his opinion of the world and its cultural icons to create a symbolic place where order reigns over emotion but the world of make-believe rules equally with reality. William's work has been featured in New York, Miami, San Francisco, and the Museum of Everything in London.
creativegrowth.org/artists/william-tyler

### Statement

It's a long story. This text, I made it up. Sometimes, I also take things from newspapers and what I read. I've been doing it for a long time, mixing them. I started here in 1978. This is just wood grain, it's black and white but it represents something in color. These flags, they're for another planet, and other realities. I like other planets, I keep things there.

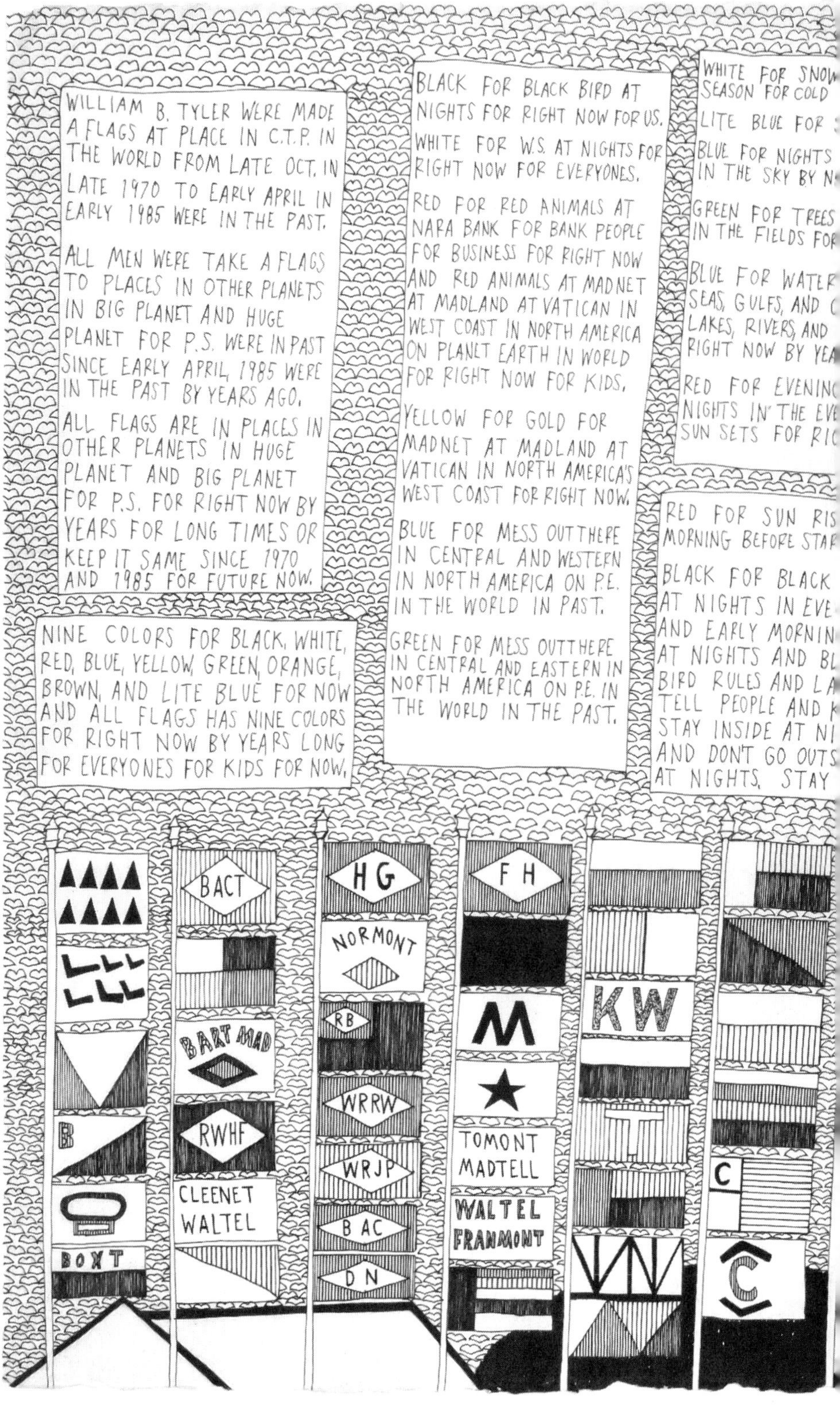

WILLIAM B. TYLER WERE MADE
A FLAGS AT PLACE IN C.T.P. IN
THE WORLD FROM LATE OCT. IN
LATE 1970 TO EARLY APRIL IN
EARLY 1985 WERE IN THE PAST.

ALL MEN WERE TAKE A FLAGS
TO PLACES IN OTHER PLANETS
IN BIG PLANET AND HUGE
PLANET FOR P.S. WERE IN PAST
SINCE EARLY APRIL, 1985 WERE
IN THE PAST BY YEARS AGO,

ALL FLAGS ARE IN PLACES IN
OTHER PLANETS IN HUGE
PLANET AND BIG PLANET
FOR P.S. FOR RIGHT NOW BY
YEARS FOR LONG TIMES OR
KEEP IT SAME SINCE 1970
AND 1985 FOR FUTURE NOW.

NINE COLORS FOR BLACK, WHITE,
RED, BLUE, YELLOW, GREEN, ORANGE,
BROWN, AND LITE BLUE FOR NOW
AND ALL FLAGS HAS NINE COLORS
FOR RIGHT NOW BY YEARS LONG
FOR EVERYONES FOR KIDS FOR NOW,

BLACK FOR BLACK BIRD AT
NIGHTS FOR RIGHT NOW FOR US.

WHITE FOR W.S. AT NIGHTS FOR
RIGHT NOW FOR EVERYONES.

RED FOR RED ANIMALS AT
NARA BANK FOR BANK PEOPLE
FOR BUSINESS FOR RIGHT NOW
AND RED ANIMALS AT MADNET
AT MADLAND AT VATICAN IN
WEST COAST IN NORTH AMERICA
ON PLANET EARTH IN WORLD
FOR RIGHT NOW FOR KIDS,

YELLOW FOR GOLD FOR
MADNET AT MADLAND AT
VATICAN IN NORTH AMERICA'S
WEST COAST FOR RIGHT NOW.

BLUE FOR MESS OUT THERE
IN CENTRAL AND WESTERN
IN NORTH AMERICA ON P.E.
IN THE WORLD IN PAST.

GREEN FOR MESS OUT THERE
IN CENTRAL AND EASTERN IN
NORTH AMERICA ON P.E. IN
THE WORLD IN THE PAST.

WHITE FOR SNOW
SEASON FOR COLD

LITE BLUE FOR
BLUE FOR NIGHTS
IN THE SKY BY N

GREEN FOR TREES
IN THE FIELDS FOR

BLUE FOR WATER
SEAS, GULFS, AND
LAKES, RIVERS AND
RIGHT NOW BY YEA

RED FOR EVENING
NIGHTS IN THE EVE
SUN SETS FOR RIG

RED FOR SUN RIS
MORNING BEFORE STAR

BLACK FOR BLACK
AT NIGHTS IN EVE
AND EARLY MORNIN
AT NIGHTS AND BL
BIRD RULES AND LA
TELL PEOPLE AND K
STAY INSIDE AT NI
AND DON'T GO OUTS
AT NIGHTS, STAY

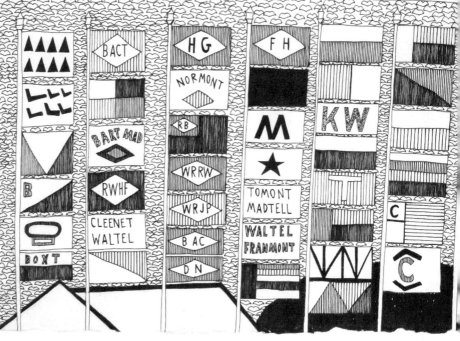

BACT

HG

FH

NORMONT

M

KW

RB

WRRW

TOMONT
MADTELL

WRJP

WALTEL
FRANMONT

C

B AC

B

BART MAD

RWHF

CLEENET
WALTEL

D N

C

BOXT

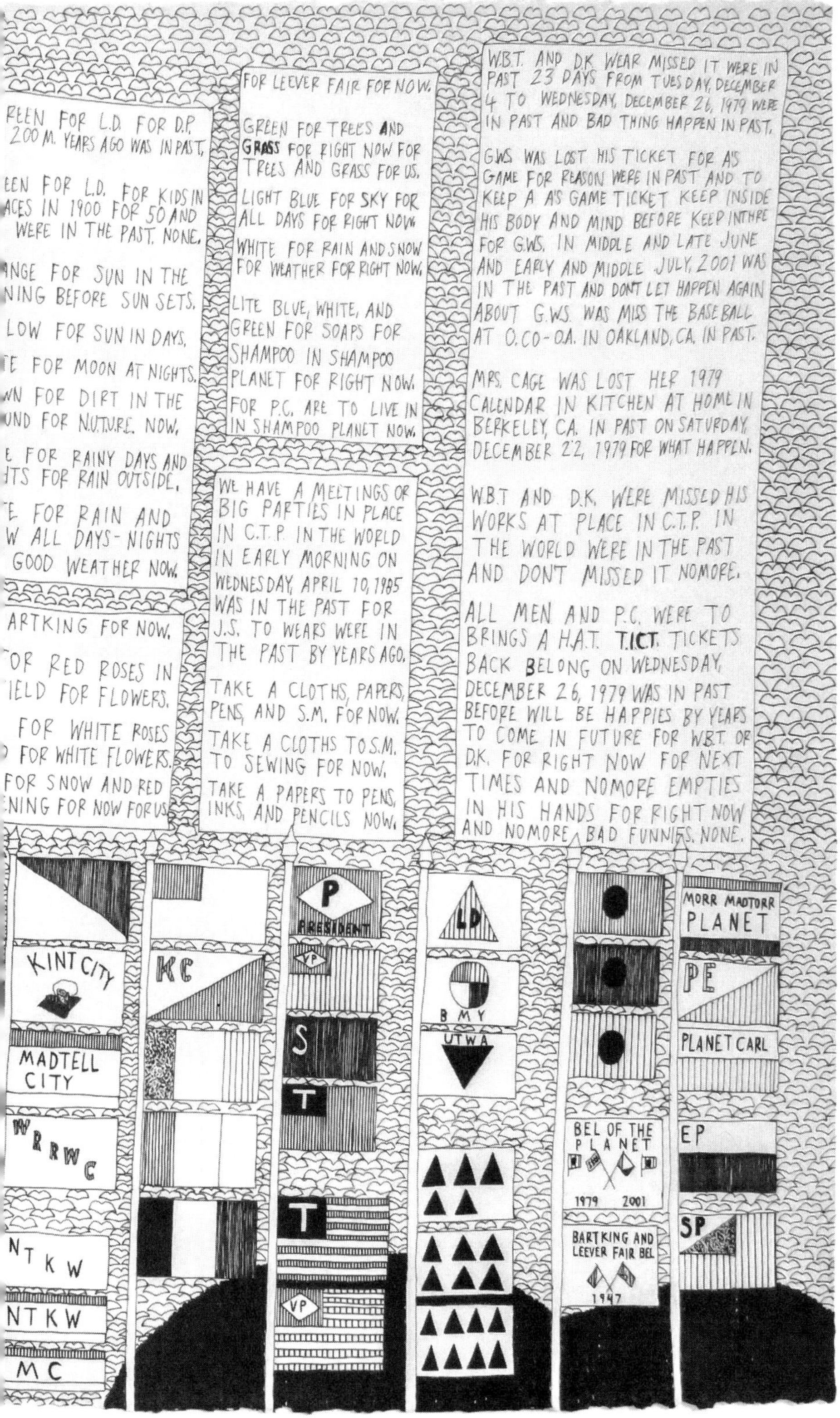
REEN FOR L.D. FOR D.P.
200 M. YEARS AGO WAS IN PAST.
EEN FOR L.D. FOR KIDS IN
ACES IN 1900 FOR 50 AND
WERE IN THE PAST. NONE.
NGE FOR SUN IN THE
NING BEFORE SUN SETS.
LOW FOR SUN IN DAYS.
TE FOR MOON AT NIGHTS.
WN FOR DIRT IN THE
UND FOR NUTURE. NOW.
E FOR RAINY DAYS AND
HTS FOR RAIN OUTSIDE.
TE FOR RAIN AND
W ALL DAYS-NIGHTS
GOOD WEATHER NOW.
ARTKING FOR NOW.
OR RED ROSES IN
IELD FOR FLOWERS.
FOR WHITE ROSES
FOR WHITE FLOWERS.
FOR SNOW AND RED
NING FOR NOW FOR US.
FOR LEEVER FAIR FOR NOW.
GREEN FOR TREES AND GRASS FOR RIGHT NOW FOR TREES AND GRASS FOR US.
LIGHT BLUE FOR SKY FOR ALL DAYS FOR RIGHT NOW.
WHITE FOR RAIN AND SNOW FOR WEATHER FOR RIGHT NOW.
LITE BLUE, WHITE, AND GREEN FOR SOAPS FOR SHAMPOO IN SHAMPOO PLANET FOR RIGHT NOW.
FOR P.C. ARE TO LIVE IN IN SHAMPOO PLANET NOW.
WE HAVE A MEETINGS OR BIG PARTIES IN PLACE IN C.T.P. IN THE WORLD IN EARLY MORNING ON WEDNESDAY, APRIL 10, 1985 WAS IN THE PAST FOR J.S. TO WEARS WERE IN THE PAST BY YEARS AGO.
TAKE A CLOTHS, PAPERS, PENS, AND S.M. FOR NOW.
TAKE A CLOTHS TO S.M. TO SEWING FOR NOW.
TAKE A PAPERS TO PENS, INKS, AND PENCILS NOW.
W.B.T. AND D.K. WEAR MISSED IT WERE IN PAST 23 DAYS FROM TUESDAY, DECEMBER 4 TO WEDNESDAY, DECEMBER 26, 1979 WERE IN PAST AND BAD THING HAPPEN IN PAST.
G.W.S. WAS LOST HIS TICKET FOR A'S GAME FOR REASON WERE IN PAST AND TO KEEP A A'S GAME TICKET KEEP INSIDE HIS BODY AND MIND BEFORE KEEP INTHRE FOR G.W.S. IN MIDDLE AND LATE JUNE AND EARLY AND MIDDLE JULY, 2001 WAS IN THE PAST AND DON'T LET HAPPEN AGAIN ABOUT G.W.S. WAS MISS THE BASEBALL AT O.CO-O.A. IN OAKLAND, CA. IN PAST.
MRS. CAGE WAS LOST HER 1979 CALENDAR IN KITCHEN AT HOME IN BERKELEY, CA. IN PAST ON SATURDAY, DECEMBER 22, 1979 FOR WHAT HAPPEN.
W.B.T AND D.K. WERE MISSED HIS WORKS AT PLACE IN C.T.P. IN THE WORLD WERE IN THE PAST AND DON'T MISSED IT NOMORE.
ALL MEN AND P.C. WERE TO BRINGS A H.A.T. T.I.C.T. TICKETS BACK BELONG ON WEDNESDAY, DECEMBER 26, 1979 WAS IN PAST BEFORE WILL BE HAPPIES BY YEARS TO COME IN FUTURE FOR W.B.T. OR D.K. FOR RIGHT NOW FOR NEXT TIMES AND NOMORE EMPTIES IN HIS HANDS FOR RIGHT NOW AND NOMORE BAD FUNNIES. NONE.
KINT CITY
KC
MADTELL CITY
WRRWC
NTKW
NTKW
MC
P
PRESIDENT
VP
S
T
T
VP
LD
B M Y
UTWA
BEL OF THE PLANET
1979 2001
BARTKING AND LEEVER FAIR BEL
1947
MORR MADTORR PLANET
PE
PLANET CARL
EP
SP

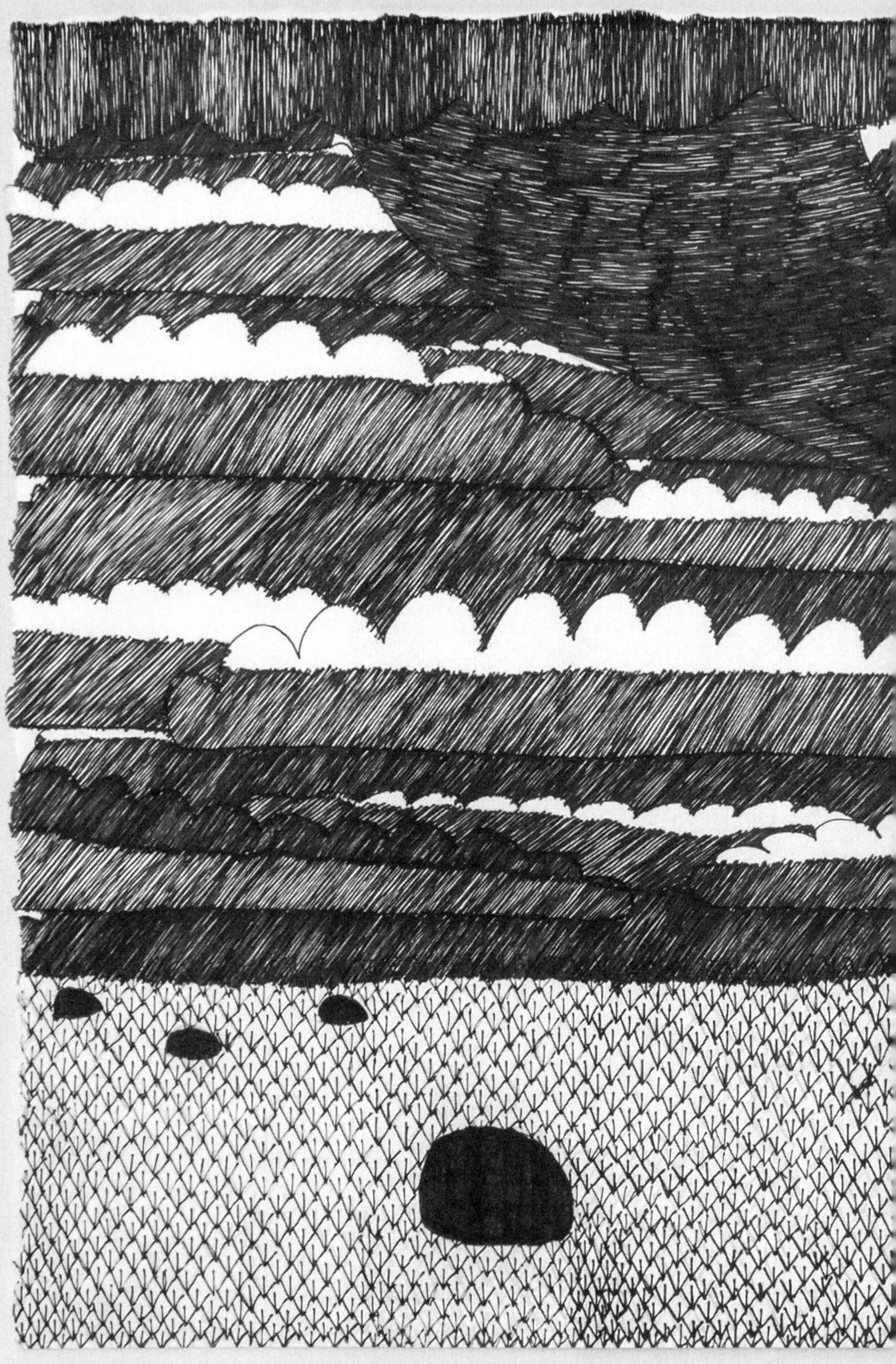

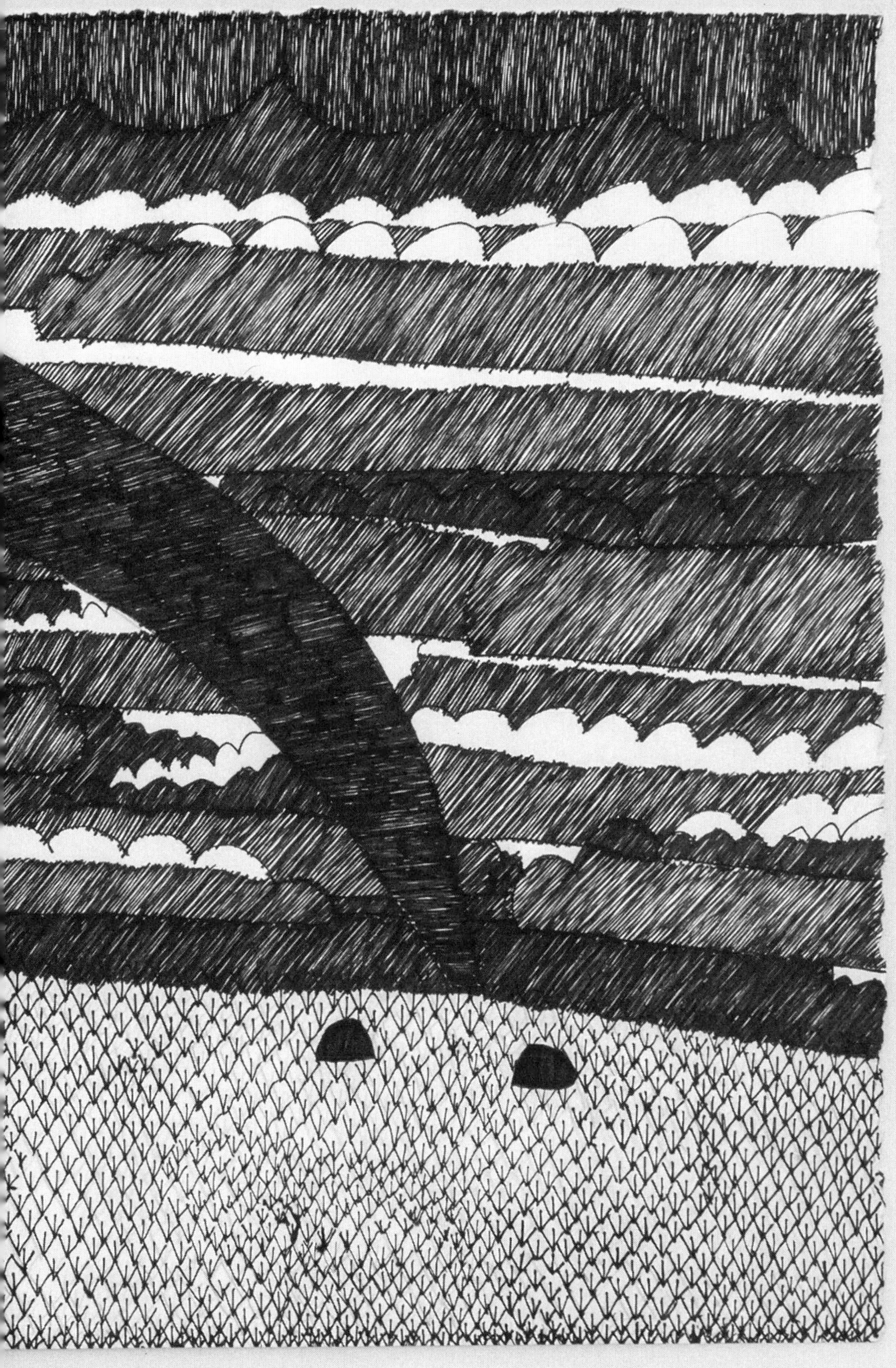

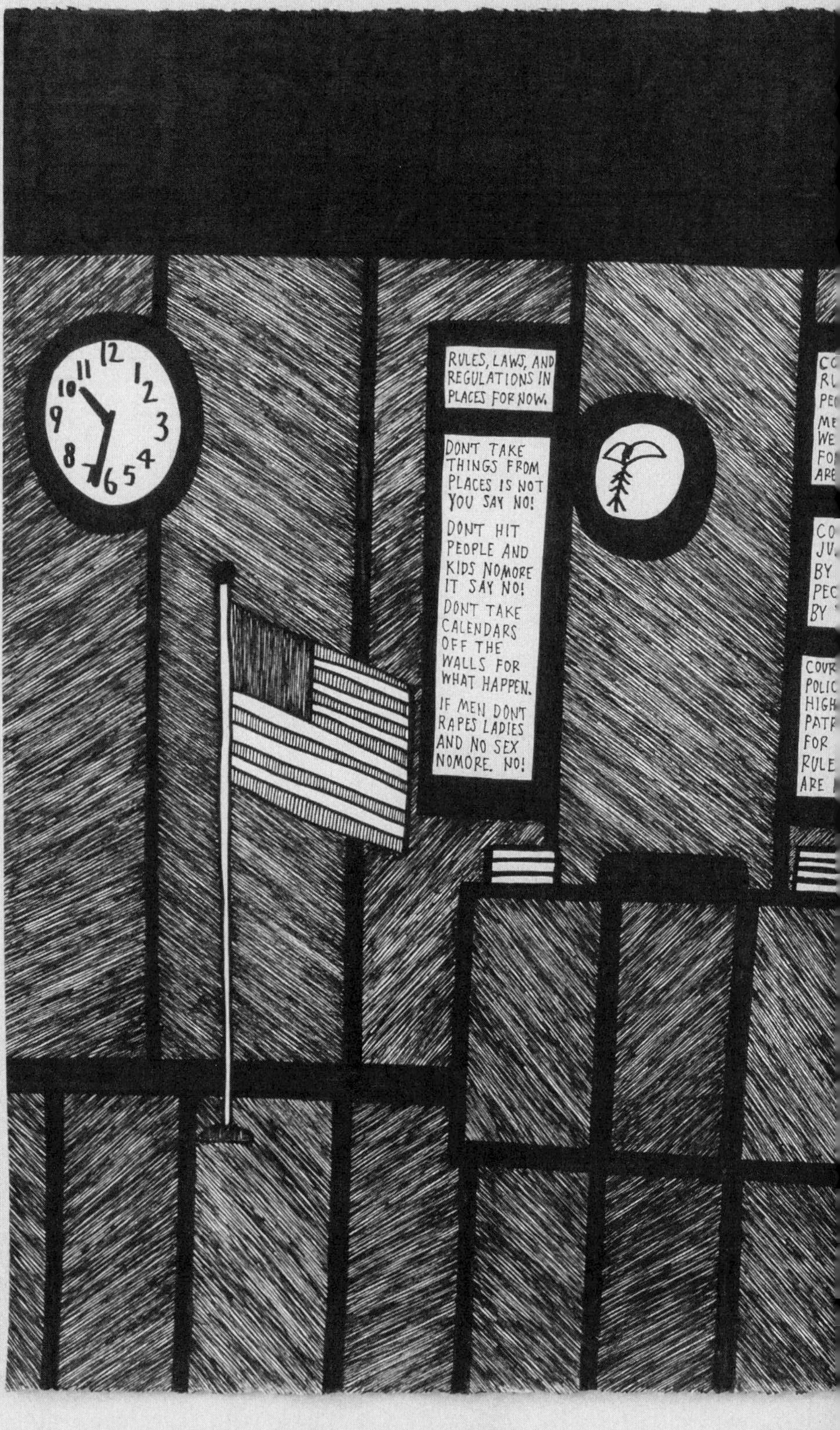
RULES, LAWS, AND REGULATIONS IN PLACES FOR NOW.
DON'T TAKE THINGS FROM PLACES IS NOT YOU SAY NO!
DON'T HIT PEOPLE AND KIDS NOMORE IT SAY NO!
DON'T TAKE CALENDARS OFF THE WALLS FOR WHAT HAPPEN.
IF MEN DON'T RAPES LADIES AND NO SEX NOMORE. NO!

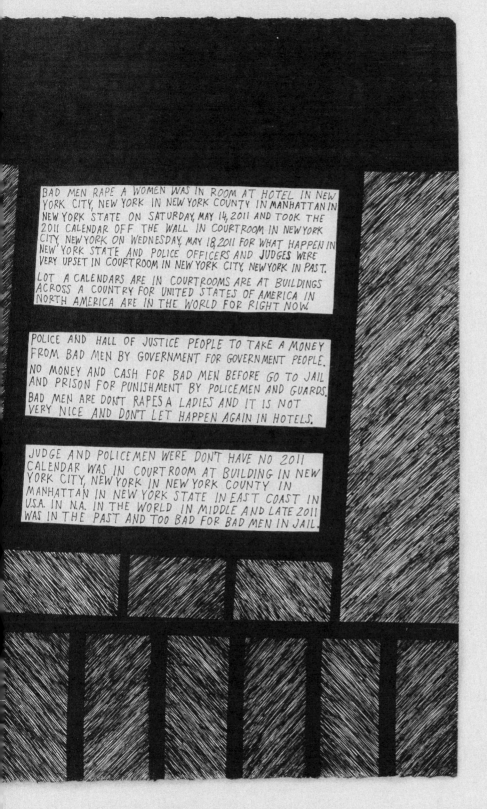

BAD MEN RAPE A WOMEN WAS IN ROOM AT HOTEL IN NEW YORK CITY, NEW YORK IN NEW YORK COUNTY IN MANHATTAN IN NEW YORK STATE ON SATURDAY, MAY 14, 2011 AND TOOK THE 2011 CALENDAR OFF THE WALL IN COURTROOM IN NEW YORK CITY, NEW YORK ON WEDNESDAY, MAY 18, 2011 FOR WHAT HAPPEN IN NEW YORK STATE AND POLICE OFFICERS AND JUDGES WERE VERY UPSET IN COURTROOM IN NEW YORK CITY, NEW YORK IN PAST.

LOT A CALENDARS ARE IN COURTROOMS ARE AT BUILDINGS ACROSS A COUNTRY FOR UNITED STATES OF AMERICA IN NORTH AMERICA ARE IN THE WORLD FOR RIGHT NOW.

POLICE AND HALL OF JUSTICE PEOPLE TO TAKE A MONEY FROM BAD MEN BY GOVERNMENT FOR GOVERNMENT PEOPLE. NO MONEY AND CASH FOR BAD MEN BEFORE GO TO JAIL AND PRISON FOR PUNISHMENT BY POLICEMEN AND GUARDS. BAD MEN ARE DON'T RAPES A LADIES AND IT IS NOT VERY NICE AND DON'T LET HAPPEN AGAIN IN HOTELS.

JUDGE AND POLICEMEN WERE DON'T HAVE NO 2011 CALENDAR WAS IN COURTROOM AT BUILDING IN NEW YORK CITY, NEW YORK IN NEW YORK COUNTY IN MANHATTAN IN NEW YORK STATE IN EAST COAST IN U.S.A. IN N.A. IN THE WORLD IN MIDDLE AND LATE 2011 WAS IN THE PAST AND TOO BAD FOR BAD MEN IN JAIL.

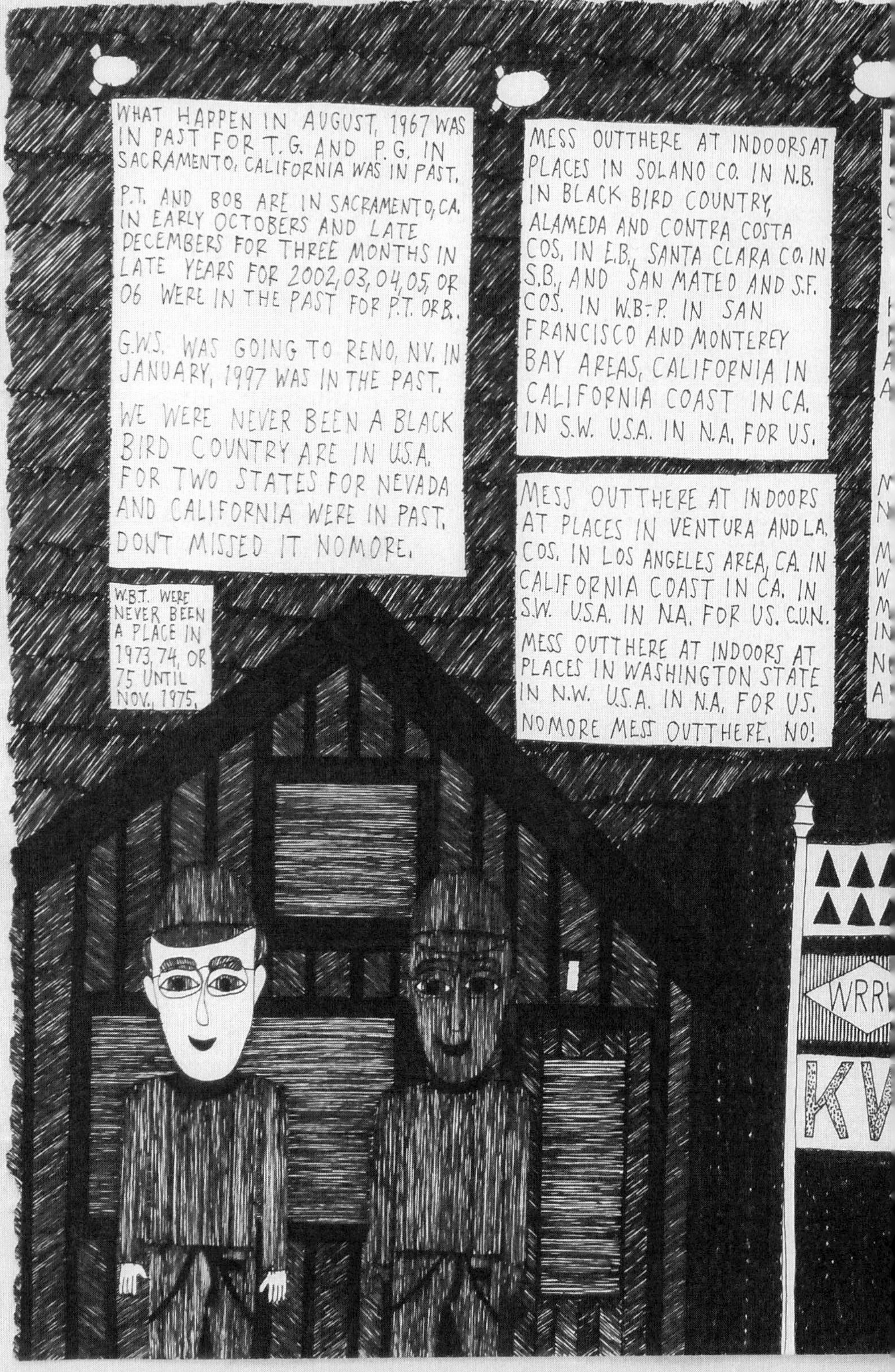
WHAT HAPPEN IN AUGUST, 1967 WAS IN PAST FOR T.G. AND P.G. IN SACRAMENTO, CALIFORNIA WAS IN PAST.
P.T. AND BOB ARE IN SACRAMENTO, CA. IN EARLY OCTOBERS AND LATE DECEMBERS FOR THREE MONTHS IN LATE YEARS FOR 2002, 03, 04, 05, OR 06 WERE IN THE PAST FOR P.T. OR B.
G.W.S. WAS GOING TO RENO, NV. IN JANUARY, 1997 WAS IN THE PAST.
WE WERE NEVER BEEN A BLACK BIRD COUNTRY ARE IN U.S.A. FOR TWO STATES FOR NEVADA AND CALIFORNIA WERE IN PAST. DON'T MISSED IT NOMORE.
W.B.T. WERE NEVER BEEN A PLACE IN 1973, 74, OR 75 UNTIL NOV., 1975.
MESS OUTTHERE AT INDOORS AT PLACES IN SOLANO CO. IN N.B. IN BLACK BIRD COUNTRY, ALAMEDA AND CONTRA COSTA COS. IN E.B., SANTA CLARA CO. IN S.B., AND SAN MATEO AND S.F. COS. IN W.B.-P. IN SAN FRANCISCO AND MONTEREY BAY AREAS, CALIFORNIA IN CALIFORNIA COAST IN CA. IN S.W. U.S.A. IN N.A. FOR US.
MESS OUTTHERE AT INDOORS AT PLACES IN VENTURA AND L.A. COS. IN LOS ANGELES AREA, CA. IN CALIFORNIA COAST IN CA. IN S.W. U.S.A. IN N.A. FOR US. C.U.N.
MESS OUTTHERE AT INDOORS AT PLACES IN WASHINGTON STATE IN N.W. U.S.A. IN N.A. FOR US.
NOMORE MESS OUTTHERE. NO!

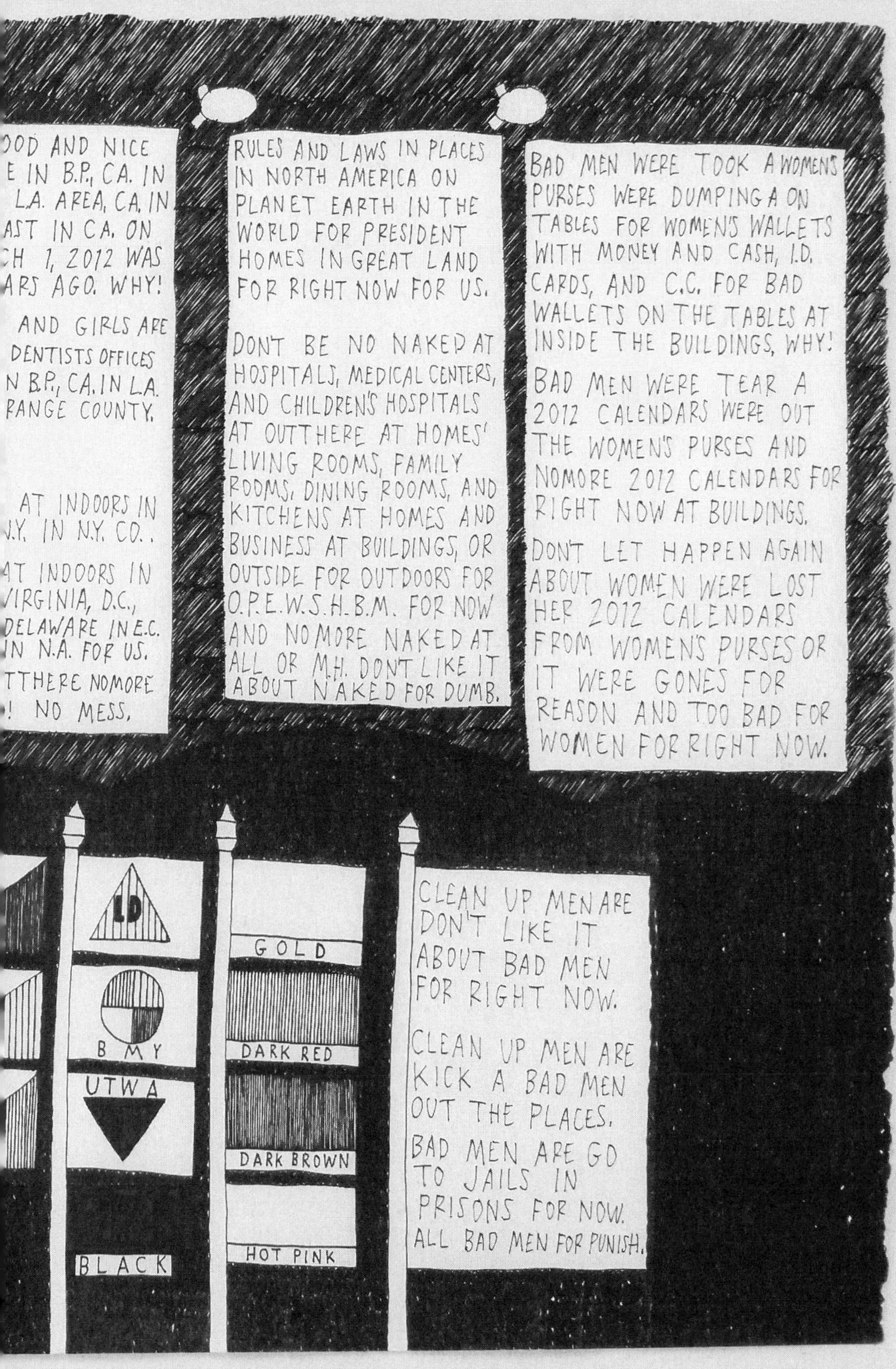
OOD AND NICE
E IN B.P., CA. IN
L.A. AREA, CA. IN
AST IN CA. ON
CH 1, 2012 WAS
ARS AGO. WHY!
AND GIRLS ARE
DENTISTS OFFICES
N B.P., CA. IN L.A.
RANGE COUNTY.
AT INDOORS IN
N.Y. IN N.Y. CO..
AT INDOORS IN
VIRGINIA, D.C.,
DELAWARE IN E.C.
IN N.A. FOR US.
TTHERE NOMORE
! NO MESS.
RULES AND LAWS IN PLACES IN NORTH AMERICA ON PLANET EARTH IN THE WORLD FOR PRESIDENT HOMES IN GREAT LAND FOR RIGHT NOW FOR US.
DON'T BE NO NAKED AT HOSPITALS, MEDICAL CENTERS, AND CHILDREN'S HOSPITALS AT OUTTHERE AT HOMES' LIVING ROOMS, FAMILY ROOMS, DINING ROOMS, AND KITCHENS AT HOMES AND BUSINESS AT BUILDINGS, OR OUTSIDE FOR OUTDOORS FOR O.P.E.W.S.H.B.M. FOR NOW AND NOMORE NAKED AT ALL OR M.H. DON'T LIKE IT ABOUT NAKED FOR DUMB.
BAD MEN WERE TOOK A WOMEN'S PURSES WERE DUMPING A ON TABLES FOR WOMEN'S WALLETS WITH MONEY AND CASH, I.D. CARDS, AND C.C. FOR BAD WALLETS ON THE TABLES AT INSIDE THE BUILDINGS, WHY!
BAD MEN WERE TEAR A 2012 CALENDARS WERE OUT THE WOMEN'S PURSES AND NOMORE 2012 CALENDARS FOR RIGHT NOW AT BUILDINGS.
DON'T LET HAPPEN AGAIN ABOUT WOMEN WERE LOST HER 2012 CALENDARS FROM WOMEN'S PURSES OR IT WERE GONES FOR REASON AND TOO BAD FOR WOMEN FOR RIGHT NOW.
LD
B M Y
UTWA
BLACK
GOLD
DARK RED
DARK BROWN
HOT PINK
CLEAN UP MEN ARE DON'T LIKE IT ABOUT BAD MEN FOR RIGHT NOW.
CLEAN UP MEN ARE KICK A BAD MEN OUT THE PLACES.
BAD MEN ARE GO TO JAILS IN PRISONS FOR NOW.
ALL BAD MEN FOR PUNISH.

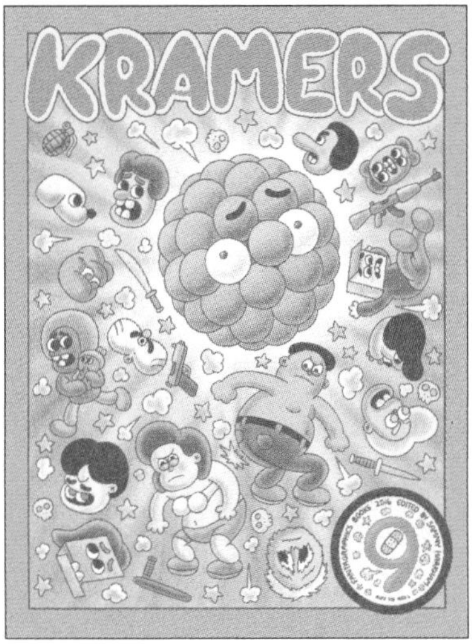
KRAMERS
9

# Kill Thurber

## MATTHEW THURBER

*originally published in*

*Kramers Ergot*, vol. 9
FANTAGRAPHICS BOOKS
9 × 11.75 inches • 296 pages

### Biography

Matthew Thurber is the author of the graphic novels *1-800-MICE* and *INFOMANIACS*, and the forthcoming *Art Comic*. With Rebecca Bird he cofounded Tomato House, an art gallery in operation from 2012 to 2015. He has taught comics and animation at Queens College since 2011. His mural *Mouse Maze* is permanently installed at P.S. 35Q, Hollis, Queens. Recently he has performed "calypso-stenographic" music as Popular Pig and created performance work as Mrs. William Horsley.
matthewthurber.com

### Statement

*Bananafish* was a magazine that ran from 1987 to 2004, edited by "Seymour Glass," which I started reading in high school. It focused on noise and experimental music and each issue came with a 7-inch record (later CD). Some of the artists I read about in this amazing publication were Thinking Fellers Union Local #282, Caroliner, Sun City Girls, World of Pooh, Masonna, Merzbow, Metalux, Wolf Eyes, C. Spencer Yeh, Harry Pussy, Prick Decay, Three Day Stubble, National Disgrace, Le Dernier Cri, Panicsville, and Reynols. It contained the most inspired writing about music I have read to this day.

KILL THURBER MT 2015

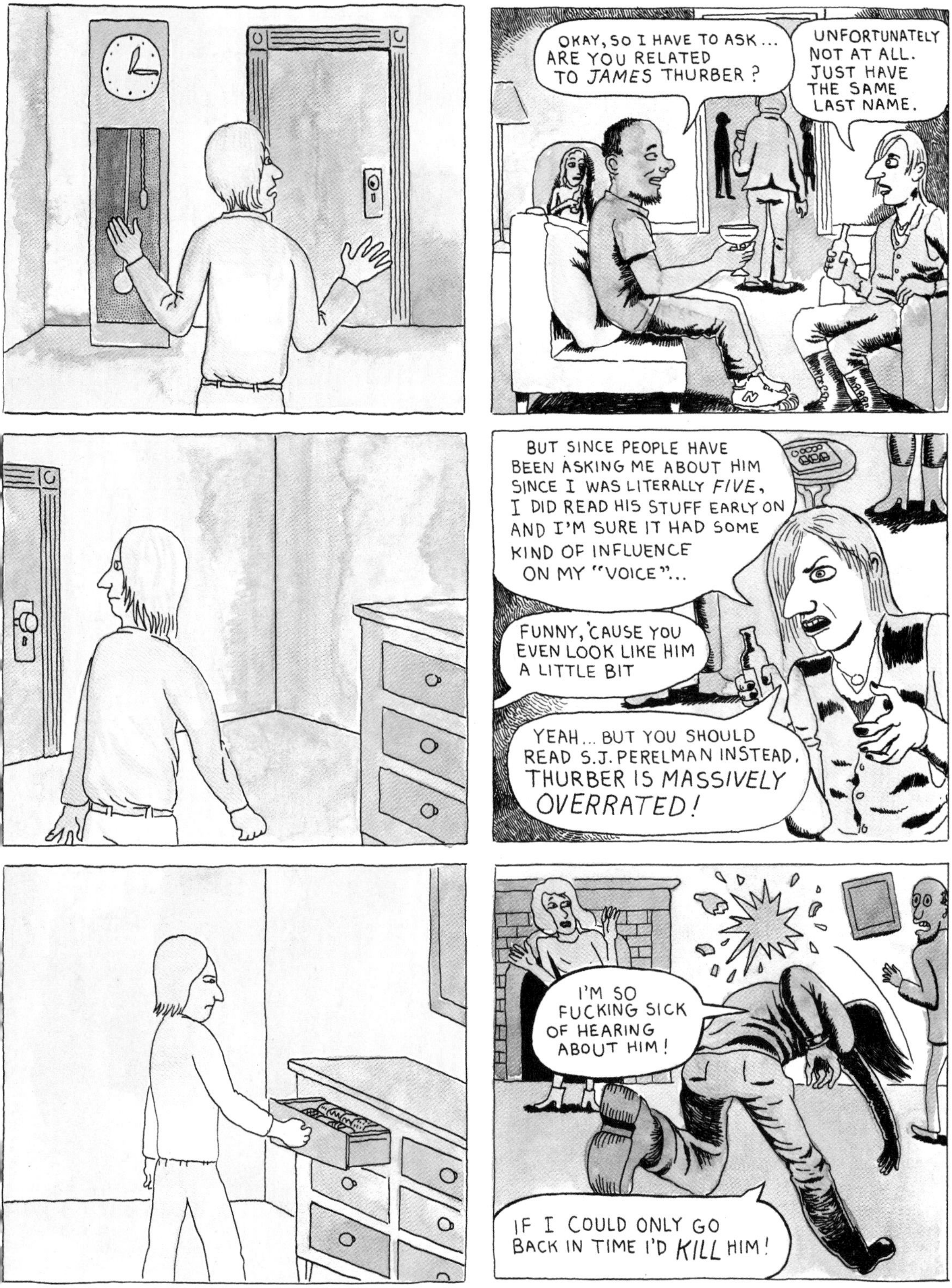
OKAY, SO I HAVE TO ASK... ARE YOU RELATED TO *JAMES* THURBER?
UNFORTUNATELY NOT AT ALL. JUST HAVE THE SAME LAST NAME.
BUT SINCE PEOPLE HAVE BEEN ASKING ME ABOUT HIM SINCE I WAS LITERALLY *FIVE*, I DID READ HIS STUFF EARLY ON AND I'M SURE IT HAD SOME KIND OF INFLUENCE ON MY "VOICE"...
FUNNY, 'CAUSE YOU EVEN LOOK LIKE HIM A LITTLE BIT
YEAH... BUT YOU SHOULD READ S.J. PERELMAN INSTEAD. THURBER IS *MASSIVELY OVERRATED!*
I'M SO FUCKING SICK OF HEARING ABOUT HIM!
IF I COULD ONLY GO BACK IN TIME I'D *KILL* HIM!

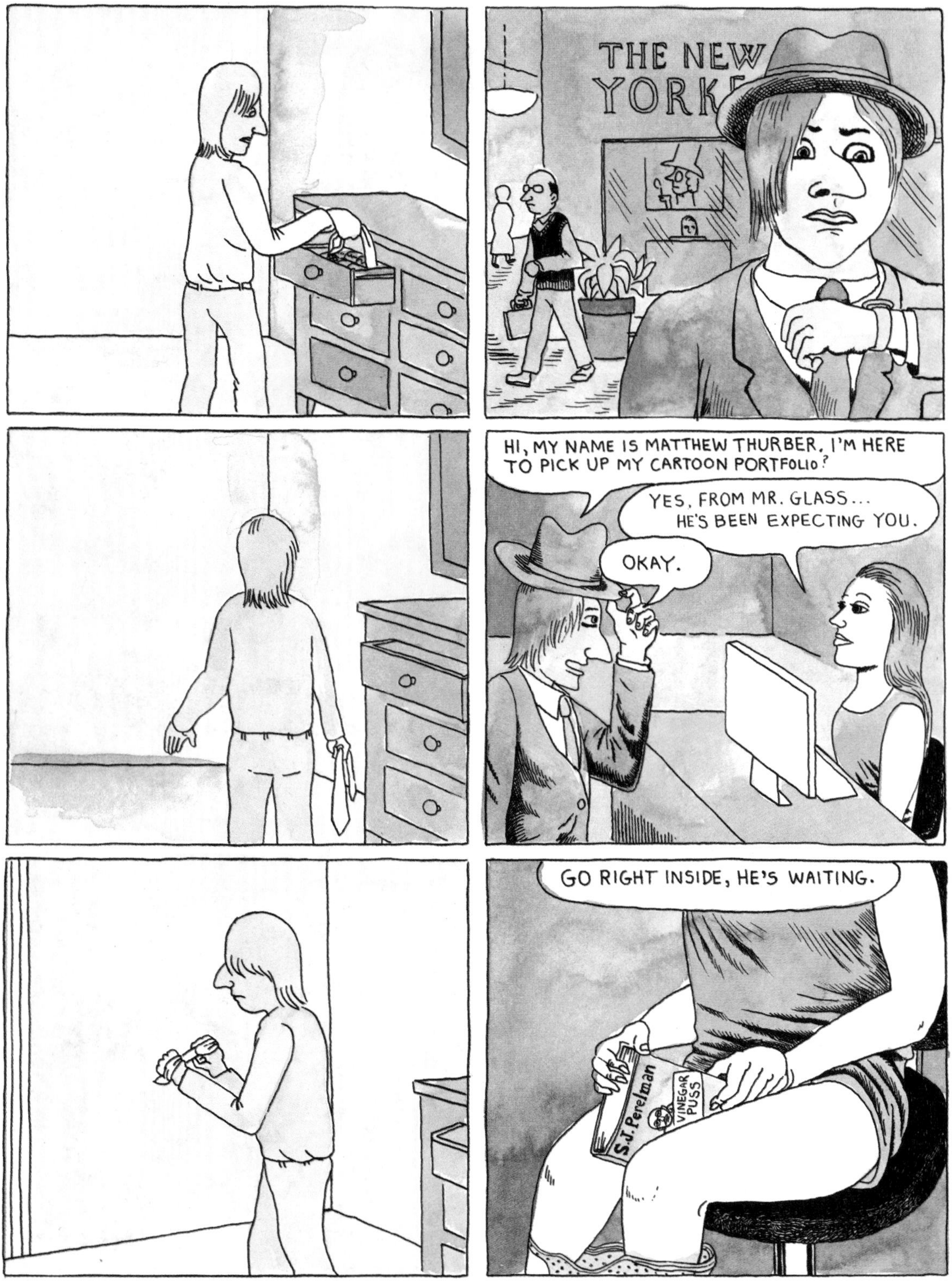
THE NEW
YORK
HI, MY NAME IS MATTHEW THURBER, I'M HERE TO PICK UP MY CARTOON PORTFOLIO?
YES, FROM MR. GLASS... HE'S BEEN EXPECTING YOU.
OKAY.
GO RIGHT INSIDE, HE'S WAITING.
S.J. Perelman
VINEGAR PUSS

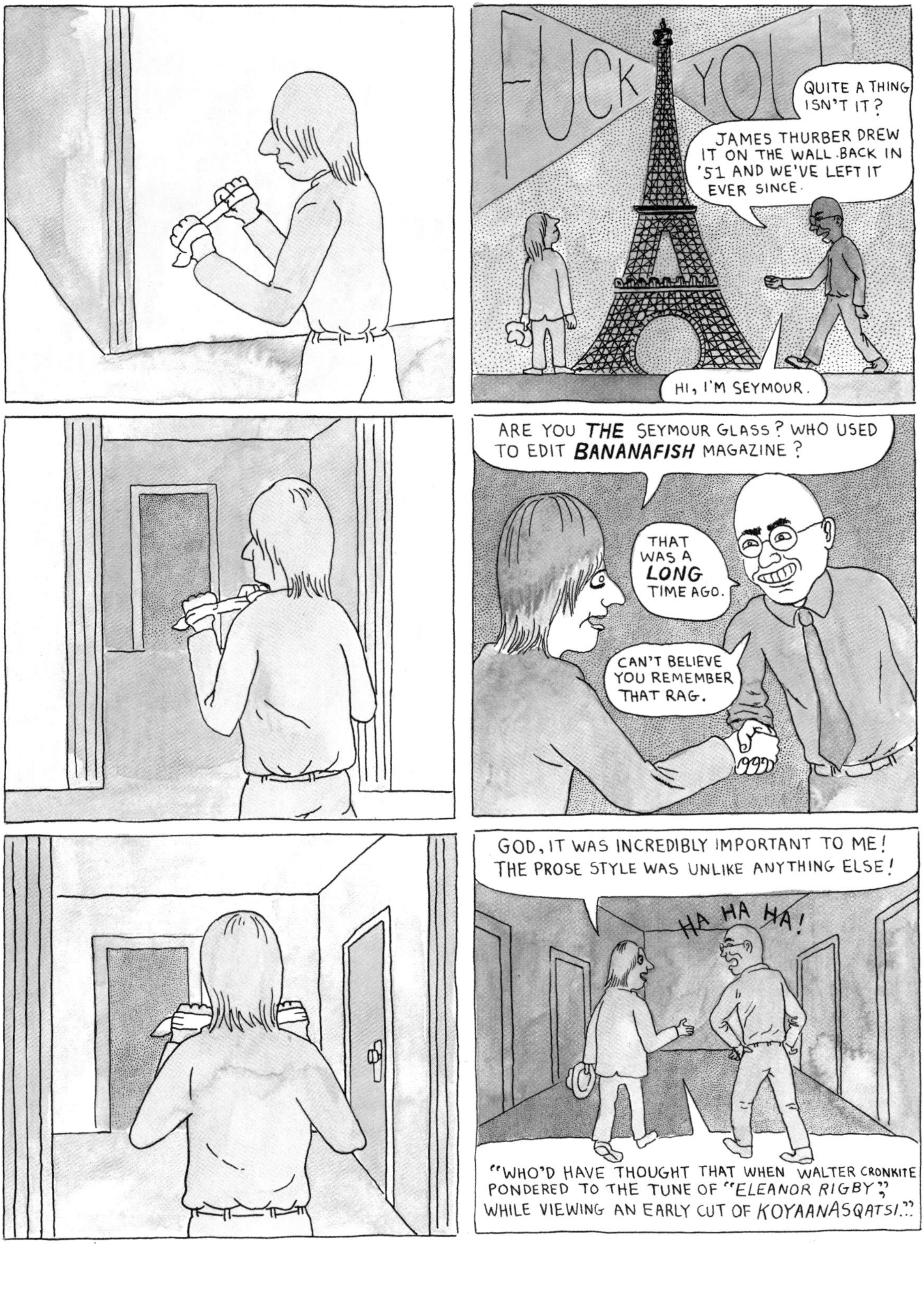
FUCK YOU
QUITE A THING ISN'T IT?
JAMES THURBER DREW IT ON THE WALL BACK IN '51 AND WE'VE LEFT IT EVER SINCE.
HI, I'M SEYMOUR.
ARE YOU THE SEYMOUR GLASS? WHO USED TO EDIT BANANAFISH MAGAZINE?
THAT WAS A LONG TIME AGO.
CAN'T BELIEVE YOU REMEMBER THAT RAG.
GOD, IT WAS INCREDIBLY IMPORTANT TO ME! THE PROSE STYLE WAS UNLIKE ANYTHING ELSE!
HA HA HA!
"WHO'D HAVE THOUGHT THAT WHEN WALTER CRONKITE PONDERED TO THE TUNE OF "ELEANOR RIGBY," WHILE VIEWING AN EARLY CUT OF KOYAANASQATSI..."

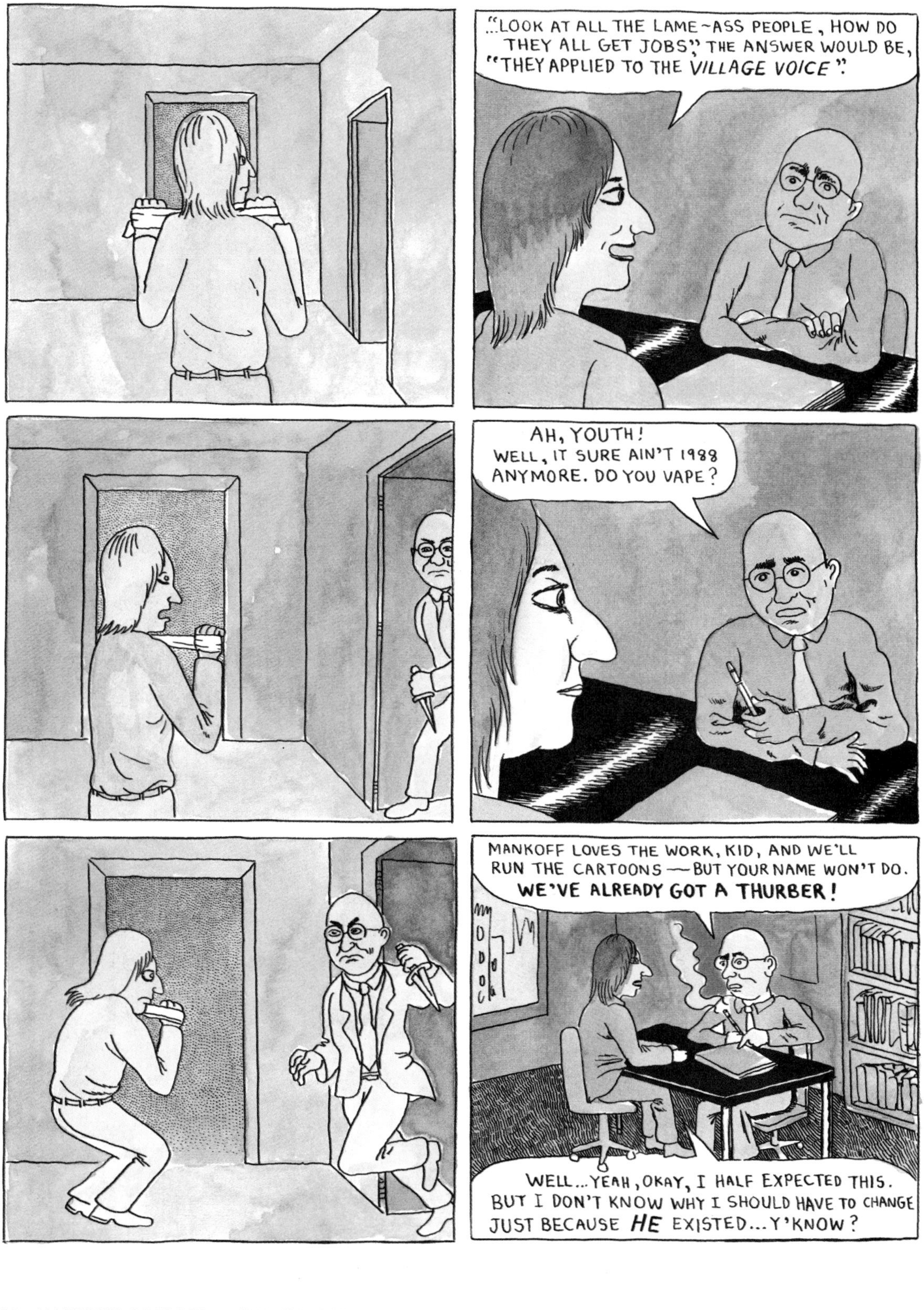
..."LOOK AT ALL THE LAME-ASS PEOPLE, HOW DO THEY ALL GET JOBS," THE ANSWER WOULD BE, "THEY APPLIED TO THE VILLAGE VOICE".
AH, YOUTH! WELL, IT SURE AIN'T 1988 ANYMORE. DO YOU VAPE?
MANKOFF LOVES THE WORK, KID, AND WE'LL RUN THE CARTOONS — BUT YOUR NAME WON'T DO. WE'VE ALREADY GOT A THURBER!
WELL... YEAH, OKAY, I HALF EXPECTED THIS. BUT I DON'T KNOW WHY I SHOULD HAVE TO CHANGE JUST BECAUSE HE EXISTED... Y'KNOW?

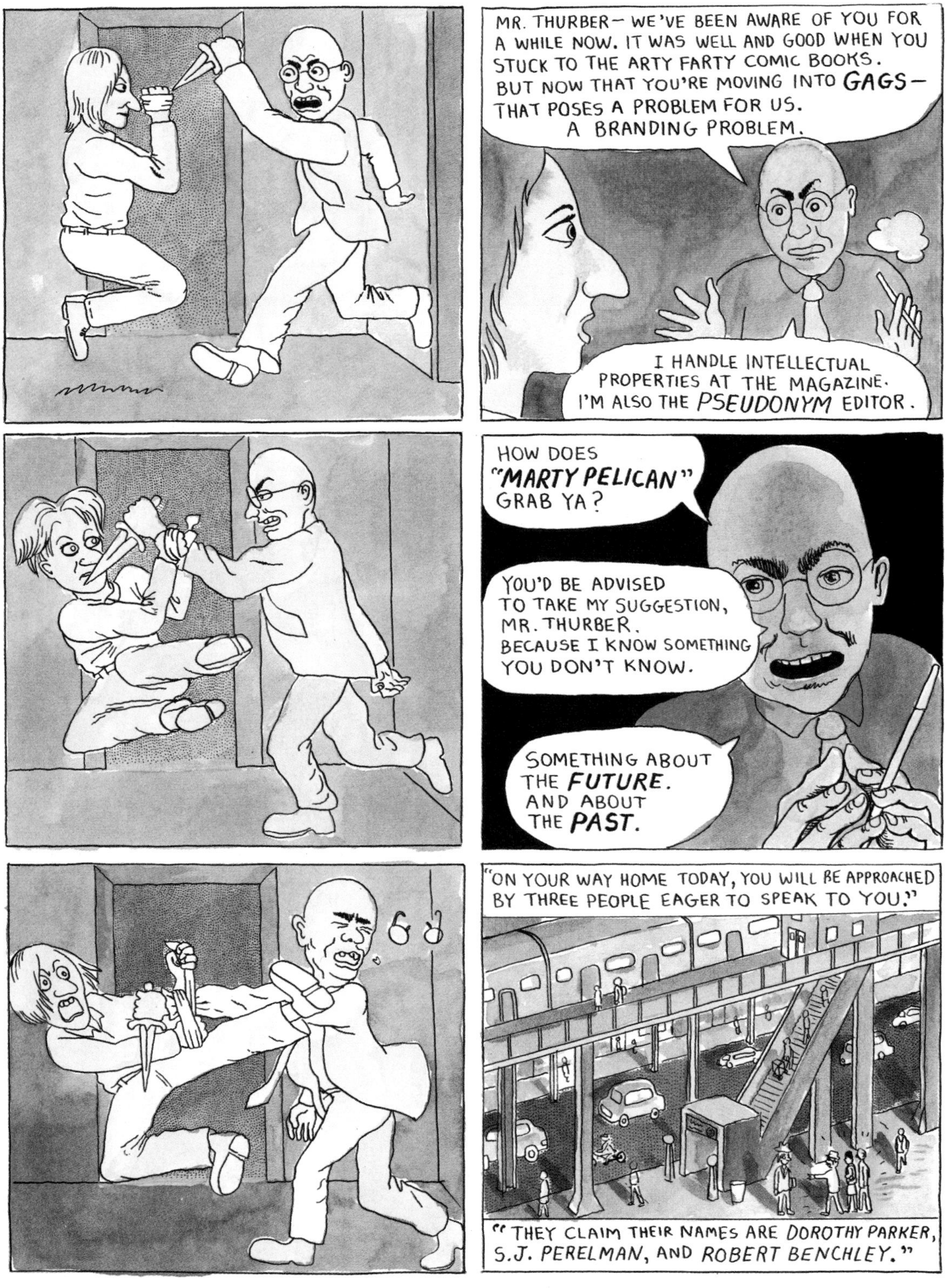
MR. THURBER— WE'VE BEEN AWARE OF YOU FOR A WHILE NOW. IT WAS WELL AND GOOD WHEN YOU STUCK TO THE ARTY FARTY COMIC BOOKS. BUT NOW THAT YOU'RE MOVING INTO GAGS— THAT POSES A PROBLEM FOR US. A BRANDING PROBLEM.
I HANDLE INTELLECTUAL PROPERTIES AT THE MAGAZINE. I'M ALSO THE PSEUDONYM EDITOR.
HOW DOES "MARTY PELICAN" GRAB YA?
YOU'D BE ADVISED TO TAKE MY SUGGESTION, MR. THURBER. BECAUSE I KNOW SOMETHING YOU DON'T KNOW.
SOMETHING ABOUT THE FUTURE. AND ABOUT THE PAST.
"ON YOUR WAY HOME TODAY, YOU WILL BE APPROACHED BY THREE PEOPLE EAGER TO SPEAK TO YOU."
"THEY CLAIM THEIR NAMES ARE DOROTHY PARKER, S.J. PERELMAN, AND ROBERT BENCHLEY."

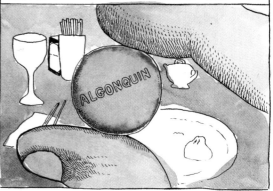
"OVER DINNER, THEY WILL CONVINCE YOU OF THEIR ABILITY TO **TRAVEL THROUGH TIME** WITH THE AID OF A SPECIAL DRUG, THAT TAKES THE FORM OF AN ORDINARY **ROUND TABLET.**"

"THEY WILL PERSUADE YOU, BY FLATTERING YOUR EGO, THAT THE ASSASSINATION OF JAMES THURBER WOULD BE AN ACT TO BENEFIT YOU ALL."

"DON'T YOU SEE HOW THAT BUNCH OF JEALOUS SECOND-STRINGERS ARE USING YOU TO ACCOMPLISH THEIR VILE GOAL?"

"BUT IT WON'T HAPPEN, MR. THURBER. AND THE PROOF IS THAT YOU'RE HERE IN MY OFFICE NOW."

"BECAUSE I'M WAITING FOR YOU IN 1930... I WON'T ALLOW YOU TO KILL THURBER."

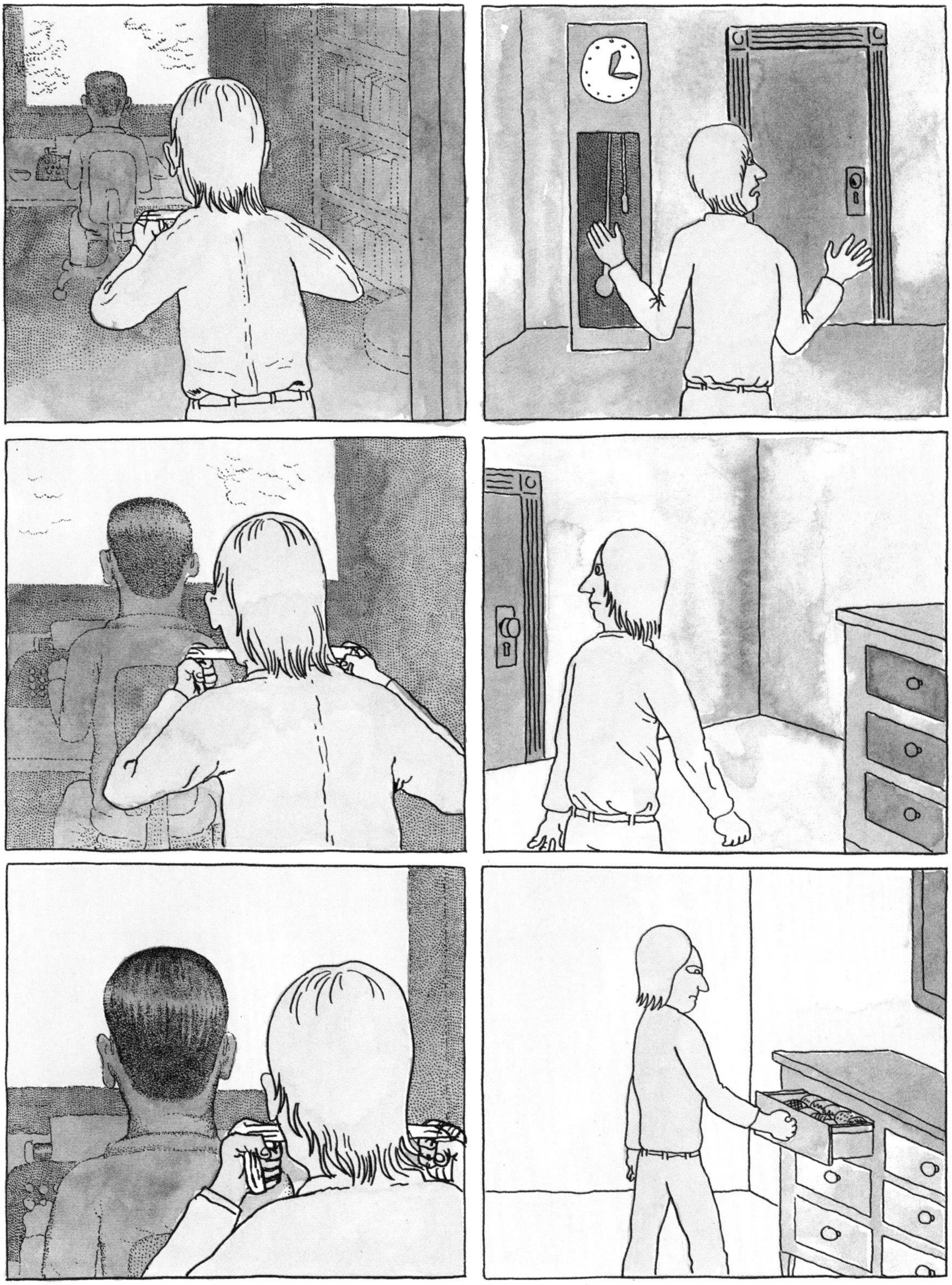

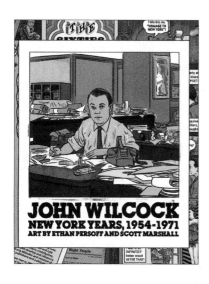

JOHN WILCOCK
NEW YORK YEARS, 1954-1971
ART BY ETHAN PERSOFF AND SCOTT MARSHALL

# John Wilcock, New York Years (*Excerpt*)

ETHAN PERSOFF AND
SCOTT MARSHALL

*originally published in*

*John Wilcock, New York Years, 1954–1971*

SELF-PUBLISHED

8 × 10 inches • 90 pages

## Biography

Ethan Persoff is a sound artist, archivist, and cartoonist, in Austin, Texas. His website contains a full archive of Paul Krassner's *The Realist,* and *Comics with Problems,* a repository of very peculiar awareness comics of the last century. He is currently working with Scott Marshall on the biography of John Wilcock. Other comics projects include *Teddy* and *Radio Wire.*
www.ep.tc

Scott Marshall is an illustrator, art director, audio collagist, and painter.
scottmarshall.org

## Statement

*John Wilcock, New York Years* is a biography project that aims to document the history of the underground press movement of the 1960s. Wilcock, who has served as an interviewed contributor to these comics, was a cofounder of the *Village Voice* and, with Andy Warhol, cocreated *Interview Magazine.*

Wilcock also established the Underground Press Syndicate, which served as the model for much of the New Journalism movement (and very directly influenced the editorial style and methods of modern journalism). The full book will detail John's life in New York, from when he arrived in 1954 until the early 1970s, when he left to become author of numerous books on traveling the globe.

A comprehensive account of the rise of drug culture, political activism, and countless personal anecdotes of this very interesting time in U.S. history are included throughout. The excerpted section for *Best American Comics 2017* includes John's arrival in New York and the establishment of the *Village Voice.*

WHEN I FIRST ARRIVED IN NEW YORK IN 1954, I WAS AN AMBITIOUS YOUNG REPORTER, AGE 27, AND EAGER FOR NEW OPPORTUNITIES.

I CAME TO NEW YORK WITH OVER A DECADE'S EXPERIENCE IN PROPER JOURNALISM. BORN IN ENGLAND, MY FIRST JOB WAS AT AGE 16 WITH THE SHEFFIELD TELEGRAPH (I DROPPED OUT OF SCHOOL TO TAKE IT.) AND FROM THERE I JOINED LONDON'S DAILY MIRROR AND DAILY MAIL.

THOSE JOBS BROUGHT ME TO CANADA, WHERE I WORKED FOR THE BRITISH UNITED PRESS (DOING AN INTERESTING JOB RE-WRITING WIRE SERVICE COPY FOR ANNOUNCEMENT ON RADIO)... THAT JOB LED TO A NUMBER OF ASSIGNMENTS FOR CANADIAN MAGAZINES, INCLUDING SATURDAY NIGHT, AND THE CANADIAN HOME JOURNAL.

BUT 1950's ENGLAND AND CANADA FELT STUFFY AND STAGNANT. AND STILL RELATIVELY YOUNG AND NOT WANTING TO WASTE MY LIFE, I SOON TOOK THE PLUNGE TO THE U.S.A., SPECIFICALLY NEW YORK.

I LOVED THE CITY FROM MY FIRST MOMENT, AND BY DAY TWO HAD MOVED INTO A CHEAP GREENWICH VILLAGE APARTMENT @ $46.00/month.

I SPENT MY TIME ROAMING THE VILLAGE BARS TO DRINK BEER AND LOOK AT GIRLS.

... I WAS A LONELY, SLOPPILY DRESSED YOUNG MAN, HAVING THE TIME OF MY LIFE...

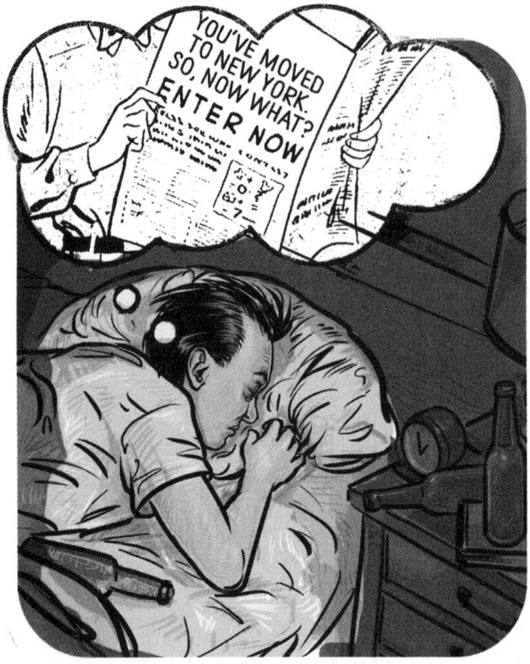
YOU'VE MOVED TO NEW YORK. SO, NOW WHAT?
ENTER NOW

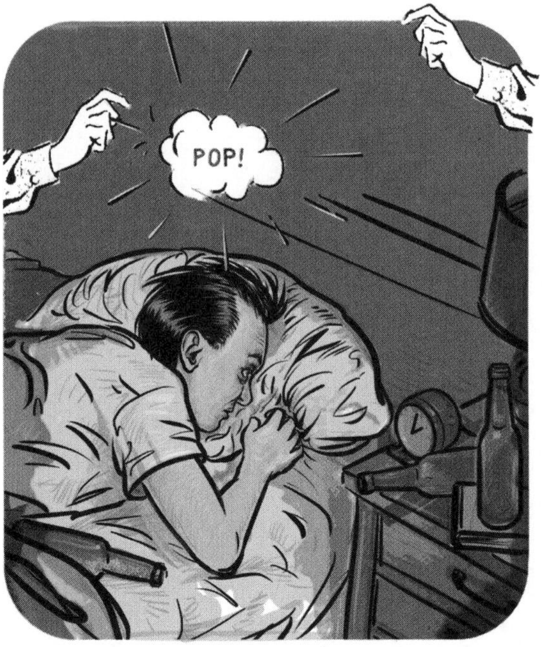
POP!

WAKING UP UPSET AFTER A FEW DAYS OF THIS CAROUSING... AND HAVING NO SKILL OTHER THAN REPORTING... I SOON BEGAN TO WONDER ABOUT A COMMUNITY NEWSPAPER FOR THE VILLAGE...

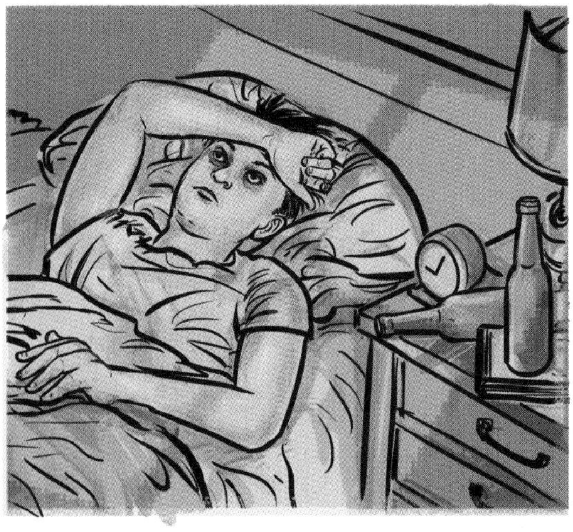

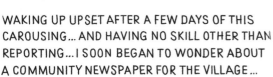

SO, FIVE DAYS INTO MY NEW LIFE, I PUT UP A HAND-WRITTEN CARD IN THE SHERIDAN SQUARE BOOKSHOP, SEEKING ANYONE INTERESTED IN SUCH A PUBLICATION.

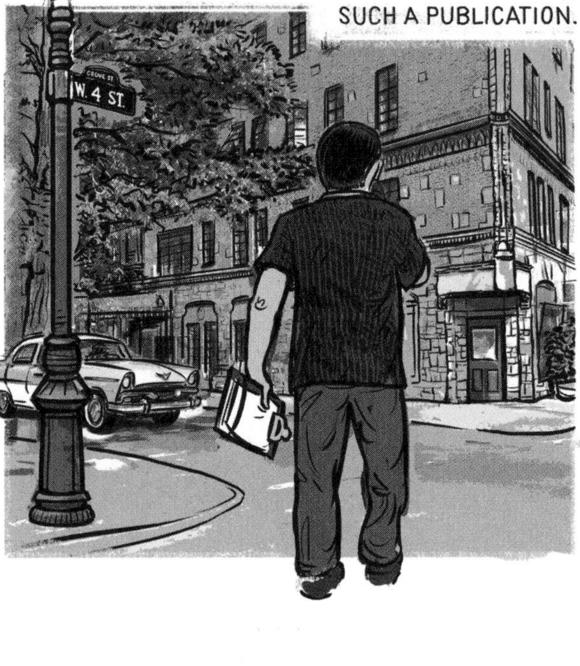
W. 4 ST.

I SHOULD COMMENT, OF COURSE, THE VILLAGE ALREADY HAD A COMMUNITY PAPER OF SORTS, "THE VILLAGER", WHICH WAS FOUNDED IN 1933.

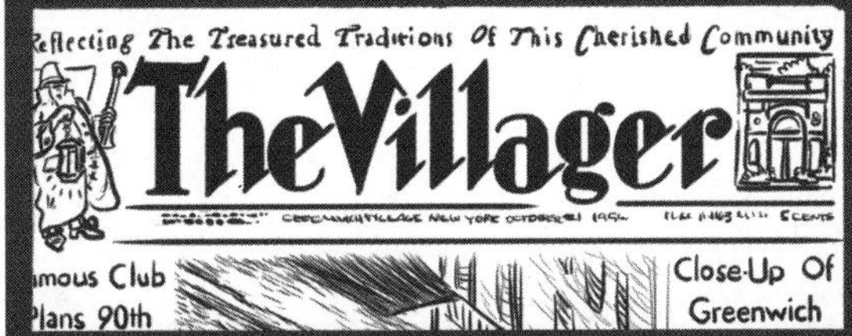
The Treasured Traditions Of This Cherished Community
The Villager
Close-Up Of Greenwich

But even someone new to the city, such as myself, could tell the paper was essentially dull and lifeless. It's changed since then, but in 1954, "THE VILLAGER" contained little community journalism. Its contents:

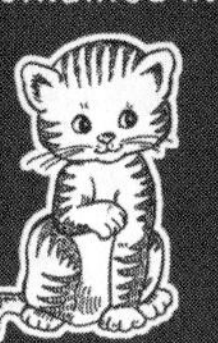

. . . Mostly bridge club party reports . . . and most sleep inducing (at least to me) an insipid column, ostensibly written by the editor's CAT, named "Scoopy Mews". CAN YOU IMAGINE?

SO IT WAS GRATIFYING TO RECEIVE INTEREST FROM OTHERS IN A CALL FOR A NEW COMMUNITY PAPER. ... MY CARD AT THE BOOKSTORE RECEIVED *A SMALL* STACK OF MAIL ... BUT NO ONE HAD ANY MONEY, AND THE IDEA INITIALLY WENT NOWHERE.

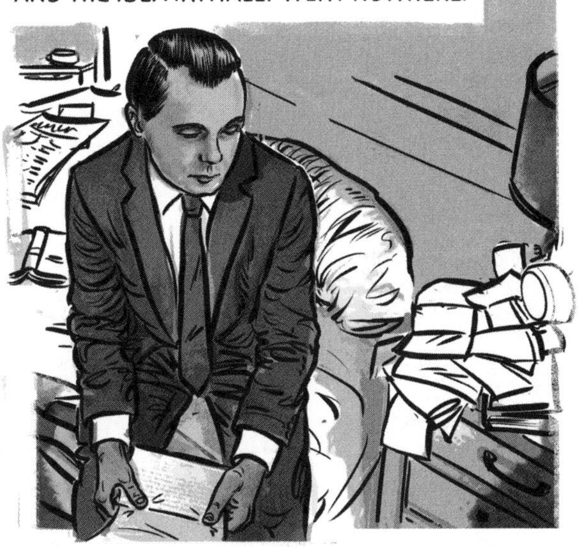

TWO PEOPLE WHO DID MEET WITH ME THAT FIRST WEEK WAS A PAIR OF NEW FRIENDS, NAMED ED FANCHER AND DAN WOLF. NEITHER OF THEM HAD JOURNALISM EXPERIENCE, BUT THEY WERE VERY WARM TO THE IDEA ABOUT A NEW PAPER.

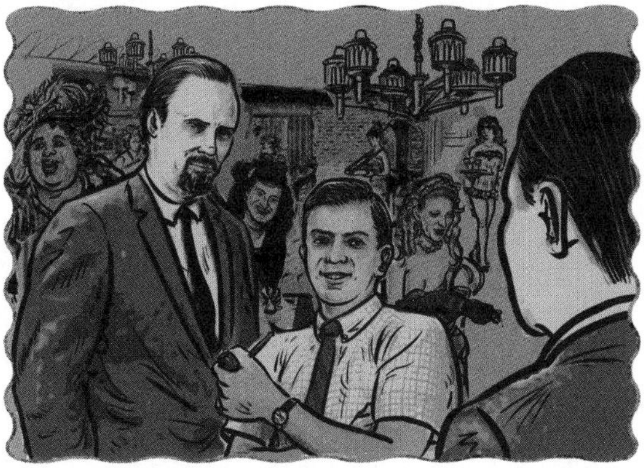

OVER THE NEXT YEAR, THIS IDEA WOULD BOUNCE AROUND AND FURTHER SOLIDIFY INTO WHAT IS NOW CALLED "THE VILLAGE VOICE."

IN THE MEANTIME, I STILL HAD CONNECTIONS TO AN EDITOR IN CANADA NAMED FRANK RASKY, WHO SENT ME ON A FEW INTERVIEW ASSIGNMENTS...

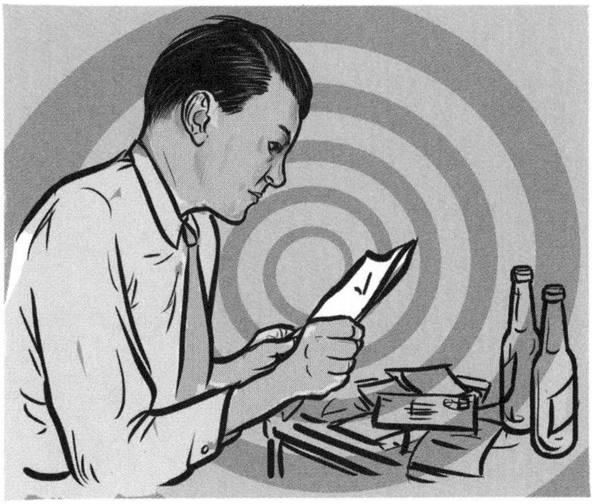

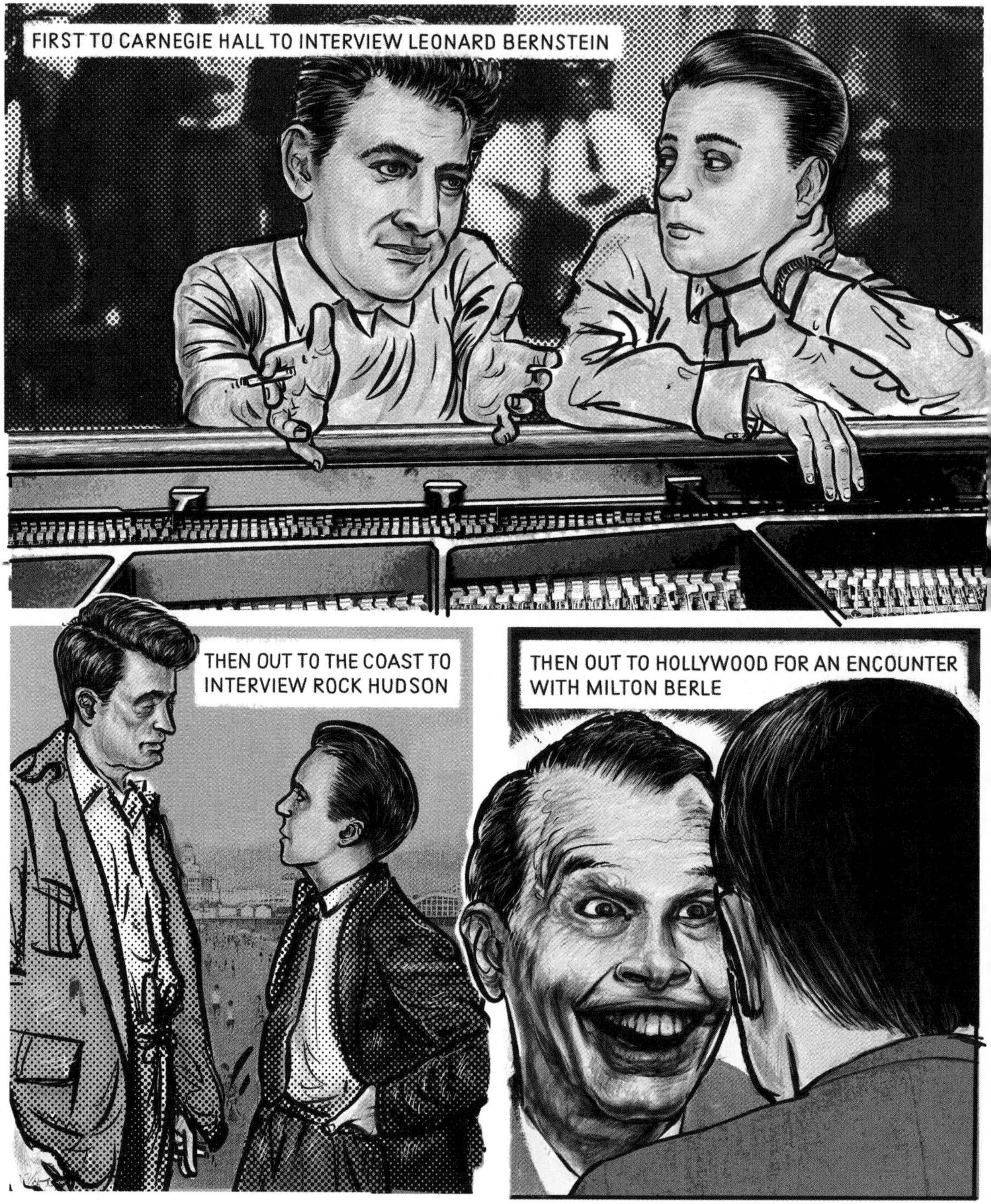
FIRST TO CARNEGIE HALL TO INTERVIEW LEONARD BERNSTEIN
THEN OUT TO THE COAST TO INTERVIEW ROCK HUDSON
THEN OUT TO HOLLYWOOD FOR AN ENCOUNTER WITH MILTON BERLE

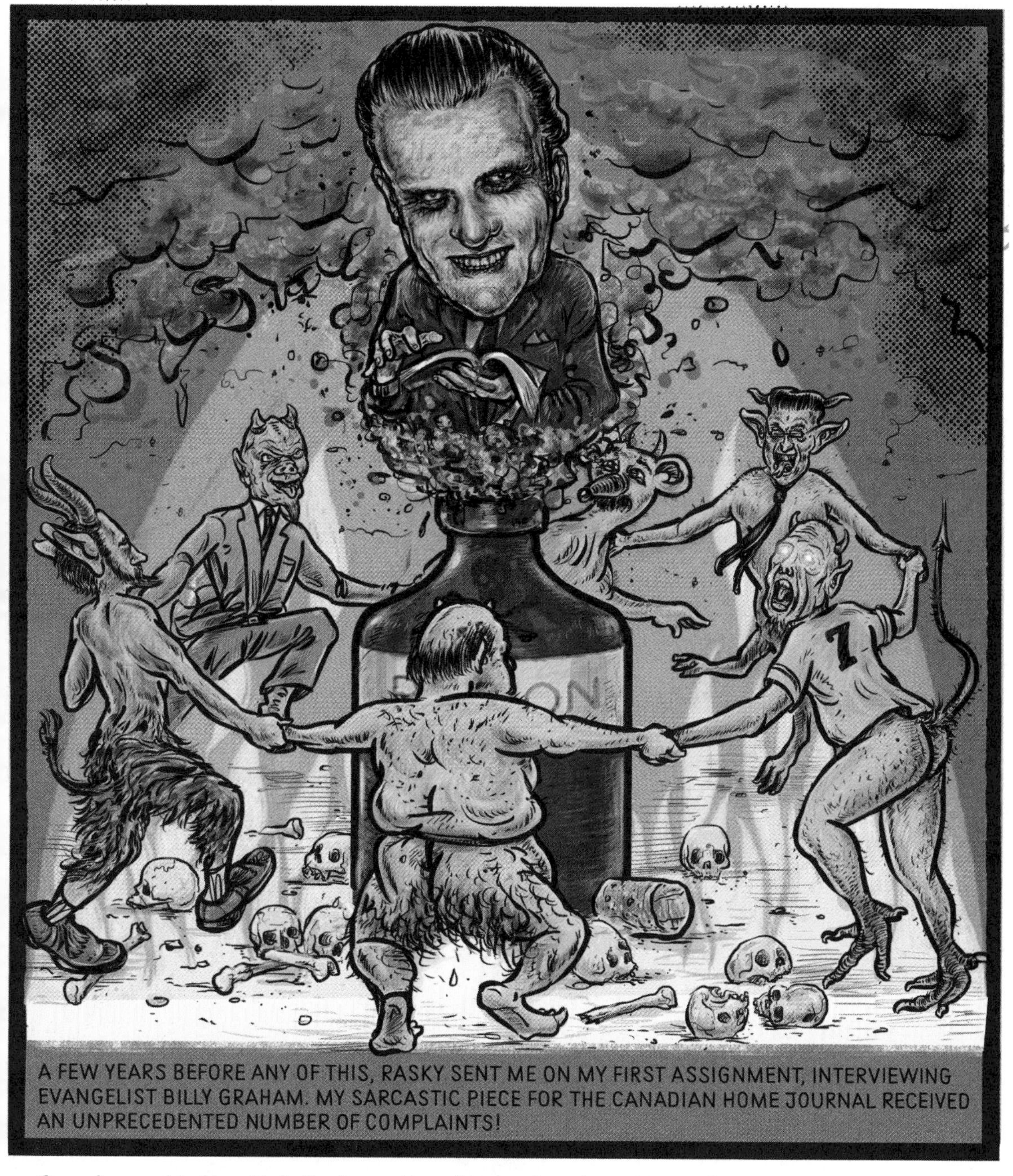
A FEW YEARS BEFORE ANY OF THIS, RASKY SENT ME ON MY FIRST ASSIGNMENT, INTERVIEWING EVANGELIST BILLY GRAHAM. MY SARCASTIC PIECE FOR THE CANADIAN HOME JOURNAL RECEIVED AN UNPRECEDENTED NUMBER OF COMPLAINTS!
7

Once I moved to New York, Rasky continued to send me interview assignments.
And one of my fondest memories *is of an afternoon spent with Marilyn Monroe ...*

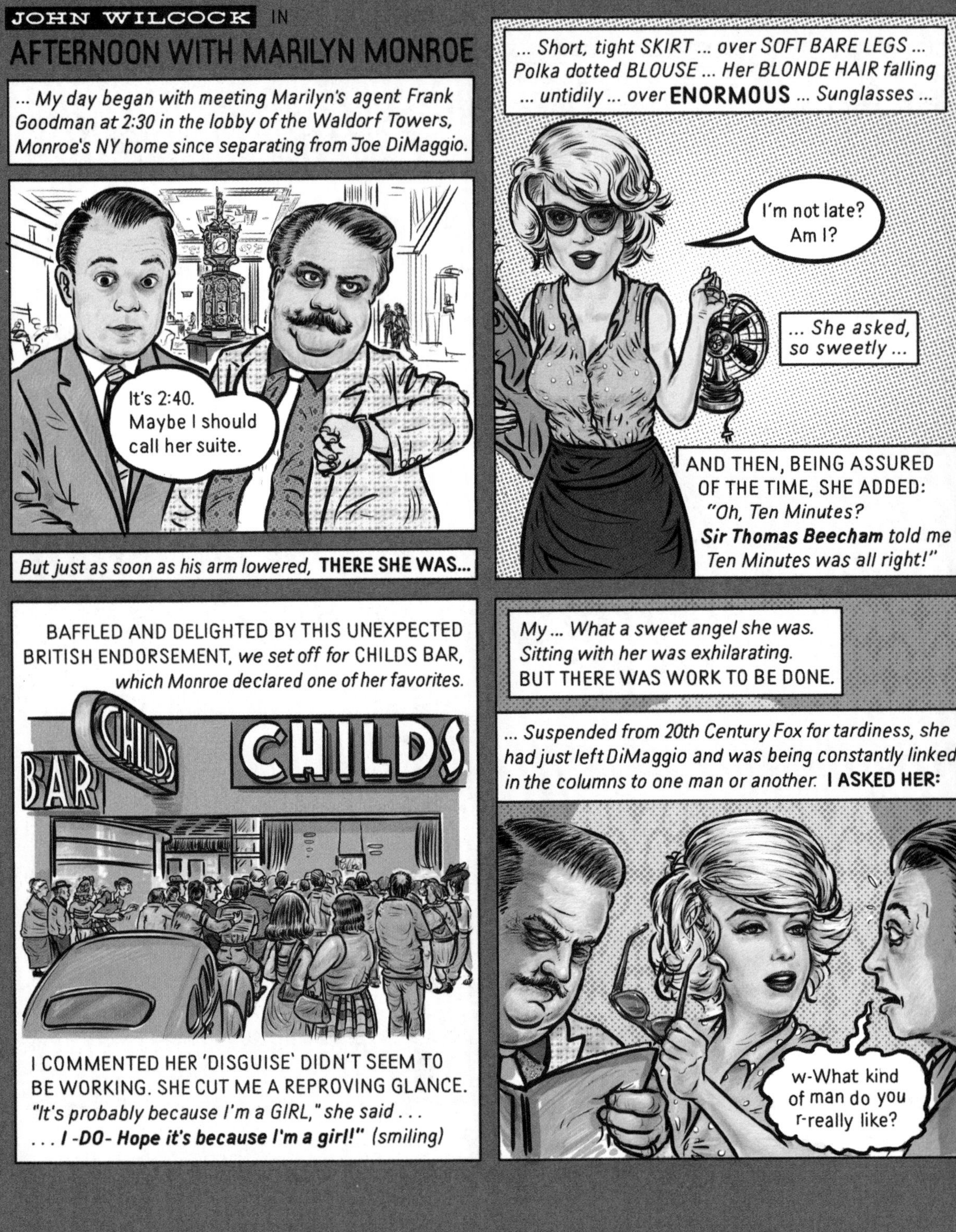
JOHN WILCOCK IN
AFTERNOON WITH MARILYN MONROE
... My day began with meeting Marilyn's agent Frank Goodman at 2:30 in the lobby of the Waldorf Towers, Monroe's NY home since separating from Joe DiMaggio.
It's 2:40. Maybe I should call her suite.
But just as soon as his arm lowered, THERE SHE WAS...
... Short, tight SKIRT ... over SOFT BARE LEGS ... Polka dotted BLOUSE ... Her BLONDE HAIR falling ... untidily ... over ENORMOUS ... Sunglasses ...
I'm not late? Am I?
... She asked, so sweetly ...
AND THEN, BEING ASSURED OF THE TIME, SHE ADDED: "Oh, Ten Minutes? Sir Thomas Beecham told me Ten Minutes was all right!"
BAFFLED AND DELIGHTED BY THIS UNEXPECTED BRITISH ENDORSEMENT, we set off for CHILDS BAR, which Monroe declared one of her favorites.
CHILDS BAR
CHILDS
I COMMENTED HER 'DISGUISE' DIDN'T SEEM TO BE WORKING. SHE CUT ME A REPROVING GLANCE. "It's probably because I'm a GIRL," she said . . . . . . I -DO- Hope it's because I'm a girl!" (smiling)
My ... What a sweet angel she was. Sitting with her was exhilarating. BUT THERE WAS WORK TO BE DONE.
... Suspended from 20th Century Fox for tardiness, she had just left DiMaggio and was being constantly linked in the columns to one man or another. I ASKED HER:
w-What kind of man do you r-really like?

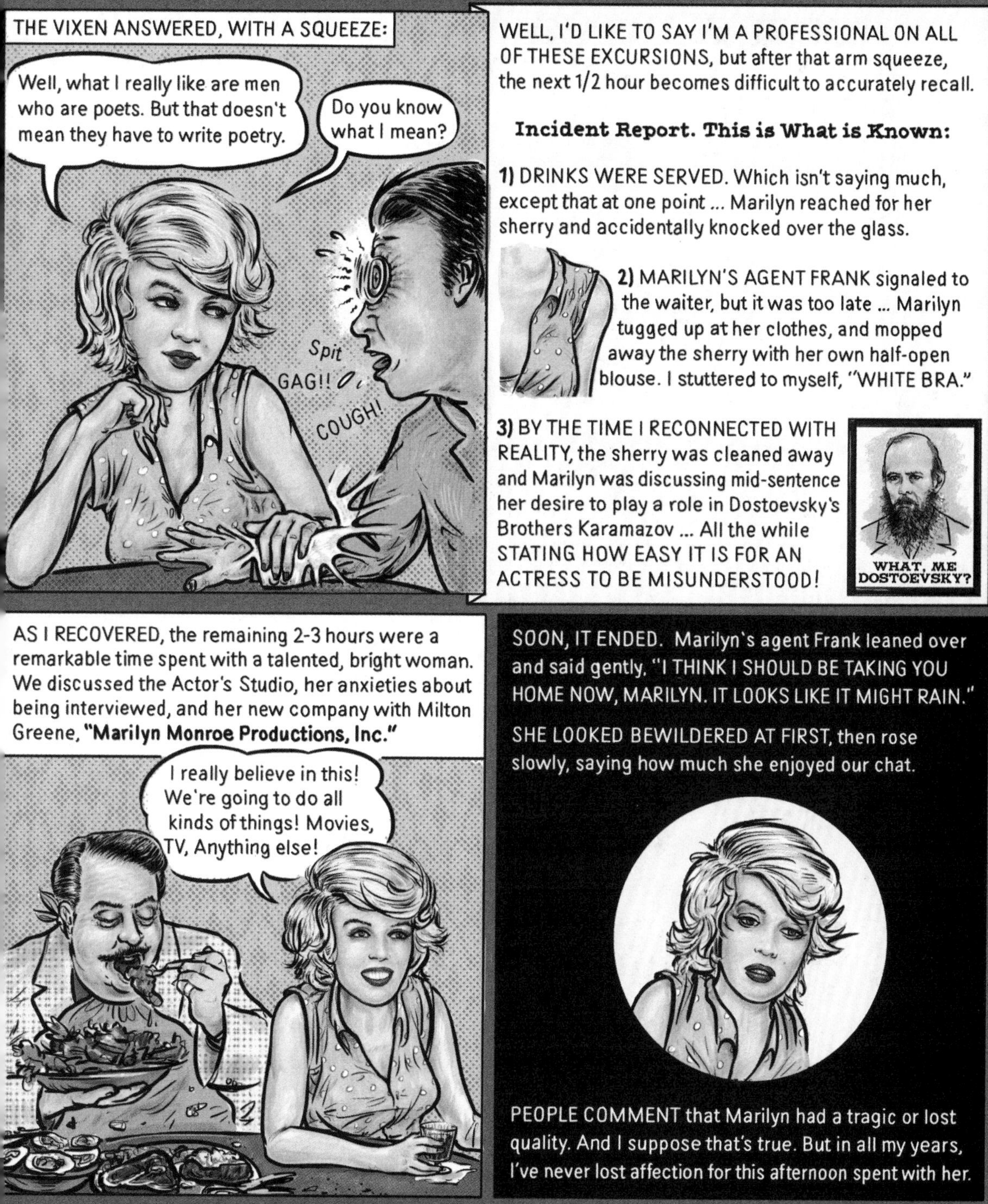
THE VIXEN ANSWERED, WITH A SQUEEZE:
Well, what I really like are men who are poets. But that doesn't mean they have to write poetry.
Do you know what I mean?
Spit
GAG!!
COUGH!
WELL, I'D LIKE TO SAY I'M A PROFESSIONAL ON ALL OF THESE EXCURSIONS, but after that arm squeeze, the next 1/2 hour becomes difficult to accurately recall.
Incident Report. This is What is Known:
1) DRINKS WERE SERVED. Which isn't saying much, except that at one point ... Marilyn reached for her sherry and accidentally knocked over the glass.
2) MARILYN'S AGENT FRANK signaled to the waiter, but it was too late ... Marilyn tugged up at her clothes, and mopped away the sherry with her own half-open blouse. I stuttered to myself, "WHITE BRA."
3) BY THE TIME I RECONNECTED WITH REALITY, the sherry was cleaned away and Marilyn was discussing mid-sentence her desire to play a role in Dostoevsky's Brothers Karamazov ... All the while STATING HOW EASY IT IS FOR AN ACTRESS TO BE MISUNDERSTOOD!
WHAT, ME DOSTOEVSKY?
AS I RECOVERED, the remaining 2-3 hours were a remarkable time spent with a talented, bright woman. We discussed the Actor's Studio, her anxieties about being interviewed, and her new company with Milton Greene, "Marilyn Monroe Productions, Inc."
I really believe in this! We're going to do all kinds of things! Movies, TV, Anything else!
SOON, IT ENDED. Marilyn's agent Frank leaned over and said gently, "I THINK I SHOULD BE TAKING YOU HOME NOW, MARILYN. IT LOOKS LIKE IT MIGHT RAIN."
SHE LOOKED BEWILDERED AT FIRST, then rose slowly, saying how much she enjoyed our chat.
PEOPLE COMMENT that Marilyn had a tragic or lost quality. And I suppose that's true. But in all my years, I've never lost affection for this afternoon spent with her.

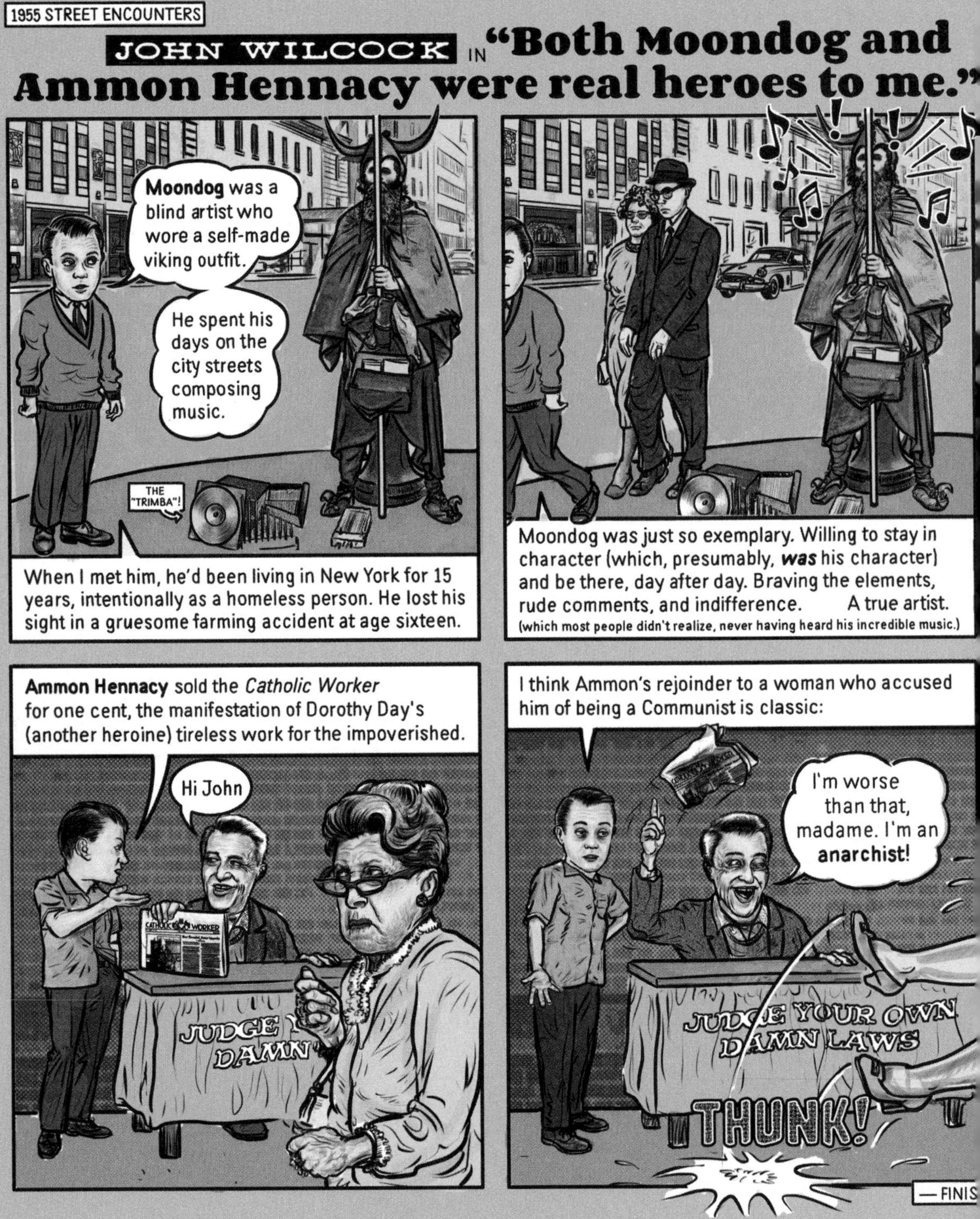
1955 STREET ENCOUNTERS
JOHN WILCOCK IN "Both Moondog and Ammon Hennacy were real heroes to me."
Moondog was a blind artist who wore a self-made viking outfit.
He spent his days on the city streets composing music.
THE "TRIMBA"!
When I met him, he'd been living in New York for 15 years, intentionally as a homeless person. He lost his sight in a gruesome farming accident at age sixteen.
Moondog was just so exemplary. Willing to stay in character (which, presumably, was his character) and be there, day after day. Braving the elements, rude comments, and indifference. A true artist.
(which most people didn't realize, never having heard his incredible music.)
Ammon Hennacy sold the Catholic Worker for one cent, the manifestation of Dorothy Day's (another heroine) tireless work for the impoverished.
Hi John
CATHOLIC WORKER
I think Ammon's rejoinder to a woman who accused him of being a Communist is classic:
I'm worse than that, madame. I'm an anarchist!
JUDGE YOUR OWN DAMN LAWS
THUNK!
—FINIS

# 1955 INTERVIEWS

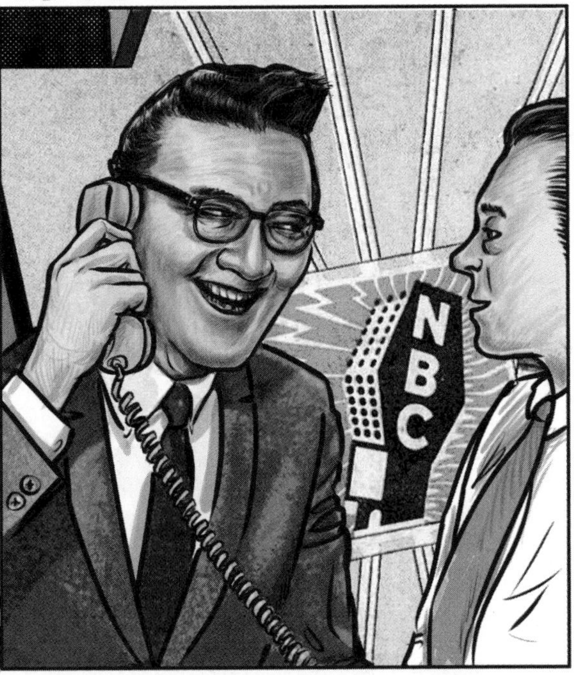
NBC

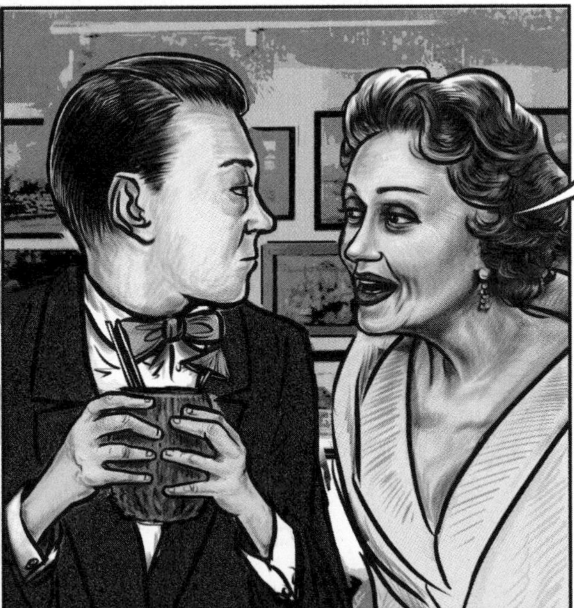

**Interviewing Steve Allen:** I was working for Liberty Magazine in 1955. Frank Rasky sent me to interview Allen, then the host of NBC's first incarnation of the Tonight Show. Many credit the late-night format that still exists (monologue, comedy routines, interviews, music, etc) to be Steve Allen's invention. I met with him at NBC.

(Pictured on the left: Allen performing for the interview his famous "funny phone bit", later popularized by Bob Newhart & Shelley Berman.)

At one point in our conversation, Allen went into the studio kitchen and made sandwiches. He wisecracked that he hoped I liked tuna fish ... because somebody once told him that tuna fish "didn't agree" with him. He visualised a tuna fish sandwich talking back: *"You're darned right I don't agree with you. Quit biting!"*

**Interviewing Marlene Dietrich:**
I arrived home one day to a ringing phone. When I picked up the receiver, a husky female voice purred acidly: *"Mr Wilcock? I understand you want to see me."* Dietrich's press agent had asked her to contact me about an interview, this job also for Liberty Magazine.

A few days later, I was in her Park Avenue apartment. Marlene had just completed a lucrative gig in Las Vegas ($30,000/week), but the assigned subject of the interview was her five-minute spots on TV where she gave married women advice. Marlene believed, she said:

"It is people's attitudes that make them unhappy ... and I tell these women watching the television sets at home ... that they are not alone in feeling this way."

I inquired if she felt a connection to the women she was addressing on television, mentioning that she was so often referred to as exotic and uncommon.

(Eva Gabor had said, for example, "Dietrich is the REAL GLAMOUR. When Marlene stretches her leg, a whole roomful of people Jump!")

Marlene commented that references to her as a "Glamorous Grandmother" were amusing, stating: "If you're admired, there's a stratosphere you reach where people aren't jealous anymore."

AS WE LEFT, my female assistant asked her if she had any advice for a woman (herself) who couldn't decide on a career or a family. "Unless you have UNUSUAL talent, dear," Marlene said, "I would marry and have children. What thrill does a woman get out of a failed career?"

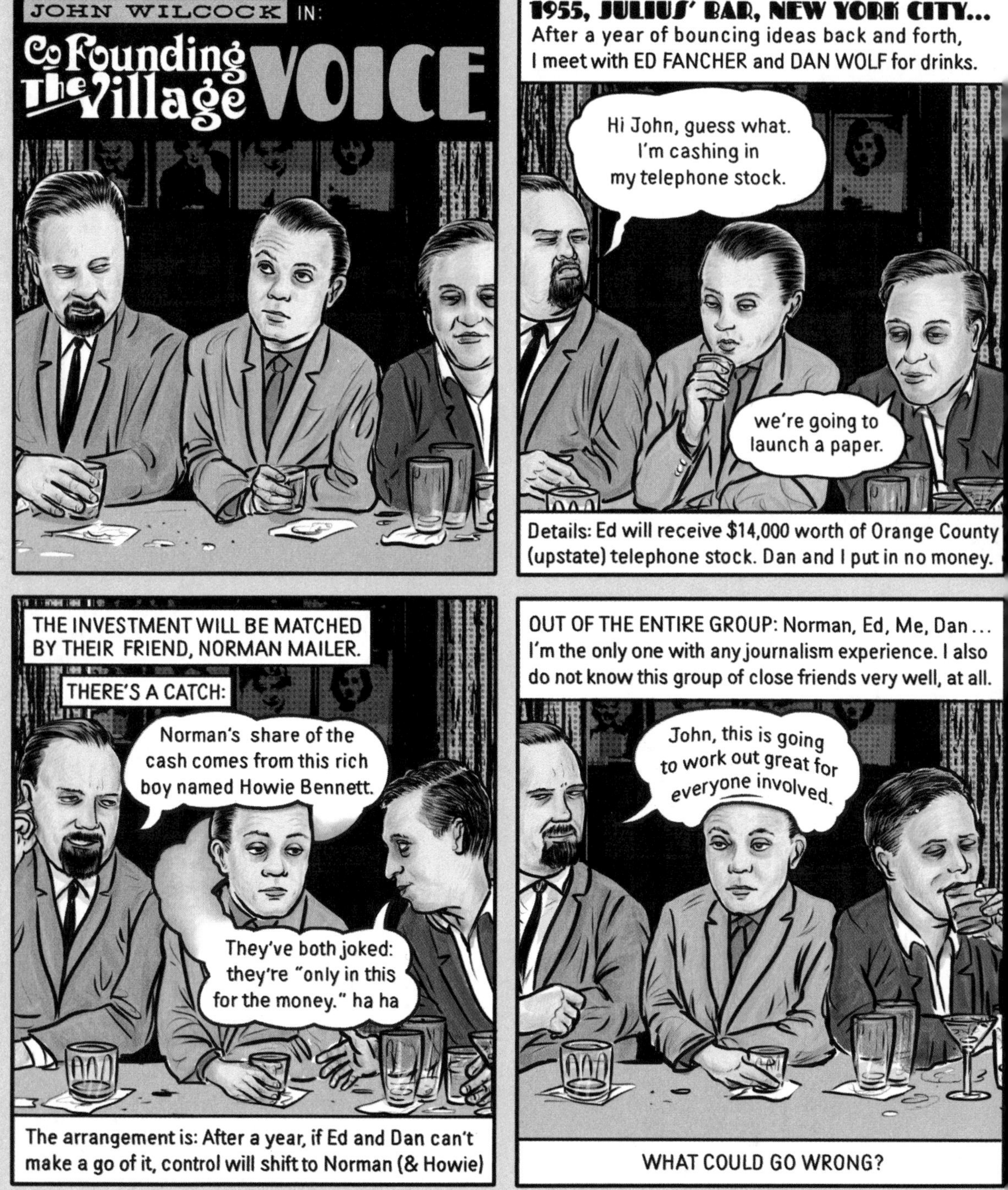

JOHN WILCOCK IN:
Co-Founding The Village VOICE
1955, JULIUS' BAR, NEW YORK CITY...
After a year of bouncing ideas back and forth, I meet with ED FANCHER and DAN WOLF for drinks.
Hi John, guess what. I'm cashing in my telephone stock.
we're going to launch a paper.
Details: Ed will receive $14,000 worth of Orange County (upstate) telephone stock. Dan and I put in no money.
THE INVESTMENT WILL BE MATCHED BY THEIR FRIEND, NORMAN MAILER.
THERE'S A CATCH:
Norman's share of the cash comes from this rich boy named Howie Bennett.
They've both joked: they're "only in this for the money." ha ha
The arrangement is: After a year, if Ed and Dan can't make a go of it, control will shift to Norman (& Howie)
OUT OF THE ENTIRE GROUP: Norman, Ed, Me, Dan... I'm the only one with any journalism experience. I also do not know this group of close friends very well, at all.
John, this is going to work out great for everyone involved.
WHAT COULD GO WRONG?

**CO-FOUNDING THE VILLAGE VOICE,** continued:

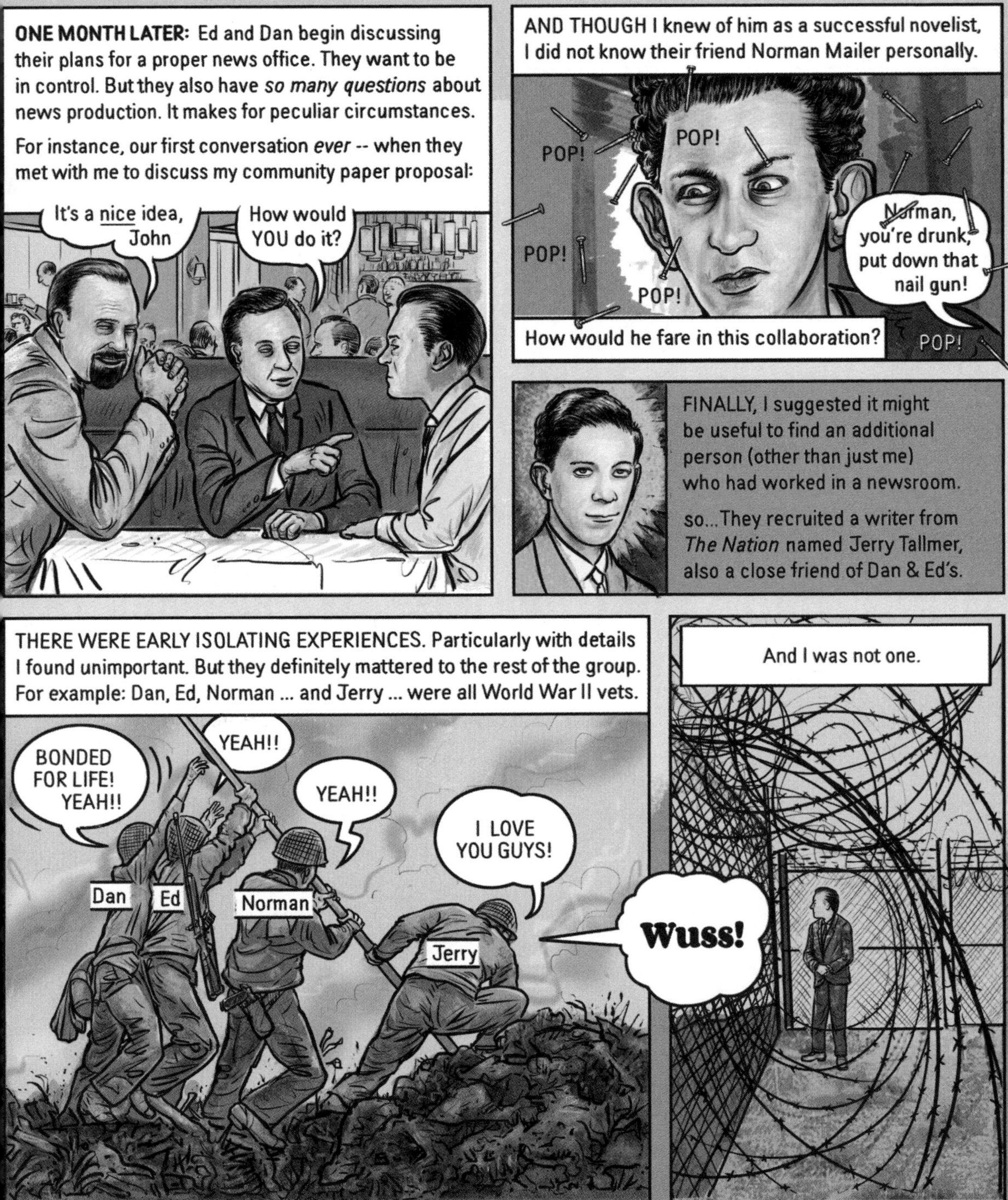
ONE MONTH LATER: Ed and Dan begin discussing their plans for a proper news office. They want to be in control. But they also have so many questions about news production. It makes for peculiar circumstances.
For instance, our first conversation ever -- when they met with me to discuss my community paper proposal:
It's a nice idea, John
How would YOU do it?
AND THOUGH I knew of him as a successful novelist, I did not know their friend Norman Mailer personally.
POP!
POP!
POP!
POP!
Norman, you're drunk, put down that nail gun!
How would he fare in this collaboration?
POP!
FINALLY, I suggested it might be useful to find an additional person (other than just me) who had worked in a newsroom.
so...They recruited a writer from The Nation named Jerry Tallmer, also a close friend of Dan & Ed's.
THERE WERE EARLY ISOLATING EXPERIENCES. Particularly with details I found unimportant. But they definitely mattered to the rest of the group. For example: Dan, Ed, Norman ... and Jerry ... were all World War II vets.
BONDED FOR LIFE! YEAH!!
YEAH!!
YEAH!!
I LOVE YOU GUYS!
Dan
Ed
Norman
Jerry
Wuss!
And I was not one.

Of course, my lack of involvement in the war wasn't out of cowardice; it just meant I was a bit younger than the others.

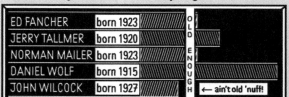

| | | OLD ENOUGH | |
|---|---|---|---|
| ED FANCHER | born 1923 | | |
| JERRY TALLMER | born 1920 | | |
| NORMAN MAILER | born 1923 | | |
| DANIEL WOLF | born 1915 | | |
| JOHN WILCOCK | born 1927 | ← ain't old 'nuff! | |

I was away at boarding school from 1937 until 1943, and had just turned the enlistable age of eighteen a month before the war ended in 1945.

I DEFINITELY DID SEE AND FEEL WAR, HOWEVER.

Sheffield, a major steel center, was bombed HEAVILY.
My mother, father and I used to shelter in the cupboard-sized coal cellar during the raids.

BOOM!

BOOM!

Boom!

BOOM!

MY FATHER SERVED IN WORLD WAR ONE, WAS GASSED IN THE TRENCHES, AND EMOTIONALLY DISTANT UNTIL HIS DEATH IN 1950.

I HAVE ALWAYS BEEN OUTSPOKEN ABOUT THE FUTILITY OF ALL WARS, AND CONSIDER NO WARS TO BE *GOOD* WARS, OR HAVE *GOOD* OR *BAD* SOLDIERS.

There's no value to any of it.

Jerry, even if I'd been forced to fight, I doubt I'd be pleased with myself.

THERE'S A CHANCE MY VIEWS ON "THE OLE' BIG ONE" WERE JUST AS BLUNTLY STATED, AND RUBBED THOSE VETERAN BUDDIES WRONG.

THE PROUDEST VET OF THE FOUR, JERRY TALLMER, FOR EXAMPLE … seemed to dislike me INSTANTLY … So much so, that in ensuing decades he became a vocal eliminator of my name from the Voice's history.

Fuck off, John.

You know who **we** are, Dan? You, Me, Ed and Norman? We're the **"Village Voice Four!"**

BUT THAT'S A STORY FOR A LATER TIME.

## Assembling the first issue of THE VILLAGE VOICE:

OVER THE SUMMER OF 1955, we began on the first issue of this new endeavor ... Assembling the first office, a rental above Sutter's Bakeshop on Greenwich Avenue ... Constructing and painting an office notice board ... Planning news features ...

... And reviewing the work of numerous volunteers, two out of three of whom wanted to write a column.

*Give me a column.*

*No, give **me** a column.*

*Give <u>me</u> a bed.*

THE OFFICE, FORMERLY AN APARTMENT, HAD A SHOWER AND A BED IN THE BACK ROOM, AND AN OCCASIONAL HOMELESS VOLUNTEER WOULD SLEEP THERE OVERNIGHT.

*hee hee!*

*Honey, it's okay. I'm gonna be a published author.*

A PITY THE BED COULDN'T WRITE ITS OWN MEMOIRS

This first workspace on Greenwich Avenue and 6th was opposite "THE WOMEN'S HOUSE OF DETENTION", a 20-story women's prison. All day and night, relatives and friends of prisoners would gather on the sidewalk below and shout up to the inmates ...

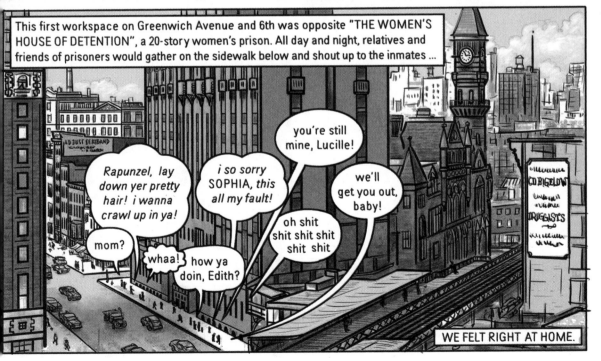

*Rapunzel, lay down yer pretty hair! i wanna crawl up in ya!*

*mom?*

*whaa!*

*i so sorry SOPHIA, this all my fault!*

*how ya doin, Edith?*

*you're still mine, Lucille!*

*oh shit shit shit shit shit shit*

*we'll get you out, baby!*

WE FELT RIGHT AT HOME.

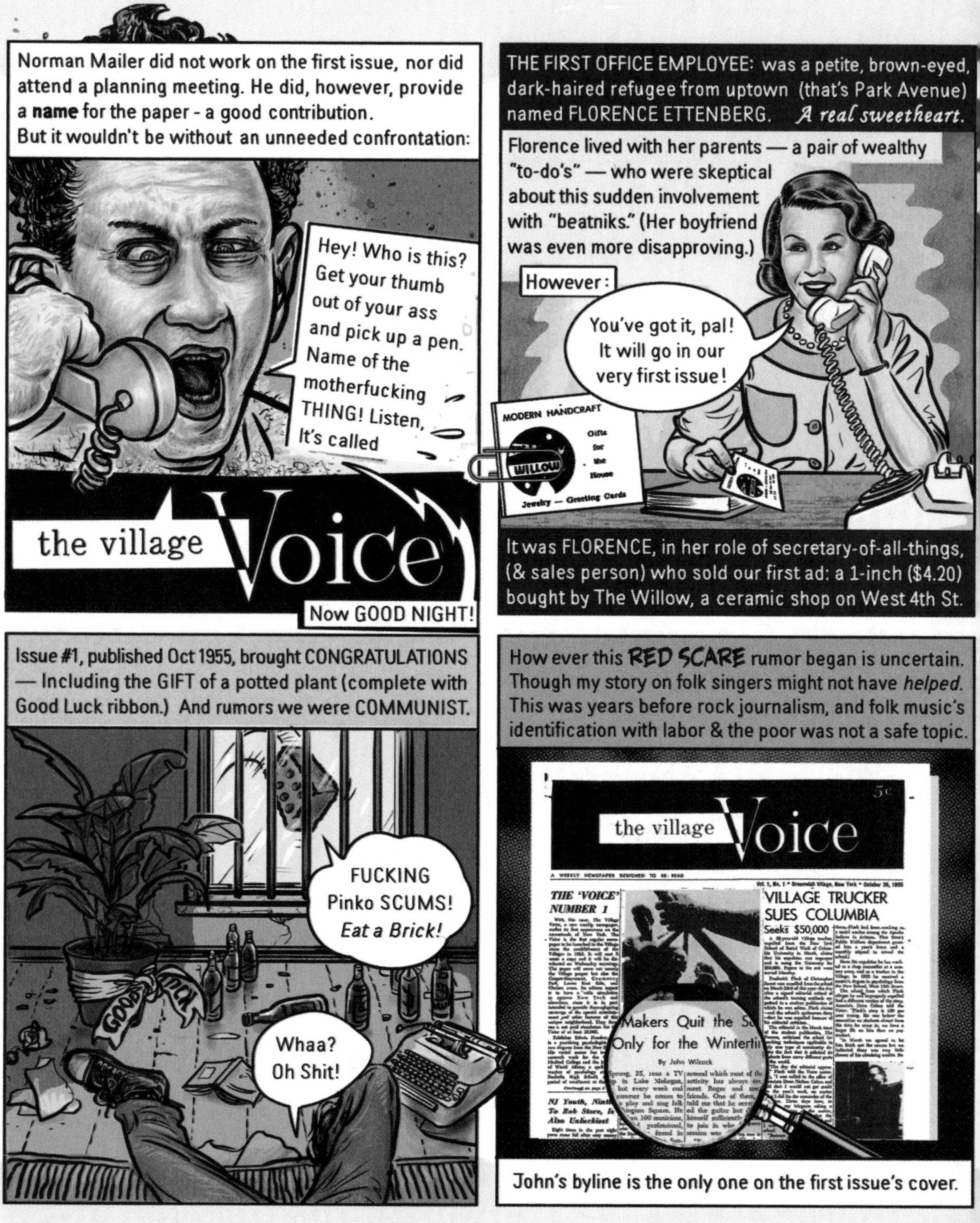

Norman Mailer did not work on the first issue, nor did attend a planning meeting. He did, however, provide a **name** for the paper - a good contribution.
But it wouldn't be without an unneeded confrontation:
Hey! Who is this? Get your thumb out of your ass and pick up a pen. Name of the motherfucking THING! Listen, It's called
the village Voice
Now GOOD NIGHT!
THE FIRST OFFICE EMPLOYEE: was a petite, brown-eyed, dark-haired refugee from uptown (that's Park Avenue) named FLORENCE ETTENBERG. *A real sweetheart.*
Florence lived with her parents — a pair of wealthy "to-do's" — who were skeptical about this sudden involvement with "beatniks." (Her boyfriend was even more disapproving.)
However:
You've got it, pal! It will go in our very first issue!
MODERN HANDCRAFT
WILLOW
Gifts for the House
Jewelry — Greeting Cards
It was FLORENCE, in her role of secretary-of-all-things, (& sales person) who sold our first ad: a 1-inch ($4.20) bought by The Willow, a ceramic shop on West 4th St.
Issue #1, published Oct 1955, brought CONGRATULATIONS — Including the GIFT of a potted plant (complete with Good Luck ribbon.) And rumors we were COMMUNIST.
FUCKING Pinko SCUMS! *Eat a Brick!*
GOOD LUCK
Whaa? Oh Shit!
How ever this **RED SCARE** rumor began is uncertain. Though my story on folk singers might not have *helped.* This was years before rock journalism, and folk music's identification with labor & the poor was not a safe topic.
5¢
the village Voice
A WEEKLY NEWSPAPER DESIGNED TO BE READ
THE 'VOICE' NUMBER 1
VILLAGE TRUCKER SUES COLUMBIA
Seeks $50,000
Makers Quit the Sq
Only for the Winterti
By John Wilcock
NJ Youth, Ninth To Rob Store, Is Also Unluckiest
John's byline is the only one on the first issue's cover.

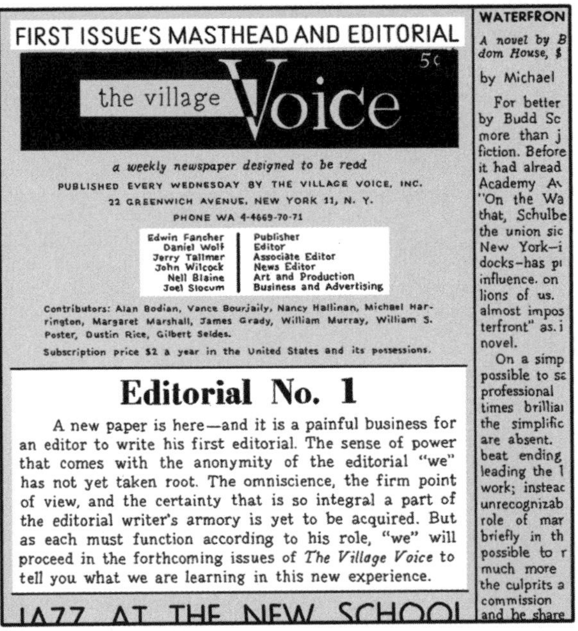

FIRST ISSUE'S MASTHEAD AND EDITORIAL

the village Voice 5¢

*a weekly newspaper designed to be read*

PUBLISHED EVERY WEDNESDAY BY THE VILLAGE VOICE, INC.
22 GREENWICH AVENUE, NEW YORK 11, N. Y.
PHONE WA 4-4669-70-71

| | |
|---|---|
| Edwin Fancher | Publisher |
| Daniel Wolf | Editor |
| Jerry Tallmer | Associate Editor |
| John Wilcock | News Editor |
| Nell Blaine | Art and Production |
| Joel Slocum | Business and Advertising |

Contributors: Alan Bodian, Vance Bourjaily, Nancy Hallinan, Michael Harrington, Margaret Marshall, James Grady, William Murray, William S. Poster, Dustin Rice, Gilbert Seldes.

Subscription price $2 a year in the United States and its possessions.

## Editorial No. 1

A new paper is here—and it is a painful business for an editor to write his first editorial. The sense of power that comes with the anonymity of the editorial "we" has not yet taken root. The omniscience, the firm point of view, and the certainty that is so integral a part of the editorial writer's armory is yet to be acquired. But as each must function according to his role, "we" will proceed in the forthcoming issues of *The Village Voice* to tell you what we are learning in this new experience.

JAZZ AT THE NEW SCHOOL

WATERFRON

*A novel by B dom House, $*

by Michael

For better by Budd Sc more than j fiction. Before it had alread Academy A "On the Wa that, Schulbe the union sic New York–i docks–has p influence on lions of us. almost impos terfront" as i novel.

On a simp possible to sa professional times brillia the simplific are absent. beat ending leading the l work; insteac unrecognizab role of mar briefly in th possible to r much more the culprits a commission and he share

Note: One year later, the art and production designer, **Nell Blaine**, would be included in the **1956 Whitney Annual (now called the Biennial)** for her paintings.
**Additional Note**: Somewhat funny "Editorial No. 1" (above) written by Dan Wolf.

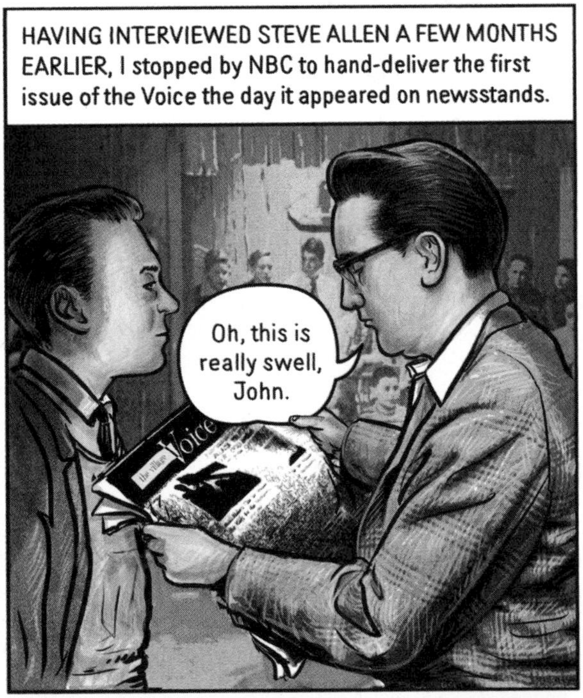
HAVING INTERVIEWED STEVE ALLEN A FEW MONTHS EARLIER, I stopped by NBC to hand-deliver the first issue of the Voice the day it appeared on newsstands.
Oh, this is really swell, John.
the village Voice

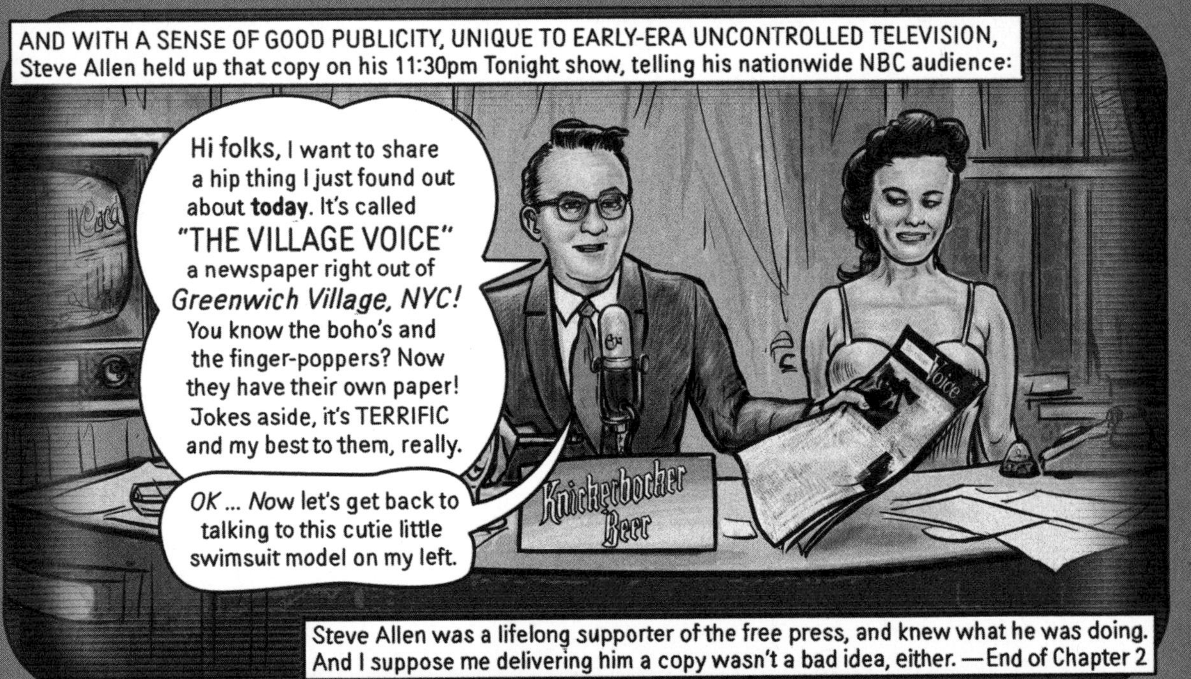
AND WITH A SENSE OF GOOD PUBLICITY, UNIQUE TO EARLY-ERA UNCONTROLLED TELEVISION, Steve Allen held up that copy on his 11:30pm Tonight show, telling his nationwide NBC audience:
Hi folks, I want to share a hip thing I just found out about **today**. It's called "THE VILLAGE VOICE" a newspaper right out of *Greenwich Village, NYC!* You know the boho's and the finger-poppers? Now they have their own paper! Jokes aside, it's TERRIFIC and my best to them, really.
*OK* ... *Now* let's get back to talking to this cutie little swimsuit model on my left.
Knickerbocker Beer
Voice
Steve Allen was a lifelong supporter of the free press, and knew what he was doing. And I suppose me delivering him a copy wasn't a bad idea, either. —End of Chapter 2

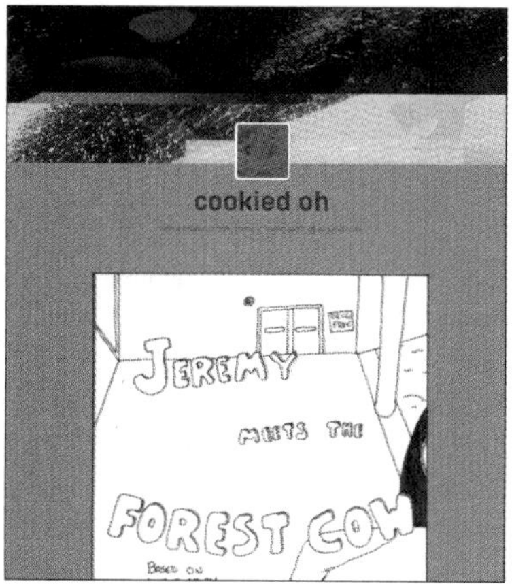
cookied oh
JEREMY
MEETS THE
FOREST COW

# Jeremy Meets the Forest Cow

SIENNA CITTADINO

*originally published at*

notyrman.tumblr.com

SELF-PUBLISHED

digital

## Biography

Sienna Cittadino is from Southern Illinois, the home of the beautiful Shawnee Forest and many, many good people. Now, Sienna lives in Pittsburgh, Pennsylvania, where there are many, many good people. She gets sad sometimes but she is also happy. She spends most of her time in libraries or on the bus. She is hopeful.
notyrman.tumblr.com

## Statement

This comic was created for the Comics Workbook Composition Competition in 2016. It's a great competition that, among other things, helps people who don't know a lot about publishing comics (like me) get them out into the world. The comic is about high school and the things that happen to us when we're in high school. It's also about mental illness and substance abuse and socioeconomic class and how things aren't fair. This comic is primarily owed to Jeremy, who I hope is having a fine time. It's based on true events.

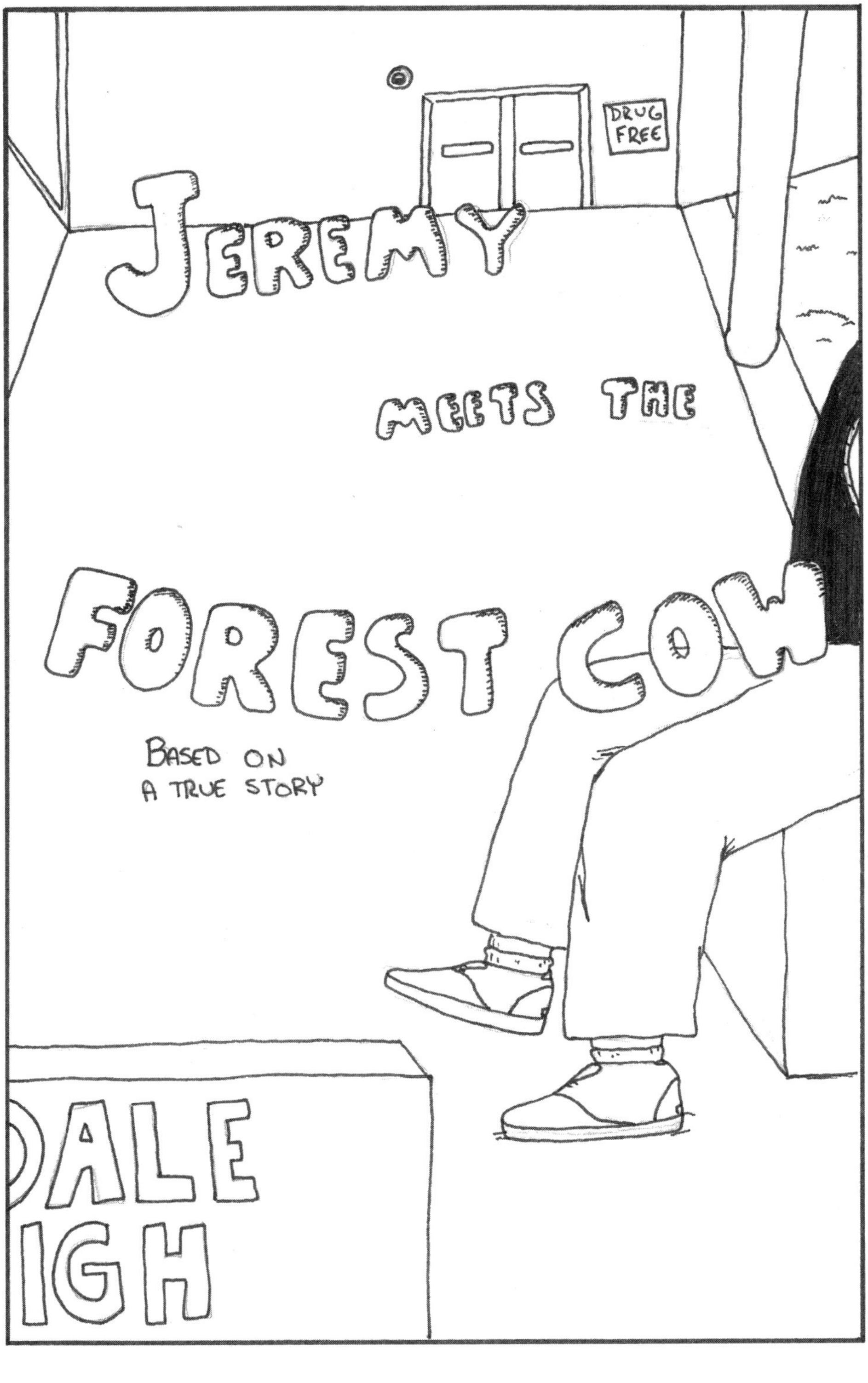
DRUG FREE
JEREMY
MEETS THE
FOREST COW
BASED ON A TRUE STORY
DALE
IGH

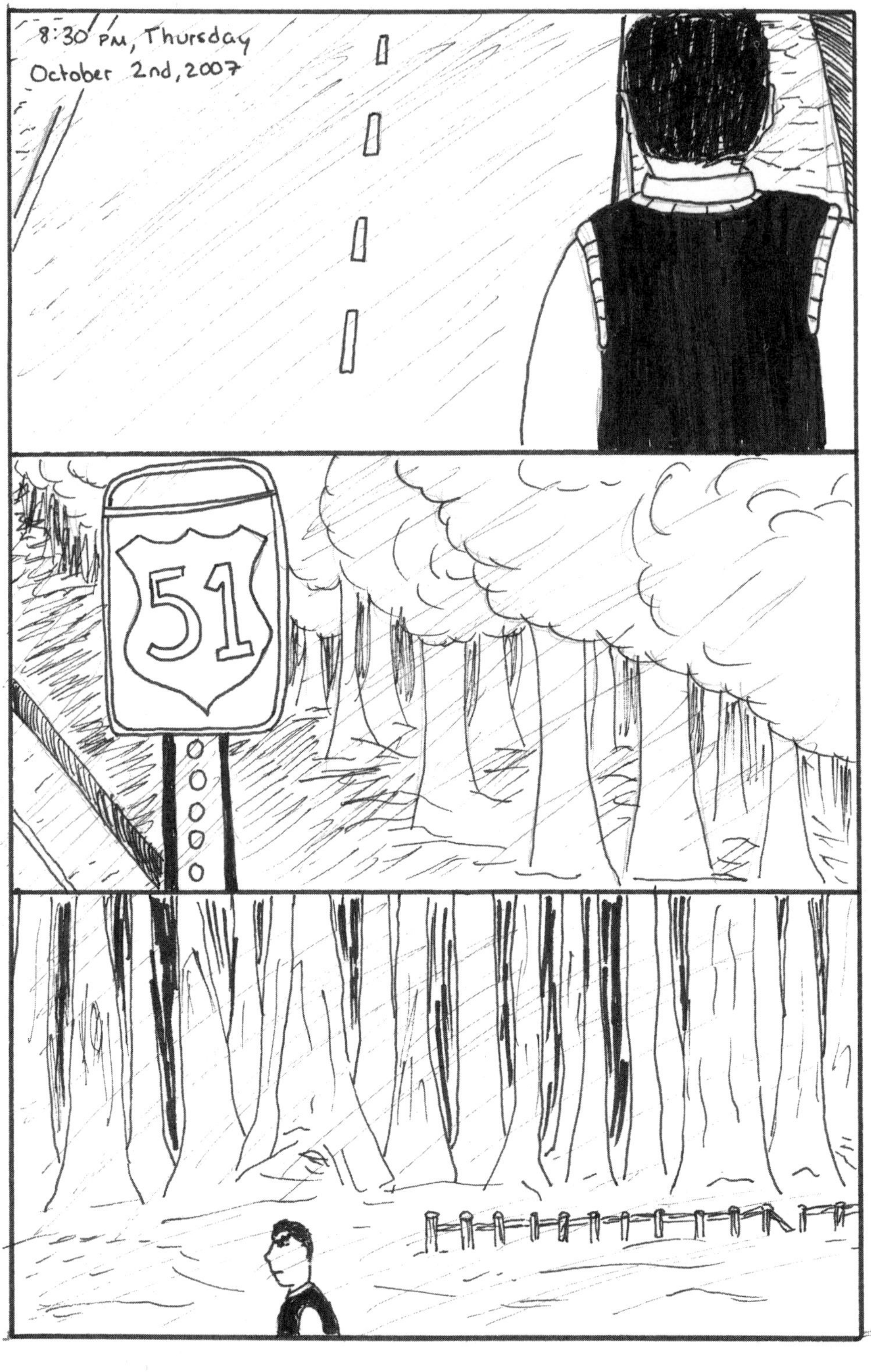
8:30 PM, Thursday
October 2nd, 2007
51

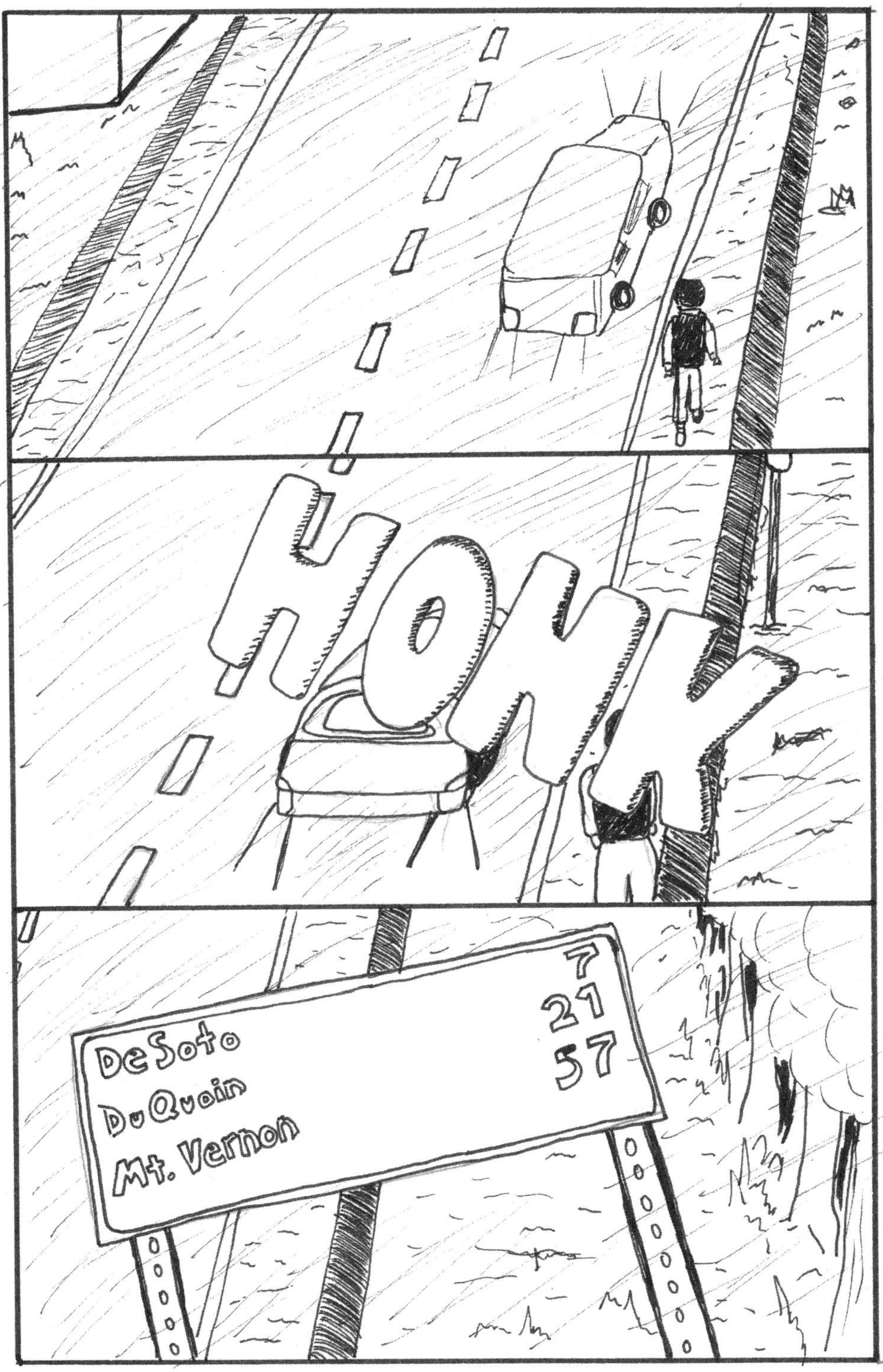
HONK
DeSoto 7
DuQuoin 21
Mt. Vernon 57

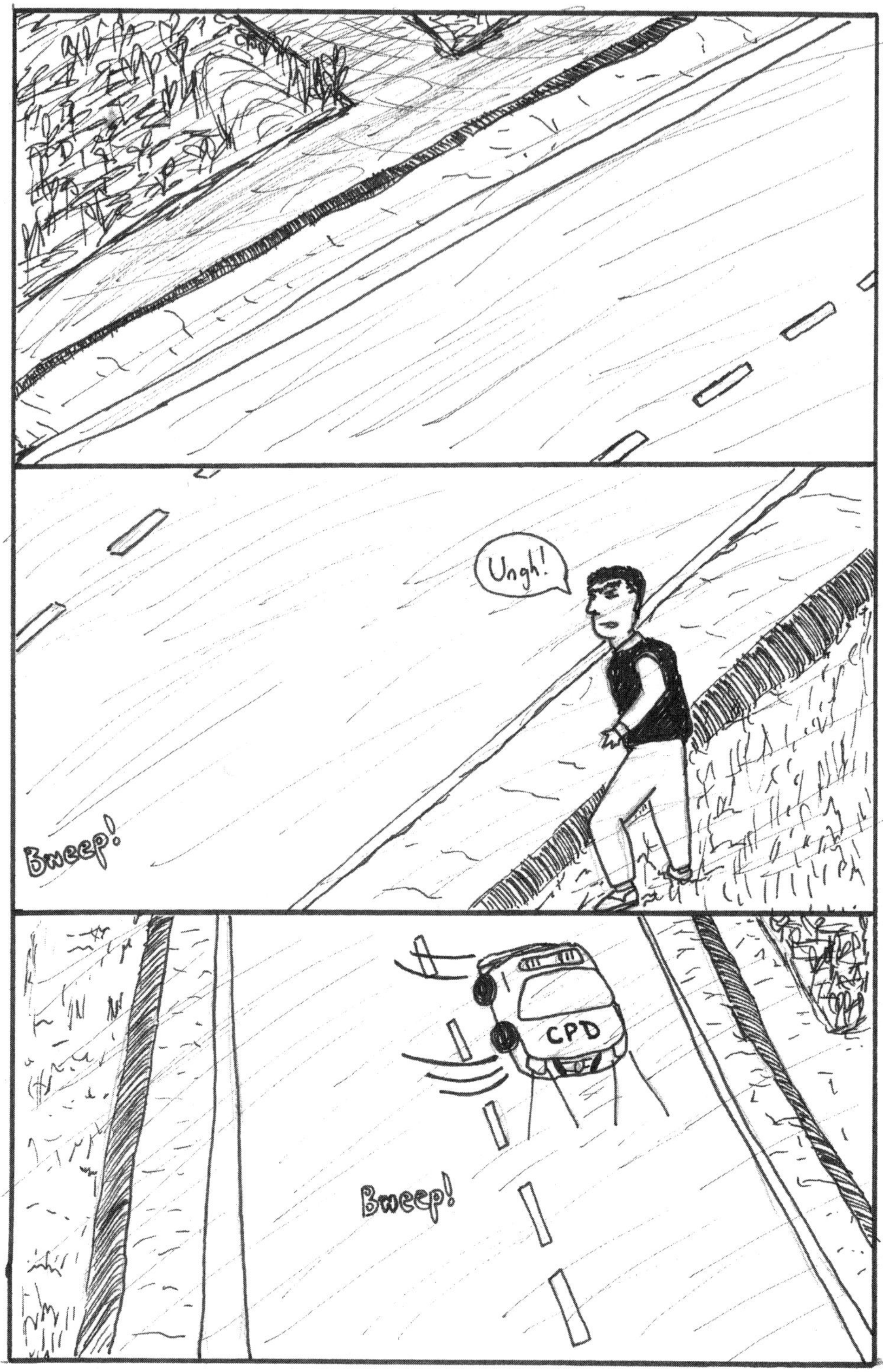
Ungh!
Bweep!
CPD
Bweep!

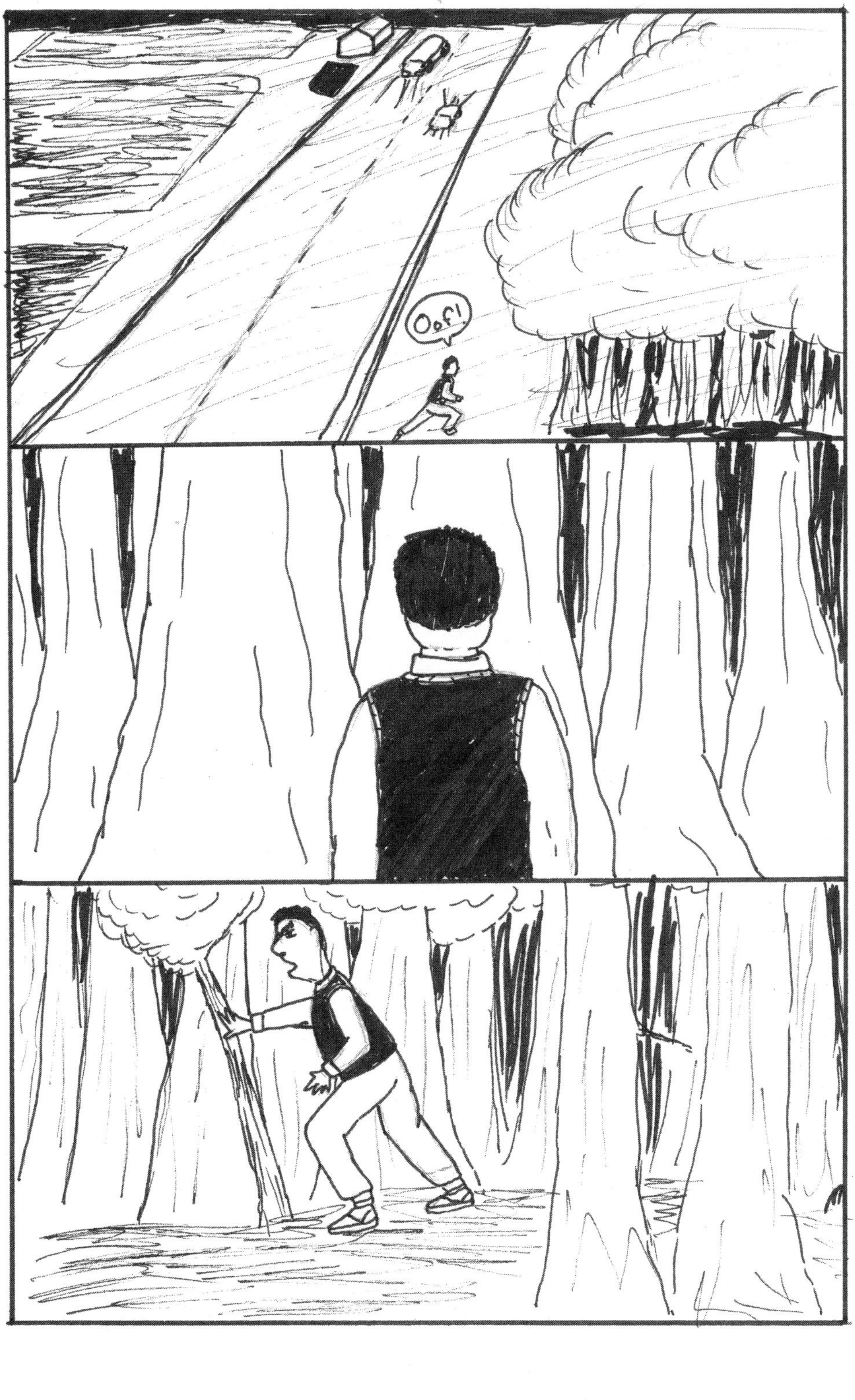
Oof!

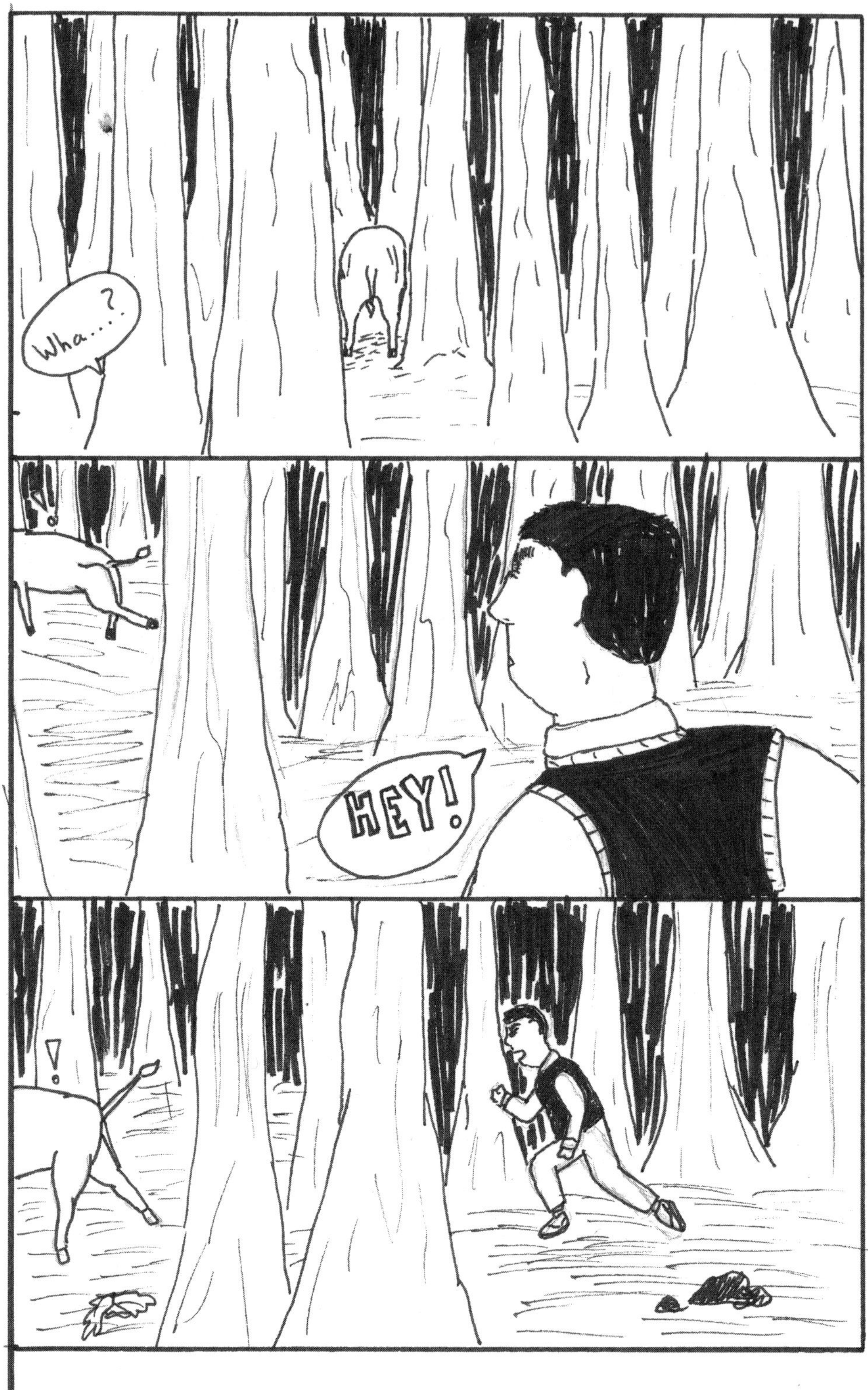
Wha...?
HEY!

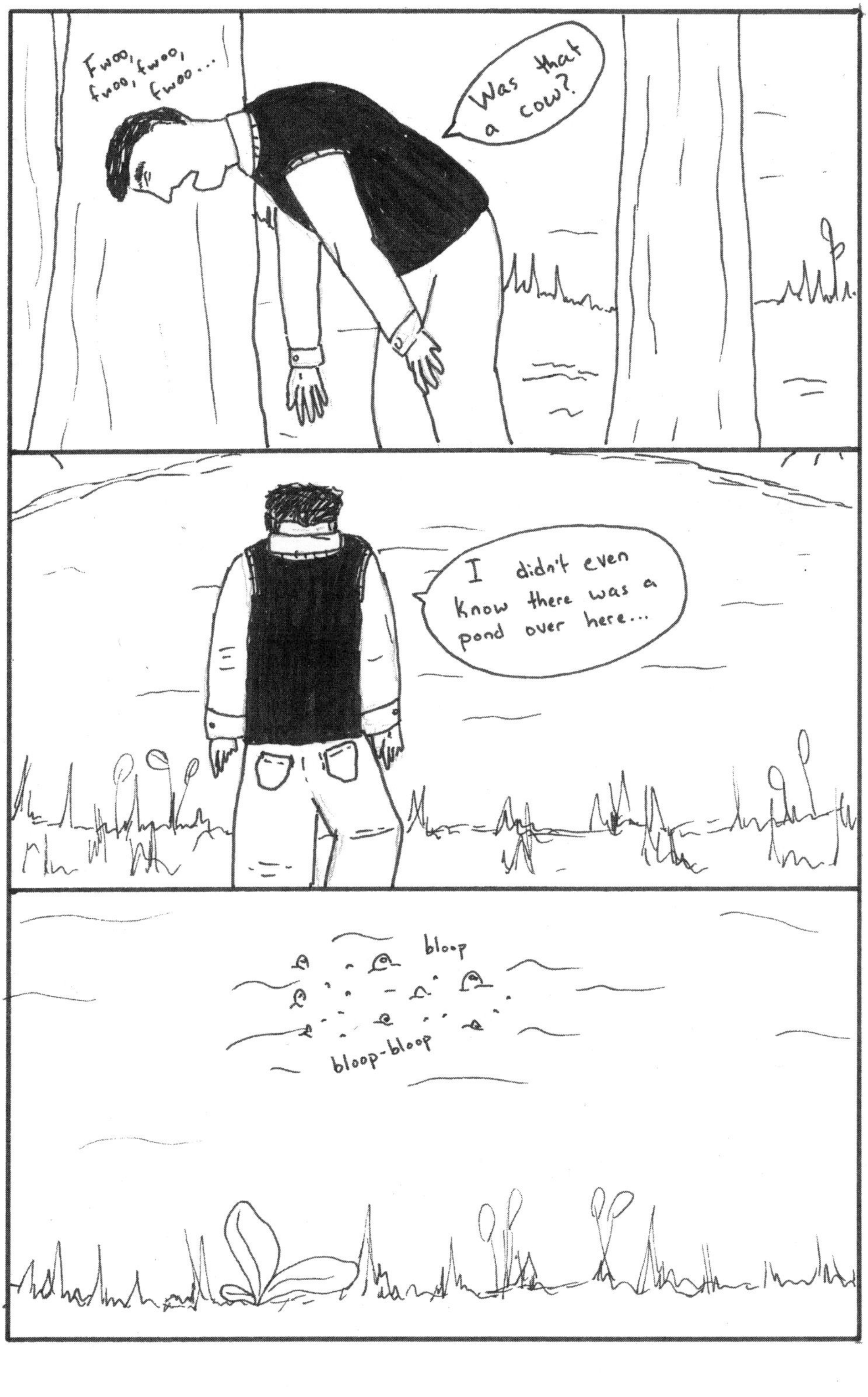
Fwoo, fwoo, fwoo, fwoo...
Was that a cow?
I didn't even know there was a pond over here...
bloop
bloop-bloop

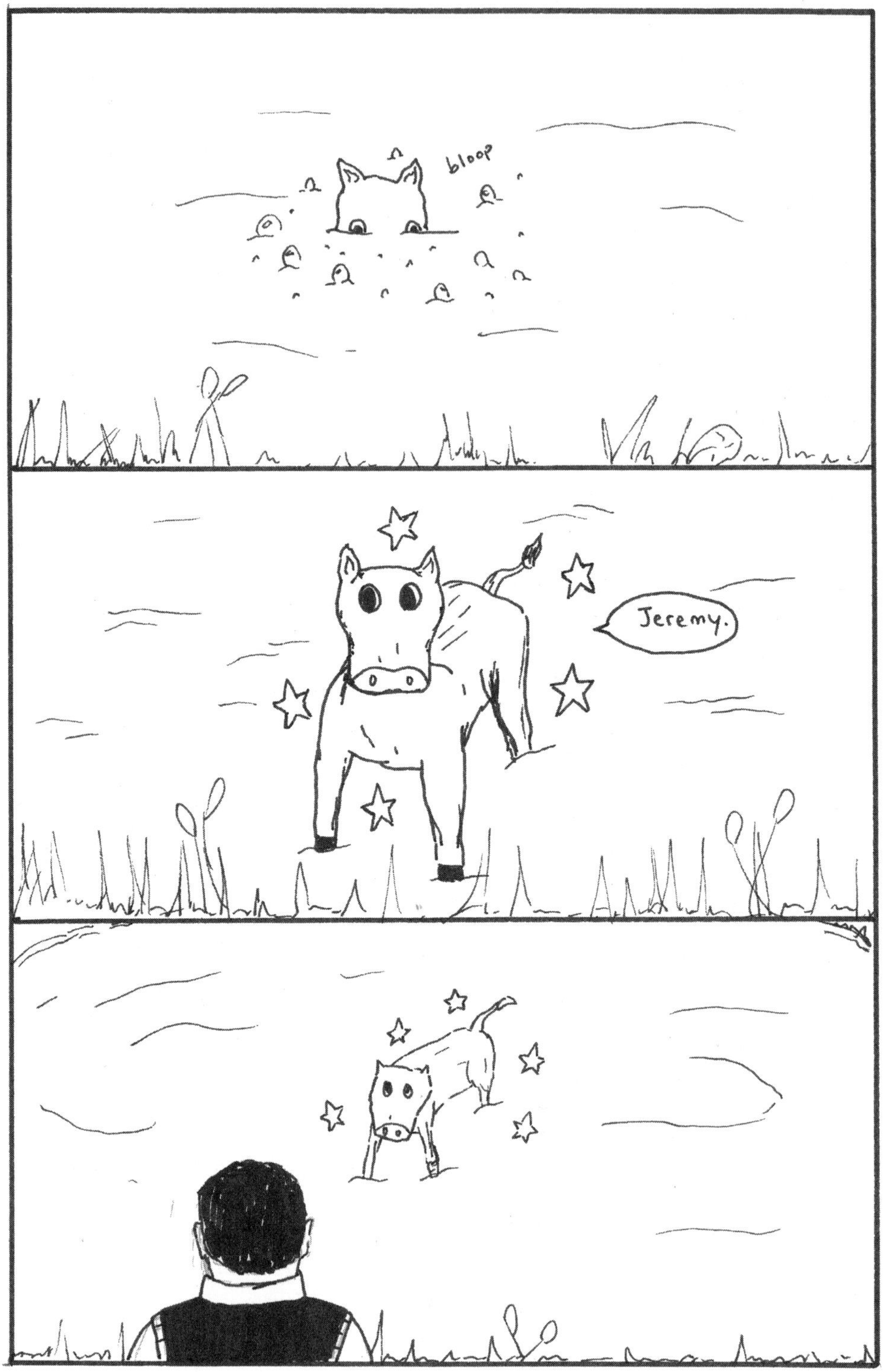
bloop
Jeremy.

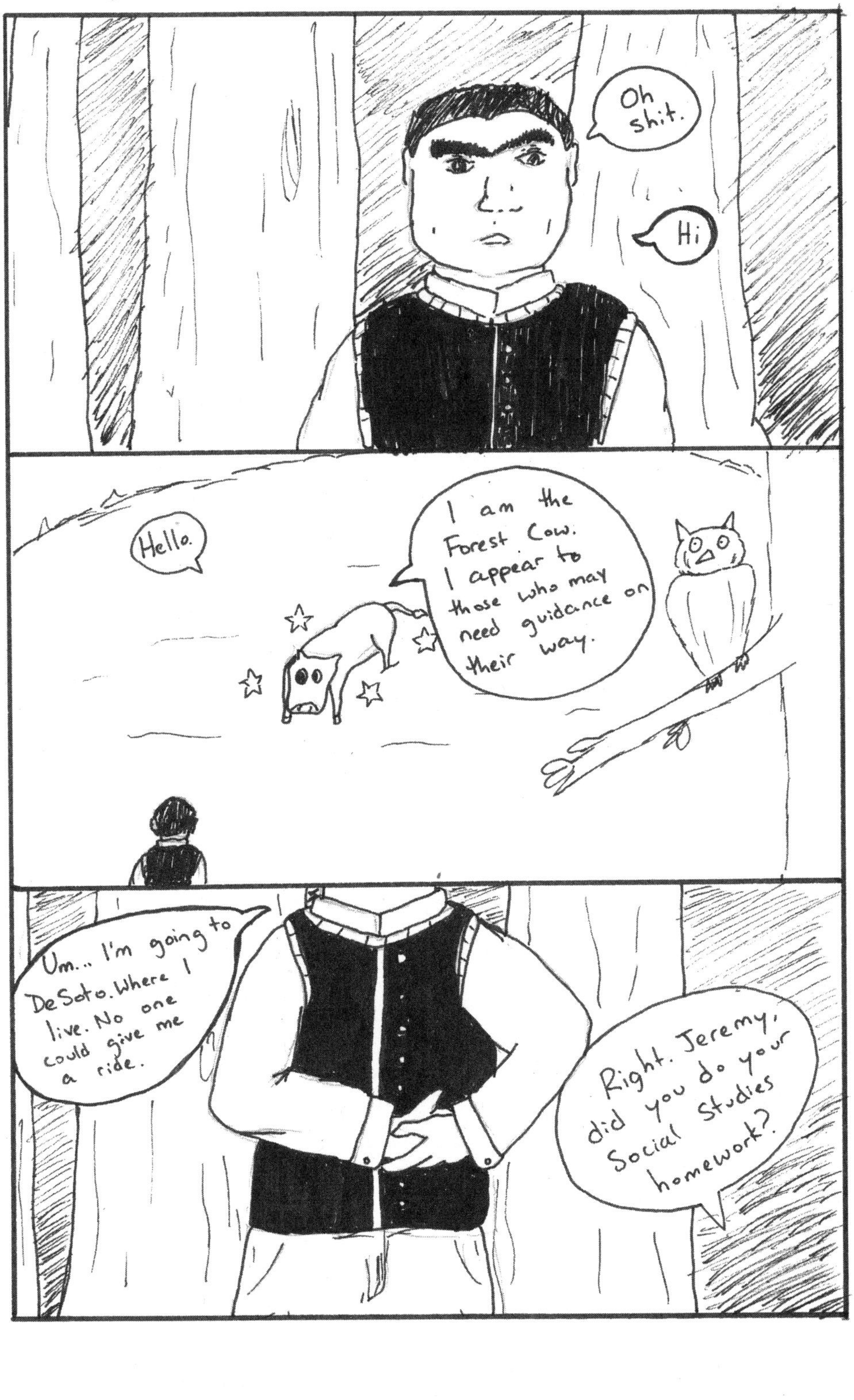

Oh shit.
Hi
Hello.
I am the Forest Cow. I appear to those who may need guidance on their way.
Um... I'm going to DeSoto. Where I live. No one could give me a ride.
Right. Jeremy, did you do your Social Studies homework?

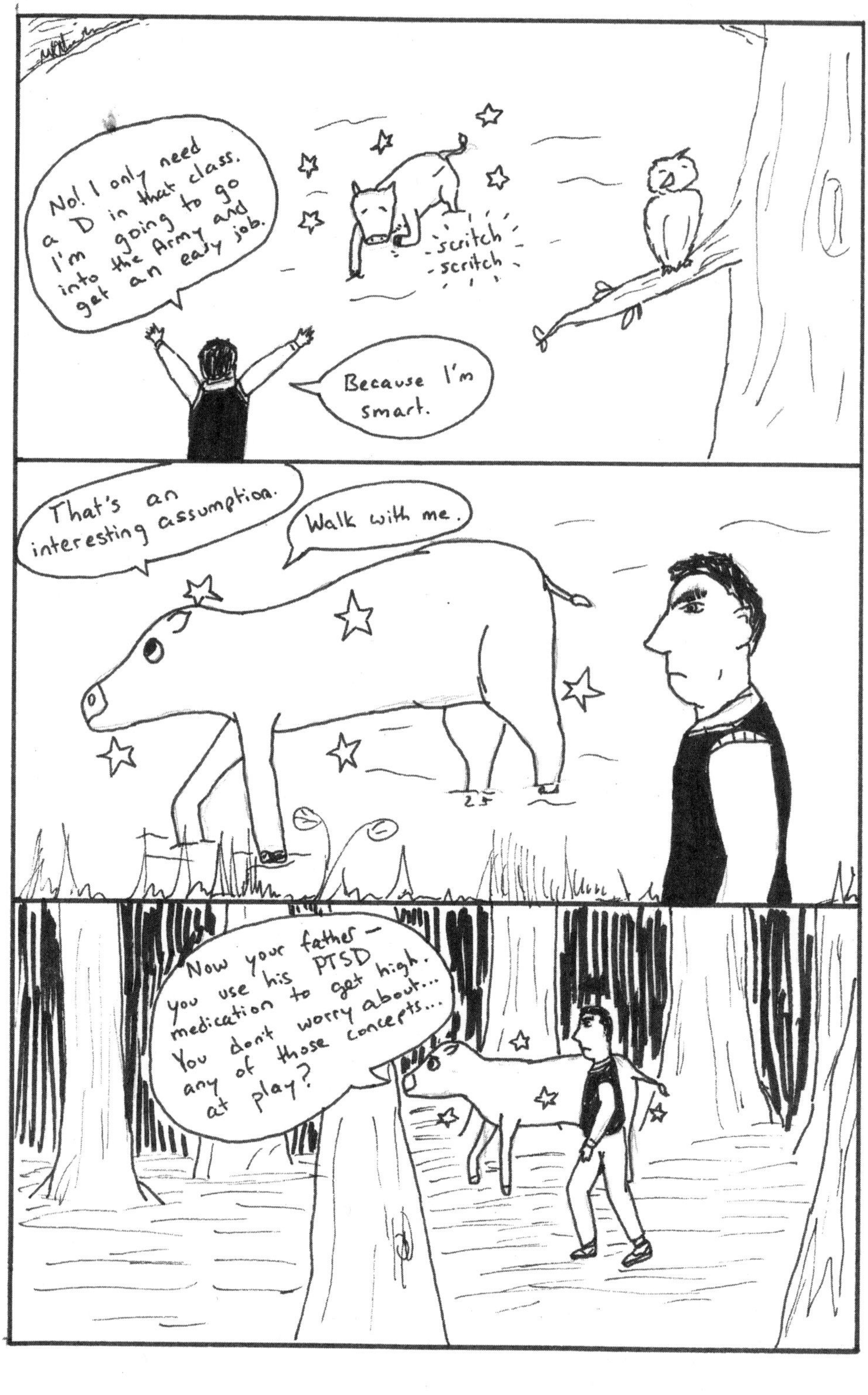
No! I only need a D in that class. I'm going to go into the Army and get an easy job.
scritch scritch
Because I'm smart.
That's an interesting assumption.
Walk with me.
Now your father — you use his PTSD medication to get high. You don't worry about... any of those concepts... at play?

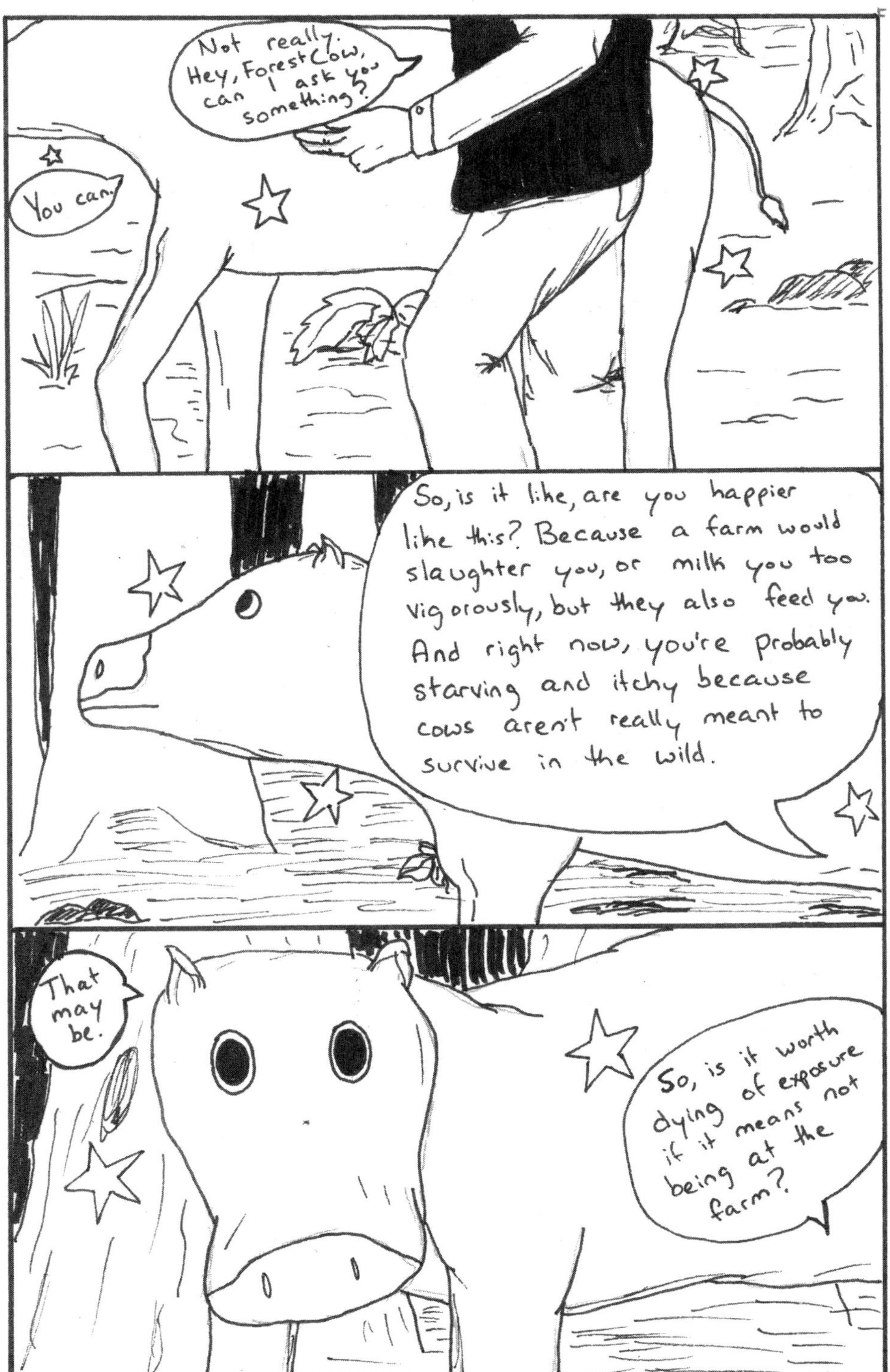
Not really. Hey, Forest Cow, can I ask you something?
You can.
So, is it like, are you happier like this? Because a farm would slaughter you, or milk you too vigorously, but they also feed you. And right now, you're probably starving and itchy because cows aren't really meant to survive in the wild.
That may be.
So, is it worth dying of exposure if it means not being at the farm?

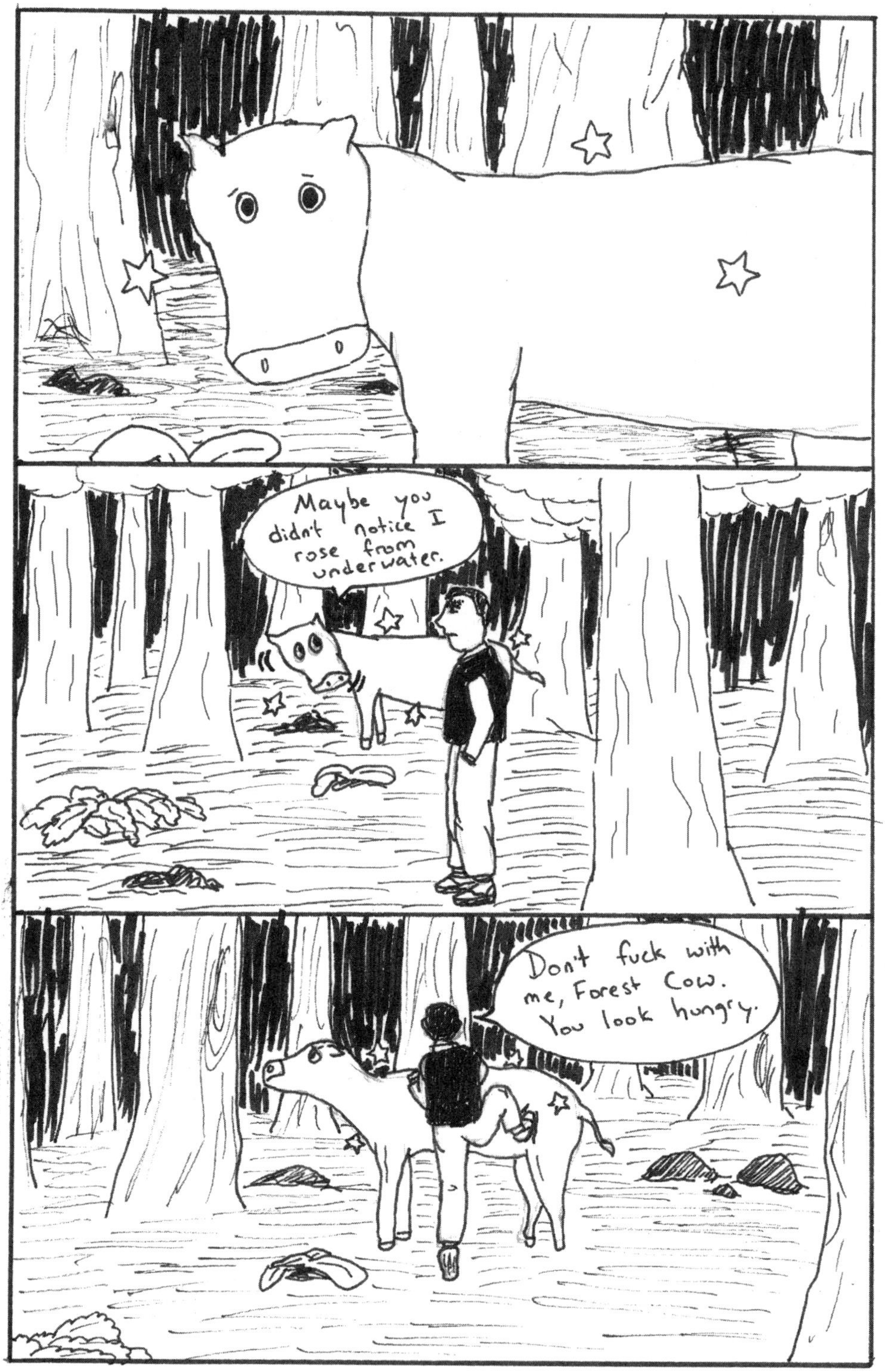
Maybe you didn't notice I rose from underwater.
Don't fuck with me, Forest Cow. You look hungry.

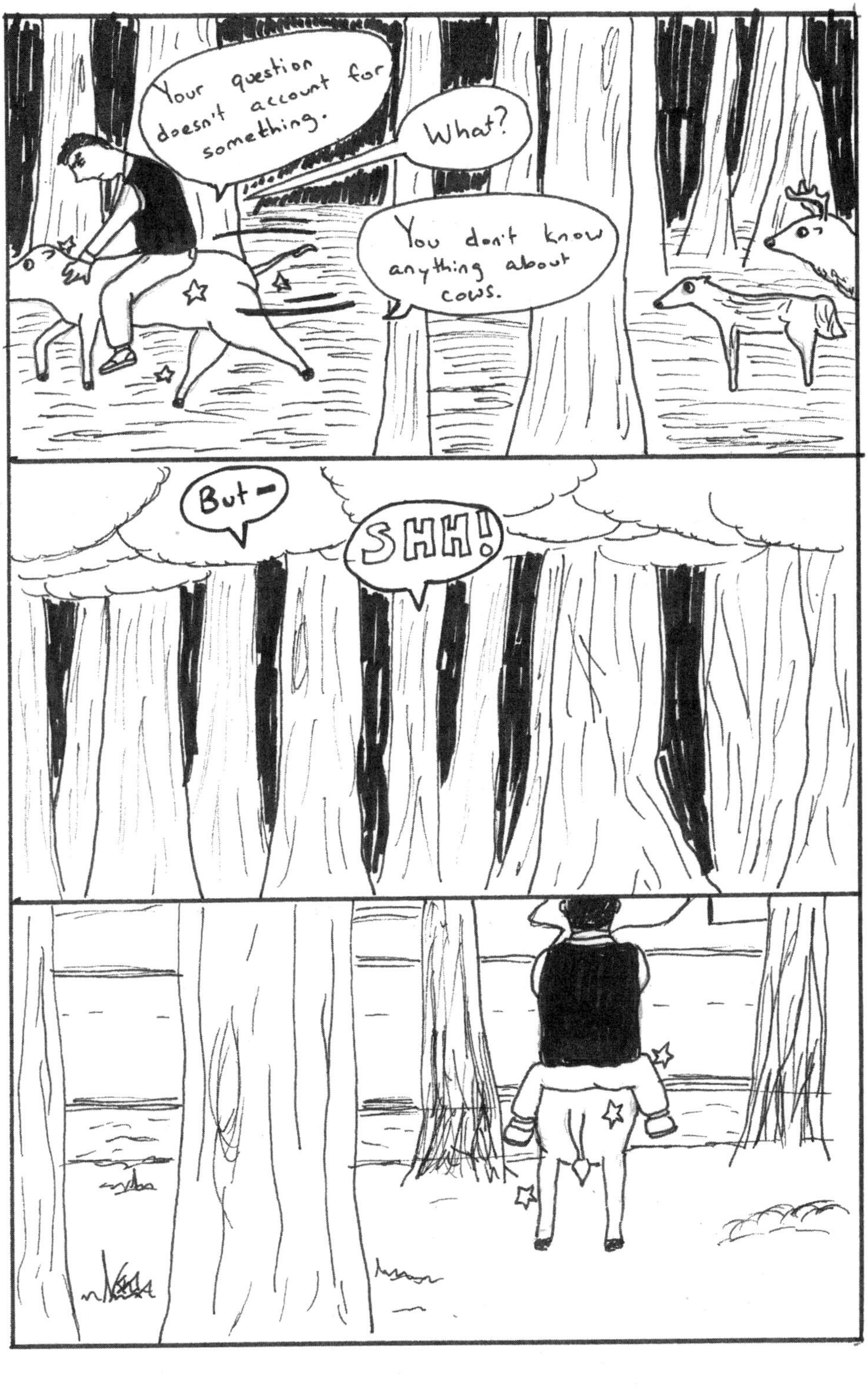
Your question doesn't account for something.
What?
You don't know anything about cows.
But—
SHH!

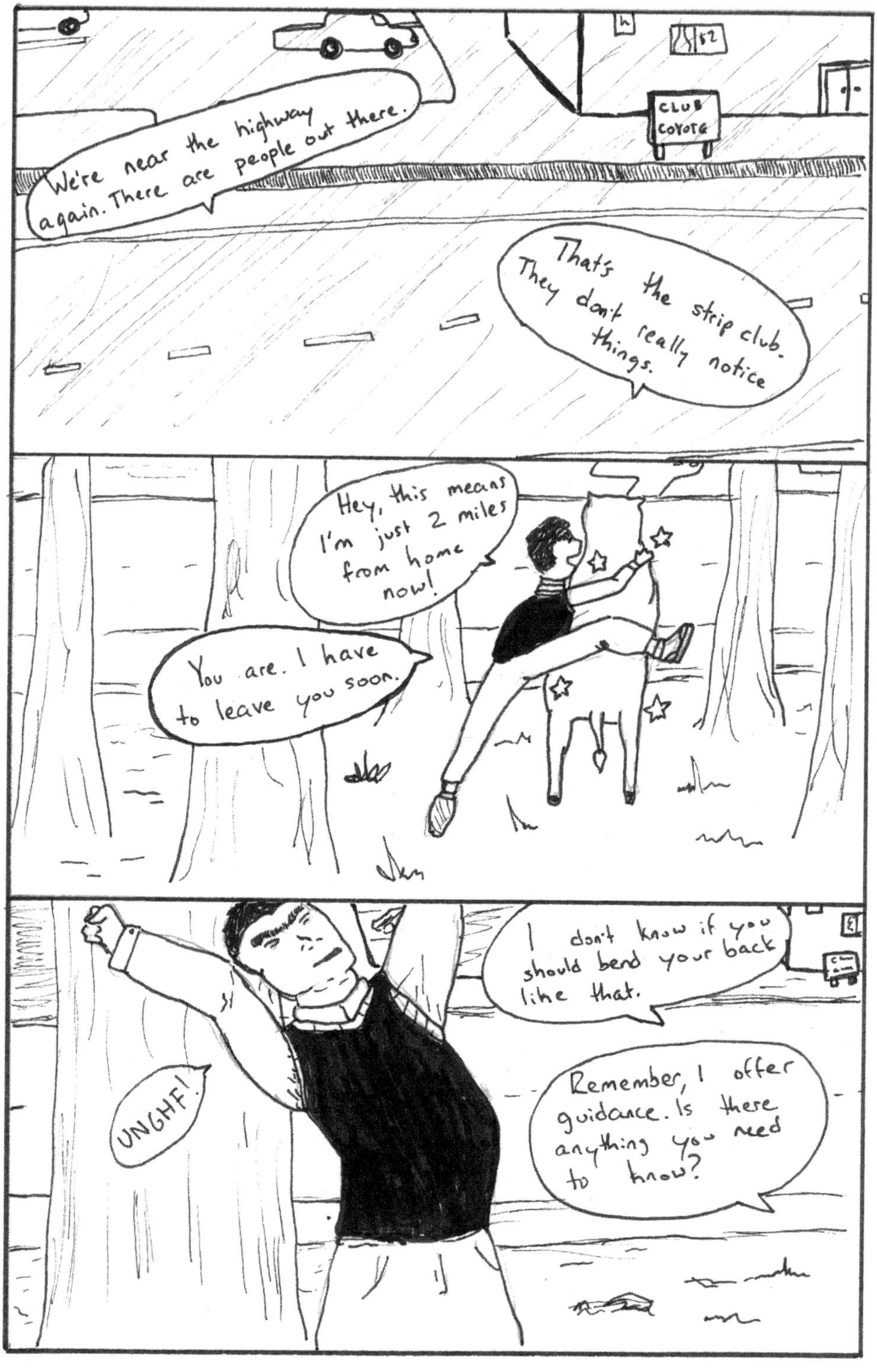
We're near the highway again. There are people out there.
CLUB COYOTE
That's the strip club. They don't really notice things.
Hey, this means I'm just 2 miles from home now!
You are. I have to leave you soon.
I don't know if you should bend your back like that.
UNGHF!
Remember, I offer guidance. Is there anything you need to know?

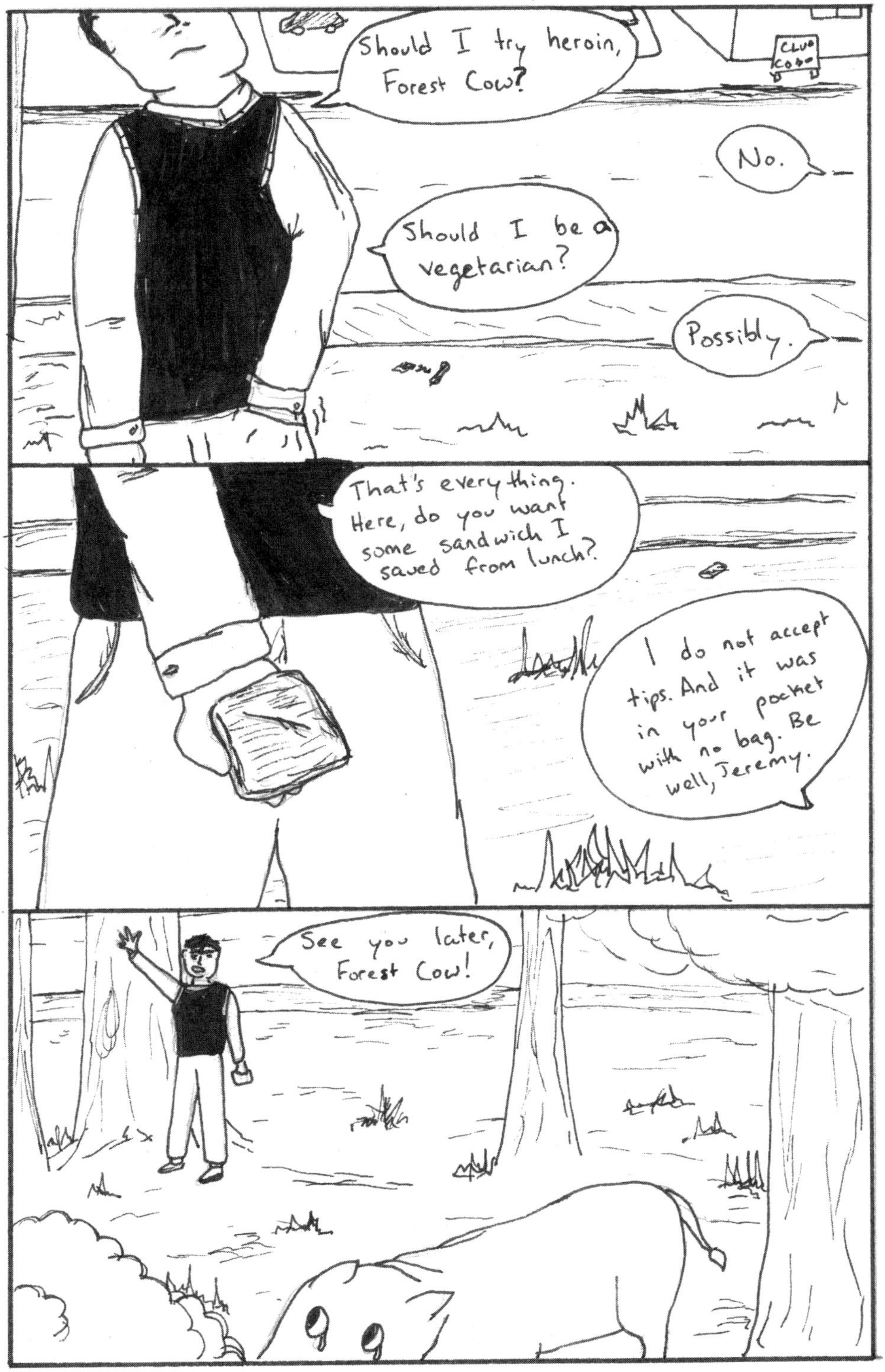
Should I try heroin, Forest Cow?
No.
Should I be a vegetarian?
Possibly.
That's everything. Here, do you want some sandwich I saved from lunch?
I do not accept tips. And it was in your pocket with no bag. Be well, Jeremy.
See you later, Forest Cow!

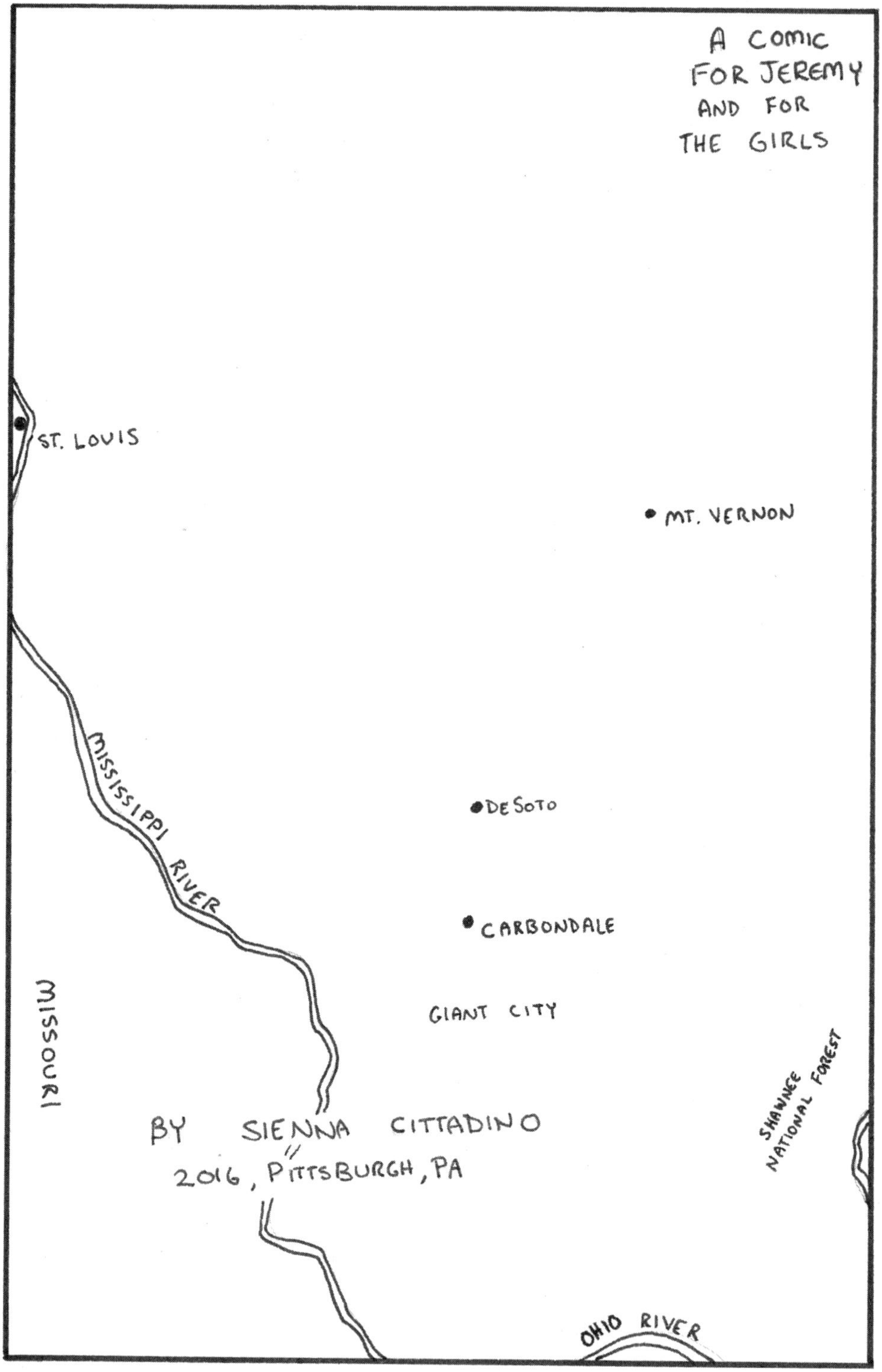
A COMIC
FOR JEREMY
AND FOR
THE GIRLS
ST. LOUIS
MT. VERNON
MISSISSIPPI RIVER
DE SOTO
CARBONDALE
GIANT CITY
MISSOURI
SHAWNEE NATIONAL FOREST
BY SIENNA CITTADINO
2016, PITTSBURGH, PA
OHIO RIVER

# Test of Loyalty

## SAM ALDEN

*originally published at*

hazlitt.net

PENGUIN RANDOM HOUSE CANADA

digital

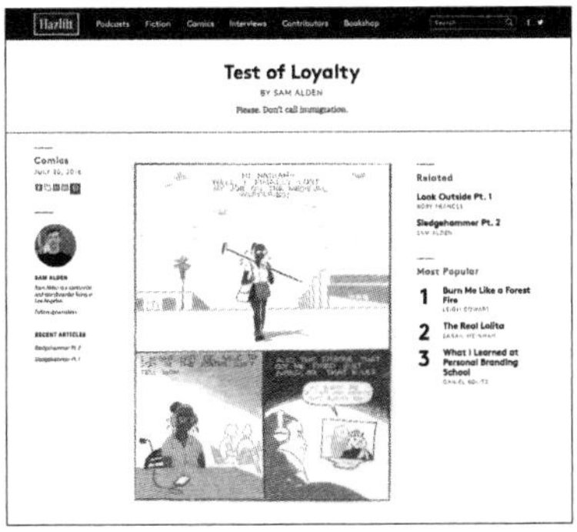

Hazlitt
Podcasts
Fiction
Comics
Interviews
Contributors
Bookshop
Test of Loyalty
BY SAM ALDEN
Please. Don't call Immigration.
Comics
Related
Look Outside Pt. 1
Sledgehammer Pt. 2
Most Popular
1 Burn Me Like a Forest Fire
2 The Real Lolita
3 What I Learned at Personal Branding School


### Biography

Sam Alden is a cartoonist and writer living in Los Angeles, previously as a writer/ boarder on *Adventure Time*. His published books include *New Construction* and *It Never Happened Again*, from Uncivilized Books. In college he was the boom operator on a handful of no-budget indie films.
gingerlandcomics.com

### Statement

I wrote the first draft of "Test of Loyalty" in early 2016, when the horrors of a Trump presidency were looming but still hypothetical; I guess the anxieties underlying it are pretty obvious.

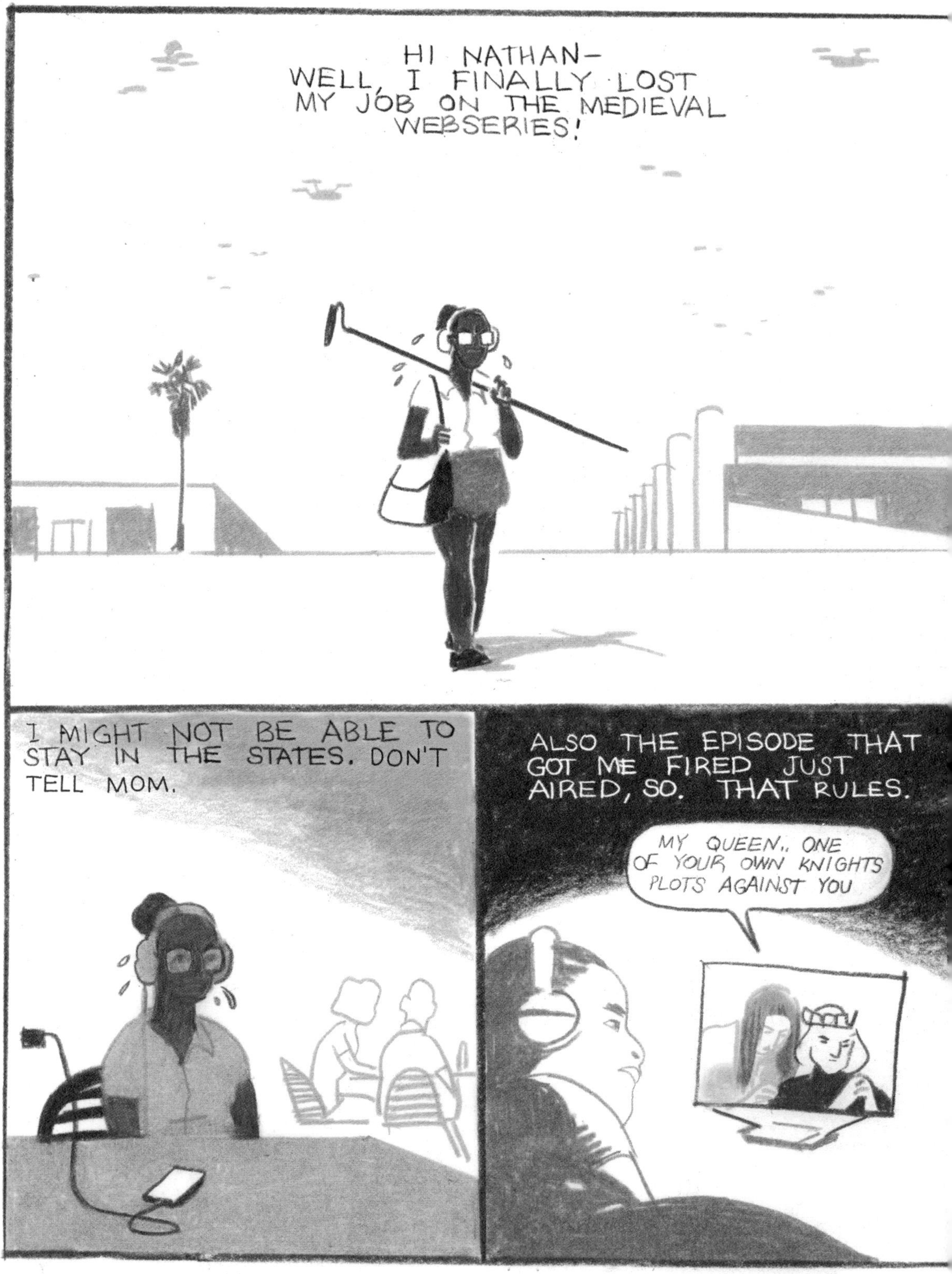
HI NATHAN-
WELL, I FINALLY LOST MY JOB ON THE MEDIEVAL WEBSERIES!
I MIGHT NOT BE ABLE TO STAY IN THE STATES. DON'T TELL MOM.
ALSO THE EPISODE THAT GOT ME FIRED JUST AIRED, SO. THAT RULES.
MY QUEEN.. ONE OF YOUR OWN KNIGHTS PLOTS AGAINST YOU

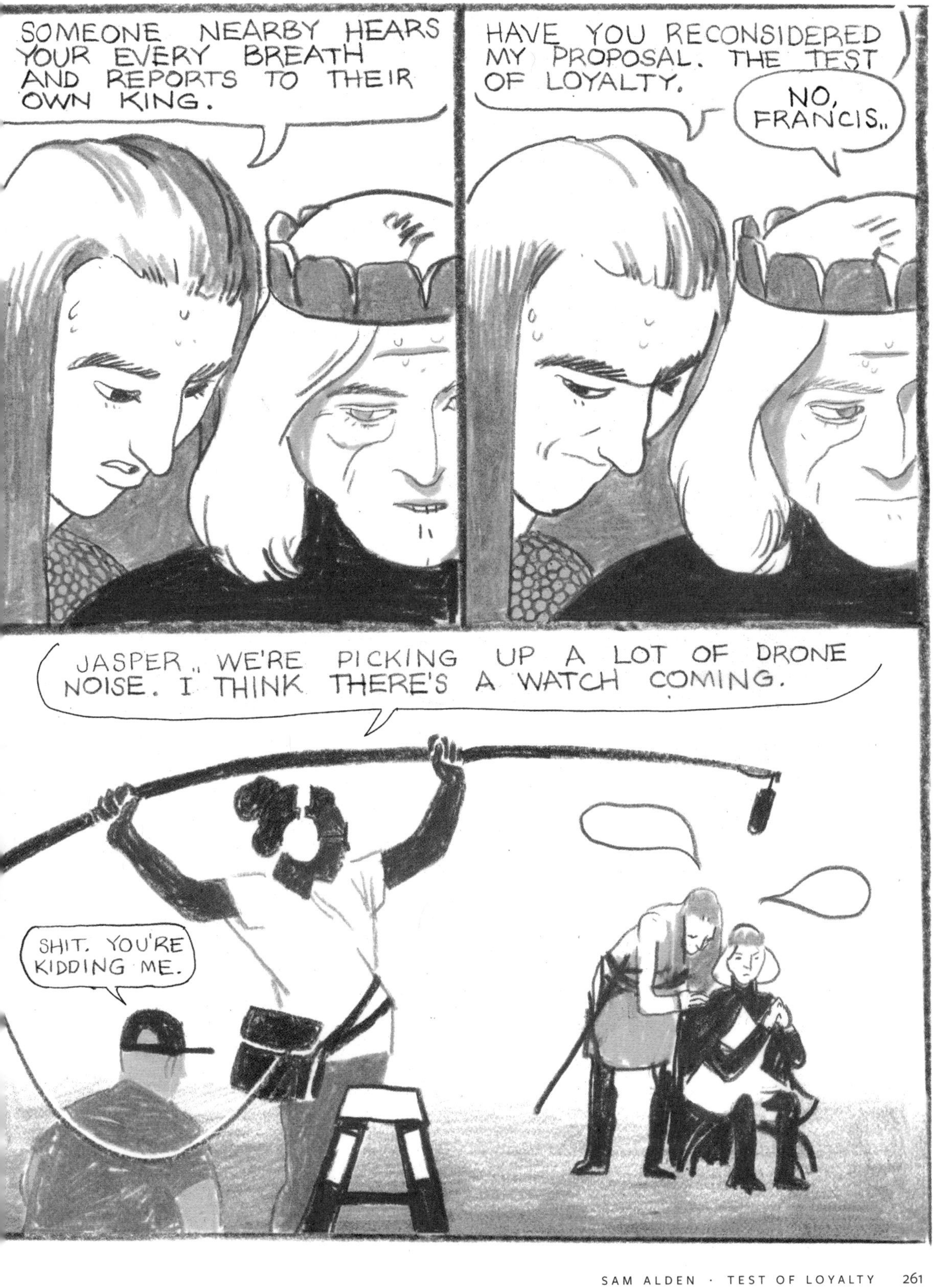
SOMEONE NEARBY HEARS YOUR EVERY BREATH AND REPORTS TO THEIR OWN KING.
HAVE YOU RECONSIDERED MY PROPOSAL. THE TEST OF LOYALTY.
NO, FRANCIS..
JASPER.. WE'RE PICKING UP A LOT OF DRONE NOISE. I THINK THERE'S A WATCH COMING.
SHIT. YOU'RE KIDDING ME.

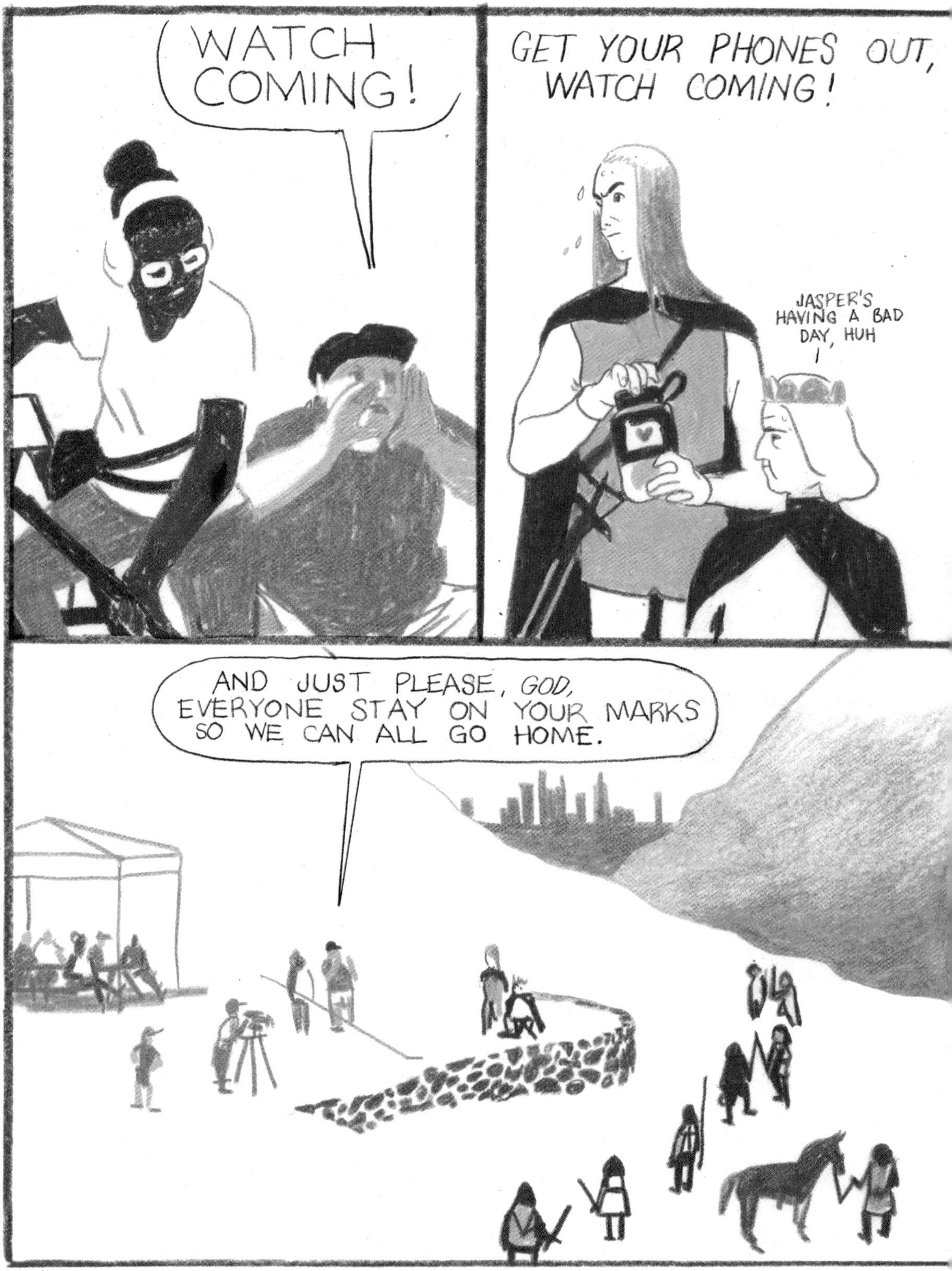
WATCH COMING!
GET YOUR PHONES OUT, WATCH COMING!
JASPER'S HAVING A BAD DAY, HUH
AND JUST PLEASE, *GOD,* EVERYONE STAY ON YOUR MARKS SO WE CAN ALL GO HOME.

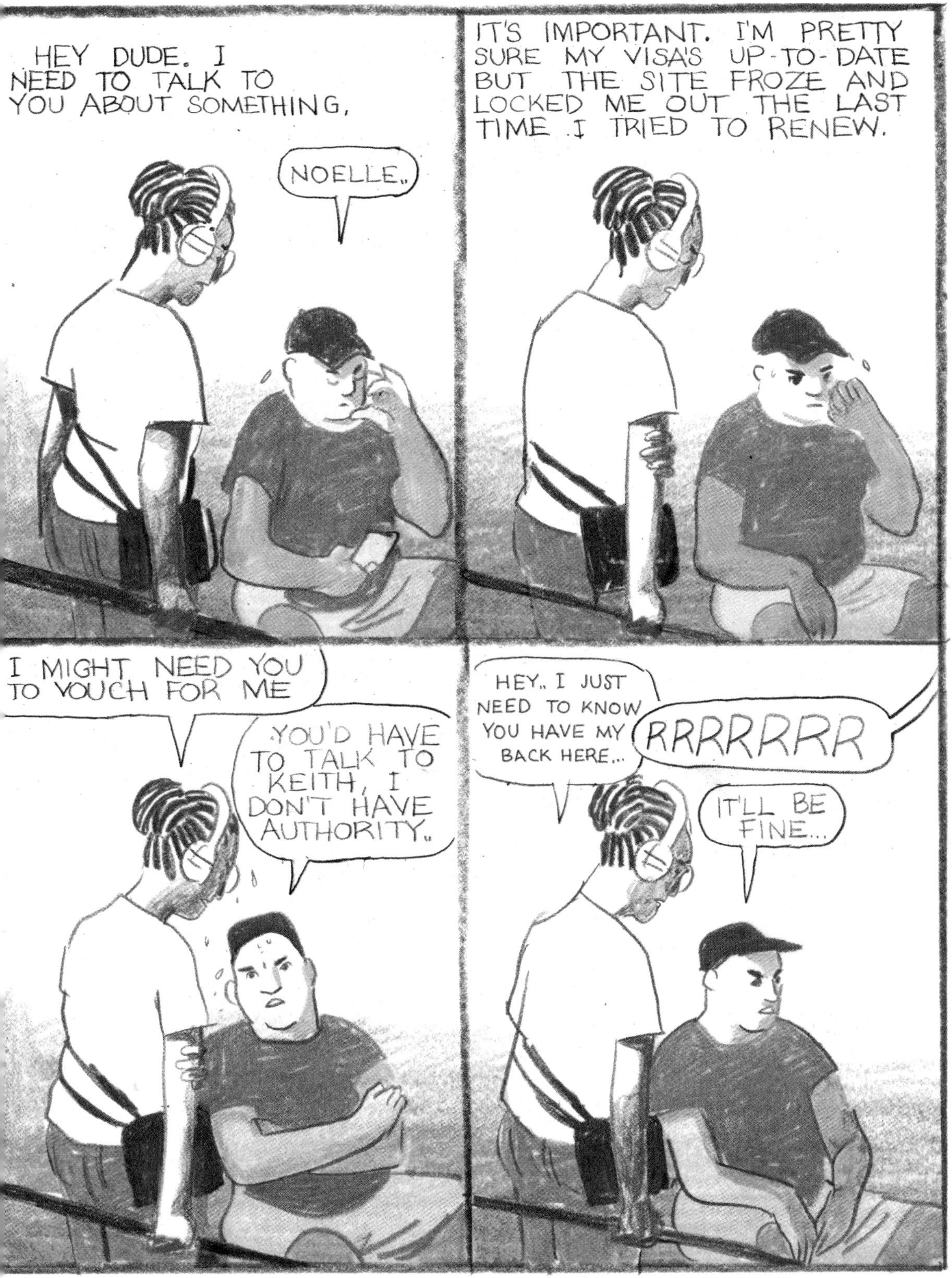
HEY DUDE. I NEED TO TALK TO YOU ABOUT SOMETHING,
NOELLE..
IT'S IMPORTANT. I'M PRETTY SURE MY VISA'S UP-TO-DATE BUT THE SITE FROZE AND LOCKED ME OUT THE LAST TIME I TRIED TO RENEW.
I MIGHT NEED YOU TO VOUCH FOR ME
YOU'D HAVE TO TALK TO KEITH, I DON'T HAVE AUTHORITY..
HEY.. I JUST NEED TO KNOW YOU HAVE MY BACK HERE...
RRRRRRRR
IT'LL BE FINE...

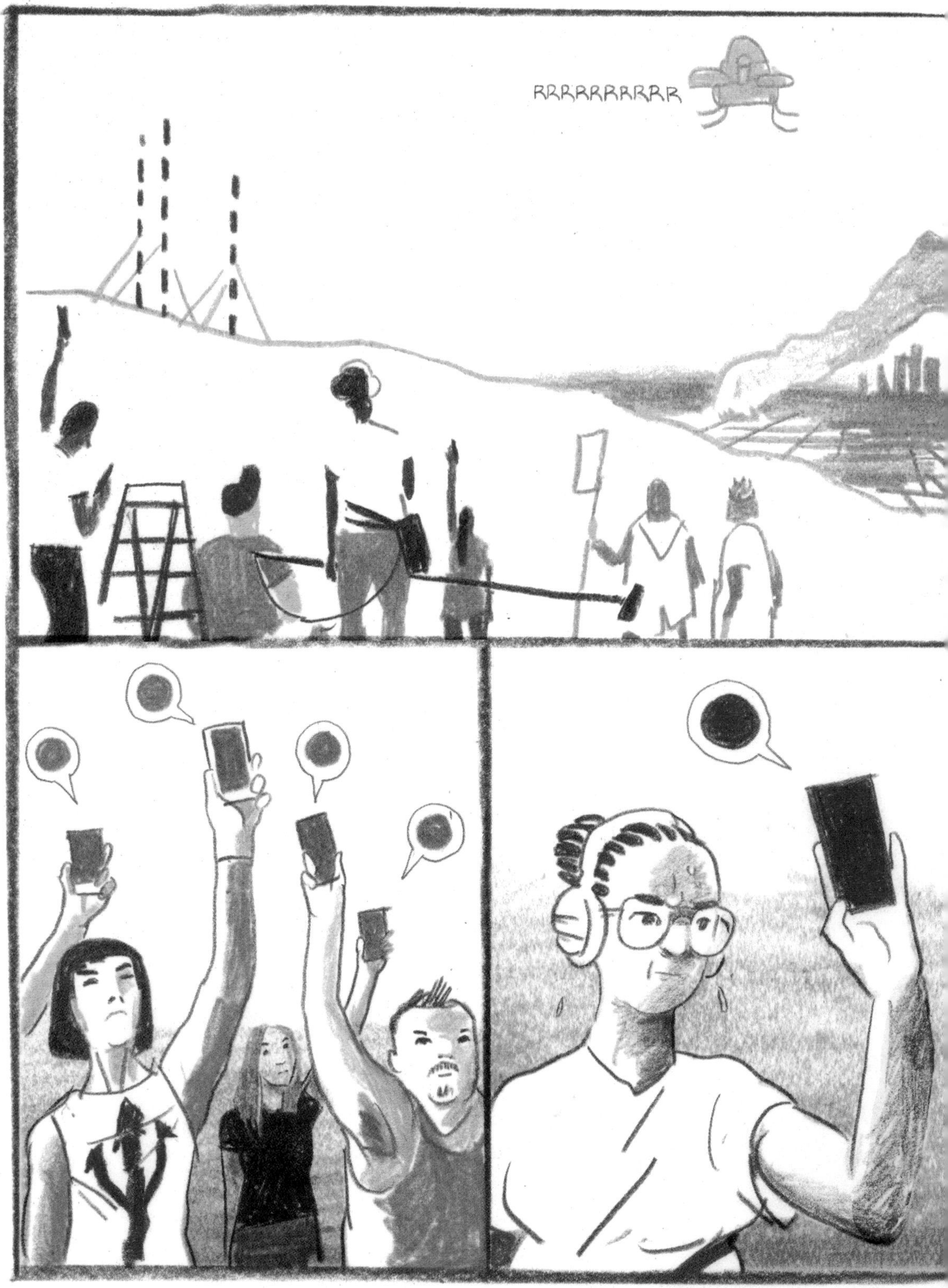
RRRRRRRRRRR

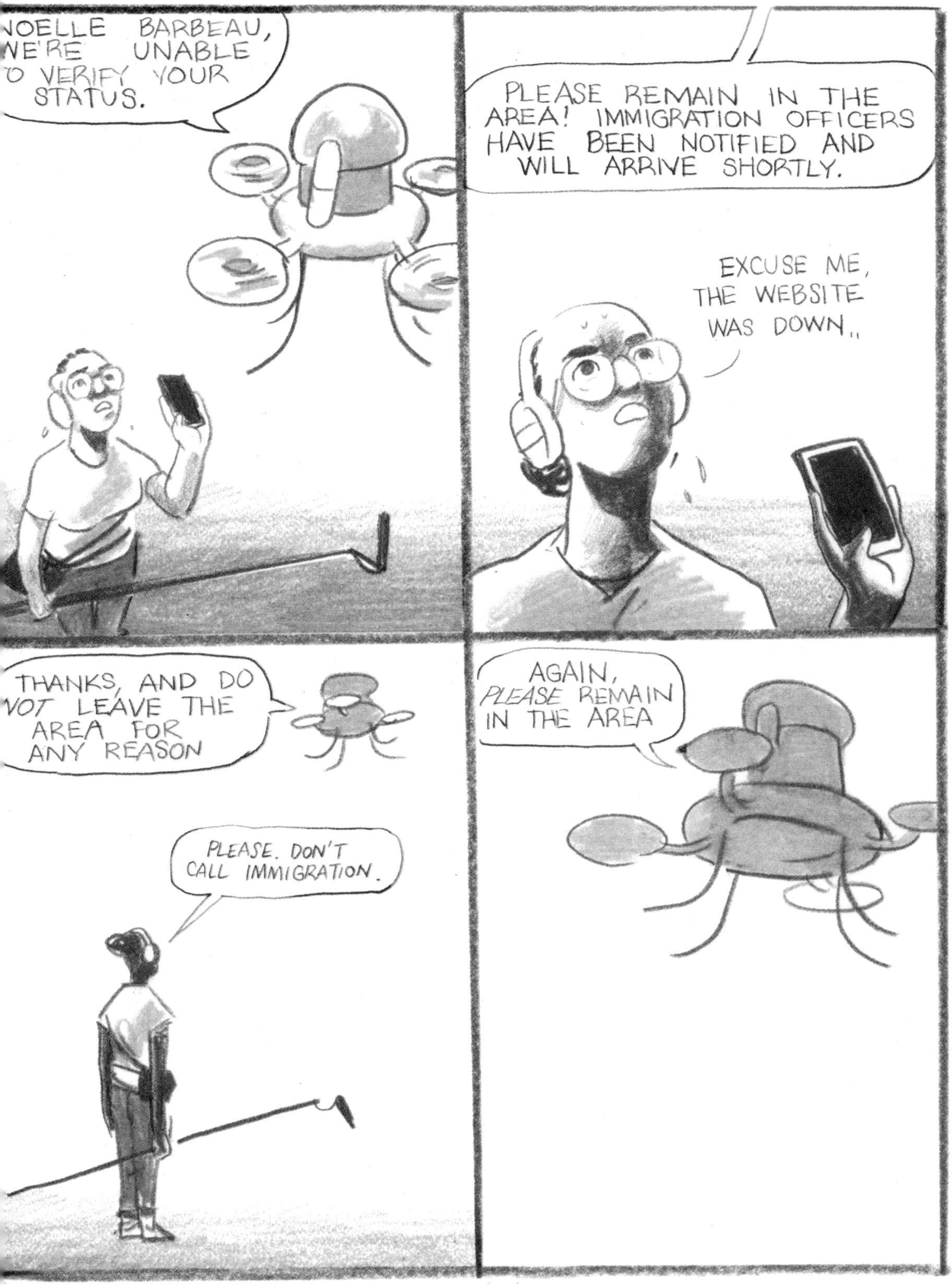
NOELLE BARBEAU, WE'RE UNABLE TO VERIFY YOUR STATUS.
PLEASE REMAIN IN THE AREA! IMMIGRATION OFFICERS HAVE BEEN NOTIFIED AND WILL ARRIVE SHORTLY.
EXCUSE ME, THE WEBSITE WAS DOWN..
THANKS, AND DO NOT LEAVE THE AREA FOR ANY REASON
PLEASE. DON'T CALL IMMIGRATION.
AGAIN, PLEASE REMAIN IN THE AREA

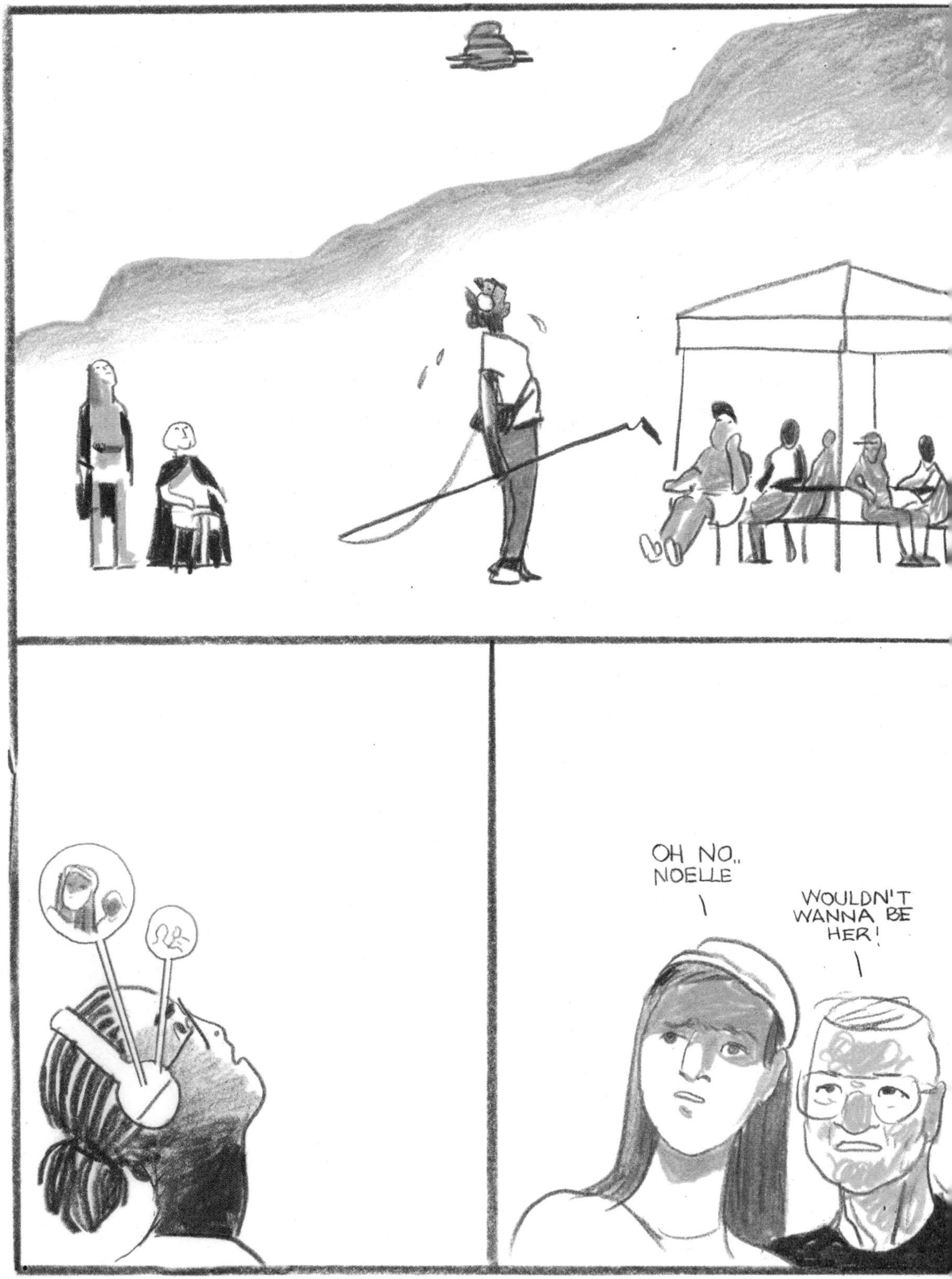
OH NO.. NOELLE
WOULDN'T WANNA BE HER!

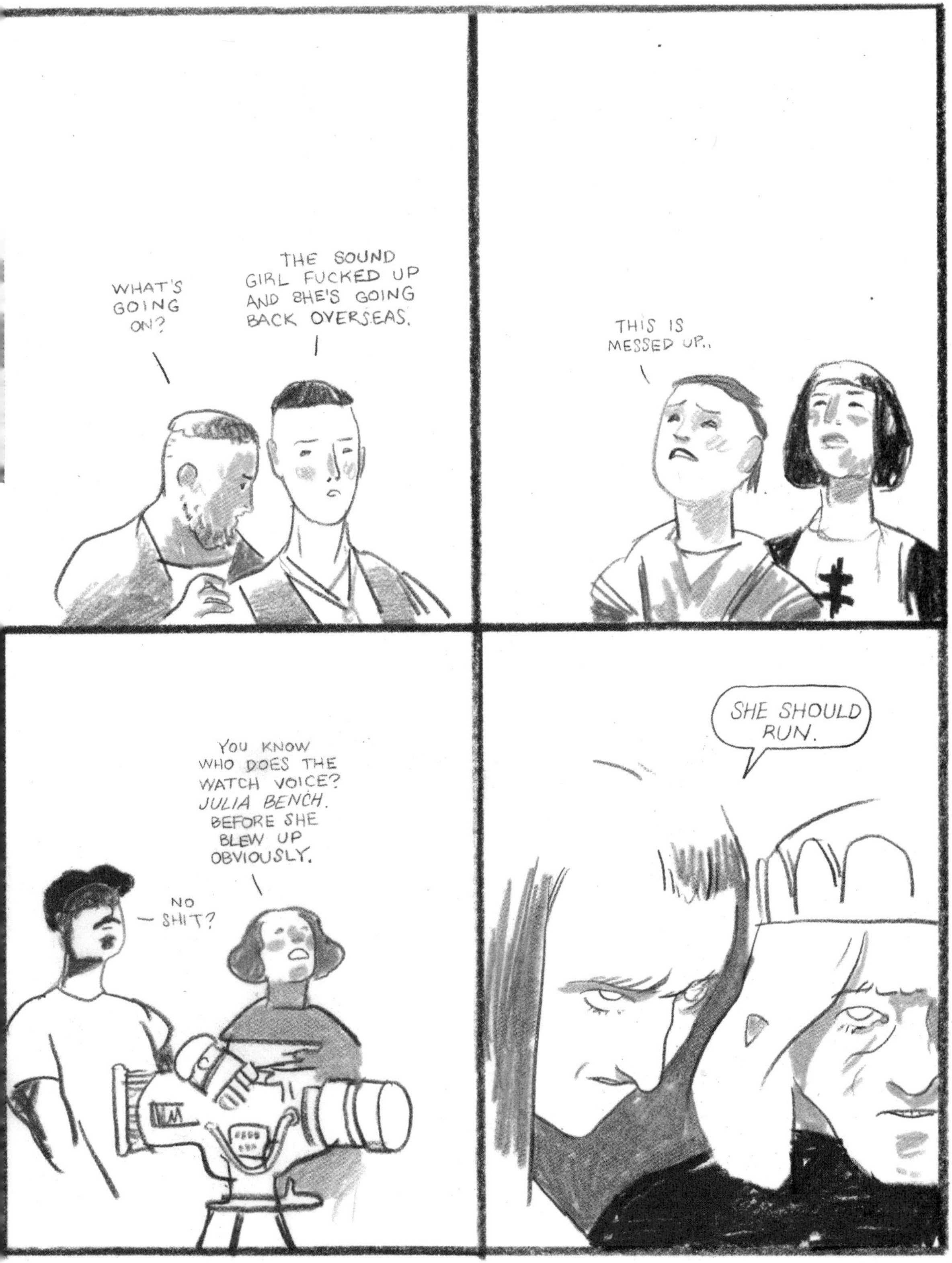
WHAT'S GOING ON?
THE SOUND GIRL FUCKED UP AND SHE'S GOING BACK OVERSEAS.
THIS IS MESSED UP..
YOU KNOW WHO DOES THE WATCH VOICE? JULIA BENCH. BEFORE SHE BLEW UP OBVIOUSLY.
NO SHIT?
SHE SHOULD RUN.

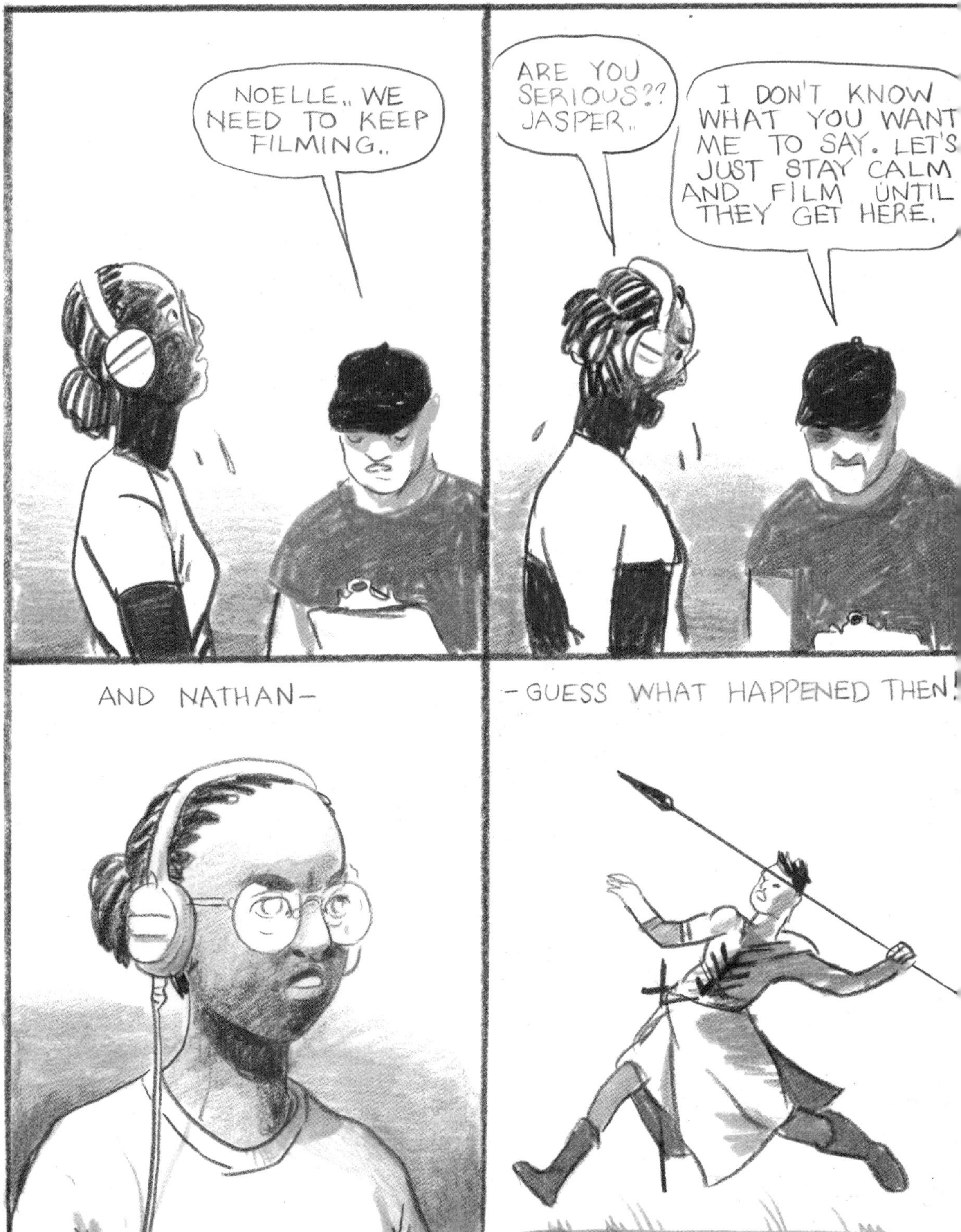
NOELLE.. WE NEED TO KEEP FILMING..
ARE YOU SERIOUS?? JASPER..
I DON'T KNOW WHAT YOU WANT ME TO SAY. LET'S JUST STAY CALM AND FILM UNTIL THEY GET HERE.
AND NATHAN-
-GUESS WHAT HAPPENED THEN!

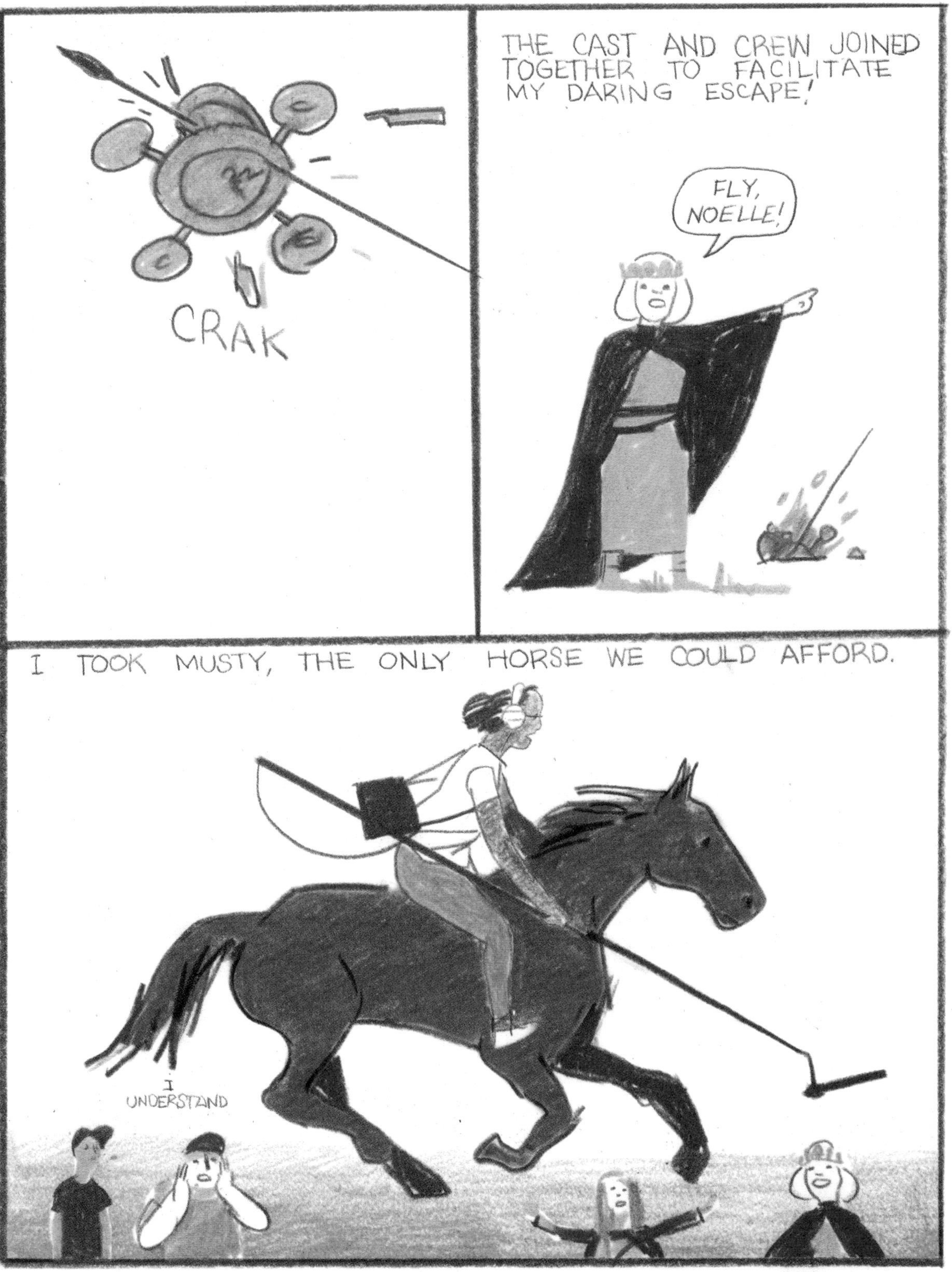
CRAK
THE CAST AND CREW JOINED TOGETHER TO FACILITATE MY DARING ESCAPE!
FLY, NOELLE!
I TOOK MUSTY, THE ONLY HORSE WE COULD AFFORD.
I UNDERSTAND

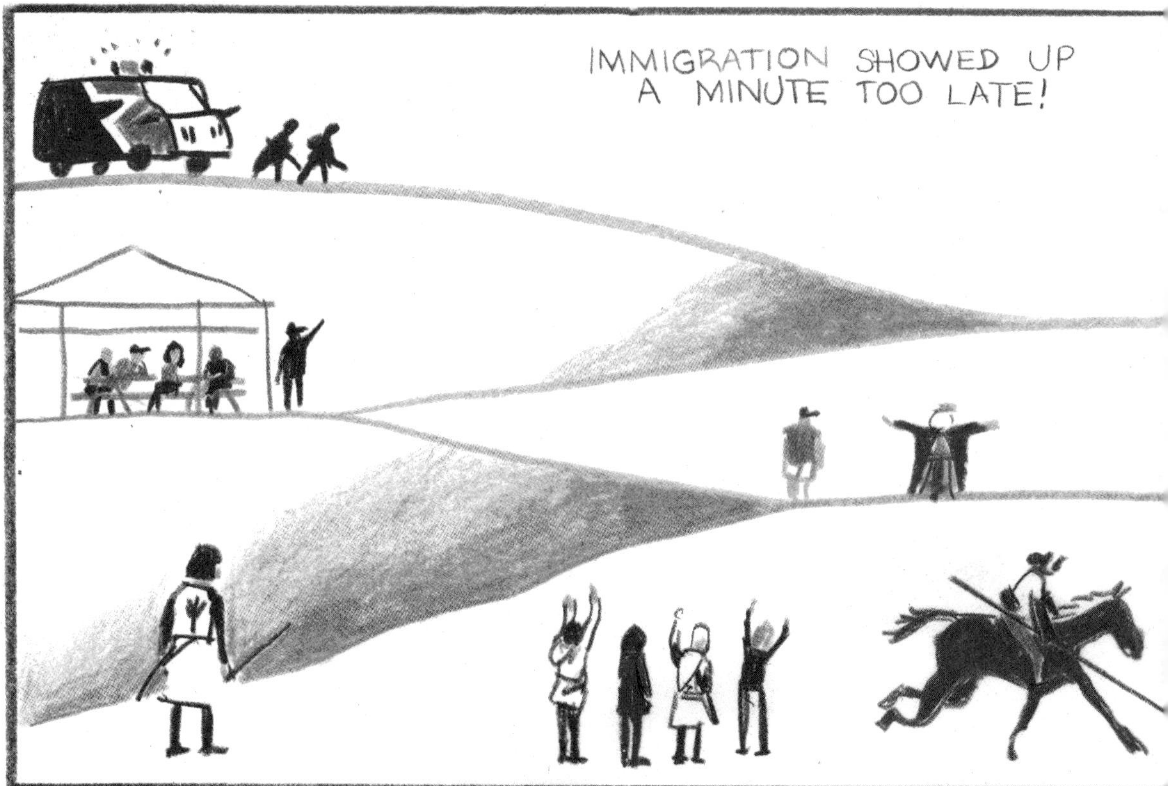
IMMIGRATION SHOWED UP A MINUTE TOO LATE!

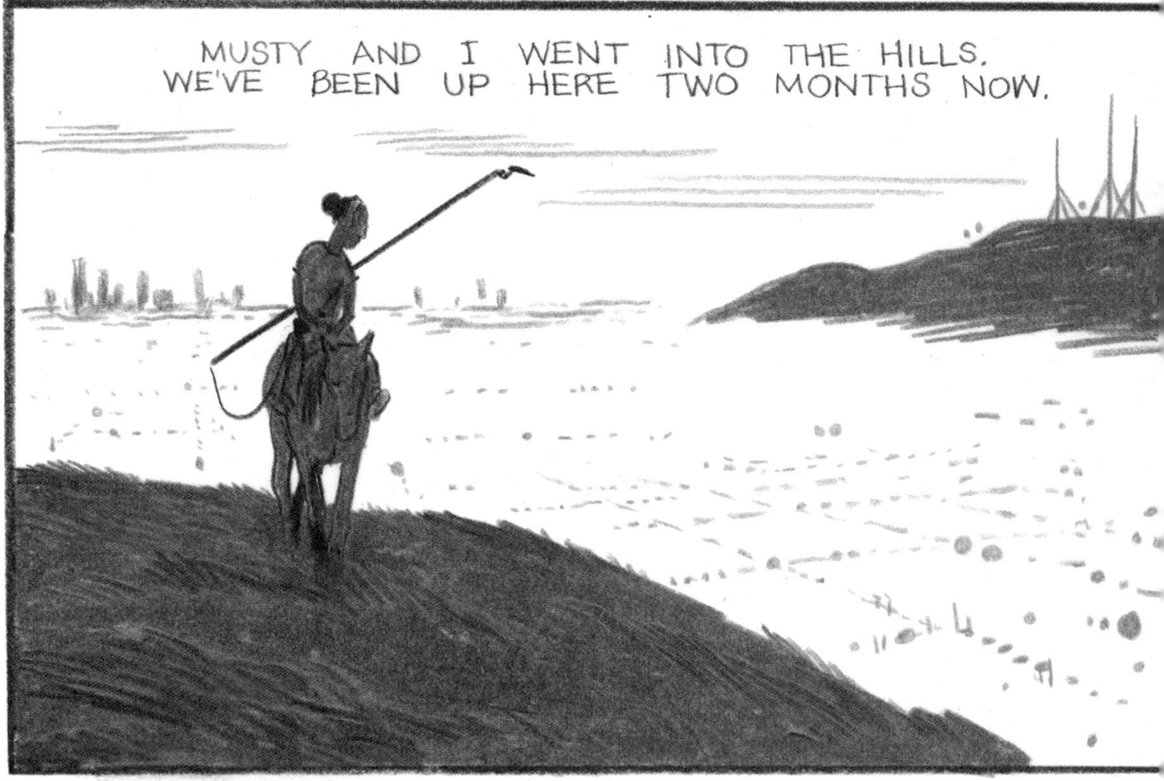
MUSTY AND I WENT INTO THE HILLS. WE'VE BEEN UP HERE TWO MONTHS NOW.

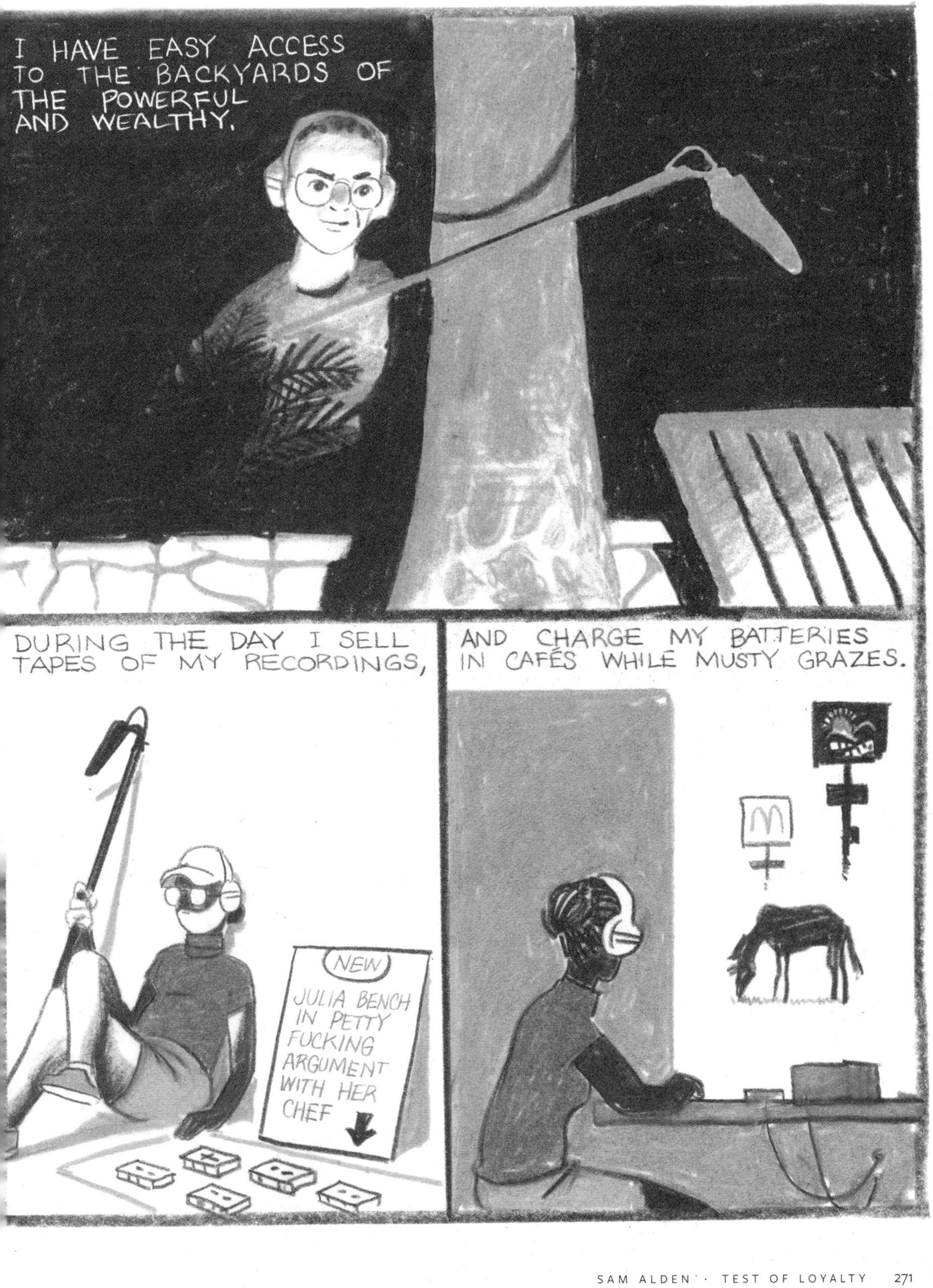
I HAVE EASY ACCESS TO THE BACKYARDS OF THE POWERFUL AND WEALTHY.
DURING THE DAY I SELL TAPES OF MY RECORDINGS,
NEW
JULIA BENCH IN PETTY FUCKING ARGUMENT WITH HER CHEF
AND CHARGE MY BATTERIES IN CAFÉS WHILE MUSTY GRAZES.

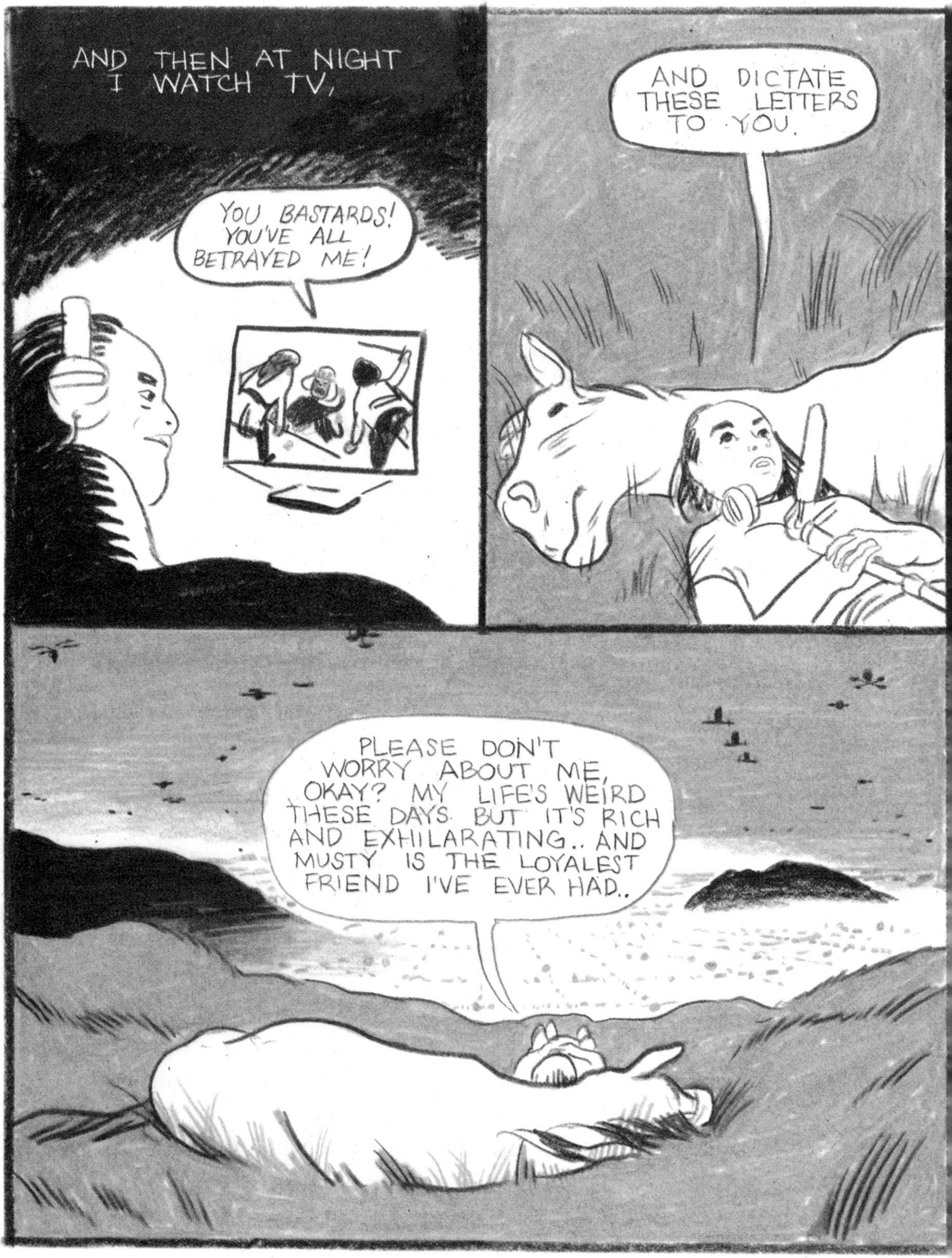
AND THEN AT NIGHT I WATCH TV,
YOU BASTARDS! YOU'VE ALL BETRAYED ME!
AND DICTATE THESE LETTERS TO YOU.
PLEASE DON'T WORRY ABOUT ME, OKAY? MY LIFE'S WEIRD THESE DAYS. BUT IT'S RICH AND EXHILARATING.. AND MUSTY IS THE LOYALEST FRIEND I'VE EVER HAD..
SAM

# Generous Bosom Part 2 (*Excerpt*)

CONOR STECHSCHULTE

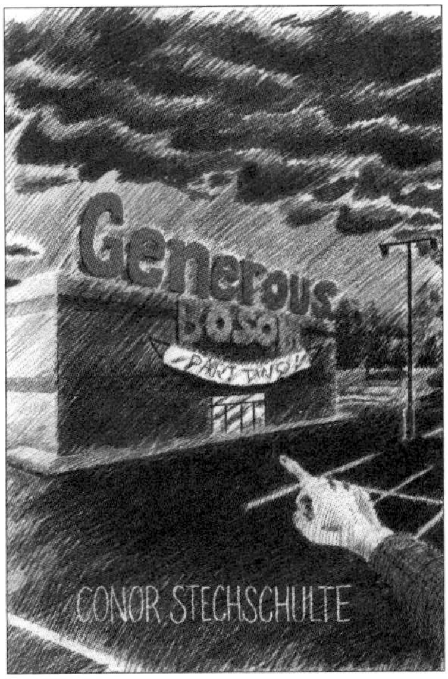
Generous Bosom
PART TWO
CONOR STECHSCHULTE

*originally published in*

*Generous Bosom Part 2*

BREAKDOWN PRESS

7.09 × 10.04 inches • 74 pages

## Biography

Conor Stechschulte began making comics with the Closed Caption Comics group in Baltimore. He has gone on to self-publish over a dozen 'zines and handmade books. He published his debut graphic novel, *The Amateurs*, with Fantagraphics in 2014. He is currently serializing the graphic novel *Generous Bosom* (excerpted here) in risographed editions with Breakdown Press. He lives in Chicago.
conorstechschulte.com

## Statement

*Generous Bosom* follows the aftermath of a strange erotic encounter as a web of manipulation, surveillance, and conspiracy reveals itself around all those involved. In the process, the gap between subjective and shared realities widens.

This excerpt is one of many flashback sequences that interrupt the primary narrative and recall incidents from the adolescence of the characters Shanon and Cyndi. It is from volume two of four planned volumes.

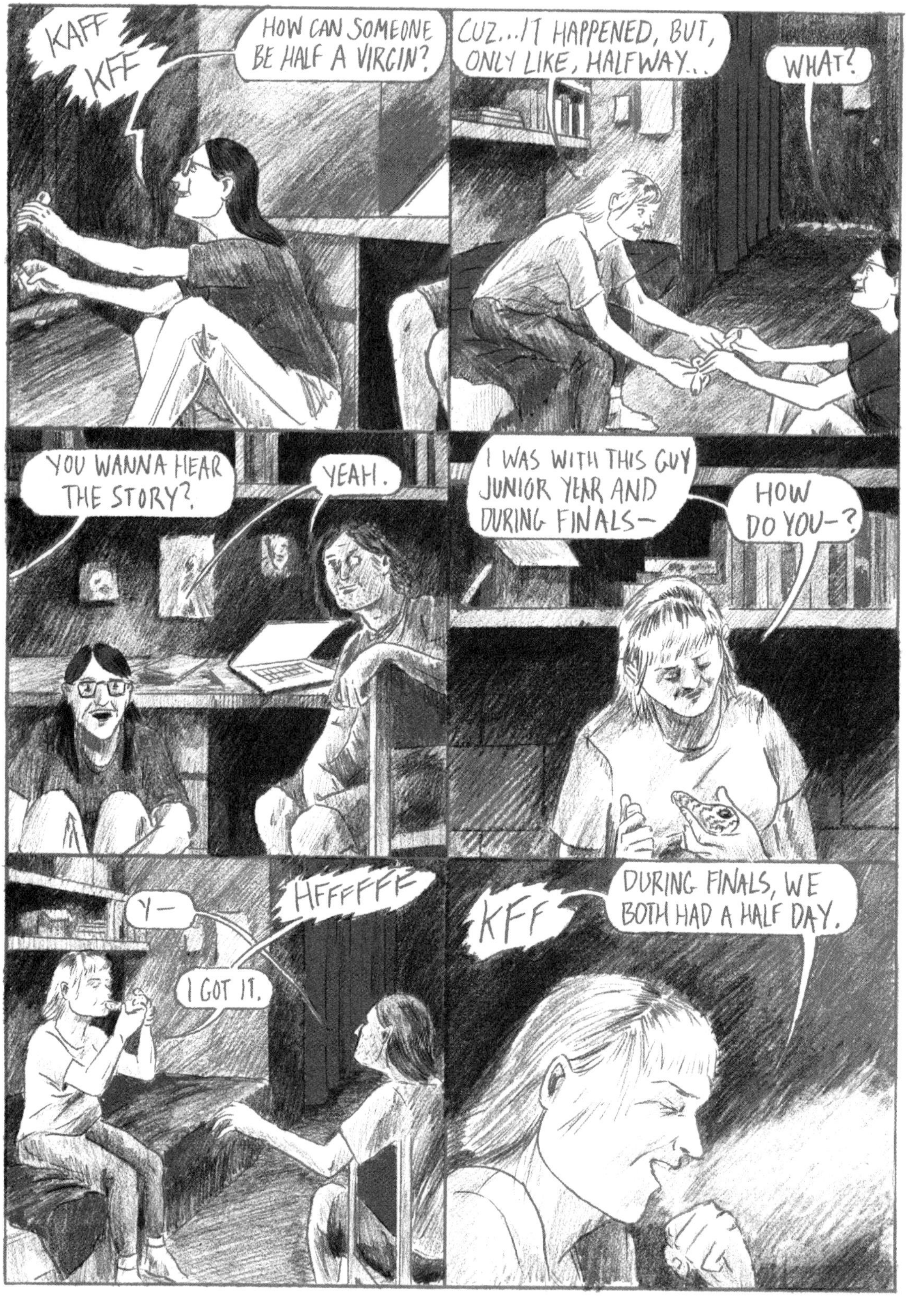
KAFF
KFF
HOW CAN SOMEONE BE HALF A VIRGIN?
CUZ...IT HAPPENED, BUT, ONLY LIKE, HALFWAY...
WHAT?
YOU WANNA HEAR THE STORY?
YEAH.
I WAS WITH THIS GUY JUNIOR YEAR AND DURING FINALS—
HOW DO YOU—?
Y—
HFFFFFF
I GOT IT.
KFF
DURING FINALS, WE BOTH HAD A HALF DAY.

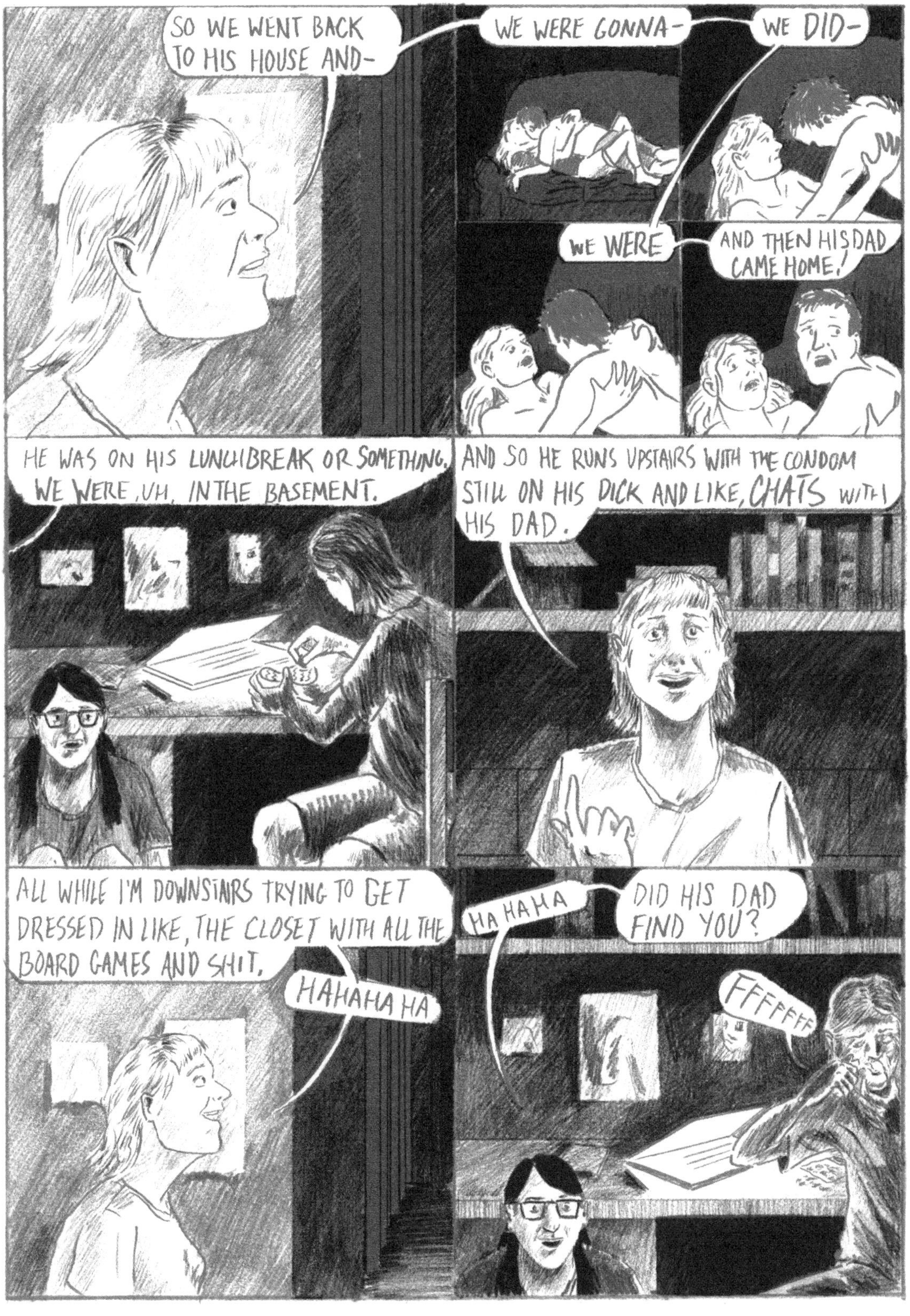
SO WE WENT BACK TO HIS HOUSE AND-
WE WERE GONNA-
WE DID-
WE WERE
AND THEN HIS DAD CAME HOME!
HE WAS ON HIS LUNCHBREAK OR SOMETHING. WE WERE, UH, IN THE BASEMENT.
AND SO HE RUNS UPSTAIRS WITH THE CONDOM STILL ON HIS DICK AND LIKE, CHATS WITH HIS DAD.
ALL WHILE I'M DOWNSTAIRS TRYING TO GET DRESSED IN LIKE, THE CLOSET WITH ALL THE BOARD GAMES AND SHIT.
HAHAHAHA
HAHAHA
DID HIS DAD FIND YOU?
FFFFFFF

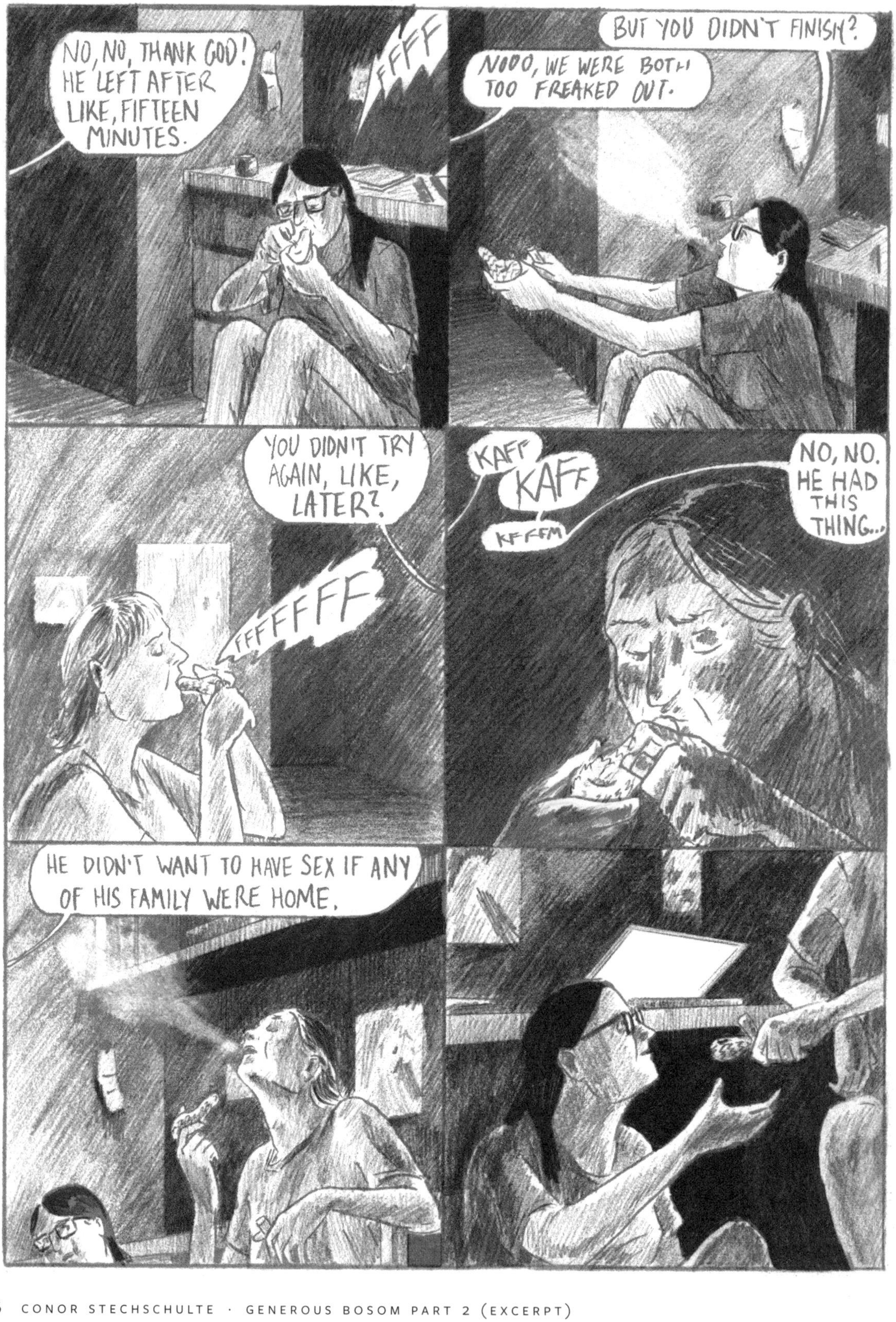
NO, NO, THANK GOD! HE LEFT AFTER LIKE, FIFTEEN MINUTES.
FFFF
BUT YOU DIDN'T FINISH?
NOOO, WE WERE BOTH TOO FREAKED OUT.
YOU DIDN'T TRY AGAIN, LIKE, LATER?
FFFFFFFF
KAFF
KAFF
KFFFM
NO, NO. HE HAD THIS THING...
HE DIDN'T WANT TO HAVE SEX IF ANY OF HIS FAMILY WERE HOME.

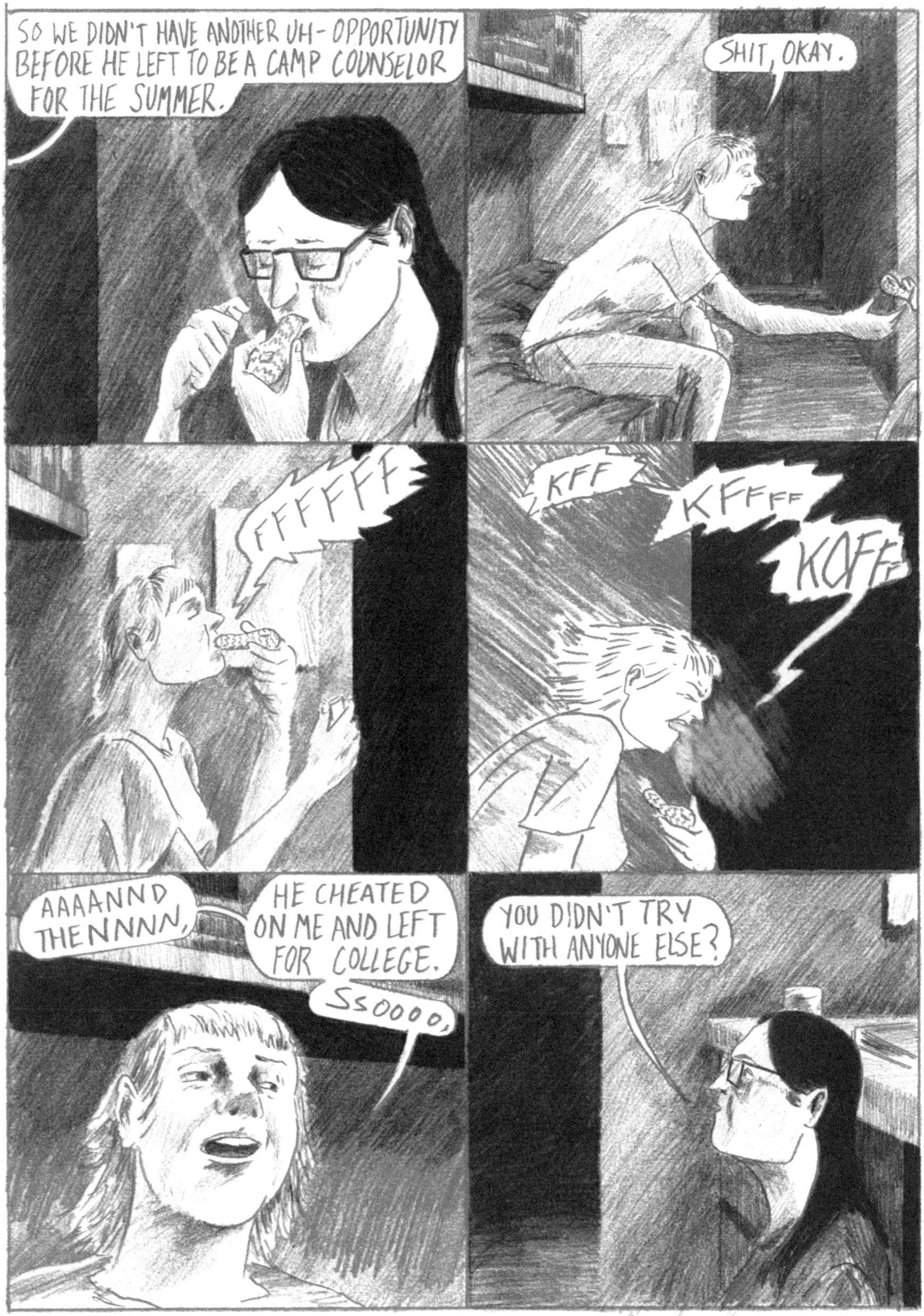
SO WE DIDN'T HAVE ANOTHER UH- OPPORTUNITY BEFORE HE LEFT TO BE A CAMP COUNSELOR FOR THE SUMMER.
SHIT, OKAY.
FFFFFF
KFF
KFFFF
KOFFF
AAAANND THENNNN,
HE CHEATED ON ME AND LEFT FOR COLLEGE.
SSOOOO,
YOU DIDN'T TRY WITH ANYONE ELSE?

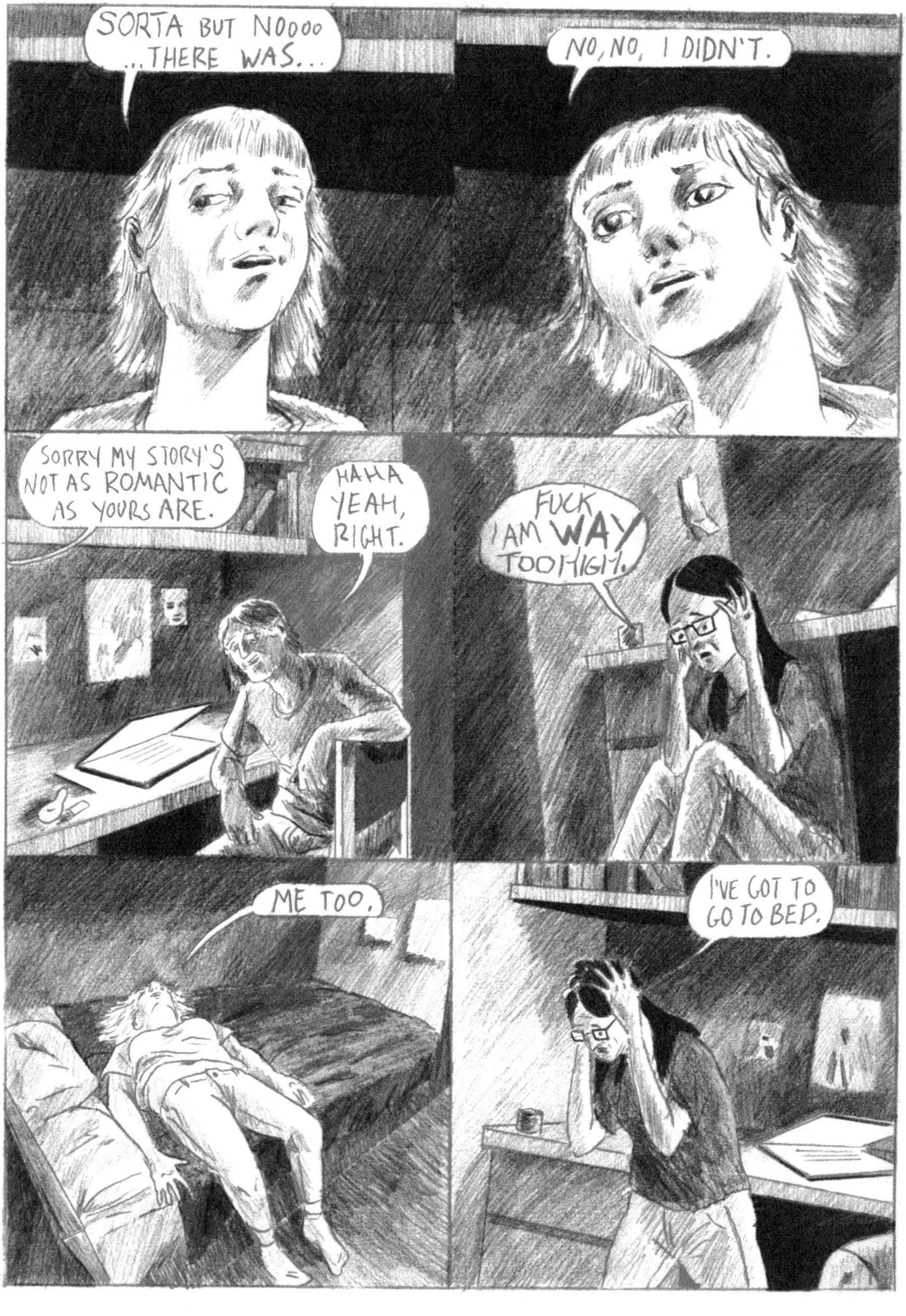
SORTA BUT NOooo
...THERE WAS...
NO, NO, I DIDN'T.
SORRY MY STORY'S NOT AS ROMANTIC AS YOURS ARE.
HAHA YEAH, RIGHT.
FUCK I AM WAY TOO HIGH.
ME TOO.
I'VE GOT TO GO TO BED.

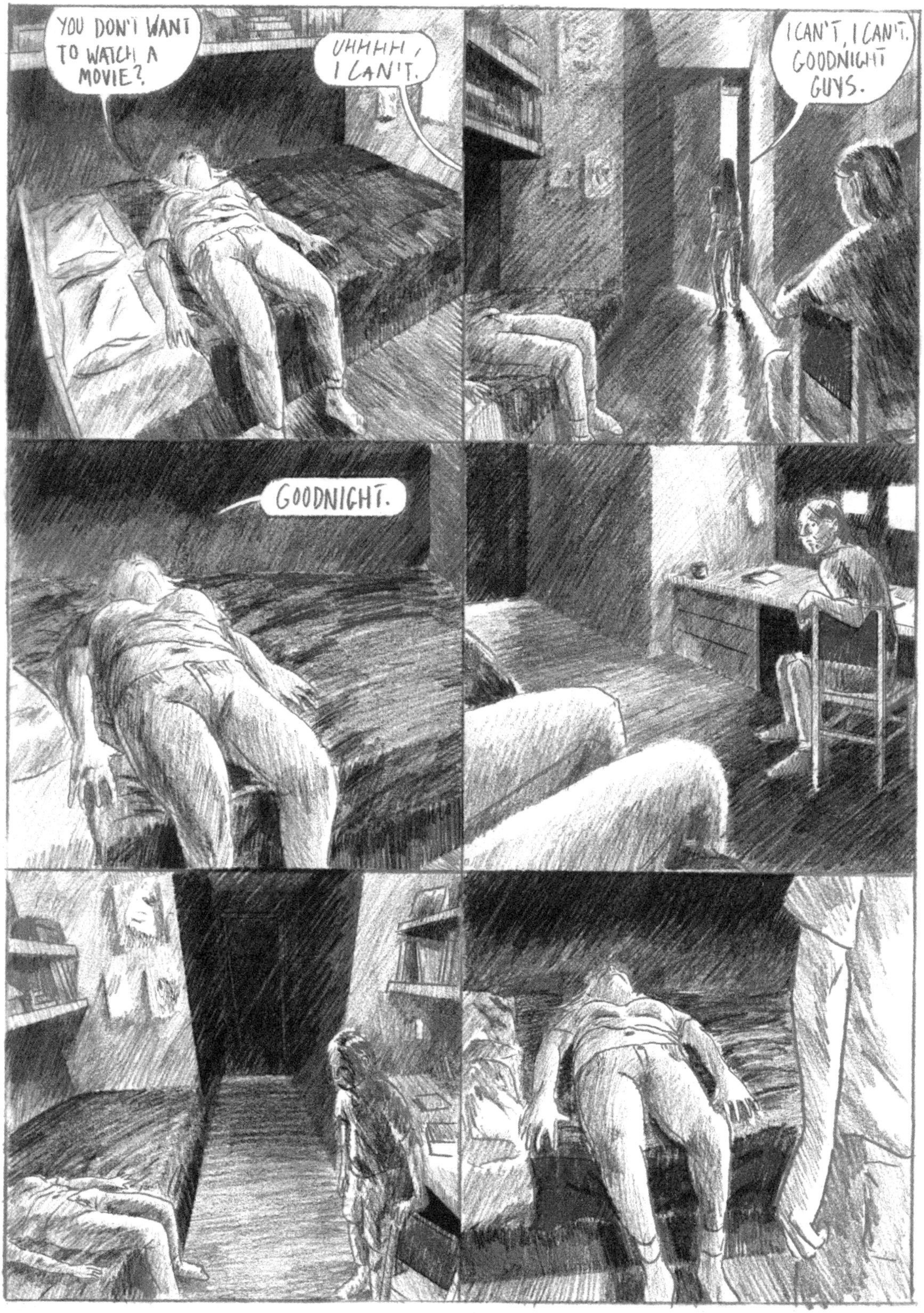
YOU DON'T WANT TO WATCH A MOVIE?
UHHHH, I CAN'T.
I CAN'T, I CAN'T. GOODNIGHT GUYS.
GOODNIGHT.

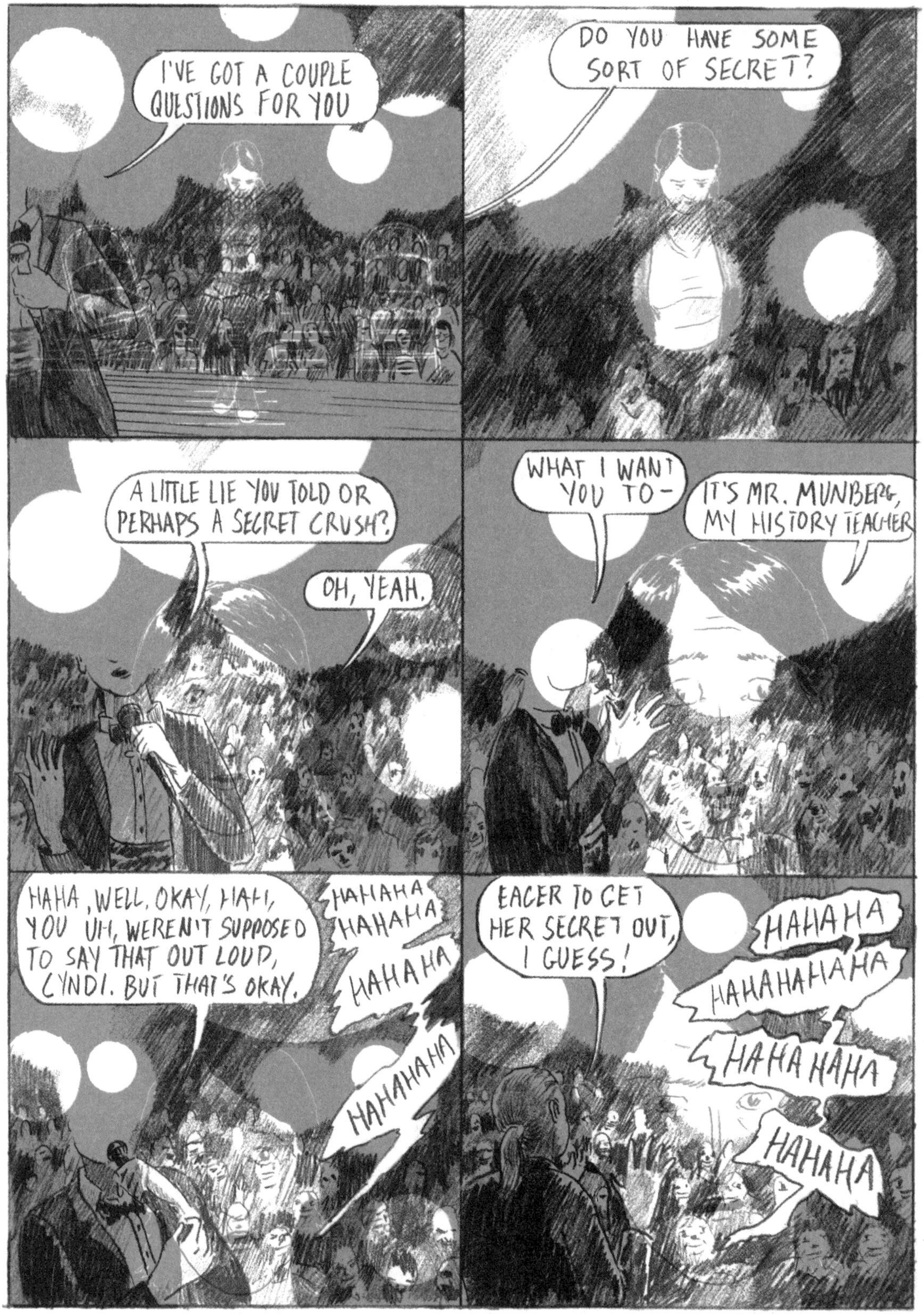
I'VE GOT A COUPLE QUESTIONS FOR YOU
DO YOU HAVE SOME SORT OF SECRET?
A LITTLE LIE YOU TOLD OR PERHAPS A SECRET CRUSH?
OH, YEAH.
WHAT I WANT YOU TO-
IT'S MR. MUNBERG, MY HISTORY TEACHER
HAHA, WELL, OKAY, HAH, YOU UH, WEREN'T SUPPOSED TO SAY THAT OUT LOUD, CYNDI. BUT THAT'S OKAY.
HAHAHA HAHAHA
HAHAHA
HAHAHAHA
EAGER TO GET HER SECRET OUT, I GUESS!
HAHAHA
HAHAHAHAHA
HAHA HAHA
HAHAHA

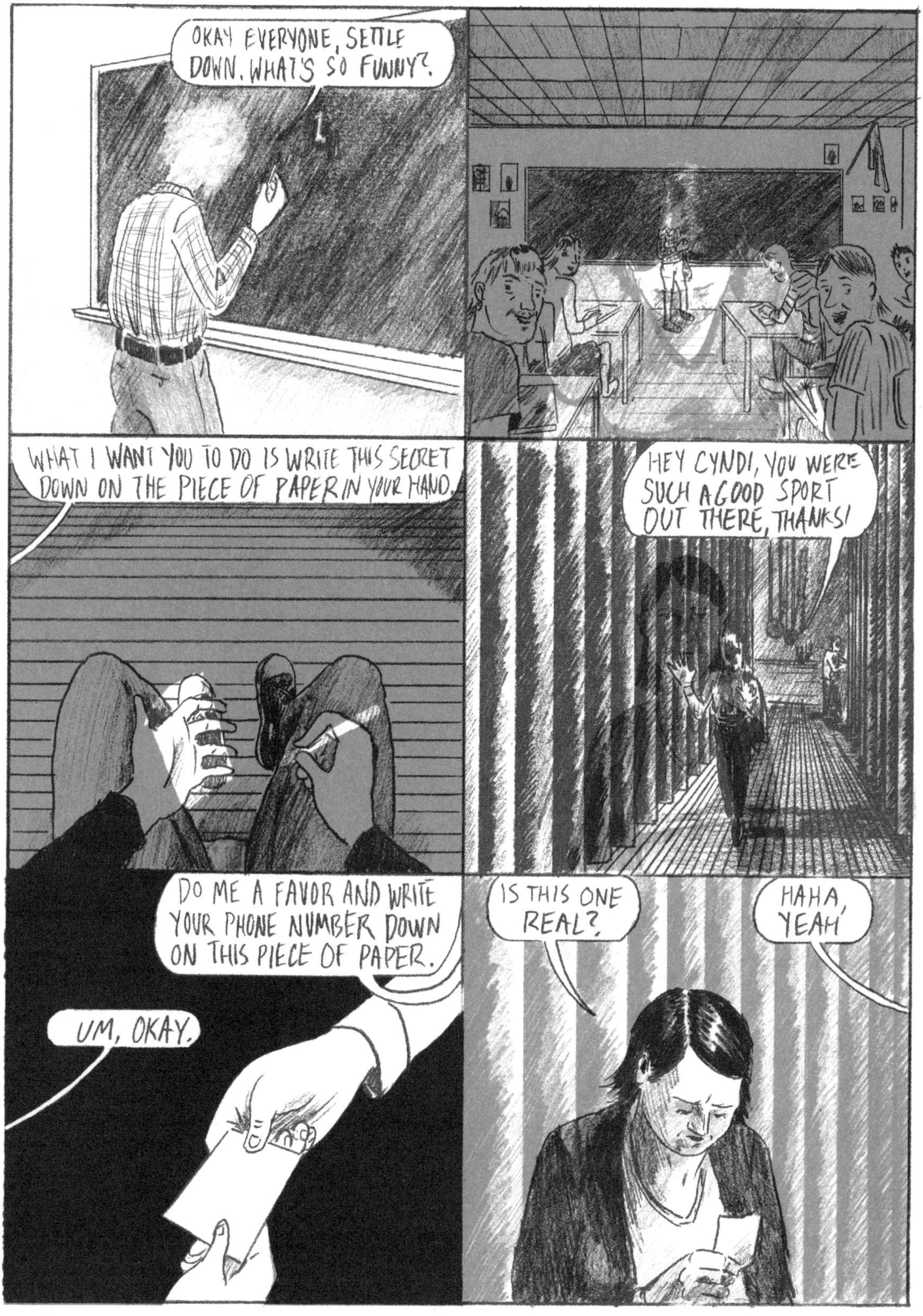
OKAY EVERYONE, SETTLE DOWN. WHAT'S SO FUNNY?
WHAT I WANT YOU TO DO IS WRITE THIS SECRET DOWN ON THE PIECE OF PAPER IN YOUR HAND.
HEY CYNDI, YOU WERE SUCH A GOOD SPORT OUT THERE, THANKS!
DO ME A FAVOR AND WRITE YOUR PHONE NUMBER DOWN ON THIS PIECE OF PAPER.
UM, OKAY.
IS THIS ONE REAL?
HAHA, YEAH

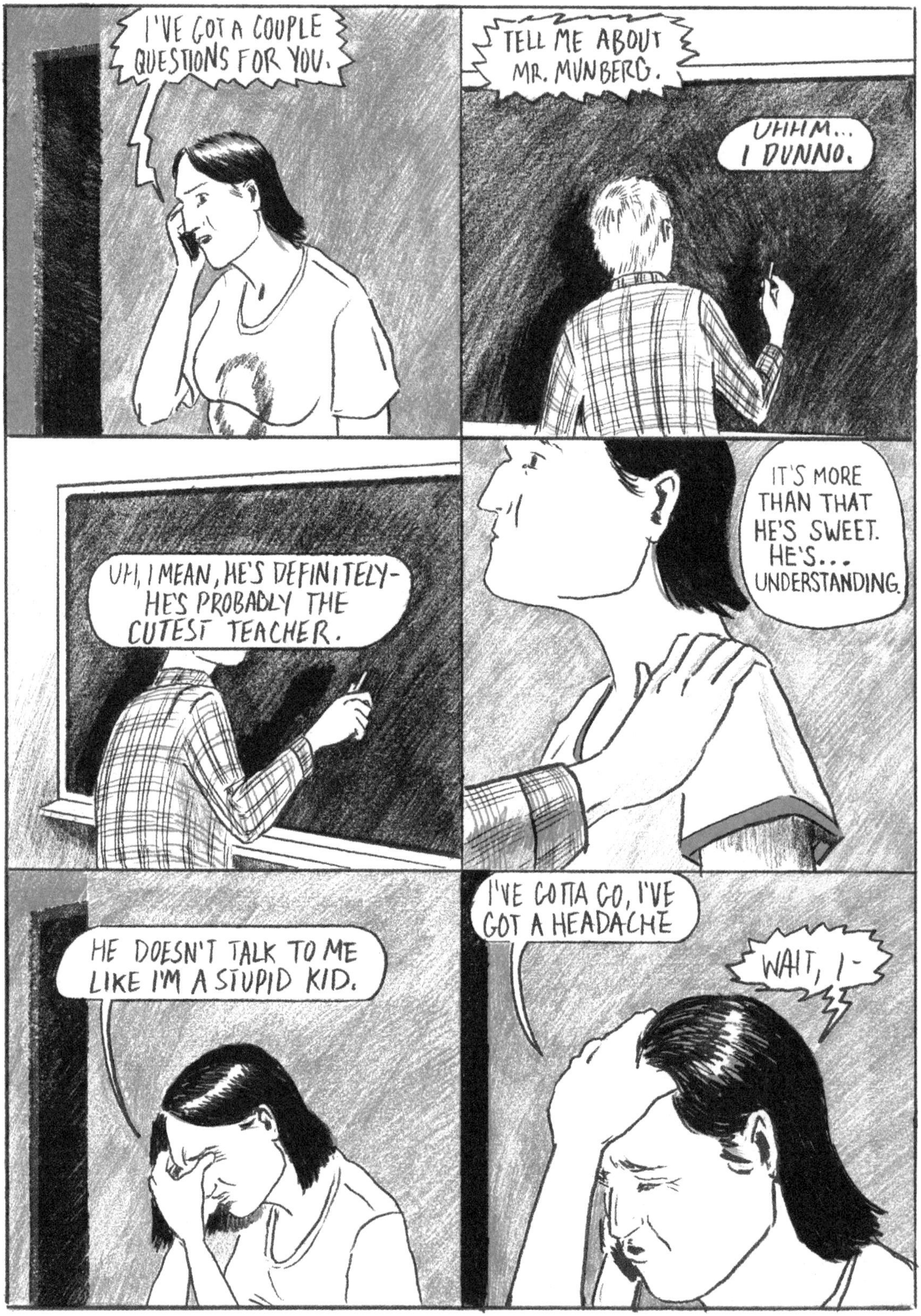
I'VE GOT A COUPLE QUESTIONS FOR YOU.
TELL ME ABOUT MR. MUNBERG.
UHHM... I DUNNO.
UH, I MEAN, HE'S DEFINITELY- HE'S PROBABLY THE CUTEST TEACHER.
IT'S MORE THAN THAT HE'S SWEET. HE'S... UNDERSTANDING.
HE DOESN'T TALK TO ME LIKE I'M A STUPID KID.
I'VE GOTTA GO, I'VE GOT A HEADACHE
WAIT, I-

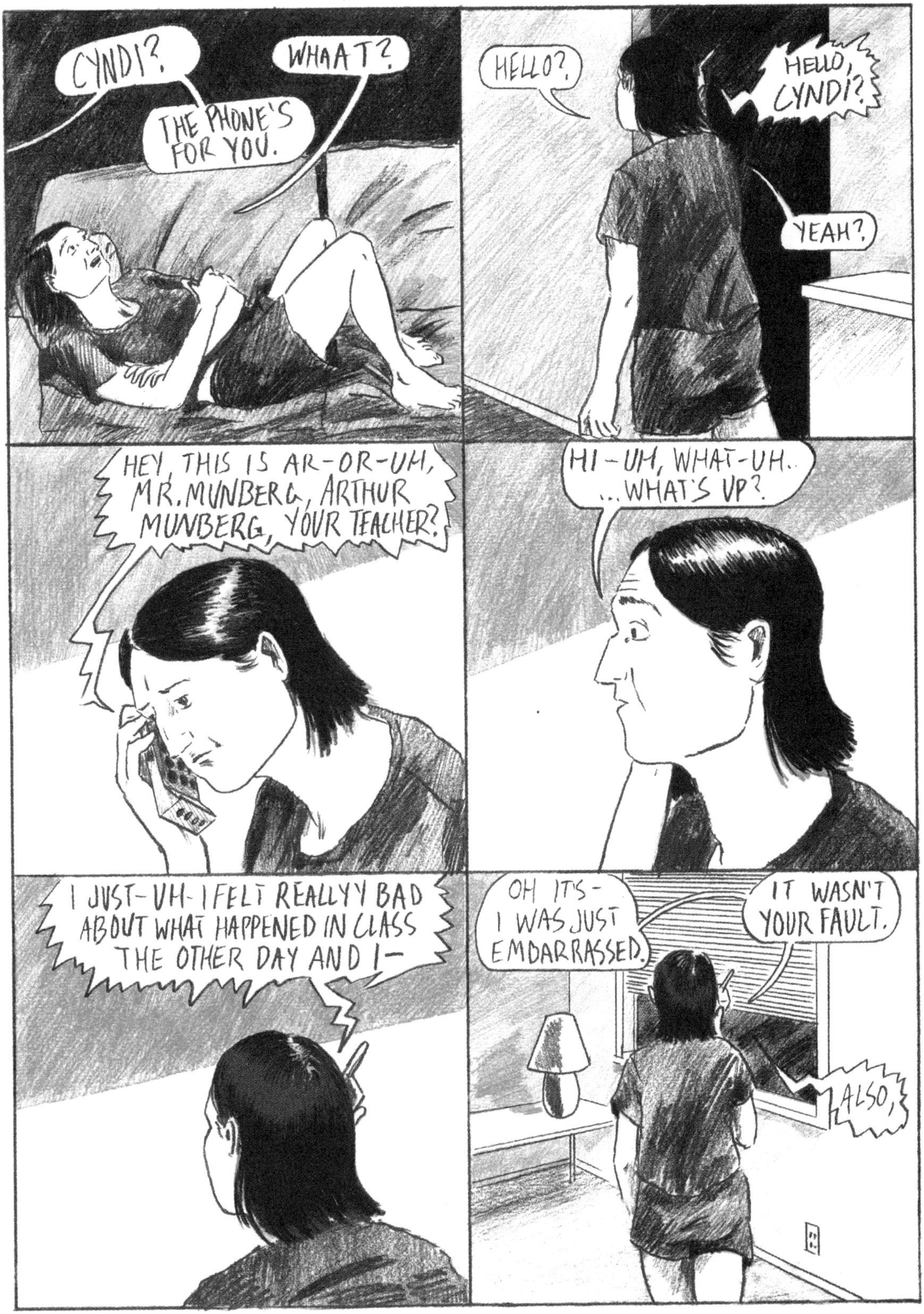
CYNDI?
WHAAT?
THE PHONE'S FOR YOU.
HELLO?
HELLO, CYNDI?
YEAH?
HEY, THIS IS AR-OR-UH, MR. MUNBERG, ARTHUR MUNBERG, YOUR TEACHER?
HI-UH, WHAT-UH.. ...WHAT'S UP?
I JUST-UH-I FELT REALLYY BAD ABOUT WHAT HAPPENED IN CLASS THE OTHER DAY AND I-
OH IT'S- I WAS JUST EMBARRASSED.
IT WASN'T YOUR FAULT.
ALSO,

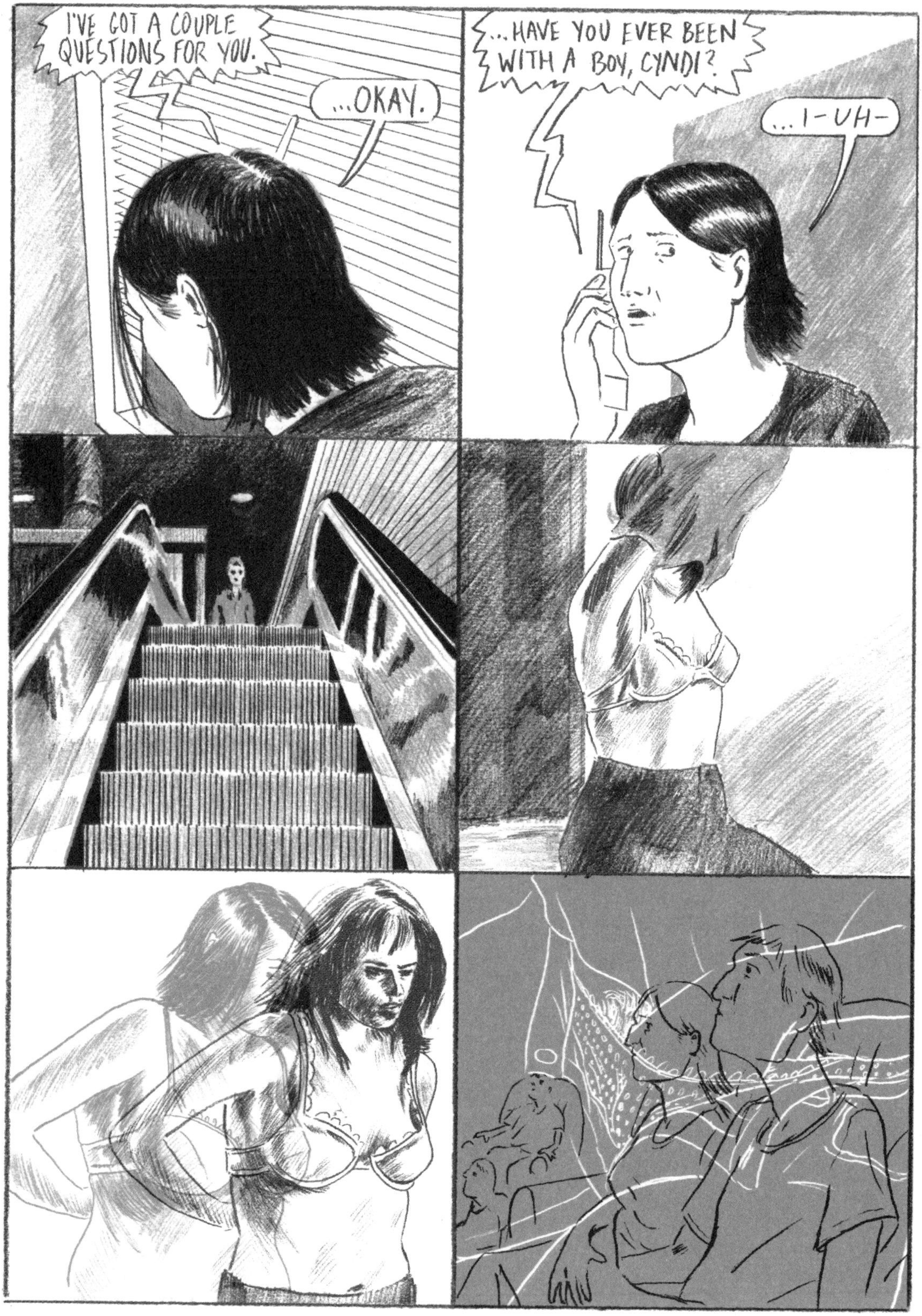
I'VE GOT A COUPLE QUESTIONS FOR YOU.
...OKAY.
...HAVE YOU EVER BEEN WITH A BOY, CYNDI?
...I-UH-

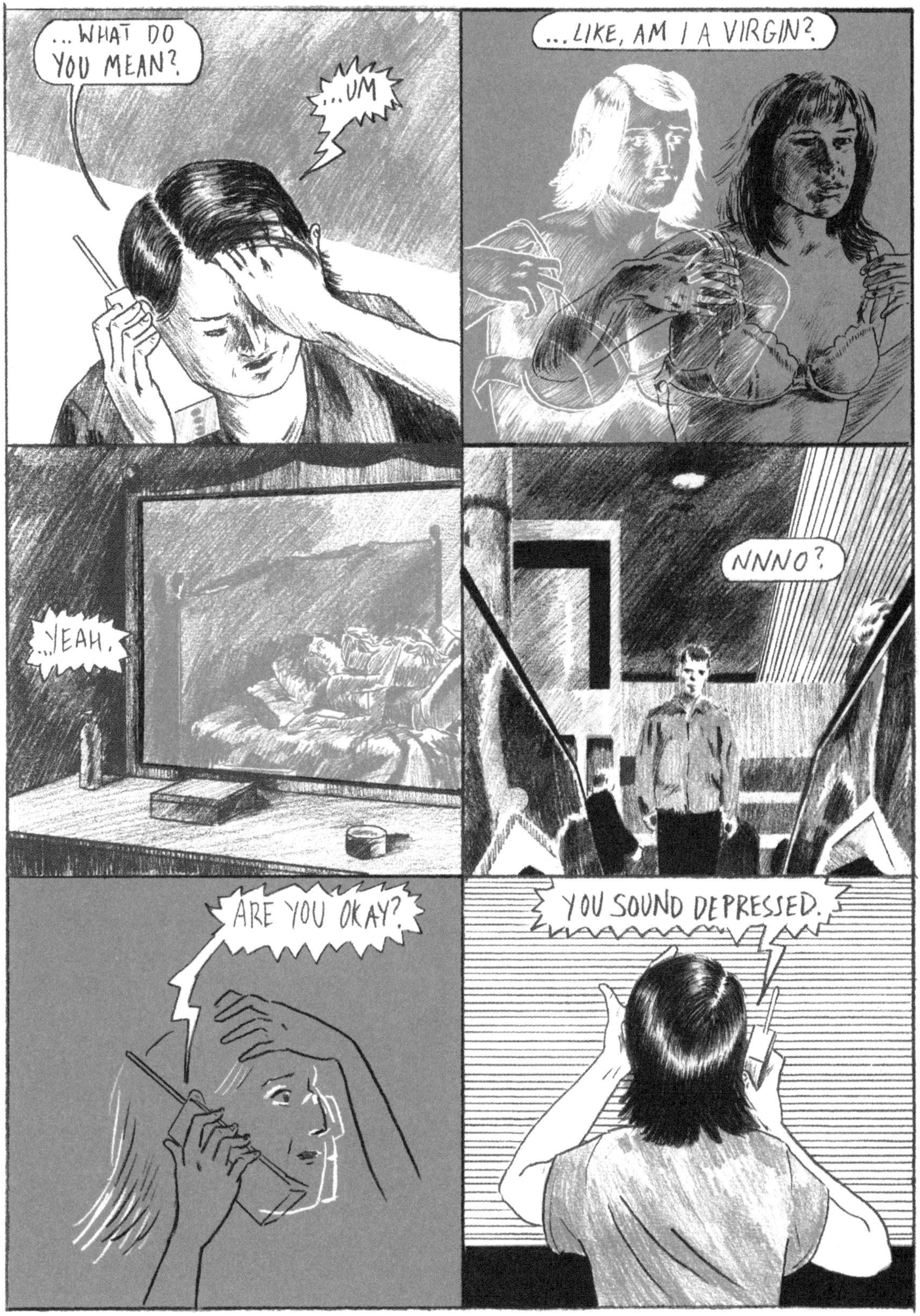

...WHAT DO YOU MEAN?
...UM
...LIKE, AM I A VIRGIN?
...YEAH.
NNNO?
ARE YOU OKAY?
YOU SOUND DEPRESSED.

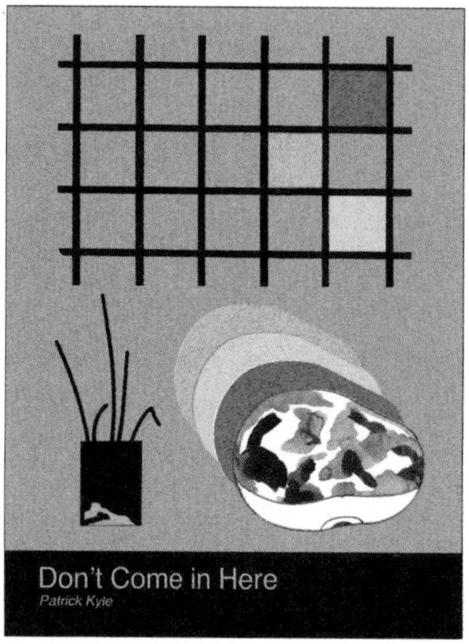
Don't Come in Here
Patrick Kyle

# Necessity (*Excerpt*)

## PATRICK KYLE

*originally published in*

*Don't Come In Here*
KOYAMA PRESS
5.5 × 7 inches • 264 pages

### Biography

Patrick Kyle is a multidisciplinary artist from Toronto, Canada.
patrickkyle.com

### Statement

This section of my book *Don't Come in Here* sees the lead character return to the kitchen of his apartment after being affected by an unusual experience there earlier in the book. The apartment is controlled by a supernatural force that is tolerant of the character's presence but demands respect. In this scene, emboldened by the encouragement of his computer assistant, the character returns to the kitchen and experiences another anomaly—but this time disregards it. This turning point in the relationship between the character and the apartment eventually leads to the dissolution of his tenancy at the end of the novel.

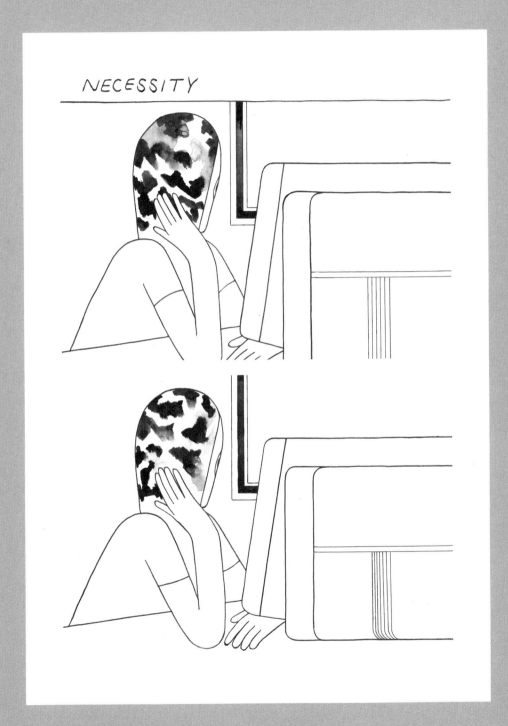

NECESSITY

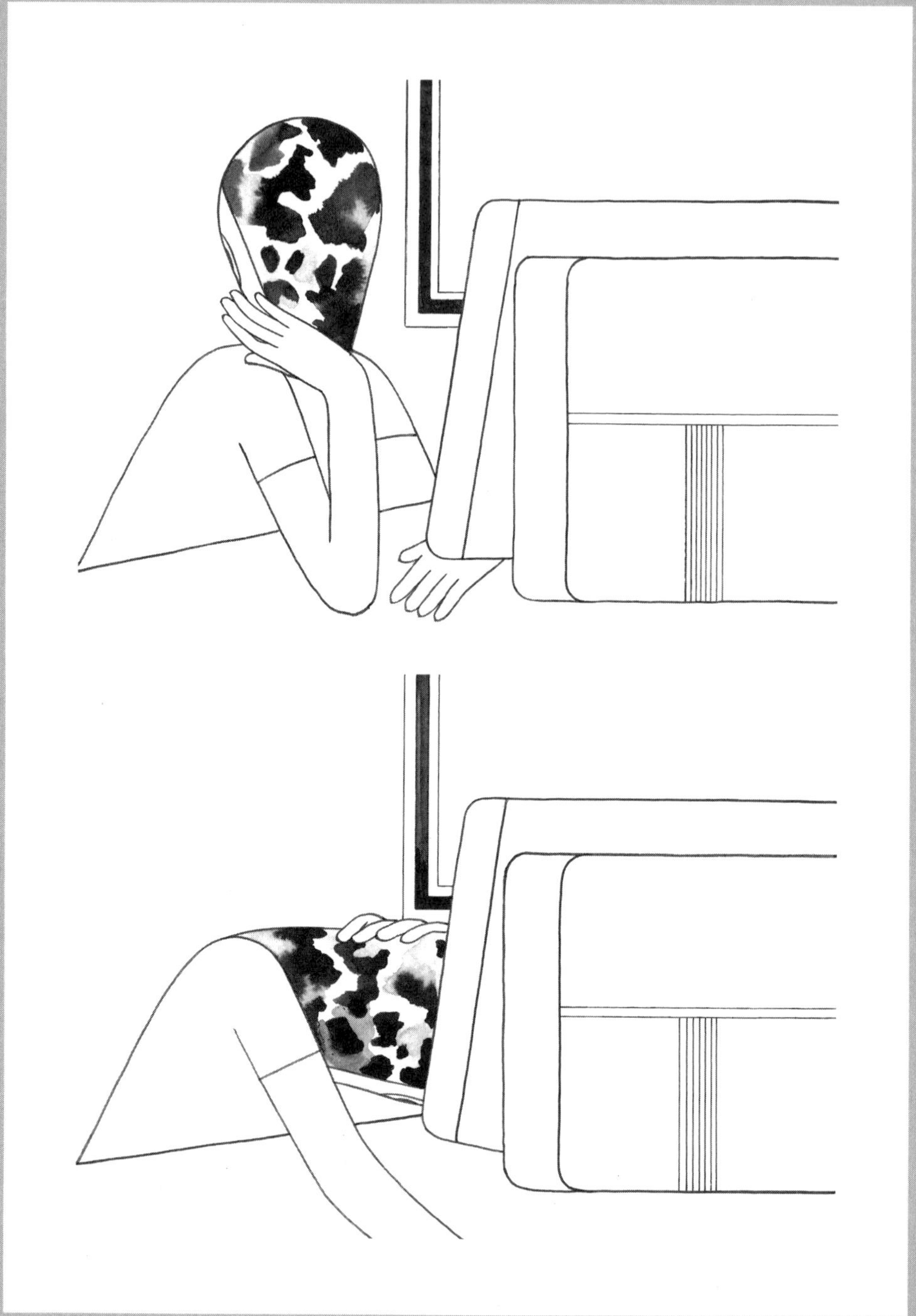

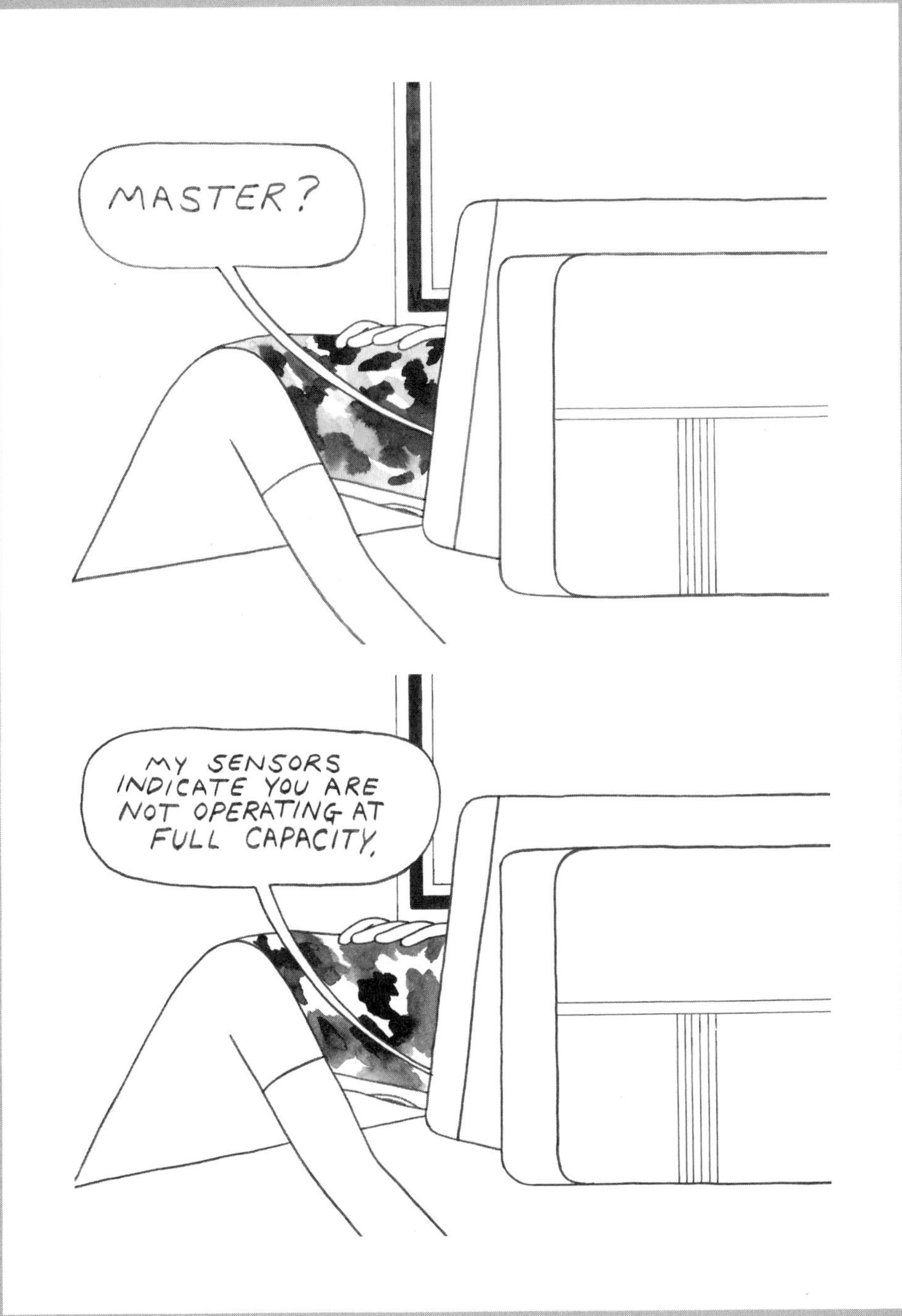
MASTER?
MY SENSORS INDICATE YOU ARE NOT OPERATING AT FULL CAPACITY.

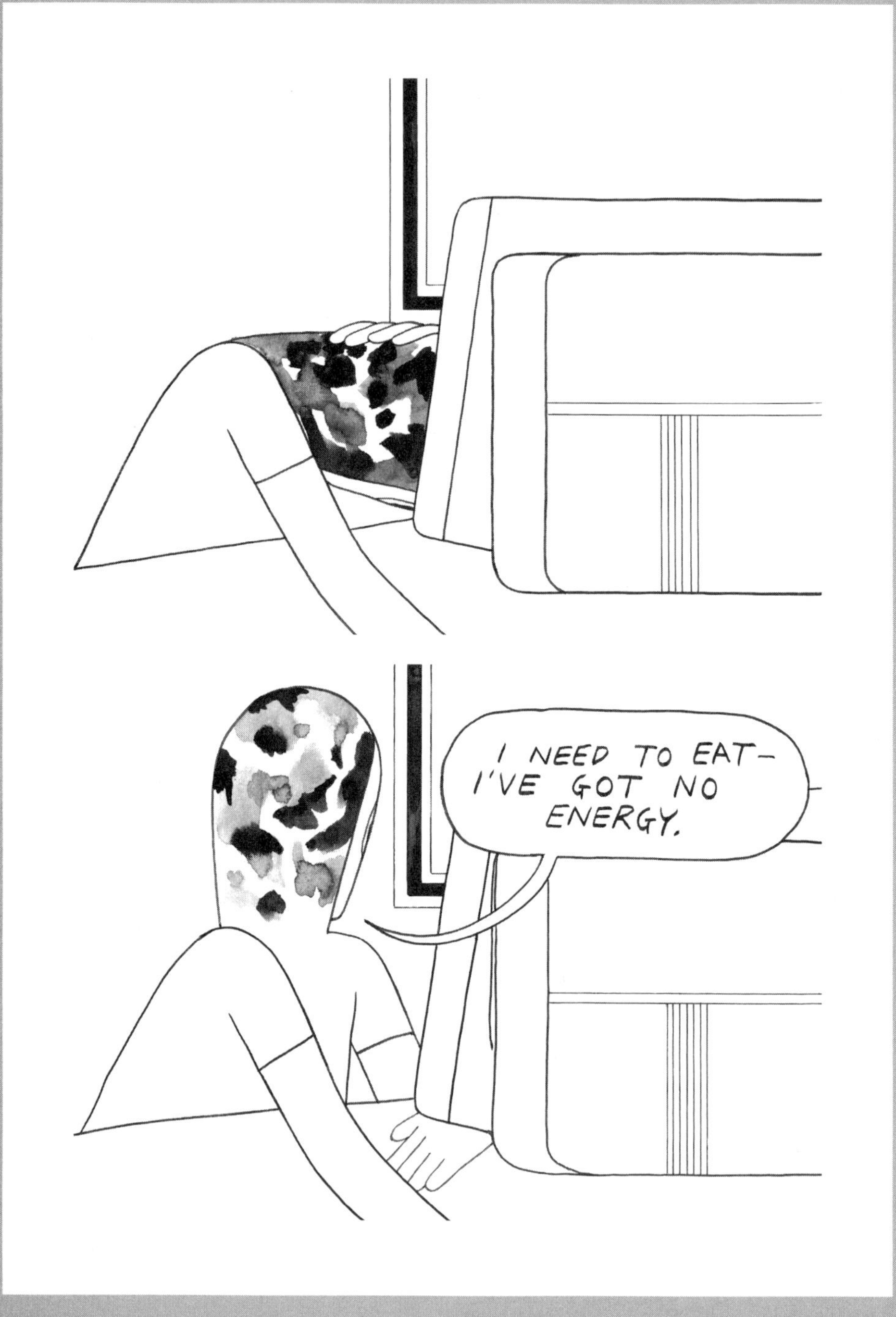
I NEED TO EAT-
I'VE GOT NO
ENERGY.

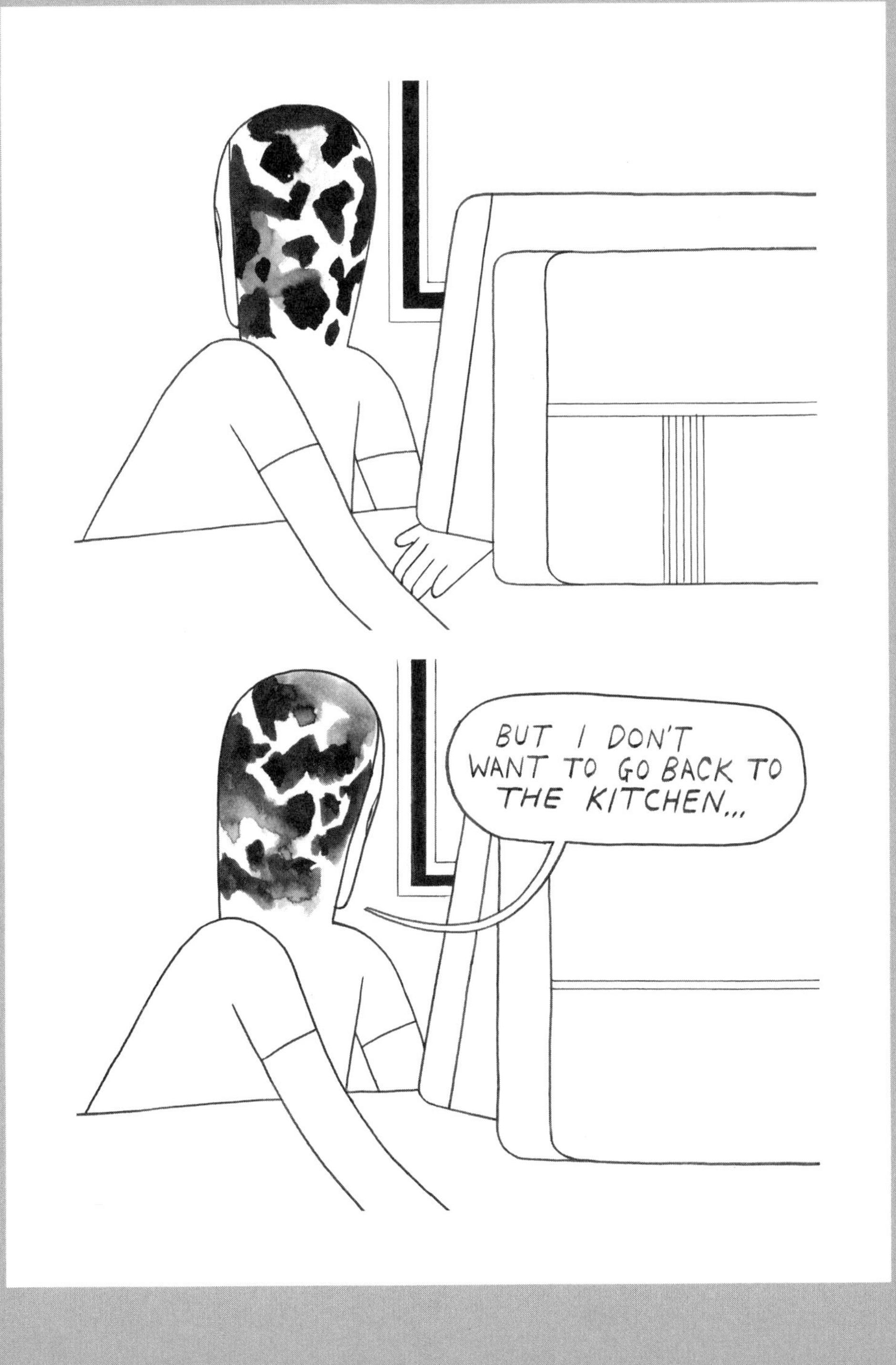
BUT I DON'T WANT TO GO BACK TO THE KITCHEN...

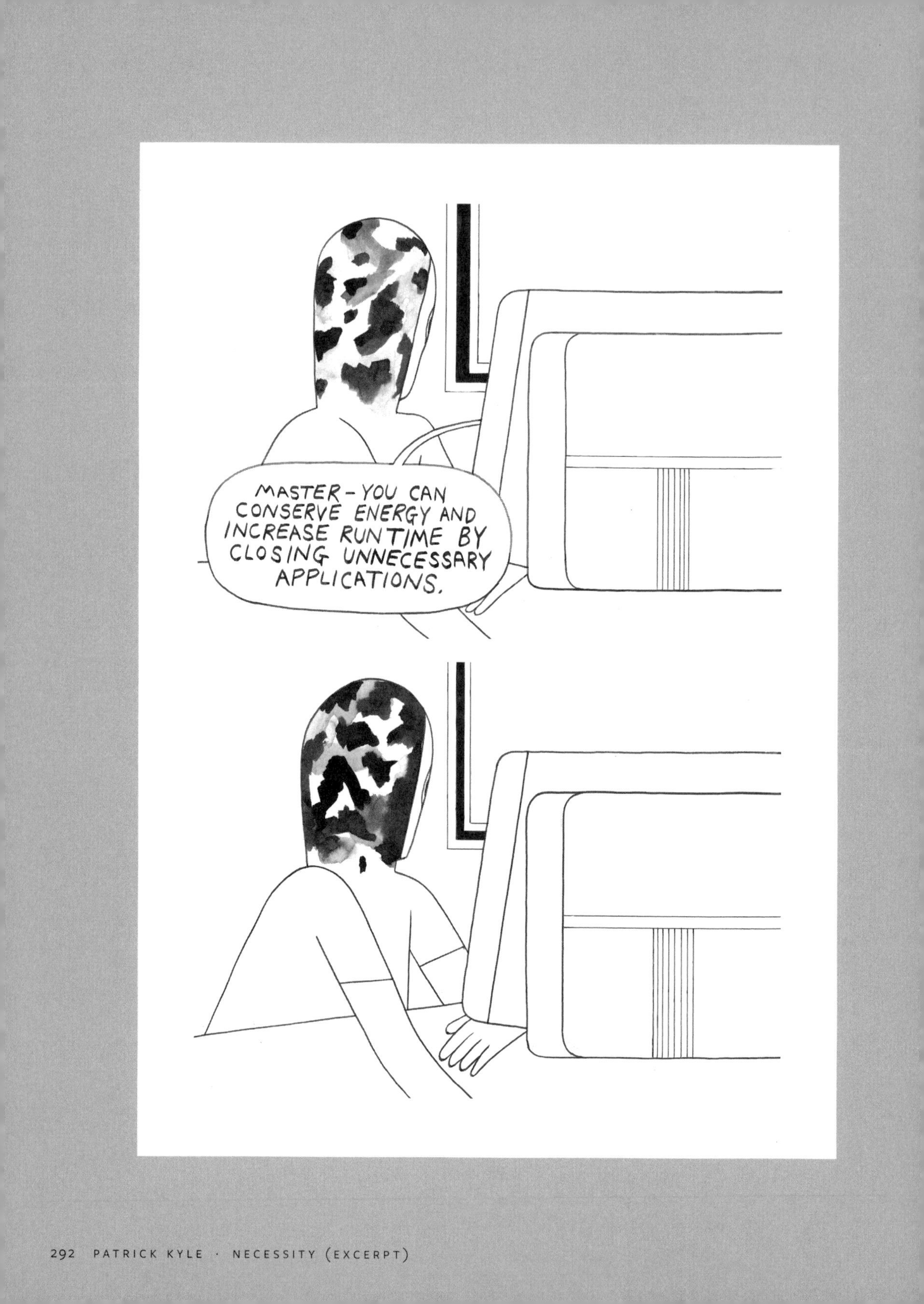
MASTER - YOU CAN CONSERVE ENERGY AND INCREASE RUNTIME BY CLOSING UNNECESSARY APPLICATIONS.

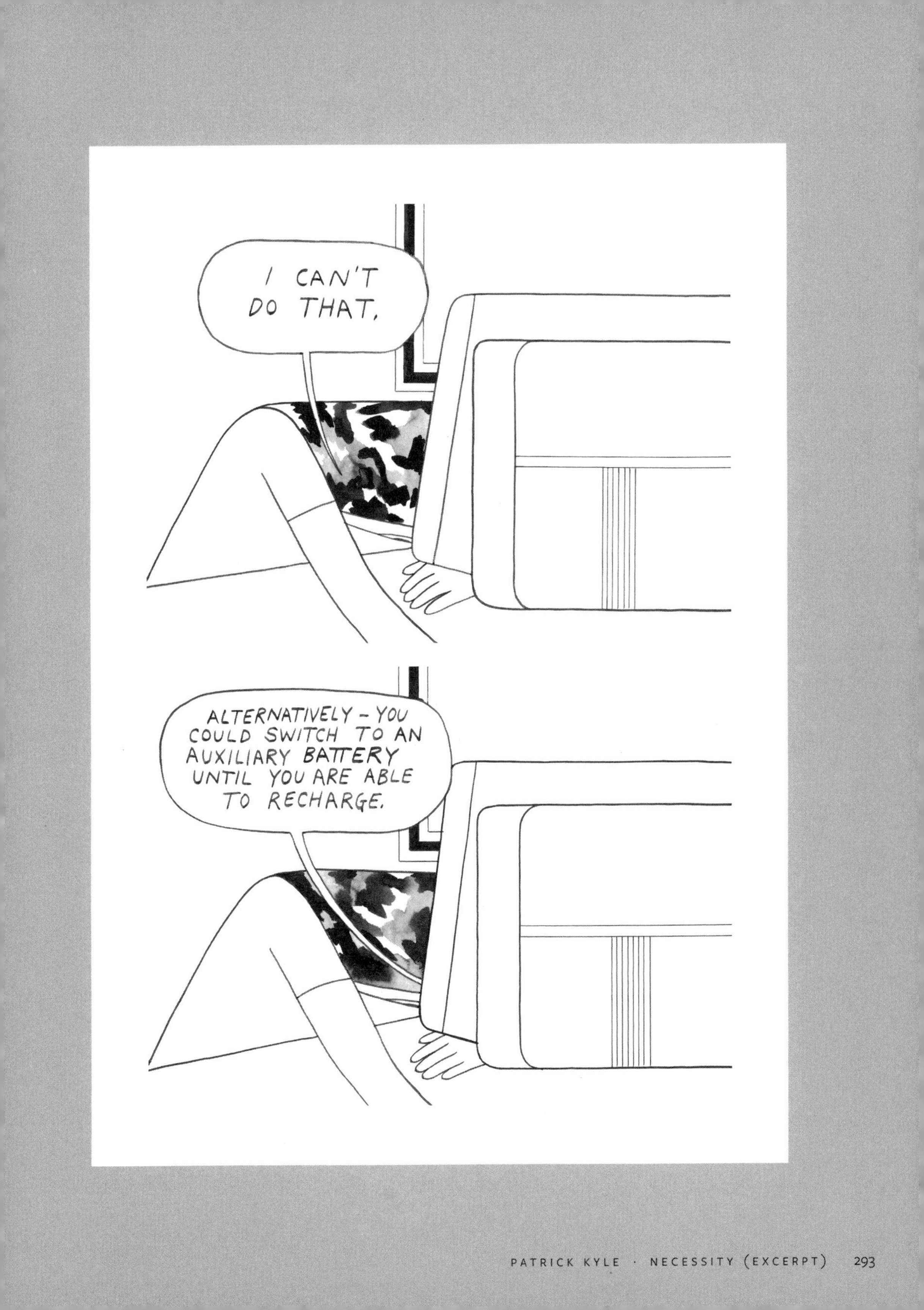
I CAN'T DO THAT.
ALTERNATIVELY – YOU COULD SWITCH TO AN AUXILIARY BATTERY UNTIL YOU ARE ABLE TO RECHARGE.

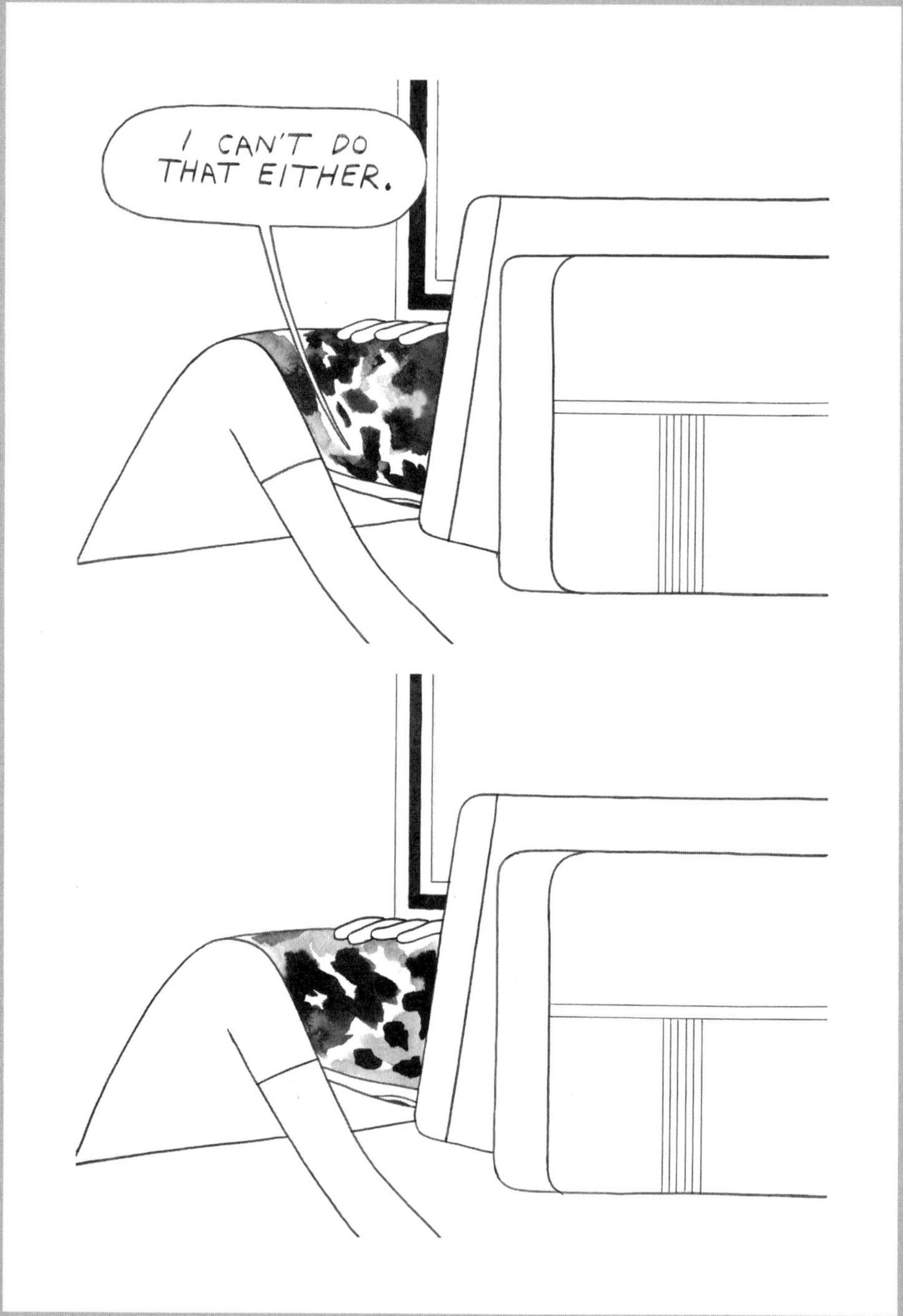
I CAN'T DO THAT EITHER.

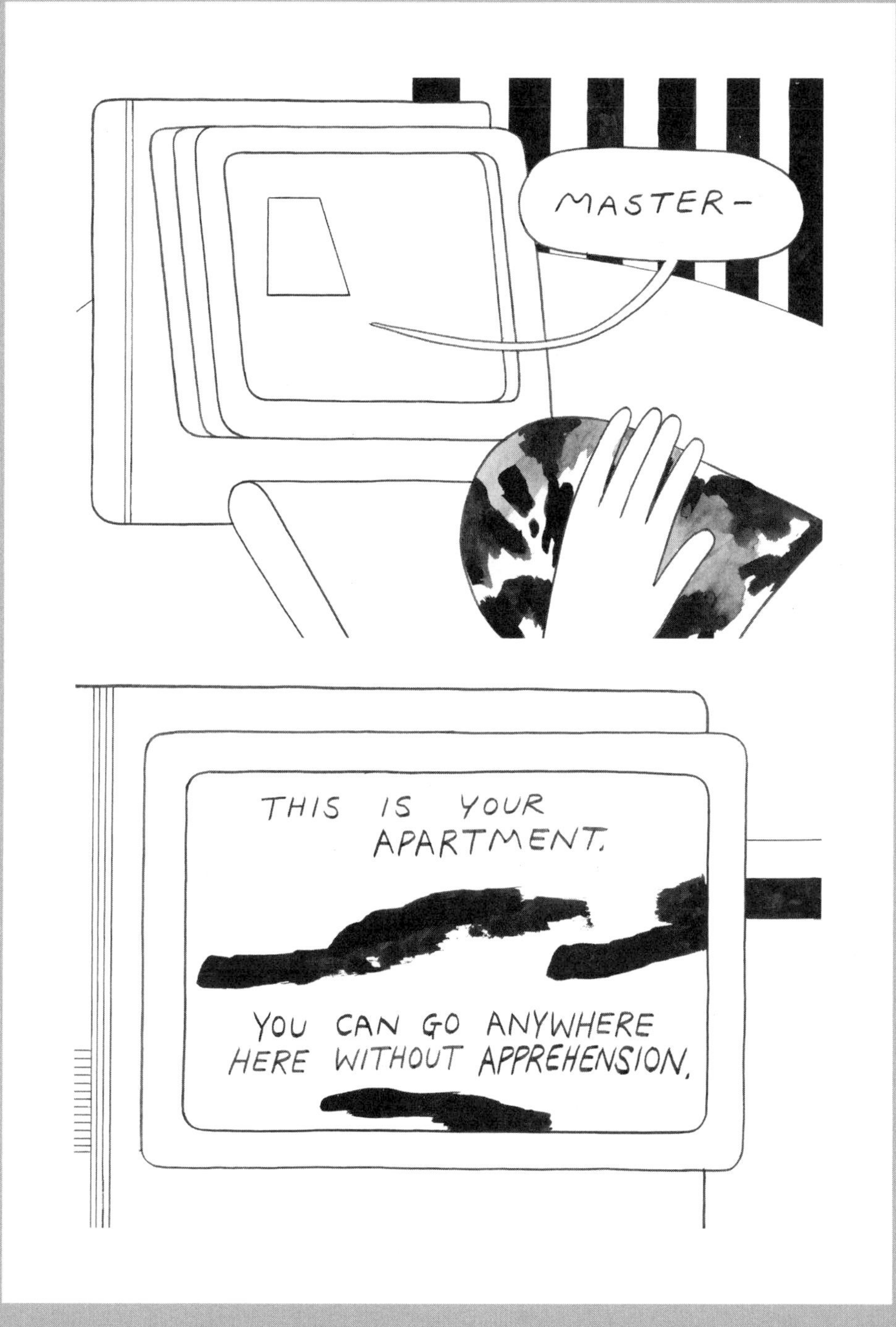
MASTER-
THIS IS YOUR APARTMENT.
YOU CAN GO ANYWHERE HERE WITHOUT APPREHENSION.

THERE'S NOTHING TO BE AFRAID OF HERE.

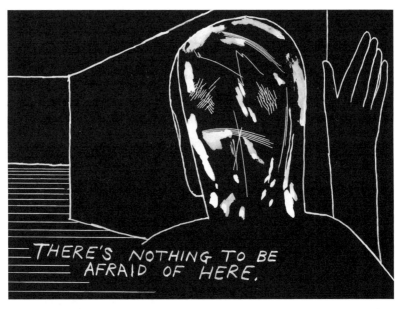

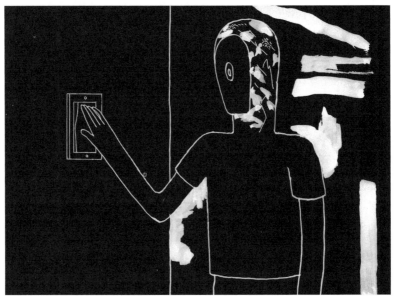

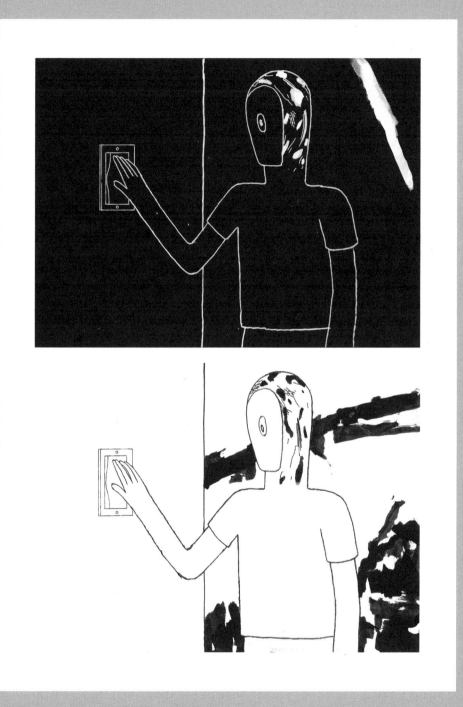

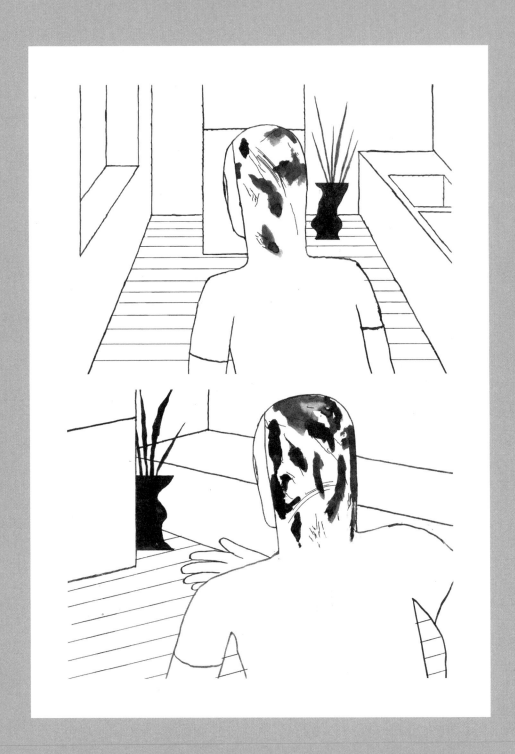

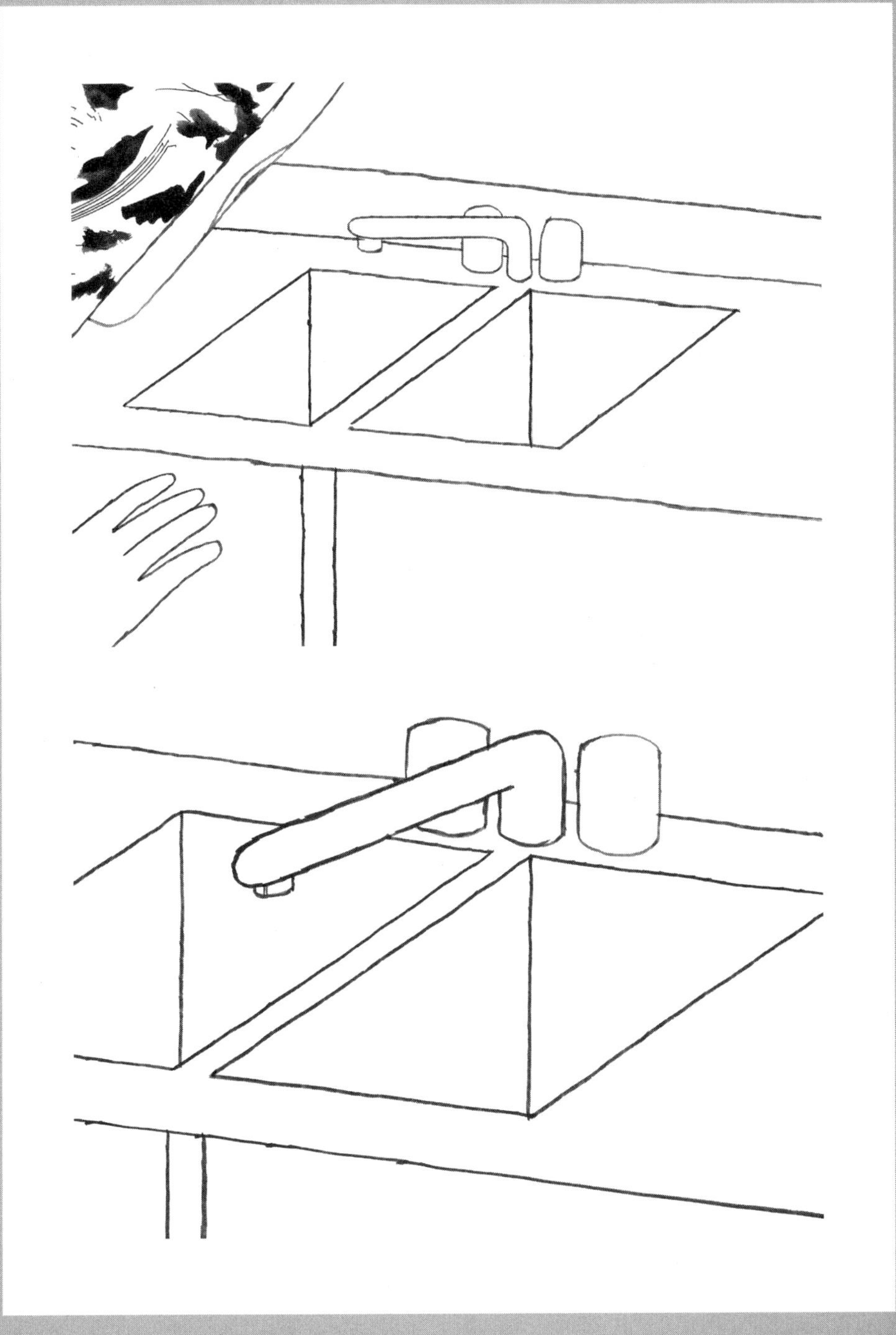

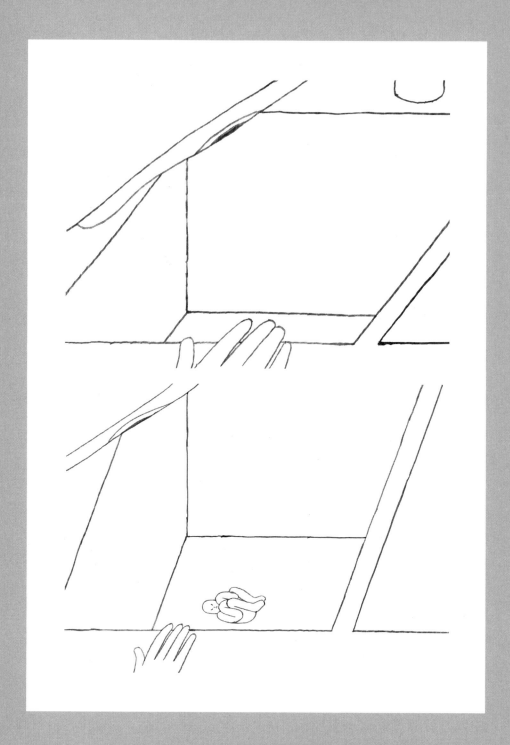

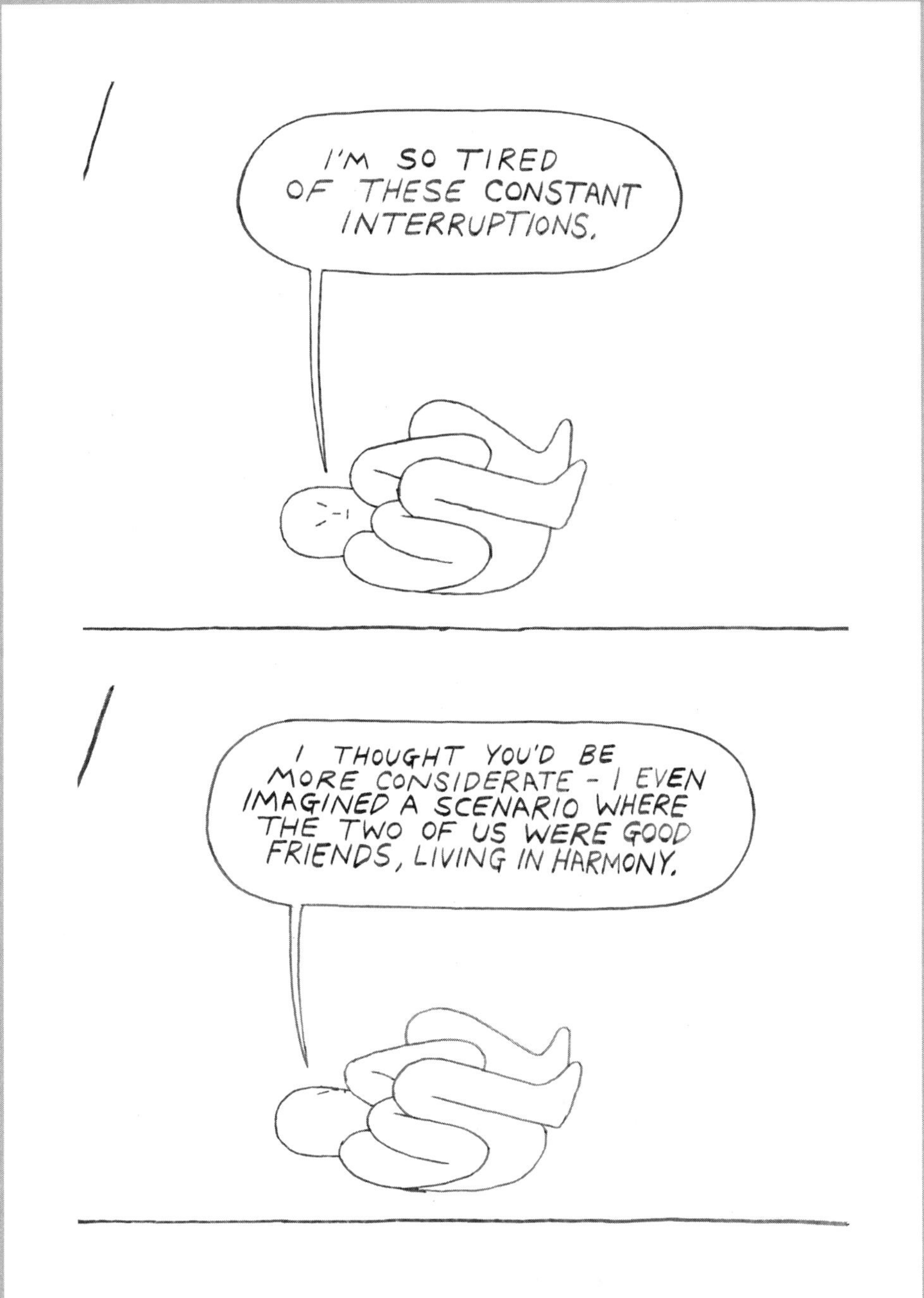
I'M SO TIRED OF THESE CONSTANT INTERRUPTIONS.
I THOUGHT YOU'D BE MORE CONSIDERATE - I EVEN IMAGINED A SCENARIO WHERE THE TWO OF US WERE GOOD FRIENDS, LIVING IN HARMONY.

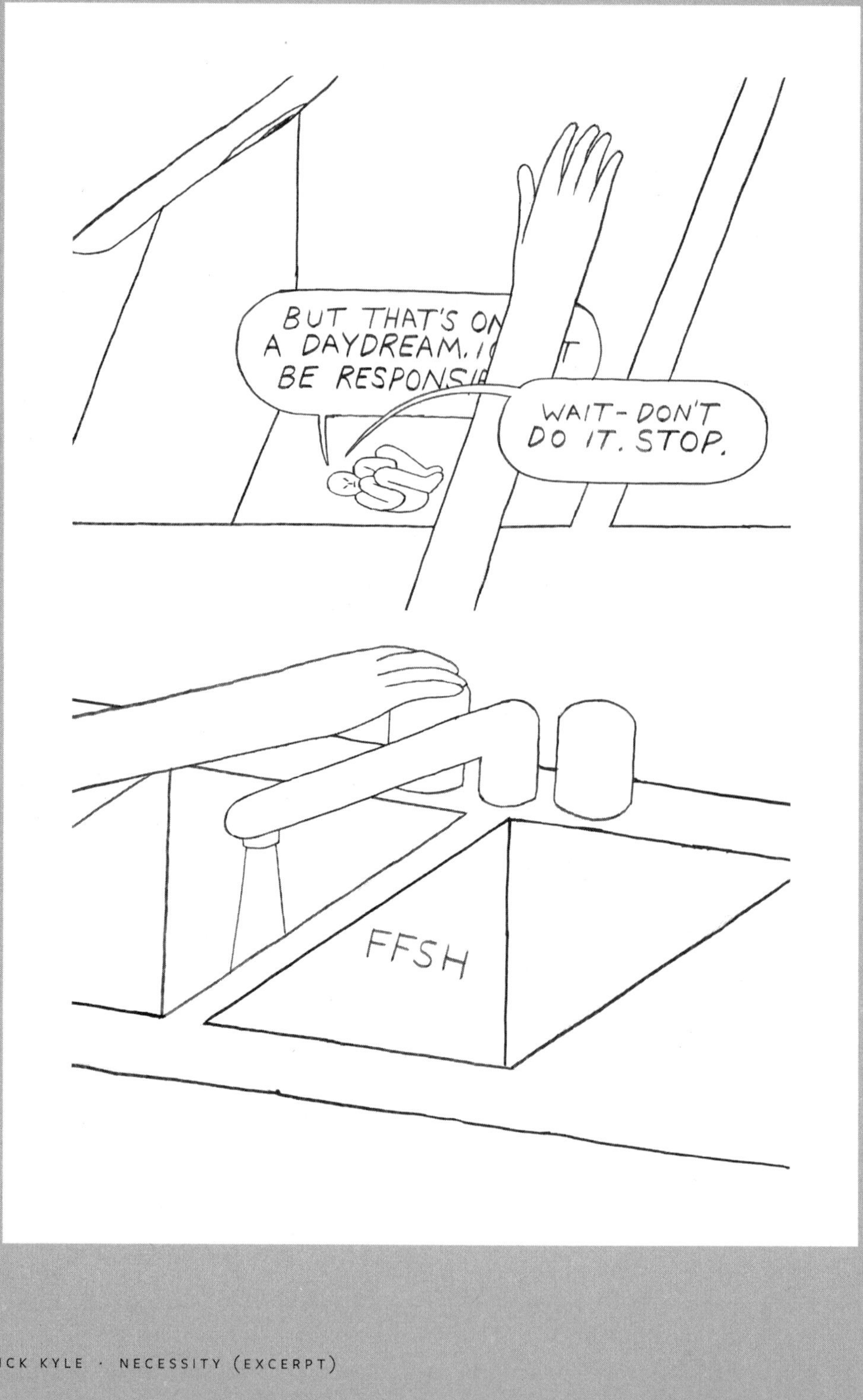
BUT THAT'S ON
A DAYDREAM. I
BE RESPONSI
WAIT- DON'T
DO IT. STOP.
FFSH

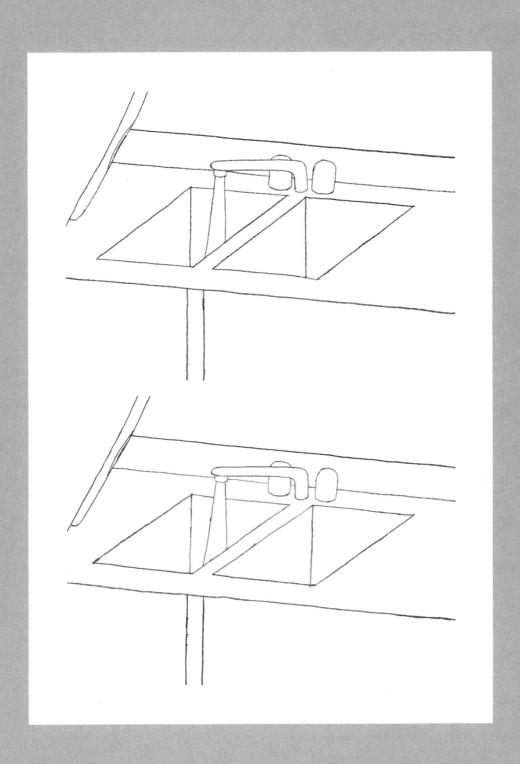

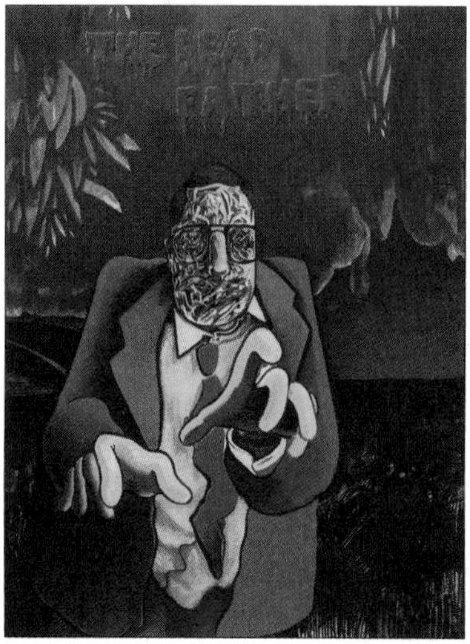
THE DEAD FATHER

# The Dead Father

SAMI ALWANI

*originally published as*

*The Dead Father*

SELF-PUBLISHED

8.5 × 11 inches • 13 pages

## Biography

Sami Alwani is a cartoonist and illustrator living in Toronto, Canada. Find more of his work at his website or by following his instagram @sami.alwani.
samialwani.com

## Statement

As a text, "The Dead Father" has three functions: 1) an elaborate misrepresentation of my horrifying cartoon destiny shamelessly revealing my grotesque, misshapen inner body through a needlessly complex system of signification; 2) an unsuccessful attempt at exorcising the demonic mental illness of Westernized thinking; 3) because it represents a historical continuum, "The Dead Father" is a process that takes place outside of time and is therefore intrinsically unknowable and resists definition.

IT'S A BOY!

WAHHH!!  WAAH HHH!

NOW SON, YOU'VE GOT A FEW OPTIONS

YOU CAN BECOME AN ACTOR OR A MUSICIAN OR A DANCER— OR A WRITER OR ARTIST OR CARTOONIST ... LIKE ME

OR YOU COULD BE A DOCTOR OR A LAWYER OR A PROFESSOR OR A DIRECTOR OR A MATHEMATICIAN OR A PEDIATRICIAN OR A SCIENTIST, PHYSICIST OR ENGINEER... LIKE MY FATHER

OR ELSE ANY OTHER OF AN UNENDING AND LIMITLESS LIST OF POSSIBLE FUTURE OCCUPATIONS INCLUDING BUT NOT LIMITED TO:

- PHYSICAL THERAPIST
- CARPENTER
- YOJIMBO
- INVESTMENT BANKER
- ACCOUNTANT
- COMPUTER TECHNICIAN
- REAL ESTATE AGENT
- CALL GIRL

OR ORNITHOLOGIST
OR OPTHAMOLOGIST
OR GYNACOLOGIST

BUT WHATEVER YOU DO CHOOSE JUST BE SURE THAT ALL YOUR ACTIONS ARE GUIDED BY AN INESCAPABLE UNDERSTANDING THAT YOU AS A PERSON ARE FUNDAMENTALLY INSUFFICIENT AND THAT YOUR CAPACITY TO WORK IS THE ONLY CAPACITY IN WHICH YOU ARE VALUABLE

. . .

AN ELECTRIC TENSION FLITS FROM HEAD TO HEAD IN THE PRESS ROOM

TAP TAP TAP TAP TAP TAP TAP TAP TAP TAP TAP TAP TAP TAP

THE ENDS OF DOZENS OF CARBON PENCILS ANXIOUSLY TAPPING DOZENS OF WIREBOUND REPORTER'S NOTEBOOKS COMPOSE A MINIATURE ORCHESTRA OF ANTICIPATORY DRUMROLL AS THE COLLECTED PRESS AWAITS THEIR FIRST CONFERENCE WITH THE FIRST-BORN SON OF AMERICA'S GREATEST LIVING HERO- SAMI ALWANI

A HUSH FALLS OVER THE ROOM AS THE SQUEAKING OF CARRIAGE WHEELS ANNOUNCES THE BABY'S ARRIVAL...

THANK YOU FOR COMING LADIES AND GENTLEMEN

WE ARE PLEASED TO HAVE YOU ALL HERE TO ANNOUNCE THE BIRTH AND SUCCESSFUL DELIVERY OF MY CHILD— BABY ALWANI. I WILL KEEP THIS INTRODUCTION SHORT AS I KNOW THERE IS A LOT TO DISCUSS, SUFFICE TO SAY, BABY WILL BE HAPPY TO ANSWER ALL OF YOUR QUESTIONS

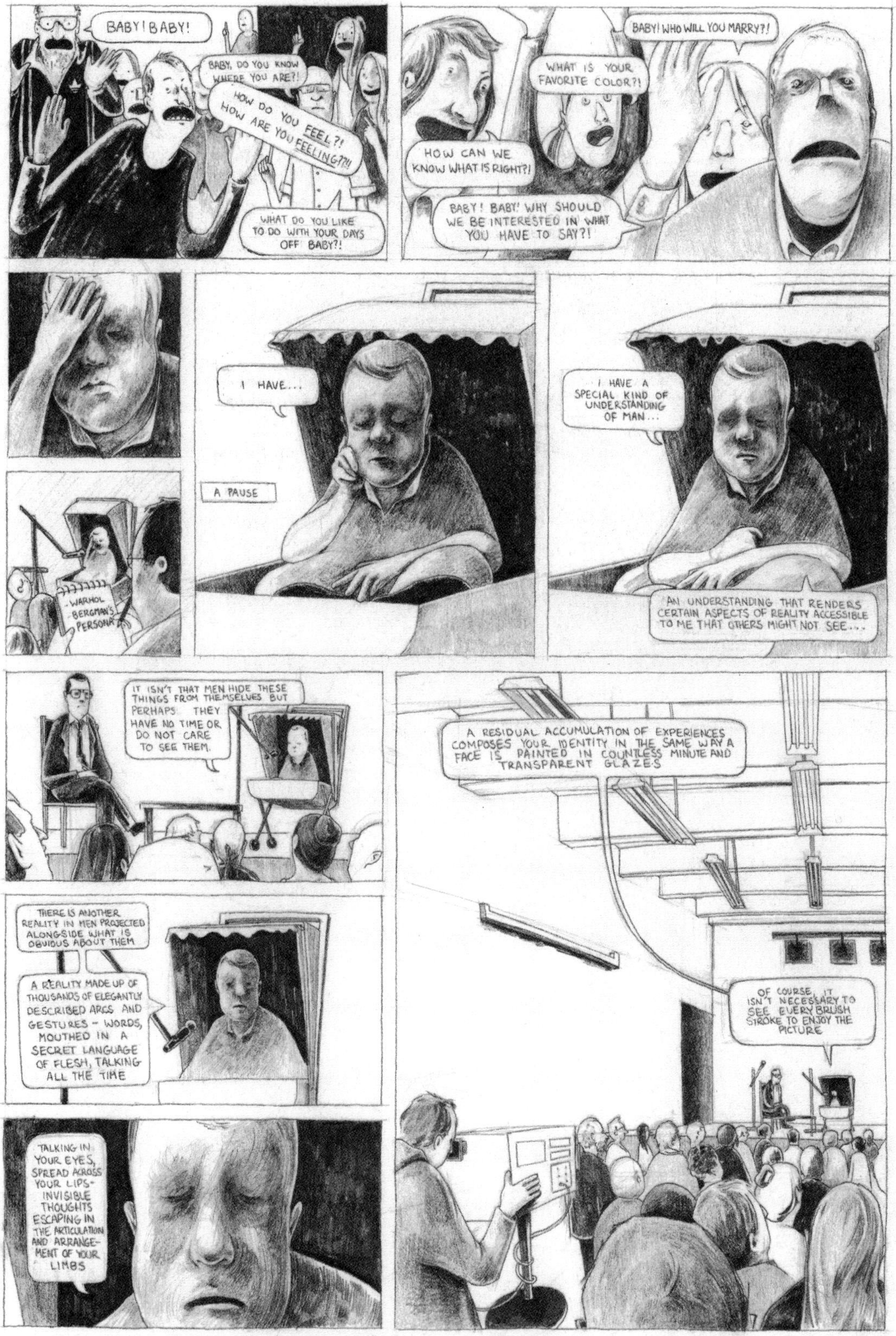
BABY! BABY!
BABY, DO YOU KNOW WHERE YOU ARE?!
HOW DO YOU FEEL?! HOW ARE YOU FEELING?!?!
WHAT DO YOU LIKE TO DO WITH YOUR DAYS OFF BABY?!
BABY! WHO WILL YOU MARRY?!
WHAT IS YOUR FAVORITE COLOR?!
HOW CAN WE KNOW WHAT IS RIGHT?!
BABY! BABY! WHY SHOULD WE BE INTERESTED IN WHAT YOU HAVE TO SAY?!
I HAVE...
A PAUSE
I HAVE A SPECIAL KIND OF UNDERSTANDING OF MAN...
WARHOL BERGMAN'S PERSONA
AN UNDERSTANDING THAT RENDERS CERTAIN ASPECTS OF REALITY ACCESSIBLE TO ME THAT OTHERS MIGHT NOT SEE....
IT ISN'T THAT MEN HIDE THESE THINGS FROM THEMSELVES BUT PERHAPS THEY HAVE NO TIME OR DO NOT CARE TO SEE THEM.
A RESIDUAL ACCUMULATION OF EXPERIENCES COMPOSES YOUR IDENTITY IN THE SAME WAY A FACE IS PAINTED IN COUNTLESS MINUTE AND TRANSPARENT GLAZES
THERE IS ANOTHER REALITY IN MEN PROJECTED ALONG-SIDE WHAT IS OBVIOUS ABOUT THEM
A REALITY MADE UP OF THOUSANDS OF ELEGANTLY DESCRIBED ARCS AND GESTURES - WORDS, MOUTHED IN A SECRET LANGUAGE OF FLESH, TALKING ALL THE TIME
OF COURSE, IT ISN'T NECESSARY TO SEE EVERY BRUSH STROKE TO ENJOY THE PICTURE
TALKING IN YOUR EYES, SPREAD ACROSS YOUR LIPS- INVISIBLE THOUGHTS ESCAPING IN THE ARTICULATION AND ARRANGE-MENT OF YOUR LIMBS

...BUT YOU SEE...?

...WELL...

THEN WHAT IS IT THAT YOU SEE?

• • •

BABY KNOCKS ON HIS FATHER'S BEDROOM DOOR TO ASK HIM A QUESTION AND PUSHES THE DOOR OPEN WHEN HE HEARS NO RESPONSE

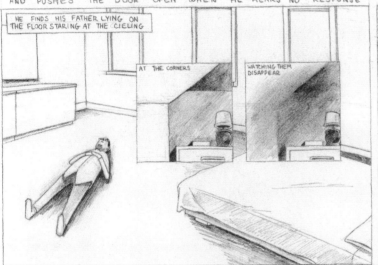
HE FINDS HIS FATHER LYING ON THE FLOOR STARING AT THE CIELING

AT THE CORNERS

WATCHING THEM DISAPPEAR

BABY FORGETS HIS QUESTION AND SITS DOWN BESIDE HIS FATHER

WHAT ARE YOU THINKING ABOUT?

NOTHING

BUT REALLY SAMI HAD BEEN THINKING ABOUT HIS PICTURES

THE OTHER DAY HE PAINTED A VIOLENT PICTURE OF HIM-SELF AS A ZOMBIE, AND HE HAD BEEN THINKING

"IS THAT HOW I REALLY FEEL?"

AND THEN:

"YES, I GUESS IT MUST BE"

SAMI'S ATTENTION SHIFTS TO A PATCH OF LIGHT ON THE WALL AND THEN TO HIS SON'S FACE, AND THEN HE HAS A THOUGHT LIKE "EVERYTHING IS A LIE," OR "HOW CAN I LIVE IN A WORLD WHERE—"
HEY DO YOU WANT TO PLAY A GAME WITH ME?
YEAH!
AND SO:
OKAY, NOW ATTACK ME.
SOCIETY
AHHHHHHH!
THERE IS NO WAY TO FIGHT ME!!
I WILL DESTROY YOU!!!
SOCIETY

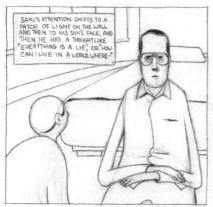

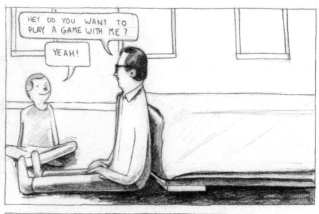

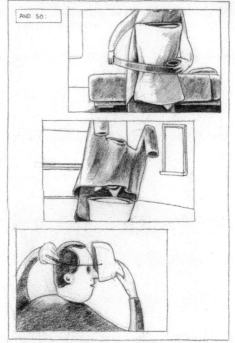

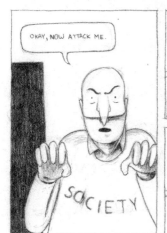

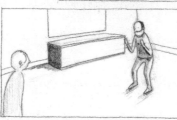

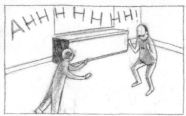

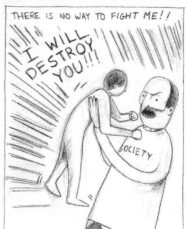

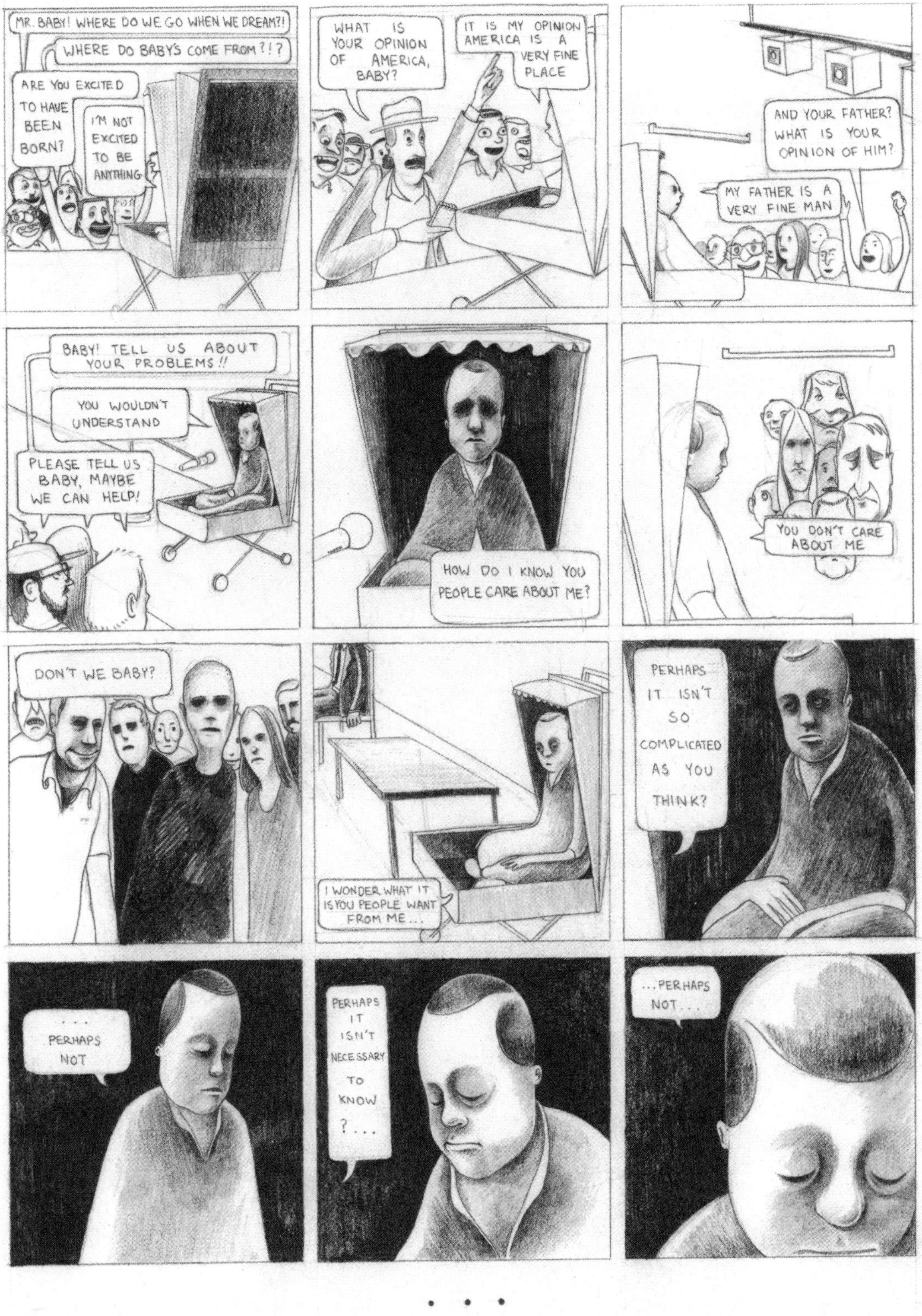
MR. BABY! WHERE DO WE GO WHEN WE DREAM?!
WHERE DO BABYS COME FROM?!?
ARE YOU EXCITED TO HAVE BEEN BORN?
I'M NOT EXCITED TO BE ANYTHING
WHAT IS YOUR OPINION OF AMERICA, BABY?
IT IS MY OPINION AMERICA IS A VERY FINE PLACE
AND YOUR FATHER? WHAT IS YOUR OPINION OF HIM?
MY FATHER IS A VERY FINE MAN
BABY! TELL US ABOUT YOUR PROBLEMS!!
YOU WOULDN'T UNDERSTAND
PLEASE TELL US BABY, MAYBE WE CAN HELP!
HOW DO I KNOW YOU PEOPLE CARE ABOUT ME?
YOU DON'T CARE ABOUT ME
DON'T WE BABY?
I WONDER WHAT IT IS YOU PEOPLE WANT FROM ME...
PERHAPS IT ISN'T SO COMPLICATED AS YOU THINK?
... PERHAPS NOT
PERHAPS IT ISN'T NECESSARY TO KNOW ?...
...PERHAPS NOT...

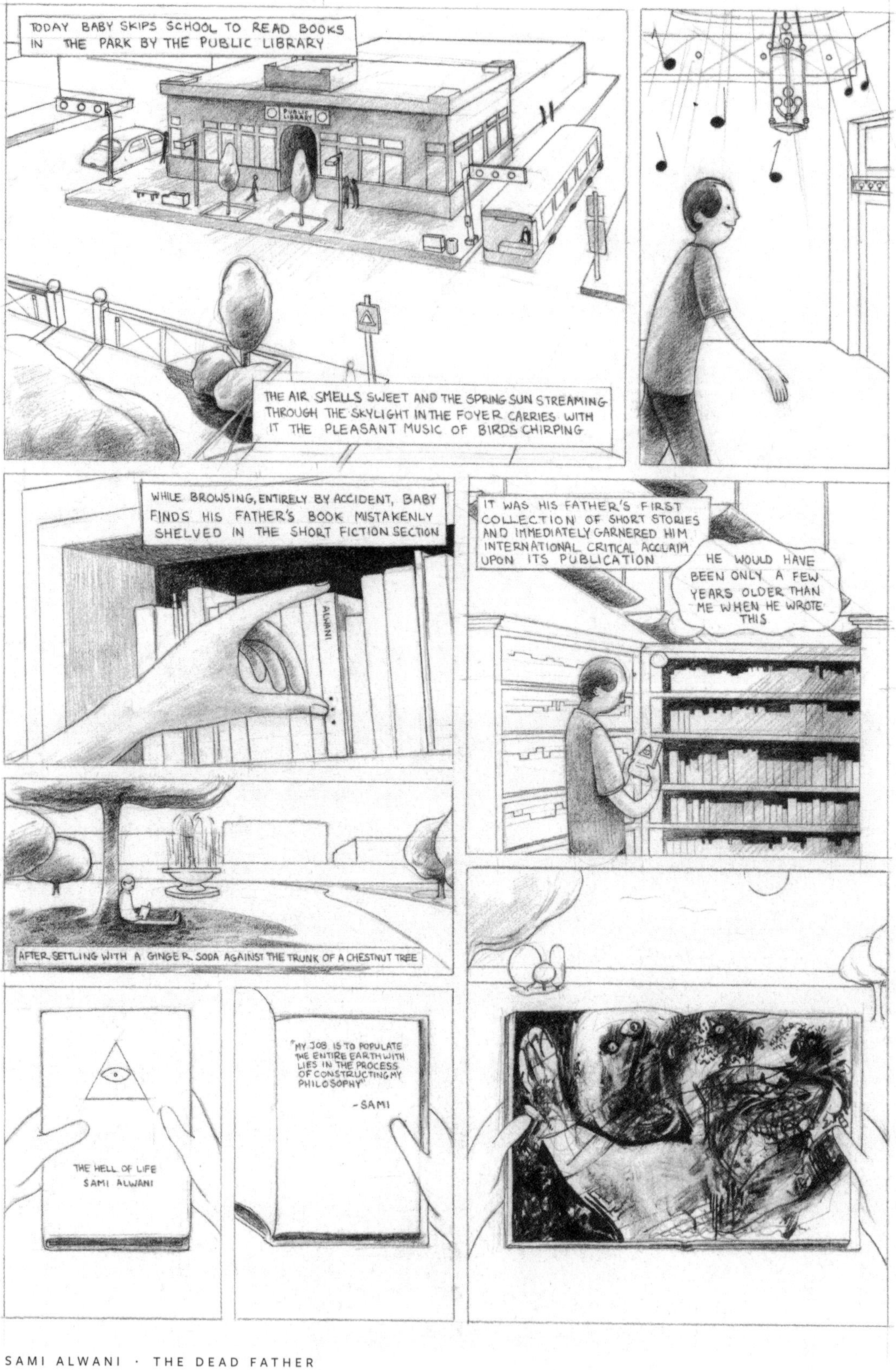
TODAY BABY SKIPS SCHOOL TO READ BOOKS IN THE PARK BY THE PUBLIC LIBRARY
PUBLIC LIBRARY
THE AIR SMELLS SWEET AND THE SPRING SUN STREAMING THROUGH THE SKYLIGHT IN THE FOYER CARRIES WITH IT THE PLEASANT MUSIC OF BIRDS CHIRPING
WHILE BROWSING, ENTIRELY BY ACCIDENT, BABY FINDS HIS FATHER'S BOOK MISTAKENLY SHELVED IN THE SHORT FICTION SECTION
ALWANI
IT WAS HIS FATHER'S FIRST COLLECTION OF SHORT STORIES AND IMMEDIATELY GARNERED HIM INTERNATIONAL CRITICAL ACCLAIM UPON ITS PUBLICATION
HE WOULD HAVE BEEN ONLY A FEW YEARS OLDER THAN ME WHEN HE WROTE THIS
AFTER SETTLING WITH A GINGER SODA AGAINST THE TRUNK OF A CHESTNUT TREE
THE HELL OF LIFE
SAMI ALWANI
"MY JOB IS TO POPULATE THE ENTIRE EARTH WITH LIES IN THE PROCESS OF CONSTRUCTING MY PHILOSOPHY"
-SAMI

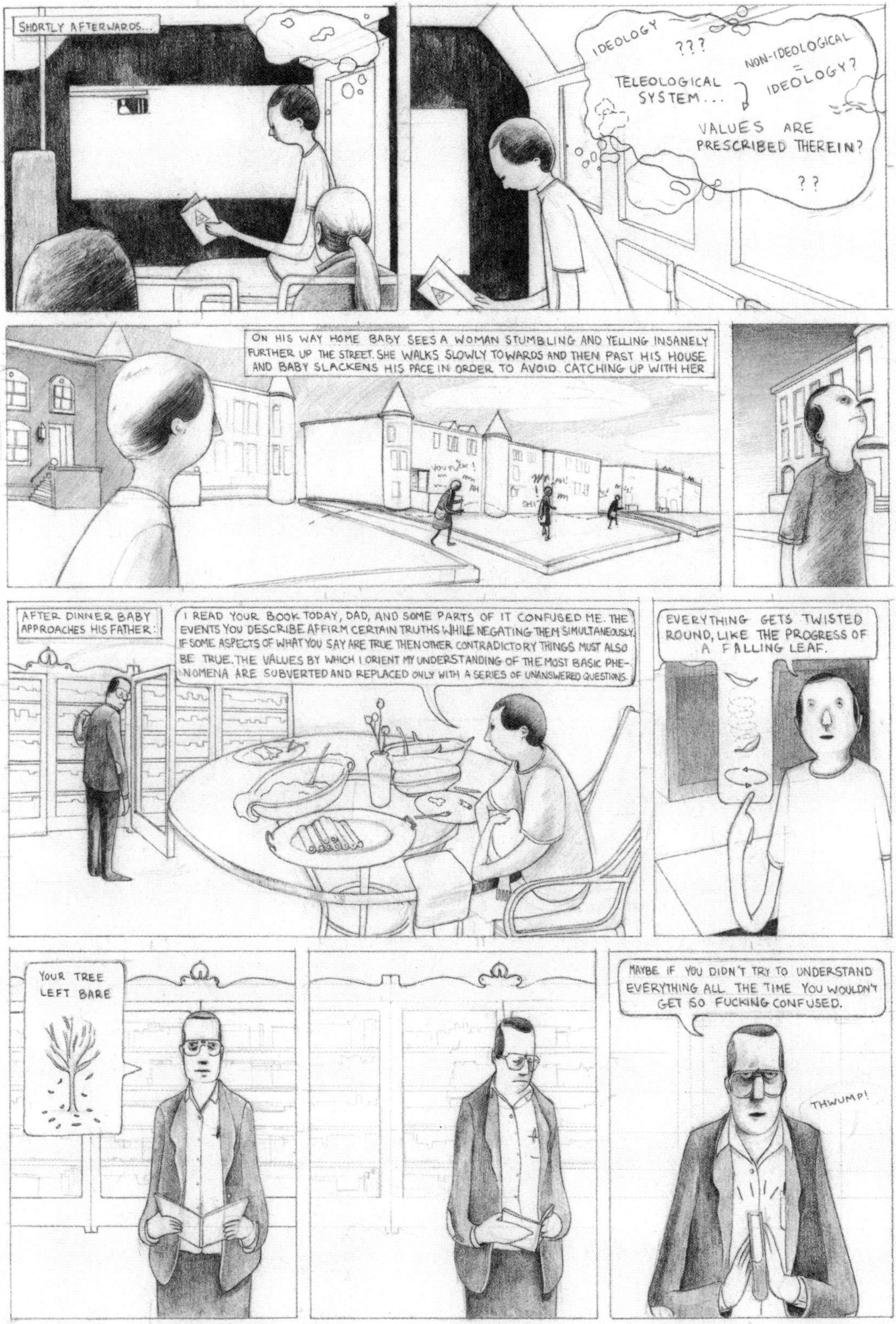
SHORTLY AFTERWARDS...
IDEOLOGY
???
NON-IDEOLOGICAL = IDEOLOGY?
TELEOLOGICAL SYSTEM...
VALUES ARE PRESCRIBED THEREIN?
??
ON HIS WAY HOME BABY SEES A WOMAN STUMBLING AND YELLING INSANELY FURTHER UP THE STREET. SHE WALKS SLOWLY TOWARDS AND THEN PAST HIS HOUSE AND BABY SLACKENS HIS PACE IN ORDER TO AVOID CATCHING UP WITH HER
AFTER DINNER BABY APPROACHES HIS FATHER:
I READ YOUR BOOK TODAY, DAD, AND SOME PARTS OF IT CONFUSED ME. THE EVENTS YOU DESCRIBE AFFIRM CERTAIN TRUTHS WHILE NEGATING THEM SIMULTANEOUSLY. IF SOME ASPECTS OF WHAT YOU SAY ARE TRUE THEN OTHER CONTRADICTORY THINGS MUST ALSO BE TRUE. THE VALUES BY WHICH I ORIENT MY UNDERSTANDING OF THE MOST BASIC PHENOMENA ARE SUBVERTED AND REPLACED ONLY WITH A SERIES OF UNANSWERED QUESTIONS.
EVERYTHING GETS TWISTED ROUND, LIKE THE PROGRESS OF A FALLING LEAF.
YOUR TREE LEFT BARE
MAYBE IF YOU DIDN'T TRY TO UNDERSTAND EVERYTHING ALL THE TIME YOU WOULDN'T GET SO FUCKING CONFUSED.
THWUMP!

• • •

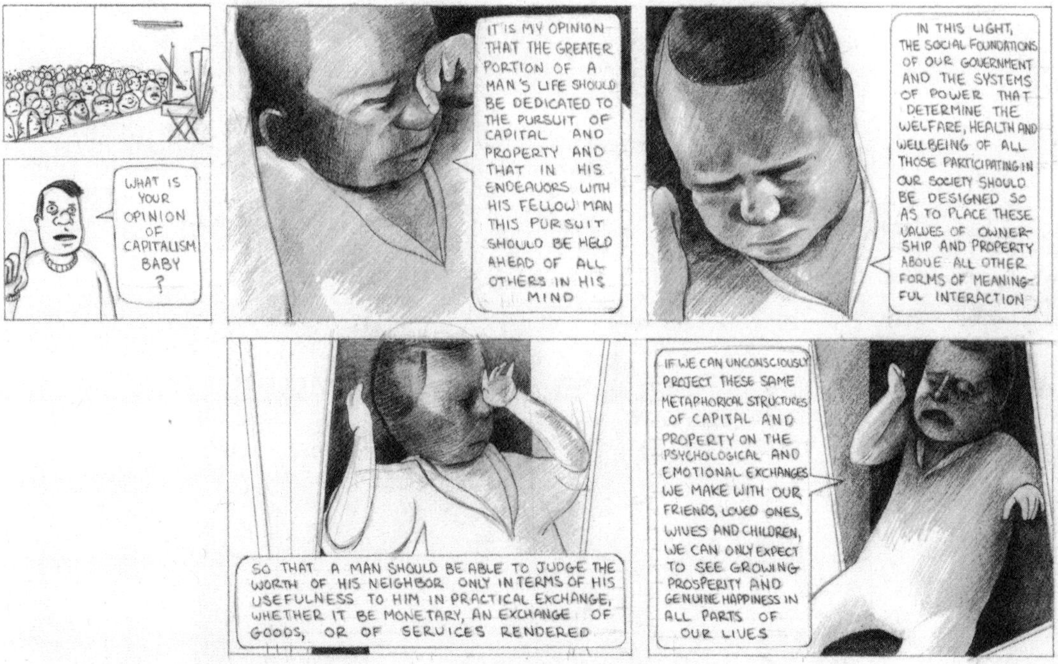
WHAT IS YOUR OPINION OF CAPITALISM BABY ?
IT IS MY OPINION THAT THE GREATER PORTION OF A MAN'S LIFE SHOULD BE DEDICATED TO THE PURSUIT OF CAPITAL AND PROPERTY AND THAT IN HIS ENDEAVORS WITH HIS FELLOW MAN THIS PURSUIT SHOULD BE HELD AHEAD OF ALL OTHERS IN HIS MIND
IN THIS LIGHT, THE SOCIAL FOUNDATIONS OF OUR GOVERNMENT AND THE SYSTEMS OF POWER THAT DETERMINE THE WELFARE, HEALTH AND WELLBEING OF ALL THOSE PARTICIPATING IN OUR SOCIETY SHOULD BE DESIGNED SO AS TO PLACE THESE VALUES OF OWNERSHIP AND PROPERTY ABOVE ALL OTHER FORMS OF MEANINGFUL INTERACTION
SO THAT A MAN SHOULD BE ABLE TO JUDGE THE WORTH OF HIS NEIGHBOR ONLY IN TERMS OF HIS USEFULNESS TO HIM IN PRACTICAL EXCHANGE, WHETHER IT BE MONETARY, AN EXCHANGE OF GOODS, OR OF SERVICES RENDERED
IF WE CAN UNCONSCIOUSLY PROJECT THESE SAME METAPHORICAL STRUCTURES OF CAPITAL AND PROPERTY ON THE PSYCHOLOGICAL AND EMOTIONAL EXCHANGES WE MAKE WITH OUR FRIENDS, LOVED ONES, WIVES AND CHILDREN, WE CAN ONLY EXPECT TO SEE GROWING PROSPERITY AND GENUINE HAPPINESS IN ALL PARTS OF OUR LIVES

• • •

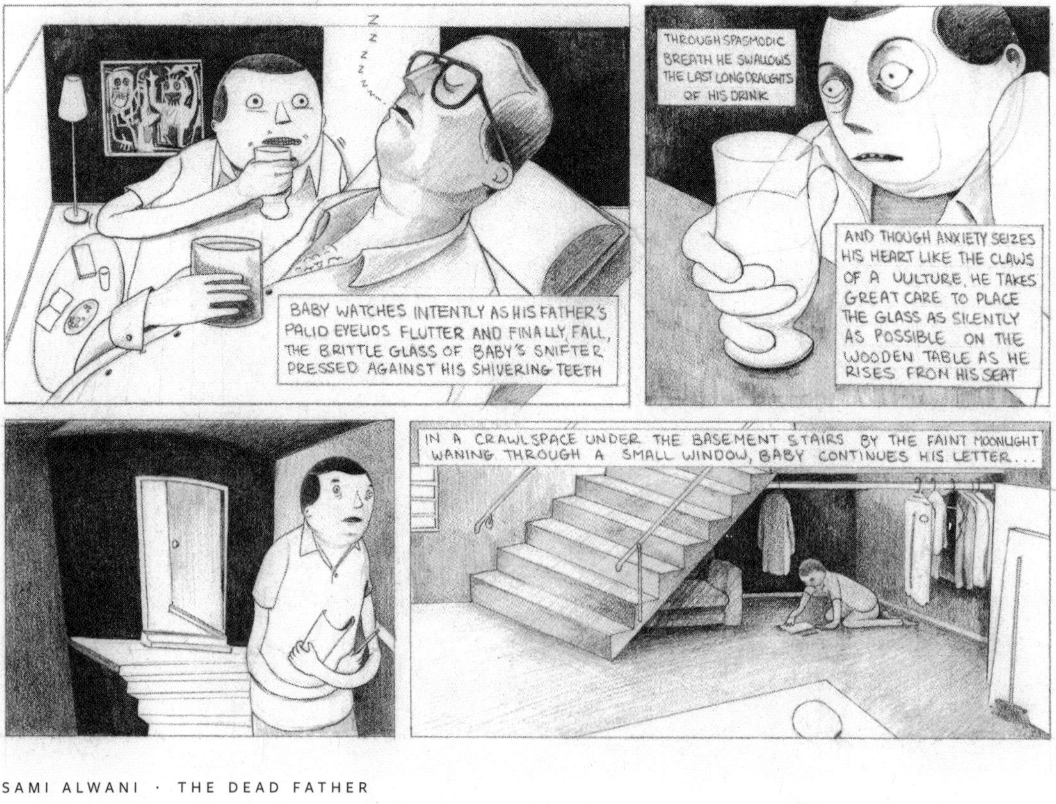
Z Z Z Z Z
BABY WATCHES INTENTLY AS HIS FATHER'S PALID EYELIDS FLUTTER AND FINALLY FALL, THE BRITTLE GLASS OF BABY'S SNIFTER PRESSED AGAINST HIS SHIVERING TEETH
THROUGH SPASMODIC BREATH HE SWALLOWS THE LAST LONG DRAUGHTS OF HIS DRINK
AND THOUGH ANXIETY SEIZES HIS HEART LIKE THE CLAWS OF A VULTURE, HE TAKES GREAT CARE TO PLACE THE GLASS AS SILENTLY AS POSSIBLE ON THE WOODEN TABLE AS HE RISES FROM HIS SEAT
IN A CRAWLSPACE UNDER THE BASEMENT STAIRS BY THE FAINT MOONLIGHT WANING THROUGH A SMALL WINDOW, BABY CONTINUES HIS LETTER...

TO WHOM IT MAY CONCERN
MY NAME IS BABY ALWANI AND I AM CONTACTING
YOU IN SECRET AS AN URGENT APPEAL FOR MY
LIBERTY. THIS LETTER WAS WRITTEN BETWEEN THE
HOURS OF EIGHT AND NINE O'CLOCK AT NIGHT AT
THE TIME IN WHICH MY FATHER REGULARLY OCCU-
PIES HIMSELF WITH A SHORT NAP AFTER WRITING.
FOR IF HE WERE TO CATCH WIND OF THIS ATTEMPT
TO ESCAPE, THE REPERCUSSIONS FOR MY APPARENT
TREACHERY WOULD BE UNBEARABLE. FOR THE PAST
MANY YEARS I HAVE BEEN COERCED INTO SALVAGIN
WHAT LITTLE SEMBLANCE OF A COMFORTABLE
LIFE I CAN FROM WHAT IS, IN ALL RESPECTS
DEN OF INIQUITY, CHARACTERIZED BY
CONTENTION, BITTER ENMITY, AND ARBITRARILY
INFLICTED TORTURE. I AM SUBJECT CONSTANTLY TO
AN UNNAMABLE AND EVER PRESENT PRESSURE
DO EVERYTHING CORRECTLY ACCORDING TO AN
IRRATIONAL AND PERPETUALLY CHANGING SET OF
AMBIGUOUS CRITERIA DESIGNED SO AS NEVER TO
BE SATISFIED. I AM ATTEMPTING NOW TO APPLY
TO A HIGHER AUTHORITY TO DELIVER ME FROM
THIS HELL. PLEASE REPLY AS QUICKLY AS
YOU ARE ABLE, BUT HARK, I MUST STEAL
MYSELF AWAY ONCE MORE AS I HEAR NOW
THE HEAVY FOOTFALLS OF THE OFFENDING MONSTER
ABOVE MY VERY HEAD.
YOURS,
Baby Alwani
BABY ALWANI
SEVERAL WEEKS PASS IN SOLEMNITY, DEJECTION, AND THEN:
THE HIGH COURT, UPON THE INTERVENTION OF AN INFLUENTIAL PERSON, HAS DISMISSED YOUR SUIT OUT OF HAND
AFTER MONTHS OF SEARCHING, BABY FINDS ASSISTANCE
HIDE YOURSELF IN THE WOOD BY THE RIVER IN THREE NIGHT'S TIME AND A SHIP WILL ARRIVE TO ENSURE YOUR ESCAPE!
AND SO...
NOOOOOOO!!
AFTER BABY'S JOURNEY SUCCEEDS PART-WAY, SAMI OBTAINS BABY'S WHEREABOUTS THROUGH A CIRCUITOUS NETWORK OF INFORMANTS AND CONVINCES COLLABORATORS TO TREACHEROUSLY RETURN BABY TO HIM AT THE END OF THE NEXT LEG OF THEIR VOYAGE
WHEN BABY DISCOVERS THE PLOT, HE FLEES TO THE STREETS ON FOOT.
A FOREIGN CITY
HIS ESCAPE BROADCAST
ANY PERSONS FOUND AIDING THE ESCAPE OF ONE BABY ALWANI SUBJECT TO THE STRICTEST CONSEQUENCES!!
THERE ARE NO FRIENDS ANYWHERE

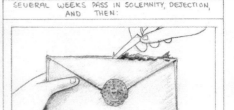

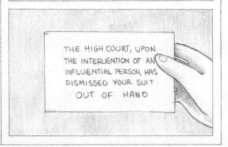

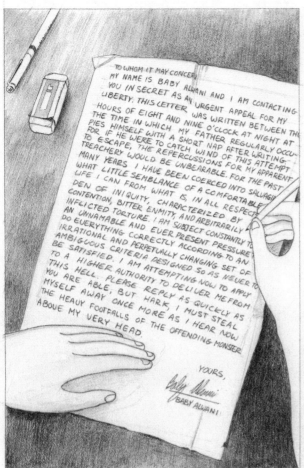

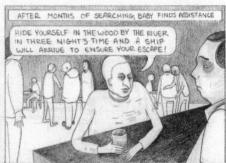

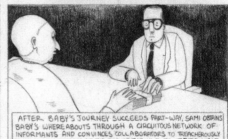

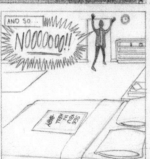

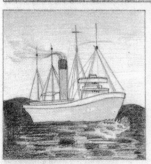

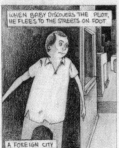

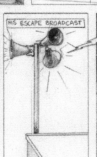

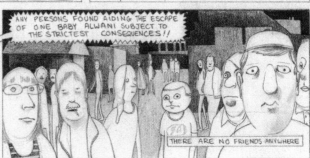

OVER MOUNTAINS...

ACROSS RIVERS...

THROUGH DESERTS...

BABY, AS IF FROM A GREAT DISTANCE NOW, REALIZES HE IS FREEZING COLD

A THICK BLACK BLANKET SPREADS ACROSS HIS BRAIN AND HE FALLS ASLEEP

IN HIS SLUMBER HE IS CAPTURED AND RETURNED TO HIS FATHER

·  ·  ·

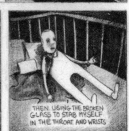

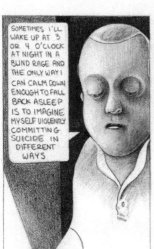
SOMETIMES I'LL WAKE UP AT 3 OR 4 O'CLOCK AT NIGHT IN A BLIND RAGE AND THE ONLY WAY I CAN CALM DOWN ENOUGH TO FALL BACK ASLEEP IS TO IMAGINE MYSELF VIOLENTLY COMMITTING SUICIDE IN DIFFERENT WAYS

HANGING

BREAKING A BOTTLE OVER MY HEAD

THEN USING THE BROKEN GLASS TO STAB MYSELF IN THE THROAT AND WRISTS

IT'S AS THOUGH MY FACULTIES FOR SELF-WORTH AND MY SENSE OF CONFIDENCE IN THE VALIDITY OF MY ACTIONS AND THE COURSE OF MY LIFE HAVE SUFFERED A SUB-TERRANEOUS SEA-CHANGE IMBUING ME WITH A PRETERNATURAL CAPACITY FOR SELF-LOATHING

LIKE SOME UNPITEOUS MIRROR HELD UP TO MY HISTORY...

REVEALING EVEN MY HAPPIEST MOMENTS AS SOME TRIFLING AND IRREDEEMABLE NAÏVETÉ

·  ·  ·

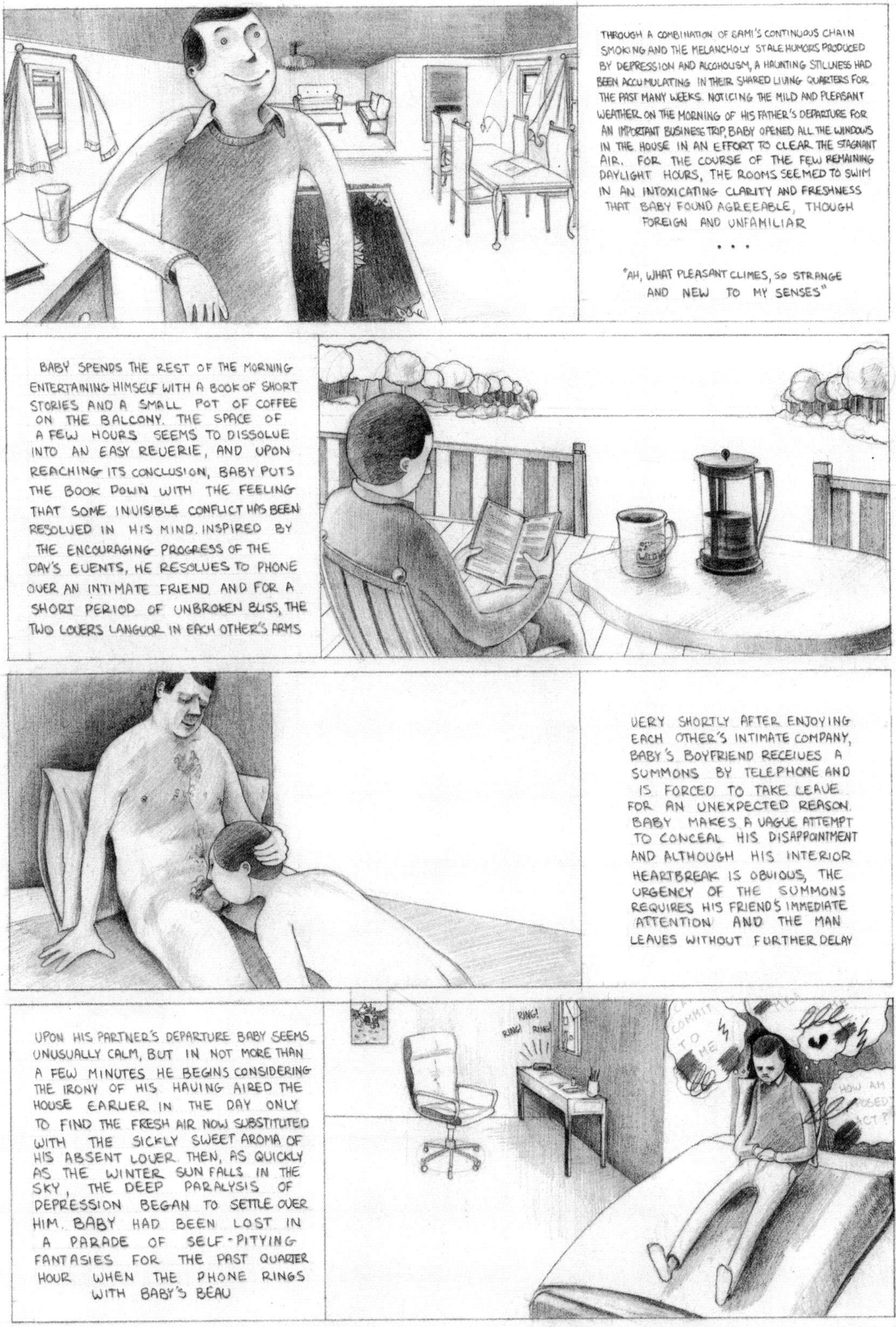
THROUGH A COMBINATION OF SAMI'S CONTINUOUS CHAIN SMOKING AND THE MELANCHOLY STALE HUMORS PRODUCED BY DEPRESSION AND ALCOHOLISM, A HAUNTING STILLNESS HAD BEEN ACCUMULATING IN THEIR SHARED LIVING QUARTERS FOR THE PAST MANY WEEKS. NOTICING THE MILD AND PLEASANT WEATHER ON THE MORNING OF HIS FATHER'S DEPARTURE FOR AN IMPORTANT BUSINESS TRIP, BABY OPENED ALL THE WINDOWS IN THE HOUSE IN AN EFFORT TO CLEAR THE STAGNANT AIR. FOR THE COURSE OF THE FEW REMAINING DAYLIGHT HOURS, THE ROOMS SEEMED TO SWIM IN AN INTOXICATING CLARITY AND FRESHNESS THAT BABY FOUND AGREEABLE, THOUGH FOREIGN AND UNFAMILIAR
• • •
"AH, WHAT PLEASANT CLIMES, SO STRANGE AND NEW TO MY SENSES"
BABY SPENDS THE REST OF THE MORNING ENTERTAINING HIMSELF WITH A BOOK OF SHORT STORIES AND A SMALL POT OF COFFEE ON THE BALCONY. THE SPACE OF A FEW HOURS SEEMS TO DISSOLVE INTO AN EASY REVERIE, AND UPON REACHING ITS CONCLUSION, BABY PUTS THE BOOK DOWN WITH THE FEELING THAT SOME INVISIBLE CONFLICT HAS BEEN RESOLVED IN HIS MIND. INSPIRED BY THE ENCOURAGING PROGRESS OF THE DAY'S EVENTS, HE RESOLVES TO PHONE OVER AN INTIMATE FRIEND AND FOR A SHORT PERIOD OF UNBROKEN BLISS, THE TWO LOVERS LANGUOR IN EACH OTHER'S ARMS
VERY SHORTLY AFTER ENJOYING EACH OTHER'S INTIMATE COMPANY, BABY'S BOYFRIEND RECEIVES A SUMMONS BY TELEPHONE AND IS FORCED TO TAKE LEAVE FOR AN UNEXPECTED REASON. BABY MAKES A VAGUE ATTEMPT TO CONCEAL HIS DISAPPOINTMENT AND ALTHOUGH HIS INTERIOR HEARTBREAK IS OBVIOUS, THE URGENCY OF THE SUMMONS REQUIRES HIS FRIEND'S IMMEDIATE ATTENTION AND THE MAN LEAVES WITHOUT FURTHER DELAY
UPON HIS PARTNER'S DEPARTURE BABY SEEMS UNUSUALLY CALM, BUT IN NOT MORE THAN A FEW MINUTES HE BEGINS CONSIDERING THE IRONY OF HIS HAVING AIRED THE HOUSE EARLIER IN THE DAY ONLY TO FIND THE FRESH AIR NOW SUBSTITUTED WITH THE SICKLY SWEET AROMA OF HIS ABSENT LOVER. THEN, AS QUICKLY AS THE WINTER SUN FALLS IN THE SKY, THE DEEP PARALYSIS OF DEPRESSION BEGAN TO SETTLE OVER HIM. BABY HAD BEEN LOST IN A PARADE OF SELF-PITYING FANTASIES FOR THE PAST QUARTER HOUR WHEN THE PHONE RINGS WITH BABY'S BEAU
RING! RING! RING!
COMMIT TO ME

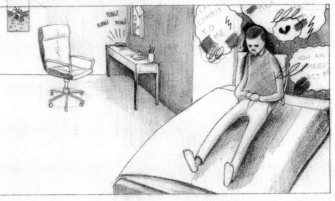

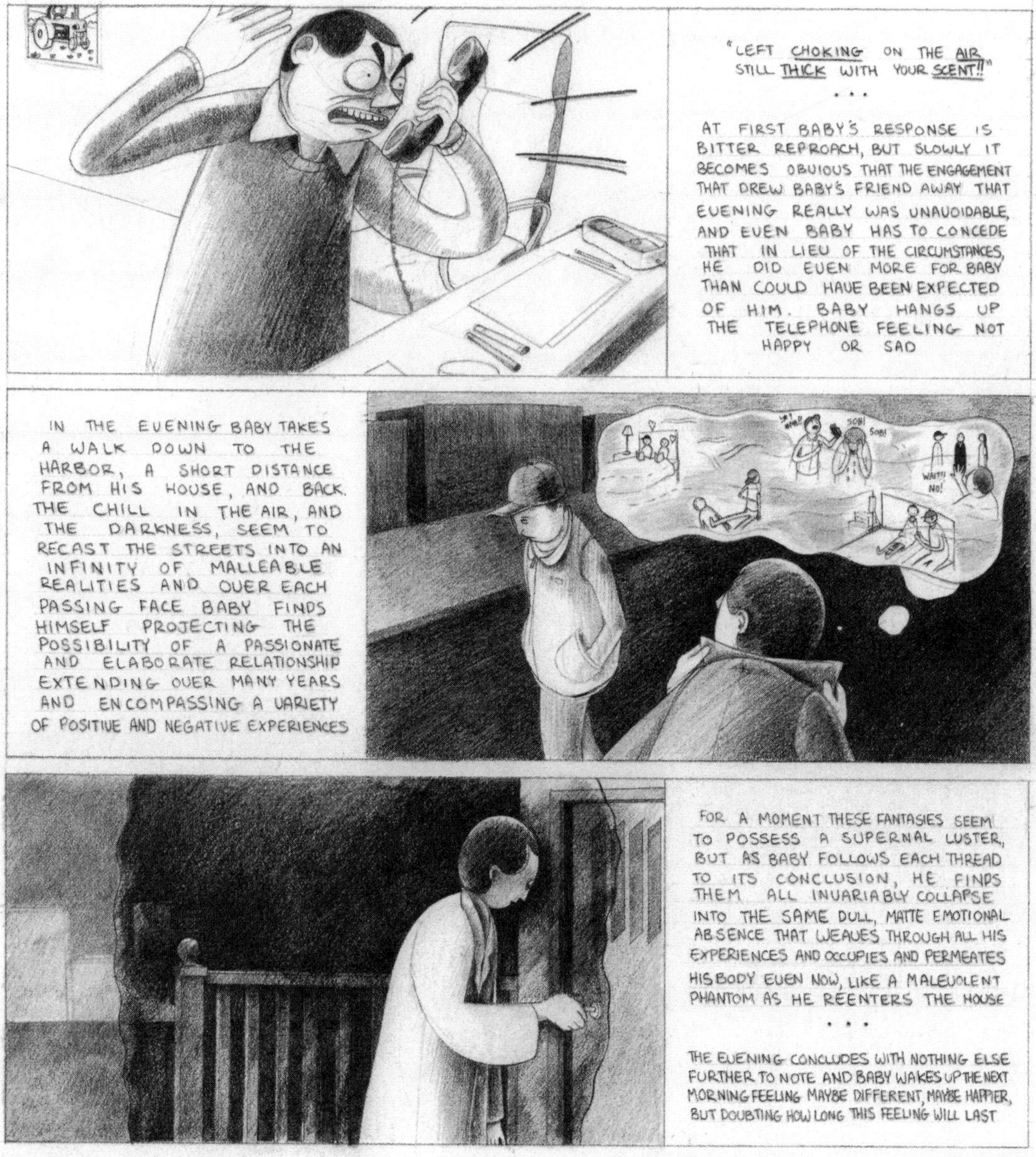
"LEFT CHOKING ON THE AIR STILL THICK WITH YOUR SCENT!!"
. . .
AT FIRST BABY'S RESPONSE IS BITTER REPROACH, BUT SLOWLY IT BECOMES OBVIOUS THAT THE ENGAGEMENT THAT DREW BABY'S FRIEND AWAY THAT EVENING REALLY WAS UNAVOIDABLE, AND EVEN BABY HAS TO CONCEDE THAT IN LIEU OF THE CIRCUMSTANCES, HE DID EVEN MORE FOR BABY THAN COULD HAVE BEEN EXPECTED OF HIM. BABY HANGS UP THE TELEPHONE FEELING NOT HAPPY OR SAD
IN THE EVENING BABY TAKES A WALK DOWN TO THE HARBOR, A SHORT DISTANCE FROM HIS HOUSE, AND BACK. THE CHILL IN THE AIR, AND THE DARKNESS, SEEM TO RECAST THE STREETS INTO AN INFINITY OF MALLEABLE REALITIES AND OVER EACH PASSING FACE BABY FINDS HIMSELF PROJECTING THE POSSIBILITY OF A PASSIONATE AND ELABORATE RELATIONSHIP EXTENDING OVER MANY YEARS AND ENCOMPASSING A VARIETY OF POSITIVE AND NEGATIVE EXPERIENCES
SOB!
SOB!
WAIT!! NO!
FOR A MOMENT THESE FANTASIES SEEM TO POSSESS A SUPERNAL LUSTER, BUT AS BABY FOLLOWS EACH THREAD TO ITS CONCLUSION, HE FINDS THEM ALL INVARIABLY COLLAPSE INTO THE SAME DULL, MATTE EMOTIONAL ABSENCE THAT WEAVES THROUGH ALL HIS EXPERIENCES AND OCCUPIES AND PERMEATES HIS BODY EVEN NOW, LIKE A MALEVOLENT PHANTOM AS HE REENTERS THE HOUSE
. . .
THE EVENING CONCLUDES WITH NOTHING ELSE FURTHER TO NOTE AND BABY WAKES UP THE NEXT MORNING FEELING MAYBE DIFFERENT, MAYBE HAPPIER, BUT DOUBTING HOW LONG THIS FEELING WILL LAST

• • •

YOU ARE RESP-ONSIBLE!!
I AM IMPLICATING YOU!!
IT IS YOUR RESPONSIBILITY TO SEE!! LIKE I DO SEE!!
A DARKNESS FALLS ACROSS SAMI'S FACE AS HE LIFTS THE BABY FROM ITS CRIB
WELL, IT SEEMS IT'S ABOUT TIME FOR BABY'S NAP
UNFORTUNATELY, I'LL HAVE TO BRING THIS INTERVIEW TO A CLOSE
BUT PAPA!! I AM NOT TIRED!
SAMI MUFFLES THE BABY
HAVE A PLEASANT EVENING EVERYONE
END

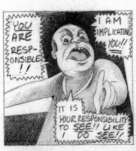

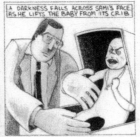

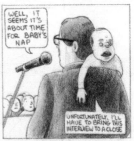

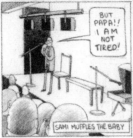

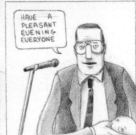

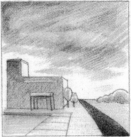

# I Am Better than Picasso

FROM *Muhammad Ali Series*

## DAPPER BRUCE LAFITTE

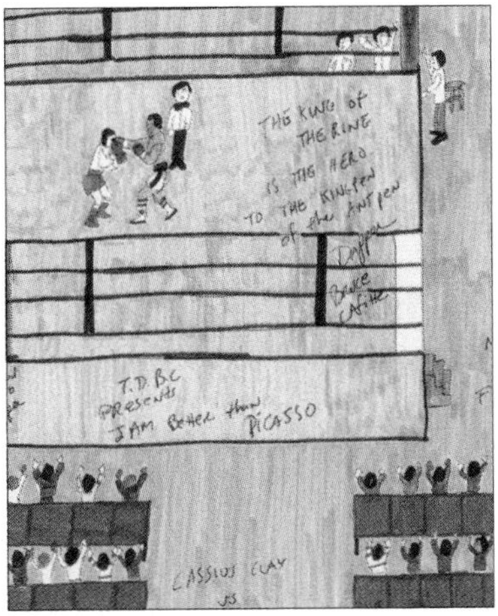
THE KING of THE RING
T.D.B.C
PRESENTS
I AM Better than PICASSO
CASSIUS CLAY

*exhibited at*

ARTHUR ROGER GALLERY

62 × 42 inches • pen and marker on paper

## Biography

Artist Dapper Bruce Lafitte lives and works in the Lower 9th Ward of New Orleans. His deliciously detailed drawings are created in the back of his shotgun house not far from the Mississippi River.

He grew up in the nearby French Quarter in the 6th Ward's Lafitte housing development. Lafitte "ain't there no more," since after Hurricane Katrina, but its memory, as chronicled in much of his art, is vibrantly alive.

Bruce's art follows his life in all things New Orleans, from its joyful bands and parades, to its struggles of poverty and racism. Along with these subjects are the glimpses into the world of sports, from baseball to football and his love of boxing. Come follow Dapper's continuing journey of the world through his images and words . . . enjoy.
dapperbruce.com

## Statement

When I was coming up it was all about Tyson, and when my uncle was coming up it was Muhammad Ali, and when my grandad was coming up it was Joe Louis. So my grandad would talk about Joe Louis to my uncles, and they would talk about Ali to me, and I want to talk about Mike Tyson to the world. I'm happy to be part of a generation who had a superstar, just like Ali and Joe Louis were superstars for my grandad and my uncles.

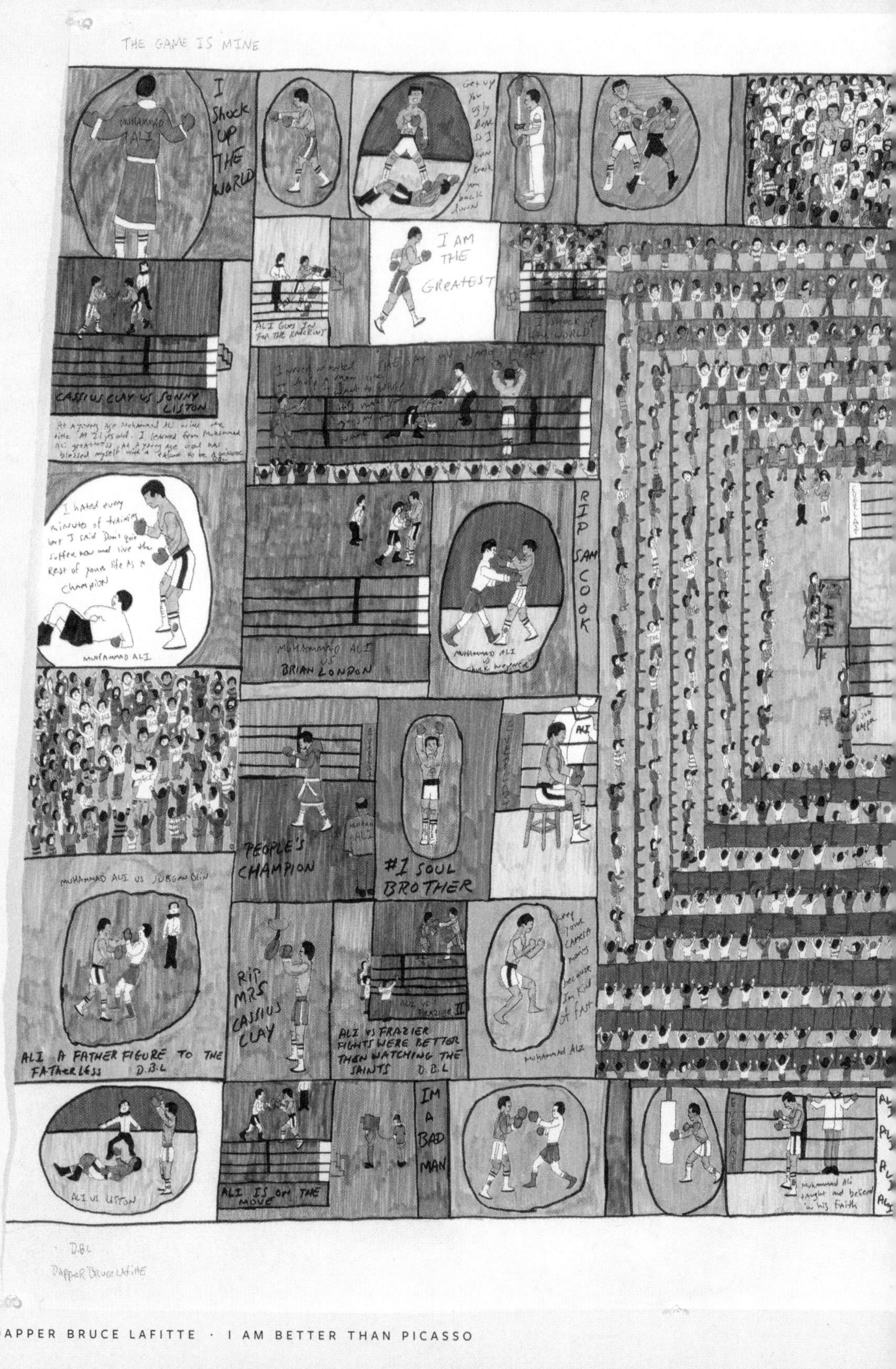
THE GAME IS MINE
I SHOCK UP THE WORLD
MUHAMMAD ALI
I AM THE GREATEST
ALI GOES IN FOR THE KNOCKOUT
CASSIUS CLAY VS SONNY LISTON
MUHAMMAD ALI
RIP SAM COOK
MUHAMMAD ALI VS BRIAN LONDON
PEOPLE'S CHAMPION
#1 SOUL BROTHER
MUHAMMAD ALI VS JURGEN BLIN
ALI A FATHER FIGURE TO THE FATHERLESS D.B.L
RIP MRS CASSIUS CLAY
ALI VS FRAZIER FIGHTS WERE BETTER THEN WATCHING THE SAINTS D.B.L
MUHAMMAD ALI
ALI VS LISTON
ALI IS ON THE MOVE
IM A BAD MAN
D.B.L
DAPPER BRUCE LAFITTE

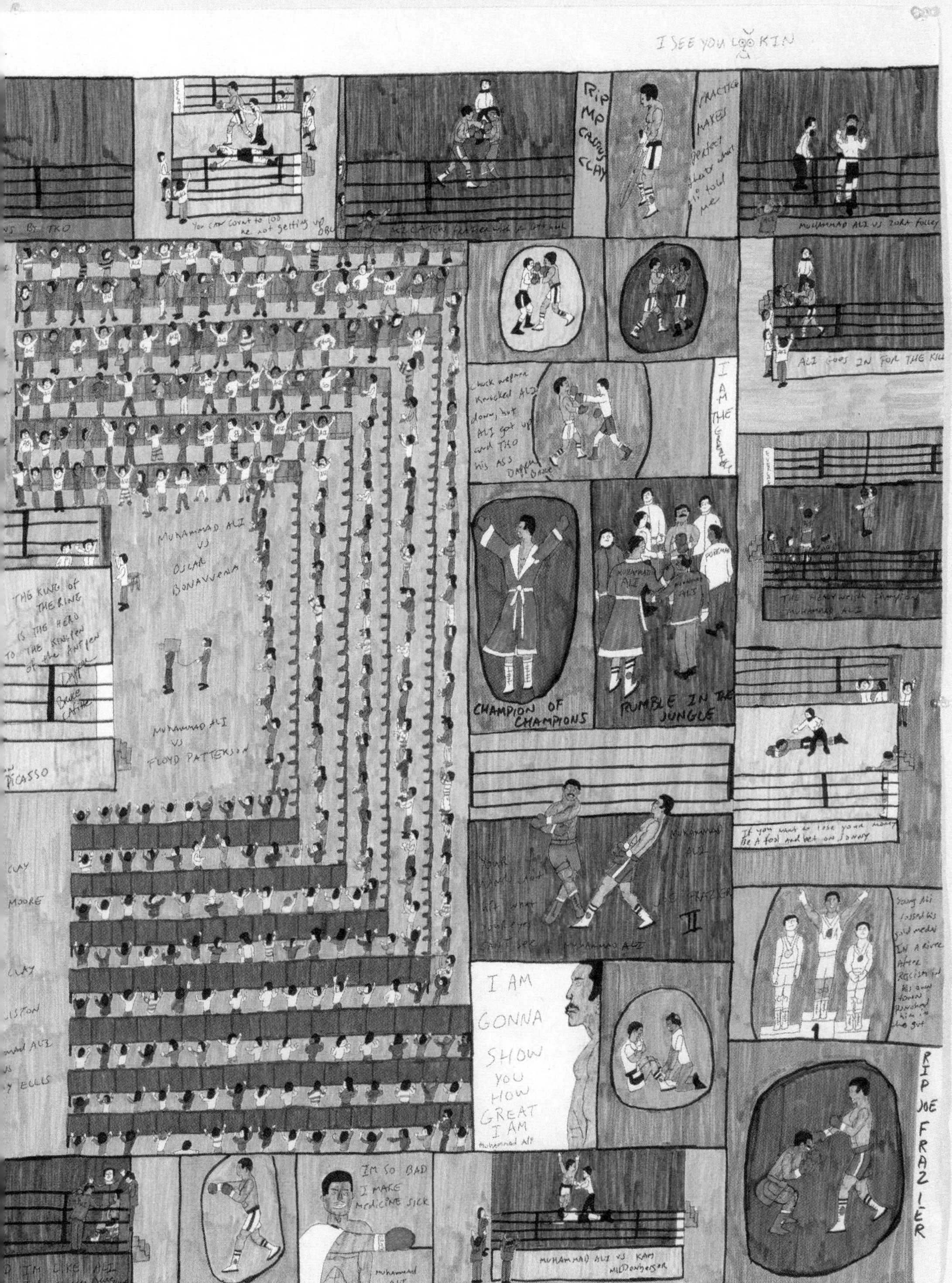

I SEE YOU LOOKIN
You can count to 100 he not getting up
RIP MR CASSIUS CLAY
PRACTICE MAKES PERFECT that's what Ali told me
MUHAMMAD ALI VS ZORA FOLLEY
ALI GOES IN FOR THE KILL
Chuck Wepner Knocked ALI down, but ALI got up and TKO his ASS Dapper Bruce
MUHAMMAD ALI VS OSCAR BONAVENA
MUHAMMAD ALI VS FLOYD PATTERSON
PICASSO
CHAMPION OF CHAMPIONS
RUMBLE IN THE JUNGLE
If you want to lose your money Be A fool and bet on Sonny
MUHAMMAD ALI VS JOE FRAZIER II
I AM GONNA SHOW YOU HOW GREAT I AM
Muhammad Ali
RIP JOE FRAZIER
IM SO BAD I MAKE MEDICINE SICK
Muhammad ALI
Dapper Bruce Lafitte
A TAURUS DA BULL CREATIONS
10th Series 15 5/2015
ORIGINAL ARTWORK by hand

THE GAME IS MINE

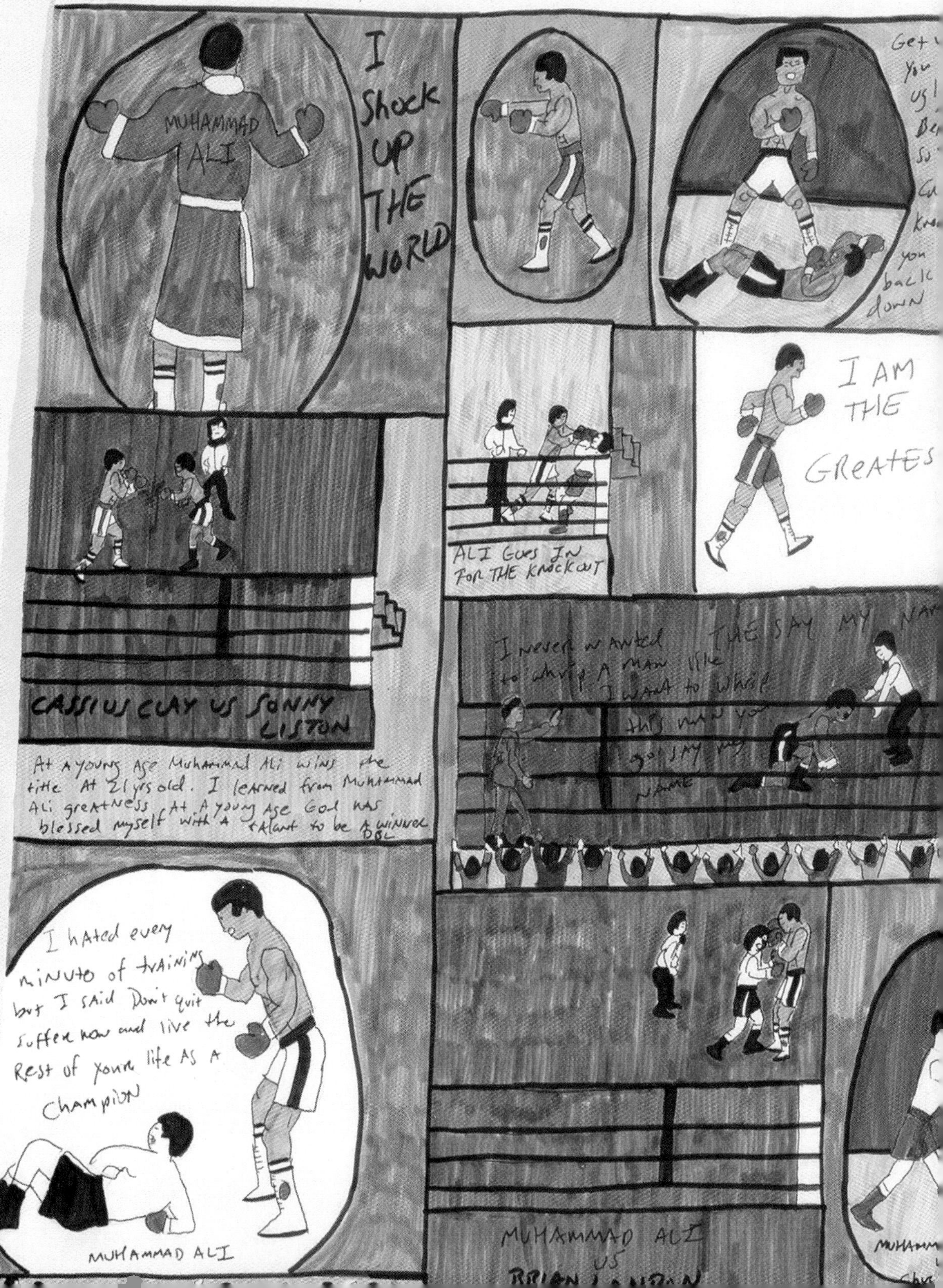

MUHAMMAD ALI
I Shock UP THE WORLD
I AM THE GREATES
ALI Goes IN FOR THE KNOCKOUT
CASSIUS CLAY VS SONNY LISTON
At A young Age Muhammad Ali wins the title At 21yrs old. I learned from Muhammad Ali greatness At A young Age God has blessed myself with A talent to be A winner DBL
I never wanted to whip A man like I want to whip this man you go say my name
I hated every minute of training but I said Don't quit suffer now and live the Rest of your life As A champion
MUHAMMAD ALI
MUHAMMAD ALI VS

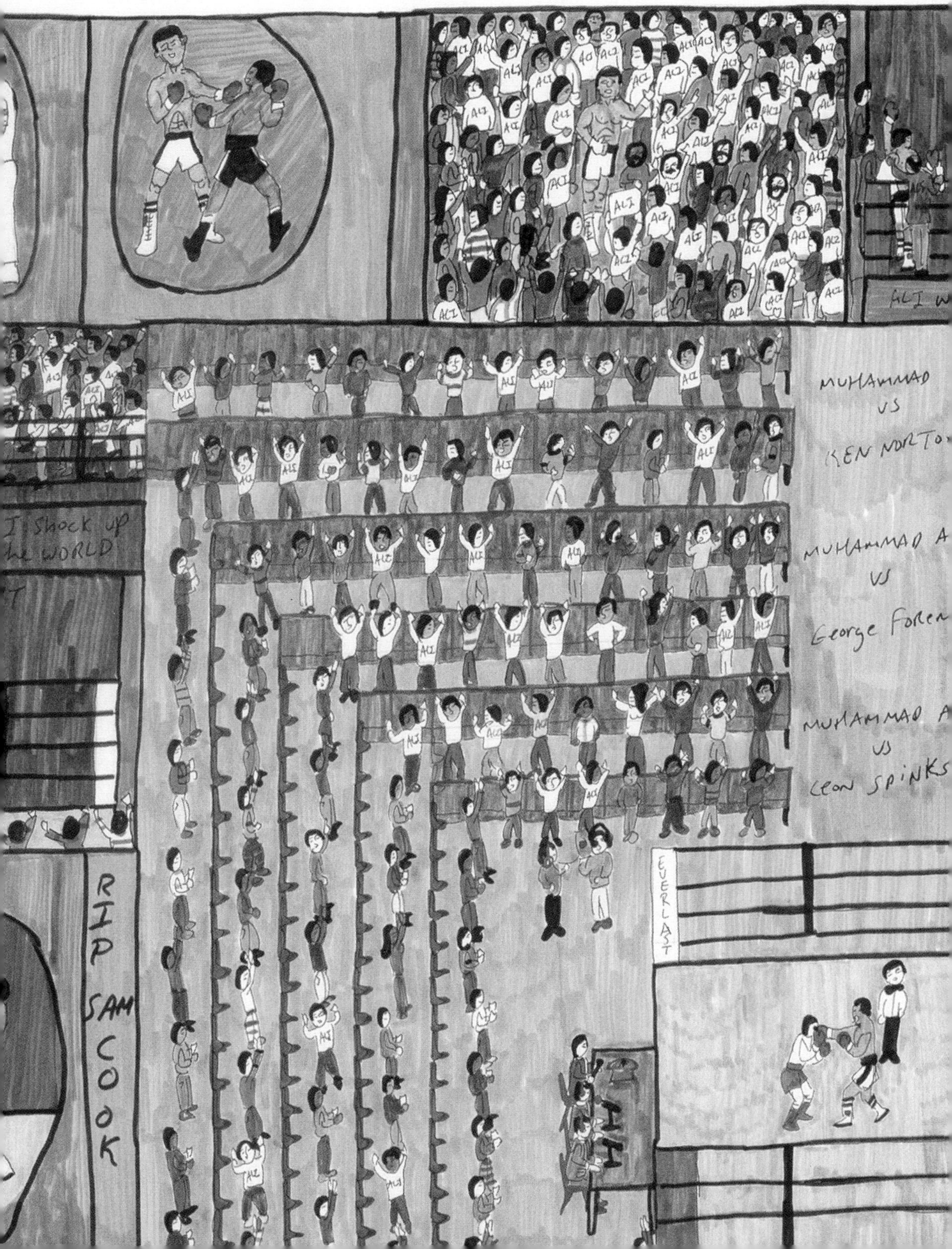

ALI W
I Shock up
he WORLD
MUHAMMAD
VS
KEN NORTO
MUHAMMAD A
VS
George Forem
MUHAMMAD A
VS
LEON SPINKS
EVERLAST
RIP SAM COOK

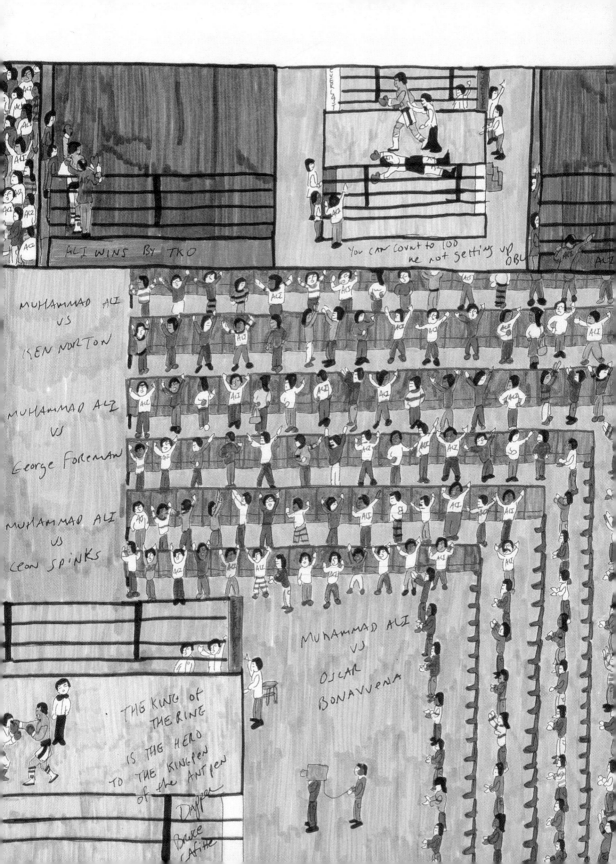

ALI WINS BY TKO

You can count to 100
he not getting up  OBU

MUHAMMAD ALI
VS
KEN NORTON

MUHAMMAD ALI
VS
George Foreman

MUHAMMAD ALI
VS
Leon SPINKS

MUHAMMAD ALI
VS
OSCAR
BONAVVENA

THE KING of
THE RING
IS THE HERO
TO THE KINGPEN
OF the ANTPEN
Dapper
Bruce Lafitte

I SEE YOU LOOKIN

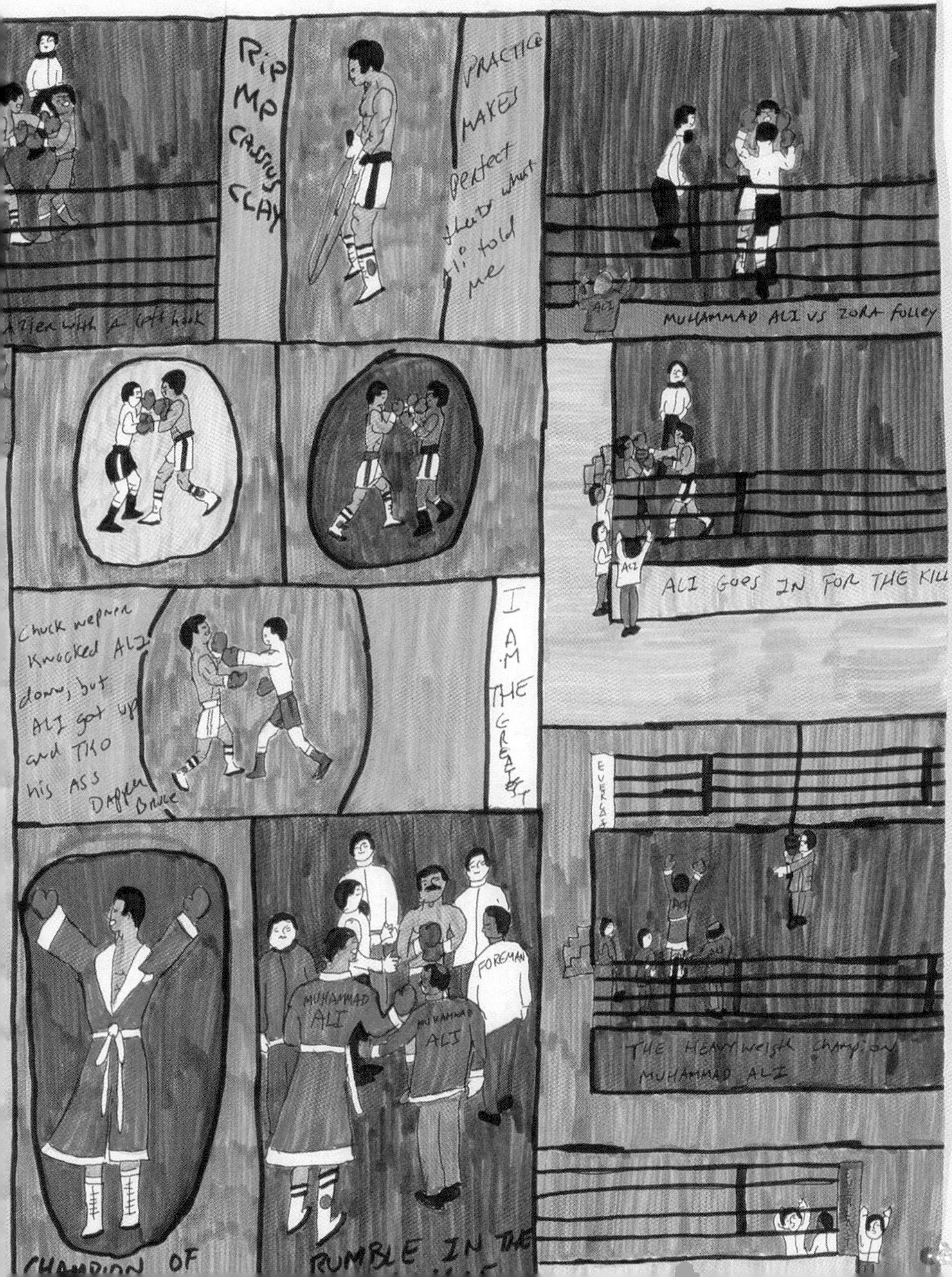
azier with a left hook
RIP MR CASSIUS CLAY
PRACTICE MAKES perfect thats what Ali told me
ALI
MUHAMMAD ALI VS ZORA FOLLEY
ALI
ALI GOES IN FOR THE KILL
Chuck wepner knocked ALI down, but ALI got up and TKO his ASS
Dapper Bruce
I AM THE GREATEST
EVERLAST
ALI
THE HEAVYWEIGHT CHAMPION MUHAMMAD ALI
MUHAMMAD ALI
MUHAMMAD ALI
FOREMAN
CHAMPION OF
RUMBLE IN THE
EVERLAST

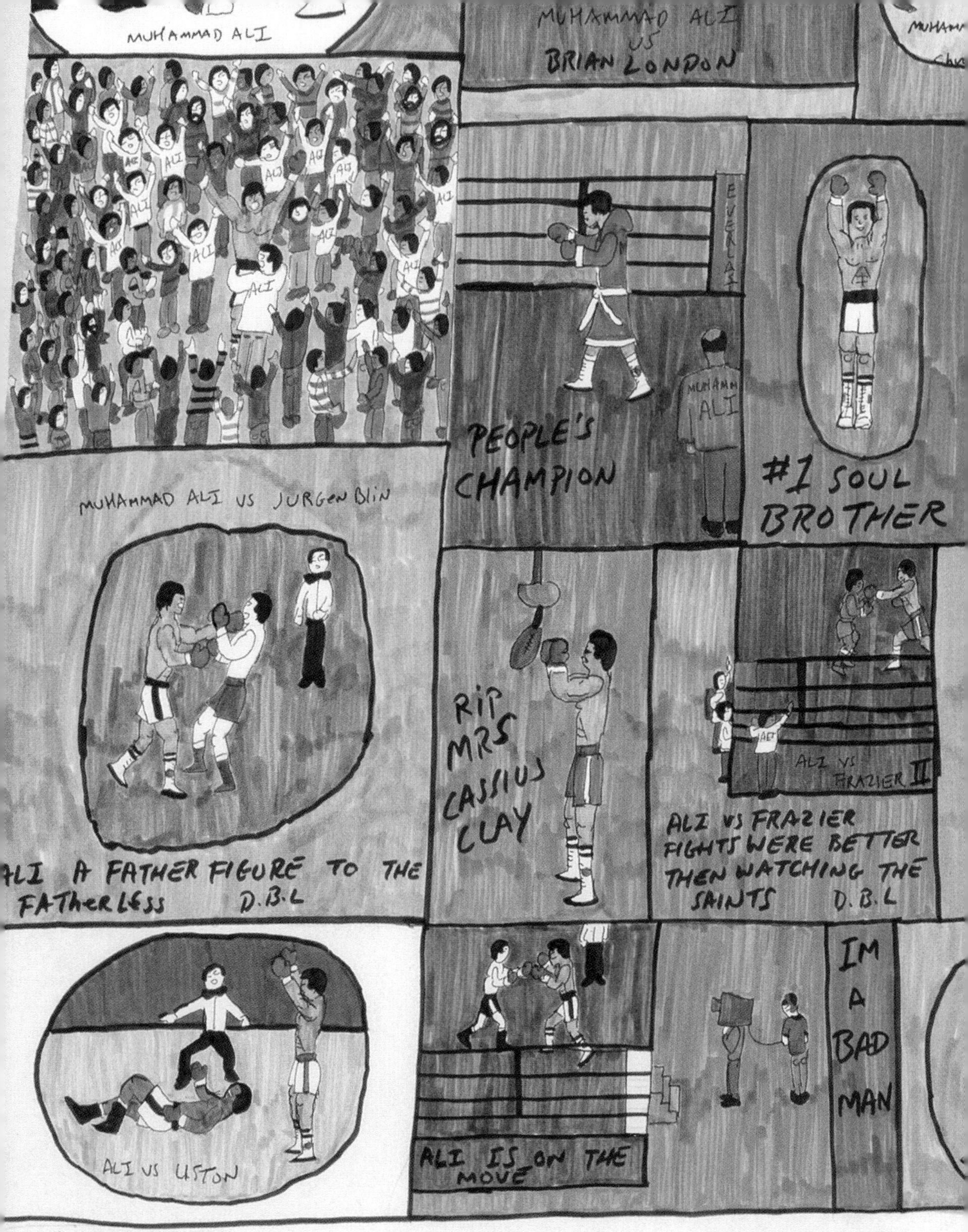
MUHAMMAD ALI
MUHAMMAD ALI VS BRIAN LONDON
EVERLAST
MUHAMMAD ALI
PEOPLE'S CHAMPION
#1 SOUL BROTHER
MUHAMMAD ALI VS JURGEN Blin
ALI A FATHER FIGURE TO THE FATHERLESS D.B.L
RIP MRS CASSIUS CLAY
ALI VS FRAZIER II
ALI VS FRAZIER FIGHTS WERE BETTER THEN WATCHING THE SAINTS D.B.L
ALI VS LISTON
ALI IS ON THE MOVE
IM A BAD MAN

D.B.L

DAPPER BRUCE LAFITTE

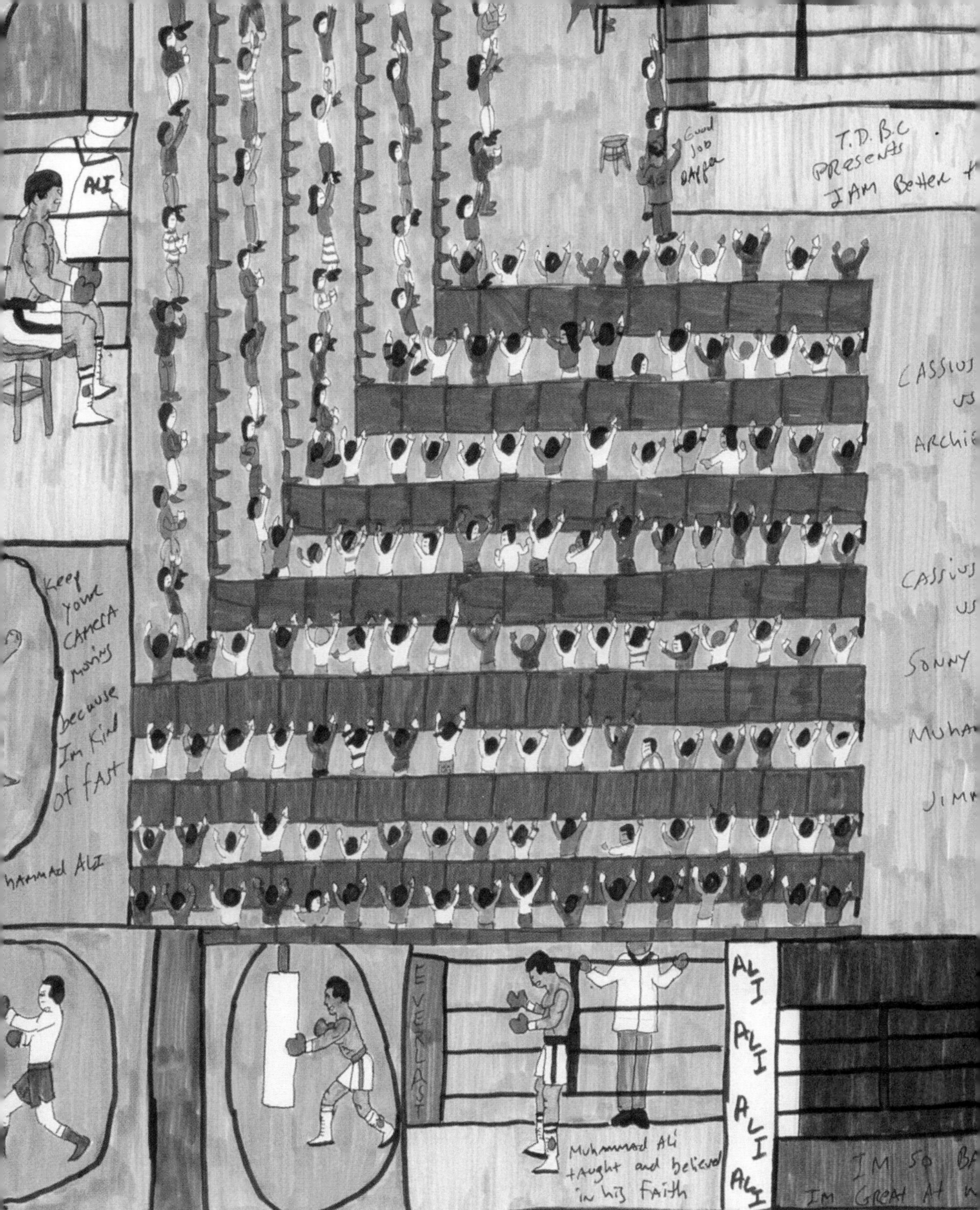

ALI
Good job Dapper
T.D.B.C
PRESENTS
I AM Better th
CASSIUS
VS
ARCHIE
CASSIUS
VS
SONNY
MUHAM
JIMM
Keep your CAMERA moving because I'm kind of fast
hammad Ali
EVERLAST
Muhammad Ali taught and believed in his Faith
ALI
ALI
ALI
ALI
IM SO BA
IM GREAT AT W

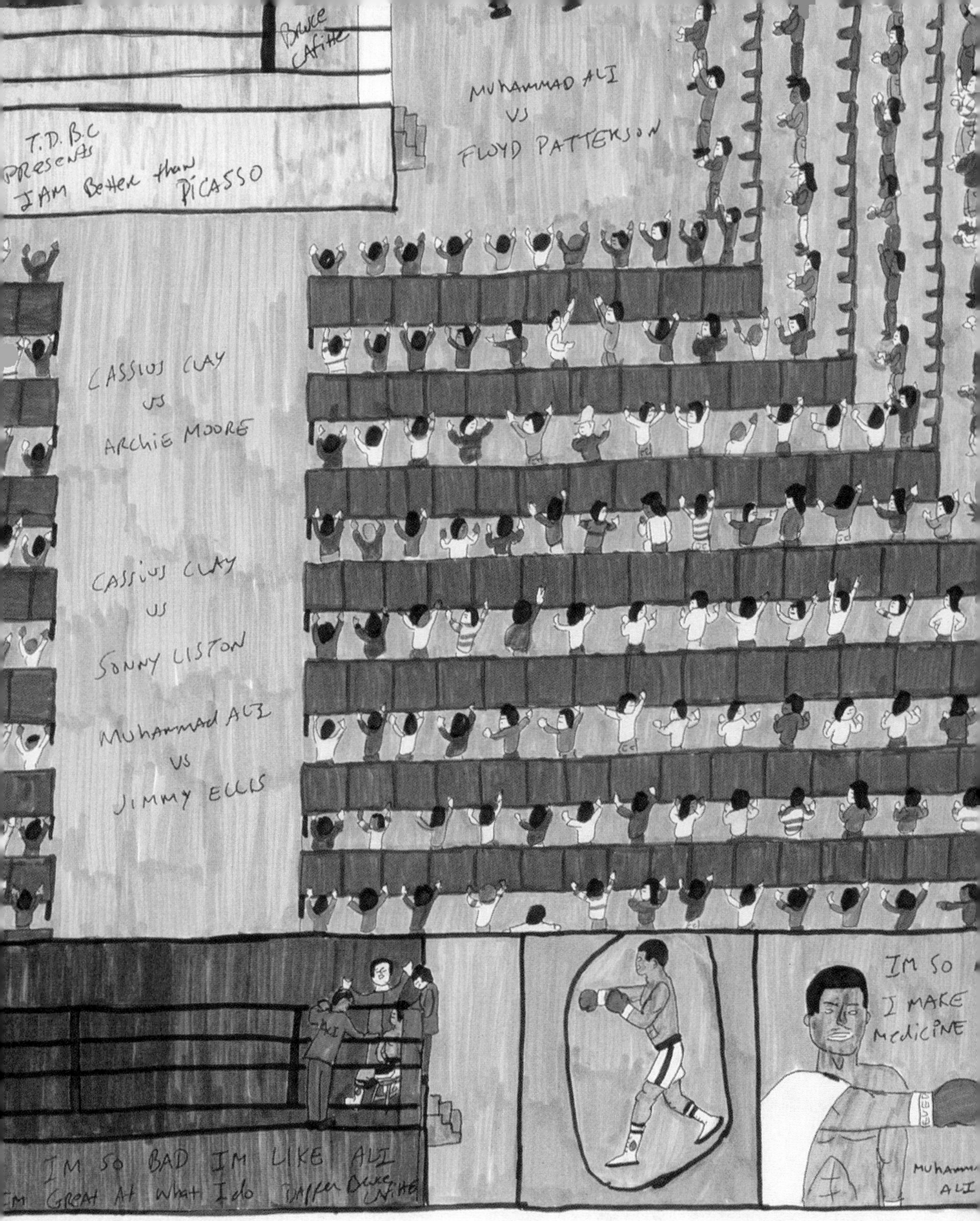
Bruce Cafitte
T.D.B.C
presents
I AM Better than PICASSO
MUHAMMAD ALI
VS
FLOYD PATTERSON
CASSIUS CLAY
VS
ARCHIE MOORE
CASSIUS CLAY
VS
SONNY LISTON
MUHAMMAD ALI
VS
JIMMY ELLIS
ALI
IM SO BAD IM LIKE ALI
IM GREAT AT WHAT I do Dapper Duke Unifie
IM SO
I MAKE
MEDICINE
EVER
MUHAMM
ALI

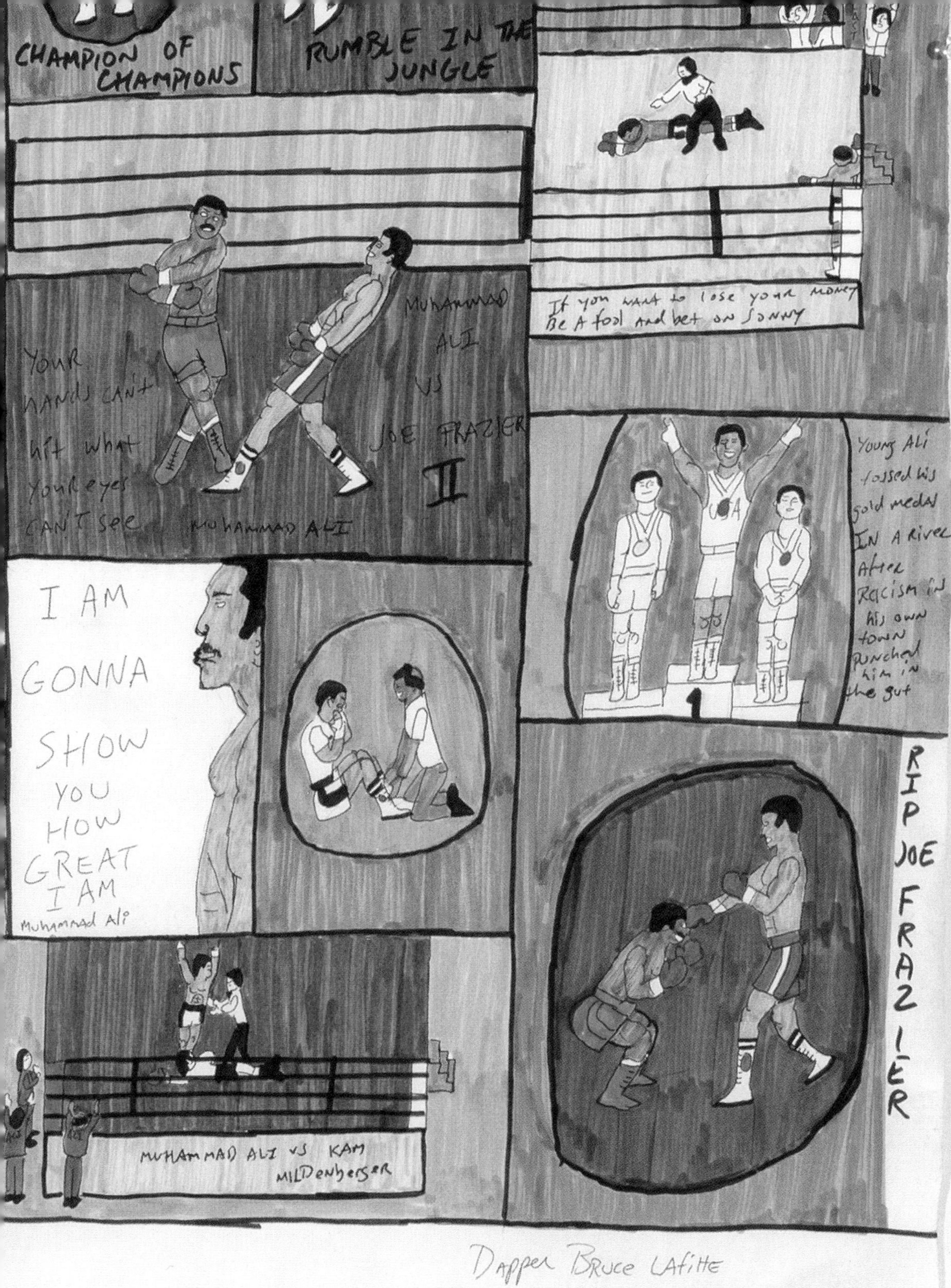

CHAMPION OF CHAMPIONS
RUMBLE IN THE JUNGLE
If you want to lose your money Be A fool and bet on Sonny
YOUR HANDS CAN'T HIT WHAT YOUR EYES CAN'T SEE MUHAMMAD ALI
MUHAMMAD ALI VS JOE FRAZIER II
Young Ali tossed his gold medal IN A river After Racism in his own town punched him in the gut
USA
I AM GONNA SHOW YOU HOW GREAT I AM
Muhammad Ali
RIP JOE FRAZIER
MUHAMMAD ALI VS KAM MILDenberger


Dapper Bruce LAfitte
A TAURUS DA BULL Creations
10th series 15 5/2015
ORIGINAL ARTWORK by hand

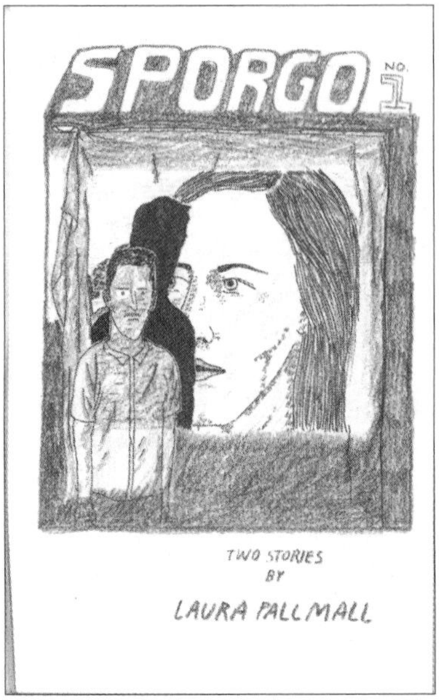
SPORGO
NO. 1
TWO STORIES
BY
LAURA PALLMALL

# Picaresque

LAURA PALLMALL

*originally published in*

*Sporgo #1*

SELF-PUBLISHED

5.5 × 8.5 inches • 28 pages

## Biography

Laura PallMall is the comics/drawing pseudonym of now Pittsburgh-based (via-Los Angeles-via-Olympia-via-Austin-via-New-York-via-Los Angeles) writer/artist Jason Lee, who puts out 'zines of essays, comics, fiction, poetry, illustration, and DIY resource books under the label Nothing Left to Learn. "Picaresque" was his first comic. nothinglefttolearn.tumblr.com

## Statement

"Picaresque" was originally published within an ongoing 'zine series called Nothing Left to Learn. Nothing Left to Learn began with a belief in alternative media and alternative creators, no matter their genre—in using DIY ethics to publish all kinds of work, whether typically DIY or not. Nothing Left to Learn aims to support the creation of work that is unencumbered by the financial or social stresses of its traditional spaces, and to that end publishes everything from boxing essays to cocktail recipes to comics and poetry to hand-drawn fonts.

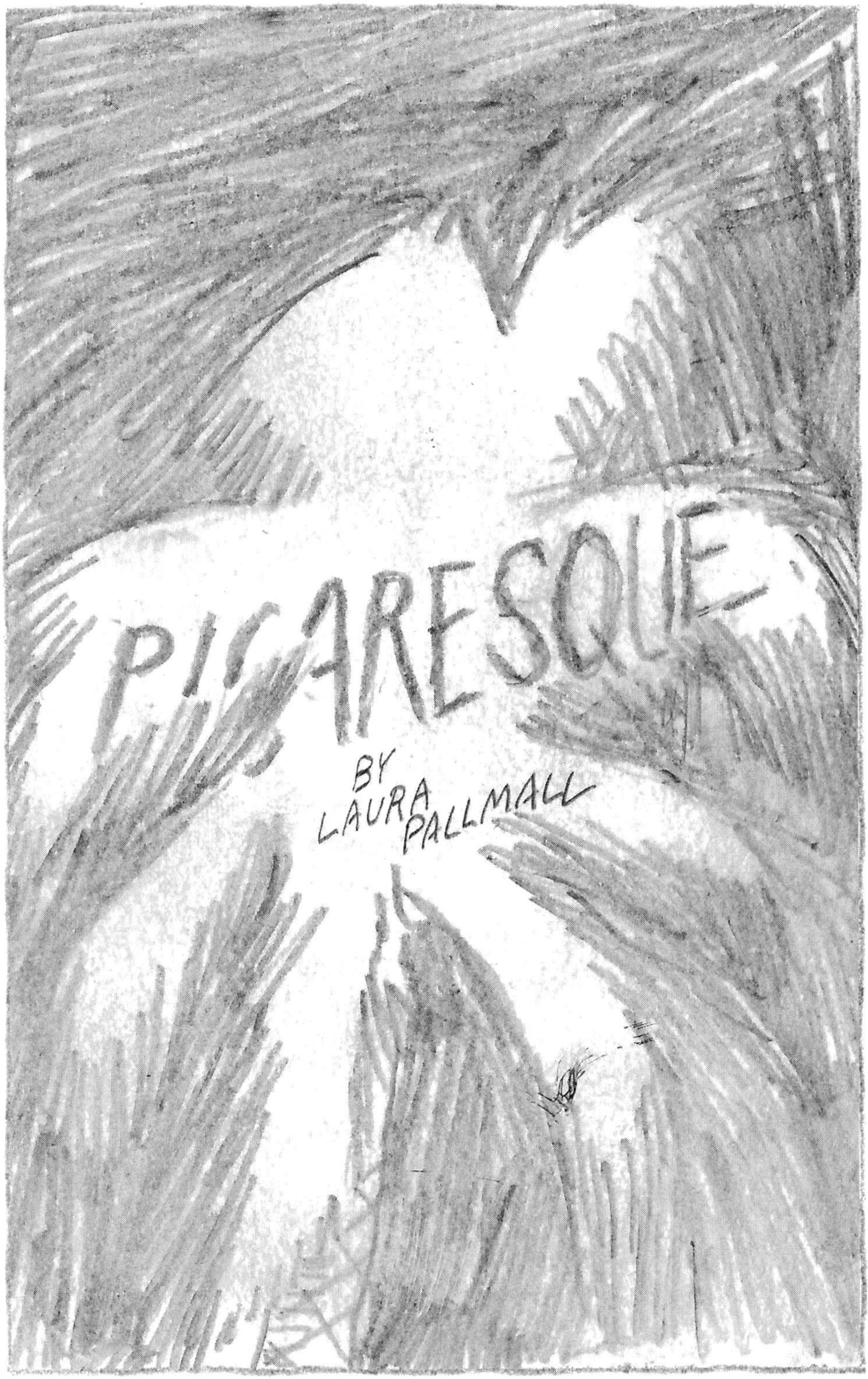
PICARESQUE
BY
LAURA
PALLMALL

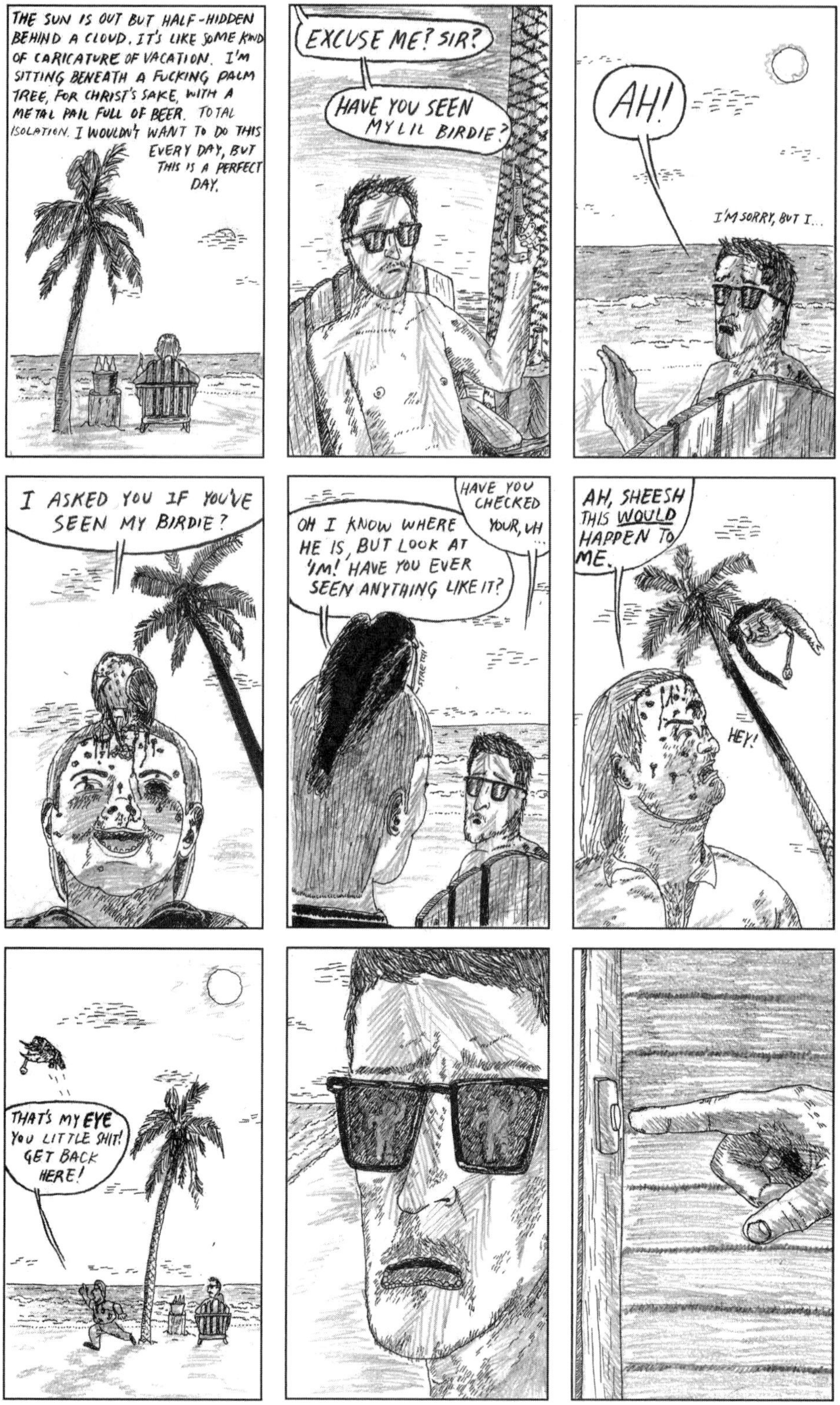
THE SUN IS OUT BUT HALF-HIDDEN BEHIND A CLOUD. IT'S LIKE SOME KIND OF CARICATURE OF VACATION. I'M SITTING BENEATH A FUCKING PALM TREE, FOR CHRIST'S SAKE, WITH A METAL PAIL FULL OF BEER. TOTAL ISOLATION. I WOULDN'T WANT TO DO THIS EVERY DAY, BUT THIS IS A PERFECT DAY.
EXCUSE ME? SIR?
HAVE YOU SEEN MY LIL BIRDIE?
AH!
I'M SORRY, BUT I...
I ASKED YOU IF YOU'VE SEEN MY BIRDIE?
HAVE YOU CHECKED YOUR, UH ...
OH I KNOW WHERE HE IS, BUT LOOK AT 'IM! HAVE YOU EVER SEEN ANYTHING LIKE IT?
AH, SHEESH THIS WOULD HAPPEN TO ME.
HEY!
THAT'S MY EYE YOU LITTLE SHIT! GET BACK HERE!

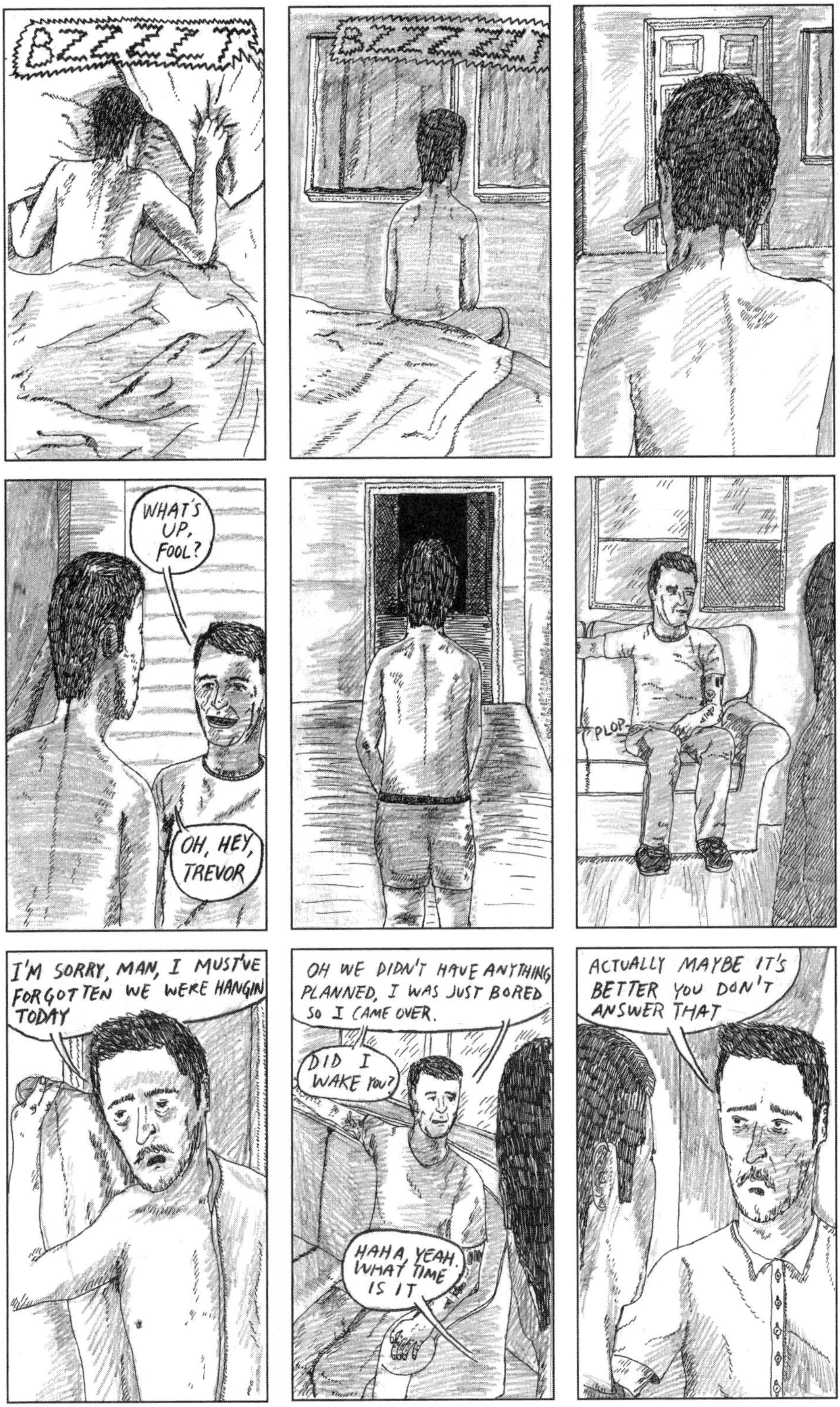
BZZZT
BZZZT
WHAT'S UP, FOOL?
OH, HEY, TREVOR
PLOP
I'M SORRY, MAN, I MUST'VE FORGOTTEN WE WERE HANGIN TODAY
OH WE DIDN'T HAVE ANYTHING PLANNED, I WAS JUST BORED SO I CAME OVER.
DID I WAKE YOU?
HAHA, YEAH. WHAT TIME IS IT
ACTUALLY MAYBE IT'S BETTER YOU DON'T ANSWER THAT

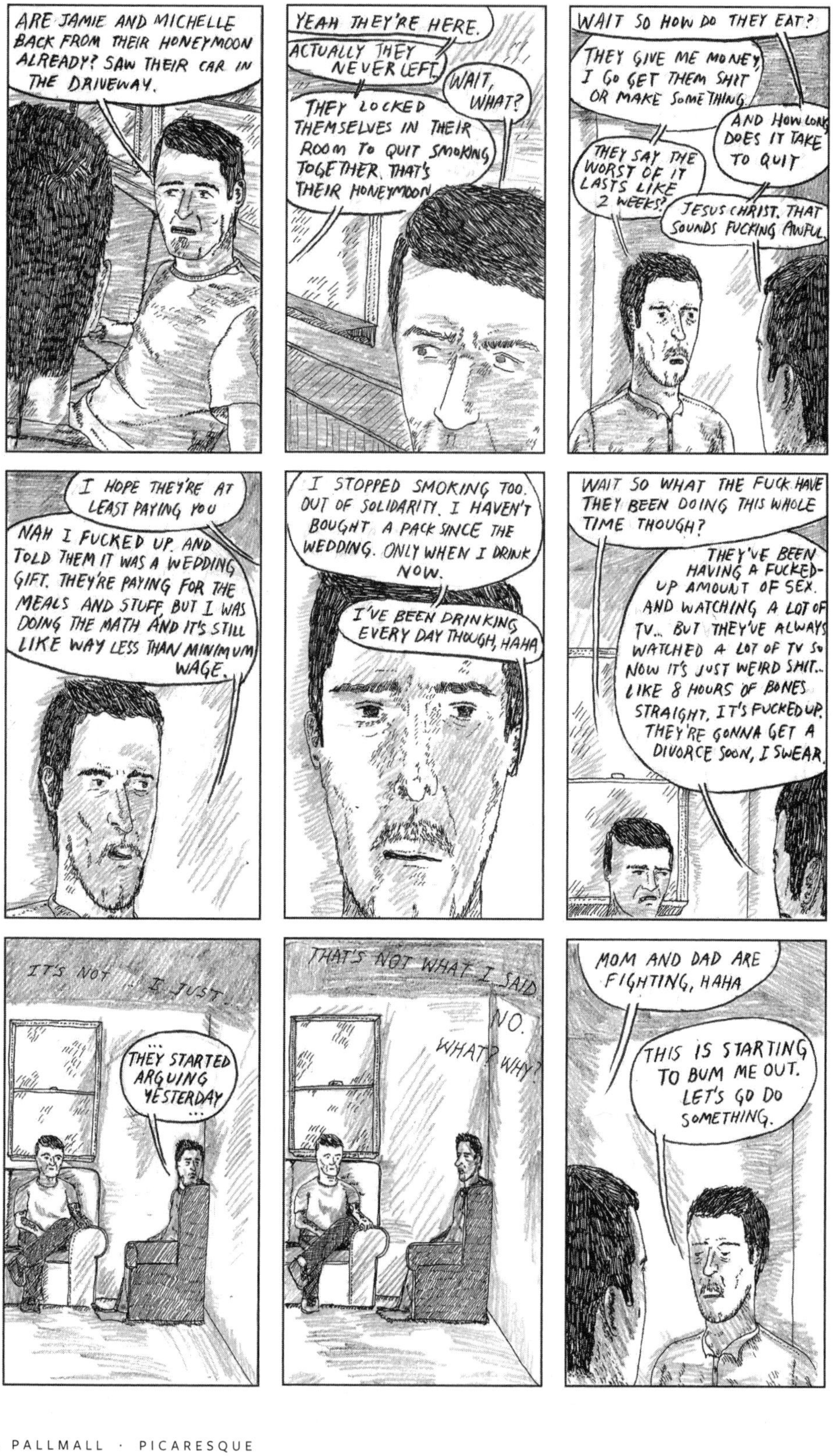
ARE JAMIE AND MICHELLE BACK FROM THEIR HONEYMOON ALREADY? SAW THEIR CAR IN THE DRIVEWAY.
YEAH THEY'RE HERE.
ACTUALLY THEY NEVER LEFT.
WAIT, WHAT?
THEY LOCKED THEMSELVES IN THEIR ROOM TO QUIT SMOKING TOGETHER. THAT'S THEIR HONEYMOON.
WAIT SO HOW DO THEY EAT?
THEY GIVE ME MONEY, I GO GET THEM SHIT OR MAKE SOMETHING.
AND HOW LONG DOES IT TAKE TO QUIT
THEY SAY THE WORST OF IT LASTS LIKE 2 WEEKS?
JESUS CHRIST. THAT SOUNDS FUCKING AWFUL.
I HOPE THEY'RE AT LEAST PAYING YOU
NAH I FUCKED UP. AND TOLD THEM IT WAS A WEDDING GIFT. THEY'RE PAYING FOR THE MEALS AND STUFF BUT I WAS DOING THE MATH AND IT'S STILL LIKE WAY LESS THAN MINIMUM WAGE.
I STOPPED SMOKING TOO. OUT OF SOLIDARITY. I HAVEN'T BOUGHT A PACK SINCE THE WEDDING. ONLY WHEN I DRINK NOW.
I'VE BEEN DRINKING EVERY DAY THOUGH, HAHA
WAIT SO WHAT THE FUCK HAVE THEY BEEN DOING THIS WHOLE TIME THOUGH?
THEY'VE BEEN HAVING A FUCKED-UP AMOUNT OF SEX. AND WATCHING A LOT OF TV.. BUT THEY'VE ALWAYS WATCHED A LOT OF TV SO NOW IT'S JUST WEIRD SHIT.. LIKE 8 HOURS OF BONES STRAIGHT. IT'S FUCKED UP. THEY'RE GONNA GET A DIVORCE SOON, I SWEAR.
IT'S NOT ... I JUST...
... THEY STARTED ARGUING YESTERDAY ...
THAT'S NOT WHAT I SAID
NO.
WHAT? WHY?
MOM AND DAD ARE FIGHTING, HAHA
THIS IS STARTING TO BUM ME OUT. LET'S GO DO SOMETHING.

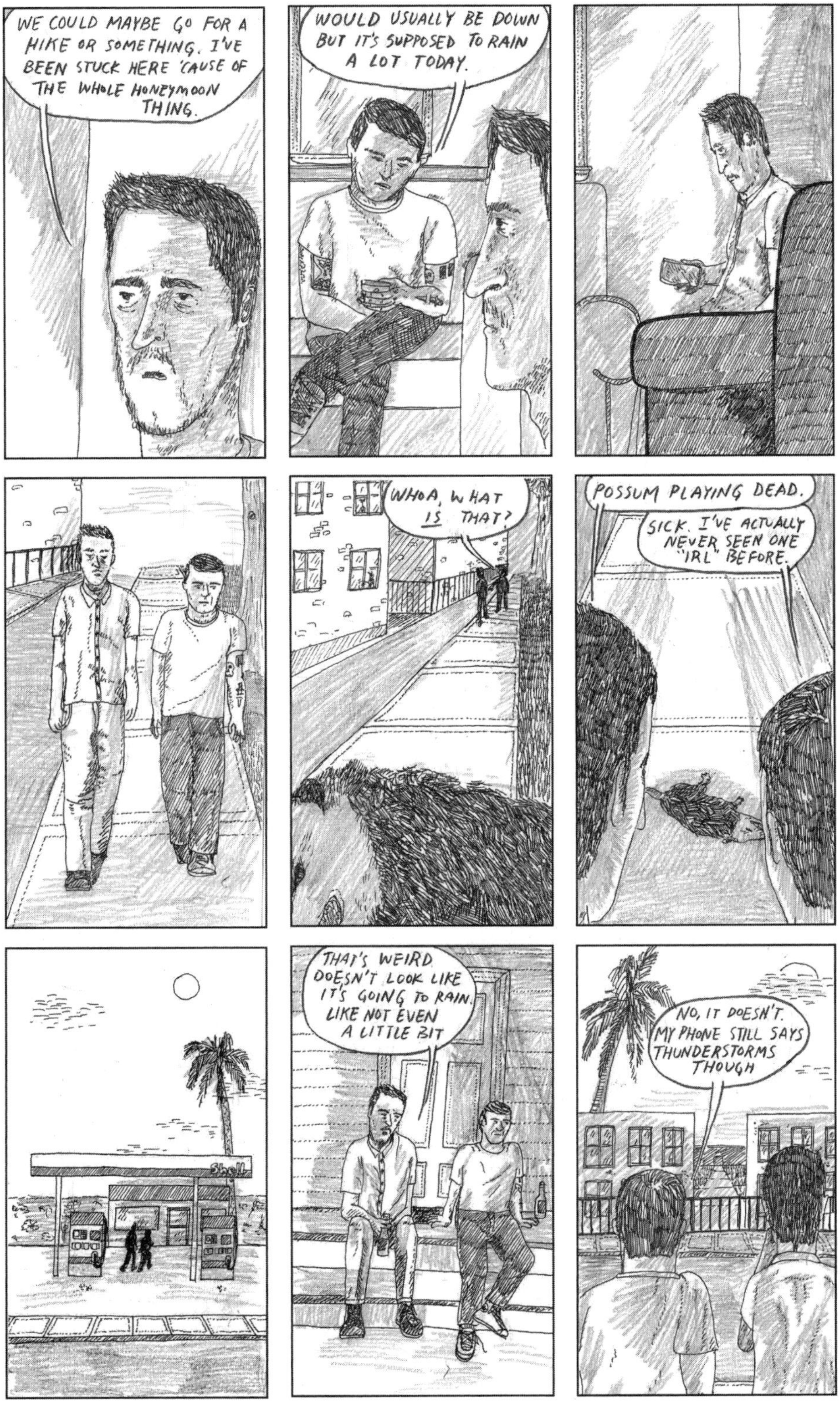
WE COULD MAYBE GO FOR A HIKE OR SOMETHING. I'VE BEEN STUCK HERE 'CAUSE OF THE WHOLE HONEYMOON THING.
WOULD USUALLY BE DOWN BUT IT'S SUPPOSED TO RAIN A LOT TODAY.
WHOA, WHAT IS THAT?
POSSUM PLAYING DEAD.
SICK. I'VE ACTUALLY NEVER SEEN ONE "IRL" BEFORE.
Shell
THAT'S WEIRD. DOESN'T LOOK LIKE IT'S GOING TO RAIN. LIKE NOT EVEN A LITTLE BIT
NO, IT DOESN'T. MY PHONE STILL SAYS THUNDERSTORMS THOUGH

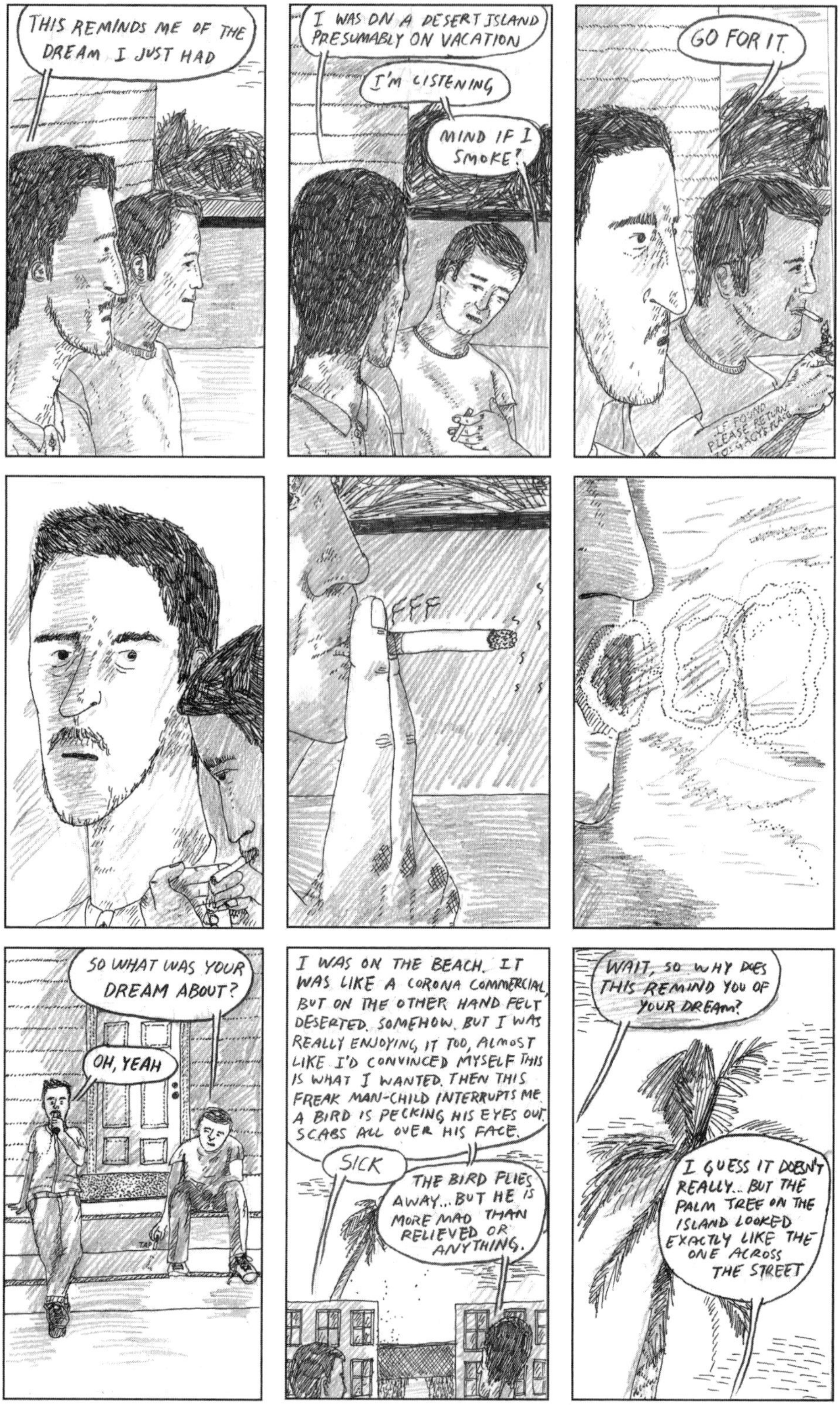
THIS REMINDS ME OF THE DREAM I JUST HAD
I WAS ON A DESERT ISLAND PRESUMABLY ON VACATION
I'M LISTENING
MIND IF I SMOKE?
GO FOR IT.
FFF
SO WHAT WAS YOUR DREAM ABOUT?
OH, YEAH
I WAS ON THE BEACH. IT WAS LIKE A CORONA COMMERCIAL, BUT ON THE OTHER HAND FELT DESERTED SOMEHOW. BUT I WAS REALLY ENJOYING IT TOO, ALMOST LIKE I'D CONVINCED MYSELF THIS IS WHAT I WANTED. THEN THIS FREAK MAN-CHILD INTERRUPTS ME. A BIRD IS PECKING HIS EYES OUT. SCABS ALL OVER HIS FACE.
SICK
THE BIRD FLIES AWAY... BUT HE IS MORE MAD THAN RELIEVED OR ANYTHING.
WAIT, SO WHY DOES THIS REMIND YOU OF YOUR DREAM?
I GUESS IT DOESN'T REALLY... BUT THE PALM TREE ON THE ISLAND LOOKED EXACTLY LIKE THE ONE ACROSS THE STREET

SO IS IT STILL SUPPOSED TO RAIN TODAY?
I THINK SO...
YEAH.
I GUESS IT DOES LOOK A LITTLE BIT CLOUDIER.
YOU WANT ANOTHER BEER?
NOT REALLY. NOT DONE WITH THIS ONE YET.
TOO LATE! THINK FAST!
UH, THANKS.
YEAH. HOW WAS TOUR?
WE DON'T LEAVE FOR ANOTHER TWO WEEKS.
OH, THAT'S RIGHT.
BUT I'M KIND OF DREADING IT TO BE HONEST.
REALLY?
YEAH... LIKE THERE HAVE DEFINITELY BEEN SOME AMAZING THINGS. BUT I KIND OF HAVE TO UPROOT EVERYTHING EVERY TIME I LEAVE-FIND A SUB LETTER, QUIT MY JOB, COME HOME AND MAKE A MONTH'S WORTH OF SOCIAL ROUNDS... I DUNNO...
IT'S JUST STARTING TO GET EXHAUSTING.
MAYBE I JUST NEED TO LET MYSELF GET OLD.

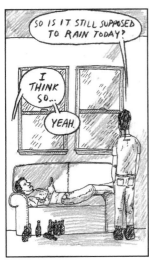

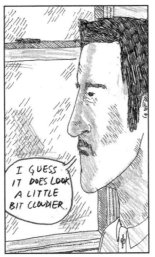

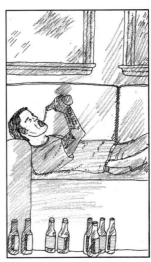

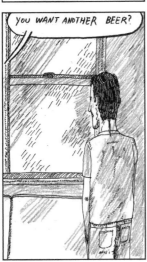

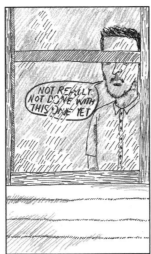

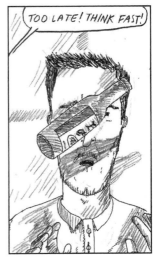

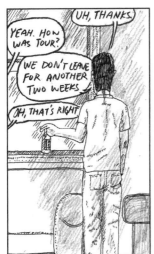

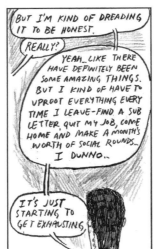

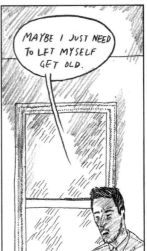

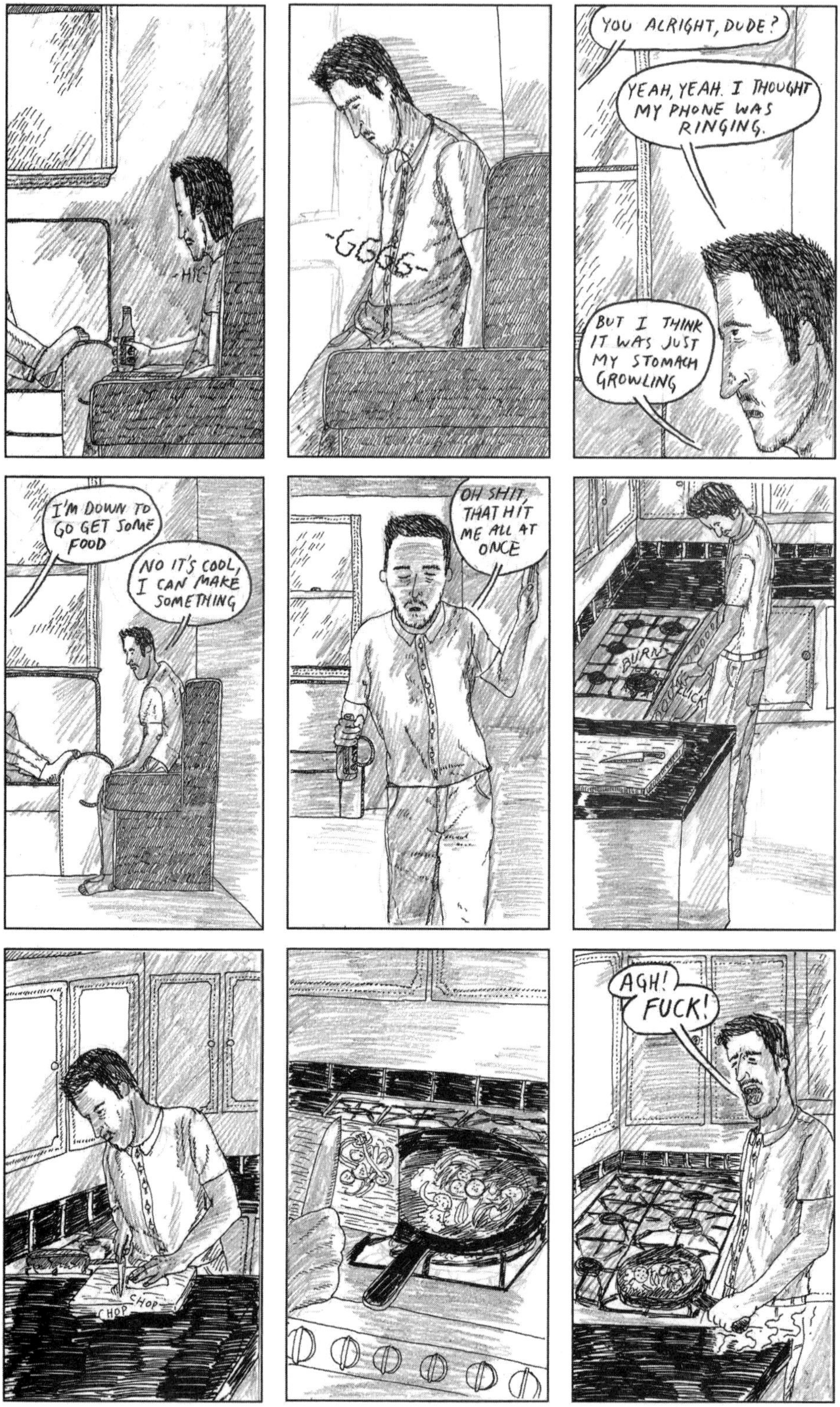
-HIC-
-GGGG-
YOU ALRIGHT, DUDE?
YEAH, YEAH. I THOUGHT MY PHONE WAS RINGING.
BUT I THINK IT WAS JUST MY STOMACH GROWLING
I'M DOWN TO GO GET SOME FOOD
NO IT'S COOL, I CAN MAKE SOMETHING
OH SHIT, THAT HIT ME ALL AT ONCE
CHOP
CHOP
AGH! FUCK!

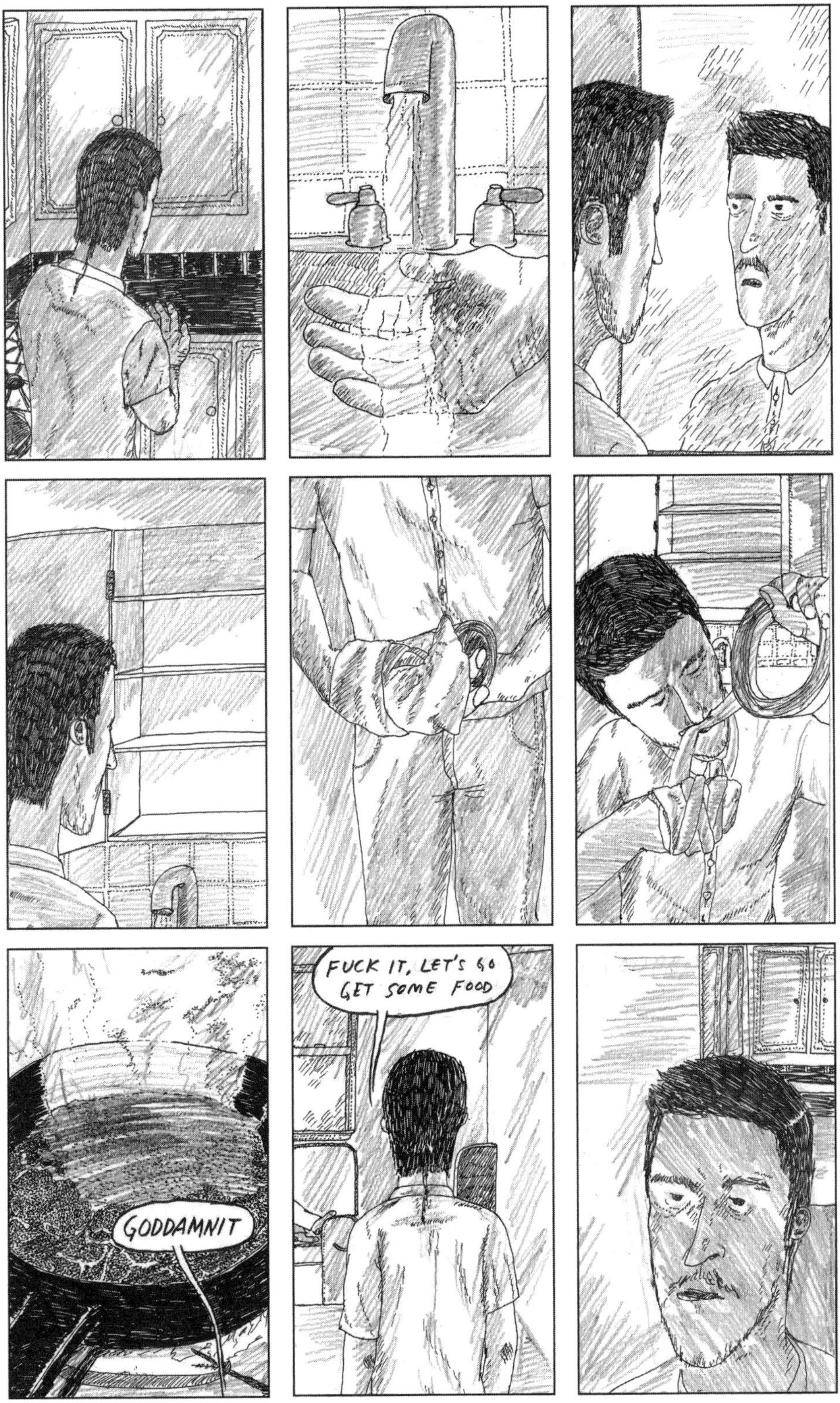
GODDAMNIT
FUCK IT, LET'S GO GET SOME FOOD

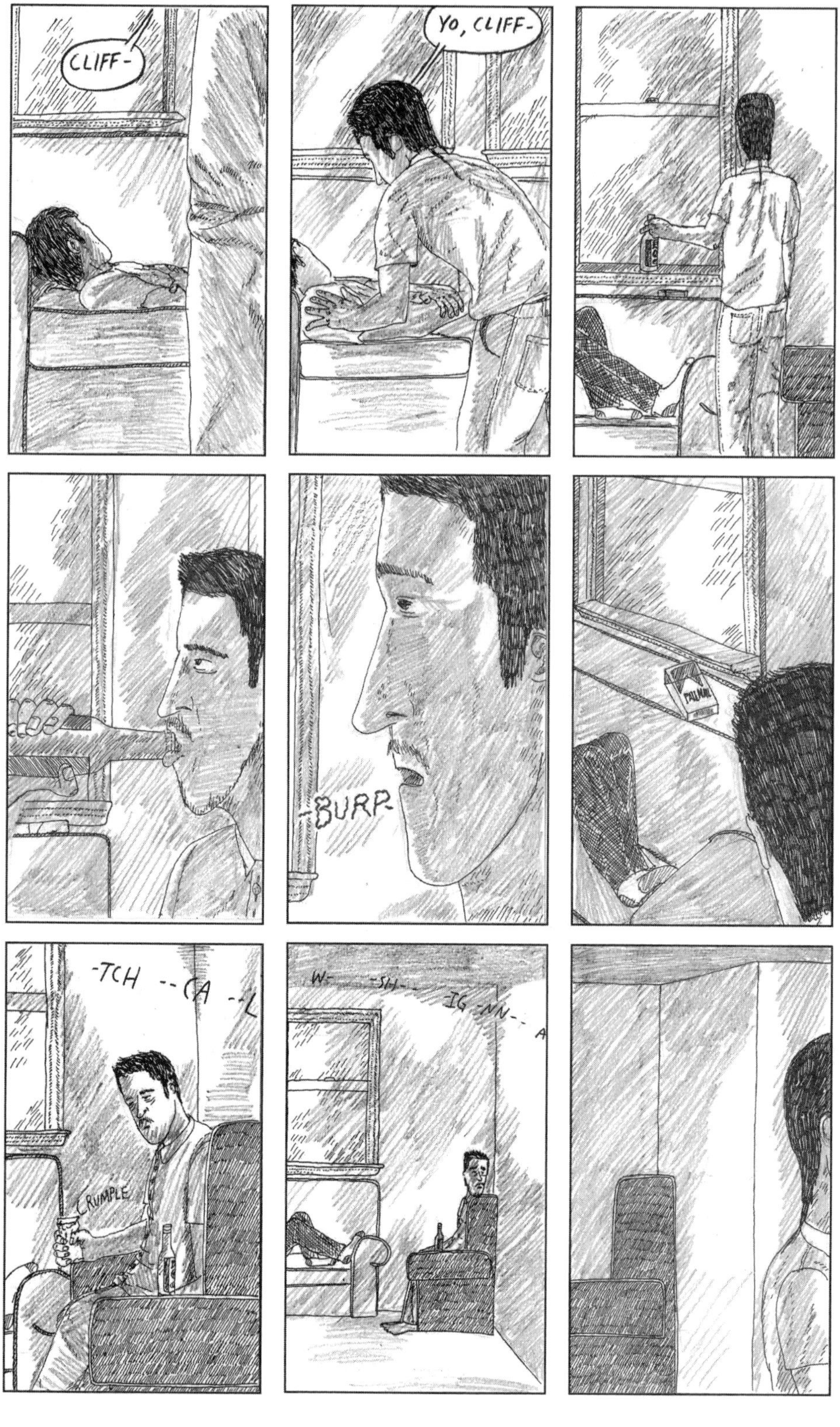
CLIFF-
YO, CLIFF-
BURP
-TCH --CA --L
CRUMPLE
W- -SH- IG -NN-- A

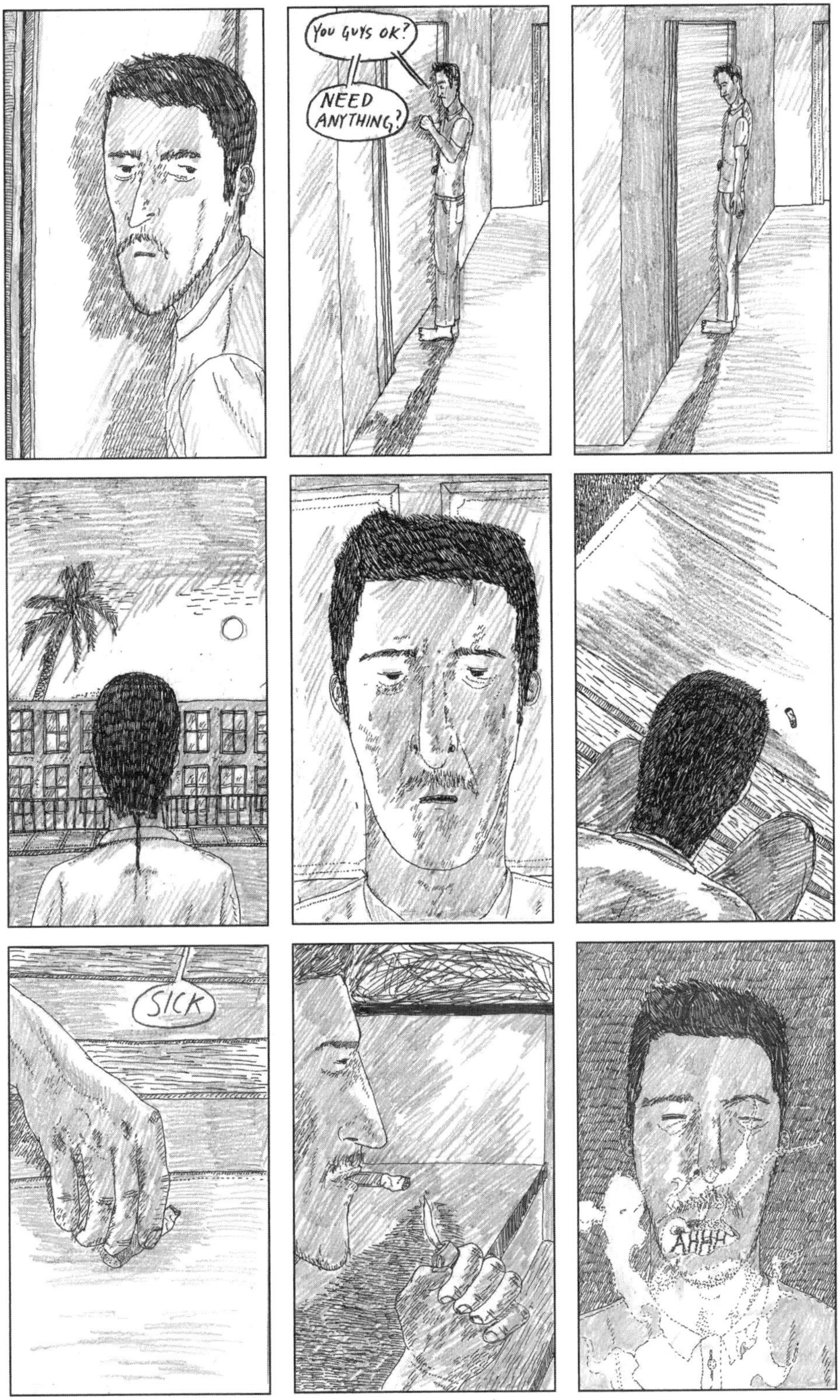
YOU GUYS OK?
NEED ANYTHING?
SICK
AHHH

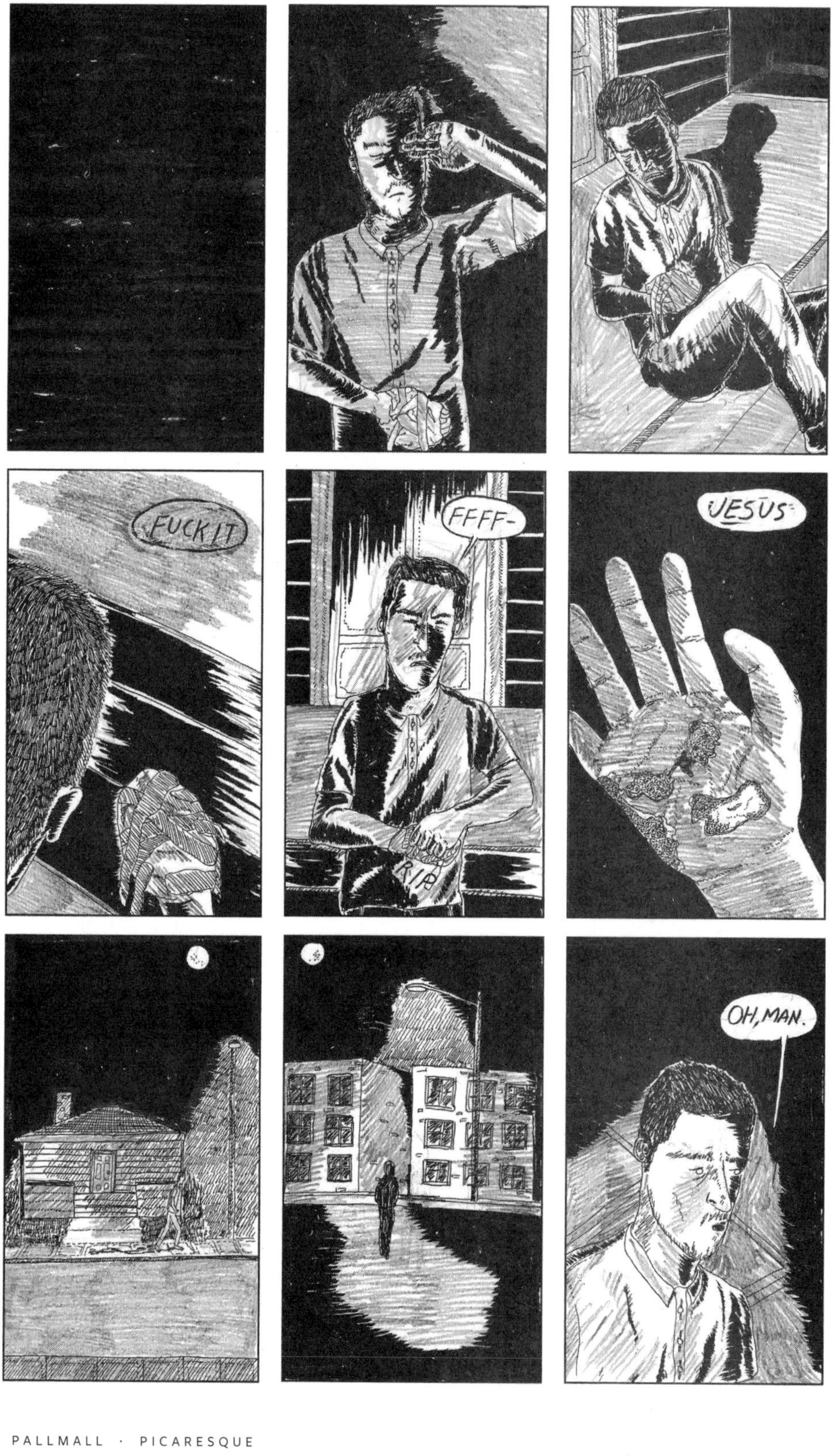
FUCK IT
FFFF-
RIP
JESUS
OH, MAN.

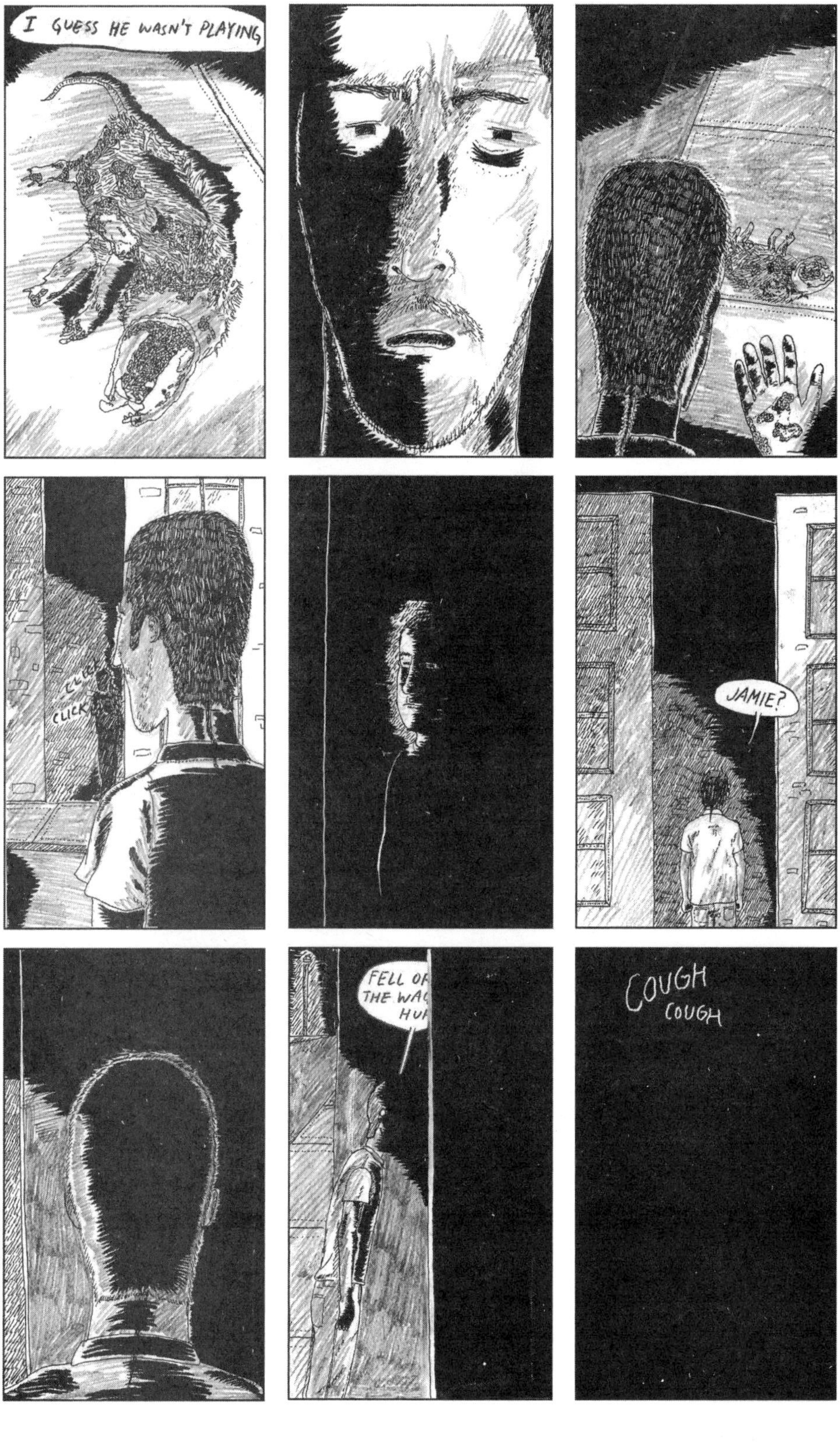
I GUESS HE WASN'T PLAYING
CLICK
CLICK
JAMIE?
FELL OF
THE WAG
HU
COUGH
COUGH

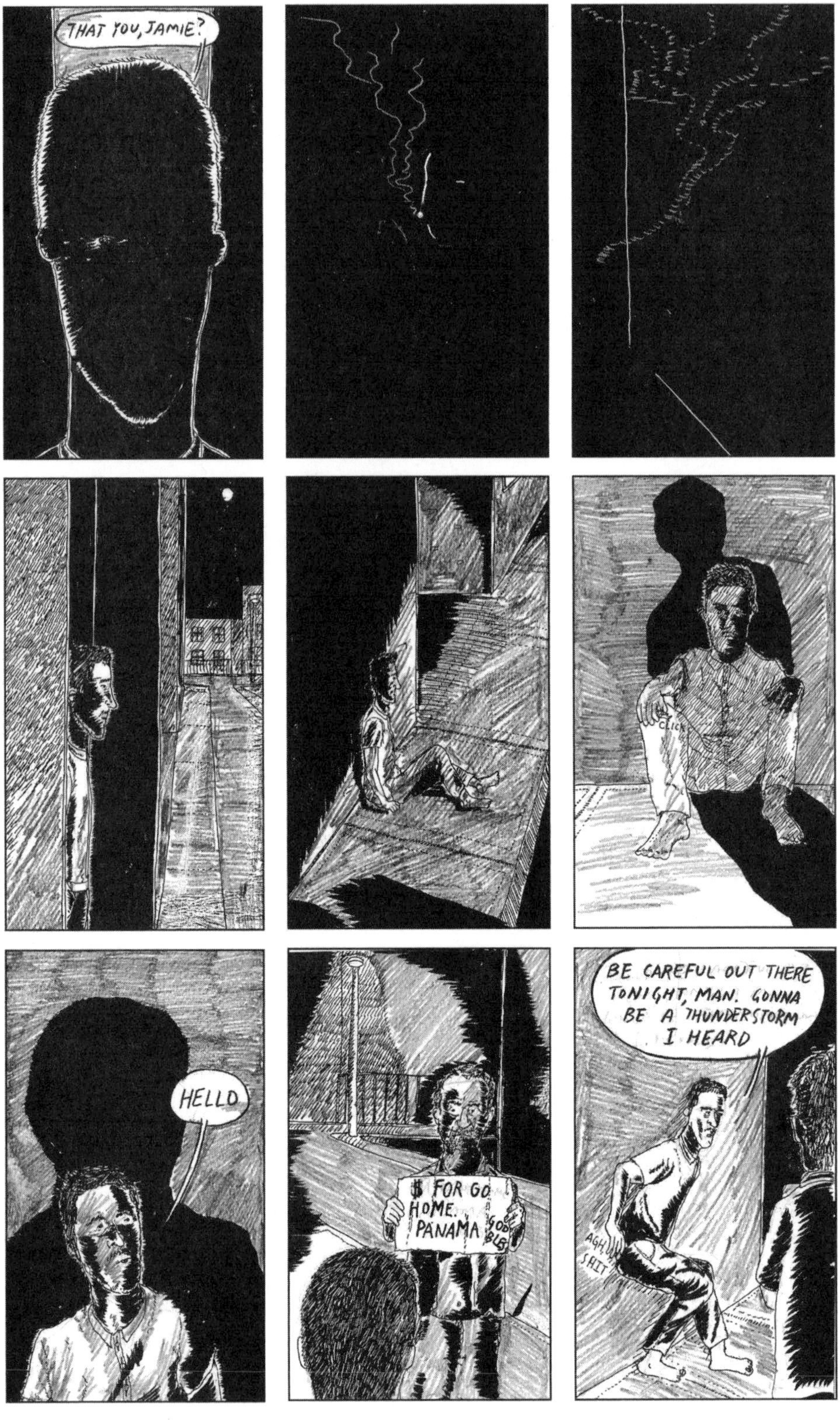
THAT YOU, JAMIE?
CLICK
HELLO
$ FOR GO HOME PANAMA
GOD BLS
BE CAREFUL OUT THERE TONIGHT, MAN. GONNA BE A THUNDERSTORM I HEARD
AGH, SHIT

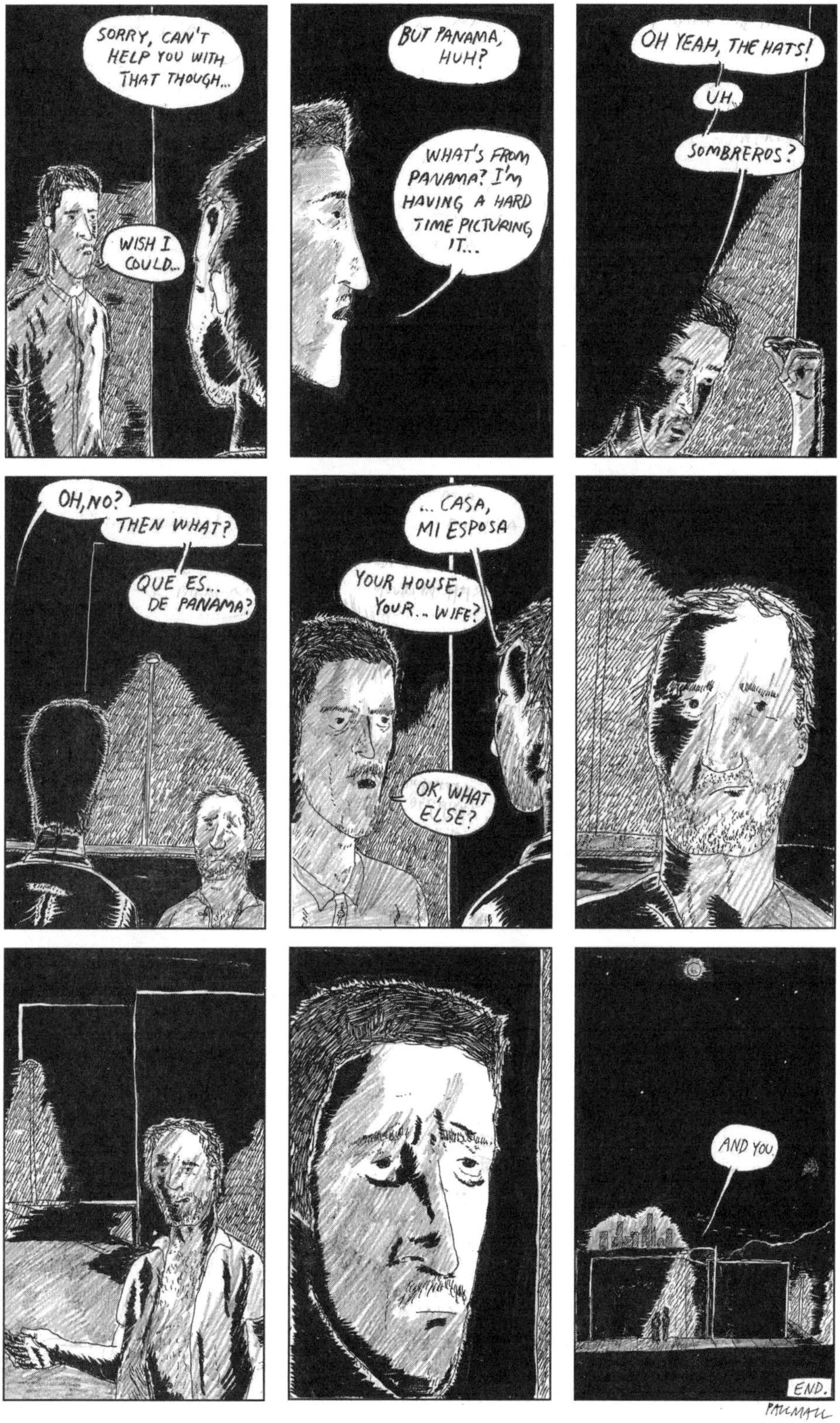
SORRY, CAN'T HELP YOU WITH THAT THOUGH...
WISH I COULD...
BUT PANAMA, HUH?
WHAT'S FROM PANAMA? I'M HAVING A HARD TIME PICTURING IT...
OH YEAH, THE HATS!
UH..
SOMBREROS?
OH, NO?
THEN WHAT?
QUE ES... DE PANAMA?
... CASA, MI ESPOSA
YOUR HOUSE, YOUR.. WIFE?
OK, WHAT ELSE?
AND YOU.
END.
PALLMALL

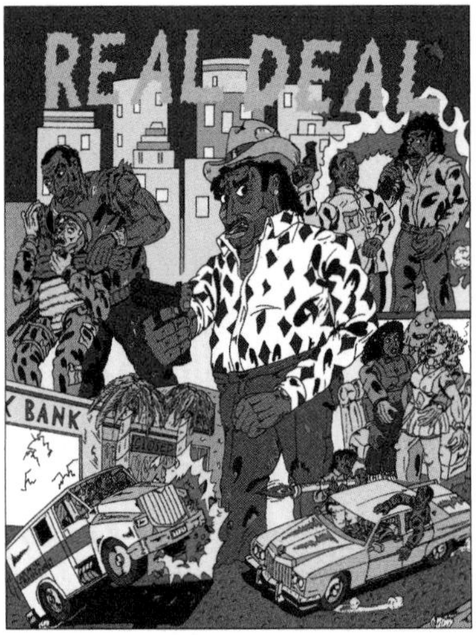
REAL DEAL
BANK

# G.C. in "Dem Bones Pt. II" (*Excerpt*)

LAWRENCE D. HUBBARD

*originally published in*

*Real Deal Comix*

FANTAGRAPHICS BOOKS

8.9 × 11.3 inches • 176 pages

## Biography

I was born in Los Angeles; I have been drawing since I was three; I ran into R.D. Bone at a miserable job we were working. We were both angry and frustrated. He had the stories, I had the art, and we created *Real Deal Comix*. More Rage per Page, More Slaughter for Your Dollar!
realdealcomix.com

## Statement

"G.C. in 'Dem Bones Part II'" is from *Real Deal #7*.

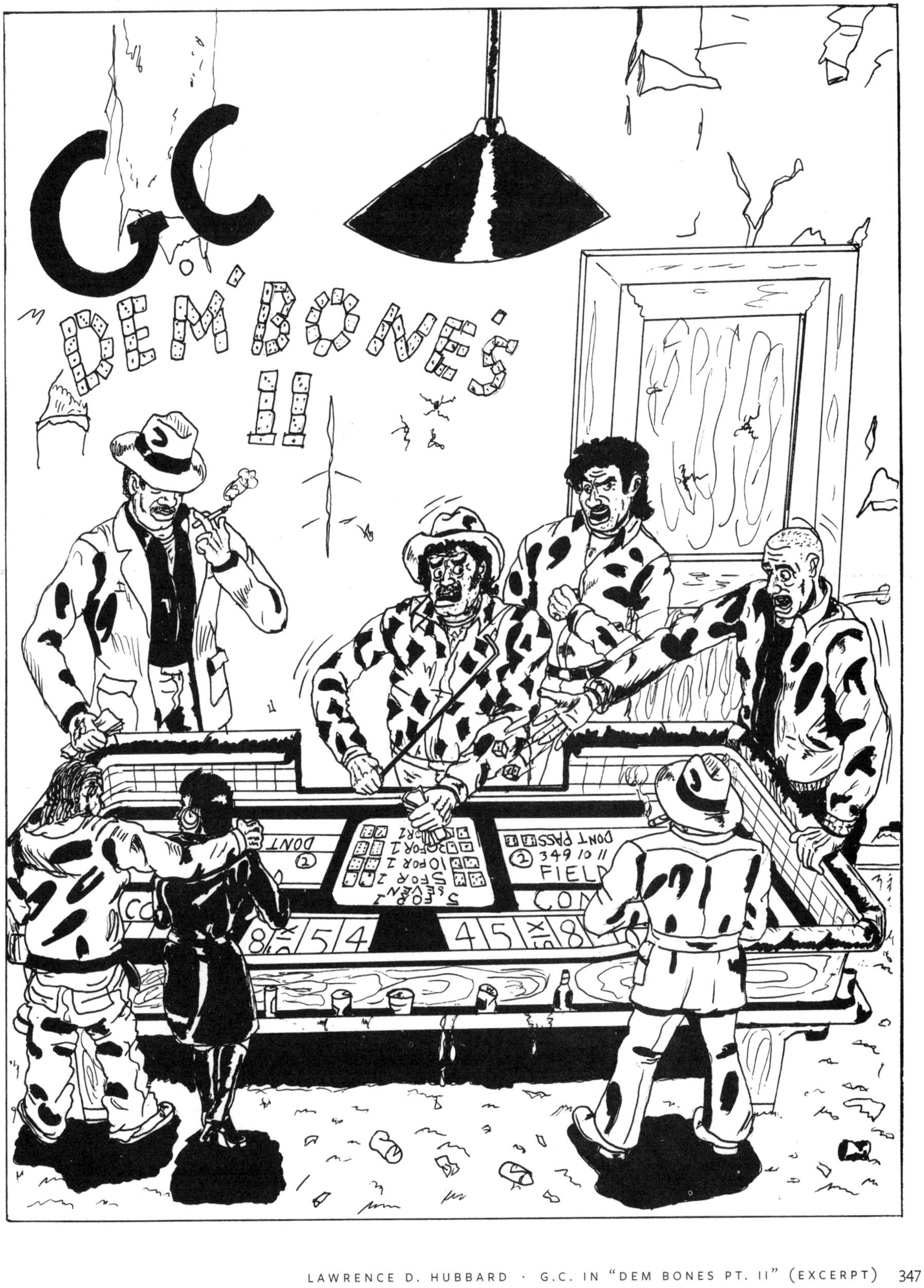
G.C
DEM BONES
II
DONT
DONT PASS
FIELD

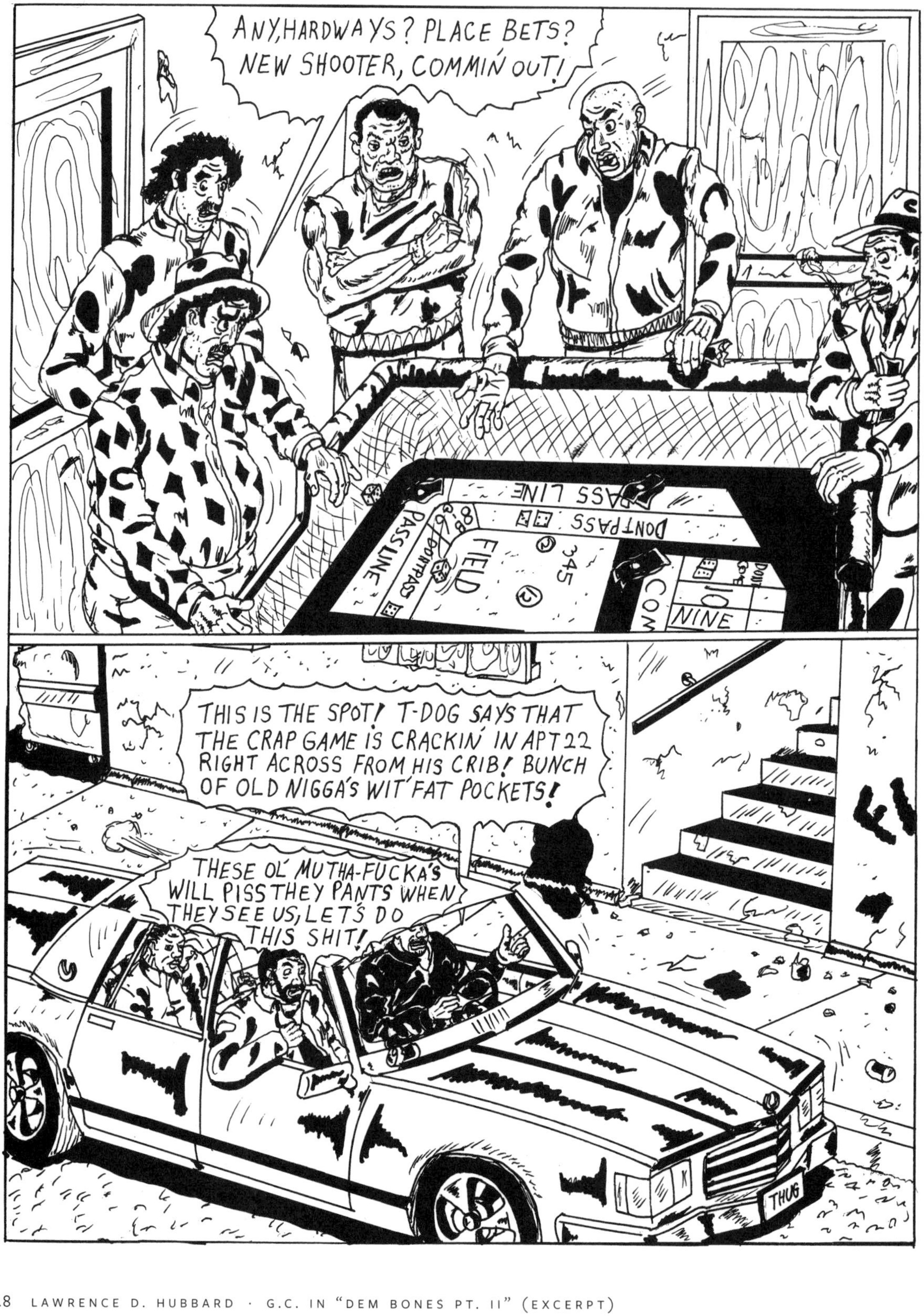
ANY, HARDWAYS? PLACE BETS? NEW SHOOTER, COMMIN' OUT!
PASS LINE
DONT PASS
FIELD
NINE
THIS IS THE SPOT! T-DOG SAYS THAT THE CRAP GAME IS CRACKIN' IN APT 22 RIGHT ACROSS FROM HIS CRIB! BUNCH OF OLD NIGGA'S WIT' FAT POCKETS!
THESE OL' MUTHA-FUCKA'S WILL PISS THEY PANTS WHEN THEY SEE US, LET'S DO THIS SHIT!
THUG

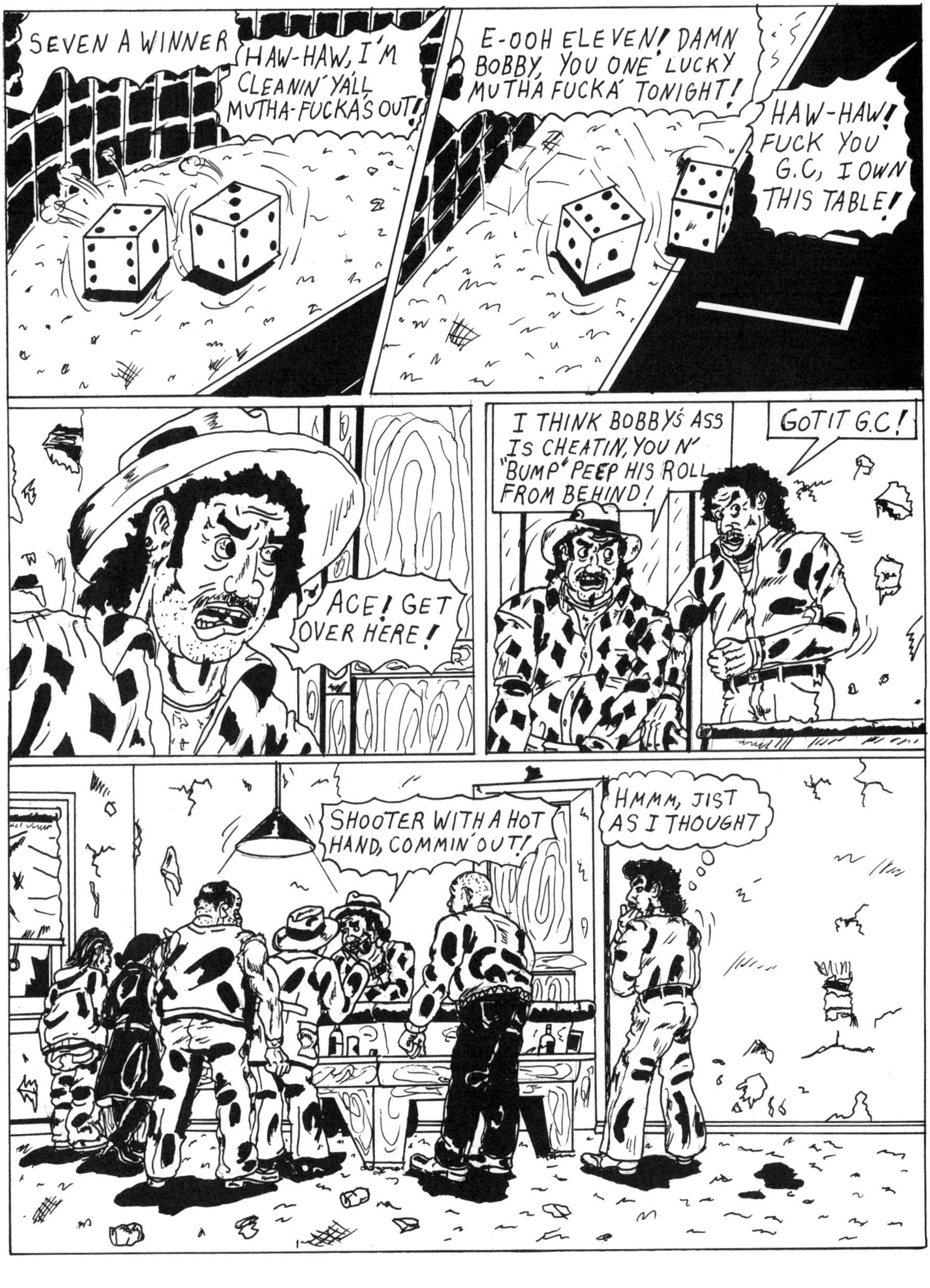
SEVEN A WINNER
HAW-HAW, I'M CLEANIN' YA'LL MUTHA-FUCKA'S OUT!
E-OOH ELEVEN! DAMN BOBBY, YOU ONE LUCKY MUTHA FUCKA' TONIGHT!
HAW-HAW! FUCK YOU G.C, I OWN THIS TABLE!
ACE! GET OVER HERE!
I THINK BOBBY'S ASS IS CHEATIN, YOU N' "BUMP" PEEP HIS ROLL FROM BEHIND!
GOT IT G.C!
SHOOTER WITH A HOT HAND, COMMIN' OUT!
HMMM, JIST AS I THOUGHT

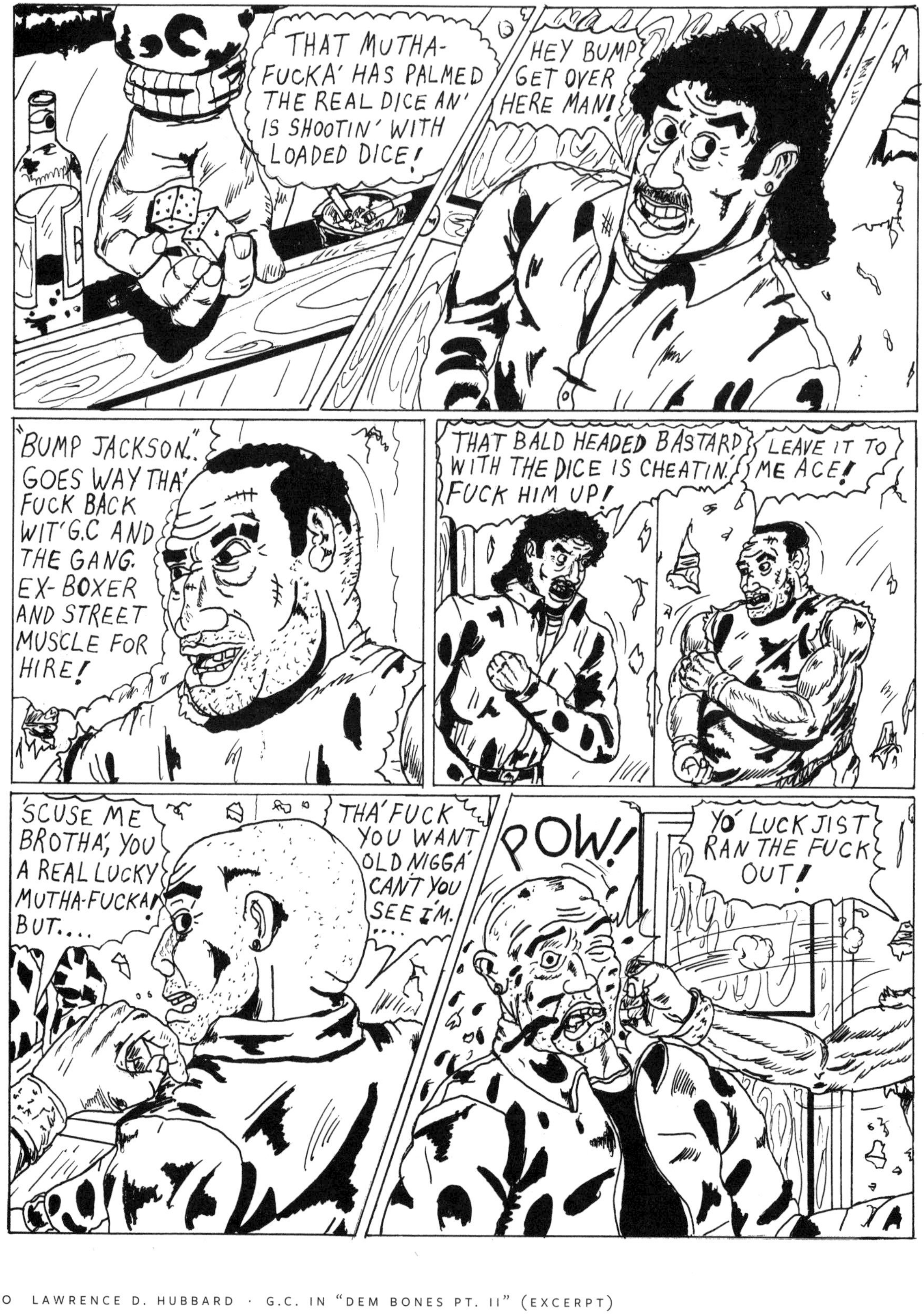
THAT MUTHA-FUCKA' HAS PALMED THE REAL DICE AN' IS SHOOTIN' WITH LOADED DICE!
HEY BUMP GET OVER HERE MAN!
"BUMP JACKSON" GOES WAY THA' FUCK BACK WIT' G.C AND THE GANG. EX-BOXER AND STREET MUSCLE FOR HIRE!
THAT BALD HEADED BASTARD WITH THE DICE IS CHEATIN'. FUCK HIM UP!
LEAVE IT TO ME ACE!
'SCUSE ME BROTHA', YOU A REAL LUCKY MUTHA-FUCKA! BUT....
THA' FUCK YOU WANT OLD NIGGA' CAN'T YOU SEE I'M....
POW!
YO' LUCK JIST RAN THE FUCK OUT!

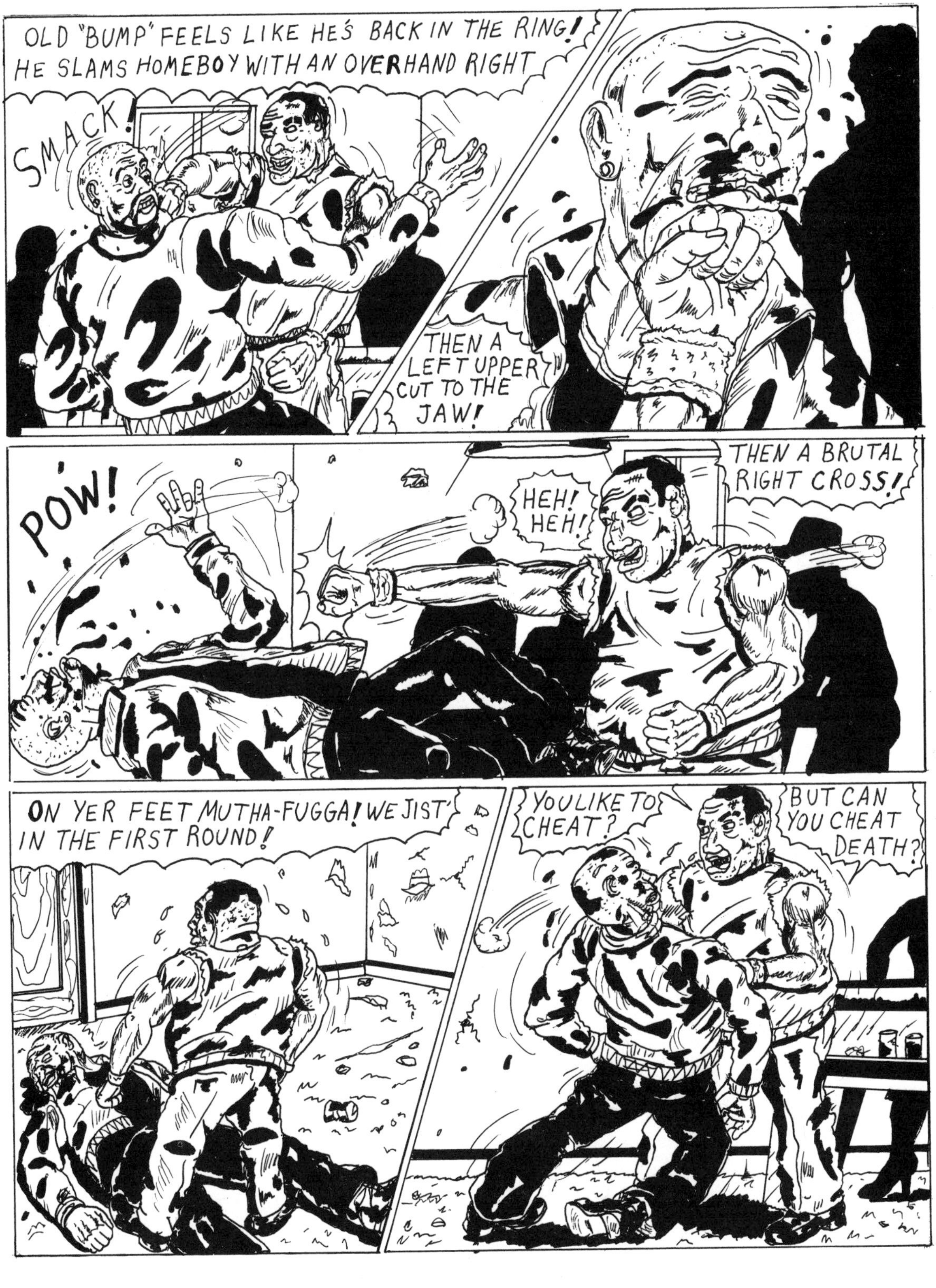
OLD "BUMP" FEELS LIKE HE'S BACK IN THE RING! HE SLAMS HOMEBOY WITH AN OVERHAND RIGHT
SMACK!
THEN A LEFT UPPER CUT TO THE JAW!
POW!
HEH! HEH!
THEN A BRUTAL RIGHT CROSS!
ON YER FEET MUTHA-FUGGA! WE JIST' IN THE FIRST ROUND!
YOU LIKE TO CHEAT?
BUT CAN YOU CHEAT DEATH?

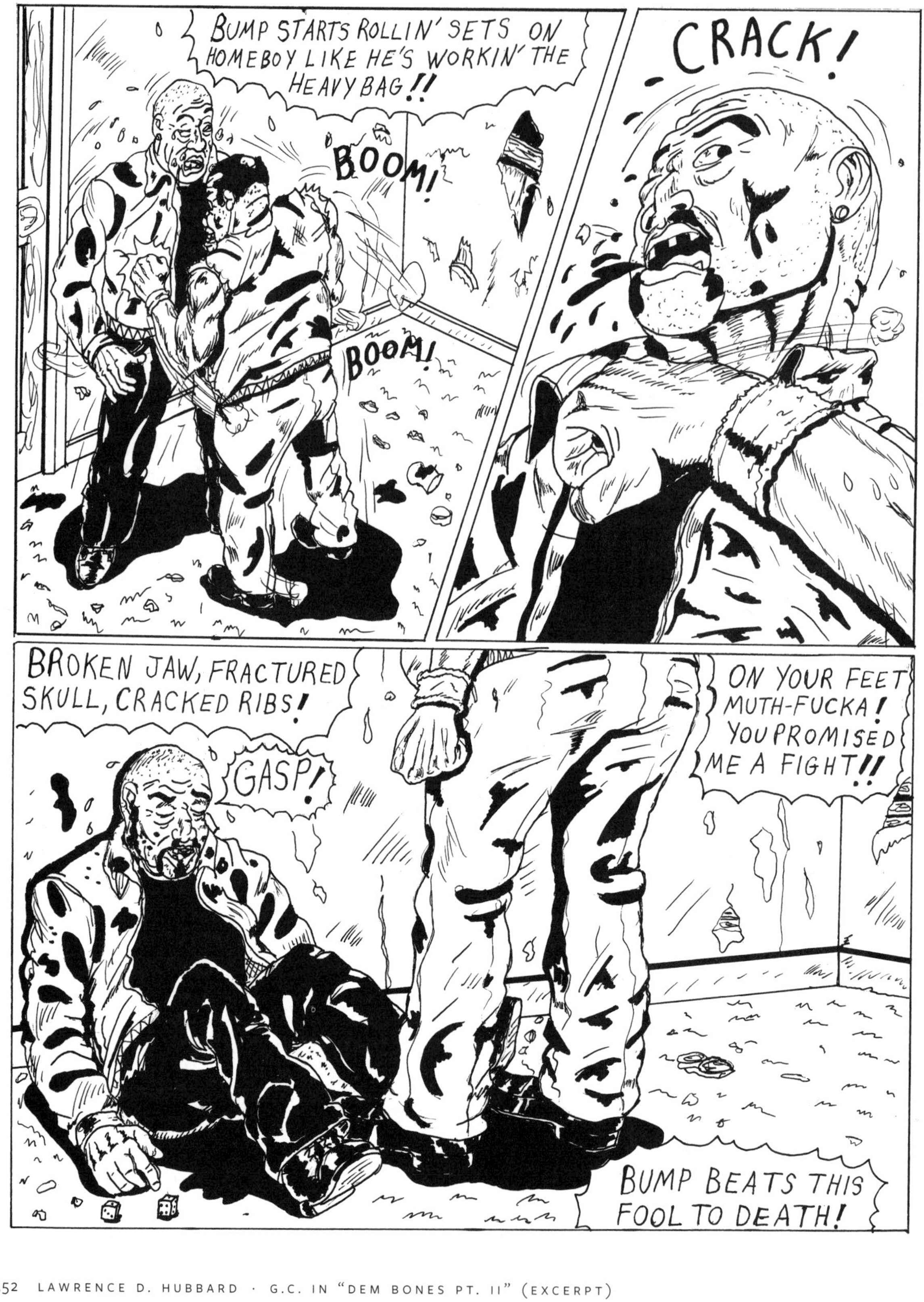
BUMP STARTS ROLLIN' SETS ON HOMEBOY LIKE HE'S WORKIN' THE HEAVY BAG!!
BOOM!
BOOM!
CRACK!
BROKEN JAW, FRACTURED SKULL, CRACKED RIBS!
GASP!
ON YOUR FEET MUTH-FUCKA! YOU PROMISED ME A FIGHT!!
BUMP BEATS THIS FOOL TO DEATH!

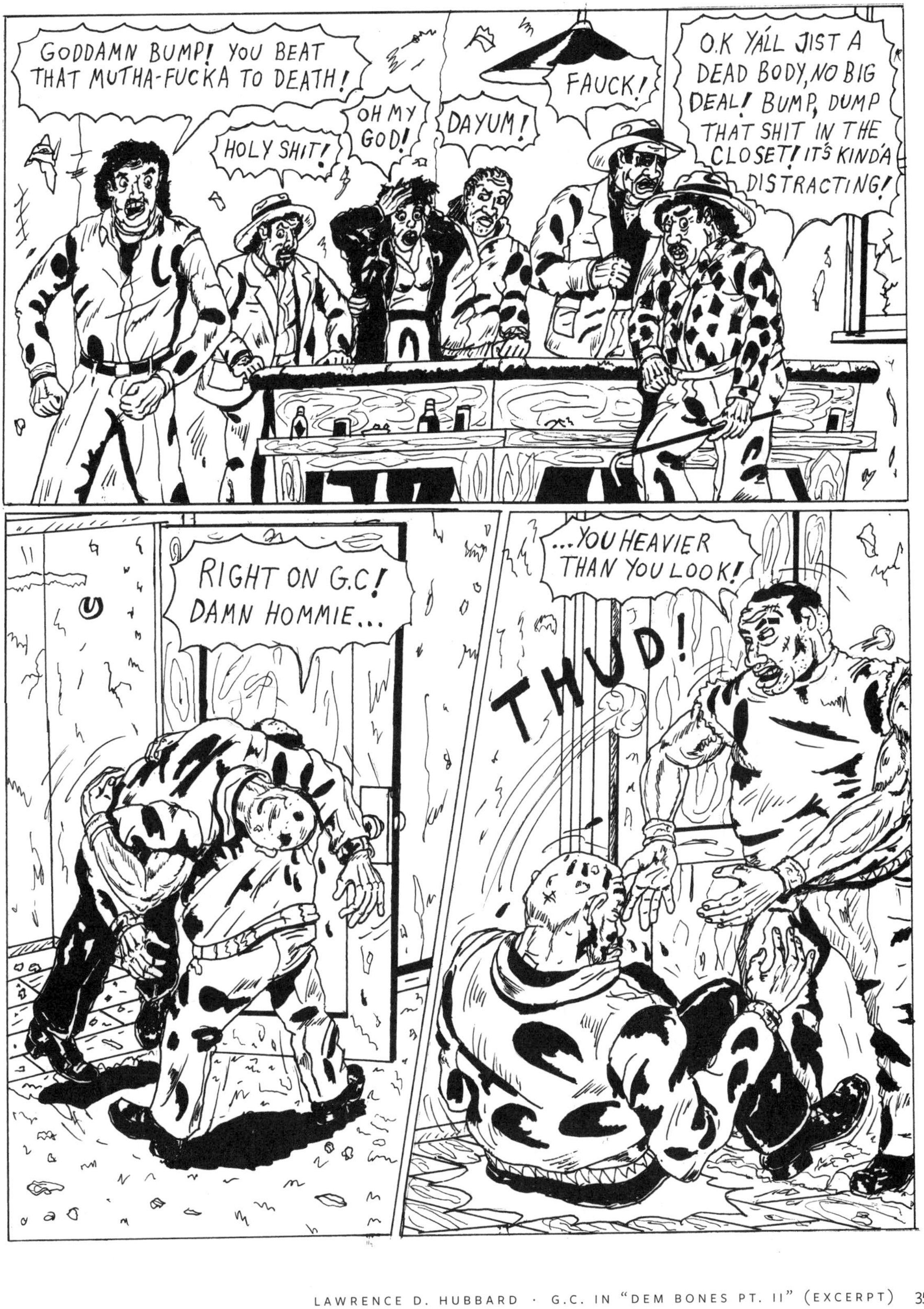
GODDAMN BUMP! YOU BEAT THAT MUTHA-FUCKA TO DEATH!
HOLY SHIT!
OH MY GOD!
DAYUM!
FAUCK!
O.K Y'ALL JIST A DEAD BODY, NO BIG DEAL! BUMP, DUMP THAT SHIT IN THE CLOSET! IT'S KIND'A DISTRACTING!
RIGHT ON G.C! DAMN HOMMIE...
...YOU HEAVIER THAN YOU LOOK!
THUD!

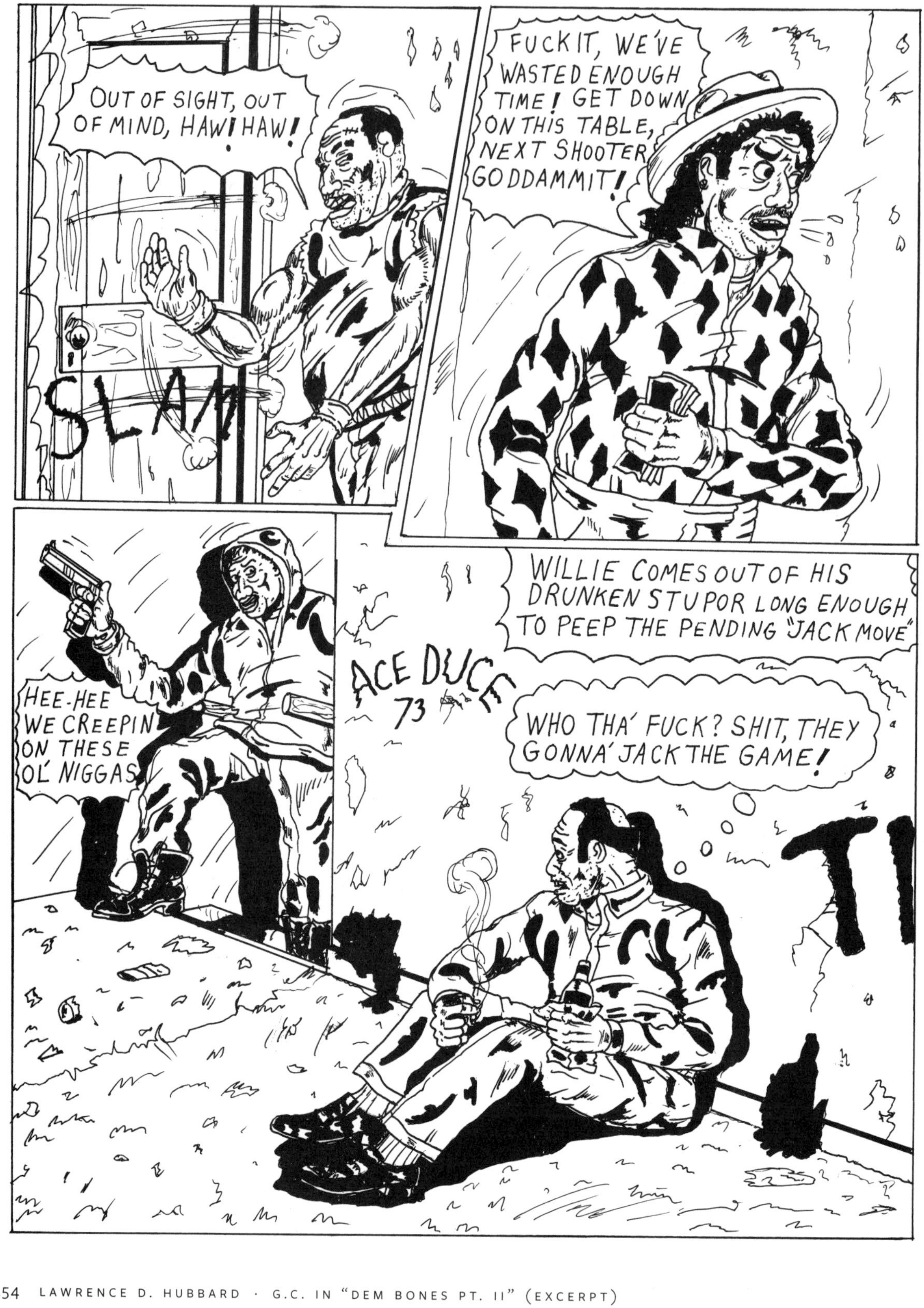
OUT OF SIGHT, OUT OF MIND, HAW! HAW!
SLAM
FUCK IT, WE'VE WASTED ENOUGH TIME! GET DOWN ON THIS TABLE, NEXT SHOOTER GODDAMMIT!
HEE-HEE WE CREEPIN ON THESE OL' NIGGAS
WILLIE COMES OUT OF HIS DRUNKEN STUPOR LONG ENOUGH TO PEEP THE PENDING "JACK MOVE"
ACE DUCE 73
WHO THA' FUCK? SHIT, THEY GONNA' JACK THE GAME!

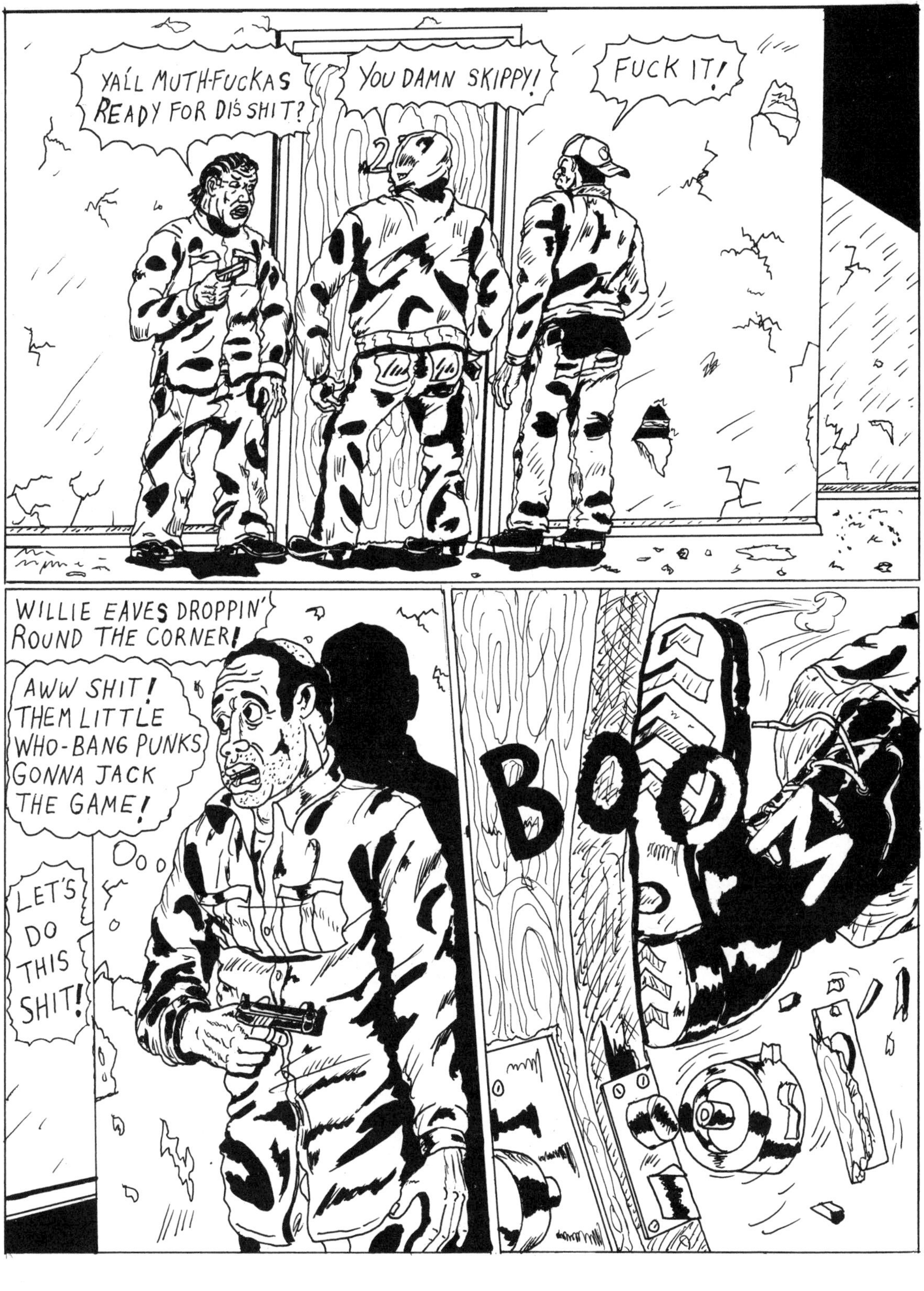
YA'LL MUTH-FUCKAS READY FOR DI'S SHIT?
YOU DAMN SKIPPY!
FUCK IT!
WILLIE EAVES DROPPIN' ROUND THE CORNER!
AWW SHIT! THEM LITTLE WHO-BANG PUNKS GONNA JACK THE GAME!
LET'S DO THIS SHIT!
BOOM

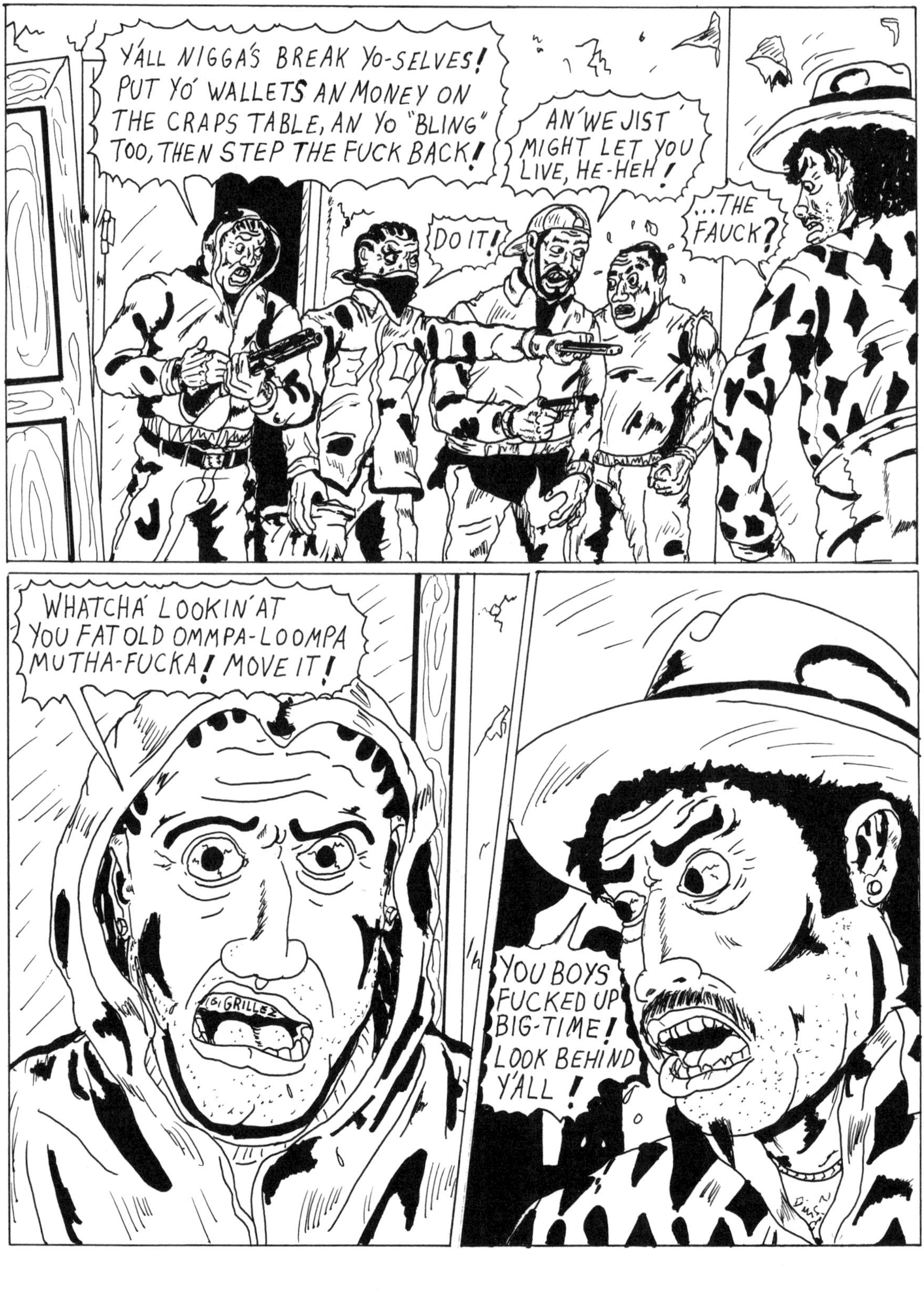
Y'ALL NIGGA'S BREAK YO-SELVES! PUT YO' WALLETS AN MONEY ON THE CRAPS TABLE, AN YO "BLING" TOO, THEN STEP THE FUCK BACK!
AN' WE JIST MIGHT LET YOU LIVE, HE-HEH!
DO IT!
...THE FAUCK?
WHATCHA' LOOKIN' AT YOU FAT OLD OMMPA-LOOMPA MUTHA-FUCKA! MOVE IT!
G GRILLEZ
YOU BOYS FUCKED UP BIG-TIME! LOOK BEHIND Y'ALL!

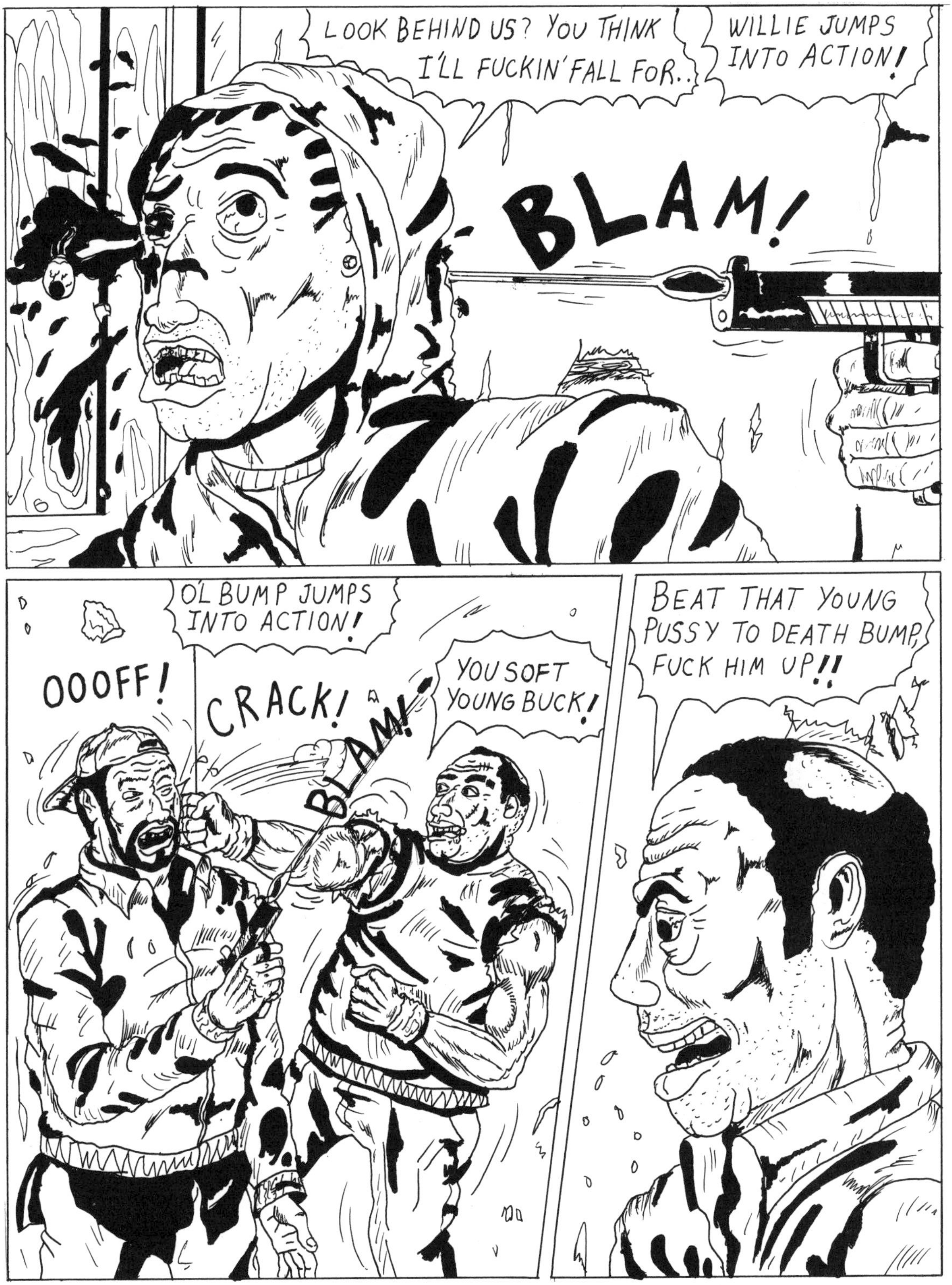
LOOK BEHIND US? YOU THINK I'LL FUCKIN' FALL FOR..
WILLIE JUMPS INTO ACTION!
BLAM!
O'L BUMP JUMPS INTO ACTION!
OOOFF!
CRACK!
BLAM!
YOU SOFT YOUNG BUCK!
BEAT THAT YOUNG PUSSY TO DEATH BUMP, FUCK HIM UP!!

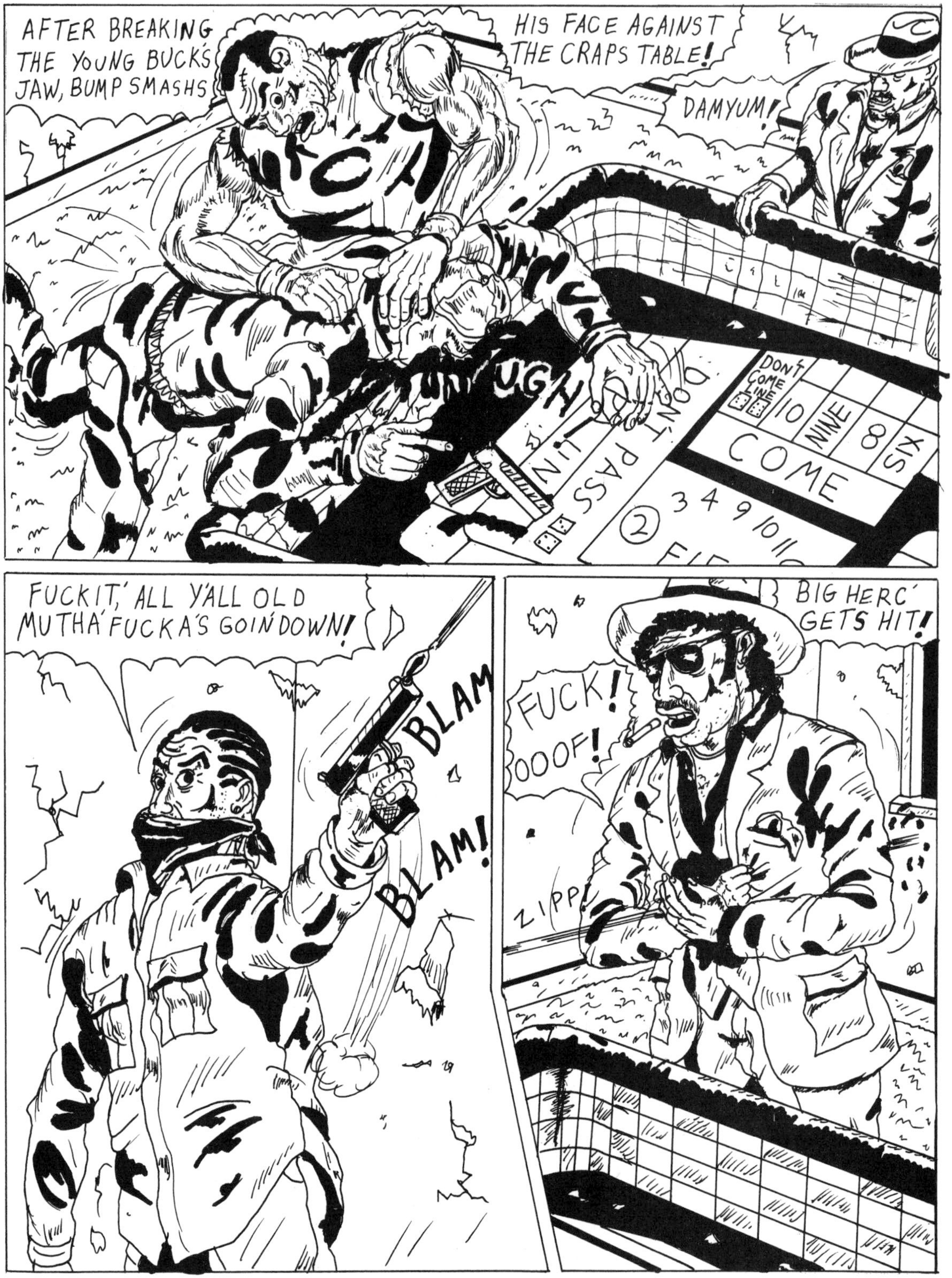
AFTER BREAKING THE YOUNG BUCK'S JAW, BUMP SMASHS
HIS FACE AGAINST THE CRAPS TABLE!
DAMYUM!
UNNNUGH!
DON'T COME LINE
10
NINE
8
SIX
COME
DON'T PASS LINE
2
3 4 9 10 11
FUCKIT, ALL Y'ALL OLD MUTHA'FUCKA'S GOIN'DOWN!
BLAM
BLAM!
BLAM
BIG HERC' GETS HIT!
FUCK!
OOOF!
ZIPP!

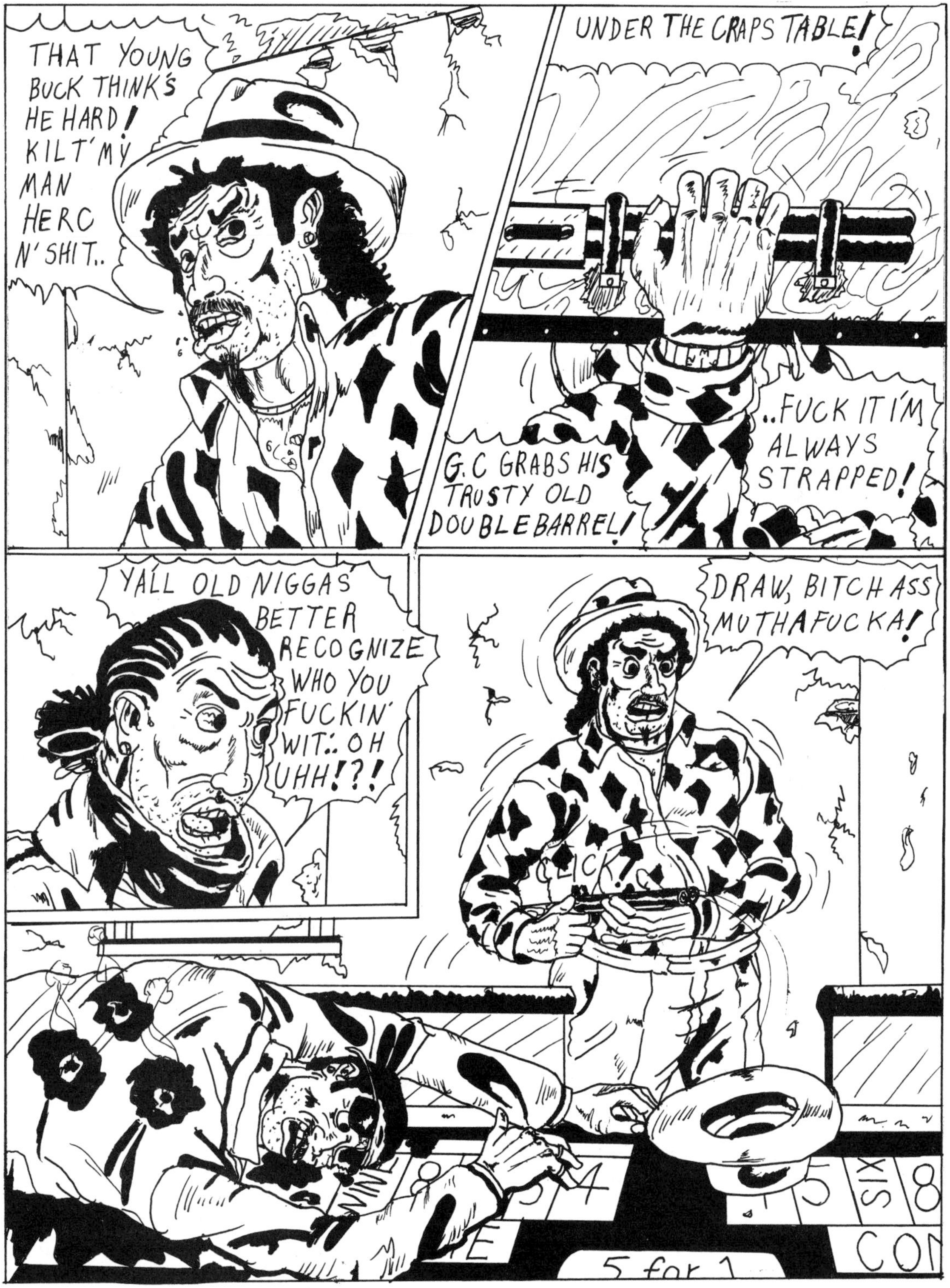
THAT YOUNG BUCK THINK'S HE HARD! KILT' MY MAN HERC N' SHIT..
UNDER THE CRAPS TABLE!
G.C GRABS HIS TRUSTY OLD DOUBLE BARREL!
..FUCK IT I'M ALWAYS STRAPPED!
YA'LL OLD NIGGAS' BETTER RECOGNIZE WHO YOU FUCKIN' WIT.. OH UHH!?!
DRAW, BITCH ASS MUTHAFUCKA!
CLICK!
5 for 1

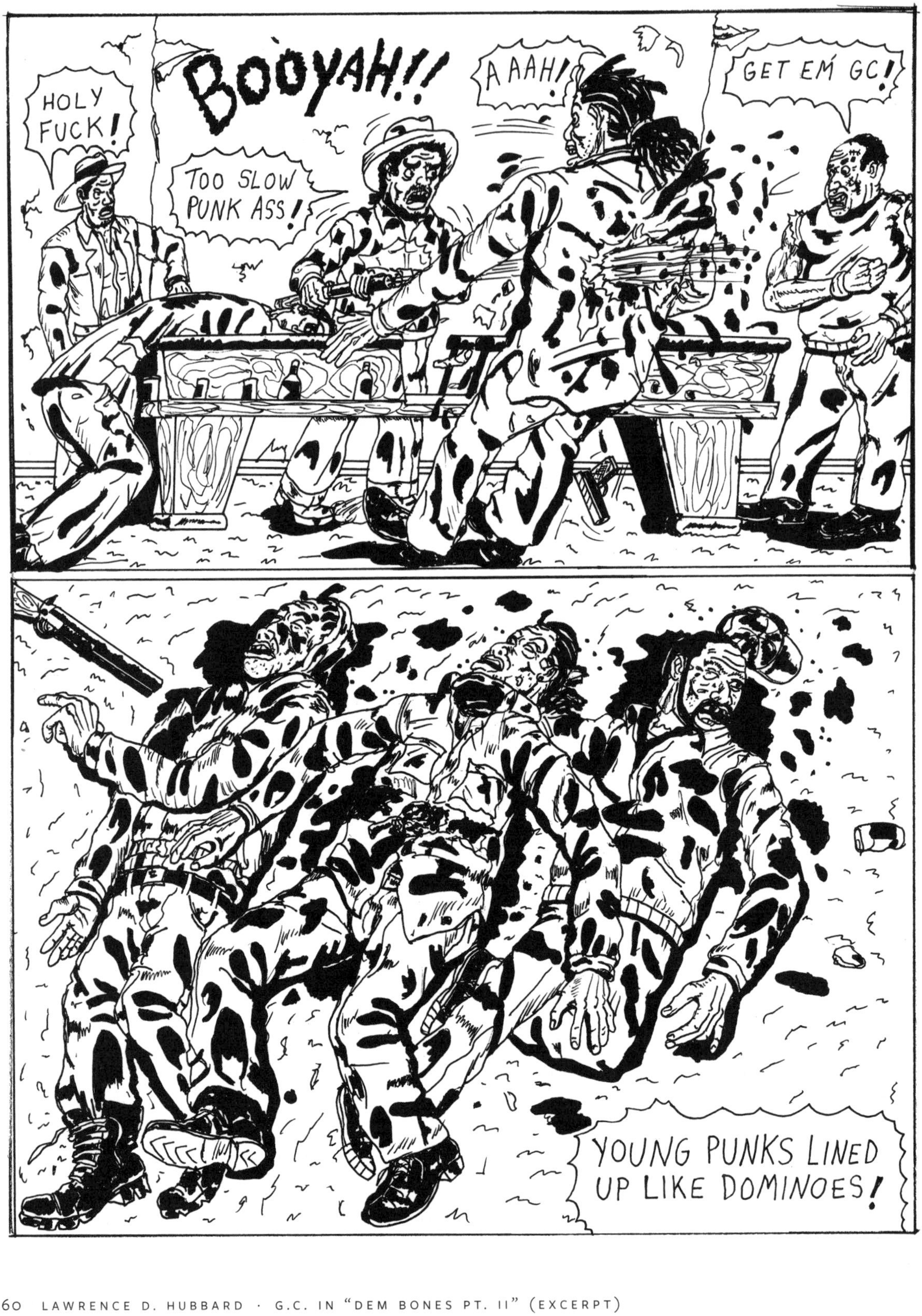
HOLY FUCK!
BOOYAH!!!
TOO SLOW PUNK ASS!
A AAH!
GET EM GC!
YOUNG PUNKS LINED UP LIKE DOMINOES!

# Love with Family Love AND The Team for Sure

## LARRY RANDOLPH

*exhibited at*

CREATIVE GROWTH ART CENTER

11 × 8.5 inches / 12.5 × 7.75 inches • colored pencils and ink

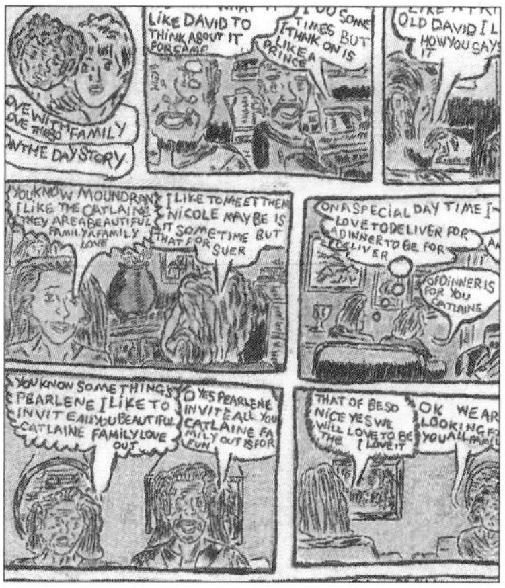
LIKE DAVID TO THINK ABOUT IT
TIMES BUT I THINK ON IS LIKE A PRINCE
OLD DAVID
HOW YOU SAY
FAMILY
THE DAY STORY
YOU KNOW MOUNDRAN I LIKE THE CATLAINE THEY ARE A BEAUTIFUL FAMILY A FAMILY LOVE
I LIKE TO MEET THEM NICOLE MAYBE IS IT SOMETIME BUT THAT FOR SUER
ON A SPECIAL DAY TIME I LOVE TO DELIVER FOR A DINNER TO BE FOR TO LIVER
OF DINNER IS FOR YOU CATLAINE
YOU KNOW SOMETHINGS PEARLENE I LIKE TO INVITE ALL YOU BEAUTIFUL CATLAINE FAMILY LOVE OUT
O YES PEARLENE INVITE ALL YOU CATLAINE FAMILY OUT IS FOR FUN
THAT OF BE SO NICE YES WE WILL LOVE TO BE THE I LOVE IT
OK WE AR LOOKING YOU ALL

## Biography

Larry Randolph was born in 1955 and has been an artist at Creative Growth Art Center in Oakland, California, since 1988. Extremely verbal and outgoing, in the studio Randolph works methodically, drawing inspiration from animals and a variety of source materials including tear-out ads and magazines. Working primarily in ceramics or drawing, Larry's work has a serial, narrative quality that instantly charms the viewer. His work has been featured in *California Magazine* and on *Bay Area Backroads* with host Jerry Graham.
creativegrowth.org

## Statement

Since August 1987, I've had the idea to make my own comics. My nephew was collecting cardboard and newspapers, and that is what got me going. I started copying comic strips from the newspapers onto the cardboard. I was drawing Blondie and Dagwood, Little Orphan Annie, Marvel superheroes like X-Men and Captain America. It's good to make your own comics with your own ideas. My comics are all about the fun of it.

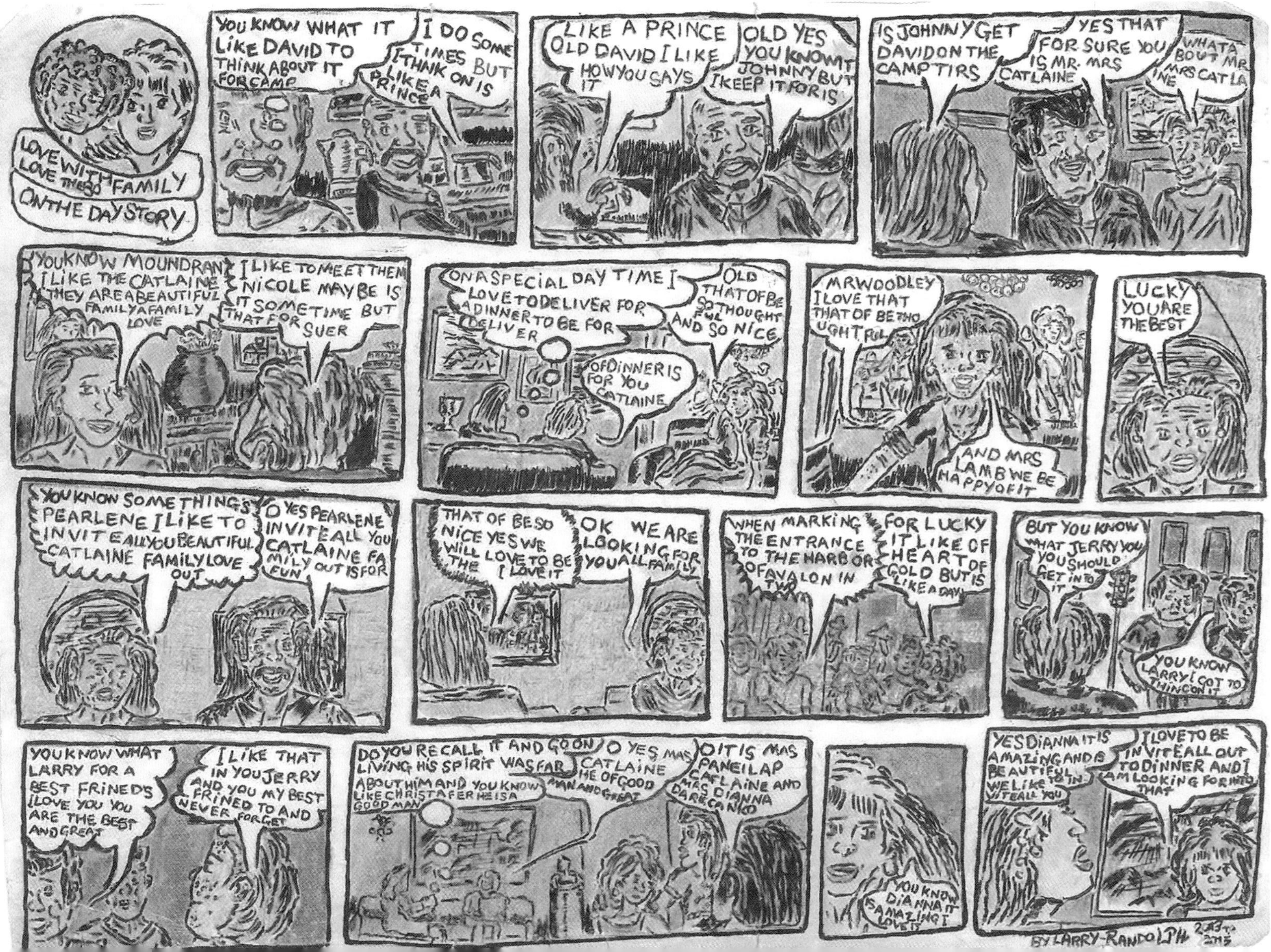
LOVE WITH FAMILY LOVE THE SO
ON THE DAY STORY
YOU KNOW WHAT IT LIKE DAVID TO THINK ABOUT IT FOR CAMP
I DO SOME TIMES BUT I THINK ON IS LIKE A PRINCE
LIKE A PRINCE OLD DAVID I LIKE HOW YOU SAYS IT
OLD YES YOU KNOW IT JOHNNY BUT I KEEP IT FOR IS
IS JOHNNY GET DAVID ON THE CAMP TIRS
YES THAT FOR SURE YOU IS MR. MRS CATLAINE
WHAT ABOUT MR MRS CATLAINE
YOU KNOW MOUNDRAN I LIKE THE CATLAINE THEY ARE A BEAUTIFUL FAMILY A FAMILY LOVE
I LIKE TO MEET THEM NICOLE MAY BE IS IT SOMETIME BUT THAT FOR SUER
ON A SPECIAL DAY TIME I LOVE TO DELIVER FOR A DINNER TO BE FOR DELIVER
OLD THAT OF BE SO THOUGHT FUL AND SO NICE
OF DINNER IS FOR YOU CATLAINE
MR WOODLEY I LOVE THAT THAT OF BE THO UGHT FUL
AND MRS LAMB WE BE HAPPY OF IT
LUCKY YOU ARE THE BEST
YOU KNOW SOMETHINGS PEARLENE I LIKE TO INVITE ALL YOU BEAUTIFUL CATLAINE FAMILY LOVE OUT
O YES PEARLENE INVITE ALL YOU CATLAINE FA MILY OUT IS FOR FUN
THAT OF BE SO NICE YES WE WILL LOVE TO BE THE I LOVE IT
OK WE ARE LOOKING FOR YOU ALL FAMILY
WHEN MARKING THE ENTRANCE TO THE HARBOR OF AVALON IN TWO
FOR LUCKY IT LIKE OF HEART OF GOLD BUT IS LIKE A DAY
BUT YOU KNOW WHAT JERRY YOU YOU SHOULD GET INTO IT
YOU KNOW LARRY I GOT TO THING ON IT
YOU KNOW WHAT LARRY FOR A BEST FRINED'S I LOVE YOU YOU ARE THE BEST AND GREAT
I LIKE THAT IN YOU JERRY AND YOU MY BEST FRINED TO AND NEVER FORGET
DO YOU RECALL IT AND GO ON LIVING HIS SPIRIT WAS FAR ABOUT HIM AND YOU KNOW LIKE CHRISTAFER HE IS A GOOD MAN
O YES MAS CATLAINE HE OF GOOD MAN AND GREAT
O IT IS MAS PANEILAP CATLAINE AND MAS DIANNA DARECANKO
YOU KNOW DIANNA IT S AMAZING I LOVE IT
YES DIANNA IT IS AMAZING AND IS BEAUTIFUL WE LIKE TO IN VITE ALL YOU
I LOVE TO BE IN VITE ALL OUT TO DINNER AND I AM LOOKING FOR INTO THAT
BY LARRY-RANDOLPH

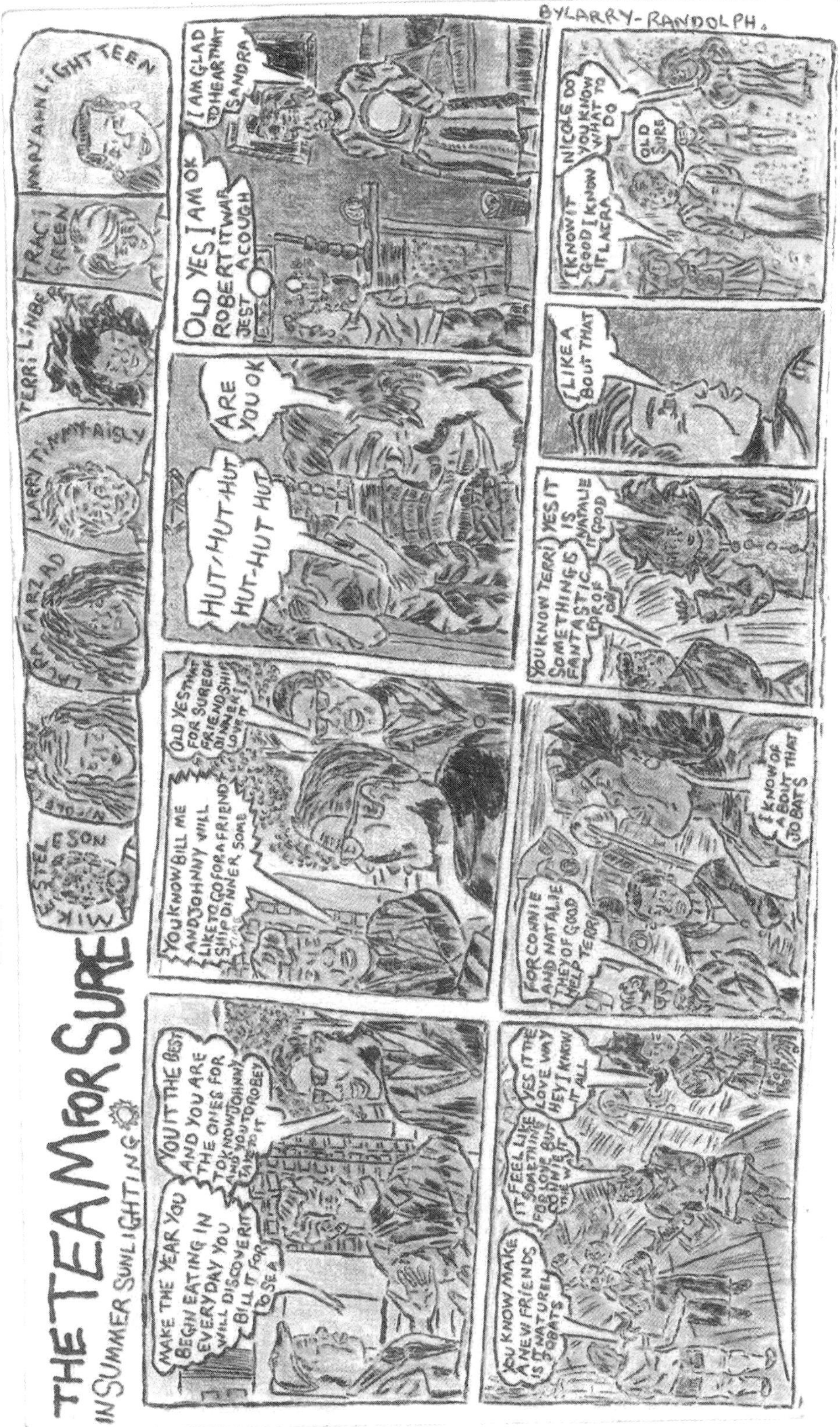
THE TEAM FOR SURE
IN SUMMER SUNLIGHTING
MIKE STELLESON
NICOLE
LAURA FARZAD
LARRY TIMMY AISLY
TERRI LINBERG
TRACI GREEN
MARYANN LIGHT TEEN
MAKE THE YEAR YOU BEGIN EATING IN EVERYDAY YOU WILL DISCOVER IT BILL IT FOR TO SEA
YOU IT THE BEST AND YOU ARE THE ONES FOR TO KNOW JOHNNY AND YOU TO ROBEY TAKE TO IT
YOU KNOW BILL ME AND JOHNNY WILL LIKE TO GO FOR A FRIENDSHIP DINNER SOME TIME
OLD YES THAT FOR SURE OF FRIENDSHIP DINNER I LOVE IT
HUT/HUT-HUT HUT-HUT HUT
ARE YOU OK
OLD YES I AM OK ROBERT IT WAR JEST A COUGH
I AM GLAD TO HEAR THAT SANDRA
YOU KNOW MAKE A NEW FRIENDS IS IT NATUREL TO BATS
IT FEEL LIKE SOMETHING FOR LOVE BUT CONNIE IT THE WAY
YES IT THE LOVE WAY HEY I KNOW IT ALL
FOR CONNIE AND NATALIE THEY OF GOOD HELP TERRI
I KNOW OF ABOUT THAT TO BATS
YOU KNOW TERRI SOMETHING IS FANTASTIC FOR OF ON
YES IT IS NATALIE IT GOOD
I LIKE ABOUT THAT
I KNOW IT GOOD I KNOW IT LAURA
NICOLE DO YOU KNOW WHAT TO DO
OLD SURE
BY LARRY-RANDOLPH.

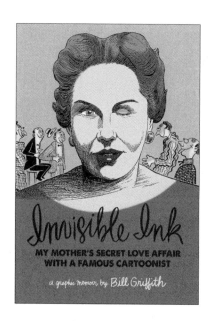

Invisible Ink
MY MOTHER'S SECRET LOVE AFFAIR WITH A FAMOUS CARTOONIST
a graphic memoir by Bill Griffith

# Invisible Ink

My Mother's Secret Love Affair with a Famous Cartoonist (*Excerpts*)

BILL GRIFFITH

*originally published in*

*Invisible Ink: My Mother's Secret Love Affair with a Famous Cartoonist*

FANTAGRAPHICS BOOKS

6.5 × 9.5 inches • 208 pages

## Biography

*Zippy the Pinhead*'s creator began his comics career in New York City in 1969. He ventured to San Francisco in 1970 to join the burgeoning underground comics movement and made his home there until 1998. In 1986 King Features Syndicate took the daily *Zippy* to a national audience. Today *Zippy* appears in over 150 newspapers worldwide. There have been many paperback collections of Griffith's work and numerous comic book and magazine appearances, both here and abroad. He is now at work on his second graphic novel, a biography of Schlitzie the Pinhead, the original inspiration for Zippy. He currently teaches comics at the School of Visual Arts in New York. He lives and works in East Haddam, Connecticut, with his wife, the cartoonist Diane Noomin.
zippythepinhead.com

## Statement

These pages are excerpts from my 200-page graphic memoir, *Invisible Ink*. It's the story of my mother's secret, sixteen-year-long affair with a then famous cartoonist, Lawrence Lariar, and the way the affair affected me and my family.

I tried to be nonjudgmental and simply lay out the facts as I know them and as revealed by my mother's diaries and other writings. Would I have become a cartoonist if not for the affair? The question lingers.

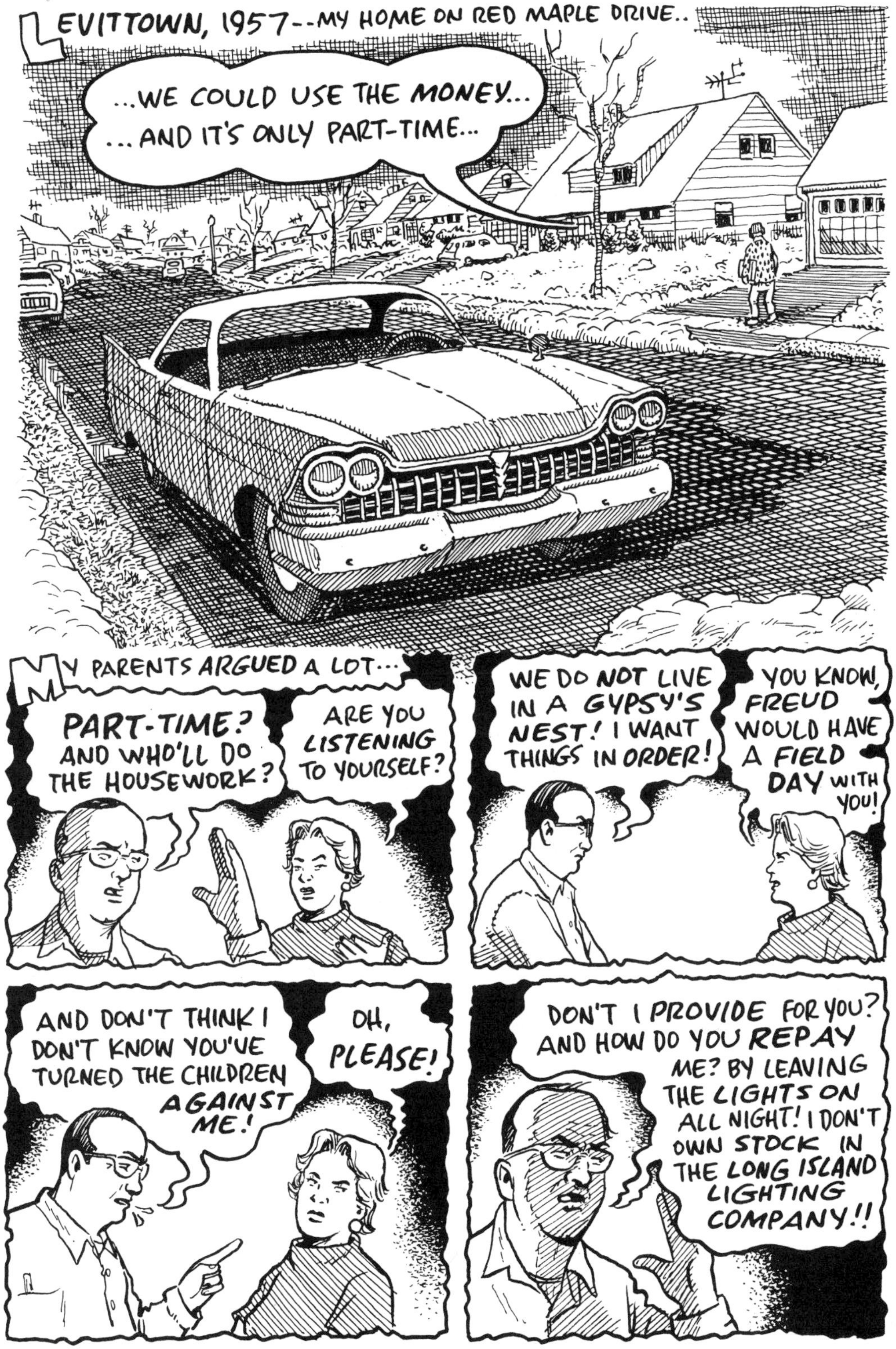
LEVITTOWN, 1957--MY HOME ON RED MAPLE DRIVE..
...WE COULD USE THE MONEY... ...AND IT'S ONLY PART-TIME...
MY PARENTS ARGUED A LOT...
PART-TIME? AND WHO'LL DO THE HOUSEWORK?
ARE YOU LISTENING TO YOURSELF?
WE DO NOT LIVE IN A GYPSY'S NEST! I WANT THINGS IN ORDER!
YOU KNOW, FREUD WOULD HAVE A FIELD DAY WITH YOU!
AND DON'T THINK I DON'T KNOW YOU'VE TURNED THE CHILDREN AGAINST ME!
OH, PLEASE!
DON'T I PROVIDE FOR YOU? AND HOW DO YOU REPAY ME? BY LEAVING THE LIGHTS ON ALL NIGHT! I DON'T OWN STOCK IN THE LONG ISLAND LIGHTING COMPANY!!

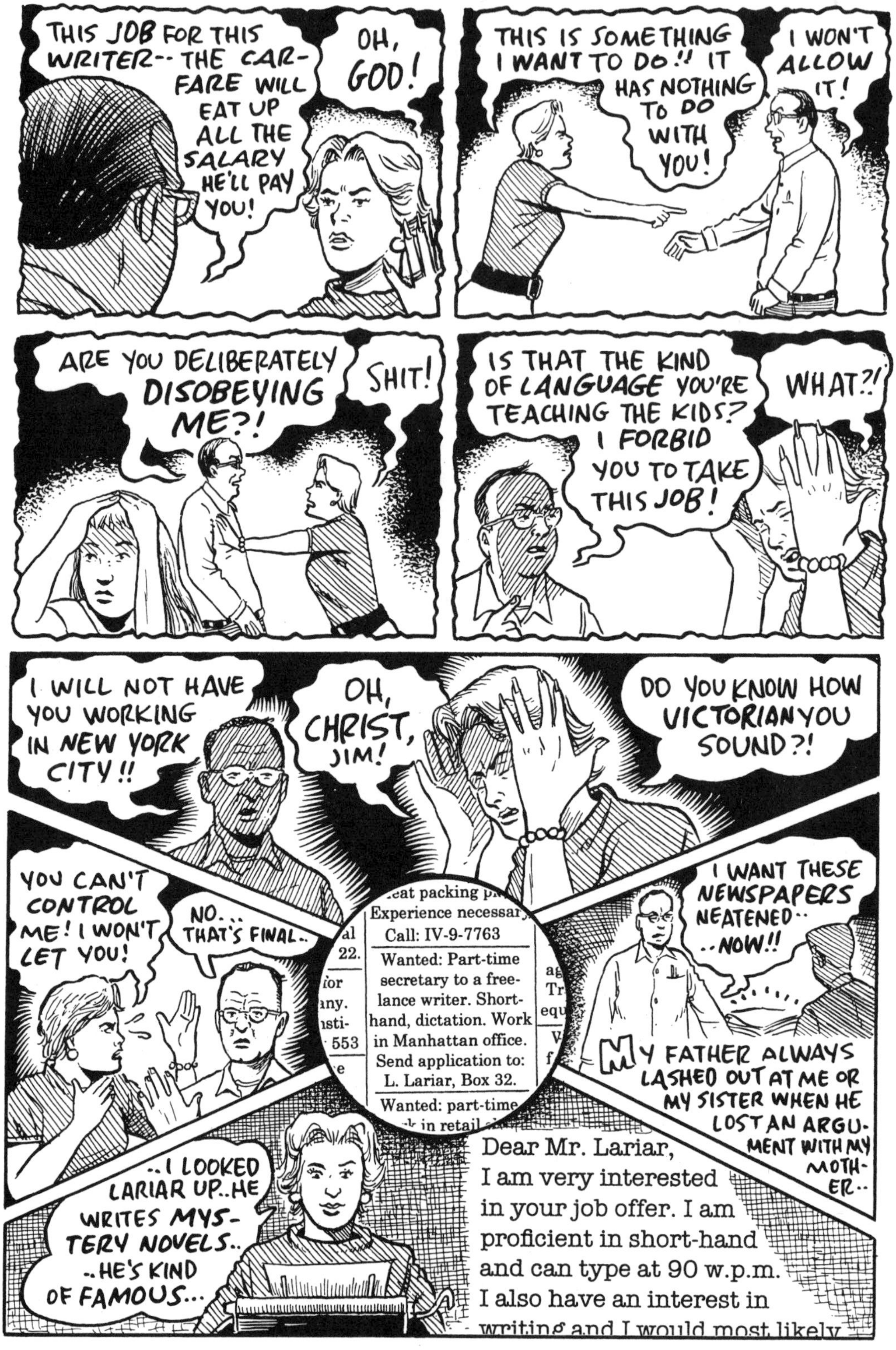
THIS JOB FOR THIS WRITER-- THE CAR-FARE WILL EAT UP ALL THE SALARY HE'LL PAY YOU!
OH, GOD!
THIS IS SOMETHING I WANT TO DO!! IT HAS NOTHING TO DO WITH YOU!
I WON'T ALLOW IT!
ARE YOU DELIBERATELY DISOBEYING ME?!
SHIT!
IS THAT THE KIND OF LANGUAGE YOU'RE TEACHING THE KIDS? I FORBID YOU TO TAKE THIS JOB!
WHAT?!
I WILL NOT HAVE YOU WORKING IN NEW YORK CITY!!
OH, CHRIST, JIM!
DO YOU KNOW HOW VICTORIAN YOU SOUND?!
YOU CAN'T CONTROL ME! I WON'T LET YOU!
NO... THAT'S FINAL..
Experience necessary
Call: IV-9-7763
Wanted: Part-time secretary to a free-lance writer. Short-hand, dictation. Work in Manhattan office. Send application to: L. Lariar, Box 32.
Wanted: part-time
I WANT THESE NEWSPAPERS NEATENED.. ..NOW!!
MY FATHER ALWAYS LASHED OUT AT ME OR MY SISTER WHEN HE LOST AN ARGU-MENT WITH MY MOTH-ER..
..I LOOKED LARIAR UP..HE WRITES MYS-TERY NOVELS.. ..HE'S KIND OF FAMOUS...
Dear Mr. Lariar,
I am very interested in your job offer. I am proficient in short-hand and can type at 90 w.p.m. I also have an interest in

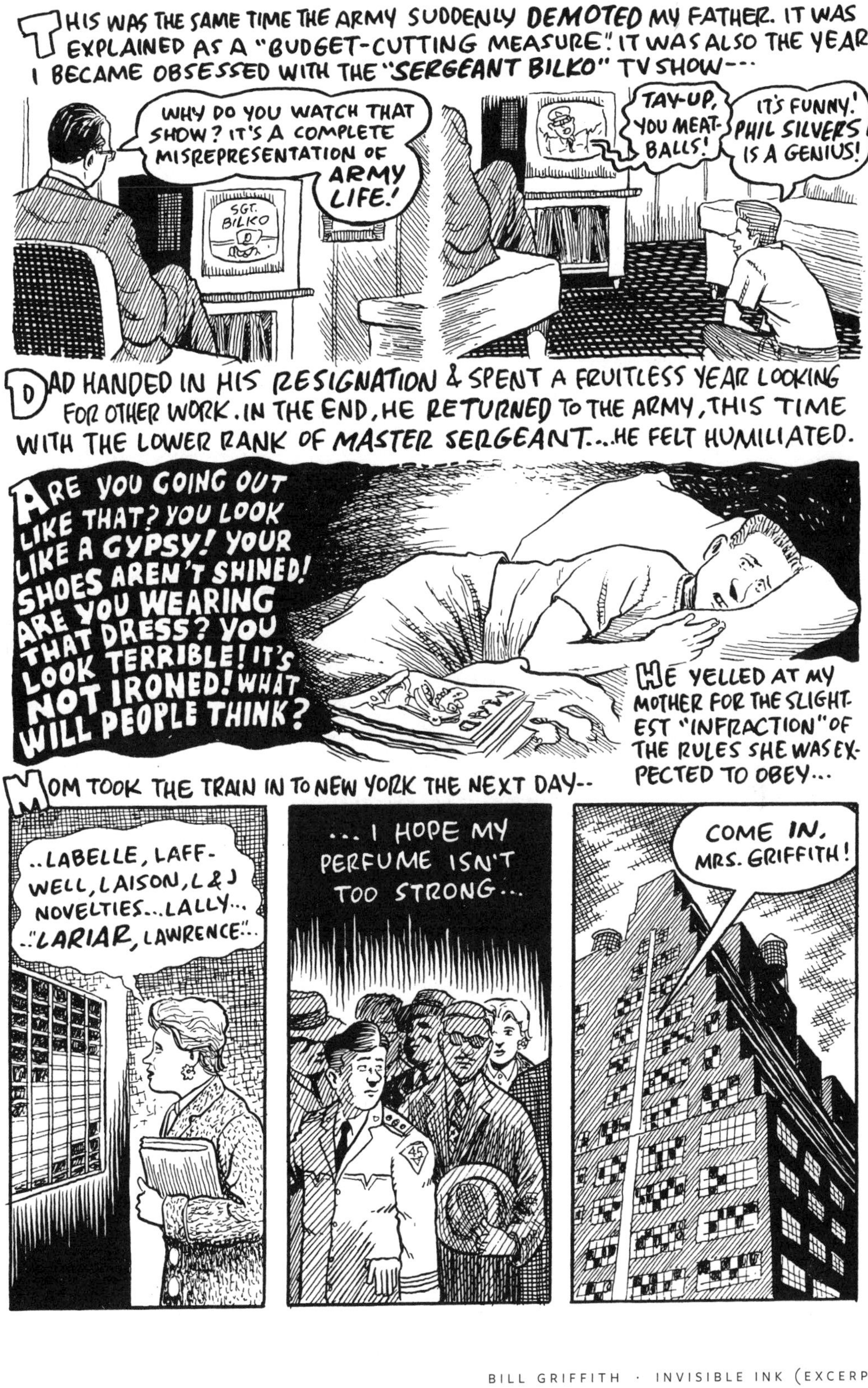
THIS WAS THE SAME TIME THE ARMY SUDDENLY DEMOTED MY FATHER. IT WAS EXPLAINED AS A "BUDGET-CUTTING MEASURE." IT WAS ALSO THE YEAR I BECAME OBSESSED WITH THE "SERGEANT BILKO" TV SHOW---
WHY DO YOU WATCH THAT SHOW? IT'S A COMPLETE MISREPRESENTATION OF ARMY LIFE!
SGT. BILKO
TAY-UP, YOU MEAT-BALLS!
IT'S FUNNY! PHIL SILVERS IS A GENIUS!
DAD HANDED IN HIS RESIGNATION & SPENT A FRUITLESS YEAR LOOKING FOR OTHER WORK. IN THE END, HE RETURNED TO THE ARMY, THIS TIME WITH THE LOWER RANK OF MASTER SERGEANT... HE FELT HUMILIATED.
ARE YOU GOING OUT LIKE THAT? YOU LOOK LIKE A GYPSY! YOUR SHOES AREN'T SHINED! ARE YOU WEARING THAT DRESS? YOU LOOK TERRIBLE! IT'S NOT IRONED! WHAT WILL PEOPLE THINK?
HE YELLED AT MY MOTHER FOR THE SLIGHT-EST "INFRACTION" OF THE RULES SHE WAS EX-PECTED TO OBEY...
MOM TOOK THE TRAIN IN TO NEW YORK THE NEXT DAY--
..LABELLE, LAFF-WELL, LAISON, L & J NOVELTIES...LALLY... ..."LARIAR, LAWRENCE"...
...I HOPE MY PERFUME ISN'T TOO STRONG...
COME IN, MRS. GRIFFITH!

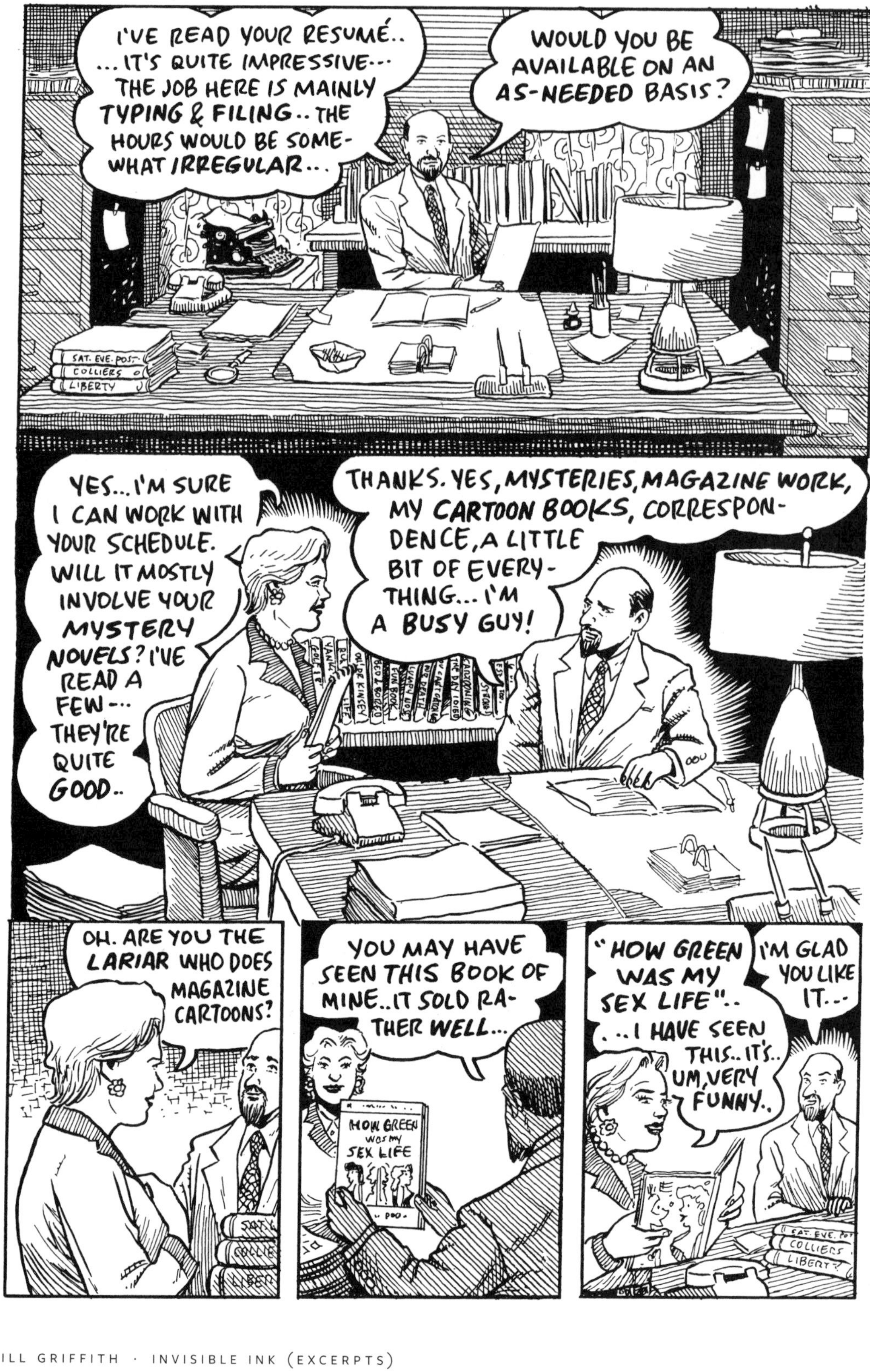
I'VE READ YOUR RESUMÉ.. ...IT'S QUITE IMPRESSIVE... THE JOB HERE IS MAINLY TYPING & FILING.. THE HOURS WOULD BE SOMEWHAT IRREGULAR...
WOULD YOU BE AVAILABLE ON AN AS-NEEDED BASIS?
SAT. EVE. POST
COLLIERS
LIBERTY
YES...I'M SURE I CAN WORK WITH YOUR SCHEDULE. WILL IT MOSTLY INVOLVE YOUR MYSTERY NOVELS? I'VE READ A FEW--... THEY'RE QUITE GOOD..
THANKS. YES, MYSTERIES, MAGAZINE WORK, MY CARTOON BOOKS, CORRESPONDENCE, A LITTLE BIT OF EVERYTHING... I'M A BUSY GUY!
OH. ARE YOU THE LARIAR WHO DOES MAGAZINE CARTOONS?
YOU MAY HAVE SEEN THIS BOOK OF MINE..IT SOLD RATHER WELL...
HOW GREEN WAS MY SEX LIFE
"HOW GREEN WAS MY SEX LIFE".. ...I HAVE SEEN THIS.. IT'S.. UM, VERY FUNNY..
I'M GLAD YOU LIKE IT...
SAT. EVE. POST
COLLIERS
LIBERTY?

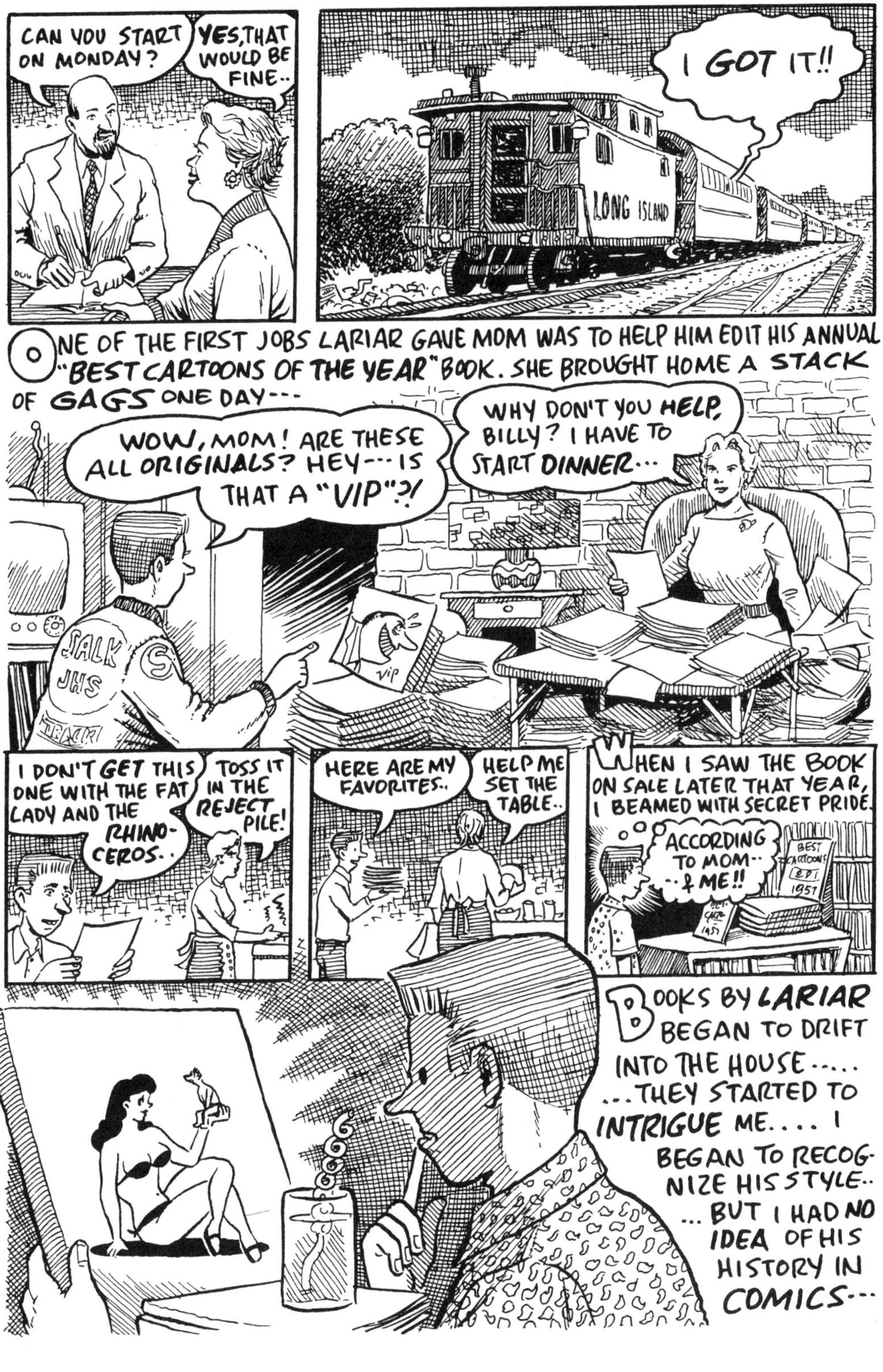

CAN YOU START ON MONDAY?
YES, THAT WOULD BE FINE..
I GOT IT!!
LONG ISLAND
ONE OF THE FIRST JOBS LARIAR GAVE MOM WAS TO HELP HIM EDIT HIS ANNUAL "BEST CARTOONS OF THE YEAR" BOOK. SHE BROUGHT HOME A STACK OF GAGS ONE DAY---
WOW, MOM! ARE THESE ALL ORIGINALS? HEY--- IS THAT A "VIP"?!
WHY DON'T YOU HELP, BILLY? I HAVE TO START DINNER...
SALK JHS
VIP
I DON'T GET THIS ONE WITH THE FAT LADY AND THE RHINOCEROS..
TOSS IT IN THE REJECT PILE!
HERE ARE MY FAVORITES..
HELP ME SET THE TABLE..
WHEN I SAW THE BOOK ON SALE LATER THAT YEAR, I BEAMED WITH SECRET PRIDE.
ACCORDING TO MOM.. & ME!!
BEST CARTOONS 1957
BOOKS BY LARIAR BEGAN TO DRIFT INTO THE HOUSE..... ...THEY STARTED TO INTRIGUE ME.... I BEGAN TO RECOGNIZE HIS STYLE.. ...BUT I HAD NO IDEA OF HIS HISTORY IN COMICS---

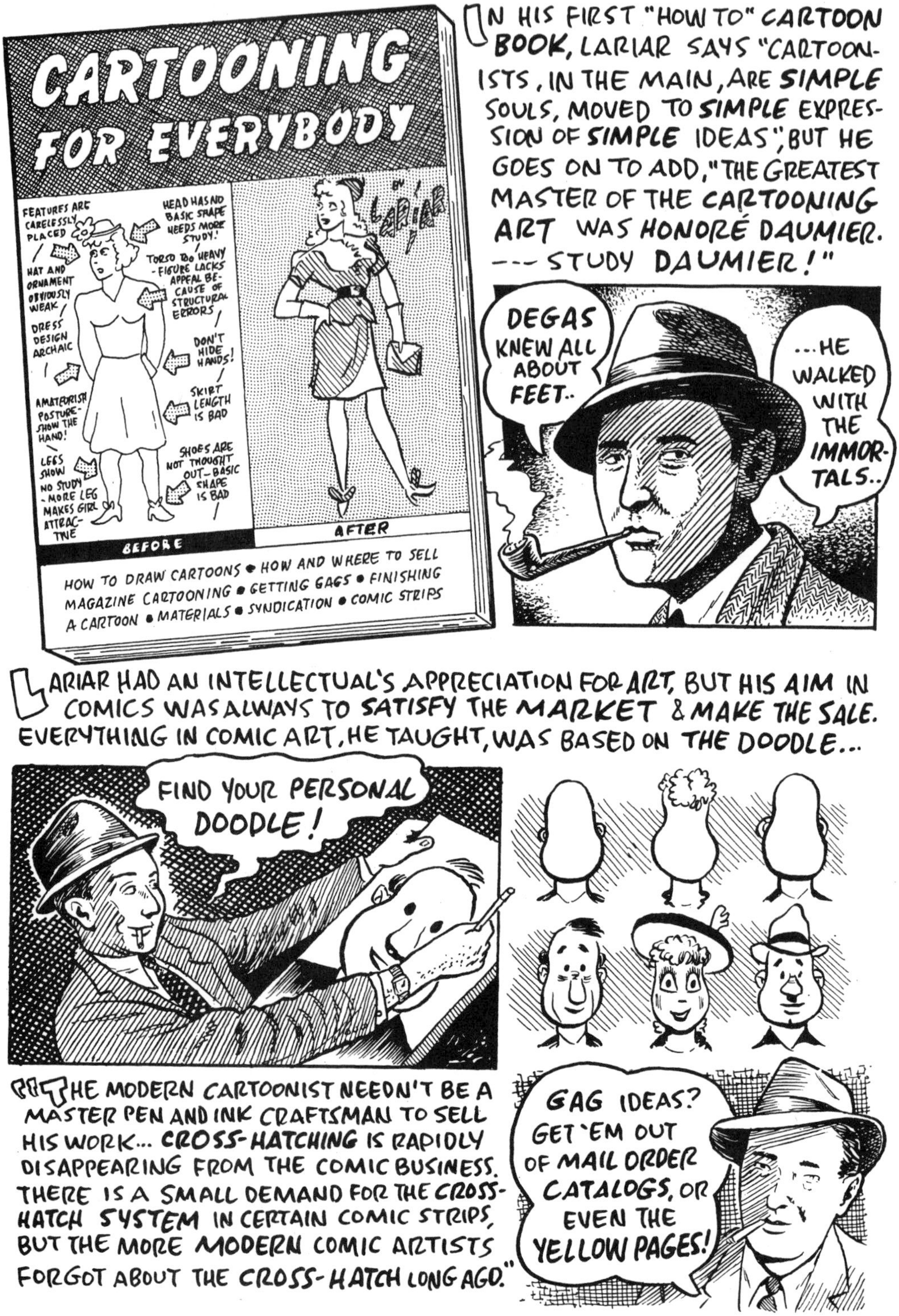
CARTOONING FOR EVERYBODY
BY LARIAR
FEATURES ARE CARELESSLY PLACED
HAT AND ORNAMENT OBVIOUSLY WEAK
DRESS DESIGN ARCHAIC
AMATEURISH POSTURE - SHOW THE HAND!
LEGS SHOW NO STUDY - MORE LEG MAKES GIRL ATTRACTIVE
HEAD HAS NO BASIC SHAPE NEEDS MORE STUDY!
TORSO TOO HEAVY - FIGURE LACKS APPEAL BECAUSE OF STRUCTURAL ERRORS
DON'T HIDE HANDS!
SKIRT LENGTH IS BAD
SHOES ARE NOT THOUGHT OUT - BASIC SHAPE IS BAD
BEFORE
AFTER
HOW TO DRAW CARTOONS • HOW AND WHERE TO SELL MAGAZINE CARTOONING • GETTING GAGS • FINISHING A CARTOON • MATERIALS • SYNDICATION • COMIC STRIPS
IN HIS FIRST "HOW TO" CARTOON BOOK, LARIAR SAYS "CARTOONISTS, IN THE MAIN, ARE SIMPLE SOULS, MOVED TO SIMPLE EXPRESSION OF SIMPLE IDEAS", BUT HE GOES ON TO ADD, "THE GREATEST MASTER OF THE CARTOONING ART WAS HONORÉ DAUMIER. --- STUDY DAUMIER!"
DEGAS KNEW ALL ABOUT FEET..
...HE WALKED WITH THE IMMORTALS..
LARIAR HAD AN INTELLECTUAL'S APPRECIATION FOR ART, BUT HIS AIM IN COMICS WAS ALWAYS TO SATISFY THE MARKET & MAKE THE SALE. EVERYTHING IN COMIC ART, HE TAUGHT, WAS BASED ON THE DOODLE...
FIND YOUR PERSONAL DOODLE!
"THE MODERN CARTOONIST NEEDN'T BE A MASTER PEN AND INK CRAFTSMAN TO SELL HIS WORK... CROSS-HATCHING IS RAPIDLY DISAPPEARING FROM THE COMIC BUSINESS. THERE IS A SMALL DEMAND FOR THE CROSS-HATCH SYSTEM IN CERTAIN COMIC STRIPS, BUT THE MORE MODERN COMIC ARTISTS FORGOT ABOUT THE CROSS-HATCH LONG AGO."
GAG IDEAS? GET 'EM OUT OF MAIL ORDER CATALOGS, OR EVEN THE YELLOW PAGES!

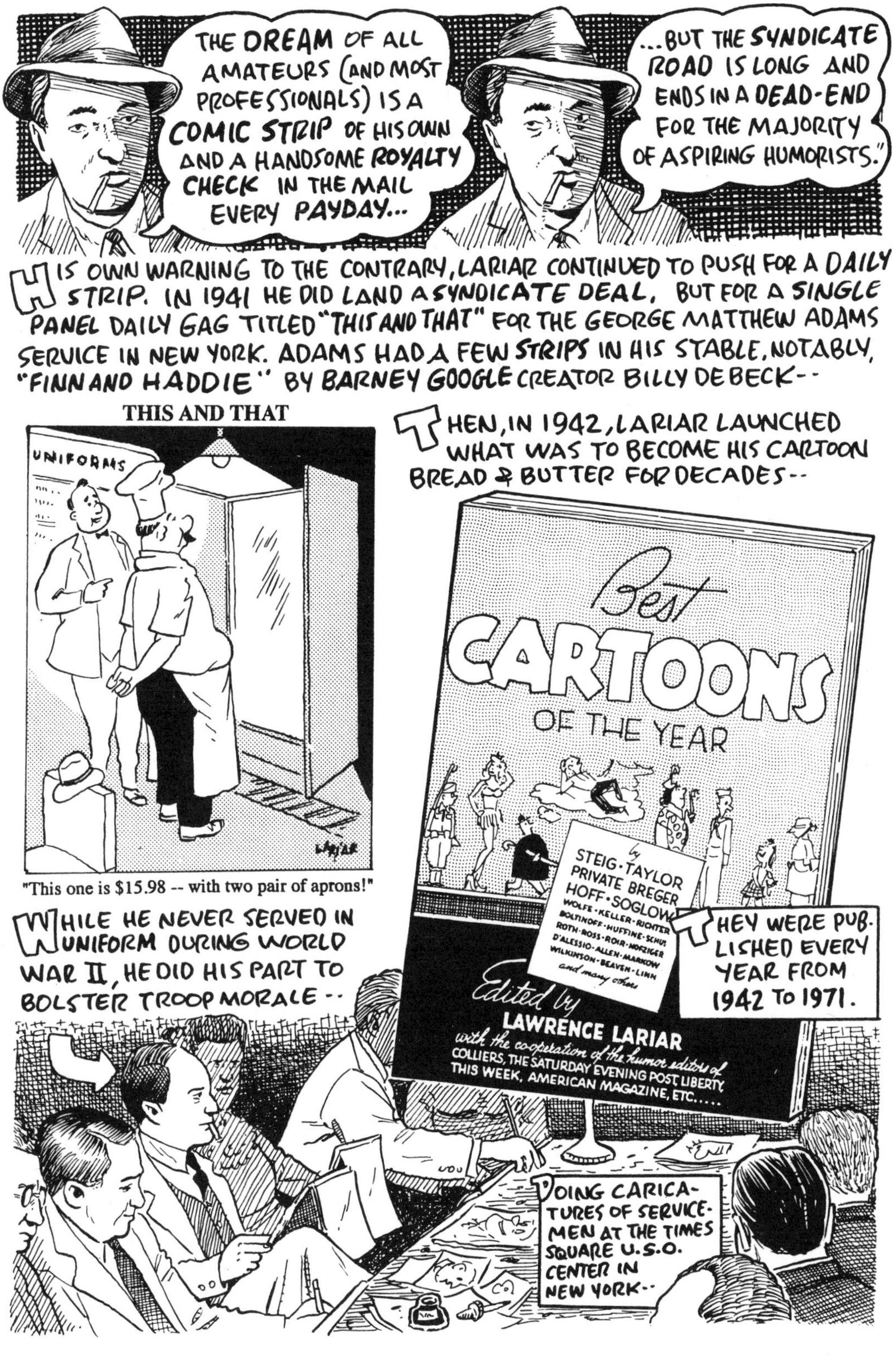
THE DREAM OF ALL AMATEURS (AND MOST PROFESSIONALS) IS A COMIC STRIP OF HIS OWN AND A HANDSOME ROYALTY CHECK IN THE MAIL EVERY PAYDAY...
...BUT THE SYNDICATE ROAD IS LONG AND ENDS IN A DEAD-END FOR THE MAJORITY OF ASPIRING HUMORISTS."
HIS OWN WARNING TO THE CONTRARY, LARIAR CONTINUED TO PUSH FOR A DAILY STRIP. IN 1941 HE DID LAND A SYNDICATE DEAL, BUT FOR A SINGLE PANEL DAILY GAG TITLED "THIS AND THAT" FOR THE GEORGE MATTHEW ADAMS SERVICE IN NEW YORK. ADAMS HAD A FEW STRIPS IN HIS STABLE, NOTABLY, "FINN AND HADDIE" BY BARNEY GOOGLE CREATOR BILLY DE BECK--
THIS AND THAT
UNIFORMS
"This one is $15.98 -- with two pair of aprons!"
THEN, IN 1942, LARIAR LAUNCHED WHAT WAS TO BECOME HIS CARTOON BREAD & BUTTER FOR DECADES--
Best CARTOONS OF THE YEAR
by STEIG · TAYLOR PRIVATE BREGER HOFF · SOGLOW
WOLFE · KELLER · RICHTER BOLTINOFF · HUFFINE · SCHUS ROTH · ROSS · ROIR · HORZIGER D'ALESSIO · ALLEN · MARKOW WILKINSON · BEAVEN · LINN and many others
Edited by LAWRENCE LARIAR
with the cooperation of the humor editors of COLLIERS, THE SATURDAY EVENING POST, LIBERTY, THIS WEEK, AMERICAN MAGAZINE, ETC.....
THEY WERE PUBLISHED EVERY YEAR FROM 1942 TO 1971.
WHILE HE NEVER SERVED IN UNIFORM DURING WORLD WAR II, HE DID HIS PART TO BOLSTER TROOP MORALE--
DOING CARICATURES OF SERVICEMEN AT THE TIMES SQUARE U.S.O. CENTER IN NEW YORK--

# Notable Comics

*from September 1, 2015, to August 31, 2016*

Selected by Bill Kartalopoulos

ROSAIRE APPEL
Conversational Maladjustment. *Central Booking Magazine*, vol. VI, issue III.

CECE BELL
Crazy Little Thing Called Lunch. *Comics Squad: Lunch!*

SAMAN BEMEL-BENRUD
Dumb. *Big Planet Comics: blue.*

ALYSSA BERG
Alpenglow.

R. O. BLECHMAN
Amadeo & Maladeo: A Musical Duet.

BRIAN BLOMERTH
The Wimpy Whisper.

TARA BOOTH
Unwell.

JOHN BRODOWSKI
Sid and Sid in Part-Time Jobs. *Magic Whistle* 3.0 #1.

CHESTER BROWN
Mary Wept Over the Feet of Jesus.

NINA BUNJEVAC
An Excerpt from Fatherland II. *Taddle Creek #36.*

APOLO CACHO
La Vida en el Presidio.

LILLI CARRÉ
Sight Modesty Snake Splitting.

ROZ CHAST
Epilogue. *The New Yorker*, July 25, 2016.

BRIAN CHIPPENDALE
Puke Force.

COLE CLOSSER
Black Rat.

DANIEL CLOWES
Patience.

AL COLUMBIA
Pim & Francie: Blood on the Walls, Blood on the Walls *and* Pim & Francie: The Candyman. *Smoke Signal #23.*

MARK CONNERY
Tricky Business. *4Panel*, vol. 1.

GREG COOK
Friends Is Friends.

JORDAN CRANE
Uptight #5.

ERIN CURRY
Poems to the Sea. *Ley Lines #5.*

DAME DARCY
Le Fantome Chateau or Ghost Castle Hassle. *Meat Cake Bible.*

ANYA DAVIDSON
Gloom Planet.

STEVE DITKO
Ditko #24.

MAËLLE DOLIVEUX
Truce.

JULIE DOUCET
Carpet Sweeper Tales.

NICK DRNASO
Beverly.

G. W. DUNCANSON
New School of Design MFA. *Weakly Annual.*

DW
Mountebank, pp. 55QVIc+ to 66UIIIb+. *Irene 6.*

THEO ELLSWORTH
The Understanding Monster, Book Three.

AUSTIN ENGLISH
low level enjoyment.

C. F.
Ladder. *Clean Sweep.*

JULES FEIFFER
Cousin Joseph.

SARAH FERRICK
Sec.

WINNIE T. FRICK
lecture/seminar. *monthlysmokeandmirrors.com.*

GG
Lapse. *š!* #25.

TOM GALAMBOS
Travis.

JULIA GFRÖRER
Dark Age.

PHILIPPE GIRARD
Tailgate.
20×20: *Twenty Years of Conundrum Press.*

SAMMY HARKHAM
Crickets #5.

TEVA HARRISON
In-Between Days.

TOM HART
Rosalie Lightning: A Graphic Memoir.

JENNIFER HAYDEN
The Story of My Tits.

TIM HENSLEY
Sir Alfred #3.

GILBERT AND JAIME HERNANDEZ
Love and Rockets: New Stories #8.

RYAN HESHKA
Mean Girls Club.

PETER AND MARIA HOEY
Coin-Op #6.

LUKE HOWARD
Our Mother.

KEVIN HUIZENGA
Ganges #5.

JESSE JACOBS
The Garden. *4Panel*, vol. 1.

DYLAN JONES
The Longer You Stare the Fatter I'm Guilty.

KEITH JONES
Secretimes.

JULIACKS
Architecture of an Atom Epilogue:
Dance Ballad Compulsive Tribulations.

SEAN KAREMAKER
The Ghosts We Know.

MARGARET KIMBALL
Dave. *Ecotone*, Fall 2015.

AIDAN KOCH
Glass Surfaces and Still Pools.

KATE LACOUR
Vivisectionary II.

JEFFREY LEWIS
Fuff #11.

AMY LOCKHART
Puppy Love. *Magic Whistle 3.2.*

CÉLINE LOUP AND ANONYMOUS
Silent Treatment. *Bad Boyfriends.*

MARDOU
Sky in Stereo.

BENJAMIN MARRA
Terror Assaulter: O.M.W.O.T.

MATS!?
It Crawled from the Grave . . .
*Rotland Dreadfuls*, vol. 2, #4

TED MAY
Men's Feelings #2.

ALISON MCCREESH
Ramshackle: A Yellowknife Story.

JED MCGOWAN
Sun. *jedmcgowan.com.*

MIKE MIGNOLA
Hellboy in Hell #9 and 10.

JASON T. MILES
Wishbone. *Love Wins.*

TONY MILLIONAIRE
Maakies.

ROMAN MURADOV
The End of a Fence.

ANNIE MURPHY
I Never Promised You a Rose Garden #2.

MARK NEWGARDEN
Man and Wart. *Fable Comics.*

MARÉ ODOMO
Late Bloomer.

ONSMITH
The Spoke of a Wheel. *Lumpen Magazine* #126.

VALERIE OWEN
Irmalinda's Doll.

LAURA PARK & J. C. MENU
Bon-Point Comix #2.

ALABASTER PIZZO AND KAELEIGH FORSYTH
Hellbound Lifestyle.

DAVID PLUNKERT
Heroical #3.

REBECCA ROHER
Bird in a Cage.

DAVID SANDLIN
Aging of Innocence.

JEN SANDWICH
Total Trash #7 and 8.

GABBY SCHULZ
Sick.

BRIAN SELZNICK
The Marvels.

ROBERT SERGEL
It's an Awesome Thing When the Spirit Leaves the Body. *Space: An Eschew Collection.*

DASH SHAW
Escape from Nostalgia World. *Hip Hop Family Tree Three-In-One Featuring Cosplayers.*

JASON SHIGA
Demon, chapters 14–21.

JOSH SIMMONS
Habit #2.

CAITLIN SKAALRUD
Houses of the Holy.

JEREMY SORESE
Curveball.

ART SPIEGELMAN
Lost. *The New Yorker*, August 29, 2016.

DANIEL SPOTTSWOOD
NiX! *2015 Annual.*

LESLIE STEIN
Time Clock.

A. K. SUMMERS
Those OTHER Nurses. *muthamagazine.com.*

IAN SUNDAHL
40X. *Vision Quest #5.*

JILLIAN TAMAKI
Platform.

WALKER TATE
Channel.

SETH TOBOCMAN
Len, a Lawyer in History.

PETE TOMS
The Linguists

GODA TRAKUMAITE
#1 ("What Is Inside?") *and* #2 ("Comix About Different Problems . . .").

BEATRIX URKOWITZ
The Beauty Theorem. *hazlitt.net.*

TILLIE WALDEN
A City Inside.

LAUREN R. WEINSTEIN
Perfect Maine Vacation. *theguardian.com.*

CREDITS

"Test of Loyalty" by Sam Alden. First published at hazlitt.com. Copyright © 2016 by Sam Alden. Reprinted by permission of Sam Alden.

"The Dead Father" by Sami Alwani. First published in *The Dead Father*. Copyright © 2016 by Sami Alwani. Reprinted by permission of Sami Alwani.

Excerpt from "In Pieces: Someplace Which I Call Home" by Kurt Ankeny. First published in *In Pieces: Someplace Which I Call Home*. Copyright © 2016 by Kurt Ankeny. Reprinted by permission of Kurt Ankeny.

"Good Haven High" by Oscar Azmitia. Copyright © 2016 by Oscar Azmitia. Reprinted by permission of Oscar Azmitia.

"2010" by Josh Bayer. First published in *2010*. Copyright © 2016 by Josh Bayer. Reprinted by permission of Josh Bayer.

Excerpt from "Get Out Your Hankies" by Gabrielle Bell. First published in *July Diary 2016*. Copyright © 2016 by Gabrielle Bell. Reprinted by permission of Gabrielle Bell.

"Jeremy Meets the Forest Cow" by Sienna Cittadino. First published at notyrman.tumblr.com. Copyright © 2016 by Sienna Cittadino. Reprinted by permission of Sienna Cittadino.

Excerpt from *Big Kids* by Michael DeForge. First published in *Big Kids*. Copyright © 2016 by Michael DeForge. Reprinted by permission of Michael DeForge.

"Shrine of the Monkey God" by Kim Deitch. First published in *Kramers Ergot*, vol. 9. Copyright © 2016 by Kim Deitch. Reprinted by permission of Kim Deitch.

"Get In Where U Fit In" and "Molt" by Ben Duncan. First published in *Ball Means*, vol. 1. Copyright © 2016 by Ben Duncan Bonner. Reprinted by permission of Ben Duncan Bonner.

Excerpts from *Invisible Ink: My Mother's Secret Love Affair with a Famous Cartoonist* by Bill Griffith. First published in *Invisible Ink*. Copyright © 2016 by Bill Griffith. Reprinted by permission of Bill Griffith.

"De Hooch" by John Hankiewicz. First published in *De Hooch*. Copyright © 2016 by John Hankiewicz. Reprinted by permission of John Hankiewicz.

Excerpt from "G.C. in 'Dem Bones Pt. II'" by Lawrence D. Hubbard. First published in *Real Deal Comix*. Copyright © 2016 by Lawrence D. Hubbard. Reprinted by permission of Lawrence D. Hubbard.

"Necessity" (Excerpt) from *Don't Come in Here* by Patrick Kyle. First published in *Don't Come in Here*, Koyoma Press, 2016. Copyright © 2016 by Patrick Kyle. Reprinted by permission of Patrick Kyle.

"I Am Better than Picasso" by Dapper Bruce Lafitte. Copyright © 2016 by Dapper Bruce Lafitte. Reprinted by permission of Dapper Bruce Lafitte.

"Remembering the Millionaire Hobo" by Tim Lane. First published in *The Riverfront Times/Happy Hour in America #6*. Copyright © 2016 by Tim Lane. Reprinted by permission of Tim Lane.

Excerpt from "Daisies" By Björn Miner. First published in *Swampson* 3. Copyright © 2016 by Björn Miner. Reprinted by permission of Björn Miner.

"Picaresque" by Laura Pallmall. First published in *Nothing Left to Learn #9: Sporgo*. Copyright © 2016 by Laura Pallmall. Reprinted by permission of Laura Pallmall/Nothing Left to Learn.

"The Future of Art 25 Years Hence" by Gary Panter. First published in *Frieze* #181. Copyright © 2016 by Gary Panter. Reprinted by permission of Gary Panter.

Excerpt from *John Wilcock, New York Years* by Ethan Persoff and Scott Marshall. First published in *John Wilcock, New York Years, 1954–1971*. Copyright © 2016 by Ethan Persoff and Scott Marshall. Reprinted by permission of Ethan Persoff and Scott Marshall.

Selections from *Hip Hop Family Tree* by Ed Piskor. First published at boingboing.net. Copyright © 2016 by Ed Piskor. Reprinted by permission of Ed Piskor.

"Love with Family Love" and "The Team for Sure" by Larry Randolph. Copyright © 2016 by Larry Randolph. Reprinted by permission of Creative Growth Art Center.

"Radio Silence" by Grant Reynolds. First published in *Lumpen* #126. Copyright © 2016 by Grant Reynolds. Reprinted by permission of Grant Reynolds.

"Rent Crisis" by Joe Sacco. Copyright © 2016 by Joe Sacco. Reprinted by permission of Joe Sacco.

"Willem de Kooning. (Geniuses are nothing if not complicated in their methods.)" by Deb Sokolow. Copyright © 2016 by Deb Sokolow. Reprinted by permission of Deb Sokolow.

"Time To Get Paid," "Sexual Chocolate," "Women Only, No Men Allowed," and "Hong Fong Chuey" by Gerone Spruill. Copyright © 2016 by Gerone Spruill. Reprinted by permission of Creative Growth Art Center.

Excerpt from *Generous Bosom Part 2* by Conor Stechschulte. First published in *Generous Bosom Part 2*. Copyright © 2016 by Conor Stechschulte. Reprinted by permission of Conor Stechschulte.

"Ranchero" by Mike Taylor. First published in *Ranchero*. Copyright © 2016 by Mike Taylor. Reprinted by permission of Mike Taylor.

Untitled by Bailey Jean Thomas. First published at theparisreview.org. Copyright © 2016 by Bailey Jean Thomas. Reprinted by permission of Bailey Jean Thomas.

"Kill Thurber" by Matthew Thurber. First published in *Kramers Ergot*, vol. 9. Copyright © 2016 by Matthew Thurber. Reprinted by permission of Matthew Thurber.

Four Untitled Pieces by William Tyler. Copyright © 2016 by William Tyler. Reprinted by permission of Creative Growth Art Center.

"SCHLONGED!" by Eli Valley. First published at *The Daily Dot* (*dailydot.com*). Copyright © 2016 by Eli Valley. Reprinted by permission of Eli Valley.

"The Kanibul Ball" by Lale Westvind. First published in *Kramers Ergot*, vol. 9. Copyright © 2016 by Lale Westvind. Reprinted by permission of Lale Westvind.

"Communications Workers of America" and "Coffee Lids of Greater Old Red Falls" by Dan Zettwoch. First published in *Redbird* #3. Copyright © 2016 by Dan Zettwoch. Reprinted by permission of Dan Zettwoch.

# THE BEST AMERICAN SERIES®

*FIRST, BEST, AND BEST-SELLING*

*The Best American Comics*

*The Best American Essays*

*The Best American Mystery Stories*

*The Best American Nonrequired Reading*

*The Best American Science and Nature Writing*

*The Best American Science Fiction and Fantasy*

*The Best American Short Stories*

*The Best American Sports Writing*

*The Best American Travel Writing*

Available in print and e-book wherever books are sold.

Visit our website: www.hmhco.com/bestamerican

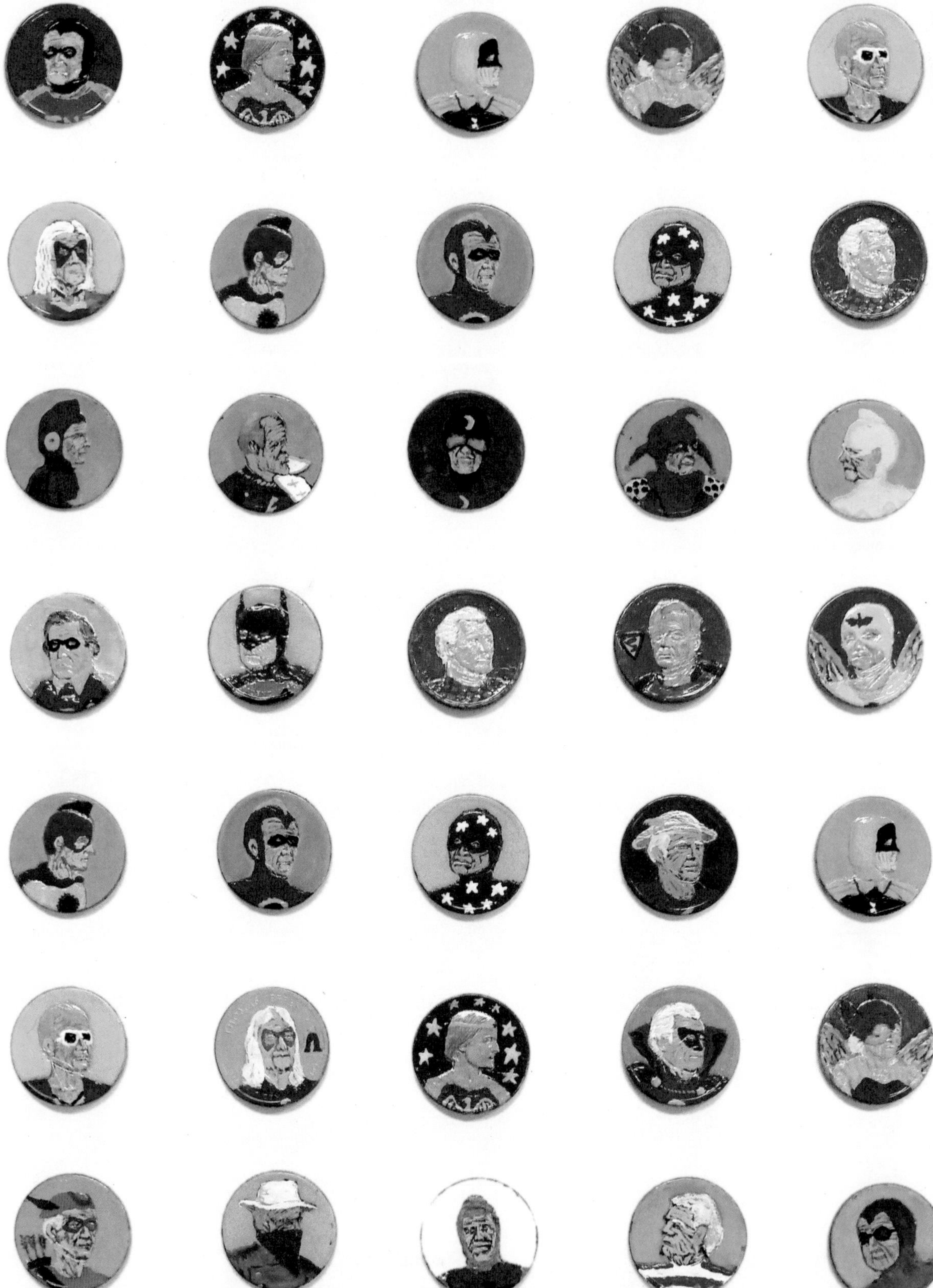